# CALIFORNIA STATE PARKS

## A Complete Recreation Guide

# CALIFORNIA STATE PARKS

## A Complete Recreation Guide

RHONDA & GEORGE OSTERTAG

THE MOUNTAINEERS

Published by The Mountaineers
1001 SW Klickitat Way, Suite 201
Seattle, Washington 98134
U.S.A.



First printing 1995, second printing 1996, third printing 1998



Published simultaneously in Great Britain by Cordee, 3a DeMontfort Street, Leicester, England, LE1 7HD

Manufactured in the United States of America

Edited by Heath Silberfeld
Maps by George Ostertag
All photographs by George Ostertag
Cover design by Watson Graphics
Book design and typesetting by The Mountaineers Books
Book layout by Virginia Hand

Cover photographs, clockwise from upper left: Redwood grove, Big Basin Redwood State Park; Marbled godwits, Silver Strand State Park; Bodie State Historical Park; Joshua tree at dawn, Saddleback Butte State Park
Frontispiece: Bowling Ball Beach, Schooner Gulch

Library of Congress Cataloging-in-Publication Data
Ostertag, Rhonda, 1957–
California state parks : a complete recreation guide / Rhonda and George Ostertag.
p. cm.
ISBN 0-89886-419-4
1. Parks--California--Guidebooks. 2. California--Guidebooks. 3. Outdoor recreation--California--Guidebooks. I. Ostertag, George, 1957– . II. Title.
F859.3.088 1995
917.9404'53--dc20 94-43339
CIP

Printed on recycled paper

# CONTENTS

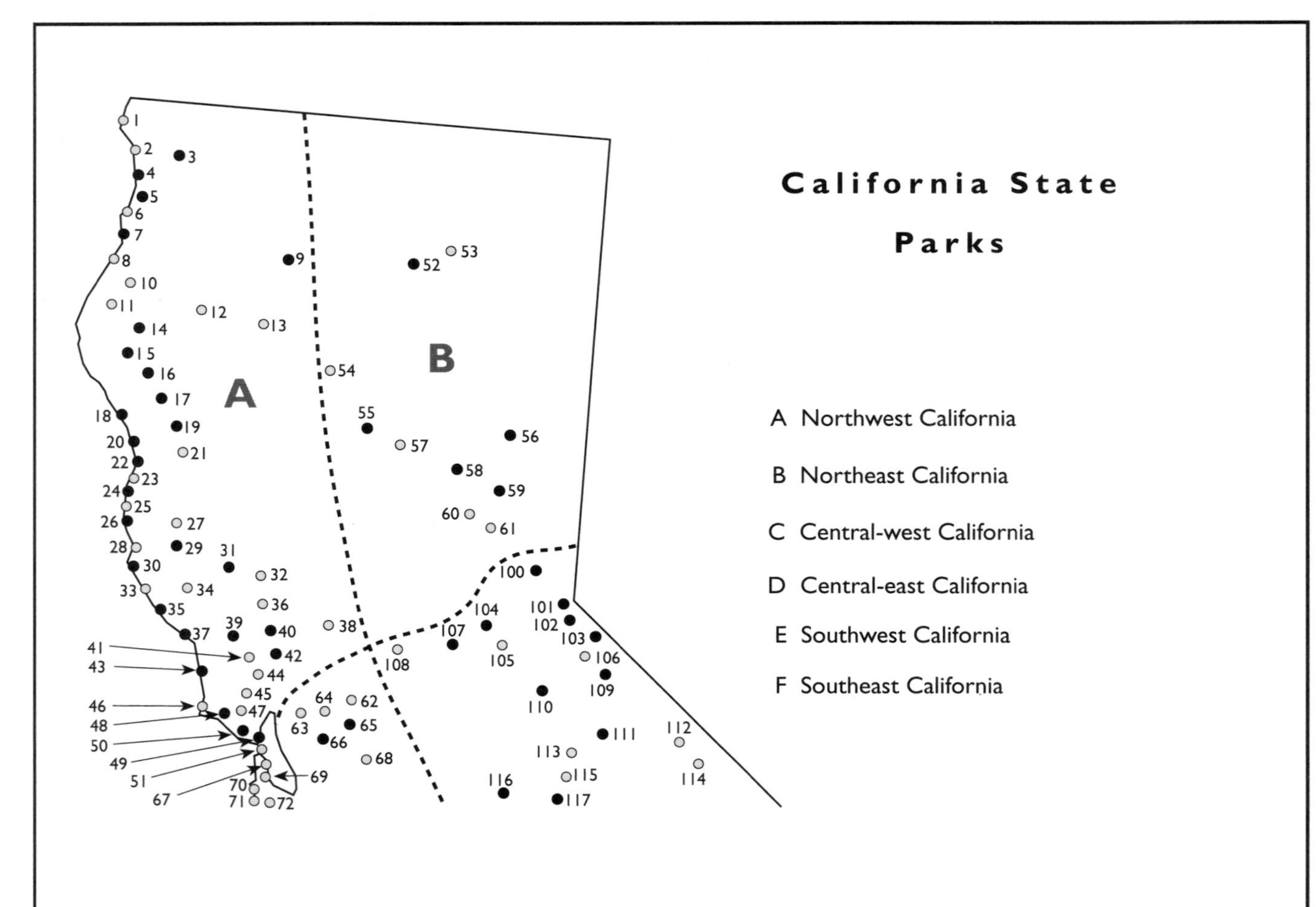
California State Parks
A Northwest California
B Northeast California
C Central-west California
D Central-east California
E Southwest California
F Southeast California
A
B

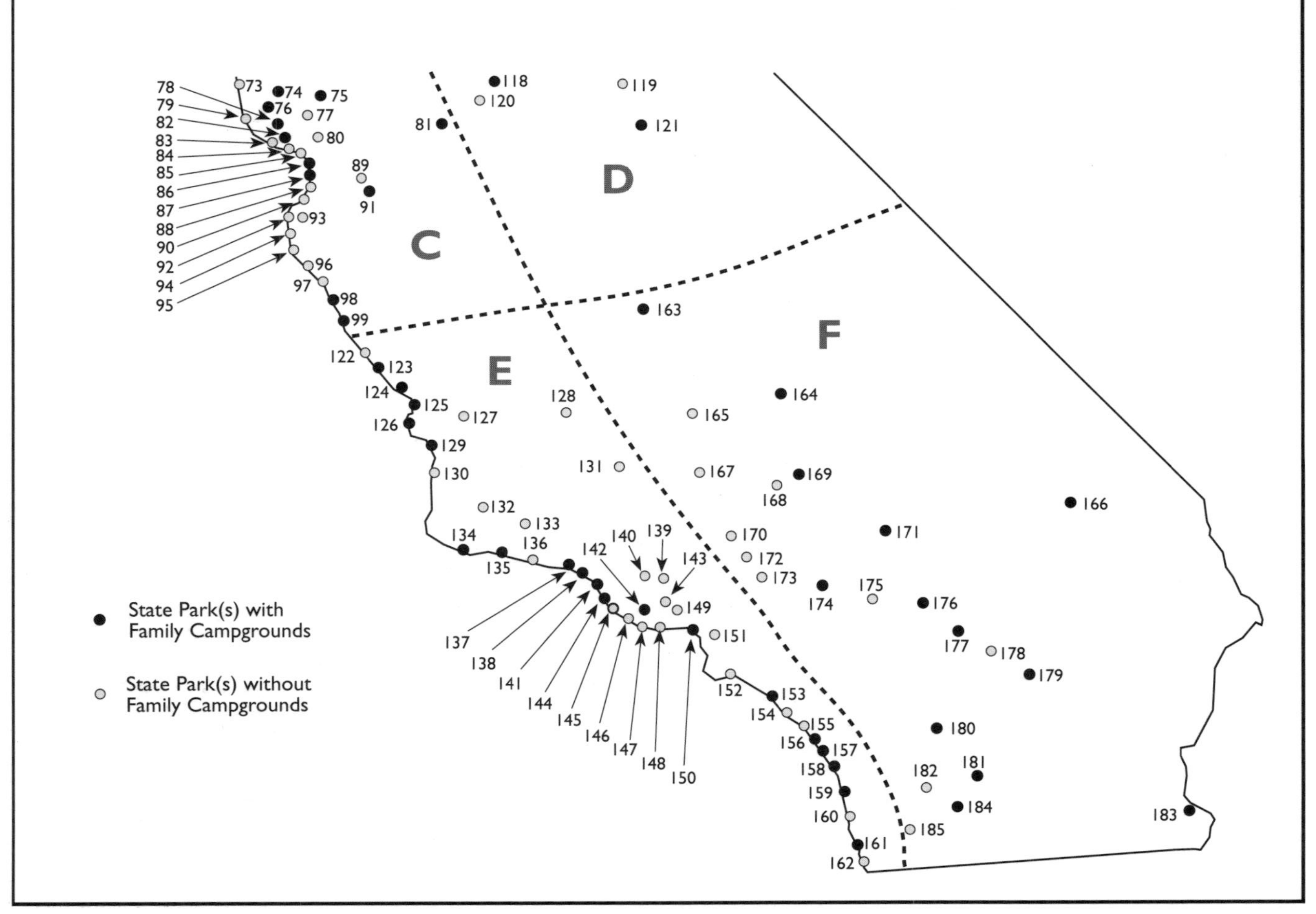
State Park(s) with Family Campgrounds
State Park(s) without Family Campgrounds
C
D
E
F
73 74 75 76 77 78 79 80 81 82 83 84 85 86 87 88 89 90 91 92 93 94 95 96 97 98 99
118 119 120 121 122 123 124 125 126 127 128 129 130 131 132 133 134 135 136 137 138 139 140 141 142 143 144 145 146 147 148 149 150 151 152 153 154 155 156 157 158 159 160 161 162
163 164 165 166 167 168 169 170 171 172 173 174 175 176 177 178 179 180 181 182 183 184 185

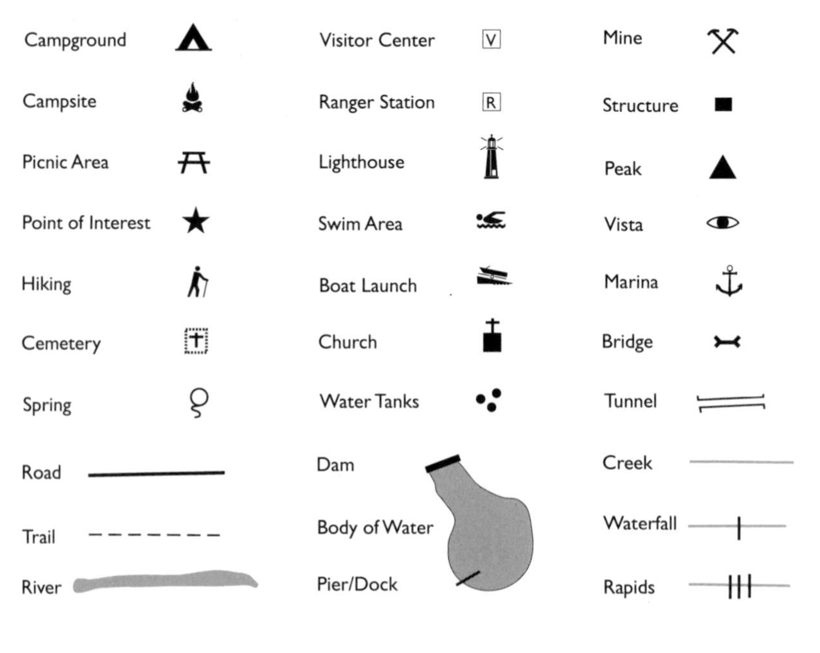

MAP SYMBOLS
Campground
Campsite
Picnic Area
Point of Interest
Hiking
Cemetery
Spring
Road
Trail
River
Visitor Center
V
Ranger Station
R
Lighthouse
Swim Area
Boat Launch
Church
Water Tanks
Dam
Body of Water
Pier/Dock
Mine
Structure
Peak
Vista
Marina
Bridge
Tunnel
Creek
Waterfall
Rapids

# INTRODUCTION

California boasts a premier state park system that showcases the diversity of its landscape and natural offerings, history, and cultural wealth. Housed and protected among its units are treasures of national merit. Management of the system balances the interests of recreationists, naturalists, and preservationists, opening an outstanding field of discovery for generations to come.

The birth of the system was marked in 1902 with the creation of Big Basin Redwoods State Park in Santa Cruz County; it both celebrates and saves an impressive stand of virgin coastal redwoods. Today, the system approaches 300 units and encompasses 1.6 million acres, nearly 1 percent of California's total land and water surface.

Several park classifications comprise the system: Generally large in size, the *State Parks* show an outstanding scenic, natural, or cultural value, with most offering sightseeing and quiet recreational pursuits, such as hiking, birdwatching, and photography. Many have campgrounds.

The *State Reserves* house California's unique or truly outstanding natural, scientific, and/or scenic offerings, while the *State Historic Parks* protect the objects, buildings, and sites important to California's heritage. Access to these park classes is frequently controlled, either in a tour setting or with restricted-use areas.

The *State Recreation Areas* and *State Beaches* are designed and managed for the recreationist. Recreation areas invite do-it-yourself fun with varying amenities for boaters, off-road-vehicle enthusiasts, equestrians, and hikers. State beaches vary in size and may be civilized and bustling with people or wild and little-traveled. Both classes may have campgrounds.

The system's few *State Wildernesses* retain their raw character and are often more remote, appealing to the adventurous. Not surprisingly, their appreciation usually requires an investment of physical energy.

*Natural or Cultural Preserves* can be found in any of the park units. These sites may hold endangered flora or other special features. The designated *Underwater Areas* within the system protect the aquatic resources found in the park, while inviting exploration.

Nearly all the parks are open year-round, with most presenting a full calendar of interpretive programs; a few, mainly the museums and historic sites, close on major holidays. Day-use hours can vary park to park and season to season. The special events at the parks cover the gamut, with everything from banana slug races to Shakespearean plays; the California Department of Parks and Recreation makes available an annual calendar of events. The living-history demonstrations offered during summer are another popular draw.

## PARK USER INFORMATION

### Fees and Passes

Most of the park units do charge day-use fees; amounts vary, depending on the offerings and level of facilities. With that being the case, frequent park users may wish to purchase an annual pass. Affixed to the vehicle, these passes offer unlimited day access to the parks during a year's time. They do not, however, provide entry to the state parks operated by local agencies, the historic parks, guided tours, museums, or vehicle-recreation areas.

Seniors, disabled individuals, and disabled veterans may obtain special passes. Separate passes are also available for boaters who frequently use the state park system and off-road-vehicle users who regularly visit the state vehicle recreation areas. Another pass program administered by the Department of Parks and Recreation is the Sno-park Program, in effect from November 1 to May 30.

If visiting several state parks on the same day, ask the entry-station ranger if that park will honor the day-use fee paid at a neighboring state park, which is commonly the case.

## Camping

Fee camping is available at many California state parks. Reservations are recommended for summer and holiday visits; year-round reservations are advisable for the coastal park campgrounds in Southern California. The MISTIX Corporation is the contractor for this service (P.O. Box 9029, Clearwater, FL 34618, or phone 1-800-444-7275). Sites may be reserved anytime from eight weeks to 48 hours in advance, but chances are better if you reserve early. A nonrefundable reservation fee of $6.75 (subject to change) is charged for each campsite reservation made.

The state parks feature several different family camp facilities: *Developed campgrounds* have improved roads, restrooms (i.e., running water facilities, commonly with coin-operated hot showers), tables, and a fire pit or grill. Some have trailer hook-ups and/or dump stations. The *primitive campgrounds* generally offer drinking water, nonflush toilets, and tables, but some have no facilities at all. *En route campsites* are simply overnight parking spaces for self-contained camp vehicles. These sites must be vacated by 9:00 A.M. the following day. The *environmental campsites* are walk-in, fend-for-yourself, primitive camp spaces; bring what you will need.

Each year, more parks offer wheelchair-accessible campsites. The MISTIX Reserved Camping flier and application form indicates which of the reservation campgrounds have these kinds of sites. For a complete list, contact the Department of Parks and Recreation. Both wheelchair users and visitors with large trailers or RVs are encouraged to make advance contact with the reservation service, as most campgrounds have only a few sites suitable for their needs.

While this book focuses on the family camp and picnic offerings, many parks also have group facilities. The MISTIX Reserved Camping flier and application form lists the parks for which MISTIX handles reservations. At other locations, group reservations are made directly through the park. For additional information, contact the parks department.

## Tours

Many of the state park system's historical areas and structures and a few of its outstanding natural resources are open to the public only through the confines of a guided tour. Separate tour fees are generally charged.

Due to the popularity of both the year-round guided tours at Hearst Castle (see Hearst San Simeon State Historical Monument—Hearst Memorial State Beach) and the December through March elephant seal tours at Año Nuevo State Reserve, make ticket reservations well in advance. Again, MISTIX handles this service.

*Elephant seals*

Drop-in visitors seeking to go on the tours often walk away disappointed, especially at Año Nuevo.

Most parks also offer a range of interpretive programs and nature walks, with the fullest calendar typically offered during the summer visitor season. For ranger- or docent-led nature walks, an early sign-up at the park office or visitor center is advisable, as group sizes are limited.

## Rules and Regulations

**Pets**. Leashed pets are allowed in the campground and picnic areas of most parks; a pet entrance fee is charged. They are not allowed on the trails or most beaches. At night, all pets must be confined to a vehicle or tent. Consider leaving pets at home.

**Fires**. Fires are restricted to the cooking structures provided; wood must be brought from home or bought at camp. In most areas, gas cook stoves also may be used. Smoking is prohibited in certain areas and parks because of the extreme hazard posed by fire.

**Collecting/harvesting/fishing.** All natural and historic objects located inside the parks are protected by state law against disturbance and collection. Driftwood gathering, seashell collecting, and rockhounding, however, may be permitted on some beaches; check with park personnel.

Unless otherwise posted, tidepool invertebrates are protected from collection. Where harvesting or fishing is allowed, consult the state's sport-fishing regulations for season, rules, and conditions that apply; a valid sport-fishing license is required.

**Firearms and fireworks.** Possessing loaded firearms and hunting are prohibited, except at the recreation areas that do allow in-season hunting. To obtain a list of these areas and current restrictions, contact the California Department of Parks and Recreation. Fireworks are prohibited at all parks.

**Off-road-vehicle use.** Off-road-vehicle (ORV) use is limited to state vehicle recreation areas. There are seven in the state park system: Carnegie, Clay Pit, Hollister Hills, Hungry Valley, Ocotillo Wells, Pismo Dunes, and Prairie City. At these areas, all off-road safety rules and regulations apply. A U.S. Forest Service-approved spark arrester is mandatory for ORVs, a helmet is required for riders, and protective clothing is advised. Vehicles must have a current, valid registration, and underaged riders must possess an All-Terrain Vehicle certificate or be properly

*Raccoon, Henry W. Coe State Park*

supervised by a safety-certified adult. Park personnel trained in emergency medical procedures routinely patrol the park.

**Boat use.** Boaters must obey posted speeds and all safety rules. Operating a boat while under the influence of alcohol or drugs is illegal. Dumping is prohibited, and where overnight use is allowed, boaters must show that the boat is fully self-contained.

**Mountain-bike use.** The state park system allows mountain bikes only on fire roads and those trails specifically designated for their use. Certain areas are closed to mountain-bike riders because of user conflict, inappropriate terrain, and sensitive habitat. Riders should watch for and heed the posted use signs. On trails where the signs are absent, do not presume you have the right-of-way.

**Horse use.** Horses are only allowed in the parks where there are appropriate horse facilities, trails of suitable width and grade, and ample open space. Riders should expect encounters with other park users, hikers, and, at times, mountain-bike riders. While horseback riders do have the right-of-way, proceed cautiously.

When visiting a park, ask about the availability of water for both you and your horse and about the rules regarding hitching, feeding, and cleaning up after your animal.

**Safety.** All outdoor participants should be aware that personal abilities vary, nature is ever-changing, and that the maintenance of roads, campgrounds, and trails (all dependent on funding) may differ from year to year. Because a trip is represented within these pages does not mean it will be safe for you. Common sense, independent judgment, and good preparation smooth the way to a safe visit.

The cornerstone to ensuring a safe and rewarding outdoor adventure is to pack the Ten Essentials:

1. Flashlight/headlamp—with extra bulbs and batteries
2. Map—the right one(s) for the trip
3. Compass—know how to use it
4. Extra food—so that something is left over at the end of a trip
5. Extra clothing—more than is needed in good weather
6. Sunglasses—especially important for alpine and snowy destinations
7. First-aid supplies—hiker should also be versed in basic first aid, with CPR skills a plus
8. Pocket knife—for first aid and emergency fire-building
9. Matches—in a waterproof container
10. Fire starter—a candle or chemical fuel for starting a fire with wet wood

The following will further promote an enjoyable outdoor experience:

- Wear sensible shoes and clothes.
- Carry water.
- Be attentive to the weather.
- Recognize your personal capabilities and limitations and those of your party.
- Be alert to trail hazards: wet or frosty footbridges, fordings, downfalls, eroded or collapsed trails, re-routes, and the like.
- Be alert to location hazards: poison oak, uneven or unstable terrain, rattlesnakes, bees, ticks, and other safety threats.
- Know that diving into any water body in the state park system is forbidden.
- Be alert along coastal beaches to high and low tides to avoid becoming stranded or surprised by a sleeper (or sneaker) wave.
- Do not expect the logs on shore to keep your feet dry, as they may dislodge with a wave and cause injury.

*Seaweed, Sonoma Coast State Beach*

*Swallowtail butterfly, Wilder Ranch State Park*

- Know that riptides occur along much of coastal California. If you get caught up in one, swim parallel with the current to shore to where you can more easily return to the beach.
- Surfers new to an area should check with a lifeguard for tips about reading and riding the waves.
- Where lifeguards are not available, take the time to familiarize yourself with water conditions and obstacles before swimming or engaging in waterplay. (Seasonal and peak-period lifeguard services are generally offered at the popular, urban coastal beaches and at the designated swimming areas at many park system reservoirs and lakes.)
- Know the demands of your individual sport or activity and pursue it responsibly.

**Etiquette.** Enjoy the parks and their offerings, but do not disturb their silence or treasures. Clean up after yourself and others, so that those who follow can experience untainted discovery.

## For Other Information

Contact the California Department of Parks and Recreation, P.O. Box 942896, Sacramento, CA 94296-0001; phone: (916) 653-6995.

Another fine source, if you are planning a visit to the California state park system, is the California State Parks Foundation, which offers a membership program and includes many benefits to help you enjoy hundreds of California state parks. For complete information about the foundation and its membership program, contact the California State Parks Foundation, P.O. Box 548, Kentfield, CA 94914; phone: (415) 258-9975.

# ABOUT THE BOOK

## Content

*California State Parks: A Complete Recreation Guide* strives to present visitors with a park snapshot and some suggestions for what to see or do while at the park. With the bounty of the state system, this guidebook can only brush the surface. But it serves as a springboard, allowing visitors to launch their own journeys of discovery and personalize their park experience.

## Organization

In this book the state of California comprises six regions: northwest, northeast, central-west, central-east, southwest, and southeast. These divisions make it possible to group the parks according to their offerings and their geographic relationships. I-5 serves as the east-west divider, and I-80 serves as the north-central divider. For the most part, the unbroken east-west county line separating Monterey and San Luis Obispo counties, Kings and Tulare counties from Kern County, and Inyo and San Bernardino counties serves as the central-south divider.

Each park description begins with an information block that specifies the usual operating hours, the site facilities, the phone number(s) for information, and directions to the park(s). At a glance, the presentation gives readers the vital information for planning a visit.

Parks listed as being year-round are overnight facilities open all day, every day; day users must vacate the park at or near sunset. Where parks maintain regular day-use hours, the times have been specified. Visitors planning early morning or late arrivals to parks where the times are not listed should phone ahead.

Parks that are closed on "major holidays" are typically closed on Thanksgiving Day, Christmas Day, and New Year's Day. Parks listed as having restrooms (running water facilities) generally have potable water available for camper and picnicker use as well.

Descriptive text follows each information block, characterizing each park and its natural, cultural, and recreational offerings. This helps readers visualize a park and assess their interest in it. The size of a park is often mentioned, but size can and does change as the system continues to grow in number and in existing acreage.

*Mushrooms, Standish-Hickey State Recreation Area*

In each "Attractions and Activities" section, visitors can read about some specific sights to see and activities to pursue while at a park. The section also tells how to find these. The activities vary and usually address both the diverse abilities and diverse time constraints of travelers.

Activities include scenic drives, walking tours, boating, fishing, climbing, birdwatching, golfing, skiing, and gold panning. Trails receive the bulk of attention, as they are common to most parks, visitors do not need special equipment to enjoy them, and they show the beauty yet remain compatible with conserving the park's natural qualities.

Some parks, such as John Little State Reserve, the John Marsh Home, and Verdugo Mountains, are not included in this book because they lack either public access or public information. Most state vehicle recreation areas are not included because they lack low-impact recreation.

Visitors may find that some of the parks described have been transferred to local governments. Over the past couple of years the state park system has been divesting itself of smaller park units that can be better and more economically managed by local interests. In some instances, the transfer is one of jurisdiction; in other cases, it involves a transfer of deed. But the beauty that prompted state park status remains intact.

## A NOTE ABOUT SAFETY

Safety is an important concern in all outdoor activities. No guidebook can alert you to every hazard or anticipate the limitations of every reader. Therefore, the descriptions of roads, trails, routes, and natural features in this book are not representations that a particular place or excursion will be safe for your party. When you follow any of the routes described in this book, you assume responsibility for your own safety. Under normal conditions, such excursions require the usual attention to traffic, road and trail conditions, weather, terrain, the capabilities of your party, and other factors. Keeping informed on current conditions and exercising common sense are the keys to a safe, enjoyable outing.

*The Mountaineers*

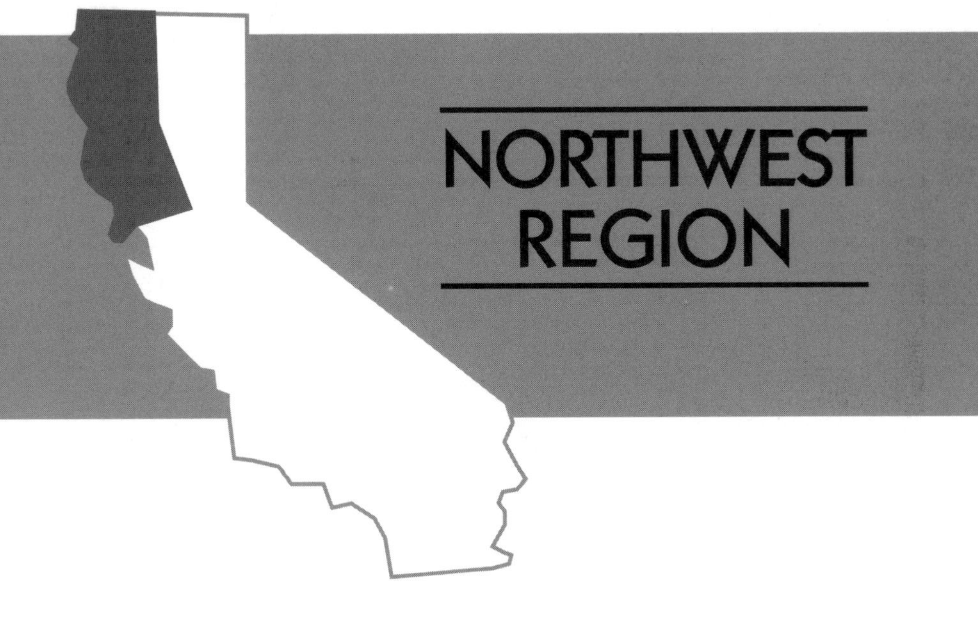

# NORTHWEST REGION

## PELICAN STATE BEACH

**Hours/Season:** Daylight hours
**Facilities:** None
**For Information:** (707) 464-9533
**Access:** On US 101, go 0.4 mile south from the Oregon-California border, or 1.3 miles north from Clifford Kamph Memorial County Park. There, turn west on an unmarked, two-lane road and take the first right to reach the undeveloped parking area in 0.1 mile.

This northernmost unit of the California state park system is easily missed with no signs along US 101, but it offers a pleasing leg-stretch for the traveler and a fine access for beachcombing and surf fishing. From the turnaround loop at the end of the road, a path gently descends 100 feet to the beach.

At this 5-acre state park, coastal scrub and wind-shaped Sitka spruce cloak the rise above a belt of dune grass and a canted beach of fine, dark sand. Drift logs and storm-stranded kelp are cast about the beach. The waves break close to shore with a crescendo, drowning out any hint of US 101. An irregular scattering of offshore rocks marks the surf zone, with a larger rock island rising to the south. On foggy, overcast days, the rough, foamy surf achieves peak beauty.

A few nearby houses come within view but do not spoil the setting's wildness. The southern end of the beach is marked by a rocky point, low bluff, and private beach access. To the north lies a concave shoreline and a long, open expanse framed by coastal hills, but public land ends shortly, as the state park only fronts about a half mile of beach.

Opposite: *Totem, Mendocino Headlands State Park*

*Drift log, Pelican State Beach*

## LAKES EARL AND TALAWA

**Hours/Season:** Daylight hours
**Facilities:** 6 environmental campsites, hike-to picnic sites, vehicle access to beach, hiker and horse trails, nonflush toilets, *bring water*
**For Information:** (707) 464-9533
**Access:** From US 101, at the north end of Crescent City, head west on Northcrest Drive, which later becomes Lake Earl Drive. State park accesses are found off Old Mill Road (a left turn 1.3 miles north of the US 101 junction) and off Kellogg Road. For the Kellogg access, go 5.8 miles north on Northcrest/Lake Earl Drive, turn left on Lower Lake Road, and go another 1.8 miles. There, Kellogg Road heads west, ending at the beach in 1.3 miles.

The Talawa and other coastal tribes occupied this lagoon area long ago. Today, adjoining California state park system and California Department of Fish and Game lands offer access to this vital habitat supporting year-round and migratory bird populations and salmon and trout during periods of high water. The large, shallow, interconnected lake bodies cover more than 2,000 acres and show a shifting shoreline. The cooperatively managed lands include open waters, marsh, coastal plain, reclaimed and existing dune, and a long ocean strand stretching north to the Smith River delta.

Open to vehicles, Kellogg Beach runs long, wide, and canted. Butting it is an extensive, natural dune field closed to off-road vehicles. A southern beach, reached via the Dead Lake Trail, offers a more reflective stay. At the coastal lakes, scopes, binoculars, and identification guides aid birdwatchers in their pursuit of bald eagle, egret, Aleutian Canada goose, scaup, wigeon, and woodpecker. Peregrine falcons may be spied in the winter.

## Attractions and Activities

**Smith River Hiker/Horse Tour.** This tour visits the Smith River, offering loop and round-trip travel options. From the trailhead parking lot, its sandy, uneven 2-track journeys north across a large coastal meadow, where the ocean roar creates a soothing backdrop. At 0.25 mile, a spur links this trail to one from the environmental camp. Bypassing the spur travelers stay along the foot of a tree-covered rise, before mounting it at 1 mile.

At 1.4 miles, the trail merges with a narrow road, following it north, rolling over old dunes, and touring a transition habitat. At 1.8 miles, bear left at the fork. Just ahead, a path crosses the dune field to the beach, offering a shorter loop option. Remain on the road, soon returning to a coastal meadow habitat, to reach the Yontocket Indian Village Cemetery at 2.7 miles.

A rustic wooden fence encircles the cemetery knoll, which overlooks the Smith River and a small wetland patrolled by hawks. Picnic tables invite a stop. The trail then dips to the floodplain of the Smith River, coming to a junction and pit toilet. Go left.

At the next junction (3.1 miles), going right leads to a Smith River overlook in 0.2 mile. Swans, ducks, and a frenzy of feeding gulls are possible sightings. To the left, the path tours grasses and dunes to top a 30-foot foredune and reach the beach at 4 miles. Return as you came, or make a loop going south on the beach and east 0.6 mile on Kellogg Road.

*Access:* From the Lower Lake Road–Kellogg Road Junction, go 0.7 mile west on Kellogg Road and turn right for the trailhead parking lot. There is adequate parking for cars and horse trailers.

**Dead Lake Trail.** This branched trail leads to Dead Lake and Dead Lake Dune, both in about 1 mile, and to the ocean in 1.4 miles.

The hike begins following an old 2-track that passes through a broad coastal meadow rimmed by Sitka spruce, shore pine, and cypress. At 0.1 mile, it passes a scenic, tree-rimmed picnic site on a low bump. During the morning, low fingers of fog may lace the meadow. A noisy chaos of squawks comes from the gulls gathered at a nearby landfill.

At 0.4 mile is a junction. The hiker gate to the left marks the start of the foot trail to Dead Lake and Dead Lake Dune. It tours a coastal scrub and Sitka spruce rise for 0.4 mile, then forks. The left fork leads to the dune, the right one to a ridge overlook of the lake.

Dead Lake Dune is a low, open sand area with tufts of dune grass and areas of packed sand. Loose, shifting sands lie farther south. Dead Lake is a dark, thin lake with a marshy, snag-dotted shore and an ocean foredune at its northwest end. An osprey nest tops one snag.

Forgoing the trek to Dead Lake and Dead Lake Dune, remain on the 2-track at 0.4 mile to arrive at the ocean. Where the trail curves right, travelers enjoy a semi-shaded tour at the edge of the woods. The trail arrives at the beach north of Point St. George, where a creek breaches the dune.

The beach here is cobble-riddled, with a ragged ocean edge. Large drift logs lay against the grass-topped dune. Gulls are numerous, bathing in the fresh water. The long open strand calls to the wanderer. Return the way you came.

*Access:* From Old Mill Road, bear left onto Sand Hill Road, opposite the Fish and Game headquarters. Trailhead parking is at the end of Sand Hill (2 miles from the Northcrest Drive–Old Mill Road Junction).

**Canoeing.** While the aquatic vegetation and mostly 4-foot lake depths discourage the use of motor-powered boats, these large, interconnected lakes are ideal for the canoeist. Paddling the shoreline and exploring the marshy lake arms promise numerous and varied bird and aquatic mammal sightings. Bald eagles often perch on the trees overlooking the lakes. Wind and open water pose a major threat, so be alert to weather changes.

*Access:* For the easiest access, from US 101 go 3.4 miles north on Northcrest/Lake Earl Drive. There, turn west on Lakeview Drive, and follow it 0.8 mile to the California Department of Fish and Game's primitive launch site.

## JEDEDIAH SMITH REDWOODS STATE PARK

**Hours/Season:** Year-round
**Facilities:** 107 developed redwood and riverside campsites, hike/bike camp, picnic area, visitor center, hiker-only trails, restrooms, showers, dump station
**For Information:** (707) 464-9533
**Access:** From Crescent City, go north on US 101 and east on US 199 to reach the park in 5 miles, the camp in 9 miles.

Named for an early-day adventurer who helped open California to discovery, this 9,500-acre park houses one of the state's premier virgin redwood forests. Situated along the Smith River, it boasts the 5,000-acre National Tribute Grove and the breathtaking Stout Memorial Grove, home to a record-size coastal redwood 20 feet in diameter and 340 feet high.

The Smith Wild and Scenic River has the distinction of being the last free-flowing major river in California. Its pristine waters draw anglers for the fall salmon and steelhead runs and for summer fly fishing. Kingfisher, dipper, and osprey frequent the river corridor.

*Howland Hill Road, Jedediah Smith Redwoods State Park*

## Attractions and Activities

**Howland Hill Road Auto Tour—Stout Grove Access.** This 6.9-mile narrow and sometimes potholed gravel road takes motorists across the interior of the park for a slow look at a splendid redwood gallery. Below the road is a side drainage to Mill Creek; above it is statuesque forest. Hemlock, fir, tanoak, and myrtle complete the complex, while rhododendron splashes it with springtime pink.

The route accesses several trailheads, including one to Stout Grove (1.2 miles from the north gate). From the parking area, follow the closed paved road downhill to the riverside grove. It is easy to see why it was the first acquisition of the park—it exhausts superlatives. A 0.5-mile loop explores the flat of 1,500- to 2,000-year-old trees, and a side trail follows the Smith River upstream for 0.5 mile. In summer, Stout Grove also may be reached by a foot trail from camp that follows the seasonal bridges across the river and Mill Creek.

*Access:* From camp, go 2.2 miles east on US 199, take a sharp right, and cross the main stem and South Fork Smith River bridges. The entrance is off Douglas Park Drive. The route ends at Elk Valley Road, south of Crescent City.

**Simpson-Reed Discovery Trail.** This 0.5-mile nature trail loop offers a first-rate introduction to the redwood forest; brochures are usually available at the trailhead. The tour showcases a number of the big trees, huge root systems, burls, fire-hollowed trunks, nurse trees, and cascading ferns. The 0.25-mile Peterson Trail connects to the loop for a figure-eight tour, adding views of a riparian area, more redwoods, and a double-anchored bigleaf maple that arches over the trail and again takes root.

*Access:* The trail is north off US 199, 2 miles west of the campground.

**Hatton Loop.** This 0.25-mile trail quickly splits into three forks. The left fork begins the Hatton-Hiouchi Trail; the right and center forks form the loop. For a clockwise tour of the loop, follow the steps up the slope, bypassing some ancient snags. A rich understory of fern, oxalis (redwood sorrel), and salal complements the soaring forest. Midway, a spur leads to a bench overlooking a beautiful, untamed grove, brimming with downfalls and greenery.

*Access:* Begin on the south side of US 199, opposite the Simpson-Reed Discovery Trail.

**Hatton-Hiouchi and Mill Creek Trails.** Passing between US 199 and Howland Hill Road, this 5.5-mile one-way tour explores redwood forest, river, and creek habitats.

As hikers head east from Hatton Loop, dead-end spurs confuse the early going, but disappear as the trail rolls across the redwood slope above US 199. The hike passes beneath single towers, snags, and family groups and requires some ducking under or skirting of logs. Traffic sounds intrude. Rhododendron, myrtle, and tanoak weave a rich midstory. At 1.25 miles, the trail changes name as it tours the Smith River upstream toward Stout Grove.

Now on the Hiouchi Trail, hikers quickly descend toward the blue-green Smith River. A side path leads to a gravel bar, while the main trail passes through a fire-hollowed redwood snag, continuing upstream. A sharp bank now separates it from the river. Before long, a scenic redwood stand straddles the trail.

At 2.25 miles, large boulders jut into the river, framing a pool used by mergansers. A memorial bench is just ahead, and mossy boulders mark the redwood-deciduous slope. Where the trail dips, hikers glimpse the Smith River–Mill Creek confluence. At 2.75 miles, approaching Stout Grove, the trail enters a shadowy, ancient forest. Stairsteps down to the left lead to a summer bridge on the river; people from camp

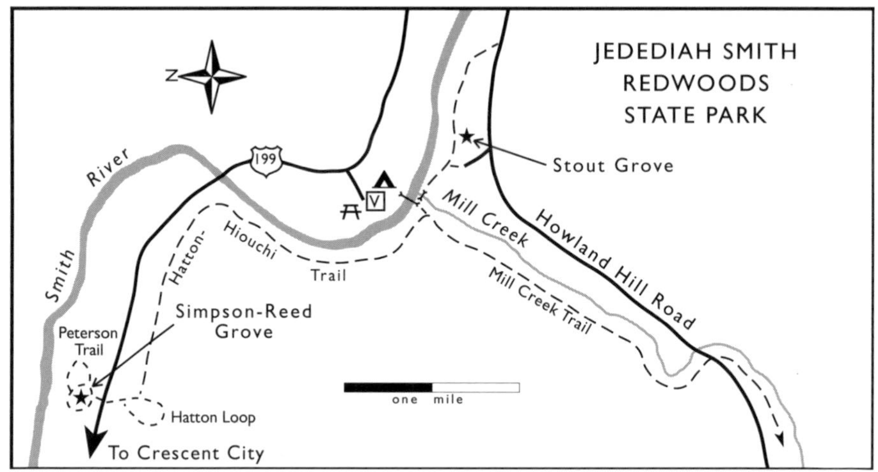


may join the hike here. Not far from the first, a second seasonal bridge over Mill Creek links up with the main Stout Grove area.

Staying on this side of Mill Creek, hikers find huge redwood sentinels marking the way. Where the route curves upstream along the creek, be alert as secondary spurs can mislead. At 3 miles, the trail climbs out of the grove, meeting a T junction; go left for a tour of the Mill Creek Trail to Howland Hill Road.

Extending the hike to Howland Hill Road, hikers tour a mixed redwood forest complex, where rhododendrons promise a showy spring display. The forest mostly denies views of Mill Creek, even where the trail contours the slope above it. On the bank at 4.5 miles, hikers first encounter the 30-foot-wide stream, coursing over a rocky bed. Maple, salmonberry, and alder line it.

Ahead, a raised path crosses a soggy riparian area. Where the trail squeezes between two tumbled giants, note the long roots of a hemlock wrapped around one. The final hike leg is in forest.

*Access:* Begin south off US 199, opposite the Simpson-Reed Discovery Trail, 2 miles west of the campground.

## Del Norte Coast Redwoods State Park

**Hours/Season:** Year-round; campground may close in winter

**Facilities:** 145 developed wooded campsites, coastal picnic area, hiker trails, restrooms, dump station

**For Information:** (707) 464-9533

**Access:** Leaving Crescent City, go 3.5 miles south on US 101 to enter the park, 5 miles to reach the campground turn.

This park brings together areas of virgin and second-growth redwood forest, the Mill Creek riparian habitat, and an especially impressive, rugged stretch of coast with plunging cliffs and pocket beaches. Where enough light penetrates the redwood canopy, rhododendron bushes thrive, showering the forest with springtime cheer. Some of these bushes grow to 30 feet tall. Tanoak, sword fern, oxalis, and salal are other floral species of the coastal redwood rain forest. In camp, huge stumps recall the former forest; this area was logged in the 1920s.

At the park's south end, west off US 101, the Wilson Creek picnic area looks out onto False Klamath Cove. It offers a convenient leg stretch, picturesque offshore and near-shore rocks, tidepools, and some good wave watching. Anglers can fish in Wilson Creek.

## Attractions and Activities

**Damnation Creek Trail.** This hike offers a workout with a round-trip distance of 5 miles and an elevation change of 1,000 feet. It is also the most celebrated trail in the park, featuring both a thick ancient redwood forest and a dramatic introduction to the coast.

The trail begins with a mild 0.4-mile rise, before the long descent to the ocean. Giant redwoods enfold the route, drawing the eyes skyward. Even the smaller trees, which provide a scale for size, are big. Ferns, rhododendron, tanoak, and oxalis accent the journey. Fire-hollowed trees, snags, and burls shaggy with leatherleaf ferns vie for notice. The noise from US 101 is the only drawback.

At 0.8 mile, the trail meets and angles right across a closed road. A trail post and cairn mark where the footpath resumes, descending the slope. Here, Douglas firs intermix with the redwoods. Where the trail overlooks the Damnation Creek drainage, at 1 mile, hikers lose the intrusion of US 101, and switchbacks come more regularly.

By 1.7 miles, Sitka spruce replaces the redwood as the star of the slope. Salmonberry is now part of the floral mix, and teasing ocean glimpses urge on hikers. The descent grows steeper, with footbridge crossings of small side creeks.

At 2.5 miles, the trail reaches an open point overlooking the ocean. The final 20 feet to the beach can be treacherous, especially when wet. Nonetheless, the ocean vista rewards, with the mouth of Damnation Creek, a small sea-carved arch below the vantage, sheer headland walls, offshore stacks, and a small, wonderfully wild, black, rocky beach.

The forest setting and shade offset the burden of the uphill return.

*Access:* The trailhead turnout is on the west side of US 101, 4.1 miles south of the Mill Creek Campground turnoff.

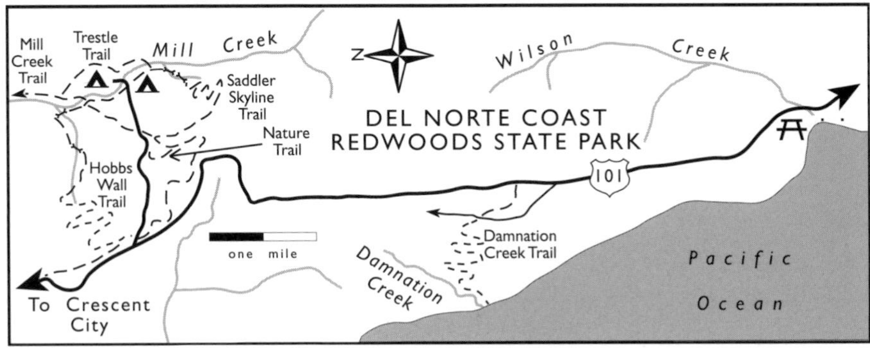

**Mill Creek–Hobbs Wall Circuit.** This 5.8-mile loop ties together several park trails for a moderate-to-strenuous riparian and forest tour, climbing and descending some 700 feet in elevation.

From camp, the hike begins by following Mill Creek downstream, touring a riparian zone of red alder, salmonberry, and sword fern. At 0.5 mile, bear left, uphill for the loop; seasonally, a summer bridge continues the Mill Creek Trail to the right. Ahead, follow the Hobbs Wall Trail across the footbridge (a shorter circuit is possible, heading left on the Saddler Skyline Trail).

The Hobbs Wall Trail continues 0.3 mile along Mill Creek, then swings left following an old skid road upstream along a side creek. Second-growth redwoods mount the slope above the grassy avenue. At 1.2 miles, look for a rusted logging cable next to the trail, just before the footbridge crossing. As the route climbs the opposite slope, the narrowing drainage brims with ferns.

At 1.6 miles, the trail again crosses the drainage (in winter, logs make the crossing possible; in summer, the drainage is likely dry). The trail then climbs with a vengeance, leaving behind the abundant ferns. At 2.3 miles, it reaches the park road near US 101. A path to its immediate right tours a memorial redwood grove; the loop crosses the park road, entering a remnant grove of ancient redwoods snug by US 101. Soon though, stumps appear, the big trees are fewer, and the second-growth trees again dominate. At 2.7 miles, hikers can see where redwoods were used to buttress US 101.

At 3.4 miles, the cushiony trail descends. Great areas of rhododendron promise a nice springtime show for the closing of the loop. At 4.2 miles, the trail levels out, meeting the Nature Trail; follow it to the right through an alder corridor to continue the tour.

Just before reaching the park road at 4.5 miles, bear right, leaving the Nature Trail via the unmarked Saddler Skyline Trail. Along the way, a few old stumps are literally jailed by the sprout rings of second-growth redwoods. The trail makes a rolling descent, crossing a couple of small drainages. At 5.5 miles, where the Trestle Trail heads right, the loop bears left toward camp. The tour ends near walk-in campsites numbers 4, 5, and 6.

*Access:* Find the Mill Creek trailhead and the start of the loop near the entrance to the campground loops.

## PRAIRIE CREEK REDWOODS STATE PARK

**Hours/Season:** Year-round

**Facilities:** 101 developed campsites, hike/bike campsites, picnic sites, visitor center, hiker and bicycle trails, restrooms, nonflush toilets, showers

**For Information:** (707) 488-2171 or (707) 488-2044

**Access:** On US 101 4.2 miles south of Klamath, take the Elk Prairie Parkway exit and go south for the park.

One of the stars of the California state park system, this 14,000-acre park in the Prairie Creek watershed preserves magnificent old-growth coastal redwoods, broad prairie meadows, a wild ocean shore, and free-roaming herds of Roosevelt elk. The park has 75 miles of trail, nearly 300 memorial groves, and miles and miles of untamed beach. Several record-size trees mark the forest, including one near the visitor center that sheltered a family for a time during the 1930s. Each

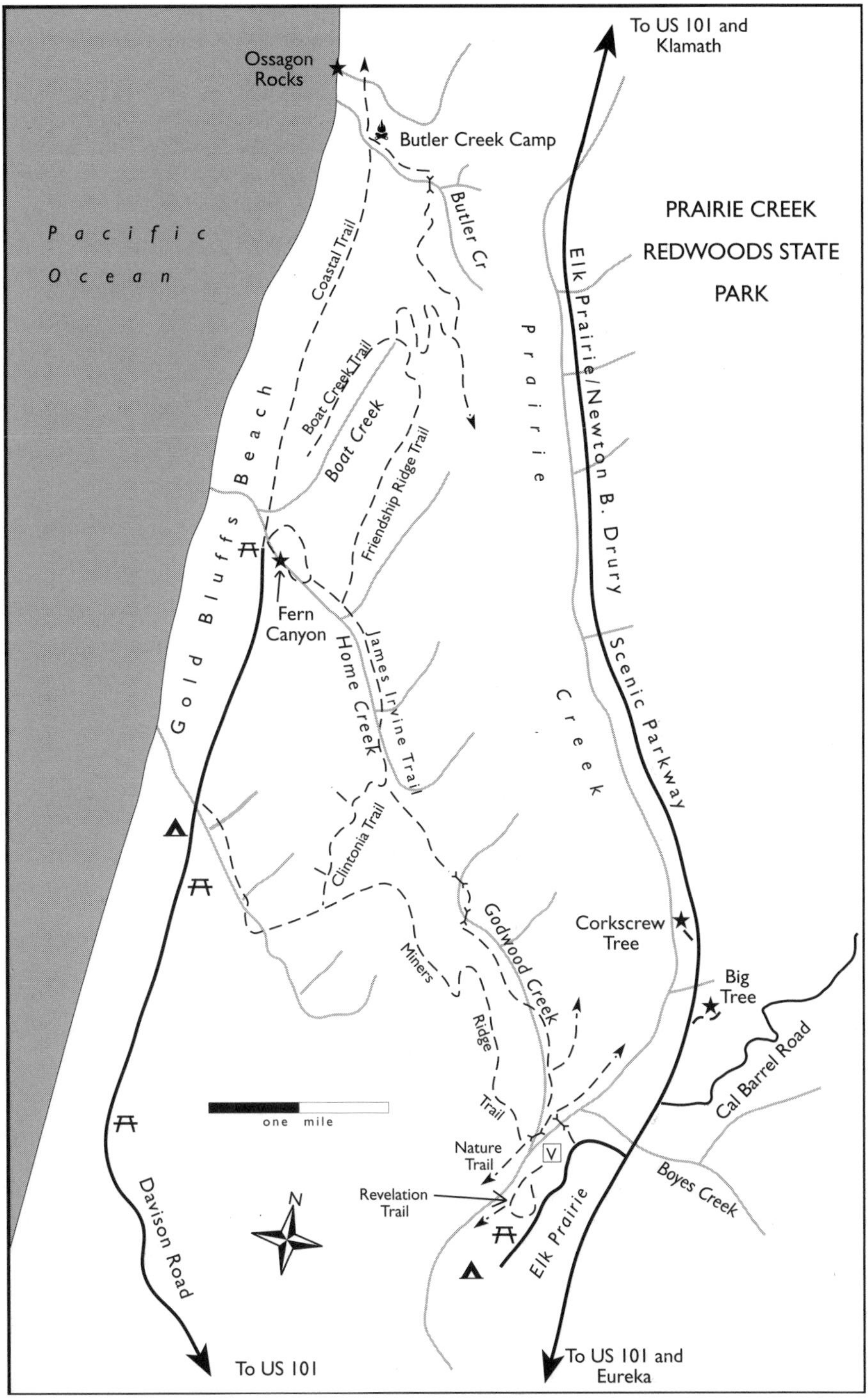

To US 101 and Klamath
Ossagon Rocks
Butler Creek Camp
Pacific Ocean
PRAIRIE CREEK REDWOODS STATE PARK
Butler Cr
Coastal Trail
Elk Prairie/Newton B. Drury Scenic Parkway
Prairie Creek
Boat Creek Trail
Boat Creek
Friendship Ridge Trail
Gold Bluffs Beach
Fern Canyon
James Irvine Trail
Home Creek
Clintonia Trail
Godwood Creek
Miners Ridge Trail
Corkscrew Tree
Big Tree
Cal Barrel Road
one mile
Nature Trail
Revelation Trail
Boyes Creek
Elk Prairie
N
Davison Road
To US 101
To US 101 and Eureka

August, the park hosts the annual Banana Slug Derby, a popular event.

At the park's rustic visitor center, located a mile north of the southern end of the parkway, travelers find a few exhibits on the elk, the coastal redwoods, and the Yurok Indians, who first occupied this area. A 30-minute video introduces the park, and at the small bookstore maps are available.

## Attractions and Activities

**Elk Prairie/Newton B. Drury Scenic Parkway.** Recently rededicated as the Newton B. Drury Scenic Parkway, this 9-mile-long US 101 bypass offers a relaxing drive through Prairie Creek Redwoods State Park. Along its length, travelers find ample opportunity to stop and sample a trail or pull into a vista parking lot, such as the one at Elk Prairie, where visitors can watch the Roosevelt elk rest and graze.

Nature trails to Big Tree and Corkscrew Tree are worth keeping an eye out for. Big Tree is 1,500 years old, stands 300 feet high, and boasts a 21-foot diameter. Its trailhead is on the east side of the parkway, 0.8 mile north of the visitor center turnoff. A paved 0.1-mile path leads to the tree. Corkscrew Tree features a strangely twisted redwood grouping. Its trailhead is on the west side of the parkway 0.5 mile north of the Big Tree turnout. To reach it, follow the earthen path paralleling the road north.

A possible side tour is 3-mile-long Cal Barrel Road. This narrow graveled side road allows a slower look at the big trees. It is open from 9:00 A.M. to 5:00 P.M. Look for it east off the parkway, 0.5 mile north of the visitor center turn.

*Access:* Take either of two marked parkway exits off US 101.

**Gold Bluffs Beach.** In 1851, the park's Gold Bluffs Beach was the site of a failed gold rush. Today, area campers and picnickers find the gold of solitude. The beautiful, broad, dark-sand beach, backed by a rolling dune-grass plain, invites wanderers, but the loose, deep sand and cant to the water provide a workout. Elk track may be seen on the beach, or the animals themselves may be spied ranging the bordering grassy plain. To the north, rounded, skyward-projecting Ossagon Rocks, located both on and near shore, suggest a possible turnaround. From the campground, the rocks represent about an 8.4-mile round-trip hike; from Fern Canyon, about 5.4 miles round trip.

Surf fishing for redtail perch and nighttime dip-netting for smelt are other favorite beach activities.

*Access:* Go 2.3 miles south on US 101 from the southern terminus of Elk Prairie Parkway, turn west on Davison Road, and proceed 3.6 miles to the start of Gold Bluffs Beach, 5.3 miles to the campground, and 6.8 miles to Fern Canyon. *The narrow, gravel road is open to conventional vehicles less than 8 feet wide and less than 24 feet long.*

**Revelation Trail.** This 0.5-mile nature trail offers the blind and wheelchair-bound an opportunity to experience the redwood-forest splendor. The seventeen interpretive stations are sensory-rich, featuring the sound, touch, and smell of the forest. A platform skirts one redwood giant, permitting an up-close assessment of its size and feel. Recorded tapes provide detailed explanations; tape players are available at the visitor center.

*Access:* Begin at the back of the visitor center.

**Fern Canyon–Friendship Ridge–Coastal Trail Loop.** This 7.5-mile loop, with a 600-foot elevation change, begins exploring the park's famous Fern Canyon, travels a Sitka spruce- and redwood-forested ridge, and returns overlooking the coastal plain.

Hikers enter Fern Canyon, traveling upstream along clear-spilling Home Creek.

*Roosevelt elk, Prairie Creek Redwoods State Park*

It is a rock-hopping, wading, crisscrossing journey. How wet you get is a matter of preference and season. Squeezing the drainage are 50-foot vertical walls, dripping and green-draped. Six kinds of fern, including five-finger ferns, plus horsetail reeds, oxalis, waterleaf, and moss contribute to the bower.

Climbing from Fern Canyon, the trail meets the James Irvine Trail at 0.5 mile. There, go right or east beginning the ridge segment of the loop, passing through a rich Sitka spruce forest. Skunk cabbage covers the drainages. At 0.75 mile, follow the Friendship Ridge Trail left for a rolling tour north. Redwoods quickly join the forest mix. While the trees are big, none are gargantuan, although some of the snags could qualify. In the distance, the ocean sounds.

By 1.75 miles, the trail contours the west slope above the Boat Creek drainage. In just over another mile, it bypasses the Boat Creek Trail, which heads left only to dead-end in 1.7 miles. Where the trail slowly switchbacks up the slope, hikers bypass a couple of memorial groves, before arriving at a ridgetop junction at 3.25 miles. Go left for the loop.

Soon after passing a memorial bench, the descent begins, and Sitka spruce and hemlock frame the lower reaches of the trail. At 5.25 miles, it enters the Butler Creek Hike/Bike Camp.

From the camp, the loop follows the Coastal Trail left, touring below the bluff. Cyclists share the mostly open trail, separated from the beach by a wetland and dune-grass plain. Killdeer and migratory ducks can be seen here, as well as elk. In places, trees mask the vertical cliff. At 6.25 miles, the first of several wet-season falls streaks the cliff wall. With Boat Creek and Home Creek crossings, the hike ends at 7.5 miles.

*Access:* Reach Fern Canyon by going 6.8 miles northwest on Davison Road (see Gold Bluffs Beach access for complete directions).

**Miners Ridge–Clintonia–James Irvine Loop.** This 5.7-mile loop with a 400-foot elevation change visits some grand redwoods, travels the historic supply route to miners, and tours the riparian bottom of Godwood Creek.

The tour begins by crossing the Prairie Creek footbridge. Each fall salmon and steelhead return to this protected water, closed to fishing. As the hike follows the Nature Trail downstream for 0.2 mile, the trees are jaw-dropping big.

Here, a clockwise tour follows the Miners Ridge Trail through ancient redwood forest. After a side drainage, it starts to climb Miners Ridge, offering new perspectives across and down to the giant trees. Deer and sword fern, red and black huckleberry, salal, and trillium decorate the floor. Benches mark the route.

At 0.75 mile, the trail tops the ridge, traveling a redwood-fir forest complex, and at 1.2 miles it tags the high point. Sunbursts, shadows, and fog create an ever-changing stage. At 2.1 miles, the trail departs the ridge and contours the slope coming to a T junction; go right on the Clintonia Trail for the loop. This tour segment travels a time-healed road lined by young hemlocks. Spurs lead from it to memorial groves. By 3 miles, second-growth Sitka spruce join the ranks, with the redwoods soon following suit.

At 3.2 miles, the loop continues on the James Irvine Trail to the right, passing through a world-class, visually rich redwood-spruce forest, with mammoth trees. On the flat, boardwalks and footbridges advance the trail along the Godwood Creek drainage. Banana slugs and wrens may be seen along the way. Remain on the James Irvine Trail.

At 5.5 miles, the loop closes at the Nature Trail; go left to return to the trailhead.

*Access:* Start at the large trailhead sign at the northeast corner of the visitor center parking lot opposite the entrance station.

**Elk Viewing.** The elk are most commonly and most easily seen at Elk and Boyes prairies off the parkway across from the visitor center; there is turnout parking. But they also may be seen in the meadow flat, as you turn west off US 101 for Davison Road, with a good number seen along the grassy dunes and coastal slope above Gold Bluff Beach.

Typically, the elk travel in groups of ten to thirty. During the fall rut, the mature bulls join the otherwise mostly female herds. The calves begin arriving in June. Keep a safe viewing distance at all times.

## Humboldt Lagoons State Park—Harry A. Merlo State Recreation Area

**Hours/Season:** Year-round

**Facilities:** Environmental and primitive boat-in camps, picnic sites, boat launches, off-road-vehicle beach access, nonflush toilets (Humboldt Lagoons); *bring water* (both)

**For Information:** (707) 488-2041

**Access:** These two park units line an 8.5-mile stretch of US 101, beginning 4 miles south of Orick. Look for the marked turns for Stone Lagoon, Dry Lagoon, and Big Lagoon Park Road.

These little-developed, connected park units offer access to two large, open-water lagoons, the Dry Lagoon marsh, miles of sandy spit, and a coastal meadow where a herd of Roosevelt elk commonly grazes. Bald, cone-shaped Sharp Point is the area's most prominent feature. The lagoon, surf, marsh, and coastal scrub habitats support a variety of resident and migratory birds, including heron, egret, brown pelican, surf scoter, and sanderling.

The beaches all have loose sand with patches of fine gravel and surf-rounded quartz. Sifting through the sands, beachgoers may find fragments of agate and black jade. Abrupt coastal knolls and onshore rocks fragment the state park strands. At Stone Lagoon, the wave slope (the beach area below the high tide line) is open to off-road vehicles.

Ice plant and other salt-tolerant floral species sporadically spread over the low dunes and lagoon shores. Some of the bald corridors through the vegetation indicate where past storms and floods have breached the spit, allowing the lagoon and ocean waters to mingle. Typically, the lagoons breach three to four times a year.

During such times, lagoon depths can drop dramatically. Records show drops of up to 6 feet in a single hour. Tides and wind, in turn, heal the breach, completing the natural cycle.

Ocean waters here are cold and treacherous, with a stiff current and sharp undertow; swimming is best restricted to the lagoons. Fishing, boating, windsurfing, and canoeing are other popular activities at these shallow coastal lakes. In winter, waterfowl hunting is allowed over their waters, while the lagoon shores remain protected.

## Attractions and Activities

**Stone Lagoon Hiking.** Here, hikers must share the sandy avenue with off-road vehicles. To the north, hikers quickly enter Redwood National Park; to the south lies 1.5 miles of open sand. When tides allow passage around the cliff jut at 1.5 miles, an additional 0.3 mile may be added, rounding a small cove to the base of Sharp Point. The quartz-veined, metamorphic rock of the cliff and onshore rocks is notably devoid of tidal life.

Return as you came or via the lagoon shore, which is closed to all vehicles. It affords a quiet, trackless return, with different discoveries of the animal and plant life common to the brackish water and the lagoon shore.

*Access:* Stone Lagoon is west off US 101, 4 miles south of Orick. *Go slow on its rough and narrow entrance road.*

**Dry Lagoon Hiking.** This coastal access fronts an 0.8-mile stretch of beach, with an impressive scatter of drift logs between the marsh and beach strand. Vehicles are not allowed here. Agate seekers walk with their heads lowered.

Inland, the sunlight glistens on the standing water of the marsh, which brims with bulrushes. Claiming the drier marsh reaches are the 2- to 3-foot-tall, ball-shaped Sitka spruce and similarly wind-shaped waxmyrtle. To the north, Sharp Point, with waves washing up the sides of its cliff, signals the end of the hike.

*Access:* Dry Lagoon is reached 6.7 miles south of Orick; go west 1 mile to the beach.

**Harry A. Merlo Hiking.** This state recreation area offers visitors a carefree stroll along the 4-mile wilderness spit of Big Lagoon. Herons can be seen along the lagoon shoreline, sanderlings along the ocean shore. The loose sand and rolling slope of the beach offer a good leg workout. Extensive Big Lagoon is deserving of its name.

*Access:* The state recreation area and spit are reached via Big Lagoon County Park. From US 101, 12.5 miles south of Orick, take the exit for Big Lagoon Park Road and head west. In 0.3 mile, go right on Big Lagoon Park Road. Walking the beach north, you quickly enter Harry A. Merlo State Recreation Area. *The county charges a parking fee.*

**Canoeing/boating/windsurfing.** Big and Stone lagoons both welcome wind- and motor-powered travel. Big Lagoon covers more than 1,400 acres and is 3.5 miles long. Much smaller Stone Lagoon has a 10-mile-per-hour boat speed and is the better-size water body for the canoeist.

*Access:* Launch sites are at Stone Lagoon Day Use and Big Lagoon County Park; an unmarked, primitive launch is west off US 101, 3.7 miles south of Dry Lagoon.

**Fishing.** Big and Stone lagoons are open year-round for fishing; trout and salmon populate these waters. Anglers must use artificial lures with barbless hooks, and in Stone Lagoon, the minimum catch size is 16 inches.

**Elk Viewing.** Look for the Roosevelt elk herd in the meadow on the west side of US 101, 0.3 mile north of the Dry Lagoon turnoff. In winter, solitary bulls with burdensome racks roam the shoulders of the highway; some fifty cows complete the herd. Calving occurs in late May and June.

# PATRICK'S POINT STATE PARK

**Hours/Season:** Year-round
**Facilities:** 124 developed forested campsites, picnic areas, small museum, bookstore, historic site, hiker trails, restrooms
**For Information:** (707) 677-3570
**Access:** On US 101, go 14.3 miles south from Orick or 5 miles north from Trinidad, and take the Patrick's Point exit. Head 0.4 mile west and turn right for the park.

This park showcases a 3-mile stretch of coastline featuring a chiseled headland, dramatic stacks and offshore rocks, secluded rocky beaches, and sandy 2-mile-long Agate Beach, where semiprecious stones may be found. This park also pays tribute to its Native American past, with a replica village built by contemporary Yuroks in the tradition of their ancestors.

Wedding Rock, Patrick's Point, and Palmer's Point all offer elevated vantages from which to spy the spouts of gray whales. Their annual migration takes them past the park, November through April. Sea lions and harbor seals are year-round passersby. Inland, the ancient sea stacks of Ceremonial and Lookout rocks overlook the park; trails lead to their summits.

## Attractions and Activities

**Yurok Indian Village.** This replica Yurok village, dubbed "Sumeg," reveals the sophistication of this coastal tribe, both in its culture and in its standard of living. Making up the village are living quarters, ceremonial dressing quarters, a sweat house, and dance pit. The sturdy square structures stand 3 to 4 feet high and are made of pole-lashed, hewn-redwood planks. Their pit and stone-floor interiors can be viewed through the circular crawlways. A leaflet available at the village identifies the various buildings and their uses. Each summer, the park celebrates Sumeg Village Days, with traditional ceremonies and dance; the public is welcome.

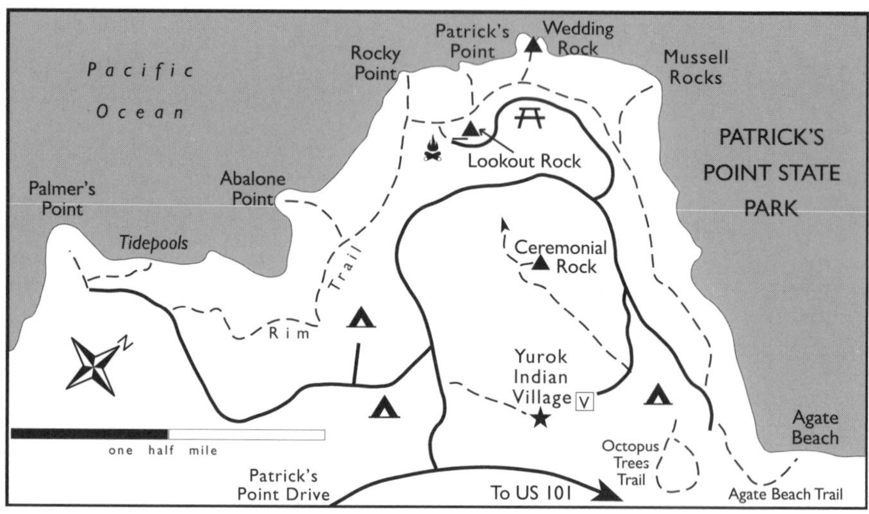

*Coastal cliff sunset, Patrick's Point State Park*

*Access:* The village is easily reached via trail from the entrance station parking lot or from Red Alder group picnic area.

**Agate Beach Trail.** A 0.3-mile trail descends via stairs and a wide footpath to this 2-mile stretch of beach. Coastal scrub and a few Sitka spruce frame the descent, with a picnic site located partway down. The trail arrives on the beach near the mouth of a small creek. The meeting of cliffs and sea quickly halts any walk south, but the beach north offers a lengthy stroll.

The sheer, golden sandstone cliffs framing the route taper in height as you approach Big Lagoon. Fine gravel patches mark the beach, calling beachcombers to kneel and sift for treasures. All-day hikers may extend the trek north, passing through Big Lagoon County Park to Harry A. Merlo State Recreation Area and walking its 4-mile spit.

*Access:* The trail begins at the northwest end of the day-use parking area at Agate Campground.

**Octopus Trees Trail.** Also called the Spruce-Hemlock Trail, this 0.25-mile self-guided loop explores the park's remnant stand of old-growth Sitka spruce, with its 300-year-old trees and typical coastal scrub vegetation. "Octopus tree" is a descriptive name for a spruce that started life atop a log, extending its roots to the ground. When its nurse tree rotted away, it was left with tentaclelike feet.

*Access:* The trail begins near sites 110 and 111 in Agate Campground; non-campers use the day-use parking lot.

**Rim Trail.** A direct north-south tour measures 2 miles, but six 0.25-mile spurs descending to coves and vista points and climbing to rock outposts build on that. Along the Rim Trail proper, the coastal vistas are few and anticlimactic relative to those found at the ends of each of the six detours. Coastal scrub and red alder, along with a few scenic wind-shaped Sitka spruce enclose the route. Grasses, salal, bracken fern, and blackberry weave the understory.

The vista detours are all earned rewards, with steep stairways descending the 100-foot walls of the headland and/or mounting the prominent points. Views north include Big Lagoon, Sharp Point, and the coast beyond, while views south focus on the park's rugged headland character and the coast curving to Eureka. Sea stacks, a jumbled rock shore, abrupt cliffs, and high-splashing waves engage at each stop. In places, the churned water creates a white foam in contrast to the dark cliff and rock.

All of the side trails to the named headland features are well-marked, except that for Abalone Point, which is worth seeking out. The spurs that head inland lead to parking and picnic areas, inviting hopscotch touring or doorway peeks at the Rim Trail offering.

For visitors with limited time, Wedding Rock is one "don't-miss" stop. Its 0.2-mile spur is quickly reached from a day-use parking lot at the northwest end of the park. A low rock wall rims the terraced vista post atop this picturesque rock. Here, visitors enjoy their final looks north up the Redwood Coast, as well as fine views south past Patrick's Point. During whale-watching season, visitors armed with thermal jugs and binoculars commonly top the rock. Winds sometimes turn back travelers before they are tired of the view.

Again, for those with limited time, the short trails at Palmer's Point are equally deserving of a look and easily reached from the end of the park road.

*Access:* The Rim Trail travels between the southwest end of the day-use parking lot at Agate Campground and Palmer's Point.

**Tidepooling.** To the north below Palmer's Point is a vast rocky expanse jutting into the water. Here, sea palms, mussels, and other intertidal life make for discovery, but be careful negotiating the rock jumble to reach the tidepool area. Loud, sharp barks sound the close presence of sea lions that frequent the offshore rocks south of here.

*Access:* Palmer's Point parking is at the park's south end. Bear right at the trail fork, descending stairs to the cove.

## TRINIDAD AND LITTLE RIVER STATE BEACHES

**Hours/Season:** Daylight hours

**Facilities:** Picnic area, hiker trails, restroom, nonflush toilets (Trinidad State Beach); none (Little River)

**For Information:** (707) 445-6547 or (707) 677-3570

**Access:** Both are off US 101. For Trinidad State Beach, exit at Trinidad and head west through town for 0.2 mile, turning north on Stagecoach Road. The main access is immediately on the left; Elk Head access is on the left in 0.7 mile. For Little River State Beach, go 3.6 miles south of Trinidad, take the Crannell Road exit, and head west to Clam Beach County Park. Park there and hike north 200 feet.

Trinidad State Beach brings together a protected cove, impressive headlands, a rocky coast, and snatches of sandy beach, with ample vantage points to enjoy them all. Centrally located in the pretty cove waters between Elk and Trinidad heads is a picturesque rock island, tree-topped Pewetole Island. Farther offshore, Flatiron Rock sometimes sports resting sea lions. Surfers arrive at daybreak to await the perfect wave, while surf fishermen perch atop the coastal rocks, casting their lines in expectation.

Trinidad's main access holds a grassy picnic area, with trailheads and a beach approach. At its turnaround, a 0.2-mile path leads to the Humboldt State University Marine Lab and visitor area complete with exhibits and an aquarium; for information, phone (707) 677-3671. The park's Elk Head Access, to the north, has a large gravel parking area, with trailheads. It is less frequented, known mainly by locals.

South of Trinidad, visitors find mile-long, undeveloped Little River State Beach adjacent to Clam Beach County Park. This beach is a broad, uninterrupted sandy avenue, welcoming hikers, horseback riders, and drivers of street vehicles. While horses are also allowed on segments of the Trinidad Beach trails, that system is too short to warrant saddling up. Together with Clam Beach, Little River is the better equestrian destination.

Low dunes topped by lupine and dune grass back the beach. Broken sand dollars, razor clams, and crab shells dot the fine sand, the few prizes of the beachcomber. The hard beach surface welcomes easy walking, but the state lands end south of the Little River.

## Attractions and Activities

**Mill Creek Trail.** This trail descends from the picnic area, passing through an area of Sitka spruce and fir. Salmonberry and sword fern frame the wide trailbed; alders line the cool, moist drainage of Mill Creek. At 0.25 mile, the trail forks. A few strides to the left lead to a small, sandy beach where the creek enters the cove. To the right stands the Mill Creek footbridge (0.5 mile).

Once across the bridge, the horse trail continues the tour north along the bluff to reach the Elk Head parking area and trailhead at 1.25 miles. This stretch of trail, along with a side loop to the west, tours both second-growth forest and red alder woodland, but neither the trail nor the side loop offers ocean vistas.

*Access:* The Mill Creek Trail leaves the picnic area near the restroom at the main Trinidad State Beach access.

**Elk Head Trail.** This is a 1.5-mile round-trip trail with multiple Elk Head viewpoints, detours to the beach, and a cliff-top vista.

Touring a raised hump, the hard-surfaced trail passes through a Sitka spruce and red alder scrub habitat. At 0.1 mile, a stairway to the left leads to the beach; the headland tour continues straight.

Along this part of the bay, rock outcrops divide the beach into three short strands; only low tides and rock scrambles allow their connection. Red alders back the beach, and the cliffs of Elk Head and Pewetole Island contribute to the view.

Forgoing the beach detour, at the 0.25-mile junction, stay straight for a clockwise tour of the headland. Where the trail enters a grassy flat, spurs radiate to vantages, offering different perspectives on the bay, Trinidad Head, the coastal bluffs, offshore rocks, and the blue horizon.

At 0.5 mile, pass through the hiker gate on the left for a 0.2-mile detour. It travels sections of trail and stairs, to an exciting vista atop a flat rock some 30 feet above the water. Here, visitors find sweeping views north and south of the rocky coast, with chance looks at sea lions (year-round) and gray whales (November through April).

Returning to the loop (0.9 mile), bear left. The trail now passes through a thick coastal scrub corridor, as it draws to a close back at the 0.25-mile junction. To end the hike, go left for the parking lot.

*Access:* This trail leaves from Trinidad's Elk Head parking area or may be reached via the Mill Creek Trail.

*Crags, Castle Crags State Park*

## Castle Crags State Park

**Hours/Season:** When snow is absent
**Facilities:** 64 developed forested campsites, environmental campsites, picnic area, vista point, hiker trails, horse trail (Pacific Crest Trail only), restrooms, showers
**For Information:** (916) 235-2684
**Access:** From I-5, 6 miles south of Dunsmuir, take the Castle Crags exit and go right for the main campground, left for the picnic area and additional camping.

Castle Crags State Park is famous for its dramatic vertical skyline of glacier-planed granitic spires. Since the days of the California-Oregon Stage, the prominent crags have attracted the attention of the Upper Sacramento Valley traveler. The park's upper reaches, which border Castle Crags Wilderness, are indisputably wild.

In addition, the forested park enjoys 2 miles of Upper Sacramento River frontage, including Soda Springs. The mineral waters of these continuously bubbling springs are captured in a foot-deep well. Some 28 miles of hiker trail explore the park, with 10 miles of the Pacific Crest Trail (PCT) open for equestrian use. The PCT passes through the park at the base of the crags.

River fishing is open from April through November. Prize rainbow trout may be caught, using a fly, bait, or lure. The fishing here is catch-and-release only. In spring, the snowmelt sends forth a fast-rushing river. By summer, the waters have receded, approaching creek size, but leaving behind some inviting swimming holes.

## Attractions and Activities

**Vista Point.** A 0.1-mile trail mounts the Vista Point knoll, which presents an exciting panorama of the region enfolding the park. Views include showy Mount Shasta to the north, jagged Castle Crags and the round top of Castle Dome just outside the park, and Grey Rocks at the crest of Flume Ridge to the southwest. Rustic benches and picnic tables suggest a lengthier stay. When ready to surrender the view, return as you came.

*Access:* On the west side of I-5, reach the point following the park road uphill away from the campground. There is parking for fourteen vehicles.

**Crags/Indian Springs Trail.** This hiker trail climbs 2 miles to Indian Springs or 2.7 miles to the base of the crags and Castle Dome. The latter hike has an elevation change of 2,200 feet.

The earthen trail enters a mixed forest, where the light-colored leaves of the dogwood and maple shower through the evergreen boughs. At the fork at 0.3 mile, bear left for the Crags/Indian Springs Trail and the start of the climb. Ahead is the junction with the PCT; cross over it, continuing uphill.

Here, the trail travels a ridge of black oak, soon replaced by a tight evergreen forest. The trail remains wide, with a steady gradient. At the 1-mile junction is a locator map; continue uphill. Starflower and iris accent the forest floor. At 1.2 miles, as the trail enters Castle Crags Wilderness, hikers encounter a steep 0.1-mile segment.

At 1.4 miles come the first tree-filtered views of the crags, Castle Dome, and later Grey Rocks. Flowering phlox colors the open pine ridge, where the trail levels out. At the saddle junction at 1.8 miles, going left 0.2 mile leads to Indian Springs, a scenic maple- and cedar-lined freshwater springs, with a mossy weeping wall; en route, hikers snare overhead views of the crags. Go right to continue out of the park to Castle Dome.

Even if you do not plan on going all the way to the dome, it is worthwhile hiking the next 0.1 mile for an open view of Castle Dome and Mount Shasta and her side volcanos. The basin below cradles a small dome feature.

As the trail to Castle Dome contours and switchbacks upslope, it passes through a scrubbier vegetation, rounding granite outcrops. At 2 miles is a great pairing of Castle Dome and Mount Shasta; more follow. Other looks include the Sacramento River drainage.

Winds wash up the slope, and vultures sail the currents. By 2.4 miles, over-the-shoulder looks capture the front ridge of Castle Crags. Ahead is a straight-on look at the imposing back wall. Low manzanita blotch the granite sands.

At the base of Castle Dome, keep an eye out for the small rock cairns pointing the way up the left side. At 2.7 miles, the trail arrives at a gap in the massive rock, affording a dizzying look down the vertical granite. The views of Shasta, an altered look at the dome, the hidden reaches of Castle Crags, and the wildness of the promontory excite; photo opportunities abound. Return as you came.

*Access:* Begin near Vista Point; the marked trailhead is on the left where the road curves to reach the parking lot.

**Indian Creek Trail.** For a clockwise tour of this 1-mile, 29-station interpretive loop, bear left at the initial fork; ask about brochures at the headquarters.

This rolling tour passes through open and choked forest, overlooks the clear-flowing, stepped waters of Indian Creek, and traverses utility corridor flats, where the tops of Castle Crags may be glimpsed. Manzanita, small oaks, ponderosa pine,

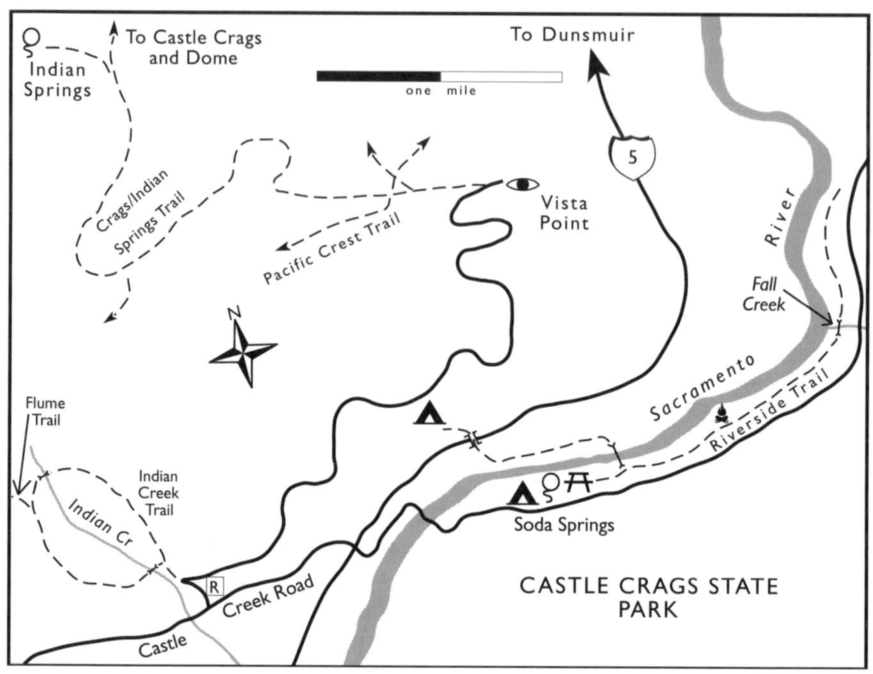


and sugar pine at times frame the route; poison oak has a patchy presence.

At 0.5 mile, where the trail tours a basalt-studded forest, the loop bears right. Some of the interpretive stations involve short side tours. At 0.75 mile, hikers may glimpse a wooden flume alongside the creek. Rusted logging remnants and a section of wooden pipe are other discoveries. Mosquitos can be a nuisance.

Midway along Indian Creek Trail, visitors may opt to hike the marked Flume Trail, which travels 0.75 mile and reaches Castle Creek Road at some environmental campsites. This trail follows a ditch and flume through dense forest. Return to the interpretive loop as you came.

*Access:* On the west side of I-5, begin opposite the headquarters/ranger station.

**Riverside Trail.** This 1.5-mile trail travels upstream along the Sacramento River, passing additional tables and potential swimming holes.

Ash and maple overhang the river, while a few azalea dot the bank. Mixed evergreens, maple, oak, and dogwood cloak the slope. At 0.1 mile, hikers come upon the suspension bridge that together with a railroad- and interstate-underpass links the park's Soda Springs and Crags areas; stay on the upstream trail.

Past the bridge, the trail contours the slope above the river. By 0.9 mile, it reaches the woody flat where environmental campsites are located. Upstream, the slope starts to rise, and at 1.2 miles a footbridge crosses Fall Creek. Here also, a flat basalt outcrop allows easy river access.

As the trail continues, columnar-planed boulders and a small rim mark the slope. Hikers gain limited looks at Castle Crags. The trail proceeds again at river level, where the tour comes to a halt at the park boundary (1.5 miles). Return as you came.

*Access:* On the east side of I-5, begin at the Soda Springs picnic area parking lot.

# Azalea State Reserve

**Hours/Season:** Year-round (best May through June)
**Facilities:** Picnic area, hiker trails (no dogs), *bring water*
**For Information:** (707) 488-2041 or (707) 677-3570
**Access:** From US 101 north of Arcata, take the North Bank Road exit. Head east on North Bank Road for 0.8 mile and turn left to reach the reserve in another 0.1 mile.

This is a cultured grove of western azaleas, manipulated to ensure both plant longevity and the production of peak blooms. In the wild, the azalea bush typically grows in disturbed areas and is replaced over time through forest succession. Here, the gardeners, or resource managers, carefully intervene in that natural process so the reserve's star feature will remain for generations of visitors to enjoy.

While the reserve presents its finest show in May and June, winter visitors may spy Steller's jays and songbirds amid the dormant, spindly armed bushes. Buds hint at next season's bounty, and blooms out of step with the season unfold, unadorned by green leaves.

## Attractions and Activities

**West Loop.** This 0.5-mile loop follows a wood-shaving path into a dense thicket of shrubs interwoven with sword fern and Himalaya berries. At a tiny drainage, the corridor opens up with alder, maple, and salmonberry. Licorice ferns adorn the mossy crooks of the trees.

At 0.2 mile, the trail passes a couple of big Sitka spruce, entering an area cleared by fire. Such gardening efforts are seen regularly at the reserve. In spring, the thousands of pinkish-white azalea blooms and their sweet, heady smell compensate for the temporary eyesores. The hike concludes by passing beneath a forked old-growth Douglas fir.

*Access:* Head north from the parking area, past the kiosk.

**East Loop.** This trail has three interlocking loops; the outer circuit measures 0.4 mile. The trail starts by entering a dense, tall grove of azalea bushes that often halt the photographer's steps. For a counterclockwise tour, head right, following the stairs out of the grove and onto the forested slope. Over-the-shoulder looks offer a different perspective on the floral showcase.

A pair of ancient, gnarled California laurel followed by an equally old, knotted fir line the start of the hillside tour. Elsewhere, second-growth fir and hemlock shade the route. At 0.3 mile, the trail descends, returning to the azalea grove for the final 0.1 mile. When wet, the trail can be slippery, so watch your step.

*Access:* Take the crosswalk from the parking area.

# Fort Humboldt State Historic Park

**Hours/Season:** 9:00 A.M. to 5:00 P.M.
**Facilities:** Picnic tables, visitor center, historic fort, logging display, restroom
**For Information:** (707) 445-6567

**Access:** In Eureka, 3.1 miles south of the CA 255–US 101 junction, turn east off US 101 onto Highland Avenue. The park entrance is on the left in 0.1 mile.

The discovery of gold on the Trinity River in 1849 led to the founding of supply settlements along Humboldt Bay and, ultimately, the establishment of Fort Humboldt in 1853. Conflicts erupting between the incoming settlers and Native Americans raised a call for army involvement.

Colonel Buchanan chose a bald, 40-foot bluff above Humboldt Bay for the fort. By the following year, fourteen buildings lined three sides of a parade-ground square kept open to the bay. The officers' quarters, barracks, surgery facility, and guardhouse were built first. A smithy, stable, and bakery later completed the fort.

Without any wars, fort life was monotonous, with soldiers answering the bells of the clock to rise, drill, eat, and sleep. Comforts were few: A moss-stuffed barrel chair was the envy of the garrison. Today, park visitors discover a silent fort amid open lawns. A few redwoods and pines, picnic tables, and pathways lend to its parklike setting.

## Attractions and Activities

**Self-guided Fort Tour.** The present-day fort consists of the hospital (built in 1862; now home to a museum), the reconstructed surgeon's quarters, and markers indicating the sites where the other buildings stood. The tidy, stark-white historic buildings recapture the orderliness of the fort of yesteryear. Long-range plans call for the fort's total reconstruction.

**Outdoor Logging Display.** A self-guided walking tour takes visitors through the history of redwood logging, beginning at a logger's cabin. Information panels provide the background. Steam donkeys, riggings, skid roads and rails, and a couple of 21-ton redwood logs (6 feet in diameter, 28 feet long) convey the magnitude of the enterprise. The third Saturday of each summer month, the park fires up some of the donkeys and locomotives, and in late April a logging competition takes place.

# WEAVERVILLE JOSS HOUSE STATE HISTORIC PARK

**Hours/Season:** Generally 10:00 A.M. to 5:00 P.M., except major holidays, Tuesdays, and Wednesdays; off-season visitors should call before coming
**Facilities:** Chinese temple, visitor center, restrooms
**For Information:** (916) 623-5284
**Access:** The park is in Weaverville's historic district on the south side of CA 299.

Shown by guided tour, "The Temple of the Forest Beneath the Clouds" is the oldest active Chinese place of worship in California. It was built by Chinese miners in 1874, with local materials, and includes a hand-carved altar front shipped from the homeland. This Taoist temple replaces an earlier one that burned to the ground.

Modeled after the rural temples of Southeast China, it is painted brick red and features ornate gables and cornices. The entryway shows a blue-painted-brick design that resembles Chinese tile. From right to left over the door are the Chinese characters for cloud, forest, and temple.

Weaverville Joss House

At the visitor center/museum, displays and artifacts relate the story of the Weaverville-area Chinese, from their leaving China to their work in the mines. The various panels describe the prejudice encountered by the Chinese, their society, their traditions, and their place in California history.

### Attractions and Activities

**Guided Temple Tour.** Walking around a spirit screen (two high wooden doors), visitors enter the darkness of the worship hall. Evil, which, according to tradition, can only pass in a straight line, is denied entry by the screens.

The atmosphere is rich in ceremony and legend. As visitors' eyes become accustomed to the dim lighting, they notice at the front of the room the carved wooden canopies housing the temple's deities.

Before the deities stands the altar, topped with incense sticks, prayer blocks, candles, wine cups, and fortune sticks. To reach the altar, worshipers must first pass the offering table, where fruit and drink are left for the gods.

Silk banners, screens, drums, gongs, and cymbals line the sides of the room. The tour guide identifies the items and describes the ceremonial role associated with each.

The tour then travels next door to the temple attendant's small, simple quarters and the courtroom where he arbitrated the disputes of the Chinese. This respected secular post was highly sought after and bid upon by various members of the Chinese community.

*Access:* Purchase tour tickets at the visitor center; the tour leaves from there at the top of the hour, every hour from 10:00 A.M. to 4:00 P.M.

## SHASTA STATE HISTORIC PARK

**Hours/Season:** Year-round; Courthouse Museum: 10:00 A.M. to 5:00 P.M., except major holidays, Tuesdays, and Wednesdays

**Facilities:** Picnic area, museum, historic buildings and sites, restrooms

**For Information:** (916) 243-8194

**Access:** In the town of Shasta (7.3 miles west of Redding and I-5), the park straddles CA 299.

The town of Shasta unites the small present-day community with the storefronts, ruins, and sites from the business district of yesteryear. A self-guided tour introduces the once-thriving mining-supply community that survived fire, only to fall victim to a dwindling gold supply and being bypassed by both stage and rail.

*Pioneer gravestone, Shasta State Historic Park*

Shasta sprang up following an 1848 gold discovery at Reading's Springs. The tent city was quickly replaced by wood-frame shops, homes, and businesses. Supplying the prospectors of the northern mines, Shasta grew to become the "Queen City of the North."

Then, in 1853, in an hour's time, fire consumed the entire Main Street district. Despite the setback, the town rallied, rebuilt, and again flourished. The red brick seen today in the ghost town's side-by-side businesses was a direct response to the danger of fire.

## Attractions and Activities

**Courthouse Museum.** Here, visitors find the restored courthouse, gallows, and frontier jail. Amid the rooms are some interesting artifacts from the Chinese era, cabinets of citizen memorabilia, mining records, and a "green box"—the safety trademark of the Wells Fargo Company. A 15-minute slide program gives visitors a sense of history and place.

*Access:* Find the courthouse near the picnic area on the north side of CA 299. Purchase admission at the site.

**Shasta Self-guided Walking Tour.** Historic Shasta's ghostly, roofless facades and common-wall shells capture the imagination and recall the bustling street of old. At the front of each enterprise is the owner's name and a description of the business. Brochures for the tour are available at the Courthouse Museum.

Grocery, dry goods, and hardware stores, a bakery, an assay office, barber shop, and a miscellany of saloons, hotels, and newspapers served the prospectors. The City Market smokehouse recessed in the hill and the Litsch Store Museum, completely restored and stocked with items of the era, are points of interest. The store is open summers only, on an irregular schedule.

At Shasta's west end are the 1855 Washington Brewery and pioneer cemetery; they may be viewed from the Trail to the Cemetery. Centrally located, the picnic area provides for a shady rest. There, an 1850s barn and antique machinery offer opportunity for study.

*Access:* Travel the sections of walkway fronting CA 299. Or, hike the Ruin Trail, which travels the slope at the back of the business district. It offers a different perspective on the ruins, but beware of poison oak.

# Grizzly Creek Redwoods State Park

**Hours/Season:** Year-round

**Facilities:** 30 developed campsites, 6 environmental campsites, picnic area, hiker trails, restrooms, showers

**For Information:** (707) 777-3683

**Access:** From the US 101–CA 36 junction south of Fortuna, head east on CA 36 for 12.4 miles to Cheatham Grove, 16.5 miles to reach the main park.

This inland park escapes the crowds of US 101. Groves of both virgin and second-growth redwood enfold the Van Duzen River corridor. Black bear, spotted owl, mountain lion, bobcat, and river otter favor the river-redwood habitat and the less-visited location. Hikers may find tracks and other signs of their presence or hear them in the distance.

Grizzly Creek is a protected spawning water for salmon. In winter, visitors can watch them wriggle upstream or rest in the deeper pools. Downstream from the Grizzly Creek confluence, anglers fish the Van Duzen River for salmon and steelhead. Bald eagles, which follow the fall and winter fish runs, can be seen perched in the overhead trees. In winter, kayakers run the rain-swollen river.

In summer, the park's shady picnic area and inviting swimming hole make it a popular draw, as do the park trails, touring both sides of the river. Usually in June, a seasonal footbridge can be placed across the Van Duzen, allowing access to the south shore loops.

Separate from the main park, Cheatham Grove is one of the state's finest virgin redwood stands. Although this grove lies nearly at the eastern edge of the coastal redwood range, many of its trees top 300 feet in height, with some pushing 2,000 years old.

## Attractions and Activities

**Cheatham Grove Trail.** This figure-eight trail is virtually flat and less than a mile long, but it "wows" visitors. Beginning next to a display of a redwood cross-section, it travels an outstanding redwood flat with scores of the giant trees. Sword fern, tanoak, laurel, and oxalis (redwood sorrel) contribute to the understory. Arrow posts guide hikers through the loops.

At 0.25 mile, the trail passes a behemoth redwood next to a splintered snag. Fire-charred redwoods, burls, and other features attract attention on this head-tilting tour, while benches offer a chance to sit and enjoy the redwood majesty. The trail invites repeat touring.

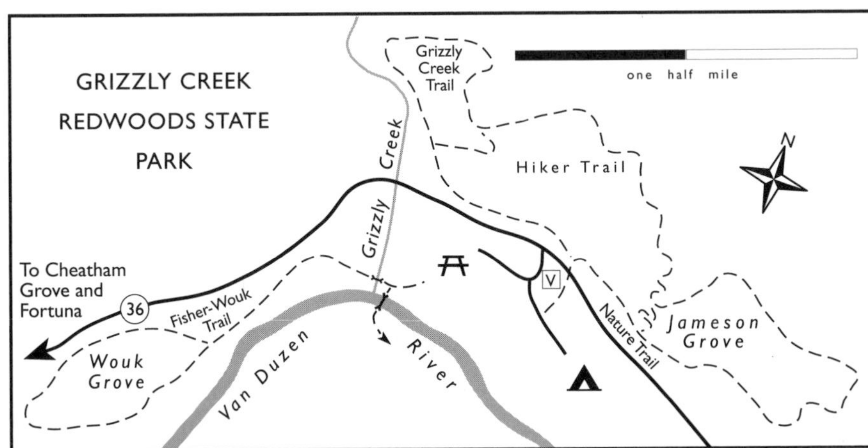

*Access:* From camp, go 4.1 miles west on CA 36 and turn right at the O'Dell Memorial Bridge. There is off-road parking for four cars.

**Jameson Grove–Grizzly Creek Loop.** This hike links three short loops for a 1.4-mile hillside tour.

Upon entering the forest, go right to begin the Nature Trail, passing through Jameson Grove. Interpretive posts identify the vegetation and describe the interworkings of a coastal redwood forest. Stairsteps advance the uphill spurts, while benches allow hikers to catch their breath. This grove has an impressive number of fire-hollowed trees.

As the trail descends, go right on the Hiker Trail at 0.7 mile for a longer tour. Here, Douglas fir and younger redwoods cloak the slope, and tanoaks introduce a leafy midstory. The trail maintains a rolling character.

At the 1-mile junction, follow the unmarked Grizzly Creek Loop to the right. A few bigleaf maples line the trail. Soon it begins descending, traveling above Grizzly Creek, but the thick forest and alder-lined drainage deny any creek views. Be careful on the boardwalks, as they can be slippery when wet.

At 1.4 miles, the Grizzly Creek Trail again meets the Hiker Trail. Go right to complete the tour amid the old-growth redwoods. In winter, mushrooms dot the forest floor with color and interesting shapes. Trillium, calypso orchid, wild ginger, and iris usher in the colors of spring. Be aware that the many vines climbing the redwoods are poison oak and may reach heights of 150 feet.

*Access:* The hike starts on the north side of CA 36, opposite camp.

**Fisher-Wouk Trail.** This 1-mile round-trip trail is reached via a summer bridge over Grizzly Creek. Where the trail forks, take the uphill branch. The hike passes along CA 36, snaring a few overlooks of the cloudy, green Van Duzen River. At 0.25 mile, it loops through a dark, inviting virgin redwood grove. Scenic family groups, a fallen redwood, and fire-hollowed trunks add to the tour. Benches invite visitors to linger in the forest coolness.

The trail eventually turns back to CA 36 and a turnout. A time-healed road completes the 0.5-mile loop, with overlooks of the redwood grove. Return as you came.

*Access:* Begin at the southwest corner of the picnic area, crossing Grizzly Creek.

## Humboldt Redwoods State Park

**Hours/Season:** Year-round

**Facilities:** 3 campgrounds with a total of 249 developed sites; 5 equestrian campsites and a group horse camp; trail camps; hike/bike campsites; picnic areas; visitor center; hiker, horse, and mountain-bike trails; restrooms; showers

**For Information:** (707) 946-2409

**Access:** Beginning 30 miles south of Eureka, seven exits off US 101 access Avenue of the Giants and the park.

Still growing, this 51,000-acre park is the largest of the state redwood parks and the third largest park in the entire state system. Running through its land is a 30-mile stretch of the Eel River and its south fork. A nearly unbroken redwood belt enfolds the waterways.

More than a third of the park features old-growth redwood, including the world's largest such grove—Rockefeller Forest. An early-day visitor dubbed it the

*Van Duzen River fishing, Grizzly Creek Redwoods State Park*

world's most beautiful, and few who have followed would dispute the claim. The Mattole Road winds through this celebrated forest for 6 miles. It offers opportunities for appreciating the views from behind the windshield of your vehicle and for walking the Rockefeller Loop and Big Trees Area trails.

The average age for the park's old-growth redwoods falls between 500 and 1,200 years, with its oldest-known tree having been 2,200 years old. Many measure over 300 feet high, with some topping 360 feet.

The park is a four-season destination. Springtime guests enjoy the wildflower bloom and canoeing the Eel River, while summer and fall guests hike, swim, pick berries, and ride horses in the tremendous Bull Creek backcountry. Winter salmon and steelhead runs draw anglers, as well as a few bald eagles, to the park. Mosquitos may be present from late spring through late summer.

## Attractions and Activities

**Avenue of the Giants Auto Tour.** Marked US 101 exits between Fortuna and Garberville announce this 32-mile scenic highway. The Avenue travels parallel to US 101 at the eastern fringe of the park, just hinting at the extent of the park's offerings. Lined by many outstanding ancient redwoods, it is a glorious tour along the Eel River and its south fork. Small towns dot the route. A brochure (available at each end and at the visitor center) points out key sights; the corresponding roadside signs precede the attractions by 200 feet.

The famed route affords access to picnic areas, the visitor center, Eel River, and named redwood groves, where visitors can stop and enjoy short walks. Following are six of the redwood walks, from north to south:

**Drury Trail.** At the north end of the park, this 2.5-mile round-trip trail escapes the attention of most parkgoers, but offers a wonderful meandering excursion amid the ancient redwoods. Mossy logs, upturned roots, and lush ground vegetation add to the walk. At one point, the trail travels next to a tumbled giant more than 10 feet in diameter. Fog and sunbursts add magic to the forest.

*Access:* Find it at mile 2.6.

**Percy French Loop Trail.** Less than a mile long, this figure-eight trail nonetheless strains the neck muscles with its impressive redwood towers. Second-growth redwoods rim the site.

*Access:* It is at mile 2.8.

**Founder's Grove Loop.** This is the most popular 0.5 mile of trail in the park, visiting both the Founder's Tree and the Dyerville Giant, which stood until 1991, when a falling neighbor claimed it. The giant had a height of 362 feet and a 17-foot diameter. Even in its present state of recline, it is imposing. A self-guided trail brochure (available at the site) introduces this grove, which honors the founders of Save-the-Redwoods League—the group responsible for the park's birth.

From the loop, hikers can extend the tour with the 0.8-mile Mahan Plaque Loop.

*Access:* Find it at mile 10.6.

**Gould–Fleishman Trail.** Opposite the park visitor center, this tour unites the 0.75-mile Gould Nature Loop (which heads right) and the 1.5-mile round-trip Fleishman Trail (heading left). Both tour the narrow corridor between the Avenue of the Giants and the South Fork Eel River, some of which was previously logged. Still, interesting discoveries about the forest and flood of 1964 await. Interpretive signs mark the nature trail.

*Access:* Find these at mile 15.2.

**Stephens Grove Loop.** This 0.8-mile loop is little traveled, having an unsigned parking lot and downfalls confusing its start, but it has a wonderful deep-woods feeling, touring a broader redwood corridor between the avenue and the South Fork Eel River. At 0.4 mile, a giant redwood 14 feet in diameter signals where the loop curves left; keep an eye out for the returning footpath. The wider path ahead leads to an old road.

*Access:* Find it at mile 24.1.

**Franklin K. Lane Loop.** This is a well-marked 0.5-mile circuit traveling through a redwood grove at the base of a deciduous slope. The loop crosses the old highway and visits a memorial plaque, but road noise does intrude.

*Access:* Find it at mile 28.1.

**River Trail to Children's Forest Loop.** A 5.4-mile round-trip seasonal hike begins at the Garden Club Grove and leads to the park's visually rich redwood grove dedicated to children. It travels above the South Fork Eel River, passing through old- and second-growth forest. When the summer footbridge is in place at Williams Grove, it is the preferred starting point, axing 3 miles off the total round-trip distance, making the forest accessible to more park visitors.

From Garden Club Grove, hikers cross a berm and summer footbridge to reach the opposite shore of the South Fork Eel River. At the junction, go left touring the forested slope upstream. Gigantic redwoods, Douglas fir, black huckleberry, and small tanoak comprise the forest. Where the slope steepens, the big trees become fewer in number. Filtered river views mark the way. The greenery increases after the initial trail stretch.

At 0.75 mile, a flatiron tree crowds the right-hand side of the trail. Soon afterward, a choked, formerly logged area claims the route. Where the forest opens up to a meadow, the trail crosses Coon Creek; its banks, too, record the long-ago logging.

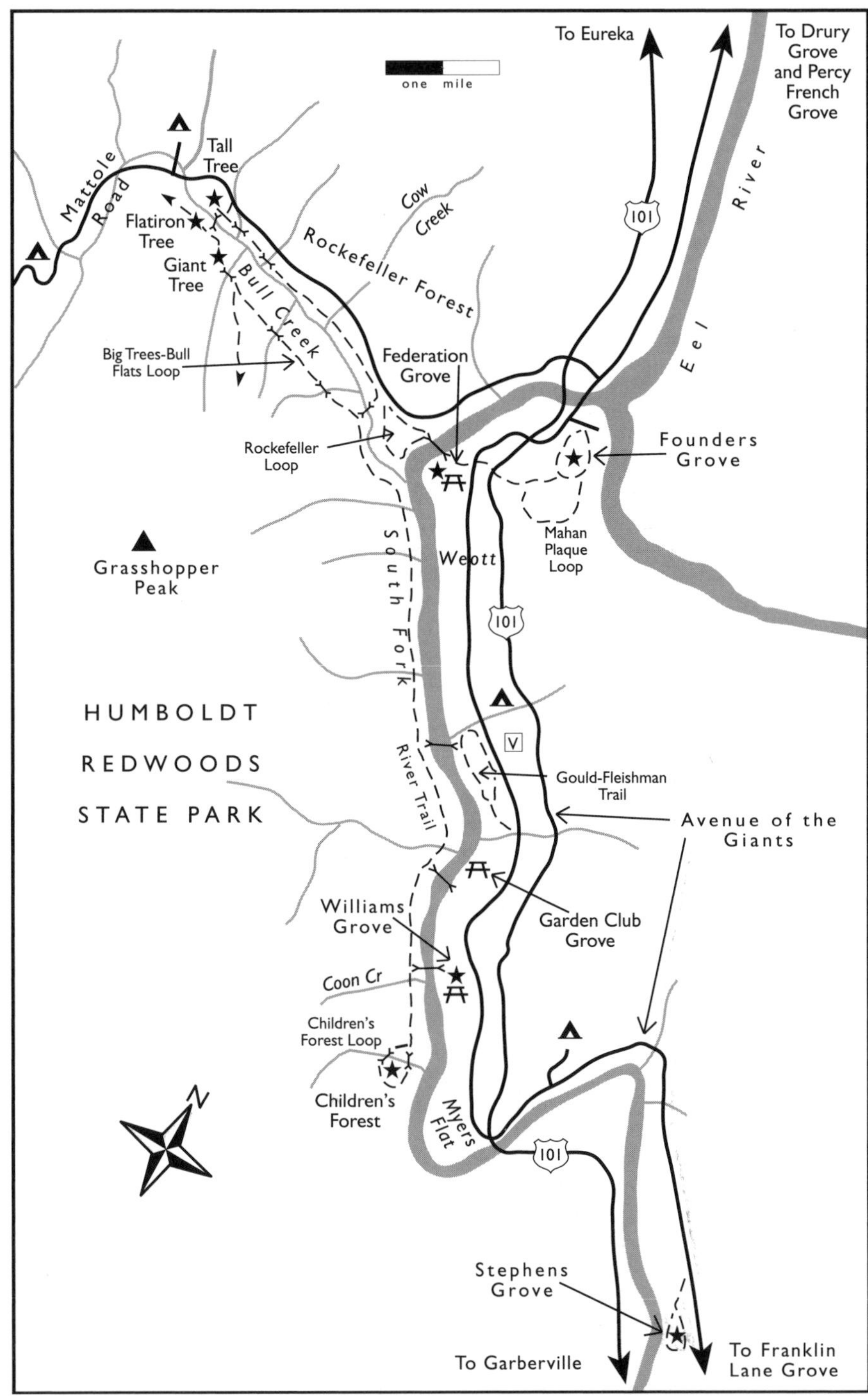
To Eureka
To Drury Grove and Percy French Grove
one mile
Tall Tree
Mattole Road
Flatiron Tree
Giant Tree
Bull Creek
Cow Creek
Rockefeller Forest
Eel River
Big Trees-Bull Flats Loop
Federation Grove
Rockefeller Loop
Founders Grove
Mahan Plaque Loop
Weott
Grasshopper Peak
South Fork
HUMBOLDT
REDWOODS
STATE PARK
River Trail
Gould-Fleishman Trail
Avenue of the Giants
Williams Grove
Garden Club Grove
Coon Cr
Children's Forest Loop
Children's Forest
Myers Flat
101
N
Stephens Grove
To Garberville
To Franklin Lane Grove

At 1.5 miles the summer bridge from Williams Grove connects, but it is not always in place. Beyond this point, the route tours second-growth forest interspersed by springboard-notched stumps. It returns to a mature redwood forest, just prior to reaching the 0.4-mile Children's Forest Loop at 2.5 miles.

The Children's Forest is a beautiful grove with shafts of sunlight piercing the stand, open looks at the many big trees, and a thick green carpet. Along it, a stone marker records the names of children who died in the early 1900s, and an ample number of goose pens (fire-hollowed trees) spark a child's imagination and invite entry. At 2.9 miles the loop closes. Retrace the first 2.5 miles, returning to the Garden Club Grove.

*Access:* Begin at the parking area for the Garden Club Grove or at Williams Grove, when its summer footbridge is in place. Both are located off the Avenue of the Giants.

**Big Trees–Bull Creek Flats Loop.** Off Mattole Road, this mostly flat 9-mile tour explores prestigious Rockefeller Forest, via the riparian corridor of Bull Creek.

Before crossing the bridge at the Big Trees Area, hikers may want to visit the area's 359-foot redwood via the 0.1-mile Tall Tree Loop. Upon crossing the bridge, a second detour to the Flatiron Tree, a redwood with an unusual oblong trunk, is also worthwhile.

With the sightseeing done, hikers are now ready to begin a counterclockwise tour of the loop, heading downstream from the Flatiron Tree junction (a left as you cross the bridge), or heading left away from the Flatiron Tree itself. At 0.3 mile, hikers come to the Giant Tree, a national champion at 363 feet tall and 53 feet in circumference. Rounding it to the right, the trail heads deeper into the redwood forest.

While it tours the creek flat, the trail is removed from Bull Creek. Only tanoak and a spattering of Douglas fir rise up amid the redwoods. Sword fern, salal, black huckleberry, oxalis, and sugarscoop paint the floor green. Log bridges cross the side creeks, some of which are dry in summer. At 2.2 miles, the trail passes through a charred triumvirate of redwoods.

The undisturbed tract is remarkable in its big-tree offerings. It frequently invites one to pause and look up, while the logs, with diameters greater than adults are tall, tend to make one reflective. At 3 miles, the trail passes through a cut in a tumbled flatiron tree. As you pass, note the shape of the rings. Beyond it, a bounty of horsetail reeds creates an out-of-focus green sea beneath the redwood towers.

At 3.5 miles, the trail comes out on a gravel bar at Bull Creek. The creek is 12 to 25 feet wide, coursing over a rocky floor. In winter, its high waters cover the bar and turn back hikers. When it is passable, hike 0.1 mile downstream on the gravel bar to pick up the trail on the right. At the 4-mile junction, go left, crossing the summer footbridge over Bull Creek, to continue the loop.

As the trail heads up the bank, hikers arrive at a junction. A detour right adds the 0.5-mile Rockefeller Loop to the tour. This scenic, dense grove offers a fine salute to the grandeur of the coast redwood.

Continuing upstream, hikers find a rolling trail passing between the alder-willow riparian shore and the redwood forest. Beware of poison oak where the trail tours close to the creek. The trek is now often sunny, with views of the creek and the rich forest across the way. At 6.5 miles, hikers cross Cow Creek.

After 7.8 miles, in places, the trail is pinched up onto Mattole Road, as the corridor between the creek and road narrows to a squeeze. By 8.5 miles though, the trail is closer to the creek, touring forest, and in another half mile the loop closes.

*Access:* Begin at the Big Trees Area parking lot on Mattole Road 4.2 miles west of the Avenue of the Giants.

# Benbow Lake State Recreation Area

**Hours/Season:** Year-round; campground: April through October
**Facilities:** 75 developed campsites, hike/bike campsite, picnic area, rental concession, hiker trails, restrooms, hot and cold showers
**For Information:** (707) 247-3318
**Access:** From Garberville, go 2 miles south on US 101 and take the Benbow Drive exit. Turn west to enter the day-use area in 0.5 mile; turn east to reach the campground in 1.4 miles.

A temporary dam constructed on the South Fork Eel River each summer, May through September, creates a 26-acre oblong, green reservoir, bringing lake recreation to the northwest corner of the state. Large, parklike lawns with planted maples frame the day-use shore. Picnic tables invite travelers to stop and have lunch. To burn off calories, a 21-station fitness trail rings the day area.

Swimmers and self-powered boaters take to the water, but the drone from US 101 intrudes on any quiet recreation. The uncrowded lake has ample room for visitors to romp, swim, and paddle around, but a rocky floor and quick drop-off make it unsuitable for wading. A concessionaire at the park rents canoes, paddleboats, and kayaks, and on a regular summer schedule, rangers conduct "canoe hikes" along the lake's edge. Other summer activities at the park include a Shakespeare festival, an arts festival, and concerts.

The first two campground loops afford good lake access; the third one, reached via the US 101 underpass, offers better shade. All sites suffer from highway noise, and only a few of the big redwoods remain.

With the removal of the dam, salmon and steelhead return up river in the fall and winter, bringing a following of anglers and eagles. Then, only a water line on the gravel bar records the sometimes lake.

## Attractions and Activities

**Pratt Mill–Pioneer Trail Loop.** This 2.7-mile tour, with a 400-foot elevation change, visits a mill ruins and a remnant grove of old-growth redwoods.

From camp, the hike begins on the Pratt Mill Trail, ascending through a mixed evergreen-deciduous forest, with stumps recording the previous woods. Where it comes to a junction at 0.5 mile, the campground loop heads left, returning near site 56. The Pratt Mill–Pioneer Trail Loop heads right on the leaf-covered, old logging road.

At 0.7 mile, hikers find the loop's one view, where a landslide stole part of the logging road. It overlooks Benbow Lake, historic Benbow Inn, and the surrounding rounded, grass- and tree-clad hills. Sometimes an osprey can be seen or heard as it sails over the lake.

At 0.9 mile, the trail bottoms out amid second-growth redwoods. Within the grove, hikers discover the rusting ruins of the old mill: half-buried equipment, old cables, and rough-cut logs supporting machinery. Past the mill, bear left for the loop, following the dirt road just above shore. Going right leads to where the canoeists anchor when they visit the mill.

The loop soon enters an area of old-growth redwoods. Where the road begins to descend, at 1.2 miles, keep an eye out for the unmarked Pioneer foot trail, which angles uphill to the left, switchbacking steeply away from the lake. Big redwood, fir, and tanoak cloak the slope.

At 1.7 miles, the trail tops out, following a onetime road through a cut-over forest. At 2.1 miles comes a steep 0.1-mile descent to a campground loop junction; small fir and black huckleberry hug the sides of the trail.

From the junction, return to camp either way. Going right, hikers descend via the old road, touring a wooded slope with a grassy floor. After skirting US 101, the hike ends near campsite 56, at 2.7 miles.

*Access:* Begin between campsites 72 and 73.

## RICHARDSON GROVE STATE PARK

**Hours/Season:** Year-round

**Facilities:** 170 developed forest or oak-meadow campsites, picnic area, visitor center, hiker trails, restrooms

**For Information:** (707) 247-3318

**Access:** From Garberville, go 7 miles south on US 101 to reach the park, which straddles the highway. Entry is on the west; an underpass connects the two parcels.

This park protects an outstanding coastal redwood grove in southern Humboldt County. On the western valley flat of the South Fork Eel River and mounting the ridge above it thrive many ancient redwoods over 1,000 years old. A self-guided nature trail tours the grove of 300-foot giants that lends the park its name. Quotes and facts reveal the wonder of the redwood forest. A walk-through tree near the visitor center lodge brings out the child in every adult.

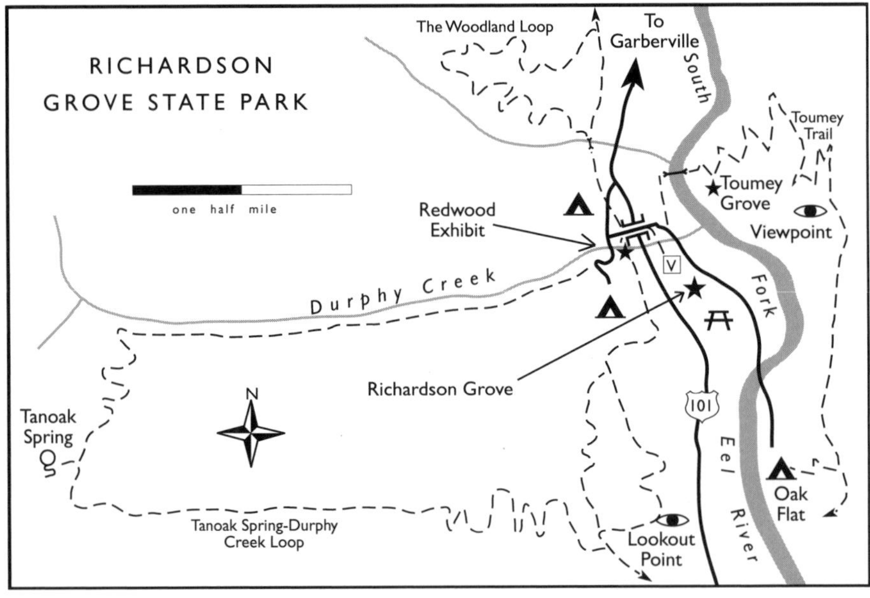

*Chain fern, Tanoak Spring, Richardson Grove State Park*

Many trees show scarring from lightning- or Indian-started fires. The Sinkyone tribe had a winter camp at what is now the south end of the park. Only US 101 mars the spell of the grove.

The Eel River receives its name from the Pacific lamprey, an eel look-alike and anadromous species that returns to these waters in late spring or early summer. Prized fish species—salmon and steelhead—run in the fall and winter. Across the river from the picnic area rises a steep, exposed slope scarred by a landslide—a marked contrast to the rich, cool darkness of the redwood flat. Swimming holes and small river beaches attract summertime guests.

## Attractions and Activities

**Richardson Grove to Tanoak Spring–Durphy Creek Loop.** This hike offers a challenging 4.6-mile round-trip tour of the park's forested western slope, climbing nearly 1,200 feet in elevation. From the day area, the hike begins north through Richardson Grove, crossing under US 101. There it swings south through the Redwood Exhibit, before climbing to Madrone Campground at 0.3 mile.

Bearing left after the campground trailhead (near sites 58 and 60), the route climbs steadily, touring a dripping redwood-Douglas fir forest with tanoak, bigleaf maple, myrtle, and madrone. A host of groundstory plants completes the stage.

At 0.6 mile sits Lookout Point, a tree-framed view of Oak Flat and the upstream floodplain of the South Fork Eel River. At the upcoming junction, go left for the full loop; a right returns to camp. Some big redwoods again line the trail. At the 0.8-mile junction, the loop bears right, and the climb intensifies.

The trail tours an impressive grove of mossy-trunked madrone, before topping the ridge at 1.75 miles. Fog may enfold the trail; tanoaks, 5 feet in diameter, border the path. The loop then switchbacks downhill, entering Durphy Creek drainage. At 2.25 miles, going straight leads to the fern bounty of Tanoak Spring; going right follows the loop, sharply descending. Tall, thick bushes of black huckleberry abound.

As the loop trail approaches the creek, the unstable sides of Durphy Canyon produce some abrupt trail rises and pitches. A redwood forest reclaims the lower slope. At 4.3 miles, the loop reaches the camp road; follow it under US 101 to end the hike.

*Access:* The hike starts at the north end of the visitor center parking area; campers may start near sites 58 and 60 in Madrone Campground for a 4-mile, open-end loop.

**The Woodland Loop.** This 1.3-mile trail climbs 500 feet, touring a mixed forest. Passing beneath redwoods and over the campground road, hikers skirt some campsites and cross a log footbridge to begin a clockwise tour of the loop. It switchbacks uphill through a mixed woodland of oak, tanoak, and madrone, rapidly leaving the redwoods behind. Sounds from US 101 carry up the slope, while utility lines stretch overhead. The trail soon tops out.

At 0.6 mile, a detour off trail onto a dirt road finds "Hikers Rest," just an old table. As the loop descends, it re-enters the redwood complex. Going right at the junction, hikers pass a couple of memorial groves, before the tour comes to an end.

*Access:* Locate the trailhead near the park entry station.

**Toumey Trail.** Reached by summer footbridges, this 2-mile trail explores the dry eastern slope of the South Fork Eel River. It visits Toumey Grove, overlooks Richardson Grove, and crosses oak hillsides. The hike may be extended, adding the Settlers Trail at Oak Flat Campground.

*Access:* Hikers may start the trail near the Group Camp entry or at Oak Flat Campground.

# Sinkyone Wilderness State Park

**Hours/Season:** Generally year-round, but winter rains can lead to park road closures

**Facilities:** 15 primitive drive-to meadow campsites, 17 primitive hike-in campsites, 3 trail camps, room rental, visitor center, hiker and horse trails, nonflush toilets, water (at visitor center area only)

**For Information:** (707) 986-7711

**Access:** *To reach the south entrance,* from the junction of US 101 and CA 1 at Leggett, follow CA 1 west for 14 miles and turn north on County 431. Usal Campground is 5.5 miles ahead. *To reach the north entrance,* in Redway, 2.5 miles west of Garberville, turn south on Briceland Road, heading toward Whitethorn, and stay on it. In 17.1 miles, the route turns to gravel. At Four Corners (in another 3.9 miles), go straight on Briceland Road / County 435 for yet another 3.3 miles to reach the visitor center. *Both entrance routes are narrow, winding, and unsuitable for motorhomes or trailers.*

This isolated wilderness features the dramatic beauty of the Lost Coast, with its sheer cliffs, near-shore rocks, high-crashing waves, and remote black sand beaches and coves. A steep inland terrain complements this untamed coast.

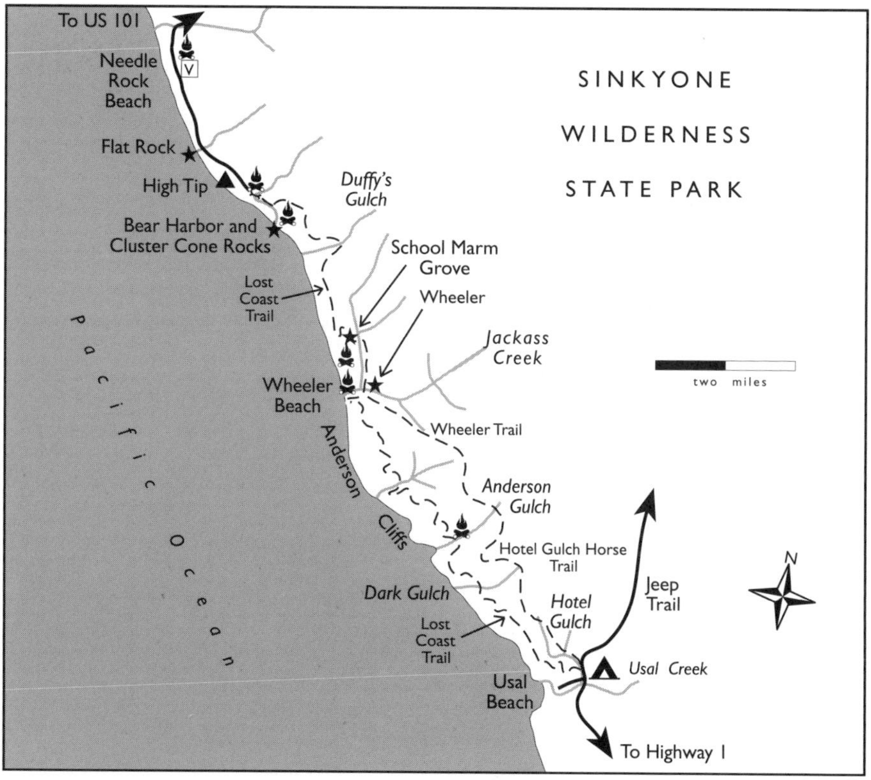

Foot trails and an abandoned dirt road tour the deep drainages, grassy seaward slope, forested ridges, and remnant redwood groves. Wildlife sightings are varied, with Roosevelt elk, deer, bobcat, skunk, raccoon, and owl. At Sinkyone Wilderness, nature excels.

Accordingly, it is difficult to imagine this uncompromising terrain as it was in the late 1800s, dotted with thriving communities engaged in logging, mill, and shipping activity; ranching; and dairying. Only a few clues linger: old foundations, a rusted rail, stumps, and a turn-of-the-century ranch house (now the visitor center). At the center, a photo album records the era.

Usal Campground, at the park's south end, is well used, despite its out-of-the-way location, or perhaps because of it. The meadow sites are within easy reach of the trails and the beach at Usal Creek. An estuary backs the black sand curvature. Pelicans may be seen there or diving for smelt in the close-breaking waves. Dip-net fishermen compete for the silvery fish.

## Attractions and Activities

**Lost Coast Trail (South).** A 10-mile round-trip sample of this 17-mile-long trail leads north to Anderson Gulch and back, offering coastal vistas and an appreciation of this rugged frontier.

The hike switchbacks uphill away from Usal Camp, touring a redwood-alder habitat. Sword fern, poison oak, nettles, and coastal grasses weave a mat beneath the trees. By 0.3 mile, hikers enjoy coastal views of Usal Creek and its beach and inland looks at Hotel Gulch. The song of the surf accompanies the hiker.

Atop the frontal ridge, the trail alternates between waist-high grasses and open stands of fir. From the saddle at 0.7 mile, the trail contours the seaward slope, passing through body-brushing grasses and vegetation; beware of ticks. Open views of the blue swells and the rugged southern coastline engage throughout. At 1.5 miles, the trail dips into a forested drainage, then resumes contouring. The thick vegetation can add to the humidity.

At 2.4 miles, where the trail climbs through an open forest corridor, keep an eye to the right for a secondary trail. It meets the Hotel Gulch Horse Trail in 100 feet for an easier return to camp. Continuing north, the trail rolls along the forested coastal ridge. At 3.2 miles, it turns inland, for a switchbacking descent into Dark Gulch. Where the trail rounds out of the gulch (4.1 miles), hikers overlook conical near-shore rocks—one with a blowhole, others iced with guano.

Coastal-ocean vistas return, as the trail again climbs and rounds the seaward slope. Views stretch north past Anderson Gulch, at sheer rock walls. By 4.7 miles, the trail drops into the gulch, where foxglove, black raspberry, waterleaf, and nettles grow. After crossing the creek, hikers come upon Anderson Trail Camp, two small flats and a pit toilet. Backpackers may wish to continue north; day hikers, return as you came.

*Access:* Begin at the Usal Campground trailhead, 0.2 mile north of the creek bridge.

**Needle Rock Beach Hike.** Opposite the visitor center, a 0.2-mile trail crosses the grassy marine terrace and descends a drainage to this black sand beach. The view is spectacular with the white tide scallops and wet black sand, the eyelet arches of Needle Rock, and the 100-foot bluffs. Cormorants perch atop the rock.

From the point of access, the beach stretches north for 0.2 mile, offering new perspectives on Needle Rock. The longer hike awaits to the south.

Touring south below the bluffs, hikers often find a clean canvas of sand, unmarked by footprints. On the bluff, vegetation alternates with exposed sandstone. By 0.9 mile, the cliffs defy vegetation. At 1.1 miles are a couple of slanted drainage cuts. Tracks may reveal that elk recently descended here, although the animals more commonly are seen at Bear Harbor Beach.

At 1.3 miles, the hike ends at Flat Rock, an extension of the cliff. Waves bash its sides, sending forth a high-shooting spray. A small punchbowl can be seen here, and turnstones often scurry about the rock. To the south, hikers can see High Tip. To the north is a fine view of Needle Rock Beach, with Chemise Mountain in the background. Return as you came.

*Access:* Begin near the Needle Rock Visitor Center.

**Lost Coast Trail (North).** This 10.5-mile round-trip sampling of the Lost Coast Trail tours a richer, more wooded wilderness than its southern counterpart. Along it, hikers find remnants of ancient redwood groves and scenic black sand beaches at Bear Harbor and Wheeler.

From the trail camp parking lot, cross the footbridge and journey south. The route bypasses a couple of walk-in camps before reaching the Bear Harbor junction at 0.4 mile. Going right leads to the beach cove in 0.1 mile; going left continues along the Lost Coast Trail.

Bear Harbor has a black gravel and sand beach with bluffs rising to its south and a low grassy point to its north. Rocks string together offshore, offering tidepooling. The length and width of the beach depend on the tide, but views south embrace Anderson Cliffs.

Continuing south, the trail journeys upstream, touring a rich laurel-Douglas fir drainage with sword fern–mantled slopes. At 0.9 mile, the trail crosses over the creek, switchbacking upslope. Where it leaves the drainage, smaller fir, laurel, and hazel frame its sides.

By 1.2 miles, the trail contours the seaward slope. Where it breaks into the open grassland, hikers have views of the coastline and the great blue expanse. Mostly though, the tour is in forest. At 1.7 miles, hikers view Bear Harbor and Cluster Cone Rocks to the north. Ahead, the trail tours amid the old-growth redwoods of Duffy's Gulch, only to alternate again between forest and grassy openings.

At 3 miles, it passes a couple of multi-armed trees and a nice redwood stand, as it switchbacks to the top of the ridge, crossing over into the North Fork Jackass drainage. Big firs dominate the slope, with redwood and tanoak intermixed. By 3.6 miles, the trail is back on the ridge. As it descends through grassland, it serves up far-stretching views north, the best of the hike.

The trail again crosses into the North Fork Jackass drainage for a forested descent to Wheeler. Beautiful big trees now rise above the trail. At 4.6 miles, it passes through the acre-size School Marm Grove, supposedly saved by a teacher and her students. Sword fern, oxalis, pathfinder, and starflower color the floor.

The trail then draws into a grassland flat, bypassing trail camps. At the creek crossing at 4.75 miles, hikers should get their water, as the water at Wheeler may be unsafe—a legacy from the old townsite.

Near a leftover wooden structure, the trail crosses Jackass Creek, soon coming to a junction. The Wheeler Trail (an equestrian route) heads left (upstream) along Jackass; the Lost Coast Trail continues downstream, touring the open flat to the beach at 5.25 miles.

While only 0.1 mile long, cliff-bound Wheeler Beach is a fine reward. Dark and broad, it cants sharply toward the surf for ideal wave watching, with pelican, harbor seal, cormorant, and murre often spied. At times, fog adds to or steals the view; it is common to this coastline in summer. Return as you came.

*Access:* Begin at the parking area for the walk-in camps, 2.4 miles south of the Needle Rock Visitor Center.

**Mountain Biking.** Mountain bikers are allowed only on the park roads and along the southern 6-mile stretch of the Hotel Gulch Horse Trail, which starts at Usal.

## SMITHE REDWOODS STATE RESERVE—STANDISH-HICKEY STATE RECREATION AREA

**Hours/Season:** Year-round (Smithe Redwoods is day-use only)

**Facilities:** 3 campgrounds with a total of 162 developed sites, picnic area, hiker trails, restrooms, showers (Standish-Hickey); restrooms, *bring water* (Smithe Redwoods)

**For Information:** (707) 925-6482

**Access:** From Leggett, go north on US 101 to reach these parks in 4 miles and 1 mile, respectively. Both straddle the highway, with their main access on the west side.

Smithe Redwoods State Reserve offers an intimate look at a stately stand of coastal redwoods. This roadside stop is small in size and has no trails. Visitors are free to roam at will and explore the trees up close. Families form human chains encircling the redwoods, just as the first area visitors did. Two walk-through stumps, leftovers from when the grove was part of a privately owned resort, allow a further assessment of the redwood's size. A wide, skipping 60-foot falls across US 101 from the north end of the parking area and easy access to the South Fork Eel River are the other park attributes.

Standish-Hickey, to the south, offers the main recreation of this pairing. This park features steep canyon bluffs, second-growth forests, and pockets of old-growth redwood and Douglas fir. It has a few miles of trail and likewise offers ac-

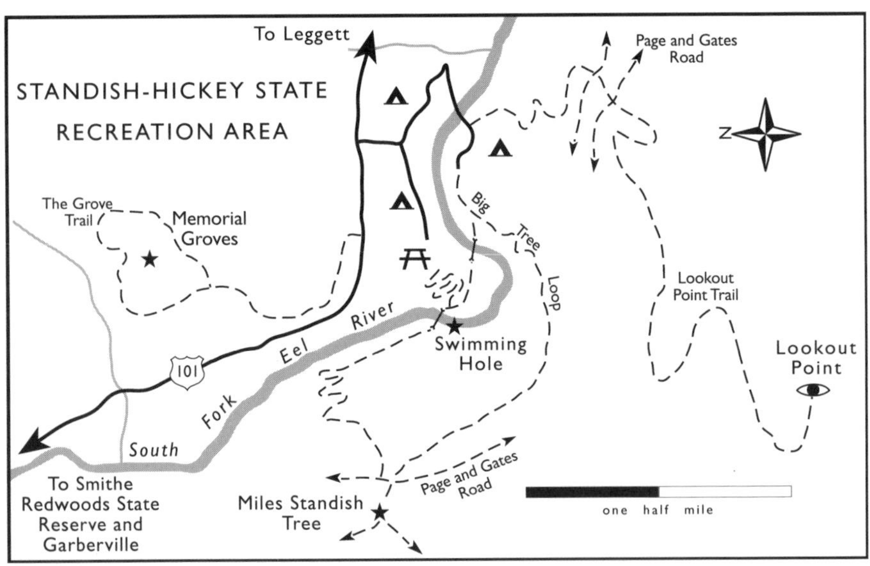

*Hiker fording the South Fork of the Eel River, Standish–Hickey State Recreation Area*

cess to the South Fork Eel River, with its deep holes, riffles, and cobbly bed. In winter, the South Fork Eel has a much altered appearance, flowing fast and full. Then kayakers and anglers join the visitor ranks; salmon and steelhead are the catches.

The area's star redwood, the 1,200-year-old Miles Standish Tree, shoots up 225 feet. Towering over the second-growth forest, it can be spotted from a distance. The Standish Tree bears the feeble chops delivered by a 1930s evangelist who, story has it, vowed to drop the biggest tree around, as well as darkening from a fire in 1947.

## Attractions and Activities

**The Grove Trail.** This 1.7-mile trail runs parallel to US 101, journeying north through Ray and Talsma meadows. After bypassing a residence, it enters a dark, second-growth woodland of madrone and tanoak, marked by charred stumps and snags. Uphill from a small drainage crossing, the 1-mile loop begins.

A clockwise tour mounts the slope, topping out at 0.5 mile. Uncut redwood groves now mark the tour, as old dirt roads crisscross the area. For the most part, arrow posts keep hikers on track; where in question, go right.

Along the way, a fire-darkened giant contrasts a surrounding forest of redwood sprouts. As the loop descends, a redwood "fairy ring" nudges the trail: young trees encircle a mature redwood like a picket fence. After a footbridge crossing, the loop closes. Return as you came.

*Access:* Look for a hiker gate in the fence on the east side of US 101, opposite the main area of Standish-Hickey State Recreation Area and north of a grocery.

**Big Tree Loop.** This 2.1-mile seasonally accessible loop travels the woodland above the South Fork Eel River, visits the record-size Standish Tree, and then closes with a couple of river crossings.

For a clockwise tour, go left, leaving the river bar, skirting the campground edge. Where the trail quickly forks, again go left, briefly switchbacking uphill, before settling into a rolling tour along the steep slope. In this uncut forest, some big redwood, tanoak, and fir rise above an understory of black huckleberry, salal, and fern. At 0.5 mile a footbridge crosses a spring-fed creek; chain fern and wild raspberry crowd its banks. At 0.7 mile, the trail tours a second-growth flat, coming out at Page and Gates Road.

For a visit to the Standish Tree, cross this road and go 0.3 mile. Big Tree Loop hooks right, never crossing Page and Gates Road. At 1 mile, hikers arrive at the impressive 1,200-year-old tree reigning over the neighborhood. A low fence rims the fully branched, time-tested specimen, protecting its roots and base. Return as you came to the loop, resuming the clockwise tour back to the river. It soon follows an abandoned dirt road through young forest.

At 1.6 miles, the trail rounds the slope above the river. After passing through a grassy meadow flat, it descends to the river bar for a South Fork crossing near the swimming hole. In summer, a temporary footbridge is generally in place; otherwise, a low-water wading or backtracking is in order. Afterward, the loop traverses the upper edge of the east-shore bar via 2-track or path, coming out at a second river crossing at its upstream end. Once on the west shore, go left to close the loop.

*Access:* Begin at the river-bar trailhead downstream from Standish-Hickey's Redwood Campground day-use parking lot.

**Lookout Point Trail.** This 3.5-mile round-trip hike offers a pleasant woodland tour to a modest overlook (elevation 1,600 feet).

From the Redwood Campground road, stairsteps uphill begin this trail, which passes through a tanoak woodland, rounding the edge of the campground and overlooking the river slope. At 0.1 mile, a landslide affords an open river view, the best of the hike. Where the trail turns inland, it settles into a moderate climb.

Second-growth redwood, tanoak, fir, and old stumps characterize the forest, with an understory of black huckleberry. At 0.4 mile, the trail crosses a dirt road, returning to forest. Ahead, where it reaches Page and Gates Road, turn right, follow the road for 100 feet, and bear left on the marked trail.

The trail now climbs along a drainage, touring a forest of 6- to 12-inch-diameter trees, with some chinquapin and madrone. At 1.1 miles, it enters a choked forest. Upon topping the ridge, hikers arrive at a fenced gap affording an overlook, at 1.5 miles. The view looks across a meadow slope with forest pockets and rural homes at the bumpy ridge across the South Fork Eel River.

The trail continues along the ridge, bypassing a twisted, old oak—a rarity on the tour. More madrone appear in the mix. At 1.75 miles, the trail ends at a similar overlook, with a view to the southeast, looking up the South Fork Eel Valley, with US 101 running through it and the forested ridge above it, but the river itself cannot be seen. Return as you came.

*Access:* Find the trailhead near the entrance to Standish-Hickey's Redwood Campground, reached by a summer road bridge.

**Swimming.** Where the South Fork Eel River flows through Standish-Hickey, it forms deep pools popular with summer guests. The favorite swimming hole is on a river curvature, 0.3 mile below the Hickey Campground campfire center and downstream from Redwood Campground. Rock outcrops below the eroded west cliff shape this good-size, nearly 20-foot-deep, sandy-bottomed pool, with a sandy east-shore beach. As the area is shadeless, sunscreen and umbrellas are worth carrying to the site.

## Westport–Union Landing State Beach

**Hours/Season:** Year-round
**Facilities:** 100 primitive coastal bluff campsites, beach-access trails, nonflush toilets, *bring water*
**For Information:** (707) 937-5804
**Access:** The park has multiple access points west off CA 1 between 0.25 and 4 miles north of Westport.

Separated by creek canyons, four bluff and beach parcels comprise this linear 41-acre park, offering a front-row seat to the beauty and spectacle of the Mendocino Coast. The park features a wild stage of offshore rocks and islands, a charging surf, 50-foot cliffs, and skinny, sea-lapped beaches. It captivates storm watchers with a fantastic show of hard-crashing, high-spraying waves.

From November through January, the bluffs afford a fine whale-watching post. Informal paths travel along the bluff edge, offering easy strolling and fine vistas and photo points. In spring and summer, wildflowers intermingle with the grasses. Scuba and free diving, along with surf fishing, appeal to the park's more active guests. In spring and summer, fishermen dip their nets for spawning surf smelt.

The camp flats are open and exposed on the grassy plateau. The sound of the ocean is a pleasing constant. To the east, the rounded coastal hills with their tree-lined drainages add to the setting.

### Attractions and Activities

**Abalone Point Trail.** Abalone Point is the park's most prominent land feature; a stairway descends to the intimate beach cove shaped by its presence. At the base of the stairs, large cobbles and rocks make up the beach, giving way to a narrow arc of sand. The cove boasts wonderful rock shapes both onshore and offshore; harbor seals slumber on the offshore rocks at the cove's north end. Oystercatchers, gulls, and cormorants are passersby, while long kelp streamers sometimes wash in with winter storms. When on the beach, be alert to the tide, and keep an eye out for sleeper waves.

*Access:* The trailhead is found in the DeHaven Creek Unit, at the kiosk, as travelers approach campsites 14 to 56.

**Pete's Beach.** This is the most reliable, amenable stretch of beach found at the park. Isolated from the road by a vegetated bluff, it offers a 0.25-mile-long, evenly wide, sandy strand suitable for strolling, sunbathing, and beach play. Sea stacks mark the surf line, while northern views include the dramatic bluff shore of Westport–Union Landing State Beach.

*Access:* An unmarked parking area 0.25 mile north of Westport provides access to this beach.

*Coast Redwood Grove, Admiral William Standley State Recreation Area*

## Admiral William Standley State Recreation Area

**Hours/Season:** Daylight hours
**Facilities:** None
**For Information:** (707) 925-6482
**Access:** From US 101 at Laytonville, go 12 miles west on Branscomb Road. The park lines both sides of the road.

Tucked away in the Coast Range, this out-of-the-way park offers an opportunity to view a little-tracked stand of virgin coastal redwood. Mature Douglas firs hold their own amid this grove of magnificent living towers. The understory bursts with madrone, black huckleberry, rhododendron, tanoak, oxalis, and fern; mushrooms scatter the forest floor. The park is undeveloped, without trails. Here, you are free to wander at will; just remember the park is only 45 acres.

While there are signs for the park, you need to be alert for them; they are set back in the redwood bounty. The entry road to one small parking area can become muddy and impassable following rain.

## MacKerricher State Park

**Hours/Season:** Year-round
**Facilities:** 142 developed pine-shaded campsites; picnic areas; hiker, horse, and bicycle trails; all-ability trails; restrooms
**For Information:** (707) 937-5804
**Access:** From Fort Bragg, go 3 miles north on CA 1, and turn west at Cleone for the main park. The Pudding Creek Day Area is found 2.5 miles south of the main entrance.

This large coastal park boasts a beautiful, grassy headland, 8 miles of beach, rolling dunes, lowland forest, and a freshwater lake—a veritable playground. Park guests engage in such activities as sightseeing, hiking, cycling, surfing, canoeing, fishing, horseback riding, and—if one is so inclined—relaxing.

The headlands offer a prime vantage for viewing the gray whale migrations December through March; a 30-foot skeleton of a gray whale is on display near the ranger station. The waters of Mackerricher support a year-round harbor seal population, with an active rookery from March through June; respect the 50-foot safety margin dictated by federal law.

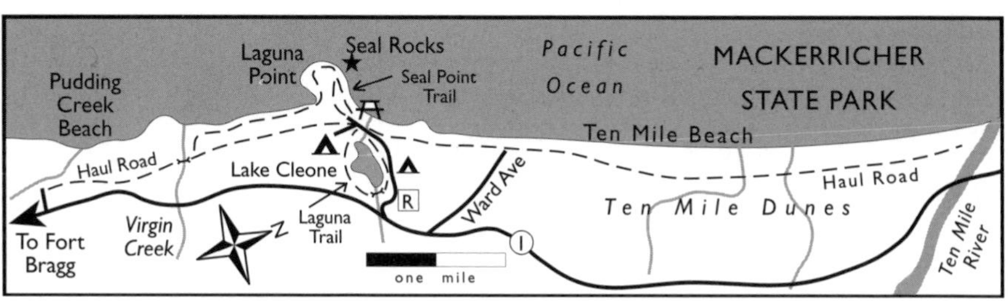

*Visitors feeding gulls, Mackerricher State Park*

## Attractions and Activities

**Laguna Trail.** Encircling Lake Cleone, nearly half of this trail's 1.25-mile length is on raised boardwalk suitable for wheelchair travel. The trail explores the marshy edge and cattail arm of the lake, travels between wind-shaped Bishop pines and alders in the riparian corridor, and snares lake overlooks, beginning midway around the lake. Lake Cleone is a scenic, quiet water plied by canoes and migrating ducks from the Mono Lake area. Periodically, it is stocked with trout. The trail ends near the outflow.

*Access:* For a clockwise tour and to travel the wheelchair-accessible portion, begin at the northeast corner of the lake area parking.

**Seal Point Trail.** This 0.5-mile all-ability loop travels a raised boardwalk along Laguna Point, offering ocean vistas and a fine introduction to the park's broad, grassy headland. The Seal Watching Station (0.25 mile) overlooks the offshore rocks where harbor seals haul out to rest; cormorants roost on other nearby rocks. Off the point, rocky tongues invite tidepool exploration. At the station, panels describe the area's natural history.

*Access:* The trail heads south from the Laguna Point Day Area.

**Headland Hiking.** Many travelers leave the boardwalk of the Seal Point Trail at the Seal Watching Station at 0.25 mile for a tour south along the headland bluff. Foot trails lead the way. In another 0.2 mile, the 15- to 20-foot bluff overlooks a blow hole, or spouting horn, where waves force the water out of a break in the top of the rocks. Just beyond, hikers discover a sea arch. In this area of the park, surf fishermen can also be seen, testing their luck off the seaward-jutting rocks.

The headland offers a pleasant, mostly flat tour with spectacular ocean and coastal vistas. Lupine, ice plant, yarrow, and bracken fern interweave the grasses. Inland from the foot trail, a horse trail and Haul Road parallel the route, offering equestrians and cyclists a similar access to this offering. At times, the foot and horse trails merge.

Isolated beaches may suggest a detour. A longer beach is found at 1.2 miles, as the trail rolls over an old dune expanse. At 1.5 miles, hikers head inland to cross Virgin Creek on the Haul Road bridge.

Continuing the tour south, hikers view the beginnings of Fort Bragg to the east, but the pull of the western horizon remains strong. At 2.2 miles, opposite a parking area/access to Haul Road, the trail comes to a beach-access trail and a bench overlooking the ocean. At 2.5 miles, the hike ends on the north side of Pudding Creek, a broad, deep, impassable drainage cut. Return as you came or follow Haul Road back to the core of the park.

*Access:* Begin by following the Seal Point Trail, which leaves the Laguna Point Day Area.

**Ten Mile Beach Hiking.** North of Ward Avenue, hikers find an uninterrupted, broad, sandy strand for carefree strolling; it stretches north to the Ten Mile River. Here, dunes replace the bluff rising above the beach.

*Access:* The strand is reached following Haul Road north from camp or heading west on Ward Avenue, at Cleone.

**Haul Road Bicycle Route.** A former logging road, 7-mile-long Haul Road stretches the length of Mackerricher from the north side of Pudding Creek to the mouth of the Ten Mile River. Closed to motor vehicles, it offers a pleasing, carefree, wind-brushed coastal tour, ideal for cyclists and joggers.

The road's southern portion passes along the eastern edge of the grassy headland, removed from the ocean. Its northern end travels above the open beach and across the shifting dunes. For the most part, the road remains intact, save for a small breach just before reaching the dunes. Where it passes through the dunes, expect patches of windblown sand to foul the going.

*Access:* Haul Road has access points within the park and at Cleone.

**Horseback Riding.** Equestrians have use of a designated trail across the headland, and they may tour the open beach north from Ward Avenue in Cleone. Horse-rental services are found just outside the park.

## Jug Handle and Caspar Headlands State Reserves—Caspar State Beach

**Hours/Season:** Daylight hours

**Facilities:** Hiker-only trails, nonflush toilets, *bring water* (Jug Handle); none (Caspar Headlands and Beach)

**For Information:** (707) 937-5804

**Access:** From CA 1, Jug Handle State Reserve is 0.1 mile north of the Caspar turnoff. For the other two parks, turn west off CA 1 at Caspar, following Point Cabrillo Drive.

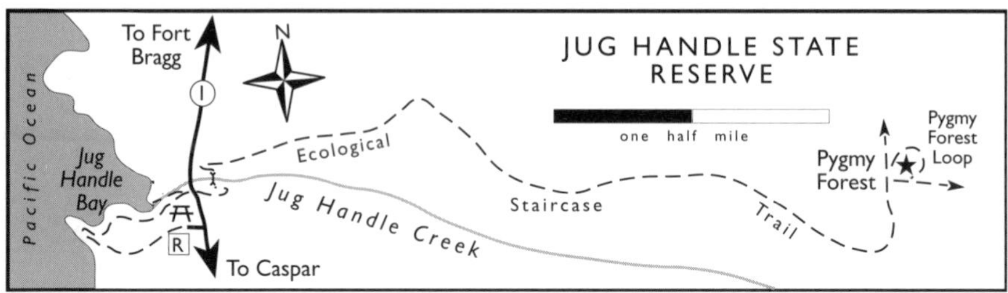


Caspar State Beach and Caspar Headlands State Reserve are two small park units, totaling less than 5 acres. Caspar State Beach is typical of a small community beach. Flanked by creeks and vegetated bluffs, its 0.2-mile sandy beach pocket opens out onto a square bay. Guest offerings include sunbathing, swimming, scuba diving, and ocean fishing.

Caspar Headlands State Reserve tops the bluff to its south. Access is by permit only; obtain both the permit and a reserve map from the Mendocino District Office, located east off CA 1, 2 miles north of Mendocino. The map is essential to avoid trespassing—the park is highly fragmented and surrounded by a housing development.

Despite offering a fine perspective of the Mendocino coastline, Caspar Headlands is one park you may choose to forgo, given its size, the need for a permit, and its having rival, more accessible offerings right next door. Nonetheless, it remains one for the curious. Picnicking and pets are not allowed.

Jug Handle State Reserve is one such rival. It offers a superior headland tour, overlooking Jug Handle Bay to the north and a matching bay to the south. Sheer cliffs and rocks shape the coves. Sea stacks and a sea arch mark the ragged coastline.

*Caspar Headlands*

A trail near the CA 1 underpass leads to the white sands of Jug Handle Beach, which is sliced by Jug Handle Creek as it reaches the sea.

In May and June, California poppy, coast lupine, Indian paintbrush, sea pink, and seaside daisy spangle the headland grasses. Wind-shaped trees border its east side. Trails tour the headland and travel inland, exploring three marine terraces—a geologic record of tectonic activity spanning more than a quarter million years. A visit to a pygmy forest caps the inland tour.

### Attractions and Activities

**The Ecological Staircase Trail.** This 5-mile, round-trip tour crosses three marine terraces, showcasing their different habitats. Interpretive brochures for the trail may be purchased at the reserve entrance.

The hike begins on the west side of CA 1, with a 0.5-mile loop exploring the headland and its vistas. Where the trail forks and returns to the parking area, go right for the headland tour alone; go left for the longer hike, crossing under CA 1.

After a quick dip and rise in the Jug Handle Creek drainage, the trail has a gentle gradient as it tours the first terrace with its meadow-transition habitat, soon passing through a single patch of adult-high bracken ferns. A fuller, mixed conifer forest announces the second terrace. Soils, weathering, and drainage determine the habitats.

By 1.5 miles, the trail has entered the third and final terrace, featuring a redwood–Douglas fir complex. While there are side paths, the trail generally remains apparent. Hikers again find a transition habitat, arriving at a firebreak road at 2.25 miles. Stay on the road to reach the Pygmy Forest Loop. It is on the right in less than 0.1 mile, just past an intersecting fire road. The compact soils here create a much different third-terrace setting.

The loop travels a congested forest of nutrient-deprived Bolander pine and pygmy cypress, with many under 5 feet in height with diameters measuring less than 2 inches. Despite their size, the trees are mature, ranging from 50 to 100 years old. Where the loop exits at a fire road, go right, followed by a left at the next intersection. This will point you back the way you came.

*Access:* The trail begins at the Jug Handle parking lot.

## Russian Gulch State Park

**Hours/Season:** Year-round; campground closes in winter
**Facilities:** 30 developed forest-riparian campsites, picnic area, hiker and horse trails, mountain-bike routes, restrooms, outdoor shower
**For Information:** (707) 937-5804
**Access:** The park is west off CA 1, 2 miles north of Mendocino.

This park brings together the drama of the Mendocino coastline and the restful beauty of a mixed conifer–redwood forest. Its coastal offerings include grassy headlands, a punchbowl and blow hole, small beach, and quiet spots where guests can watch the waves crash into the rocks and cliffs. Divers anchor their boats in the park's protected coves, and harbor seals often rear their shiny heads. At Russian Gulch Beach, restrooms and an outdoor shower serve swimmers and divers. A scenic highway bridge on CA 1 arches over the beach setting, while seaward views feature the headlands.

Inland, fern-hairy slopes, a 36-foot ribbonlike falls, and alder-showered Russian Gulch unite with western hemlocks and second-growth redwoods in a rich canyon setting. Springboard-logged stumps, nurse trees, tree-family sprout clusters, and the tall, straight redwood columns capture the eye and hold the imagination.

## Attractions and Activities

**Fern Canyon Trail.** This 6-mile round-trip trail begins open to foot and mountain-bike travel, with cyclists turned back at the start of the waterfall loop at 1.5 miles.

The hike travels an 8-foot-wide paved fire lane upstream alongside narrow-spilling Russian Gulch. Forest and ferns race up the canyon, while alder, hazel, and California laurel frame the creek. Nightshade, nettle, and salmonberry riddle the riparian zone. The redwoods first appear at 0.4 mile, as some thickly vegetated weeping walls mark the route. The canyon now narrows.

At 1.5 miles, picnic tables signal the junction for the waterfall loop. Here, cyclists should turn around, or lock up their bikes and continue on foot. Go left, clockwise, for the shortest route to the falls.

The trail makes a moderate ascent as it draws deeper into the canyon. Its foot-path width allows a more intimate study of the area. At 2.3 miles, hikers view the thin, white stream of Russian Gulch Falls. A fern-decorated vertical log accents the flow. The trail then dips to a bridge and another perspective on the falls, before mounting the slope and leaving the creek at 2.4 miles.

The loop next switchbacks uphill, touring the drier forest of the upper slope. Rhododendron bushes appear in the mix. After the 3-mile mark, the trail tops out, and a slow descent follows. Where the trail approaches a side creek, the descent quickens. The loop closes at 4.5 miles. Retrace the initial 1.5 miles to end the tour.

*Access:* This trail heads upstream from the trailhead parking area at the end of the campground road.

**Headland Trail.** This 1-mile circuit tours the perimeter of the park's north headland, offering first-rate vistas of the surf-carved rocks and cliffs. At the southwest end of the headland, a blow hole fed by a small sea cave calls visitors over for a closer look. Larger sea caves and arches in the bluff urge the hiker onward. Waves thunder into the cliffs, sending a showery spray shooting skyward.

Midway, side trails lead inland to a large punchbowl, where the roof of a sea cave collapsed long ago. Plants now drape the bowl. Remarkably, the sea has scoured the floor clean, carrying the rocks and debris out through the narrow arch opening.

*Access:* An interpretive panel identifying the seascape features of the Mendocino coastline marks the start of the tour at the headlands parking area.

**South Trail–South Headland Loop.** For an alternative, more private look at this stunning coastline, bear right on the South Trail as it leaves the beach road. The trail

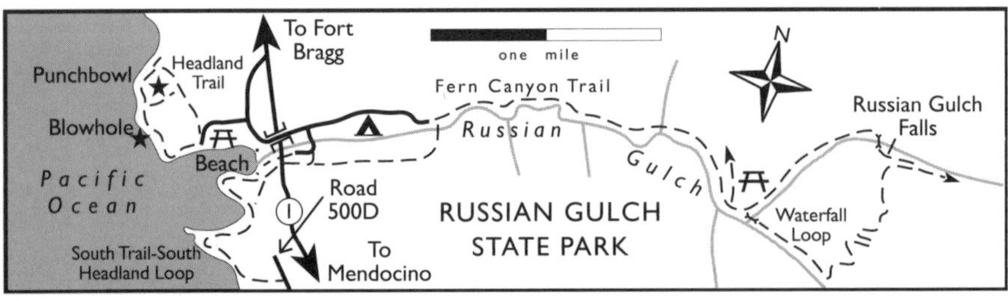

climbs 0.3 mile, passing under the bridge, topping the pine-forested south headland. Beneath a stately, multi-branched fir a 1-mile loop starts; stay right for the more pleasant tour along the headland edge. A bench seat overlooks Russian Gulch Beach.

The loop offers a rolling tour on a conifer-needle bed. Below the trail, hikers see a calmer cove punctuated by rocks. Wind-shaped trees both frame and add to the view; sunset photographers may find one to lend an interesting silhouette to the orange horizon. Occasionally the noise from CA 1 rises above the roar of the ocean, intruding on the tour.

*Access:* Leave the beach road opposite the Group Camp. Or reach the trail off Road 500D, west off CA 1 just south of the park.

## Mendocino Headlands State Park

**Hours/Season:** Daylight hours
**Facilities:** Picnic sites, visitor center, hiker trail, restrooms
**For Information:** (707) 937-5804
**Access:** Reach the park off Heeser Drive and Main Street in Mendocino.

This park represents perhaps the premier headland attraction for this coastal segment of California. It wraps around three sides of Mendocino, a coastal village with old-time charm. The white storefronts, Victorian homes, and old-fashioned water towers complement the scenic seaboard, while the protected headland, in turn, preserves the town's historical window on the ocean.

Spring wildflowers and winter gray-whale watches are seasonal attractions, while the secluded beaches, blue-green waters, blow holes, islands, arches, and grottos possess year-round appeal for photographers and artists. South of the headland, Big River Beach invites sunbathers and swimmers; it is reached by a rough road off CA 1 or via the Headlands Trail.

At the north end of town, a picnic area and restroom are found along Heeser Drive, west of its junction with Lansing. The small Ford House Visitor Center and another public restroom are located in town. At the Ford House, visitors can view films and exhibits on early Mendocino, "dog-hole" shipping (where chutes deliver logs to waiting boats in small coastal coves), logging, and the area's natural history. Out the back door is a picturesque water tower.

### Attractions and Activities

**Headlands Trail.** This 6-mile round-trip trail travels the perimeter of wave-sculpted Mendocino Headland, offering spectacular ocean and coastal vistas and opportunities for beach and town detours.

A north-to-south tour begins at the park picnic area. From there, it passes through a cluster of wind-shaped cypress. Where it comes out, a headland point awaits discovery. Below stretches a large, inaccessible gravelly beach. Views to the north include Point Cabrillo Lighthouse. To the south is the long arm of the sea.

Beyond the point, the trail hugs the headland rim, as a broad, open grassy expanse spreads toward town. Seaweeds pulse in the water, and oystercatchers announce their presence in high pitches. At 0.6 mile, the trail offers a good look at an offshore island, with its collection of rocks separated by channels. Past the parking area ahead, a brief detour onto a small jut offers a better vantage on the island's sea arch. Many such rock features mark the coastline.

At times, a rocky foot replaces the steep-dropping cliff; here, surf fishermen leave the trail. When tides are low, hikers can glimpse the tidal life on the base of the offshore rocks. Colors catch the eye, but binoculars are needed for detail. At 1.25 miles, the trail is opposite Goat Island, a long, vegetated ridge with a couple of caves or arches carved in its sides. Twin arches mark a smaller broken-off feature between it and the headland. Just beyond, hikers discover a sea bridge carved in the headland bluff.

At 1.4 miles is another parking area and a plaque honoring the Mendocino sister-city relationship with Miasa, Japan. Soon, a deep channel sculpts the headland, and the broad grassland buffer between town and the trail disappears. By 2 miles, the headland is notably lower, as the trail passes closer to the ocean.

Ahead, where a punchbowl opens up in the headland, carved totems face out to sea. Benches overlook the ocean at 2.4 miles, where a stairway descends to Portuguese Beach—a narrow, sandy strip stretching below the bluffs of town. Secondary paths now wander toward town. Many days, the warm inland temperatures draw a stiff, chilly ocean breeze across the headland.

By 2.8 miles the trail is rounding the ragged rim, overlooking Big River to the south. Its broad, sandy beach spreads north from the river mouth. Ahead, Bishop pines create a sheltered vista point, and a well-placed log offers seating. At 3 miles, hikers come to the stairway descending to Big River Beach. This marks the turn-around point for the Headlands Trail.

*Access:* Begin at the picnic area west of the Heeser-Lansing Junction.

## VAN DAMME STATE PARK

**Hours/Season:** Year-round

**Facilities:** 74 developed forest and meadow campsites, en route beach-parking campsites, 10 hike-in canyon campsites, picnic area, visitor center, hiker trails, mountain-bike routes, all-ability trail, restrooms, indoor and outdoor showers

**For Information:** (707) 937-5804

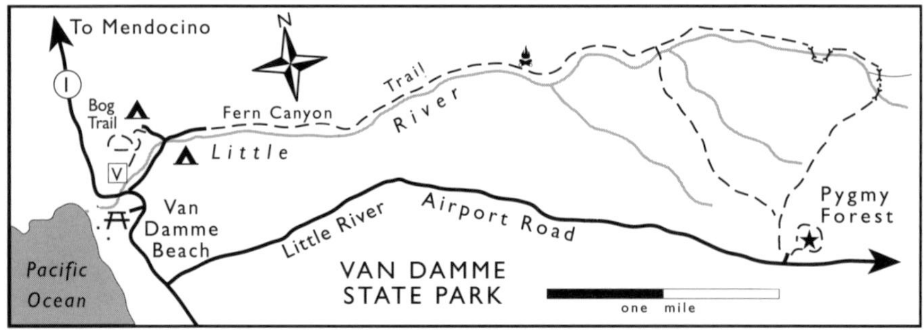

*Pygmy forest boardwalk, Van Damme State Park*

**Access:** From Mendocino, go 2.5 miles south on CA 1. Turn east for the main park, west for the beach.

This park's treasury includes an underwater preserve, a small beach, a pygmy forest, and a rich, redwood-fern canyon threaded by Little River—a winter spawning water for salmon and steelhead. The park is a popular destination for scuba and abalone divers. Landlubbers can catch a glimpse of the undersea attraction by touring the visitor center's "Living with the Sea" diorama and entering its lifelike depiction of an underwater surge channel. The visitor center also offers film presentations, park information, and publications for sale.

## Attractions and Activities

**Fern Canyon Trail.** This trail offers travelers either a 9.8-mile round-trip tour or a 4.9-mile shuttle. From the canyon campground, follow the gated, paved road upstream along creek-size Little River. At this point, hikers, joggers, and cyclists share the route, becoming immersed in the canyon bounty.

Cascades of sword fern splash green down the hillsides. Redwood, hemlock, and fir trees line the canyon, while alder, salmonberry, and thimbleberry crowd the stream. Dusted with needles, the one-lane road offers a pleasant tour with a gradual grade. At 1.75 miles, it passes the hike-in campsites and pit toilets.

At 2.5 miles, the paved route ends at a broad, open flat with junctions. Here, cyclists and hikers part company. Cyclists may either bear right on the dirt fire lane that leads to Pygmy Forest or return as they came. Hikers will want to follow the foot trail to the left, for a scenic tour, venturing deep into Fern Canyon.

As the canyon becomes more squeezed, its richness becomes amplified, and the discovery more intimate. Douglas fir and second-generation redwoods enfold the steadily climbing trail and keep the canyon dark and cool. The hike now offers more looks at Little River—narrow, shallow, and smooth-flowing, overlaced by logs. Footbridges allow dry crossings.

At the canyon head, at 4 miles, the fern bounty attains its peak. Afterward, the trail switchbacks out of the drainage, bypassing an imposing, fire-hollowed redwood stump at 4.25 miles. It must measure some 8 to 10 feet in diameter, with next-generation redwoods ringing it. The grade relaxes, and before long the trail leaves the forest.

A dirt lane replaces the footpath where hikers enter an open corridor of tanoak, manzanita, chinquapin, and pines. At the dirt-road junction ahead, go left to reach the Pygmy Forest parking area and trailhead at 4.9 miles; to the right is the bike route. Round-trip hikers return as you came, or follow the bike route back to the junction flat, chiseling 1.2 miles off the round-trip distance.

*Access:* Trailheads are located at the east end of the canyon campground and at the Pygmy Forest parking area.

**Pygmy Forest Trail.** This 0.25-mile wheelchair-accessible loop travels a raised boardwalk through a unique environment of stunted old-growth trees, with 1-inch diameters and average heights of 4 feet. A few scraggly towers top out at 7 feet. The compact, mineralized soils bring about this congested forest of gnarled, lichen-etched pygmy cypress and Bolander pine. Rhododendron, tanoak, blackberry, salal, and waxmyrtle fill in the ranks. Despite their size, the trees produce a good cone crop.

*Access:* Go 0.5 mile south on CA 1 from the main park, and turn east on Little River Airport Road. In 2.7 miles, look for the marked turn on the left, just past the intersection.

**Bog Trail.** Below the Highland Meadow Campground, this 0.6-mile loop tours the edge of a bog, where forest and wetland meet. Ferns frame the trail, while dense grasses, water plants, and alders claim the bog. Footbridges and boardwalks traverse the soggier reaches; beware, they can be slippery when wet or frosty.

*Access:* This trail begins near the Group Camp.

**Mountain Biking.** Cyclists may travel the 2.5-mile paved portion of the Fern Canyon Trail that leaves from the canyon campground. They may also tour the 1.2-mile gated dirt fire road heading north from the Pygmy Forest parking lot. These trails tie together for a 7.4-mile round-trip ride.

## MONTGOMERY WOODS STATE RESERVE

**Hours/Season:** Daylight hours
**Facilities:** 1 picnic site, hiker trail, nonflush toilet, *bring water*
**For Information:** (707) 937-5804
**Access:** In Ukiah, at the corner of North State Street and Orr Springs Road, go west on Orr Springs Road to reach the park in 12.1 miles, the trailhead in 13.2 miles.

A scenic drive along narrow, two-lane Orr Springs Road wraps around and over oak- and madrone-studded grassland hills to reach this remote pocket of redwood solitude and splendor. As the road tours the park, trees interlace over the creek that flows beside it. A short walk along the reserve's nature trail leads to the park's single creekside picnic site, but equally inviting spots elsewhere suggest that visitors lay out a blanket, spread a picnic lunch, and spend some time.

## Attractions and Activities

**Montgomery Woods Nature Trail.** This 2-mile round-trip hike visits five outstanding ancient redwood groves along Montgomery Creek. The tour's merit suggests a slow investigation. Normally, brochures are available at the start of the trail. Following winter rains, the creek sometimes floods the canyon bottom, requiring hikers to wade.

Near the closed bridge at the end of the parking turnout, hikers bear left, following a creekside trail upstream. Redwoods, California laurel, black huckleberry, tanoak, and ferns frame the creek bottom, while a rich tanoak woodland claims the canyon slopes. At 0.1 mile, the trail crosses a footbridge to travel an old road along the opposite bank. The picnic site is tucked away just below the grade near the first memorial-grove marker.

Continue following the steep road. It tops out at 0.3 mile and then descends, entering the impressive Grubbs' Memorial Grove, where light-colored sword and chain ferns contrast with the dark redwood trunks. Many giants contribute to the forest ranks. Just ahead, the hike's interpretive component begins, as the trail explores the redwood splendor of the canyon bottom.

At 0.5 mile, hikers pass along a fine gallery of chain ferns. Soon after, a foot trail replaces the old road. Downfalls briefly claim the route preceding the log crossing of the drainage at 1 mile; steps cut into the redwood log make it easy to mount.

The loop now follows the base of the opposite slope downstream, affording hikers a different perspective on the virgin redwood canyon. Where the trail forks at 1.4 miles, take either route, as they again merge. Near the fork, moss and ferns drape a large boulder outcrop, and newts share the trail.

With a couple of footbridge crossings, the loop draws to a close past the upturned root at post 13. Stepping through an aisle cut through a redwood log, hikers return to Grubbs' Memorial Grove near the memorial-grove sign. Return as you came.

*Access:* The trail begins at the parking turnout next to a road bridge, 1.1 miles past the park entrance sign.

# GREENWOOD CREEK STATE BEACH

**Hours/Season:** Daylight hours
**Facilities:** Picnic sites, visitor center (expected to open in 1994), beach-access trail, nonflush toilets, *bring water*
**For Information:** (707) 937-5804
**Access:** The park is on the west side of CA 1 at Elk, 6 miles south of the CA 128–CA 1 junction.

This small bi-level park offers coastal overlooks and beach access. It has multiple picnic sites set back and directly on the 150-foot bluff, with still others dotting a grassy flat just above the beach where Greenwood Creek cuts to the ocean. A few cypress trees and woody shrubs claim the otherwise open bluff.

A 0.5-mile trail descends from the bluff to the beach. Where it forks at 0.1 mile, the path to the right leads to a cliffside picnic site; the one to the left descends, passing through the lower picnic flat, to arrive at the southern end of the beach. Three rock islands or stacks characterize the broad cove. Sea arches mark the two southern rock islands. Seabirds and harbor seals bob in the nearby waters.

Cliffs frame the park's canted, 0.3-mile strand, made up of coarse sand and gravel patches. An irregular tideline washes to shore, leaving behind foamy scallops. The breaking waves and hush of the backwash create a pleasing sound mix. Storm-tossed seaweed and logs add to the winter wildness of the beach. In winter, anglers fish Greenwood Creek for steelhead; year-round, the ocean calls to them to try their luck.

In Elk, the town's original mill office serves as a park visitor center. It has interpretive displays on the area's Native American heritage, early-day redwood logging, and the mill's history.

## Hendy Woods State Park—Navarro River Redwoods

**Hours/Season:** Year-round; Navarro River's Paul M. Dimmick Campground closes in winter

**Facilities:** 92 developed forested campsites, hike/bike campsite, picnic area, hiker trails, mountain-bike route, all-ability trail, restrooms, showers (Hendy Woods); 25 primitive campsites, restroom or nonflush toilets, *bring water* (Paul M. Dimmick, Navarro River Redwoods)

**For Information:** (707) 937-5804

**Access:** Both are reached via CA 128. For Hendy Woods, go 2.8 miles west of Philo and turn south on Philo-Greenwood Road. The park entrance is in 0.6 mile. CA 128 passes through Navarro River Redwoods, an 11-mile linear park. Enter the park 1.8 miles west of Navarro or 1 mile east of the CA 128–CA 1 junction.

These two parks showcase the Navarro River and virgin and second-growth redwoods. Hendy Woods is best explored on foot. Although many of its trails are also open to equestrians, the state park lacks the necessary parking to accommodate horse trailers. Navarro River Redwoods is primarily a car-touring destination, with roadside turnouts suggesting opportunities to stop and poke around on foot, spread a picnic lunch, or cool one's ankles in the river.

Fall steelhead runs draw anglers to the Navarro River. As special fishing conditions may exist, check current state regulations. In winter and spring, kayakers and canoeists make their way to these parks. At Hendy Woods, the river is accessed most easily at the day-use area. At Navarro River Redwoods, the many river corridor turnouts and Paul M. Dimmick Campground (5.9 miles west of Navarro or 7.7 miles east of the CA 128–CA 1 junction) serve the river user. Enormous stumps remain throughout the camp.

### Attractions and Activities

**CA 128–Navarro River Redwoods Car Tour.** For 11 miles, a congested corridor of second-growth redwoods shadows CA 128, while alders overhang a parallel creek course and, later, the Navarro River. Amid the forest are huge redwood stumps, some jailed by second-generation trees. A couple of memorial groves dot the route. Sword fern, tanoak, and California laurel interweave between the tall, straight trunks. Horsetail reeds thrive in places.

A distinct water-and-mud line on the trees hints at past flood heights. On a rock cliff above CA 128 (9 miles west of Navarro), travelers may spy a small marker also noting the 1964 flood height. Turnouts are frequent. For the most part, the park is sandwiched between the road and the river.

*Access:* Find the car tour between Navarro and CA 1.

*Hermit's hut, Hendy Woods State Park*

**Gentle Giants All-Access Trail—Upper Loop Tour.** This easy 1.5-mile hiker circuit tours Big Hendy, an extensive, first-rate grove of virgin coastal redwoods—the last of its kind in the Anderson Valley. Following the wide, surfaced all-ability trail, hikers are quickly bowled over by the grandeur of the forest. At 0.2 mile, multiple tour options present themselves. Follow the Upper Loop, heading left, to travel the outermost circuit; major junctions are well marked.

Redwood sorrel, vanilla leaf, ferns, tanoak, and laurel contribute to the forest bounty. Benches suggest frequent stops and lingering looks. Fire-charred and fire-hollowed trees, jagged snags, fallen giants, upturned roots, and dozens upon dozens of the big-diameter trees cause fingers to point and necks to crane.

At 0.9 mile is an unmarked junction. Bear left, heading toward a bench, to continue the Upper Loop; to the right is the open field leading to the day-use area. Where the Upper Loop ends at 1.4 miles, follow the all-ability trail back to the parking area.

*Access:* The trail begins at Hendy Woods day-use area.

**Little Hendy Grove Trail.** This lopsided figure-eight trail is 1 mile round-trip. It visits a much smaller grove of virgin redwoods, with a few notably striking trees. From the campground loops, the trail passes through a woodland corridor with tanoak, laurel, and black huckleberry, reaching Little Hendy Loop at 0.2 mile.

A clockwise tour of the 0.5-mile redwood loop begins to the left. It remains in woodland, descending to a footbridge, where hikers enter the cool darkness of the redwood grove. Off the redwood loop branches a 0.1-mile woodland loop, completing the figure-eight. It tours a slope above the redwood drainage bottom.

*Access:* Begin at Hendy Woods Campground: near site 73 in Wildcat Loop, near site 11 in Azalea Loop.

**Hermit Hut Trail.** This 0.3-mile round-trip walk begins with a steep 0.1-mile uphill charge on an old skid road, passing through second growth. At the T junction, go left and keep an eye on the right-hand side of the road. In less than 0.1 mile, look for the hermit's hut in a burned-out redwood snag; a faint path leads to it.

The hut, a partially collapsed lean-to, still displays its redwood limb supports and bough thatching. A crawl space in the base of the snag reveals the cramped inside quarters and remnants of flooring. The Boonville Hermit, who died in 1986, lived here some eighteen years. Gradually, nature is reclaiming his home.

*Access:* Follow the path leading from the hiker/biker campsite at Hendy Campground's Wildcat Loop to the park road and turn left. The trailhead is marked only by a post stating no dogs or bikes allowed.

**Hendy Fire Road.** This gravel-surfaced, single-lane road shows a slow, steady climb and is open to foot, mountain bike, and horse travel. Second-growth redwood, laurel, tanoak, fir, and madrone frame and semi-shade the route. Where the fire road forks in a few places, stay on the primary route. Side trails branch to Hendy Grove and the Navarro River. If you decide to take one of these, heed the posted use signs. All trails are closed to mountain bikes and some prohibit horses.

By 0.8 mile, the fire road affords filtered looks at the river, and by 1.2 miles the climbing grade becomes more marked. Grouse sound in the distance. A gate at 1.7 miles signals the end of the park fire road, but travelers may continue. The state park and the rancher next door have a mutual-access agreement. Respect private property, and leave gates as you find them.

Loop tours are possible by traveling both state park and private ranch lands. Before beginning such a trip, ask the park ranger for a map.

*Access:* The gated fire road leaves the Hendy Woods park road between the campground and day-use area.

## Manchester State Beach

**Hours/Season:** Year-round

**Facilities:** 46 primitive inland campsites, 8 environmental campsites, hiker trails, nonflush toilets, water

**For Information:** (707) 937-5804

**Access:** Just north of Manchester, turn west off CA 1 onto Kinney Road to reach the main entrance in 0.6 mile.

This park encompasses a 5-mile beach, dune fields, marsh and ponds, a coastal plain, lagoon, and two year-round creeks, serving beachcomber, hiker, birder, and surf and freshwater angler. Winds often sweep this coastal stretch; the many drift-log shelters along the beach hint at their tenacity and frequency. Alder Creek, the park's north boundary, hosts winter steelhead runs.

The grassland campsites are mostly open, interspersed with a few cypresses and pines. Westward views stretch across the field and low dune toward the ocean. Eastward looks are of the Coast Range.

In the grassy areas at Manchester State Beach and other coastal parks, ticks are a concern from January through May.

### Attractions and Activities

**Beach-Inland Loop.** This 5-mile loop offers an exploration of beach, bluff, grassy dune, and coastal plain.

The hike begins heading north on the beach. Grass-topped dunes rising 8 to 10 feet border the early distance. Drift logs pile at the foot of the dunes; other logs protrude from the sandbanks. Makeshift wind shelters dot the beach. Looks south are of Point Arena Lighthouse.

The dark, coarse sand becomes easier to walk on and hikers will not sink in as much after 0.5 mile. At 1 mile is a seasonal pond outlet. When swollen by winter rains, it defies fording, turning back hikers. Other times of the year, the outlet presents an easy crossing or is absent altogether.

As the tour resumes north, bluffs replace the dunes; gradually they grade up to 100 feet tall. The beach is still clean, with sloping, dark sand. Its abrupt drop provides a casting edge for surf fishing. Atop the bluff sits a condemned beach house, now part of the park. At Alder Creek Access at 1.9 miles, the loop turns inland, following the road ascending away from the beach. Hikers may choose, however, to continue on the beach for a 1-mile round-trip detour, hiking the loose sand of the spit to the Alder Creek outlet and back.

Forgoing the detour, hikers pass a parking area overlooking Alder Creek at 2 miles. Remain on the road for another 0.1 mile, and take the gated route on its west side to continue the loop.

It follows this closed route west and south along the open bluff for an inland return. At 2.5 miles, hikers bypass the hazardous, condemned house; stay out. Beyond the house is the Osprey environmental site, complete with table, fire ring, and pit toilet. Lupine and wild strawberry grow in the coastal field.

At the 2.7-mile junction, a left leads to still more such campsites snugged amid the cypress trees. To the right, the overgrown trail that continues the loop heads south at the edge of the dune. Posts help hikers stay on course; grasses brush the legs.

At 3 miles, hikers reach the Sea Grass environmental site, near the pond outlet mentioned at 1 mile. The route now travels south atop the dune, overlooking the marsh. After passing through an area of old fence posts, it veers east, touring above a small pond at 3.5 miles. Buffleheads ply the water, while frogs croak from unseen places. Bulrushes rim the pond.

Next, the trail angles southeast across the plain with its knee-high shrubs, grasses, and lupine. Here, deer, rabbits, and hawks are possible wildlife sightings. At 4 miles is a trail fork: to the left is a KOA campground; to the right is the park and the rest of the loop.

Where the trail again quickly forks, stay right. At 4.25 miles, it cuts through a cypress hedgerow, arriving at the parking area for the environmental sites. Again, go right, following the narrow, paved lane toward the beach. A mowed path replaces it as it crosses the campground road, bringing the loop to a close at the beach day-use area at 5 miles.

*Access:* Begin the loop at the Kinney Road day-use parking area, crossing the dune to the beach.

**Stoneboro Road Beach Access.** This 0.75-mile trail to the park's southern beach segment crosses a rolling field of grass-topped dunes. Loose sands work the legs. At 0.6 mile, the path dips into an open, sandy bowl, suggesting dune play. Where the trail meets the beach, a long strand invites in either direction.

A 2-mile hike north leads to the mouth of Brush Creek and the heart of the park; a 0.5-mile hike south offers fine looks at the long, flat peninsula of Point Arena, with its lighthouse and few cypress trees. The beach is similar to that farther north, with drift-log debris along its upper reaches and coarse, open sand.

*Access:* From the junction of Kinney Road and CA 1, go south on CA 1 for 1.7 miles. There, turn west onto Stoneboro Road and go 1.6 miles for beach parking.

**Birdwatching.** The park's varied terrain brings variety to birdwatching. Northern harriers soar over the vegetated dunes and coastal plains; tundra swans winter here and at Garcia River (0.5 mile south of the park); ducks, herons, and shorebirds frequent the ponds; and seabirds skim atop and dive in the ocean. The informal lagoon overlooks, reached by taking Barnegat Drive and Bristol Road off Stoneboro Road, promise additional sightings. Scopes and binoculars are recommended.

# Clear Lake State Park

**Hours/Season:** Year-round
**Facilities:** 147 developed campsites, picnic areas, visitor center, boat launch, swimming area, hiker trails, restrooms, pay showers
**For Information:** (707) 279-4293
**Access:** At Kelseyville, turn north off CA 29, following the signs through town for Clear Lake. In 3 miles, turn east on Soda Bay Road to reach the park in another mile.

The park occupies 565 acres on the southwest shore of Clear Lake—the largest natural lake fully contained within California's borders. The lake is 19 miles long, with 100 miles of shore. Furrowed hillsides, riparian and tule shores, and residential and resort areas frame the sparkling blue water and its many coves. The park borders Soda Bay, named for the bubbles released by a below-surface carbonated spring.

Clear Lake offers great wet fun, with boating, fishing, swimming, and waterskiing; summertime water temperatures warm to 76 degrees. Picnicking, hiking, and birdwatching also engage parkgoers. The visitor center, alongside Kelsey Creek Diversion, boasts both natural and cultural displays, a fine aquarium with Clear Lake fish species, films, and a gift shop. Its broad porches and many benches offer a place to relax and enjoy the area. Heron, gull, jay, woodpecker, and kingfisher are common passersby. Deer often nibble the surrounding grasses.

Next door to the center is Cole Creek Launch, with its extensive parking area and fish-cleaning station. A 10-minute mooring time is allowed, with boat-slip rentals available. Arching over Cole Creek, a scenic footbridge links the launch and the picnic area flat.

*Campsite breakfast, Clear Lake State Park*

The park has four camp areas, with open or oak-shaded sites; some are lakeside. While shower facilities are within access of all, Lower Bayview campers have a longer walk. Due to the size of Lower Bayview's parking spaces, it is recommended for tent camping only. Upper Bayview Campground is the most remote. A separate swimming area faces out on Dorn Cove. It has an open, gravelly beach, some 30 feet wide and 200 feet long. Dense willows frame the cove's sides.

### Attractions and Activities

**Indian Nature Trail.** This 0.5-mile round-trip self-guided trail travels the tree- and chaparral-clad slope above the park road, visiting twenty interpretive stations. The park brochure contains descriptions corresponding to the numbered markers. Along the trail, visitors discover not only the plant varieties of the park but also learn how the plants were used by the Pomo Indians for food, making baskets or tools, and stunning fish. The tour actually passes through an ancient village site. Elsewhere, a mortar hole and obsidian provide visible clues to the past. Midway, a spur leads to a bench overlooking the valley and the ridge to the southwest. Beware of poison oak along the trail and throughout the park.

*Access:* The trail begins north of the entrance station.

**Dorn Trail.** This 1.5-mile hiker loop travels the wooded rise at the heart of the park, offering limited vistas.

Heading uphill from the park road near the visitor center, hikers quickly come upon the loop junction. To the right, a counterclockwise tour climbs, contours, and switchbacks to the top of the ridge (0.3 mile), crossing a grassland peppered by oaks, California buckeye, and moss-capped boulders. In spring, the buckeye are showered with blooms. By late summer, the leaves have dried, and heavy fruit hangs on the tree. At the ridgetop junction, a left continues the loop.

Soon, a bench offers limited views west, and laurels join the mix, piquing the nostrils with their medicinal fragrance. As the trail resumes, it makes a rolling descent. More benches present views north of the lake and the folded hillside of the far shore. Hawks, crows, woodpeckers, and songbirds add to the hike, as does the occasional deer. At 0.7 mile, again go left. A mild descent follows, passing through a fuller woodland denying views.

Stay left, as spurs branch to the park road. At 1 mile the final bench sits amid a scenic moss-decorated outcrop. The trail continues rounding and descending the rise, closing the loop at 1.5 miles.

*Access:* Begin on the trail angling uphill opposite the entrance road to the visitor center. Alternative starts are at Upper and Lower Bayview campgrounds and the beach.

**Fishing.** A kiosk near Cole Creek Launch identifies the lake fish: largemouth bass, bluegill, channel catfish, black crappie, and Sacramento perch. Anglers looking for an edge should consult the park brochure. It gives hints on when, where, and how to fish for each.

## Anderson Marsh State Historic Park

**Hours/Season:** 10:00 A.M. to 4:00 P.M. Wednesday through Sunday
**Facilities:** Picnic area, historic ranch house, hiker trails, nonflush toilets, *bring water*
**For Information:** (707) 994-0688 or (707) 279-4293

**Access:** The park is on the west side of CA 53, 2 miles south of the town of Clear Lake.

This park unit offers visitors a unique look at a nineteenth-century ranch operation—one of the few remaining in Lake County. In 1885, John Anderson started a dairy here; later his family switched to cattle ranching. Enclosed within the park borders is a 500-acre tule marsh, which serves as a vital wildlife nursery for the Clear Lake area. Cache Creek, Clear Lake's only outlet, travels at the northern edge of the broad, grassy ranch lowland. Elsewhere, oak knolls mark the property.

Today, visitors can take a guided tour through the Anderson ranch house, encircle the weathered-board barns and corral, and picnic beneath the stately walnut and oak trees. They also can hike the web of trails stringing from the ranch house to Cache Creek to Anderson Marsh and beyond to McVicar Wildlife Sanctuary, a neighboring Audubon Society natural area.

## Attractions and Activities

**Ranch House Tour.** The two-story wooden house surrounded by a white picket fence maintains a simple elegance—functional and homey. Visitors can see where it was built onto at various times. A covered porch wraps around two sides, protecting the lower story windows and doors. Inside, the house is being refurbished and furnished to convey the comforts and necessities of ranch living at the turn of the century. On the tour, visitors learn about ranch life and the family who lived here.

**Cache Creek–Anderson Marsh Loop.** This 3-mile circuit tours the various park habitats, offering bird and wildlife observation.

A counterclockwise tour follows the mowed track toward Cache Creek and its sidewater oxbows. Mustard, grasses, and mullein line the open way. As it curves west, paralleling the creek upstream, willows, cottonwoods, and oaks mark the meadow-riparian edge. Occasionally, hikers see deer drinking at the creek or western pond turtles sunning on semi-submerged limbs.

Where the trail meets another mowed track at 0.4 mile, bear right for the loop. Ahead, a newly installed footbridge arcs over the creek, as the trail system continues to grow. Throughout the tour, cross-meadow views engage. Sometimes a ring-necked pheasant bursts from the thick grass. By 0.9 mile, the trail continues briefly next to Cache Creek proper; it is lined by residences and private docks on the opposite shore. After 1.25 miles, the trail leaves the creek, approaching an oak rise.

At 1.5 miles, the Ridge Trail heads left, bypassing a picnic table and chemical toilet. For the loop, continue straight, following the Marsh Trail, as it rounds the oak hillside. Where animals have burrowed, hikers may spy bits of obsidian. Ahead, short spurs branch to rock outcroppings, where shallow grinding depressions made by early Indians may be seen. While interesting, the examples are not outstanding.

Soon the trail overlooks the seasonal marsh. Poison oak thrives beneath the trees, while a couple of woodpecker-drilled snags catch the eye. At the 2.1-mile junction, go left for the loop. Just ahead is a four-way junction on a low saddle. There, go right, passing through an area of smaller-trunked oaks.

For much of the remaining way, the trail stays near the border fence. At 2.4 miles, it bypasses a picnic table and chemical toilet. After edging along a grassland flat for 0.2 mile, turn right at the fence corner to return to the ranch house.

*Access:* Begin north of the ranch house following the mowed track parallel to CA 53 past the windmill and blackberry vines.

**Birdwatching.** The park's 500 acres of marsh represent more than half of the re-

*Woodpecker-drilled snag, Anderson Marsh State Historic Park*

maining wetland along the Clear Lake shore. This critical, productive habitat affords exceptional birdwatching, with wintering bald eagles (December through March), white pelicans (returning after a forty-year absence), blue herons, ducks, and coots. The park's grassland, oak woodland, and riparian areas further expand the bird count and species identification list.

## Schooner Gulch

**Hours/Season:** Daylight hours
**Facilities:** Beach-access trails, nonflush toilets, *bring water*
**For Information:** (707) 937-5804
**Access:** From Point Arena, go 3.6 miles south on CA 1. South-facing roadside parking is found along CA 1 opposite Schooner Gulch Road.

This park accesses two beach segments isolated by a headland point. The northern one, Bowling Ball Beach, is a "don't miss" destination. It owes its name to a series of unusually round boulders revealed at low tide. Its eroding cliffs and other odd rock features further recommend it. Bowling Ball Beach is better for walkers, while its rocky counterpart, Schooner Gulch, is preferred by anglers. The waters offshore represent a protected underwater area.

Bishop pines dot the dividing headland's grass and fern flat. While the site welcomes picnickers, from January through May visitors need to beware of ticks and check pant legs often.

### Attractions and Activities

**Bowling Ball Beach Trail.** This 0.2-mile trail bears right, crossing the grass and fern plateau, for a steep bluff descent to the beach. The narrow footpath can become slippery when wet. It arrives at the beach amid a drift-log jumble near a small creek drainage.

Pretty Bowling Ball Beach features a flat, hard-packed, light-colored sandy strand. The curvature of the cliffs cuts it off at about 1 mile. The amount of beach and how far one can walk depend on the tide. Low rocks and kelp beds lie just offshore.

Hiking north 0.25 mile leads to the main area of "bowling balls," revealed at low tide. It is worth consulting a tide table and timing your visit to see them. Above the beach, the mudstone cliffs reveal a vertical layering, and visitors can see where the boulders have eroded and are eroding from their walls.

In another 0.25 mile, a section of cliff features some amazing, vertically aligned, orange disk-shaped rocks, measuring 5 to 8 feet in diameter. Elsewhere, pockmarks, undulating patterns, and accordion ribs characterize the cliff. In places, the ribs bend, extending into the ocean, creating a perch for seabirds.

A short walk south on Bowling Ball Beach finds interconnected sea caves in the rusty, leached cliff.

*Access:* Take the northern trail on the west side of CA 1.

**Schooner Gulch Beach-Access Trail.** This 0.2-mile trail descends through a corridor of second-growth redwoods, with alder and pines appearing later. At 0.1 mile, hikers find a spur to a pit toilet and a connecting trail to Bowling Ball Beach. Stay straight, negotiating the drift-log scatter. Ahead, Schooner Gulch feeds into the sea; gravel and logs are piled in its mouth. A log crossing or fording is necessary to reach the small beach, hugged by cliffs.

*Access:* Take the southern trail on the west side of CA 1.

## Mailliard Redwoods State Reserve

**Hours/Season:** Daylight hours
**Facilities:** 1 picnic table, *bring water*
**For Information:** (707) 937-5804
**Access:** On CA 128, go 20 miles west of Cloverdale or 7.3 miles east of Boonville and turn south on Fish Rock Road. Go another 3.1 miles to enter the park.

This park unit is suitable either for the CA 128 traveler looking for a place to stretch or for a true state park buff, but for most its offerings are too limited to consider it as a destination.

The park's 242 acres of virgin and second-growth redwoods along the headwaters of the Garcia River are best appreciated while driving Fish Rock Road and taking advantage of the shoulder turnouts or the lone picnic site on the right, 0.8 mile into the park. Salmon and steelhead spawn in the small, protected waterway, closed to fishing. Tanoaks weave a midstory beneath the redwood high-rises, and firs are among the forest mix. Quiet reigns supreme.

## Salt Point State Park—Kruse Rhododendron State Reserve

**Hours/Season:** Year-round (Kruse Rhododendron State Reserve is day-use only)
**Facilities:** 2 campgrounds with a total of 109 developed pine-forested sites, 10

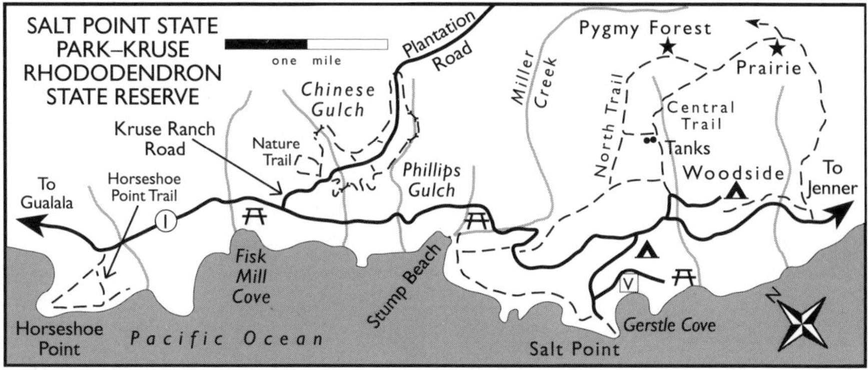


hike/bike campsites, 20 walk-in campsites, RV/trailer overflow lot, picnic area, visitor center, diver's boat launch, hiker and horse trails, mountain-bike routes (open May through October), restrooms (Salt Point); hiker trails, non-flush toilets, *bring water* (Kruse Rhododendron)

**For Information:** (707) 847-3221 or (707) 865-2391

**Access:** Reach Salt Point's main entry off CA 1, 18.5 miles south of Gualala or 15.5 miles north of Jenner. Kruse Rhododendron State Reserve is east off CA 1, 2.7 miles north of Salt Point's Gerstle Cove turnoff.

These adjoining parks bring together an exciting rocky coastline, small beach coves, an underwater marine reserve, patches of rhododendron, stands of second-growth redwood, a pygmy forest, and coastal meadows. Divers, anglers, picnickers, hikers, equestrians, and other nature enthusiasts share in the discovery.

Sentinel Rock at Fisk Mill Cove offers an elevated look at the coast, while Gerstle Cove's 0.1-mile Salt Point Trail affords a fine overlook of the marine reserve and the offshore rocks frequented by harbor seals. The many rhododendrons attain their glory April through June.

## Attractions and Activities

**Gerstle Cove to Stump Beach Hike.** This 1.6-mile one-way trail heads north on a 2-track, crossing the western edge of a grassy bluff dotted by sandstone outcrops. Lupine and Douglas iris grow amid the coastal grasses; rabbits and quail startle upon approach. At the 0.3-mile fork, stay west to enjoy the rocky shoreline splashed by the surf. The ragged foot of the low bluffs provides surf fishermen a casting advantage, but be ever watchful of the waves.

At 0.7 mile, where the track merges with one from the east, CA 1 is visible. Ahead, a tall rock outcrop blocks the coastal view, and the grassy flat between the trail and the coastline broadens. By 1.3 miles, the trail overlooks Stump Beach, just a small sandy area facing out on a boxy cove; sea caves mark the north wall.

At 1.4 miles, an erosion gouge north of the jeep track presents the descent to Miller Creek and Stump Beach. In winter, a creek wading or CA 1 detour is necessary to reach the beach. The hike ends at Stump Beach parking at 1.6 miles.

Hikers may extend the trek to Fisk Mill Cove (3.75 miles one-way). For this, near the bottom of the Stump Beach stairway, take the path heading north ascending and rounding a small side drainage. The route begins well, but atop the bluff it degenerates into a maze of paths, requiring continual choosing. Keep north.

*Visitor Center at Gerstle Cove, Salt Point State Park*

*Access:* Take the 2-track north from Gerstle Cove parking.

**Horseshoe Point Trail.** This 1.3-mile loop follows 2-tracks, touring the coastal bluff meadow south of Horseshoe Point.

At 0.1 mile, go right at the fork. Where the trail quickly splits into three prongs, take the center route, mounting a small, broad-topped knoll (0.3 mile) for a Sonoma Coast overlook. Grasses, bracken fern, iris, and other wildflowers top the knoll; pines rim its east edge. The jeep trail then rounds the north side of the knoll, tagging the saddle between the knoll and the rocky rise ahead. Quail are often flushed from the shrubs.

From the saddle, the loop journeys south, traveling just inland from shore. The area's low rock outcrops serve the surf fishermen. At 1 mile, follow the jeep track that curves east; it ascends the slope, passing between areas of pines, to close the loop. A second route continues south.

*Access:* Start at the gate on the west side of CA 1, 1.2 miles north of the turn for Kruse Rhododendron State Reserve.

**Pygmy Forest Loop.** This 5-mile hiker/horse trail travels mostly on fire roads. It begins framed by fir, pine, waxmyrtle, tanoak, black huckleberry, and redwoods.

Go 0.1 mile from the Woodside hike/bike area and bear right for the described tour. The vegetation becomes more shrubby and dense, with fewer tall trees. Next to the water tanks at 0.4 mile, head left on the fire road for a steady uphill.

At 0.7 mile, the loop meets and follows the North Trail to the right toward Pygmy Forest. Stumps record long-ago redwood logging, while a tanoak leaf mat disguises the fire road. Still the route climbs. At 1.1 miles, it tops out and enters the naturally stunted forest. Bordering the path are 15-foot-tall old-growth pines and 4-foot-tall, single-branched pygmy cypress. Shrubs weave between the 1- to 2-inch-diameter trees.

At 1.4 miles, hikers depart Pygmy Forest, touring a transition habitat, and the road narrows to trail width. After a descent, the trail comes out at a main dirt fire road at 1.9 miles. For the described loop, go left on it, reaching the open prairie in 0.2 mile. The trail next tours the edge of this long, mixed-grass plain, where deer, fox, or hawk may be spied. Bypassing the spur junction to Sea View Road, hikers leave the prairie at 2.6 miles.

Now, the loop arcs west, starting the major downhill portion of the journey. Second-growth redwoods again frame the route, with the Bishop pines returning, as it nears CA 1.

At 3.9 miles, horseback riders and hikers part company. Riders descend to CA 1; hikers bear right on the footpath, touring a utility corridor back to Woodside Campground and the start of the loop. At 4.5 miles, where the trail enters the campground, follow the road or the utility corridor toward the campground exit to close the loop.

*Access:* From CA 1, south of the Gerstle Cove turnoff, turn east for Woodside Campground. The trail (a gated fire road) heads northeast from the hike/bike parking lot.

**Chinese Gulch–Phillips Gulch Loop.** This 3-mile hiker-only loop introduces the natural offering of Kruse Rhododendron State Reserve. Although the entire trail is mostly or semi-shaded for a comfortable tour, visitors should carry water.

At the information board, go left on the 0.2-mile nature trail. The area it tours is exposed from a past fire and recent downfalls, creating a finer rhododendron display. Salal, tanoak, huckleberry, and wild grasses, along with pines and fir, contribute to the vegetation.

At the junction, go left on the Chinese Gulch Trail, touring a fuller forest. The rhododendrons now have a spotty presence, often growing tall and spindly while reaching toward the light. Stairsteps descend to the footbridge crossing of Chinese Gulch at 0.5 mile; Plantation Road passes nearby. Ahead, the trail ascends a narrow draw. Second-growth redwoods with 3- to 4-foot-diameter trunks, snags, and stumps contribute to the forest. Benches dot the route.

After switchbacking uphill, hikers come to a junction at 0.8 mile; go left, staying on the Chinese Gulch Trail. The loop continues its rolling journey, with subtle changes occurring in the forest mix. At 1.5 miles, after crossing a county road, hikers begin the return leg, along the Phillips Gulch Trail.

Tanoaks dominate, with rhododendrons still spotting the mix. As the trail descends, it follows an old skid-road corridor. After a couple of footbridges, at 2 miles the loop curves right, following a foot trail away from the skid road.

At the 2.3-mile junction, go left, staying on the Phillips Gulch Trail to complete the loop. The trail switchbacks downhill to the gulch bridge crossing (2.75 miles), only to switchback up the opposite slope. The hike ends at the reserve parking area.

*Access:* From the Junction of CA 1 and Kruse Ranch Road, go east 0.4 mile on Kruse Ranch Road to the reserve. *With limited parking and turning space, this road is not recommended for trailers or motorhomes.*

**Diving.** At the northern parking area for Gerstle Cove, a paved trail descends to the tidepools and water. Divers use this trail to portage and launch their inflatable rafts. All cove marine life is protected in an underwater reserve; the area is closed to collecting and fishing. The reserve boasts a variety of life, colorful and fragile. Even from the bluff overlooking the cove, visitors can spy the anemone, starfish, and algae in the tidepools and shallows.

*Access:* Take the Salt Point State Park, Gerstle Cove Campground turnoff and follow the park road to Gerstle Cove Parking.

# ROBERT LOUIS STEVENSON STATE PARK

**Hours/Season:** Daylight hours
**Facilities:** 2 picnic tables, historical marker, hiker trails, mountain-bike route, *bring water*
**For Information:** (707) 942-4575
**Access:** From Calistoga, go 8 miles north on CA 29 for the park. Dirt parking areas are on both sides of the road.

This slightly out-of-the-way, primitive addition to the state park system has won favor with mountain-bike riders and hikers. The park celebrates the most prominent feature rising above the Napa Valley—Mount St. Helena (elevation 4,343 feet). The peak is noted for its grand vistas. Robert Louis Stevenson, who honeymooned here in 1880, popularized the mountain in his book *The Silverado Squatters.*

On weekends and summer days, finding a parking space can be a challenge. Park personnel regularly patrol the summit fire road by vehicle.

## Attractions and Activities

**Mount St. Helena Summit Trail.** While cyclists must follow the 5.25-mile summit fire road the entire way, hikers have the option of touring the Stevenson Memorial Trail, which links up with it, for a shortened 5-mile one-way hike to the summit. Each of the routes has a 2,100-foot elevation change.

The Stevenson Memorial Trail remains mostly shaded, touring a complex of fir, oak, madrone, and tanoak, with greasewood and manzanita in the more open areas. Even-climbing switchbacks advance the trail. At 0.8 mile is the Robert Louis Stevenson Memorial.

This simple salute to the writer rests beside the flat where his honeymoon cabin stood. Atop the memorial's crystal-spangled mined-rock pedestal is an opened marble book bearing Stevenson's personal account of the mountain. On a nearby slope, a chute of broken rocks hints at a onetime mine.

From the memorial, the trail climbs steeply and ruggedly to meet up with the fire-road bicycle route at 0.9 mile. Here, hikers should take a moment to note where they came out, as the return to the foot trail is unmarked and easy to miss. When ready, bear left on the fire road, joining the legion of mountain bikers en route to the summit.

The single-lane dirt road is semi-shaded where big trees claim the lower slope, but is mostly open for the bulk of the climb. After the first mile, low pines, manzanita, laurel, small oaks, and greasewood vegetate the slope, with rock outcrops interspersing the chaparral cover.

Here, too, the road offers an early vista, featuring Mount Diablo, Calistoga, and the Napa Valley. Secondary trails descend to old mining sites—some with steep shafts. Be alert, should you do any off-trail exploration.

At the 1.6-mile switchback rises Bubble Rock, a pockmarked outcrop (bicyclists, add 0.25-mile to the given distance readings). After 2 miles, a few pines afford patchy shade. Between 3 and 3.4 miles, the trail tours the moister north slope, marked by a return of firs. Here, too, the climb intensifies. Views are of the side peak to the north and the distant Sierra to the east.

At 3.5 miles is a road junction. To the left is the route up South Peak (elevation 4,003 feet); to the right lies Mount St. Helena's summit. The 0.5-mile detour topping South Peak offers a fine Napa Valley vista. Forgoing the detour, travelers find the route flattens as it rounds the rugged drainage between South Peak and Mount St. Helena.

At 4 miles, the climb resumes, and at 4.6 miles, a side road heads up a neighboring ridge with towers. Stay on the main fire road to reach the summit. Larger trees, including a sugar pine, soon line the road. At 4.8 miles, the fire road makes a sharp charge for the summit, coming out at a tower (5 miles).

Best views are to the west and north, but summit visitors can piece together a full 360-degree vista. Panoramas sweep from the Sierra crest to the ocean's glare. Mounts Diablo and Tamalpais, Snow Mountain, South Peak, and Mount St. Helena's own rugged north flank add to the view. Return as you came.

*Access:* From the parking areas, bicyclists go 0.25 mile north on CA 29 and take the gated dirt fire road heading west. Hikers find the start for the Stevenson Memorial Trail at the west-side parking area.

**Wild Lilac Trail.** This hiker-only trail follows an abandoned road and pieces of foot trail for a 1.7-mile round-trip hike, with a 300-foot elevation change. Along it, hikers find the best looks at Mount St. Helena's South Peak.

The trail switchbacks through a woodland of Douglas fir, tanoak, laurel, and maple, soon arriving at a rocky road. Go left on it, continuing the climb. At 0.3 mile, a clearing offers a preview look at South Peak; at 0.4 mile, a bald knob serves up a bold look at South Peak and the side peak to its north.

Pulling away from the vista knob, the trail next tops a saddle, where hikers gain a 90-degree view southwest from Calistoga to the coastal ridges. Two descending slopes frame the view, while utility lines detract from it.

At the T junction at 0.6 mile, go right. The trail is now a footpath, ascending the slope. Stay on the path, as poison oak is well represented in the vegetation. A couple more openings offer looks west, before the trail tops a rise, reaching the park boundary. From the boundary, return as you came.

*Access:* This trail leaves from the east trailhead parking area.

## Fort Ross State Historic Park

**Hours/Season:** 10:00 A.M. to 4:30 P.M., except major holidays (fort); March 15 through November 30 (campground)

**Facilities:** 20 developed coastal canyon campsites, picnic areas, visitor center, historic fort, hiker trails, restrooms and flush toilets

**For Information:** (707) 847-3286

**Access:** Entry to the fort is west off CA 1, 11 miles north of Jenner; the campground is 9.4 miles north of Jenner.

Centerpiece to the park is the reconstructed nineteenth-century Russian fort, which sits atop a wind-washed plateau overlooking the ocean and Fort Ross Cove. It was established in 1812, to protect Russian interests, promote fur hunting, and grow foodstuffs to supply the Alaskan outposts. In 1841, the resulting decline in the number of sea otters made further hunting uneconomical, and the Russians withdrew.

In addition to the fort, the park has 3,157 acres of undeveloped upland, stretching to the coastal ridge. Within this acreage, visitors are free to roam at will or hike along the old logging roads. Its redwood canyons, once logged by the Russians, now hold some of the oldest second-growth redwoods in the world. Coastal vistas

*Cannon and Russian Orthodox Church, Fort Ross State Historic Park*

are far-sweeping. Wildflower meadows and an abandoned Russian orchard are other possible discoveries.

The visitor center is a good place to begin a stay. There one can learn about the history of the fort and its residents and about the May-Tee-Nee Indian settlement, which stood on this site when the Russians arrived. Interpretive panels, exhibits, and a film unfold the tale.

## Attractions and Activities

**Fort Ross Walking Tour.** A 0.25-mile paved, all-ability trail travels the edge of a cypress grove and traverses the grassland bluff to reach the fort gate. An impenetrable 10-foot-tall solid wall topped by 2.5-foot-high pickets encloses the compound. Inside, signs indicate the sites of former structures and describe the historic use of each of the reconstructed redwood buildings. Examples of maritime joinery can be seen in the sturdy units.

The Fort Ross settlement consisted of fifty-nine buildings, only nine of which were inside the stockade. The Commandant's House, built in 1836, is the only structure still possessing the original Russian materials. In its rooms are historical panels.

The Officials Quarters (next door), the chapel, and the Kuskov House all contain rooms reflecting the lifestyle, furnishings, and supplies of the day. True to the past, the rooms are kept dimly lit, and indoor and outdoor shutters double-protect the windows. Entering the cannon-fortified blockhouses at the corners of the compound, visitors can view the fort's defense.

The original chapel collapsed in the 1906 earthquake and was twice restored before it burned down in 1970. The present-time restored chapel accurately reflects the appearance of the original Russian Orthodox church, with its two dome towers, chandelier, and simple altar and pulpit. The bell outside its door was recast, using the metal from the original bell.

Exiting the west gate, visitors can cross the bluff, descending a dirt lane to Fort Ross Cove. A sign indicates that the Russians had their first shipyard, bathhouse, cooperage, tannery, and smithy on this site. Drift logs and cobbles mark the upper edge of the scenic 0.1-mile-long dark-sand curvature.

At the southeast corner of the cove, a trail mounts the bluff and journeys south along it, accessing fantastic views of the rugged, rocky shore and offering over-the-shoulder looks at Fort Ross. It ends at the park campground in 1 mile. So, from Fort Ross Cove, hikers may opt to continue to the campground, return as they came, or follow a fragment of old CA 1 back to the visitor center parking area.

*Access:* The tour begins at the visitor center.

**Bluff Trail.** This 0.25-mile walk west along a 2-track and foot trail crosses an open, grassy bluff marked by a few white sandstone outcrops. It overlooks Fort Ross Cove, and offers a different perspective on the fort—one that photographers will want to investigate. In the late 1800s, when a lumberman owned the fort, a flexible loading chute ran between the bluff and the cove. Now, cows graze the bluff plateau. While no formal trail exists, hikers are free to continue north along the bluff. When ready, return as you came.

*Access:* Leave the southwest end of the visitor center parking lot, and look for the hiker gate on the west side of old CA 1.

## Woodland Opera House State Historic Park

**Hours/Season:** 9:00 A.M. to 5:00 P.M. Tuesday through Friday (box office); phone for the times of weekend evening performances and docent-led tours
**Facilities:** Historic building, restrooms
**For Information:** (916) 666-9617
**Access:** On Main Street in Woodland near the Second Street intersection.

In downtown Woodland, an open plaza allows visitors to admire the red brick exterior of this historic 1896 opera house. The plaza benches, garden boxes, and antique lightposts capture the flavor of the era. This was actually the town's second opera house; the original one on this site was lost to fire.

Inside, visitors find a fully restored 644-seat Victorian opera house, complete with balcony, orchestra pit, and box and general seating. The velvet drapes, wallpaper friezes, imported carpet, carved pillars, and chandelier suspended from a star-spangled dome draw visitors back in time.

The guided tours journey upstairs and backstage. In the ladies' retiring room, visitors can see the swooning couch, costume trunks, and a memorabilia case filled with old programs and billboards advertising the performances. Backstage and in the basement are some of the more interesting discoveries, including the original gas lighting panel for the stage, old-time props, and dressing room graffiti left by the traveling troupes.

The opera house closed in 1913 and remained vacant until its restoration in the early 1980s. As it was untouched during those years, the restoration is highly accurate, and the theater retains features not seen in most others like it. The necessary modernizations to meet state codes blend with the old-time elegance and bring comfort to the players and audiences that once again fill the Woodland Opera House.

## Armstrong Redwoods State Reserve—Austin Creek State Recreation Area

**Hours/Season:** 8:00 A.M. to one hour after sunset (Armstrong Redwoods); year-round (Austin Creek)
**Facilities:** Picnic area, visitor center, pack station, hiker trails, restrooms (Armstrong Redwoods); 24 developed wooded campsites (no reservations), 4 trail camps (permits required), hiker and horse trails, mountain-bike routes, restrooms, nonflush toilets (Austin Creek)
**For Information:** (707) 869-2015

**Access:** At Guerneville, turn north off Main Street (River Road/CA 116) onto Armstrong Woods Road and go 2.2 miles to enter Armstrong Redwoods State Reserve. Pass through the reserve to the picnic area and take the winding mountain road another 2.5 miles to reach Bullfrog Pond Campground at Austin Creek State Recreation Area. *The route to the campground is closed to all trailers and to vehicles over 20 feet.*

These adjoining parks bring together the deep-woods grandeur of a remnant ancient redwood grove and the breakaway adventure of the enfolding rolling hills.

In its 700 acres, Armstrong Redwoods Reserve boasts some truly fine ancient trees, as well as second-growth redwoods. In the 1870s, Colonel Armstrong, a lumberman, realized the splendor of the area's ancient coastal redwoods would be lost forever and turned his attention from cutting to preserving the big trees. From his natural park comes the reserve of today. The Parson Jones Tree, the tallest one here, tops out at 310 feet; the Colonel Armstrong Tree is the oldest at 1,400 years.

In addition to its nature trails touring the Armstrong Grove, the park has a fine picnic area amid the big trees. Its Forest Theater, while no longer used for outdoor performances, offers a fine place to sit and quietly enjoy this natural redwood amphitheater.

Next door, at 4,200-acre Austin Creek State Recreation Area, the remote grassland hills, mixed open forests, and plunging wooded drainages serve up a striking contrast to the cool darkness of Armstrong Redwoods Reserve. Deer, wild turkey, hawk, and raccoon are commonly spied. Solitude can be found. It is this wildness and peace that attracted and inspired world-renowned ceramic artist Marguerite Wildenhain. Her Pond Farm home and workshop are now part of the park.

While horses are allowed on all Austin Creek trails, riders must access the park through Armstrong Redwoods Reserve. A riding concession/pack station operates adjacent to the reserve, offering guided day and overnight trips into the recreation area.

## Attractions and Activities

**Armstrong Redwoods Nature Trail–Discovery Trail Loop.** A 1-mile loop tours the core of Armstrong Redwoods Reserve, visiting two of its named trees. A brochure for the nature trail component may be purchased at the visitor center (open 10:00 A.M. to 4:00 P.M.). Along the Discovery Trail, guide wires and Braille signs help the park's sight-impaired visitors enjoy the grove.

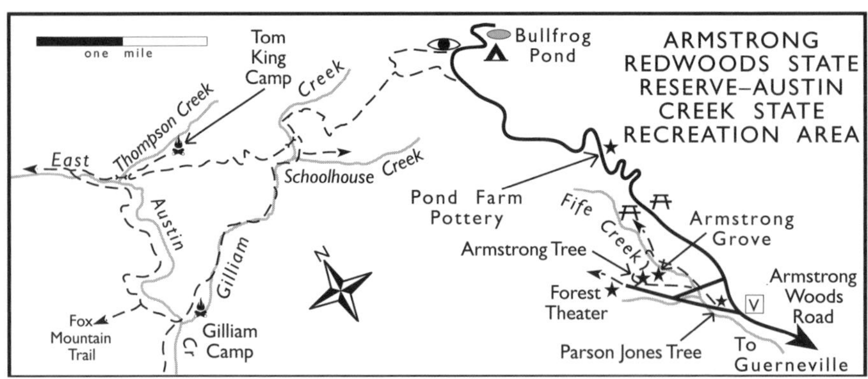

*East Austin Creek, Austin Creek State Recreation Area*

The loop begins following the Pioneer Trail/Nature Trail, which starts next to the Parson Jones Tree, an impressive giant named for Armstrong's son-in-law. A 1,000-year-old log cut, its rings paired to historical events, also sits near the start. Bigleaf maple, laurel, hazel, and tanoak weave the midstory, while oxalis, trillium, sword fern, orchids, and moss decorate the forest floor. A low rail fence lines the earthen lane. Snags, "fairy rings" (sprout circles), and upturned roots contribute to the tour.

Where the trail crosses a connecting road, keep right to follow the nature trail numbers. Ahead, Burbank Circle features some fine big trees on either side of the trail. After passing one with a fire-hollowed goose pen, hikers pace off the length of a fallen redwood. At 0.4 mile, go left for the Nature Trail, continuing toward the Armstrong Tree. Light and shadow play amid the trunks.

At 0.6 mile, bear right a couple of steps to view the Armstrong Tree, which marks the end of the Nature Trail and the start of the Discovery Trail. The tree is noteworthy, standing taller than a thirty-story building.

When ready to continue, retrace those couple of steps, and resume the loop, now following the Discovery Trail. It points out features to touch and smell and offers a ramp leading hikers up to a redwood. At 0.8 mile, the Discovery Trail ends at the connecting road, mentioned earlier. Follow the road across Fife Creek and go right, retracing the initial 0.2 mile of the hike.

*Access:* From the Armstrong Redwoods Reserve visitor center, hike north past the entry kiosk, taking the left fork of the park road. The trailhead is on the right within 0.1 mile.

**East Austin and Gilliam Creeks Loop.** This strenuous 9.2-mile hiker/horse loop travels ridge and drainage in Austin Creek State Recreation Area, offering fine park overviews. Where it travels service roads, mountain bikers share the route.

A foot trail sharply descends from the vista point and tours a ridge, the north side of which is oak woods, the south side grassland. Keep to the ridge backbone, bypassing a couple of side trails. As the hike continues, madrone, manzanita, laurel, fir, and even some redwood intermingle with the oaks. At 0.4 mile, the trail rapidly descends the grassy slope to meet a service road at 0.5 mile. Bear right on it, continuing the steady descent. Wild turkeys range the grasslands that slope above and below the open route.

By 1.3 miles, a mixed woodland claims the way. The loop junction is where the road reaches riffling Gilliam Creek (1.9 miles). Bear right, crossing the creek, for a counterclockwise tour. Before long, the service-road route is climbing steeply along a side drainage. It then zigzags up the ridge. Overlooking the open grassland slope, travelers find views out over Gilliam Creek.

At 2.9 miles, the trail tops out, exchanging the previous view for ones of the Thompson and East Austin creek drainages; the crowns of the redwoods tower above the other trees. A steep, steady descent follows. At 3.4 miles, the trail to the right leads to Tom King Camp. After crossing Thompson Creek near its East Austin Creek confluence, the loop follows East Austin Creek upstream. Redwood and fir join maple and laurel in shading this much larger creek, coursing over cobbles.

Coming to the junction at 4 miles, bear left for the loop, soon fording East Austin Creek. Here, azaleas spot the banks. The trail now climbs the forested slope, staying parallel to but above East Austin Creek as it follows the waterway back downstream. In less than a mile, the trail tops out. Stay left on the service road bypassing the Fox Mountain Trail. At 5.4 miles, the loop leaves the road, following the foot trail descending left toward Gilliam Camp and Schoolhouse Creek. Again, the loop crosses East Austin Creek, this time near its confluence with Gilliam Creek.

At 5.6 miles, Gilliam Camp occupies a creek flat just below the trail. Its facilities are picnic tables, fire rings, and an outhouse. The trail rolls along the slope above Gilliam Creek and then, between 6.1 and 6.7 miles, crisscrosses it some nine times. Maples, laurels, and firs frame the route. Newts, fish, frogs, and crayfish animate the small, pretty, trickling waterway. By the way, all park streams are closed to fishing.

By about 7 miles, travelers can see the service road across the way. At the upcoming junction go left, crossing Schoolhouse Creek to close the loop alongside Gilliam Creek at 7.3 miles. Retrace the initial 1.9 miles, ending the tour.

*Access:* Begin at the vista parking area at the entrance to Bullfrog Pond Campground.

## BALE GRIST MILL STATE HISTORIC PARK—BOTHE–NAPA VALLEY STATE PARK

**Hours/Season:** 10:00 A.M. to 5:00 P.M., except major holidays (Bale Grist Mill); year-round (Bothe–Napa Valley)

**Facilities:** Picnic sites, historic mill and granary, hiker trail, restrooms (Bale Grist Mill); 50 developed wooded campsites (of which 9 are walk-in), picnic area, visitor center, swimming pool (open summers only), hiker and horse trails, restrooms, showers, dump station (Bothe–Napa Valley)

**For Information:** (707) 963-2236 (Grist Mill); (707) 942-4575 (Bothe-Napa)

**Access:** From St. Helena, go 3 miles north on CA 29 for the mill, 4.6 miles north for Bothe–Napa Valley.

Trail and highway link these side-by-side state parks. At Bale Grist Mill, visitors can rediscover a bygone era in Napa Valley, when grain—not the grape—was the agricultural mainstay. At Bothe–Napa Valley, they can picnic beneath the trees, establish an overnight base for a wine-country stay, or journey the back reaches.

In its 1,900 acres, Bothe–Napa Valley features a varied, rugged terrain, with redwood-lined drainages, areas of rich evergreen-deciduous forest, and harsh hillsides of chaparral and brush. From atop its ridges and saddles, visitors gain state park and Napa Valley vistas.

## Attractions and Activities

**Bale Grist Mill Tour.** Built in 1846, Bale Grist Mill has been meticulously restored to its former appearance and operational status. On weekends, visitors can witness the actual milling process.

It is a sensory-rich experience, with the floor vibrating, the waterwheel groaning, and the stones gnashing. From the cooking demonstration in the adjoining granary wafts the aroma of fresh-baked breads and cookies. Docents in period dress explain the working of the mill and bake old-time recipes, using the stone-milled flours and wood-stoked stoves. Sampling the eats is yet another recommendation for the experience, and bags of the park-milled flour may be purchased for home use.

About the mill are 25- and 50-pound sacks of grist (grain ready to be milled), worn millstones, grain shovels, and the various whisks used to clean the grindingstone furrows. Displayed in saucers are the raw grains. On the second floor, visitors can view the elevators, hoppers, bins, and sifter of the milling process.

At the granary, movable history panels describe the mill and its colorful

*Bale Grist Mill*

founder, Dr. E. T. Bale. In the early days, this room served as the community's social center. In that tradition, the exhibits are pushed aside and a barn dance is held here one Saturday a month.

Outside, visitors can stroll around the rustic frontier mill, with its western facade, weathered-wood sides, and small paned windows. The 36-foot-diameter waterwheel and a segment of a flume and trestle add to its charm, as does its wooded setting. On the grounds, visitors may see a remnant of an original halved and hollowed redwood trunk that carried water to the wheel.

*Access:* Reached via CA 29 or via the History Trail from Bothe–Napa Valley State Park.

**History Trail.** This wooded, moderate 1.2-mile trail links Bale Grist Mill and Bothe–Napa Valley parks.

Hiking north from "Old Bale," travelers bypass the remains of the mill's water system, before they leave the Mill Creek drainage. They then ascend a ridge that runs parallel to CA 29.

Where the trail steeply descends from the ridge, hikers pass through an old pioneer cemetery and visit an early-day church site. Graves dating back to the mid-1800s are scattered amid the forest of Douglas fir, laurel, and tanoak. Some of the older ones are encircled by white picket fences. Both new and broken stones can be seen. In the vicinity, a plaque indicates the site of Napa Valley's first church. In another 0.1 mile, the trail arrives at the Bothe–Napa Valley State Park picnic area.

*Access:* Begin north of the mill or leave from the south end of the Bothe–Napa Valley picnic area.

**Redwood Trail–Coyote Peak Loop.** This 4.7-mile hiker loop shows the variety of the park terrain and offers views from atop Coyote Peak (elevation 1,170 feet).

From the day-use area, the trail begins as a wide earthen path, touring a mixed forest. Quickly, it angles left across the authorized vehicle road to follow Ritchie Creek upstream. Bypassing a couple of park residences, the route bears right on a narrow gravel road to resume the upstream tour. The campground now occupies the far shore.

At 0.5 mile, the Redwood Trail heads left; the Ritchie Canyon Trail heads right. While both follow the creek upstream, go left for the hiker loop. The Canyon Trail offers horseback riders an equally pleasant excursion.

Ritchie Creek varies from 5 to 10 feet wide, spilling over cobbles. Groups of redwood spot the drainage, and a complement of maples adds to the tour. Wild grape drapes some of the firs; poison oak scales others.

The forest becomes more varied as it draws away from the creek, adding oak, tanoak, hazel, laurel, and madrone. At 0.9 mile, go past the Coyote Trail junction for a counterclockwise tour. Ahead, the trail eases back toward the creek. At 1.6 miles, a rock-hop crossing is needed to round a small slide area. Soon, the Redwood Trail merges with the Ritchie Canyon Trail as it crosses over the creek on a concrete bridge.

From the bridge, take the foot trail immediately on the left (the unmarked South Fork Trail) for the loop. It follows a side drainage upstream, crossing over it at 1.9 miles. This drainage features a rich evergreen-deciduous complex, with the redwoods being more continuous. The climb grows steeper, as the trail again follows a side fork. At 2.1 miles, where the South Fork Trail curves to the right, take the Coyote Peak Trail uphill to the left.

As this trail climbs and rounds out of the drainage, the redwoods are left behind. At the saddle at 2.4 miles, live oak, manzanita, and greasewood dominate, and the tour becomes hot and exposed. Overlooking the greasewood slope, hikers now view the forested drainage of Ritchie Creek.

Taking the short, rugged summit spur to the right, hikers top Coyote Peak at 2.6 miles. Here, the demarcation between the forested northeast slope and the drier west slope is pronounced. Mount St. Helena commands the view north, while the valley vineyards spread east.

Returning to the Coyote Peak Trail, hikers soon round out of the manzanita and greasewood and back into the forest. The trail width, surface, and grade improve. After rounding the head of a drainage at 3.4 miles, the trail follows it downstream for a relatively steep, fast descent, meeting the Redwood Trail at 3.8 miles. Go right, retracing the initial 0.9 mile to the trailhead.

*Access:* Begin at the horse-trailer parking lot in the day-use area, next to the authorized vehicle road. A sign indicates this is the trailhead for Ritchie Creek trails. Campers may start at the 0.5-mile junction.

## Annadel State Park

**Hours/Season:** 9:00 A.M. to sunset

**Facilities:** Picnic sites (no fires); hiker, horse, and mountain-bike trails; hitching posts; nonflush toilets; water

**For Information:** (707) 539-3911

**Access:** From CA 12 just east of Santa Rosa, turn south on Los Alamos Road, go 0.2 mile, and turn right on Melita Road to merge onto Montgomery Drive. In 0.7 mile, turn left onto Channel Road and proceed into the park. *Dogs are not allowed.*

Just an hour from San Francisco, this undeveloped park presents residents and visitors with a wild, open space to explore on foot, horse, or bicycle. Its 5,000 acres offer ample opportunity for discovery with oak woodlands, mixed forests, broad meadows and rolling hills, a fine marsh, riparian and chaparral habitats, and man-made Lake Ilsanjo. Routes allow for a variety of tours, but even with the primary junctions marked, it remains a good idea to carry the park map and a compass for navigating this intricate system. Travelers should keep to the named

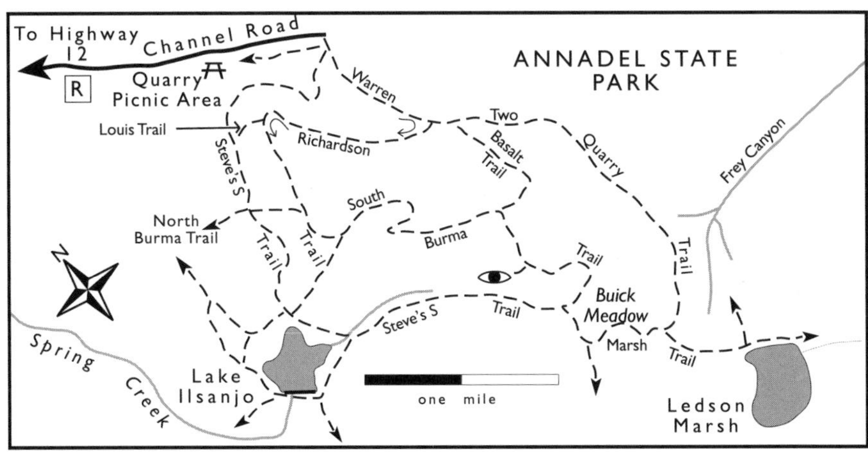

trails, as secondary routes damage the park resources. Anglers find sport on Lake Ilsanjo, with black bass and bluegill being the sought-after prizes. Birdwatching, nature study, and photography also engage guests.

Long ago, Native Americans worked obsidian quarries in the area. The sharp, black-glass rock was prized for tools and weapons. In the late 1800s and early 1900s, cobblestone quarries met a demand for street paving; moss-reclaimed quarry sites can be seen along the park trails. At the park, beware of poison oak and ticks year-round.

## Attractions and Activities

**Warren Richardson–Ledson Marsh Loop.** Open to all, this 7.5-mile loop is a moderate, rolling fire road and single-track tour.

It begins on the Warren Richardson Trail, passing through mixed forest and a boulder-studded oak woodland. In the morning, deer may be seen grazing in the woods; wildflowers adorn the roadside. At the end of a long meadow slope stand a picnic table, bench, and hitching post. Here, switchback right, staying on the Richardson Trail. Ahead, second-growth redwoods filter into the mix and a couple of small quarry pits can be seen, as the semi-shaded trail climbs steadily. Past the North Burma Trail junction (1.7 miles), the Richardson Trail overlooks Lake Ilsanjo and the broad meadow to its north.

In another 0.2 mile, the South Burma Trail continues the tour, heading left. Less groomed, with areas of washout and rocks, this single-track route passes through mixed forest, oak grassland, and a chaparral-transition habitat. At 3 miles, a 0.1-mile spur leads to a tree-obscured view and an isolated picnic site.

Forgoing the detour, travelers soon approach pretty, relaxing Buick Meadow, where hawks circle overhead. At 3.5 miles, the loop bears left on the Marsh Trail, rounding the far side of the meadow before returning to forest. The Marsh Trail then skirts a pocket meadow, a cobblestone quarry, and a larger meadow cradled by oak hillsides, coming to the 4.2-mile junction, where it bears right. Tables, a pit toilet, and hitching post mark the junction site. Ledson Marsh is 0.3 mile ahead.

Bulrushes claim the center of the marsh; they are often rimmed by open water until late summer. Areas of cattails add to the shoreline. Ducks and coots weave amid the wetland stalks. In spring, a chorus of frogs may entertain guests. For the loop, return to the 4.2-mile junction and follow the Two Quarry Trail.

With a comfortable grade, the trail descends through forest. At 5.5 miles, the Two Quarry Trail bears left just before the gate at Frey Canyon Overlook. Where it parallels the park boundary, the fire road becomes heavily cobbled and uneven. Upon leveling out, it improves. From the Warren Richardson Trail junction at 6.8 miles, retrace the first 0.7 mile to the trailhead.

*Access:* Start at the east end parking lot.

**Steve's S Trail–Lake Ilsanjo Loop.** This 4.9-mile round-trip hike tours forest, meadow, and lakeshore.

Crossing over the Warren Richardson Trail, the Steve's S Trail heads uphill, touring a mixed forest of fir, madrone,

*Grassland meadow, Annadel State Park*

and laurel. Small ferns and mossy rocks spot the floor, while bird songs add to a morning tour. At 0.5 mile, the trail crosses over the ridge slope, and the ascent moderates. Where it meets the single-track route of Louis Trail, turn right edging the open grass meadow. At the 1.2-mile junction with the North Burma Trail, go left a few feet and take the immediate right to resume the next segment of the Steve's S Trail, as it heads uphill.

Before long, the trail descends, touring an area of live and deciduous oak, manzanita, and laurel. Overlooking the big meadow bowl, hikers can just make out the lake at the head of the basin. After edging along the meadow, hikers come to the Lake Ilsanjo loop junction at 1.7 miles. Go straight, crossing over the Warren Richardson Trail for a clockwise tour of the 26-acre lake.

A 1.5-mile circuit travels dirt fire roads, the dam, and a fisherman's foot trail, staying close to the lake, but the mostly wooded shore filters out all but glimpses of the dense bulrush rim and the open water. Picnic areas and individual sites are located around the lake. Side trails branch to shore. Coots, pied-billed grebes, and herons are sometimes seen as hikers reach the shore. The north end of the lake holds greater accessibility. The loop closes via the Warren Richardson Trail at 3.2 miles. Retrace the initial 1.7 miles to end the tour.

*Access:* Start at the east end parking lot, taking the hiker trail at its far corner.

## SUGARLOAF RIDGE STATE PARK

**Hours/Season:** Year-round
**Facilities:** 48 developed oak-shaded campsites, picnic area, visitor center, horse concession, hiker and horse trails, mountain-bike routes, flush and nonflush toilets, water
**For Information:** (707) 833-5712
**Access:** Go 9 miles east of Santa Rosa or 11 miles west of Sonoma on CA 12 and turn north on Adobe Canyon Road. Reach the entry station in another 3.3 miles.

Threaded by Sonoma Creek, this park represents a small piece of wilderness in the rugged coastal mountains of Northern California. Although its mountain vistas sweep the San Francisco Bay Area and the sprawl of the neighboring valley communities, its steep terrain and chaparral-woodland habitat suggest isolation and a sense of adventure. In the off-season, deer openly range the meadow slopes, and gray fox, bobcat, and even a mountain lion may be seen. Springtime brings a flurry of wildflowers to the slopes and drainages. But beware: Poison oak is well represented in the park.

By summer, Sonoma Creek may be dry, but the relative coolness of its shaded canyon lingers. Lining Sonoma Creek are a few coastal redwoods, straining the limits of the tree's growing range. These trees are neither stout, nor tall, but prove interesting due to their mere presence.

Miles of trails and service roads crisscross the rugged terrain, inviting hiker, equestrian, and mountain-bike rider to probe the park recesses. The junctions are well posted with trail names and permissible uses. The park brochure shows the mileage between junctions, allowing visitors to plan their time and customize trips.

In the campground, oak-shaded sites rim a broad central meadow above Sonoma Creek. Next door is a small visitor center with a few displays. With limited day parking, the road entering the park can become congested with spillover traffic, so plan to arrive early.

## Attractions and Activities

**The Creekside Nature Trail.** The park brochure contains the descriptions that correspond to this seventeen-station, 0.75-mile nature trail that travels along Sonoma Creek, stitching together the picnic area and campground. The brochure identifies the vegetation and the role some of the plants played in the lives of the Wappo Indians who lived here prior to the Spaniards' arrival.

The route bypasses the campfire center, and post 11 suggests a short detour to a westward-facing bench offering looks at Mount Hood. In winter, Sonoma Creek may defy completion of the trail or suggest a wading. After the crossing, the closing leg of the tour heads right on the Hillside Trail. It bypasses a water tank and crosses another drainage before reaching the campground at its turnaround loop.

*Access:* For a clockwise tour that follows the sequence of descriptions in the brochure, begin at the picnic area parking lot above the campground.

**Bald Mountain Loop.** This 7-mile loop has a 1,500-foot elevation change and utilizes hiker-only trails, where possible. As it is but one of several loops touching the mountain's summit (elevation 2,729 feet), horseback riders and mountain bikers can plot out similar tours.

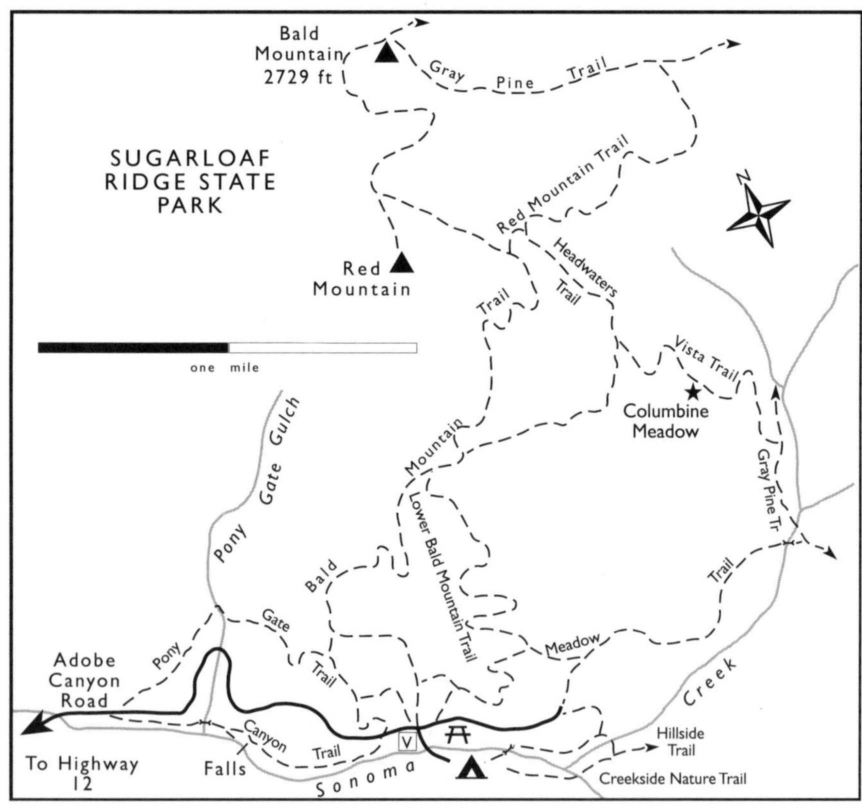

From the day-use parking area, hike up the open, grassy slope a couple of hundred feet to a junction. For the loop, go right. In quick succession, the trail tours a woodland edge, chaparral, and meadow slope. At the 0.3-mile junction, follow the Lower Bald Mountain Trail uphill to the left to reach the paved service road of Bald Mountain Trail (0.9 mile). Here, the loop heads right. Over-the-shoulder looks take in the Sonoma Creek drainage and the bumpy skyline of brushy Sugarloaf Ridge.

For the next 1.4 miles, stay on the Bald Mountain Trail, a steeply climbing, mostly open road, with occasional reprieves afforded by the patchy presence of laurel, madrone, and mixed oak. Greasewood and manzanita dominate the chaparral complex. In the road cuts, visitors may note some blue-green rock—it is serpentine, a fault indicator. The St. John's Mountain Fault crosses the area.

At 2.3 miles, the paved road continues to a microwave station atop Red Mountain, while the loop follows the steep dirt road uphill to the right, touring the grassy slope of Bald Mountain. Approaching the summit, follow the Gray Pine Trail to the right to reach the mountain's open, rounded top (2.7 miles).

Display boards identify the surrounding landmarks and bear the quotes of Jack London and Robert Louis Stevenson, area writers. Boxy Mount St. Helena, the Napa Valley, and Sierra Ridge may be seen panning north, while the San Francisco Bay Area, Mount Diablo, and Sugarloaf Ridge punctuate the view south. Winds wash the summit.

From the summit, follow the Gray Pine Trail east for a rolling ridge descent, bypassing some splendid old oaks. At 3.5 miles, the loop follows the footpath of the Red Mountain Trail downhill to the right for a pleasant high chaparral walk, with some final looks at Bald Mountain. Afterward, trees enfold the trail.

In less than a mile, the loop follows the Headwaters Trail left for a scenic, sharp, wonderfully tree-shaded 0.5-mile descent, following a small drainage. Passing through an area of mossy boulders, hikers come to the Vista Trail junction; go left. This trail edges around small, pretty Columbine Meadow and later flattens as it begins following Sonoma Creek. Where it comes out at a broad meadow, the loop follows the Gray Pine Trail right to meet the Meadow Trail, a service road, at 5.9 miles (in winter, this may require wading Sonoma Creek).

Going right on the Meadow Trail, visitors pass a pleasant picnic site beneath a tall landmark maple and cross a bridge. Deer sometimes roam the grassy slopes above the trail. At 6.7 miles, the loop enters the Group Camp area; continue following the Meadow Trail, which is now a footpath, over the rolling slopes back to the Lower Bald Mountain Trail junction. There, head left, retracing the route to the trailhead.

*Access:* Begin at the day use/picnic area parking lot above the campground.

**Pony Gate–Canyon Loop.** Counterclockwise, this 1.6-mile loop climbs the coastal live oak and grassland slope above the park entrance road. At 0.25 mile, the route heads left, crossing an unnamed drainage. At 0.4 mile, again go left, staying on the hiker-only Pony Gate Trail.

Openings offer looks at the Sonoma Creek drainage and Sugarloaf Ridge, as hawks and vultures sail over the grassland slope. Where the trail descends, it shows a steep gradient. Live and white oak, laurel, and small fir shade its course. At 0.7 mile, the trail crosses Pony Gate Gulch. After a brief uphill, the route descends a time-healed grade to meet the park road at 1 mile.

Go right on the park road to pick up Canyon Trail on the opposite side in less than 0.1 mile. Here, the trail follows Sonoma Creek upstream; coastal redwoods and large Douglas firs line the drainage. The redwoods are 2 to 2.5 feet in diameter and lack a towering presence; lichen and charring etch their trunks.

After the Pony Gate Gulch footbridge, a 50-foot detour upstream finds a 25-foot

*Bald Mountain interpretive sign, Sugarloaf Ridge State Park*

winter waterfall spilling over a boulder jumble. The main trail follows the stairsteps up the slope, bidding farewell to the redwoods and large firs. Woodland and areas of moss-covered boulders characterize the final climb. A nice stand of madrone graces the trail's exit at the park road.

*Access:* Begin at the Upper Pony Gate trailhead parking turnout, 0.2 mile downhill from the park entry station.

## SONOMA COAST STATE BEACH

**Hours/Season:** Year-round

**Facilities:** 2 campgrounds with a total of 128 developed sites, 31 inland environmental tent sites, picnic areas, visitor center, hiker and horse trails, restrooms, nonflush toilets, showers at Bodega Dunes Campground

**For Information:** (707) 875-3483

**Access:** Find the various park accesses off CA 1, between Bodega Bay and the bluffs 4.8 miles north of Jenner. The visitor center is in Jenner.

Stretching 16.6 miles, this park celebrates the rugged majesty of the Sonoma coastline. It features scalloped 100-foot bluffs, grass and coastal scrub plateaus, isolated black sand coves and strands, and offshore rocks, islands, and arches. Within its borders, it brings together ocean, bay, lagoon, and riparian shores.

While the untamed waters do not welcome swimming or waterplay, they do provide an eye-startling backdrop for one's stay. Sometimes surfers—an unstoppable lot—may be seen waiting for the more predictable waves off Miwok and North Salmon Creek beaches. At certain times of the year, Salmon Creek breaks through to the ocean. Other times, it forms a backwater lagoon and an unbroken 3-mile-long beach.

In December and January and again in March and April, rangers and volunteers lead whale-watching tours at Bodega Head. The harbor seal, a year-round resident, can be seen with its pups in spring. The mouth of the Russian River and Russian Gulch Cove often reward with harbor seal sightings.

Sonoma Coast State Beach has numerous marked and unmarked accesses. Some have parking lots, others have only roadside parking. Foot trails access the remote beaches and cross the plateau to overlooks; opportunities for solitude abound. In spring, lizardtail, bush lupine, sea pinks, Indian paintbrush, monkey-flower, and a host of other wildflowers decorate the bluff. Equestrian trails travel Bodega Dunes and Bodega Dunes Beach south of its boardwalk. Lighter colored sands claim these southern park reaches.

## Attractions and Activities

**Goat Rock.** This is one of the most popular year-round destinations in the park. To Goat Rock's south, beachgoers find tide-dependent hiking, rounding rocky points to Blind Beach; views are of Arch Rock. To its north stretches an uninterrupted loose-sand strand. It passes Whale Point and continues along the Russian River spit, where it is backed by low scrub dunes. Strings of pelicans skim the waves, and occasionally a harbor seal stops to study the beachgoer.

Goat Rock itself is an impressive landmark, a massive, towering block outcrop connected to land. Waves splash far up its sides, while riprap protects the parking lot extending to its base. For obvious safety reasons, Goat Rock proper is closed to the general public, but ocean fishermen enjoy success casting from the riprap sides of the parking-lot extension.

*Access:* Find the Goat Rock Access west off CA 1 about 2 miles south of Jenner, 2.3 miles north of Wright's Beach Campground.

**Vista Trail.** This paved 1-mile all-ability loop tours the grassy plateau and the bluff's edge, accessing wheelchair-accessible picnic tables and offering ocean overlooks. A platform midway offers an exceptional coastal view stretching south. The view includes the Russian River, Goat Rock, Duncan Point, and Bodega Head, with Point Reyes National Seashore far to the south.

*Access:* Find the Vista Trail parking lot west off CA 1, 4.8 miles north of Jenner.

**Kortum Trail.** This trail travels 4.2 miles, touring coastal plateau, ravine, and beach, between the Goat Rock Access and Wright's Beach Campground. While it is ideal for shuttle hiking, round trips grant new perspectives.

North to south, the trampled grass trail angles across the coastal plateau ascending toward a small rise. After rounding the foot of a rock outcrop, hairy with light-green lichen, it crosses over a small saddle. A short uphill spur tops the rise for views north and south, including Arch Rock and a distant Point Reyes. The trail then briefly travels along a fence, before turning right and descending back across the plateau to the bluff edge. Where the path bypasses a large, cliff-faced outcrop, hikers may spy a perched hawk. An equally massive offshore rock dominates the sea.

As the hike resumes south, views are of Bodega Head and Point Reyes, with ocean views to the west. Short detours to the edge reveal views of the dramatic coastal cliffs, inaccessible beaches, scenic coves, and rocks strung offshore. Small drainages mark off distances. At a fence crossing, hikers add Wright's Beach to the previous view. While the primary trail remains slightly inland, all paths journeying south ultimately end at the Shell Beach parking lot (2 miles).

From there, the tour bypasses the handicapped parking spaces and crosses a footbridge over a gulch brimming with coyote bush, wild blackberry, and fern. Now, cedar posts more regularly mark the route, often pointing hikers inland to the footbridge crossings for the various drainages. Deer sometimes spook from their hiding places.

In splashy display, the waves continue their assault on the offshore rocks. At 2.5 miles, the trail angles left, entering Furlong Gulch, gaining access to its scenic cove with a conical rock just offshore. The bluff tour resumes following the reinforced steps up the opposite slope. Ahead, some private homes line the upper plateau, but the power of the sea draws attention.

At 3.4 miles, the trail makes its final descent from the bluff. Coarse, loose, black sand characterizes the canted beach stretching south beneath the cliffs; a white lacy tideline contrasts the blackness. Near the start, an onshore rock reveals an eroded window. Except following winter storms, only kelp and a few sticks scatter the beach. Always, hikers must be alert to sleeper waves. Before long, the campground and Duncan's Landing come into view. At 4.2 miles, the hike ends at Wright's Beach Day Use.

*Access:* A southbound tour begins off the Goat Rock Access Road, just uphill from the Blind Beach parking area.

**Bodega Head Trail.** This 1.4-mile trail rounds rugged Bodega Head between its east and west parking areas, affording some striking coastal views.

Bypassing the outhouses at its east parking area, the trail contours the headland rise, overlooking Bodega Bay. Bush lupine, coyote bush, grasses, and yarrow cloak the slope. Views south include Tomales Bay and Point Reyes. On a low rock out from the headland, sea lions haul out to sun and seabirds roost. The main trail continues encircling the headland while secondary routes branch to other vantages on the colony. Scopes and binoculars are needed.

A ragged rocky foot extends from the base of the sharp cliff. At 0.4 mile, the trail bypasses a small beacon and begins to climb. Deer, pelicans, and oystercatchers

*Bodega Head coastline, Sonoma Coast State Beach*

may also be sighted. Far below, on the near-shore rocks, travelers can glimpse sea palms and the colorful intertidal life during low tides.

At 0.8 mile, the trail delivers a haunting view, overlooking a sheer vertical cliff. Cormorants roost on a sharp edge. Peering across the headland at low tide, travelers again gain looks at Bodega Bay and its mudflats.

Where the trail overlooks a fluted area of cliffs, a rock arch can be seen. At 1.1 miles, the cliffs isolate a pretty sandy beach marked by near-shore and onshore rocks; another arch feature lies offshore from it. Views north are of Mussel Point. The trail, now much less defined, descends to the west parking area, coming out near its outhouse. If a shuttle was not prearranged, return as you came.

*Access:* Begin at the east (upper) parking lot, taking the left fork where East Shore Road approaches Bodega Head.

## JACK LONDON STATE HISTORIC PARK

**Hours/Season:** 10:00 A.M. to 5:00 P.M. (winter), 7:00 P.M. (summer); 10:00 A.M. to 5:00 P.M., except major holidays (museum)

**Facilities:** Picnic areas, museum, historic ranch, hiker and horse trails, mountain-bike roads, restrooms, nonflush toilets

**For Information:** (707) 938-5216

**Access:** Between Santa Rosa and Sonoma on CA 12, turn west for Glen Ellen and the park. From Glen Ellen, the park is 1.5 miles west via London Ranch Road.

At this 800-acre park, visitors get to know Jack London—the adventurer, writer, rancher, and person. Here, they can visit the cottage where he wrote, view his innovative ideas at Beauty Ranch, hike to Wolf House (which was to have been his family mansion), and stand beside his simple grave. In the House of Happy Walls, visitors can examine an incredible collection of Jack London's mementos, letters, belongings, and photographs.

### Attractions and Activities

**House of Happy Walls.** Modeled after Jack London's Wolf House, this two-story, volcanic rock and hardwood structure was home to Charmian London after her husband's death. Upon entering it, visitors are greeted by vivid images of the man. A riding saddle, fencing gear, and boxing gloves adorn one of the window nooks, while memorabilia from the South Seas and the voyage of the *Snark* (London's custom-built sailing ship) fills another.

London's first rejection letter, as well as his handwritten list of contacted publishers, are on display. Glass cases filled with exotic souvenirs from Jack and Charmian London's travels line the stairway to the second floor. At the top is a re-creation of Jack London's small bed chamber, complete with a wake-up card on the door.

*Access:* At the parking area for the museum and visitor center, take the wide, paved 0.1-mile trail heading uphill.

**Grave and Wolf House Ruins.** From the museum, a wide trail passing through woods and meadow leads to Jack London's grave and the Wolf House ruins. To visit both requires a 1.5-mile round-trip walk; drinking fountains, chemical toilets, and benches line the route.

*Wolf House ruins, Jack London State Historic Park*

The grave occupies a small knoll where two pioneer children were buried. In an offhand comment, London described how he would like to be buried there, with a large boulder from Wolf House rolled atop his ashes. In a silent ceremony in 1916, Charmian complied with his wishes. Rustic, lichen-etched fences rim the plots.

At the Wolf House ruins, visitors find an imposing, fire-gutted shell of red lava rock and unpeeled redwood. Just when the mansion was ready for occupancy, fire swept through it, and London died before it could be rebuilt. Visitors today can walk around its exterior and climb to a platform overlooking the second-floor reflection pool. Architectural sketches show the ambitious floor plan.

*Access:* The trail begins next to the House of Happy Walls.

**Beauty Ranch Self-guided Trail.** A 0.6-mile round-trip tour explores the ranch of Jack London. Descriptions of the ranch structures and their uses can be found in the park brochure.

Heavy stone buildings left over from a nineteenth-century winery and those later added by Jack London comprise the heart of the ranch. Inside the Sherry Barn, which housed London's prized stallions, is the old Oakland Street Watering Wagon he used to tend the eucalyptus grove that now shades the picnic area. Views are of Sonoma Mountain. About the ranch, woodpeckers abound.

At the white wooden cottage, where he and Charmian shared their lives, visitors can look into the window of Jack London's porch study. A photograph depicts how it looked in his day. An ancient oak stands at the side of the house, a winery ruin can be found at the back. Private vineyards neighbor the park, keeping a sense of its agricultural start.

Uphill a short way, visitors come upon London's Pig Palace, an impressive stone establishment serving seventeen pig families with separate pens and runs and a central feeding station. Just beyond are the 40-foot stone silos built to store fodder. Return as you came or follow the mowed path to the ranch road leading to the lake.

*Access:* At the parking area for Beauty Ranch, take the path that leads to and through the picnic area.

**Lake and Viewpoint Trail.** A 3-mile round-trip tour visits the 5-acre reservoir and redwood bathhouse, where the Londons entertained guests, and a vista point on the Sonoma Mountain hillside. The tour can be extended to the boundary for a 7-mile round-trip option.

There are lake routes open to all users. Cyclists and horseback riders must keep to the dirt road leaving the ranch headquarters. At 0.6 mile, hikers may bear right on the forested foot trail for a shadier trek; signs mark its junctions. By road or by trail, visitors reach the lake in about a mile. A small, curved concrete block dam holds back the water. Cattails rim much of the shore, while redwoods claim the slope above it. Coots and ducks paddle the water.

Continuing up the road another 0.5 mile, travelers come to the Mays Meadow Vista, overlooking an open grassy slope. Views are to the southeast of the local ridges and valley. Continue the climb, or return to the ranch.

*Access:* Begin at Beauty Ranch parking area; it has ample room for horse trailers.

# PETALUMA ADOBE AND SONOMA STATE HISTORIC PARKS

**Hours/Season:** 10:00 A.M. to 5:00 P.M., except major holidays
**Facilities:** Picnic tables, visitor centers, historic buildings, bookstore/gift shop, restrooms
**For Information:** (707) 762-4871 (Petaluma Adobe); (707) 938-1519 (Sonoma)
**Access:** Going east from Petaluma on CA 116, turn north on Casa Grande, go 2 miles, and turn right on Adobe Road. Petaluma Adobe is at the corner of Casa Grande and Adobe Road. In Sonoma, the Vallejo House is at the corner of Third Street West and Spain Street; the other Sonoma State Historic Park buildings are located off Spain Street at the Central Plaza.

Only a half-hour's drive apart, together these two park units relate the story of General Mariano Vallejo and Northern California, at the turning point from Mexican to American rule. Petaluma Adobe records the peak of Vallejo's career (1834–1846), during Mexico's supremacy. Sonoma State Historic Park takes up the tale with the collapse of Mexican rule and Vallejo's empire, following the raising of the Stars and Stripes. Exhibits and self-guided walking tours introduce each park.

## Attractions and Activities

**Petaluma Adobe Self-guided Tour.** Atop a lawn-covered knoll, this two-story, three-sided, U-shaped adobe enfolds a central courtyard. The original complex had a fourth side and was twice as big. Some 85 percent of the adobe and 25 percent of the timber are original. Wide verandas encircle the structure, covering walkways and protecting the gray mud brick from the rain. In the veranda rafters, swallows nest. Where the brick is exposed, visitors can see how the adobe was worked together with straw.

Within the courtyard are adobe ovens (*hornos*), thatch-roofed cooking areas, wooden carts, and a smithy fire and bellows. Burros, sheep, and chickens fill the barnyard. Through window grates and screened entries, visitors can look into the past and see how the rooms were used and how the people lived and worked. The three Vallejo family rooms at the adobe were modest in size and furnishings, while the general's primary residence in Sonoma—"La Casa Grande"—was reportedly one of the most elegant private homes in all of California.

From Petaluma Adobe, Vallejo and his majordomo oversaw a cattle and agricultural empire that spanned 100 square miles and employed more than 2,000 Native Americans.

**The Vallejo Home.** After the Bear Flag Revolt in 1846, Vallejo lacked the political, military, and financial clout to keep his empire and eventually lost it all, but he remained a vital civic leader in Northern California. "Lachryma Montis" (mountain tear), is the general's final residence. Centerpiece to the property was a free-flowing spring, suggesting its name. While in residence here, Vallejo served as mayor of Sonoma.

Vineyards and fruit trees surround the 1850s Victorian Gothic home. An arborway travels the length of the spring-fed pool, and a fountain ornaments each entry to the house. Many of the family furnishings remain in place. The home carries an air of dignified elegance.

Its produce warehouse, later a residence known as the "Swiss Chalet," now serves as a visitor center. Among the exhibits are Vallejo's French-built carriage and a piece of redwood pipe from the 1870s, when he sold spring water to the city of Sonoma.

**Sonoma Walking Tour.** A tour of the Central Plaza area visits buildings from the mid-1800s that are owned privately and by the state park system. Here, visitors can trace Vallejo's role from the secularization of this Spanish mission settlement to the growth of Sonoma under United States rule.

The low adobe living quarters at the Mission is the oldest building in Sonoma. The present church was built between 1840 and 1841 by General Vallejo for the town parishioners. The chapel interior is decorated with the traditional patterns used by Christianized Indians; it has an uneven red brick floor. Outside the white walls, benches under a thatch-roofed veranda look out at the Central Plaza.

The historic two-story Sonoma Barracks adobe now holds a fine museum and interpretive store filled with educational books and gifts. A first-floor exhibit features the Mexican army sleeping quarters. In the breezeway is a Spanish cannon, which is fired on special occasions. At the barracks, park rangers are available to provide flintlock-firing demonstrations and show slide programs on historical topics. Another popular demonstration is bread baking at the adobe ovens.

Other possible Sonoma Walking Tour stops are the servants' wing (all that remains of Vallejo's La Casa Grande), the Toscano Hotel with its period furnishings, and the Blue Wing Inn, a onetime Gold Rush gambling hall now filled with private shops. The shaded plaza offers a restful spot to break for lunch or take an admiring look at the area.

## TOMALES BAY STATE PARK

**Hours/Season:** 8:00 A.M. to sunset

**Facilities:** Hike/bike camp, picnic areas, hiker trails, restrooms, nonflush toilets, outdoor shower

**For Information:** (415) 669-1140

**Access:** From CA 1, 0.3 mile south of Point Reyes Station, turn west on Francis Drake Boulevard, go 6.1 miles, and bear right on Pierce Point Road to reach the park in 0.6 mile. The Millerton Point unit is west off CA 1, 4.6 miles north of Point Reyes Station.

On Point Reyes Peninsula, the main park unit occupies the quiet west shore of Tomales Bay. It extends protected calm-water-bay beaches and a small network of tranquil trails, passing through a dense hardwood woodland and a virgin stand of Bishop pine. Four modest-size beaches serve park visitors: Heart's Desire is the most accessible and developed; Indian, Shell, and Pebble beaches are reached via short, easy trails. Shell Beach, isolated by a parcel of private land, is alternatively reached via Camino del Mar Road northwest of Inverness.

The beaches are gently sloping strands of clean, light-colored sand, scattered with fine shell fragments. They offer outstanding swimming, wading, and waterplay for the entire family. While the park has no launch facility, guests may portage, put in, and take out their boats away from the swimming areas. Clammers find suitable sands for pursuing their sport within the park.

Millerton Point on the east shore of Tomales Bay is more wind buffeted and subject to fog. It features a coastal grassland, tide-dependent beach, and marshy shore. While it has a small primitive picnic area, the point is mostly undeveloped. Visitors are free to roam at will; old 2-tracks offer tried routes. From a pickleweed spit, hikers view the long sweep of Tomales Bay (through which the San Andreas Fault passes) and have cross-bay views of the Point Reyes Peninsula, including wooded Inverness Ridge, the maritime village of Inverness, and main Tomales Bay State Park.

## Attractions and Activities

**Indian Nature Trail.** This 1-mile self-guided round-trip trail tours a rich hardwood woodland above the bay. Along it, plaques identify the vegetation and explain how the species served the Miwok Indians as a food, medicine, or ceremonial item. Bishop pines claim the upper slope. At 0.2 mile is a loop junction; stay right to continue the nature trail.

*Pebble Beach, Tomales Bay State Park*

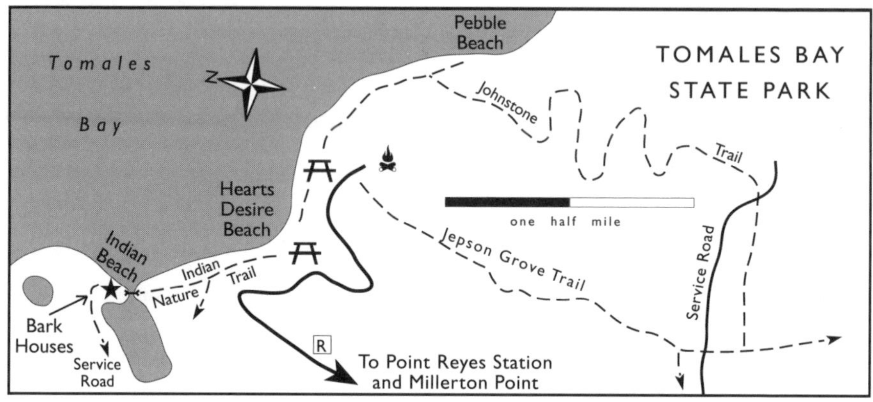


Where the trail arrives at Indian Beach, it crosses a boardwalk over the neck of a side bay to reach the main sunlit curvature of sand. There, hikers find three replica "Kotchas"—bark-covered tepees—the family dwelling of the Miwok Indian. Strolling the beach north, hikers bypass a second side bay or marsh. Pickleweed, saltgrass, and rushes claim its edge. In the off-season, shorebirds frequent it. The beach stretches more than 0.25 mile to a small point offering a fine view of the extensive gulf of Tomales Bay.

Return as you came or cross to the service road at the foot of the slope and follow it and a short segment of trail back to the junction at 0.2 mile. An outhouse is located above the start of the service road.

*Access:* Begin on the trail heading north from Heart's Desire Beach, bypassing the comfort station.

**Jepson Grove–Johnstone Loop.** This well-marked 2.75-mile loop has a 100-foot elevation change as it passes through woodland, tours the park's premier Bishop pine grove, and visits Pebble Beach.

The trail climbs through a congested hardwood forest with oak, laurel, and madrone interspersed with Bishop pines nearly from the start. Evergreen huckleberry, waxmyrtle, coffeeberry, and sword fern contribute to the green profusion. The trunks of the oaks have a pink hue, owing to a lichen, visible only on close inspection. A more commonly seen lichen drips from the upper branches.

As the trail makes its steady ascent, hikers have ample time to admire the rounded, spread crowns of the Bishop pine. Where a bench marks the route, toyon, hazel, and poison oak appear in the mix. At the 0.75-mile junction, go left for the Johnstone Trail.

The trail crosses over a restricted-use paved road and tops out. It then descends through a broad chaparral opening, with coyote bush and bracken fern. Areas of Bishop pine border the opening. At the upcoming junction, the loop heads left toward Pebble Beach, re-entering forest. While the species remain similar, the understory is less congested. Flocks of band-tailed pigeons, woodpeckers, and vultures divert the eyes skyward.

Crossing back over the paved access road, the trail becomes more enclosed. The branchwork tangle affords only limited glimpses at Tomales Bay, and the pines remain dominant. At 2.2 miles, the trail crosses a small alder-lined creek. At the T junction beyond it, go right to reach Pebble Beach in 200 feet; the loop continues left.

Thin Pebble Beach is perhaps 250 feet long, facing the quiet bay; a pit toilet is its only amenity. A scenic tree-topped cliff marks the shore to the south. Orange lichen adorns the exposed rock. Harbor seals and grebes may be spied on the bay, while a tiny marsh backs the beach.

Resuming the loop, hikers find oak, laurel, and madrone shaping the forest. The tour ends at the park picnic area.

*Access:* Begin across from the parallel parking spaces, where the main park road approaches the hike / bike camp and picnic area.

**Birdwatching.** On both sides of the bay, park birders find a great variety of inland, bay, and marsh species. At Millerton Point, an active osprey nest tops a tall post; visitors should maintain a respectful distance.

## Olompali State Historic Park

**Hours/Season:** 10:00 A.M. to sunset

**Facilities:** Picnic tables, historic buildings, hiker and horse trails, nonflush toilets, water

**For Information:** (415) 892-3387

**Access:** Reach the park off US 101 South, 2.6 miles north of Novato. From US 101 North, go past the park, turn left on San Antonio Road, and go south on US 101 to the entrance.

This 700-acre park is in its infancy. While visitors can explore its oak and grassland hillsides, stroll amid the closed ranch buildings, and picnic beneath the towering live oaks, the park's future calls for much more. Plans include a visitor center, restoration of the existing buildings, rebuilding of a conservatory, revitalization of the formal gardens, and construction of a replica Miwok Indian village.

This site lays claim to a colorful human history dating back some 4,000 years. Much of that time, it was the home of the Olompali, the largest of the Miwok tribes. It was here that the Indians advanced trade with the Europeans, and it was here that a bloody skirmish occurred during the Bear Flag Revolt.

Later, the area hosted cattle raising, dairying, and agricultural experimentation. This onetime home of the Jesuits was also once a commune, where the rock group the Grateful Dead stayed. But in 1969, a fire brought an end to the saga, clearing the way for the present-day park.

Mount Burdell is the high point in the park, elevation 1,558 feet. At the peak, the park adjoins a 1,600-acre Marin County open space, broadening opportunity for discovery. Views east overlook the Petaluma River as it empties into San Pablo Bay.

### Attractions and Activities

**Self-guided Walking Tour.** This tour takes visitors through the ranch grounds while identifying the structures and relating some of the cultural history. A brochure, available at the start, is a must for appreciating the area.

Among the ruins is part of the old Ynitia adobe, home of the Olompali leader who held the original Mexican land grant. It is protected in a covered, shingle-sided building with viewing windows. Elsewhere on the grounds, visitors can discover a grinding rock, a pot used by Ynitia for rendering tallow, and the rock walls and foundations cut and laid by Chinese laborers.

In the orchard and formal gardens, visitors find trees and plantings from around the world; some are quite unusual. Making up the core of the tour are the many boarded-up buildings from the Burdell ranching era (1866–1943).

*Access:* Begin at the informational board, upon entering the ranch grounds.

**Loop Trail.** This 3-mile loop travels both former ranch road and trail, exploring a wooded hillside and offering limited vistas. Following the road through the old ranch area, bear left at the Burdell Barn. Here, a trail sign indicates the route is open to hikers and equestrians. The Petaluma River estuary is visible below to the east. Vultures soar overhead and roost on the snags.

As the road climbs past the tin-sided dairy barn and a massive eucalyptus, at 0.3 mile, travelers find the loop junction. Go straight for a counterclockwise tour.

The sometimes-rutted dirt road passes alongside a rich laurel drainage, below an oak-savanna slope graced by a scenic rock wall. The route is mostly shaded, with a few California buckeye seen amid the mix, as well as some beautiful snarled trunks. Lizards scurry across the sunny patches on the road.

Bypassing a small, fenced-off reservoir, the loop briefly follows the creek upstream. Ferns line the drainage, while a leaf mat claims the woodland floor. At 0.8 mile, the loop heads left away from the creek, touring a thick, mixed woodland with live and deciduous oaks, laurel, and madrone. Deer, flickers, and Steller's jays favor this woody shelter.

At the four-way junction at 1.1 miles, the loop tops out and bears left. The route to the right is the proposed trail to the top of Mount Burdell. It would replace the present one that streaks uphill from here, subjecting the slope to erosion. Oaks dominate, as the loop contours the steep wooded slope. Laurel and fern crowd the head of the upcoming drainage.

The descending trail then switchbacks and contours a drier, open area of white oak and manzanita, where hikers gain glimpses of the Petaluma River area. Wildflowers and poison oak grow in the understory.

By 2.6 miles, a plain rail fence lines the route, as noise from US 101 carries upslope. A fine ranch overlook concludes the tour, as the trail approaches the footbridge near the dairy barn. Hikers may either cross and pass through the ranch or take the path to the right to return to the parking area.

*Access:* Begin at the parking lot, entering the ranch.

## SAMUEL P. TAYLOR STATE PARK

**Hours/Season:** Year-round

**Facilities:** 60 developed redwood-slope campsites; horse camp; picnic area; hiker, horse, and bicycle trails; mountain-bike routes; restrooms; showers; dump station

**For Information:** (415) 488-9897

**Access:** Reach the park off Sir Francis Drake Highway, going 5 miles east from CA 1 at Olema or 10 miles west from San Anselmo.

Historically, the site of a papermill, resort, and private campground—one of the first recreational campgrounds in the nation, the park continues to woo its guests with outdoor fun. The rolling hills marked by broad grassy slopes and mixed wooded drainages, together with the park's redwood-forested north-facing slopes and scenic Papermill Creek, create a varied 2,700-acre realm for recreation. Slicing the park, Sir Francis Drake Highway is the lone detractor, its noise echoing up the slope.

A paved or hard-surfaced 3-mile segment of the Cross-Marin Bike Trail

*Valley fog from Barnabe Peak, Samuel P. Taylor State Park*

traverses the park, offering a comfortable, carefree bicycle ride for the entire family. On the open slopes across the way, a network of fire roads challenges the mountain biker with hard-earned climbs and well-won descents. Still other trails serve hikers and equestrians with sunlit, vista-packed tours and deep-wood retreats. Picnickers enjoy a wonderful setting, with scenic stone fireplaces and beautiful big redwoods, interspersed by fir, laurel, maple, and tanoak. In other reaches, parts of Papermill Creek are suitable for an ankle-cooling wade or even splashing around, but the wide, smooth-flowing creek is closed to fishing.

## Attractions and Activities

**Salmon and Steelhead Runs.** Papermill Creek supports spawning runs of silver salmon and steelhead, a dramatic spectacle of nature. The salmon return mostly in November and December, but can be seen as late as February. The steelhead generally make their appearance in February and March. The salmon display red and bronze bodies as they spawn, flopping about in the creek; a red stripe characterizes the steelhead's speckled body.

On Papermill Creek, Samuel Taylor built one of the first spawning ladders on the West Coast, guiding fish around his mill pond. Today, this protected waterway also preserves the habitat of the endangered California freshwater shrimp.

**Pioneer Tree Trail.** This 2.5-mile loop tours the ancient and second-growth redwoods along Wildcat Canyon and Papermill Creek, visiting one of the park's oldest trees.

Taking the first path uphill to the right after leaving Redwood Grove group picnic area, hikers are immediately immersed in the full, rich forest of Wildcat Canyon.

Tanoak, hazel, laurel, and maple join the towering old-growth redwoods. In a few feet, a trail from the campground arrives on the right. Ahead is the first of several benches. After overlooking a massive redwood overlaying the drainage, hikers cross the canyon to ascend the opposite slope. The noisy passage of a raven often interrupts reflection.

At 0.6 mile, the trail rounds out of Wildcat Canyon to travel the slope well above Papermill Creek. After bypassing a couple of side trails that are now closed to use, the trail tops out in an area marked by more second-growth redwoods. Before long, the forest transitions to a fir-tanoak-laurel complex. Here, watch for a marked spur on the right for the Pioneer Tree (1.3 miles).

Just off the trail, the Pioneer Tree is a striking old redwood with a fairy ring of mature ones jailing it. It sports a tall, thin fire hollow at its base and is remarkably congested with low branches. The lone representative of its kind in the area, it stands out.

As the tour resumes, more poison oak is present. Approaching the Irving Creek drainage at 1.5 miles, the trail switchbacks downhill, re-entering the redwoods above Papermill Creek. After the trail bottoms out, it reaches a junction near the bike-trail bridge. Go left on the Cross-Marin Bike Trail to close the loop at 2.5 miles.

*Access:* Begin at the Redwood Grove group picnic area, rounding the gate at the end of the road.

**Barnabe Peak Loop.** Nearly 9 miles long, this loop explores grassland and woodland, snagging grand vistas just below Barnabe Peak (elevation 1,466 feet). Bring plenty of water for the tour.

From Madrone Group Camp, the closed road climbs, angling west across the open grass-and-scrub slope. In a short way, bear left, briefly passing through an oak and laurel drainage. Beyond a vista rock outcrop, the road comes to a T junction with a bigger fire road (0.6 mile). Go right for the peak.

The route climbs steadily, passing through the grassland and fall-flowering shrubs. Deer and quail are commonly sighted. Small animal burrows may be detected amid the woven grasses, while dew accents the spider webs on dead stalks. By 0.75 mile, the Marin County fire lookout (closed to the public) comes into view.

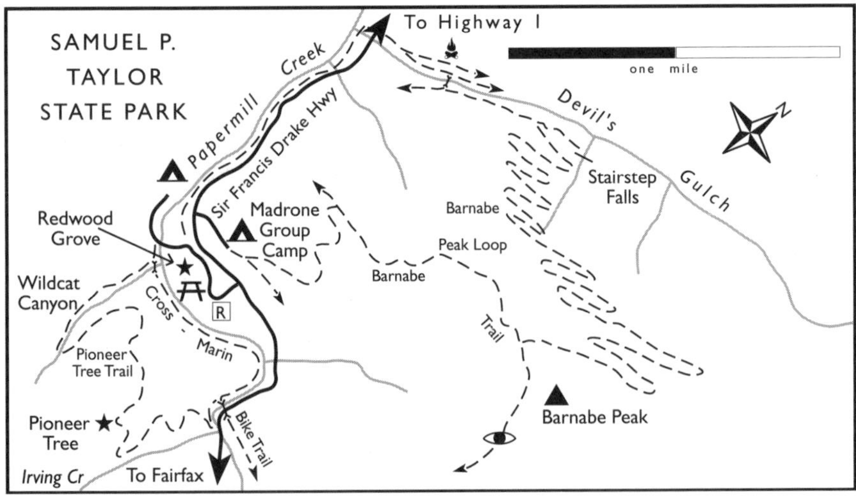

As the trail wraps and climbs, it tops small rises and edges laurel-evergreen drainages. Views broaden with the ascent.

At 1.75 miles, the foot trail heading left to Devils Gulch marks the loop junction for hikers. But, to first claim the ridge vista, continue climbing on the fire road. At 2.1 miles, the road reaches the ridge at a T junction with yet another fire road. To the right cyclists find the return leg for their loop; it meets the Cross-Marin Bike Trail east of the entrance station.

Views from Barnabe Peak Ridge include the high-class lookout, the park lands, the serial ridges to the east and northeast (particularly spectacular when fog fills the drainages), Mount Tamalpais, Tomales Bay, and the ocean. As one heads right, Kent Lake is added.

Returning to the 1.75-mile junction, hikers find a well-wooded tour, distinguished by long switchbacks. On extremely warm days, hikers may opt to reverse the tour. Laurel abounds, punctuated by some big Douglas fir. From 4.5 to 4.9 miles, the trail features more fir and maple, with trillium and starflower adding spring accents. By the time the trail reaches the lower slope, the canopy is mostly deciduous.

At the switchback at 5.9 miles, the main trail continues left; the path to the right leads to Stairstep Falls, a wet-season destination, in 0.2 mile. The 40-foot falls consists of an upper drop and a stepped base. In late season, it shows only a dark stain and faint trickle, but the drainage remains pretty.

Resuming the tour, hikers are soon contouring above Devils Gulch. The bridge at 6.9 miles leads to the horse camp; a beautiful redwood stands sentinel. From the bridge crossing, the loop follows Devils Gulch briefly downstream, then meets and descends the gated horse-camp road to cross the highway at 7.25 miles. The hike ends heading upstream along the narrow corridor between the highway and tree-overhung Papermill Creek. It reaches the picnic area at 8.3 miles; the return to Madrone Group Camp adds another 0.5 mile.

*Access:* Begin on the gated dirt fire road at the upper northwest corner of the Madrone Group Camp parking area.

## China Camp State Park

**Hours/Season:** Year-round; 10:00 A.M. to 5:00 P.M. (museum)

**Facilities:** 30 developed walk-in campsites, picnic areas, historic fishing village, unpaved launches for small boats, hiker and horse trails, mountain-bike roads, restrooms, nonflush toilets

**For Information:** (415) 456-0766

**Access:** From US 101 at the north end of San Rafael, exit at North San Pedro Road and go east to enter the park.

Along the southwest corner of San Pablo Bay, this park preserves a picturesque, historic Chinese fishing village—a quiet reflection of Chinese culture in early California. In the 1880s, it supported a population of 500 Canton Chinese. When anti-Chinese sentiment escalated, restrictive legislation pushed the villagers out, leaving behind a ghost of the former settlement.

Artists and photographers are enchanted by the village, recording it on canvas and film. From the bay bluff, visitors gain an excellent overlook of the village, its pier across the muddy shallows, and the Chinese fishing boat moored at its end.

Besides China Camp, the park's 1,640 acres host a variety of recreational pur-

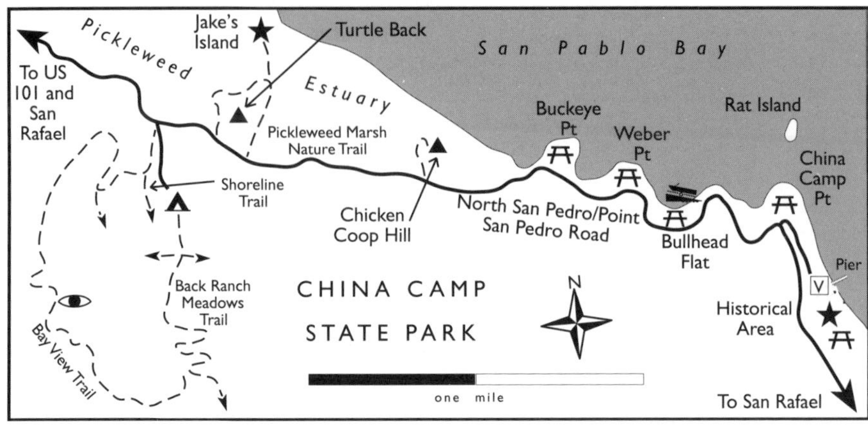


suits, including picnicking, fishing, sunbathing, swimming, windsurfing, hiking, and horseback riding. Upland and estuarine habitats provide a diversity of nature study. Atop Bullet and Chicken Coop hills and from the various picnic area points, visitors enjoy vistas of the estuary, San Pablo Bay, Mount Burdell, and the Sonoma Mountains.

At the park's west end is a small, pleasant walk-in campground. Campers with self-contained recreational vehicles are welcome to use its parking lot on an overnight basis, but the gate is locked at night.

For the San Francisco Bay area, the park enjoys uncommonly good weather, sheltered by San Pablo Ridge.

## Attractions and Activities

**China Camp.** Today, visitors can stroll amid the abandoned wooden shanties that abut a peaceful cove on San Pablo Bay. In the dimly lit museum warehouse, photographs, panels, exhibits, and artifacts relate the story of China Camp and its people.

Grass shrimp were harvested by traditional means, using sampans and nets. Outside, baskets, yokes, wheelbarrows, drying tables, and crates vividly recall the shrimp-fishing venture. Along the beach, visitors will discover an old set of tracks and pulleys used to bring the boats to shore.

At the village, a small, old-fashioned luncheon counter and bait stand is open on weekends. Its interior recalls the past.

*Access:* Find it off North San Pedro/Point San Pedro Road, at the east side of the park.

**Back Ranch Meadows–Bay View Loop.** This 3.5-mile loop travels fire road and multi-use trail along a wooded slope of San Pablo Ridge, affording limited, but worthwhile, views.

Leaving the laurel-shaded campground near site 12, travelers follow a rough, eroded fire road for a steep uphill climb. After crossing over the Shoreline Trail, which traverses the park, they then enter a complex of manzanita, madrone, toyon, and oak. The roadway is mostly exposed to the sun. Deer, squirrels, and lizards are co-travelers, with hawks and vultures claiming the sky.

The road offers a hefty workout. At 0.75 mile and again at 1 mile, the utility corridor creates a gap affording views of the salt marsh, tidal sloughs, and San Pablo Bay. At 1 mile, go right on the Bay View Trail to continue the loop.

The loop contours a similarly wooded slope, but is better shaded, owing to the width of the trail. Where it rounds several drainages, there are small-diameter redwoods and laurels. At 1.8 and 2.1 miles, open views north feature Jake's Island and Turtle Back; both are estuary hills. At 2.3 miles, travelers come upon a picnic table, as the trail slowly descends.

It next travels on or just below a ridge, coming to a fire road, which continues the loop downhill. At 3 miles, travelers may opt to either stay on the fire road, which comes out at the curve on the campground road, or resume on the Bay View Trail, which now heads left.

Taking the Bay View Trail, they cross over a small drainage, entering a mixed manzanita-madrone forest. The Shoreline Trail holds a parallel course on the lower slope. At 3.3 miles, the Bay View Trail meets and ends at the Shoreline Trail. To the right leads to camp; going left 0.2 mile leads to the entry station, closing the tour.

*Access:* Head through the campground toward sites 1 to 15; day users must park outside the campground entrance and hike the 0.3 mile to the camp parking lot.

**Pickleweed Marsh Nature Trail.** This 0.75-mile nature trail rounds three sides of Turtle Back, skirting the tidal flat, sloughs, and channels of a vast pickleweed marsh. Signs identify the hill's vegetation: mixed oak, laurel, toyon, and madrone. A briny scent pinches the nose, and egrets and herons may be spied.

About midway around Turtle Back, a 0.2-mile spur heads north to tree-covered Jake's Island, a small rise isolated by the estuary. Tides can make it impassable; even at ideal times, rubber boots or old sneakers may be in order. The soft mud records the tracks of deer, skunk, and raccoon. To return, visitors must hike along the road or retrace their steps.

*Access:* Find the main trailhead on the southeast side of Turtle Back, east of the entrance to Back Ranch Meadows Campground; parking is roadside.

**Fishing.** The park affords some fine shore and boat fishing, but anglers must confine their sport to periods of high tide. Most of the bay is less than 6 feet deep, and the level fluctuates some 4 feet between high and low tide. Flounder, perch, striped bass, and sturgeon are among the catches.

## MOUNT TAMALPAIS STATE PARK

**Hours/Season:** Year-round

**Facilities:** 16 walk-in tent sites at Pantoll Station, en route lot for RVs under 25 feet, environmental camp, horse camp, picnic areas, visitor center, outdoor theater, hiker and horse trails, mountain-bike routes, restrooms, nonflush toilets

**For Information:** (415) 388-2070

**Access:** From US 101, exit onto CA 1 North for Stinson Beach, Muir Woods, and Mount Tamalpais and stay on it for 3.4 miles. Turn right on Panoramic Highway and go 5.1 miles to Pantoll Ranger Station. *The winding mountainous roads to and through the park are not recommended for trailers or RVs over 25 feet.*

Mount Tamalpais, "Mount Tam" (elevation 2,571 feet), is the most famous natural skyline feature overlooking San Francisco Bay. It has long been a destination of area residents and visitors. From 1896 to 1930, the "Crookedest Railroad in the World" traveled up its flank through 281 curves. In 1929, a wildfire swept the mountain, consuming much of the line; but hikers, riders, and cyclists can still travel most of its former route.

Muir Woods National Monument is an island surrounded by this 6,300-acre state park; the state park, in turn, is encompassed by the Marin Water District Lands and Golden Gate National Recreation Area. Together, these public lands create an extensive, interlocking trail network that includes more than 50 miles in Mount Tamalpais State Park. These trails cross coastal grassland slopes, dip into cool redwood ravines, travel leafy woodlands, and conquer the rugged chaparral hillsides of Mount Tam.

## Attractions and Activities

**East Peak Summit Auto Tour.** A paved road climbs within 0.3 mile of the East Peak summit, affording a grand Pacific Coast–San Francisco Bay vista. A visitor center, snack stand, picnic tables, and restroom serve the traveler. From the parking lot, a steep, rugged trail climbs to Gardner Lookout, but the nicer tour and actually better views are gained rounding the peak on the Verna Dunshee Trail (see trail description). Views span the Farallon Islands to the Sierra crest.

*Access:* From Pantoll junction near the ranger station, go 1.4 miles north on Pantoll Road to Ridgecrest Boulevard and follow it northeast 2.9 miles to the East Peak parking lot.

**Cushing Memorial Theater.** A worthwhile stop en route to or from the East Peak summit is this 1930s-built open-air mountain amphitheater, reached via a short trail. Its rows of stone seating—enough for 3,500 people—contour the slope

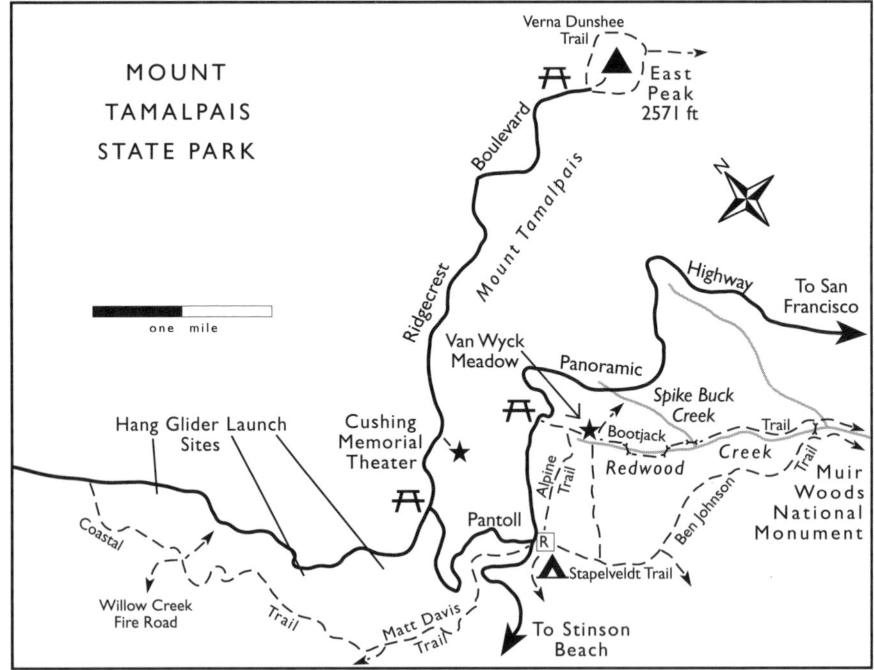

above an earthen flat, where productions are staged. It brings to mind ancient Greece or Rome. Each spring, the performance of a traditional play takes place here.

*Access:* Reach the marked parking turnout off Ridgecrest Boulevard 0.1 mile northeast of its intersection with Pantoll Road.

**Verna Dunshee Trail.** This 0.7-mile paved circuit encircles chaparral-clad East Peak, slowly unraveling a 360-degree vista. Counterclockwise, the first stop is near some picnic tables. A locator board identifies the San Francisco Bay area features and points south. The Golden Gate Bridge, Seal Rock, Alcatraz and Angel islands, and Mount Diablo are some of the pinpointed locales.

Unfortunately, the other compass directions lack such identifying boards, but visitors will be able to see the Sierra (on clear days) rising above the Central Valley to the east, Mount St. Helena to the north, and Middle Peak to the west. The loop ends near the snack bar. Benches dot the circuit.

*Access:* The hike begins at the East Peak parking lot, rounding the south slope of the peak.

**Matt Davis–Coastal Trail.** This mildly rolling hiker trail contours the park's coastal slope at its 1,500-foot elevation for 4.2 miles. Along the way, it offers views of the Golden Gate, the coastal mountains to the south, Stinson Beach, Bolinas Lagoon, and Point Reyes.

The hike begins following the Matt Davis Trail, ascending a rock-studded slope above Panoramic Highway. Dwarf mountain mahogany vegetates the sides of the trail. Where it enters a twisted-oak woodland, hikers find a good, wide trail. Moss decorates the oaks, while Douglas fir and laurel add to the woodland mix. Prior to reaching the 1.6-mile junction, the route breaks into the open a couple of times, offering early views of the San Francisco Bay area and Point Reyes. At 1.6 miles, where the Matt Davis Trail heads southwest (left) toward Stinson Beach, bear right following the Coastal Trail.

*Coastal Trail, Mount Tamalpais State Park*

The Coastal Trail tours the open grassy slope with brief dips into tree-shaded drainages. Coastal vistas are nearly continuous and now include Bolinas Point, Bolinas Lagoon, and Stinson Beach. Downhill views are of the foothill slope of Mount Tam. At 2.4 miles, hikers bypass a rusted car wreck hooked around a California laurel.

Along the route, the rising thermals may carry colorful winged humans, as well as vultures and hawks. Members of the Marin County Hang Gliding Association hold a special permit to use the park. They alone are allowed this privilege. While the general public may not hang glide in the park, they may enjoy the spectacle. Deer and gray squirrels are other trail companions. In spring, wildflowers dot the grasses.

At the 3.2-mile junction, hikers cross over the Willow Camp Fire Road, remaining on the Coastal Trail. Its rolling-grassland character has changed little. A short distance ahead, a memorial bench honors the Eagle Scout who built this trail segment. Views stretch north to Point Reyes. The hike ends at Ridgecrest Boulevard. If a car shuttle is not possible, return as you came.

*Access:* From Pantoll, cross the Panoramic Highway, climb the steps, and head west on the Matt Davis Trail. The hike ends east of the McKennan Gulch trailhead, off Ridgecrest Boulevard.

**Stapelveldt–Ben Johnson–Bootjack–Alpine Loop.** This 4.4-mile loop has an elevation change of 1,300 feet. Touring the Redwood Creek drainage, it travels both state park and Muir Woods National Monument lands.

Passing behind the Pantoll Station walk-in camp, hikers cross over a ridge for a steep woodland descent. Fir, oak, tanoak, and spotty black huckleberry frame the trail. Laurel and sword fern thrive in the drainage. At the 0.4-mile junction, take a sharp right, just before the footbridge.

By 0.5 mile, the redwoods begin to appear. With the trail's descent, hikers discover more and more of the big trees. Fire-hollowed redwoods, family groups, and imposing sentinels capture the eye. Tanoaks fill the midstory. At the 1-mile junction is a bench; go straight on the Ben Johnson Trail as it enters Muir Woods National Monument. In places, boughs and trunks lace over the trail, requiring ducking. Beside the trail is a walk-through tree.

Redwood Creek now drops faster than the trail. Douglas fir, laurel, and ferns fill out the forest. The monument trail is wide and well groomed, the trek cool and shady. At 2.1 miles, go past the Hillside Trail, and cross the footbridge over Redwood Creek. In winter, steelhead may be seen fighting the current. At the upcoming junction, go left for an uphill return on the Bootjack Trail, re-entering the state park.

At 2.3 miles is an impressive memorial stand of orange-sided redwoods. The trail now travels along the creek bank, with overlooks of pools and cascades. In a couple of places, the trail forks only to again merge.

At 2.8 miles a footbridge crosses Spike Buck Creek; afterward, the trail climbs steeply. Crossing over Redwood Creek, it briefly tours an oak flat before returning to the drainage, stairstepping up the slope. Redwoods continue to line the way.

At 3.7 miles, hikers reach Van Wyck Meadow, a small grassy flat with a large central boulder. Continue straight, remaining on the Bootjack Trail, which rounds the meadow, climbs, and goes left at the next junction. Redwoods still claim the upper drainage.

At 4 miles, go left on the Alpine Trail, following it back to Pantoll Station. The forest becomes more mixed, as the trail climbs. The loop closes at 4.4 miles.

*Access:* The trail begins near the entrance to Pantoll Ranger Station, on the south side of Panoramic Highway.

# ANGEL ISLAND STATE PARK

**Hours/Season:** 8:00 A.M. to sunset

**Facilities:** Picnic areas, visitor center, historic areas, pier, boat slips, mooring buoys, concession-run deli, hiker trails, bicycle roads, restrooms

**For Information:** (415) 435-1915

**Access:** Reach the park at Ayala Cove via private boat or public ferry service from Tiburon, San Francisco, or Vallejo. For costs and schedules, phone the Angel Island State Park Ferry Company in Tiburon, (415) 435-2131, or the Red and White Fleet, which operates out of San Francisco and Vallejo, (800) 229-2784. *Bicycles may be taken on the ferries, but space is limited. Dogs, rollerskates, and skateboards are not allowed on the island.*

This San Francisco Bay island has had a varied history, beginning with the arrival of the Coast Miwok Indians, who sailed their tule reed canoes to its shores. In 1775, the Spanish anchored here while charting San Francisco Bay; the island bears the name they gave it. Through the years, it has served as a cattle ranch, a quarantine and immigration station, and a military installation. Today, only the automated Coast Guard light station remains.

Open grassland and stands of native oak, laurel, and madrone contribute to the island mosaic. In spring, the upland meadows present a myriad of wildflowers: blue-eyed grass, California poppy, wild geranium, iris, and Indian paintbrush, while the ceanothus colors and scents the chaparral. Deer roam this mountain island. Hummingbird, flicker, and hawk are commonly seen, as are seal and sea lion, scoter, and grebe. Bay area vistas appear nonstop.

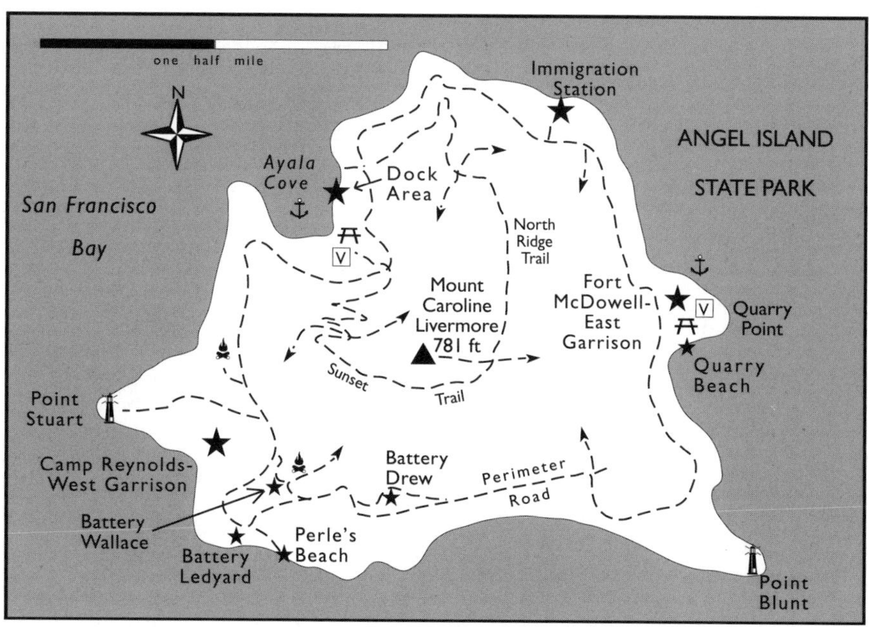

## Attractions and Activities

**Beaches.** The island has some fine sandy beaches for sunning and strolling, with those at Ayala Cove and Quarry Point being sheltered from the afternoon winds. While the waters off Quarry Point invite waterplay, swimming at Angel Island is not recommended, due to strong, changeable currents, the cold water, and no lifeguards. Swept by wind and looking out at the agitated waters, Perle's Beach has a wildness about it.

**Perimeter Road Tour.** This 5-mile paved or gravel road encircles the island, stitching together military sites, beaches, and coves; it is open to foot and bicycle travel. On weekends, a fee-shuttle service to the historic sites is available from 11:00 A.M. to 3:00 P.M., and docents are regularly stationed at the quarantine and immigration stations, Camp Reynolds, and Fort McDowell, where guided tours are available. Tables, drinking fountains, and restrooms mark the route.

From the Ayala Cove landing, head toward the two-story white building, formerly the *Quarantine Station and Hospital,* now the visitor center. Inside are exhibits, a topographic model of the island, maps, and an informed staff ready to point out areas to visit. Following the paved route up through the tree-shaded picnic area behind it, visitors come to the Perimeter Road (0.4 mile).

Go right for a counterclockwise tour. As it rounds the island staying 150 to 200 feet above shore, it offers early overlooks of Ayala Cove. Oak, toyon, laurel, pine, and buckeye vegetate the slope.

At 1.2 miles, travelers come to the *Camp Reynolds–West Garrison* area, which served as a military camp from the Civil War through World War II. A brief detour west to Point Stuart offers views of the San Francisco skyline, Golden Gate, Sausalito, and Tiburon, and an overlook of the West Garrison beach. Following the dirt road downhill at 1.2 miles leads to the garrison's tidy white residences and service buildings, rimming a parade ground above the beach. Plaques and the park brochure identify some of the buildings; a museum at the head of the parade ground is open during peak visitor times.

Keeping to the Perimeter Road, at 1.4 miles travelers begin bypassing side routes to the island's three gun batteries (concrete bunkers). Battery Wallace is secluded in the woods uphill to the left, while Battery Ledyard lies below the road, recessed into the slope at Point Knox. At 1.6 miles, a roadside bench overlooks Ledyard and the Golden Gate Bridge. Here, too, a dirt road descends to Perle's Beach, a 0.1-mile-long, wide sandy strand, backed by a slope of eucalyptus. Past the quarry site (1.9 miles), a side road heads left to the third battery, Drew. Island vegetation tops this boxy structure.

At the 2.8-mile junction, bear right keeping to the Perimeter Road. Ahead a bench affords a 180-degree cross-bay view of San Francisco and Oakland. Past the onetime Nike Missile Base, stay left, as Point Blunt is off limits to the public.

At 3.6 miles, travelers reach the *Fort McDowell–East Garrison–Quarry Beach* area. The abandoned structures with glassless, haunting windows claim a good portion of the shore and slope above it. Descending toward the open court, visitors find two routes passing between the structures. Living quarters mainly line the upper route, while imposing, sterile, concrete structures line the lower one. Among these building are the mess hall, post exchange, and administration buildings. Near the new ferry landing, the Guardhouse Museum has displays on the area and its history. At its back remain the old cells.

As the Perimeter Road resumes rounding a slope of native woodland and eucalyptus, visitors next come to the *Immigration Station Area* at 4.1 miles. This historic area best lends itself to a self-guided tour. A legend at the entry identifies the buildings, and plaques on the structures and sites give bits of history. Here, Chinese immigrants and World War II prisoners were housed. At the Detention Barracks Museum, visitors see the poems and messages left by the detainees. Above the beach is the original bell and a marble memorial dedicated to the Chinese people. Behind the barracks, visitors can still see the menacing barbed wire and guard tower.

As the Perimeter Road tour draws to a close, it offers looks at Richmond Bridge and Tiburon. At 4.8 miles, hikers may take the steep stairway and trail descending to the Ayala Cove landing. Cyclists must keep to the road, returning near the visitor center.

*Access:* Begin at Ayala Cove.

**North Ridge–Sunset Trail Loop.** This 4.5-mile loop tops Mount Caroline Livermore (elevation 781 feet) for a fine overview of the San Francisco Bay area.

The hike begins with a quick, breath-stealing ascent from the Ayala Cove landing to Perimeter Road. Across the road, the North Ridge Trail continues the climb to Mount Livermore. It passes through an oak grassland with patchy ceanothus, offering looks west at scenic, protected Ayala Cove. The trail is wide and well graded. As it ascends and enwraps the slope, areas of chaparral divide the woodland. The poison oak vines wriggle up the oaks, while the bay breeze brings refreshment.

At 0.8 mile, the North Ridge Trail bears left crossing over a dirt fire road, and at 1.2 miles, it tours a grassland rise marked by a couple of pines, then alternates between woodland and grassland. Views are of the summit and Tiburon. Soon, a rich area of ceanothus commands the trail. After briefly traveling a pine-clad slope, it comes out at a paved road (2.1 miles). Go right for the summit. Angling left, hikers find the earthen Sunset Trail (the return leg of the loop), descending from the road.

After a steep, 0.2-mile climb, hikers claim the summit flat. Views build with the climb, and strolling the flat, visitors pull together a full 360-degree look at San Francisco Bay. A few picnic tables occupy the top, and directional boards identify the landmarks.

Returning to the 2.1-mile junction, take the Sunset Trail to close the loop. This trail rounds the island's mountaintop, passing through grassland. Open views accompany the first 0.5 mile of descent. At 3 miles, the trail angles right, crossing over a fire road. A slow, switchbacking descent amid a laurel and oak woodland follows.

At 3.5 miles, the trail tags one last open viewpoint of the Golden Gate Bridge and Mount Livermore, looking across Point Stuart. Meeting the Perimeter Road at 4.1 miles, hikers cross over it, taking the road straight ahead to return to Ayala Cove near the visitor center.

*Access:* Begin at the northeast corner of the Ayala Cove Ferry Waiting Area, past the restrooms.

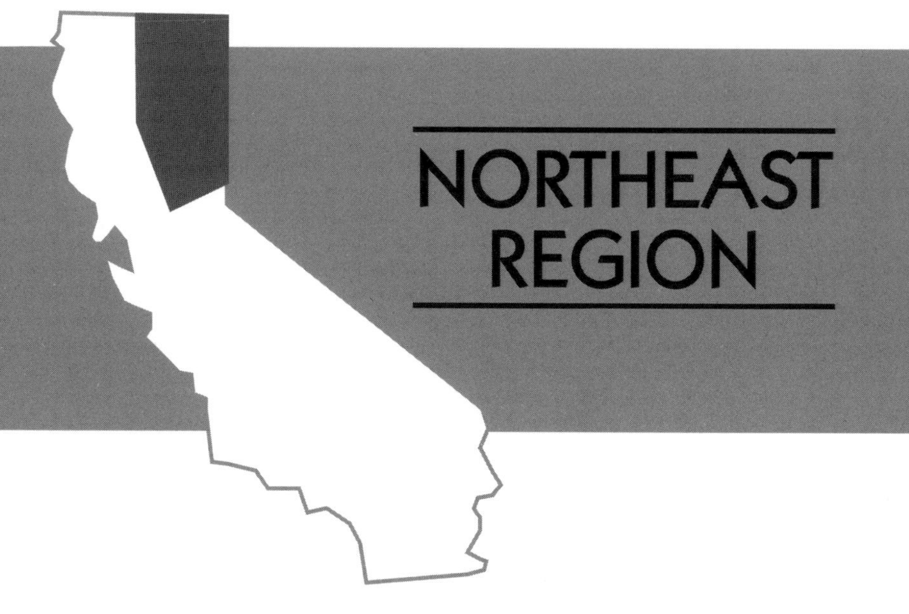


## McArthur–Burney Falls Memorial State Park

**Hours/Season:** Year-round
**Facilities:** 128 developed canyon-rim campsites, environmental camp, picnic area, visitor center, store and snackbar, marina, boat launch, swimming area, hiker trails, restrooms, pay showers, dump station
**For Information:** (916) 335-2777
**Access:** From the junction of CA 299 and CA 89 (northeast of Burney), go 5.5 miles northwest on CA 89.

Centerpiece to this quiet 875-acre forest park is 129-foot Burney Falls—revered by the Pit River Indians, who first occupied this area, and by the parkgoers who have since followed. Fed by an underground reservoir, this split-drop waterfall makes a consistent, dramatic year-round statement. Daily, some 100 million gallons of water spill over it.

The park also enjoys open forests of ponderosa pine, mixed fir, and oak and has frontage on PG&E's 9-mile-long Lake Britton.

### Attractions and Activities

**Lake Britton Day Use.** Here, the park has a marina, a semi-shaded picnic area overlooking Burney Creek Cove, and a protected swimming area. A few pines and oaks shade the long sandy beach, while the buoy-roped lake area offers ample space for swimming and waterplay. At the marina, visitors may rent paddleboats, canoes, and motorboats; the reservoir accommodates all users. Its waters generally are kept

Opposite: *Osprey nest, Ahjumawi Lava Springs State Park*

high for weekend recreation and pulled down for power needs during the week.

*Access:* To reach the lake, continue north on the park road from the falls area or hike the Rim or Burney Creek trail.

**Fall Creek Loop Trail.** This 1.2-mile self-guided interpretive loop tours the creek canyon, offering different perspectives on Burney Falls. Plaques relate the natural history of the area. Benches dot the route.

The tour begins following a paved walk to the falls vista deck, offering a tree-framed view of majestic Burney Falls, the jewel-like secondary falls flanking it, and its deep canyon pool. The trail remains paved as it switchbacks into the canyon, affording more looks at the falls. Black swifts may be spied flying through the mist. These seabirds nest in the waterfall cliff from March through the autumn months.

By 0.3 mile, the trail nears the creek. The main trail continues downstream, while an upstream spur leads to a straight-ahead view of the waterfall. Crossing the foot of a talus slope, hikers overlook a fast-rushing section of the creek. White alder, dogwood, maple, and Douglas fir frame it. At the end of the pavement at 0.5 mile, the loop crosses the bridge over Burney Creek, while the route ahead leads to Lake Britton.

As the loop turns upstream, ascending the opposite canyon wall, a few more plaques introduce the vegetation and describe the falls, but the vistas are now mostly obstructed. Waterleaf, columbine, and mountain misery are among the forest floor cover. A bench at 1 mile overlooks the top of the falls.

After crossing the footbridge back over the creek, hikers arrive at a gravel parking area. Go left on the pedestrian trail to close the loop. To the right is the Headwaters Trail.

*Access:* Begin at the trail kiosk located above the falls, opposite the entry station and a tree-ring exhibit.

*Fly fishing, Burney Creek, McArthur–Burney Falls Memorial State Park*

**Headwaters Trail.** This 0.5-mile trail follows the shore of Burney Creek upstream to the site of its headwater—an underground spring and reservoir. During the dry season, there is no creek above this point.

This is the trail traveled by fly fishermen to their favorite pools. Its rolling route passes through open forest and the oak and shrub habitat of the basalt slope. As the forest buffer between the trail and the creek narrows, views come more frequently.

At 0.5 mile is the headwater pool, a broad, slow place on the creek, cut off by some willows; it is more interesting than scenic. Across the bridge, a trail leads to the environmental camps. Return as you came, or cross the bridge and return via the Fall Creek Loop.

*Access:* Begin at the gravel parking area upstream from Burney Falls.

**Pioneer Cemetery Trail.** This 0.8-mile trail follows a former wagon road away from camp, touring an open forest of pine and cedar above a grassy floor. Signs and arrows point the way.

At 0.3 mile, oak woodlands spot the open flat, and at 0.6 mile, the trail descends. During construction of the dam on Lake Britton, the cemetery's historic wooden markers were consumed by fire. Now, a single marker lists the pioneer dead, and only a few headstones remain. Lilacs, oaks, and pines dress the site.

Following the route away from the cemetery leads to Cemetery Cove on Lake Britton, at 1 mile. Here, visitors find a quiet retreat, looking out on the main lake. The open bank welcomes shore fishing, while ponderosa pines offer shade. Return as you came.

*Access:* Start at Pioneer Campground, near site 75.

**Fishing.** Both the creek and Lake Britton are noted for their fishing. The lake supports bass, bluegill, catfish, crappie, and trout. At Burney Creek, both native and planted trout offer sport. Anglers mainly fish the slower creek stretches above Burney Falls. Waders are recommended, as the branches prevent bank fishing in most places.

## Ahjumawi Lava Springs State Park

**Hours/Season:** Year-round

**Facilities:** 9 environmental campsites, hiker trails, nonflush toilets (at Crystal Springs and Ja She Creek), *bring or purify water*

**For Information:** McArthur–Burney Falls Memorial State Park, (916) 335-2777

**Access:** This park can only be accessed by boat. To reach the public launch that serves it, from CA 299 at McArthur, turn north on Main Street and go 3.7 miles. A dry-weather dirt road leads to PG&E's Rat Farm Launch. The park occupies the opposite shore.

Both the park and the band of Pit River Indians who resided here share the name "Ahjumawi," meaning "where the waters come together." This park boasts one of the nation's largest spring-fed freshwater systems, uniting Big Lake, Horr Pond, the Tule and Fall rivers, and Ja She and Lava creeks—a grand "coming together" of bubbling clear, aquamarine and cobalt water. The waters originate from lava springs; recent flows cover more than two-thirds of the park's 6,000-acre wilderness.

Isolated by a roadless area, water, and private lands, this park promises its seekers solitude, escape, and wilderness discovery. Among the attractions are pressure ridges, lava tubes, a spatter cone, unmatched birding, and superb vistas of Mounts Shasta and Lassen, Burney Mountain, and the Thousand Lakes Wilderness Area. Rock mortars offer clues to the dozens of Indian villages that once lined these shores. As all artifacts are protected, do not disturb them. In spring and summer, the hordes of mosquitos can be a drawback; come prepared.

## Attractions and Activities

**Lava Springs Trail.** This is the shoreline trail. Coming ashore from Rat Farm, visitors meet it midroute. Hiking west on the trail leads to Horr Pond, the environmental camps, Crystal Springs, Ja She Creek, and the trailheads for Spatter Cone Loop. Hiking east, visitors tour the Big Lake shore to Big Lake Spring.

**Westbound Tour.** The old jeep track begins about 0.1 mile inland from shore. Locator maps dot the way, with park brochures available near the camps.

Early views are of Mount Lassen; later, hikers gain looks at regal Mount Shasta. A harmonious blend of bird songs fills the air, while sightings include white pelican, grebe, osprey, heron, red-winged blackbird, and tern. Juniper and white oak cloak the low rise, while cattails and tule rushes rim Horr Pond. This large water body marked by scenic coves, inlets, and grassy islands is ideal for canoeing.

At 1 mile, hikers pass the first environmental camps and one end of Spatter Cone Loop; continue west. Although the jeep track of the shoreline trail can become faint, the line of travel is clear. Shrubs, sagebrush, and areas of basalt soon claim the way.

On the right at 1.6 miles is the other end of the Spatter Cone Loop; again continue west. Swallows, woodpeckers, cedar waxwings, and orioles may make you raise your binoculars. Where the trail drifts inland, the trees offer some shade.

At 2.1 miles, near Crystal Springs, hikers come upon the next set of camps. Here, rock channels frame where the springs percolate from the lava flow; elsewhere they pour freely.

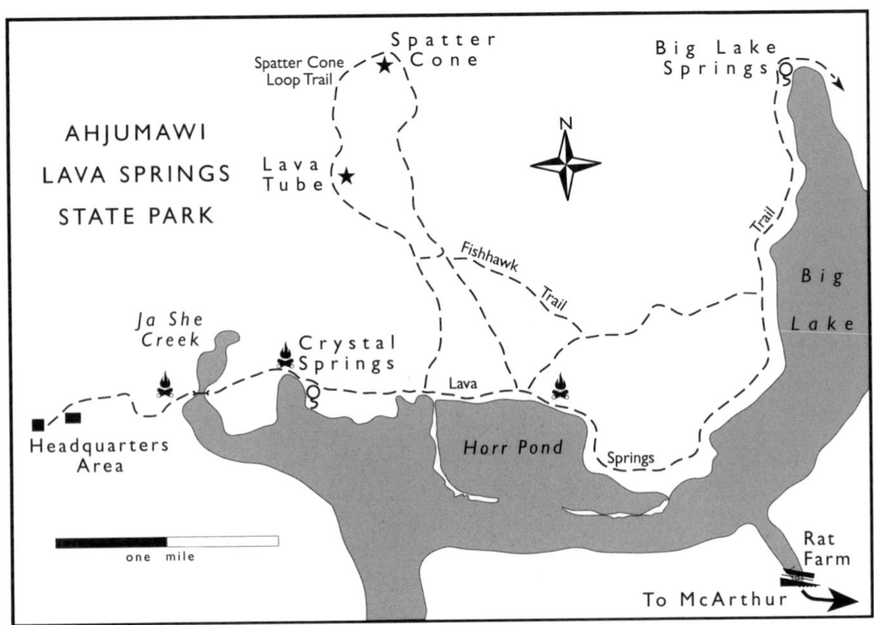

At 2.7 miles a bridge crosses Ja She Creek, one of the prettiest places in the park, with its looking-glass pool. Visitors can watch the fish swim and snatch bugs from the surface. They also can admire the reflection of the surrounding red-trunked ponderosa pines and snags.

The last set of camps is at 3 miles, but the trail continues west, journeying inland, passing through grassy flats and a forest stand, before halting at an old ranch house and barn at 3.75 miles. Barn owls sometimes spook from the rafters upon approach. At this point, return as you came.

**Eastbound Tour.** Hikers find an even more fickle jeep trail to follow, as the trail alternately tours grassy shore or inland lava flow, rounding Big Lake to its headwater spring.

Again, the tour offers wonderful birdwatching and listening. Oaks intermix with the juniper above the trail. At 1.3 miles, the trail crosses over a grinding rock, with worn mortars. Afterward, it resumes rolling, passing from flow to shore.

At 2.1 miles, it begins passing springs, with Big Spring at 2.3 miles. Like Crystal Springs, its sides have been rock lined. As the route deteriorates further beyond this point, it is best to turn around here.

*Access:* Both tours begin on the east side of Horr Pond, directly across from the PG&E Rat Farm Launch.

**Spatter Cone Loop Trail.** Keep an eye out for the start of this clockwise tour. Heading north off the Lava Springs Trail, it begins faint, semi-hidden by downfalls. Soon the trail grows easy to follow, as a lava-studded earthen jeep track replaces the loose rock.

A few pines pepper the open white oak-juniper forest, while patches of bluedicks, skyrockets, and balsamroot accent the floor. Broken lava bowls can be seen alongside the trail, as can several woodrat nests.

At 0.5 mile, mountain mahogany lines the route and an enormous osprey nest can be seen atop a juniper on the right; it has branches stacked 4 feet high. As hikers continue, more nests can be seen. In spring, the screech of an osprey may suggest you hurry along, so as not to disturb the nesting pair.

The rolling tour continues. At 0.8 mile, hikers have the option of going right for a shorter loop or left for the full tour. Going left they find a lava tube below the trail on the right at 1.25 miles. Here, a gaping black hole, with a rubble floor, greets the intrepid. A flashlight is needed to study the crusty, porous walls and lavacicles.

In another mile, hikers reach a spatter cone, a small crater with built-up sides of molten rock. Views are of Mount Shasta and a ridge to the east.

By 2.4 miles, the trail overlooks a younger, less vegetated lava flow to the northeast. At 3.3 miles, the spur for the shorter loop arrives on the right. Stay left to complete the tour.

Past Fishhawk Trail, more trees fill out the area, with yellow lichens adorning the low, dead branches. The loop then tours flow and forest, drawing to a close. It returns to the Lava Springs Trail near environmental campsite 7.

*Access:* Hike 1.6 miles west on the Lava Springs Trail and bear right for the start of the loop; this is the westernmost trailhead.

## William B. Ide Adobe State Historic Park

**Hours/Season:** 8:00 A.M. to sunset
**Facilities:** Picnic area, historic building, restroom
**For Information:** (916) 529-8599

*William B. Ide Adobe*

**Access:** In Red Bluff, from the intersection of Main Street and Adobe Road, go 0.8 mile east on Adobe Road.

This day-use picnic area and historic site occupy a bench above the Sacramento River. Various trees, including blue and live oak, shade the picnic area, while some majestic valley oak stand near the historic adobe. Although the adobe was most likely built by another pioneer, Abraham Dibble, this structure stands in memorial to William B. Ide and is typical of the frontier structure of his day.

The adobe home was built in the 1850s, during the American period of California history. William B. Ide was a vital player in opening California to United States rule. He participated in the overthrow of the Mexican leadership during the Bear Flag Revolt, June 14, 1846, and was afterward named the first and only president of the Bear Flag Republic. The republic stood less than a month, for that July the Stars and Stripes were formally raised over California.

The single-room adobe, heated by a fireplace, holds simple, utilitarian furnishings: a dining table, bed, old chests and trunks, work tables, and a spinning wheel. The interior walls reveal the natural look of mud brick. The window ledges support candles in interesting holders.

In addition to the adobe, there are several outbuildings. A well, a fruit press, and a collapsed wooden wagon further recall the era.

# Woodson Bridge and Colusa–Sacramento River State Recreation Areas—Irvine Finch River Access—Bidwell–Sacramento River State Park

**Hours/Season:** Year-round; 6:00 A.M. to 9:00 P.M. (Irvine Finch and Bidwell-Sacramento)

**Facilities:** 41 developed oak-shaded campsites, nature trail, restroom, showers (Woodson Bridge); picnic sites, launch, nonflush toilets, water (Irvine Finch); picnic sites, launch/take-out sites, nature trail, nonflush toilet, water (Bidwell-Sacramento); 14 developed parklike campsites, en route campsites, picnic sites, launch, nature trail, restroom, showers (Colusa-Sacramento)

**For Information:** (916) 839-2112 (Woodson Bridge); (916) 342-5185 (Irvine Finch and Bidwell-Sacramento); (916) 458-4927 (Colusa-Sacramento)

**Access:** These four Sacramento River units are off I-5 between Corning and Williams. For *Woodson Bridge State Recreation Area*, take the South Avenue exit south of Corning, and head east 6 miles. For the *Irvine Finch River Access*, take the CA 32 exit at Orland and go east 10.6 miles; access is on the south side of CA 32. For *Bidwell–Sacramento River State Park*, take the CA 32 exit at Orland and go east 12.2 miles, turning south on River Road; day-use areas mark the next 4 miles. For *Colusa–Sacramento River State Recreation Area*, take the CA 20 exit at Williams and go 9.1 miles east; where CA 20 turns right in Colusa, go straight 0.2 mile to the park.

All four state parks offer boating, river running, and fishing access to the Sacramento River, with camping at the two recreation areas—Woodson Bridge and Colusa–Sacramento River. Ancient valley oaks, cottonwood-riparian areas, orchards, and farmland frame this broad river, marked by gravel bars. Across from Woodson Bridge is a natural preserve bordered by Koptka Slough and the Sacramento River. As it can only be accessed by water, wildlife thrive in its isolation.

Throughout the corridor, feathered sightings include vulture, heron, egret, merganser, and Canada goose. River otter, raccoon, and deer provide other encounters enjoyed by the river traveler. Along the side waters, the turtles sunning on snags capture attention.

Woodson Bridge boasts one of the prettiest campgrounds in the state, with its big valley oaks. It also has a small, hike-to gravelly beach for swimming and wading; summer water temperatures seldom top 60 degrees Fahrenheit. Although the park lacks a picnic area and boat launch, visitors find these services next door at Tehama County Park.

Irvine Finch is a fine, developed river access, primarily serving river travelers, although it does offer road travelers a view of the river and basic conveniences.

The nicest picnic area is at Bidwell–Sacramento River State Park, at the Indian Fishery day-use area where tables are scattered on a broad, oak-shaded bluff that overlooks a side slough. A bluff nature trail offers picnickers a nice woodland stroll, with channel overlooks. Near the start (heading south from the parking area), a marker on an oak indicates the high-water line from the flood of 1986.

At Colusa–Sacramento River State Recreation Area, travelers enjoy a pleasant parklike setting, with lawn and planted shade trees; it represents a successfully reclaimed landfill. From the boat launch, an abandoned road segment journeys upstream a half mile, passing through a cottonwood-riparian area. It offers campers and day visitors a place to roam, ending at the river.

## Attractions and Activities

**Woodson Bridge Nature Trail.** This easy 0.8-mile loop has twenty interpretive stops, which identify the vegetation and points of note. Brochures are generally available at the trailhead.

The trail passes through riparian scrub; an open, tall-grass field with small oaks; a woodland of crooked-armed ancient oaks; and a blackberry thicket. A few sycamores dot the way. Discoveries may range from crows nagging an owl from its roost to the unseen rustlings of mice in the brush. At the junction with the beach trail, go left over the park road. Close the loop following the footpath to the left.

*Access:* Begin near the campfire center at Woodson Bridge.

**Fishing.** Boat and bank fishing are popular at all sites. Catfish, striped bass, shad, and steelhead may be caught on the river, with largemouth bass and bluegills taken from the quiet side waters. Red-and-white bobbers dangle from the branches, recording the frustration of past shore anglers.

**River Running.** Irvine Finch is an ideal river put-in site for inner tubers, rafters, and kayakers. It has off-road parking and a couple of lattice-shaded picnic tables overlooking the water. Downstream, the broad gravel bar at Bidwell-Sacramento's Big Chico Creek Day Use offers a convenient take-out point for a half-day river tour, but it has no developed facilities.

# Plumas Eureka State Park

**Hours/Season:** Year-round; 8:30 A.M. to 4:00 P.M., May 1 through September 30 (museum); typically May 1 through October 15 (campground)

**Facilities:** 67 developed forested campsites, picnic areas, visitor center/museum, historic mining area, alpine ski area and lodge, hiker trails, Nordic trail, restrooms, showers, dump station

**For Information:** (916) 836-2380

**Access:** From the CA 70–CA 89 junction, southwest of Portola, go 0.8 mile south on CA 89 and turn west on County Road A-14 to reach the park headquarters in another 5 miles.

This park is a celebration of its High Sierra location. It features granite peaks and crags, high-elevation forests, wildflower meadows, clear-coursing streams, and grand wilderness vistas. While the park contains only man-made lakes, it is a popular gateway to the neighboring Lakes Basin Recreation Area. The park also has a rich hard-rock mining legacy. Its museum, historic mining areas, and Eureka Peak piece together the story.

At Plumas Eureka, visitors find a full calendar of activity, with hiking, fishing, picnicking, and camping in summer, and Nordic and alpine skiing in winter.

This location was one of the first areas in the Western Hemisphere to host competitive alpine skiing. A museum displays race notices dating back to 1869, as well as an example of the single 12-foot-long, 20-pound ski then used in the sport. Throughout winter, County Road A-14 is kept cleared to the museum and ski area.

## Attractions and Activities

**Mining Complex Walking Tour.** A self-guided tour begins at the museum, where visitors learn from displays and exhibits about hard-rock mining at Eureka

Peak. Working models of a stamp mill and an arrastra vividly demonstrate how the gold-bearing quartz was processed. The museum was originally the miners' bunkhouse; across the way are other tidy red mining-company buildings.

A blacksmith shop contains a forge and tools, and a stable now holds a collection of mining machines. About the complex grounds, visitors can see worn 3-foot-diameter Chile wheels (primitive millstones used to crush the rock), tram buckets, a jaw crusher, and even a hydraulic monitor. The standout feature, though, is the 1878-built Mohawk Mill.

This multi-story, Pelton wheel-powered mill was gravity operated. Ore, brought by aerial tram, entered the facility at its upper level. As the rock passed to each successive lower level, it was further processed; a display details the operation. Through a screened door, visitors can peer inside at some of the equipment still in place. A trail continues past the mill, leading to the tram terminal ruins and a powderhouse recessed in the hill. From the trail, visitors also gain a better look at the mill.

*Access:* Begin at the museum.

**Moriarity House Guided Tour.** On a variable schedule, docents lead tours through this 1890s company house where the mine foreman and his family lived. Visitors view the parlor, a bedroom, utility room, and kitchen. Among the interesting features are the whittled cigar-box picture frames, odd kitchen gadgets, and the innovative miner's lunch bucket. Docents relate stories about life at the mine and at home and about the Moriarity family.

*Access:* Sign up at the museum; the house is located across County Road A-14 from the museum and other buildings.

**Eureka Peak Loop.** This 4-mile loop with a 1,300-foot elevation change travels from Eureka Lake to the park's highest peak.

Cross the lake's dam and spillway to enter the forest for a steep, steady climb. Four varieties of pine and white and true fir make up the open forest, while manzanita, kinnikinnick, and sticky laurel dress the floor. Lichens on tree trunks hint at a 10-foot snowline. At 0.6 mile, the trail breaks out onto a rocky chaparral slope—a fine short hike destination. Views are of pointy-topped North Peak, the Sierra ridges to the east, and the Eureka Lake basin. The feel and sound of the wind contribute to the location's wildness.

Choosing to continue, hikers re-enter a forest with a lupine floor, coming to the loop junction at 0.75 mile. Going left begins a clockwise tour, contouring the slope and crossing a 5-foot-wide mountain stream (or trickle, depending on season) at 1

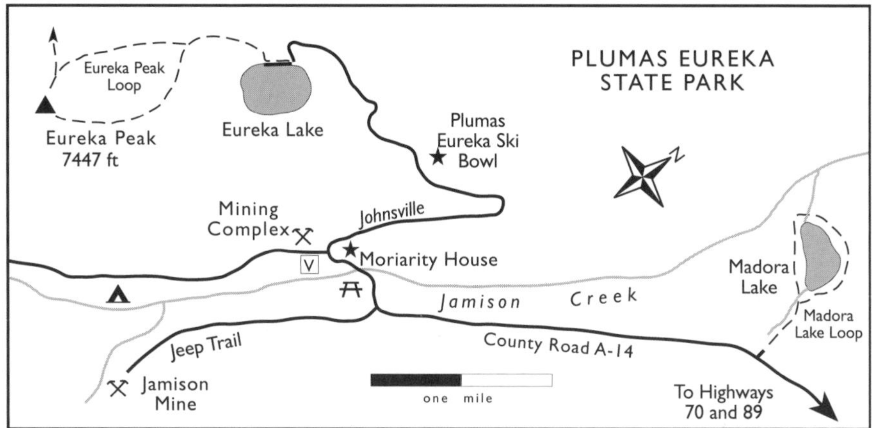

mile. As the trail approaches the ridge, it turns, passing through the forest at the foot of a rocky slope. After skirting a meadow decorated with leopard lilies in August, it switchbacks past the false peak (North Peak). Mountain hemlock and whitebark pine claim the upper slope.

At 1.6 miles, the trail tops the main ridge and heads right, serving up a superb 180-degree eastern view of the forested expanse and Eureka Lake. Afterward, it begins rounding the forested bowl on the ridge's north flank. At 2 miles, hikers gain views south, and at 2.2 miles, the trail splits the two summit crags of Eureka Peak; posts mark the tops.

The short trail to the top of the left crag requires bushwacking. The route to the top of the right one is easier, with a short path and brief rock scramble to the top. A United States Geological Survey marker is found there, and looks north reveal Lassen Peak. Each summit crag affords a 360-degree view, limited only by the top of the other. A snowfield on the north side of Eureka Peak lingers through summer; the drop to the south is abrupt. Dark lichens etch the rocks.

The loop now descends on an old jeep trail. The trees are wind-shaped, absent their south-facing limbs. Entering a dry meadow, sprinkled with lupine and forget-me-not, hikers lose the view. At 2.5 miles, the trail heads right, leaving the jeep road; a sign and parallel rows of rocks indicate the turn. It briefly follows the lower rim of the bowl, offering views north, before a steep descent and cut to the right begins the final downhill. The trail passes through forest and open areas to close the loop at 3.25 miles. Return as you came.

*Access:* Begin at Eureka Lake, 1.3 miles up the narrow, winding high-clearance road from Ski Bowl. The road is currently open for driving when passable. Visitors without high-clearance vehicles must hike this distance.

**Madora Lake Loop.** This 1.8-mile loop is an easy walk to a scenic park reservoir.

The hike begins in a thick forest of fir, pine, and cedar. Upon reaching Lundy Ditch, follow the 2-foot-wide channel downstream to the loop junction at 0.3 mile. False hellebore, columbine, and other wildflowers color its meadow banks; ponderosa pines dominate the skyline.

Cross over the ditch for a clockwise tour. The loop travels a forest with a dry meadow floor, removed from the west shore of Madora Lake. Tree-filtered glimpses reveal a marshy, cattail edge. A couple of old-growth pines rise above the trail as it draws closer to the open water near the dam.

At the outlet, hikers enjoy a full-length view down the lake; lichen-painted snags pierce the water. Bypassing a picnic table, the trail travels closer to the east shore, passing through forest and overlooking the shallow water. At 1.3 miles, the trail leaves the lake, traveling the edge of a meadow. The loop closes at 1.5 miles; return as you came.

*Access:* Find the trailhead on County Road A-14, 2.1 miles northeast of the headquarters–Johnsville junction.

**Fishing:** At Madora and Eureka lakes and in the park's clear-water streams, anglers have success catching trout with both bait and flies, using light line and gear. Bait is best early in the season, while flies work better in the fall. Occasionally, the park creeks are planted by the California Department of Fish and Game.

**Alpine Skiing.** The Plumas Eureka Ski Bowl has old-fashioned poma lifts and a small rustic lodge operated by a nonprofit ski club. Located at the historic site of the miners' longboard snowshoe races, Ski Bowl features a 1,100-foot slope. Runs rate from beginner to advanced, with most being intermediate. At the lodge, located over the hill from the parking area, visitors find lockers, a warming fire, restrooms, and a food service, but no lessons, rentals, or repairs. As snow conditions allow, the bowl operates from mid-December through April, staying open Wednesday, Saturday, Sunday, and holidays from 10:00 A.M. to 4:00 P.M. (Saturdays, it opens at 8:30 A.M.). For more details, phone (916) 836-2317 or the park at (916) 836-2380.

*Access:* Reach it off County Road A-14, a mile past Johnsville.

**Nordic Skiing.** The park has one formal Nordic trail through Jamison Canyon. This 3-mile trail mostly follows old or existing roads, passing through Camp Lisa and the park campground. Below Eureka Peak, skiers need to beware of possible avalanches. A map of the route is available at the headquarters.

*Access:* Begin off County Road A-14, near the entrance to Jamison Mine Road or at the museum; orange ski markers indicate the route from the former.

## BIDWELL MANSION STATE HISTORIC PARK

**Hours/Season:** Tours hourly from 10:00 A.M. to 4:00 P.M., except major holidays
**Facilities:** Visitor center, historic mansion, restrooms
**For Information:** (916) 895-6144
**Access:** The mansion is at 525 Esplanade Drive, next to the university in downtown Chico.

*Carriage shed, Bidwell Mansion State Historic Park*

Shown by guided tour, this restored 1860s-built, three-story, Italian Renaissance country manor was the home of John Bidwell—California pioneer, founder of Chico, activist, statesman, and agriculturist. In the late 1840s, Bidwell purchased land along Chico Creek with his gold-rush earnings, planted it with crops, and stocked it with livestock. A log cabin, and later an adobe house, served as his bachelor residence.

As Rancho Chico grew into a diverse, prosperous, and innovative agricultural empire, Bidwell won recognition and status. He also became involved in politics, and while a United States Congressman he met Annie Kennedy, who became his wife. The mansion is the home he had built for her.

The large, newly constructed visitor center next door is the place to begin a visit. It introduces the Bidwells through exhibits and displays.

### Attractions and Activities

**Guided Mansion Tour.** The 26-room mansion is furnished with original Bidwell items and period pieces. The rooms reveal the personalities and interests of the owners. The dining room is notably absent of wine decanters. John Bidwell was the 1892 Prohibitionist Party candidate for president.

His office contains an elaborate Audubon display of stuffed birds and a painting of his bachelor adobe. Among the many library volumes are several books devoted to women's suffrage and temperance. Upstairs, visitors view a never-used ballroom and a sewing room, where Annie Bidwell gave the ranch Indians sewing and Bible instruction.

Tall windows, rather than doors, access the veranda. A gravity-operated system brought running water to the bedrooms. Human hair wreaths, an alcohol-powered fan, and a life-size portrait of John Bidwell, in which his gaze seemingly follows you, are just a few more of the many treasures on display. Notable guests to the home included President Rutherford B. Hayes, Susan B. Anthony, and John Muir.

**Self-guided Grounds Tour.** The carriage shed in back of the mansion houses several original Bidwell vehicles, including a Tally-ho, a Rockaway, and a Depot wagon. The landscaped grounds blend directly into the parklike grounds of the campus of Chico State University.

## LAKE OROVILLE STATE RECREATION AREA

**Hours/Season:** Year-round; 9:00 A.M. to 5:00 P.M. (visitor center)

**Facilities:** 212 developed campsites (75 with hook-ups), en route campsites, boat-in campsites (bring water), picnic areas, visitor center, bookstore, historic sites, fish hatchery, marina, boat launches and rentals, swimming areas, hiker and horse trails, fitness trail, restrooms, nonflush toilets, showers, dump station

**For Information:** (916) 538-2200

**Access:** From Oroville, go 7 miles east on CA 162 to reach the recreation area. Other lake accesses are found off CA 70, going 11.5 miles north of Oroville.

The tallest earth-filled dam in the nation captures the Feather River waters in Butte County to form this boaters' playground. When full, the reservoir's surface covers 15,800 acres; its shoreline stretches 167 miles. Canyon walls of mixed oak, Digger pine, and chaparral enfold the reservoir. When lake levels drop, a steep rim of reddish rock encircles it.

The roomy lake, its far-reaching river arms, and its forebays (water held below the dam for use at Thermalito Powerplant) accommodate all kinds of boating fun. There are areas for speedboats and waterskiing, sailboats and sailboards, fishing boats, houseboats, and even canoes.

The lake has two designated swimming areas with beaches and nearby picnic areas. One is at Loafer Creek, the other at North Forebay. Natural oaks intersperse the planted shade trees at Loafer Creek.

Swallowed by the captured waters were an estimated 145 ancient Maidu Indian villages, as well as historic Bidwell Bar, where gold was discovered in the mid-1800s. Only the 1856 suspension bridge and tollhouse were spared. They can now be viewed at the Bidwell Canyon picnic area.

## Attractions and Activities

**Kelly Ridge Visitor Center.** At the park visitor center, a 47-foot open-air tower offers unobstructed looks at the reservoir and pine-filtered views of the surrounding countryside. Views encompass the present-day Bidwell Bar Bridge and Middle Fork Feather River; Sutter Butte, the smallest complete mountain range in the world; the valley and Coast Range to the west; and the foothills to the east.

Inside the visitor center are exhibits on the area's natural and cultural history and on the ambitious state water project. Films and photographs add to the information, and a small bookstore sells park brochures, maps, and books to help visitors plan their stay.

*Access:* From CA 162, 6.8 miles east of Oroville, turn north on Kelly Ridge Road to reach the visitor center.

**The Dam and Spillway.** Along Oro Dam Boulevard, motorists find numerous

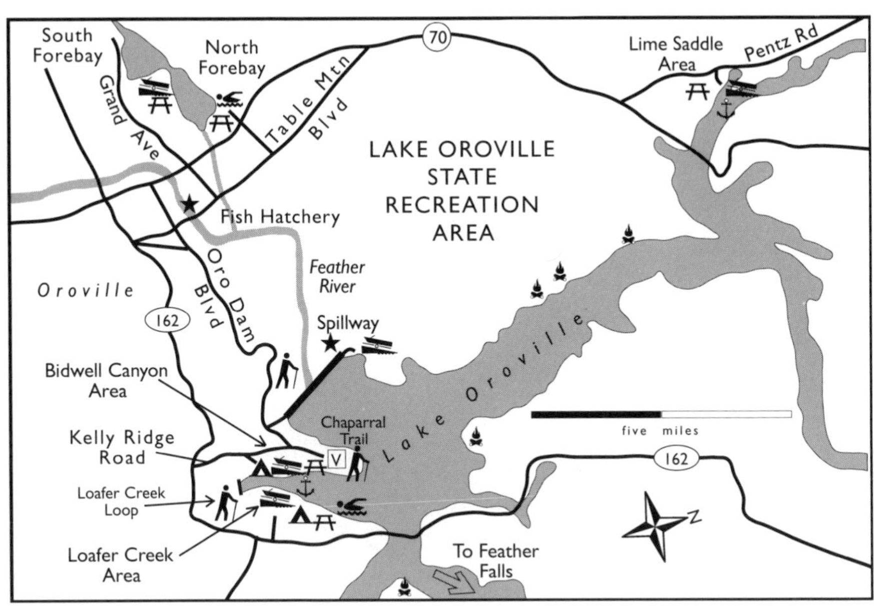

pullouts for viewing the funnel-shaped, grassy-sided, tall earthen dam. After the winter rains, locals and visitors alike make the journey to watch the thunderous plunge of water coming over the spillway. The force fills the canyon with towering billows of white spray. A two-lane road crosses the dam leading to still other parking areas, where visitors can overlook Oroville Valley, the canyon lake, and the spillway.

*Access:* From Oroville, head east on Oro Dam Boulevard.

**Feather River Fish Hatchery.** Situated alongside the Feather River, this split-level salmon and steelhead hatchery offers a self-guided tour of its gathering tanks, rearing ponds, spawning facility, fish ladder, and underwater windows.

The lower level holds the main operation. A chicken-wire mesh over the concrete pens protects the fish from osprey and kingfisher. Large windows in the spawning building allow visitors to observe the seasonal activity that occurs there. The upper level has a diversion channel, fish ladders, and underwater windows for viewing the fish migrations, as well as an overlook of the Fish Barrier Dam.

*Access:* From the junction of Grand Avenue and Table Mountain Boulevard in Oroville, go 0.3 mile south on Table Mountain Boulevard and turn west.

**Chaparral Nature Trail.** This 0.2-mile, self-guided trail tours an oak grassland and chaparral transition complex below the Kelly Ridge Visitor Center. Brochures may be purchased at the center.

The circuit introduces the common area vegetation and explains the habitat adaptations. The route twice meets the long-distance Dan Beebe Hiker/Horse Trail, which tours the south shore from Loafer Creek to Oroville. Keep right for the nature-trail loop. Where hikers meet the park road, cross over it and follow the paved path back to the visitor center.

*Access:* Start at the visitor center's inner courtyard.

**Loafer Creek Loop.** This 4.6-mile round trip offers a good area sampling. For the most part, it passes through natural habitat and is nicely remote.

The trail parallels the park road to the boat launch, quickly entering a woodland. There, live and deciduous oaks, manzanita, toyon, and low-growing poison oak shield it from the lake waters. The route is rolling, semi-shaded, and absent of views. At the small drainage at 0.5 mile though, visitors may catch a quick glimpse of the reservoir. In late May, mariposa lilies sprinkle through the grasses.

At 0.8 mile the loop junction is marked by a yellow-capped post. Going right for a counterclockwise tour, pass through a more open area with a few Digger pines. Wild turkey, deer, and jackrabbits may be seen. Ahead, the trail alternately tours grassland and open woodland, with looks at Kelly Ridge across the way. The grasses grow knee to waist high, and the oaks are multi-trunked.

At 2 miles, the trail comes out at a fire road below Saddle Dam. Cross over the road and follow the 2-track along an often dry reservoir extension. At the gravel pad at the end of the dam, bear left toward Brooks Orchard and stay left. At 2.3 miles (past post 13), turn left per the arrow. The woodland at the sides of the trail now grows more congested, and poison oak is again common.

The trail continues its rolling way, bypassing a campground at 2.8 miles. At 3 miles, bear left, staying on the loop; the trail straight ahead leads to Brooks Orchard. Where the trail meets a main park road at 3.3 miles, yellow-capped posts point hikers across the road and to the right on a gated gravel fire road.

At 3.75 miles, leave the fire road, taking the narrow footpath to the right. The loop closes just ahead at 3.8 miles; go right to finish the hike.

*Access:* Find the trail's start at the Loafer Creek area where the park road forks to the picnic area and boat launch.

**Boating.** The lake has both developed launch sites and primitive cartop-boat ramps. Primary launch sites are at Loafer Creek (seven-lane ramp), Bidwell Canyon (seven-lane ramp), the Spillway (thirteen-lane ramp), Lime Saddle (five-lane ramp), South Forebay (four-lane ramp), and North Forebay (two-lane ramp for wind- and self-powered boats only). Marinas are found at both Bidwell Canyon and Lime Saddle; boat rentals are available only at Bidwell Canyon.

The narrow upper reaches of the lake tributaries have a 5-miles-per-hour boat speed limit. The nighttime boating speed limit is also 5 miles per hour. As state lands rim the lake, boaters may access the shoreline where they please. Overnight boating is allowed for approved self-contained boats.

Exploring the Middle Fork Feather River, when the reservoir is full, boaters can get within 0.25 mile of the spectacular 640-foot Feather Falls, located on the Fall River upstream from its Middle Fork confluence. The waterfall begins narrow, then fans out. Photographs of it can be seen at the visitor center.

**Fishing.** While both boat and shore fishing are popular at the forebays, boat fishermen have greater success in steep-sided Lake Oroville. Bass and rainbow trout are the most common catches, with a few German brown trout, kokanee salmon, and catfish also taken. Some 1 million fish have been planted in the lake.

The waters are open to fishing year-round; check current regulations for size and limit restrictions. About the lake, park signboards offer updated fishing hints, as conditions can change almost daily.

## MALAKOFF DIGGINS STATE HISTORIC PARK

**Hours/Season:** Year-round; 10:00 A.M. to 5:00 P.M. daily during summer, on weekends spring and fall (museum)

**Facilities:** 30 developed forested campsites, 3 cabins (reserved through the park office), picnic sites, visitor center/museum, historic area, hiker trails, restrooms, nonflush toilets

**For Information:** (916) 265-2740

**Access:** In Nevada City, take CA 49 north for 10.4 miles and turn right on Tyler Foote Crossing Road, which becomes Backbone Road. Go 12.2 miles and turn right on unpaved Derbec Road. At the T junction, again go right to enter the park.

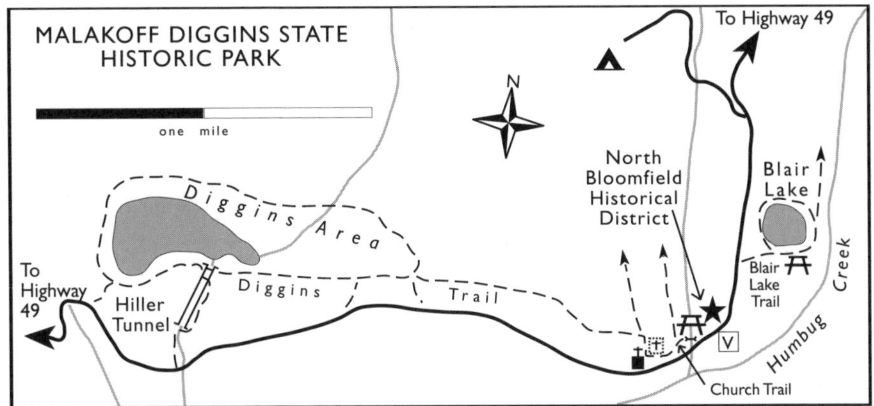

*Water monitor, Malakoff Diggins State Historic Park*

This park in Northern California's Mother Lode country showcases what was the world's largest hydraulic mining site. Today, visitors can walk the streets of old North Bloomfield, once a bustling mining town, or they can hike around and through the "diggins"—a pit 7,000 feet long, 3,000 feet wide, and 600 feet deep that has been carved out by the forced columns of water. Its time-eroded, badlands-character temples and columns remind some of Utah's Bryce Canyon. Probing the dark recess of Hiller Tunnel calls to the more adventurous. It was part of an extensive network of tunnels, ditches, flumes, and reservoirs that supplied water to miners.

Cummins Hall Museum launches a park visit, with its exhibits, photographs, and videos introducing hydraulic mining and recording mining-town life in the late 1800s.

## Attractions and Activities

**North Bloomfield Walking Tour.** At the park, a couple of blocks of original, restored, and reconstructed buildings recall old North Bloomfield; a self-guided brochure (available at the museum) identifies them. In the 1870s, the town boasted a population of 1,700 and accommodated numerous businesses, including five hotels, two breweries, and a daily stage service. The town also had a sizeable Chinese community.

Today the tidy white wooden structures reveal some of the enterprises and record the lifestyle of the townspeople. Ostrom Livery Stable, Kings Saloon, and the neatly stocked Smith and Knotwell Drug Store are among the places where visitors can look back in time. True to towns of this era, the Volunteer Fire Department and Bell Tower were vital to North Bloomfield. Scattered throughout town are mining relics.

*Access:* Begin at the Cummins Hall Museum; guided tours may be arranged there.

**Blair Lake Trail.** A 0.1-mile walk up a gated dirt road leads to a former mining site turned reservoir turned swimming and fishing hole. Ponderosa pines and cedars offer shade. A 0.3-mile trail rings Blair Lake, stringing together picnic sites and benches, while a wooden raft entices swimmers out to its middle. The lake has only bank access, and cattails claim portions of shore. Black bass, bluegill, and catfish are the catches. Rounding the lake, visitors bypass one of the old mining ditches that threaded this area.

*Access:* Find the trailhead and small parking turnout 0.1 mile north of the museum.

**Diggins Trail.** From North Bloomfield, a mostly forested 0.7-mile trail leads to the 3-mile Diggins Loop, which tours both the interior and rim of the mining pit.

At the west end of the picnic area, cross the bridge and go straight following the Church Trail toward the Diggins; the trail to the right leads to the campground. Leaving the flats of town, the trail ascends a manzanita slope. At the cemetery (0.2 mile), bear right, rounding the fenced enclosure to take the wide, evergreen-needle path ahead; a sign indicates "no dogs."

At the unmarked junction at 0.3 mile, go left for the Diggins. Manzanita, mountain misery, small oaks, and a few wildflowers decorate the rolling way. Some discarded mining rock marks the forest floor. As the trail travels below the park road, it offers a tree-filtered glimpse at the pit hillsides. An open manzanita corridor then ushers hikers to a jeep road. Cross it to reach the Diggins Loop (0.7 mile).

Going left for a clockwise tour on the South Side Trail, hikers travel inland from the rim, skirting some small mining pits. At 0.9 mile, the trail bears right, heading downslope; a small rock barrier indicates you do not go straight. At the bottom of the slope, a detour left leads to a bench and rock monument in 0.1 mile. The plaque notes the landmark ruling of 1884 that ended the boom days for the North Bloomfield Mining and Gravel Company. Once back on the loop, stepping a few feet right provides a Diggins overlook; views are of its bottom wetland and eroded hillsides.

The route continues rounding the water-carved pit. Stay straight at the upcoming junction, bypassing an area of rusted cable and pipe. At 1.7 miles, a side trail on the right leads to an opening of Hiller Tunnel, semi-hidden by the angle of the drainage and the vegetation; flashlights, sturdy shoes, and a hat are needed for a dry-season tour of the tunnel. Slippery rocks and low ceilings hamper travel in this dark passage. A short distance farther, a left leads to the other Hiller Tunnel opening and Hiller Tunnel trailhead; keep right for the loop.

The trail now enters the Diggins basin with its eroded orange and beige cliffs.

Red-winged blackbirds occupy its wetland of cattails, rushes, willows, and reeds. After the boardwalk crossing of a wetland arm, a short detour left leads to an old monitor (water cannon).

Ahead, the loop rounds the foot of the north wall, where the badland slope continues to erode, swallowing up young trees and stealing the line of the trail. Stay between the base of the slope and the willow edge, rounding toward the giant cottonwood at the head of the basin. Posts sometimes mark the way.

At 3.3 miles, the Diggins Loop curves right, crossing the basin to ascend a slope littered by rusted hydraulic pipes. The trail next follows a drainage, bearing right at 3.5 miles and again at 3.6 miles. Now, climbing along a thin secondary drainage, hikers close the loop. From the loop junction, follow the spur straight ahead, cross the jeep road, and take the path angling left to return to the townsite and headquarters (4.4 miles).

*Access:* From the picnic area in North Bloomfield, take the trail crossing the small footbridge beyond the restrooms. An alternate start is the Hiller Tunnel trailhead.

**Gold Panning.** Along a 1-mile stretch of Humbug Creek, contemporary prospectors may dip for gold. A miner's pan is the only equipment allowed. Ask at the visitor center about the exact boundaries, the rules for where you may scoop your sediments, and the limits on clouding the water.

## South Yuba River Project

**Hours/Season:** Year-round

**Facilities:** Picnic sites, information center, historic covered bridge, hiker and wheelchair-access trails, nonflush toilets, *bring water*

**For Information:** (916) 273-3884

**Access:** Trailheads are located off CA 49 6.1 miles northwest of Nevada City and at Bridgeport. From Grass Valley, go about 7 miles west on CA 20 and turn north on Pleasant Valley Road to reach the Bridgeport Visitor Center in another 7.5 miles.

A joint California State Parks–Bureau of Land Management project, this long-distance trail will one day follow a 20-mile stretch of the South Yuba River from Malakoff Diggins State Historic Park to Bridgeport. The trail incorporates parts of the 1859-built Excelsior mining ditch, wooden flumes, and a segment of stagecoach route.

South of the river bridge on CA 49, the Independence Trail represents the first wheelchair-accessible wilderness trail in the United States. Prior to the fire of 1988, it followed the Excelsior ditch for 9 miles. The trail segments, flumes, and platforms lost in the fire are slowly being restored. Touring the park trails in March and April, wildflower fanciers receive a treat.

Picnicking, sunning and swimming, fishing, and gold panning are other river pastimes. Recreational panning is allowed in the state park unless otherwise posted, but special equipment may not be used. Rainbow and brown trout are the river catches, while Lake Englebright anglers pull out bass and suckers.

### Attractions and Activities

**Covered Bridge.** Within the park, at 232 feet, is the longest single-span wooden covered bridge in the country. Built in 1862, it was part of the Virginia Turnpike

Company Toll Road, which served the mines of the Nevada Comstock Lode. Today, it serves hikers and photographers.

*Access:* Located next to the Bridgeport Visitor Center.

**Bridgeport Area Trails.** Trail segments follow the river on both sides and in both directions.

*South Shore Trails.* The trails traveling the south shore lead to small beach areas. The 0.4-mile trail upstream leads to the more scenic one, with boulders and a pleasant, deep hole. Two routes journey downstream; one is a 0.1-mile wheelchair-accessible trail.

*North Shore Trail, Downstream.* This trail travels 1 mile to Point Defiance and Lake Englebright.

To begin, pass through the covered bridge and turn left, contouring the steep, densely vegetated canyon slope. Moss and lichen decorate the boulders; poison oak is present. At 0.1 mile is a beach access; at 0.4 mile, the trail tours above a sandy bar. Where the route is open, visitors overlook a swift green band of water.

By 0.6 mile, the trail is above the reservoir, Lake Englebright. Here, houseboats sometimes anchor along shore. After the trail crosses over an old jeep track, willows clog the way. Pushing through, hikers come out at the Point Defiance Boat Camp. Return as you came.

*North Shore Trail, Upstream.* This trail starts at the parking lot on the opposite side of the road and offers the best hike for the Bridgeport Area. It begins touring the edge of an open, grassy bench overlooking the river and riparian shore. At 0.2 mile, the fork ahead leads to the river; the main trail bears left.

Soon, it contours the slope some 50 feet above the water, entering the more defined canyon. Overlooks feature areas of riffles, cascades, and pools confined by the polished gray rock of the riverbed. The steep slope defies access. California buckeye and toyon intermix with oak and Digger pine. Deer, woodpeckers, lizards, and quail may be among the wildlife sightings.

At 0.75 mile, the trail crosses a footbridge and old road as it rounds an alder-lined side drainage. At 1.1 miles side trails descend to the river, and at 1.2 miles the trail leaves the state park lands. Hikers may continue, but there is a washout to skirt at 1.3 miles, and beyond it the trail becomes more overgrown.

*Access:* All begin at the Bridgeport Visitor Center area.

**Independence Trail.** This trail contours the slope well above the South Yuba River, offering a side trail to the river and Jones Bar at 0.25 mile and a river overlook at 0.4 mile. At 2.5 miles, it meets Jones Bar Road, which allows a 4-mile loop tour. The route is generally wheelchair accessible to the picnic platform just beyond the Rush Creek Falls Vista (1 mile).

A low-clearance hiker tunnel leads to the start of the trail. Initially, it is wide, groomed, and all-ability, with toe boards and railings for the sight-impaired. Picnic tables and outhouses are spaced along the early distance. The trail alternately travels the levee wall and ditch floor of the historic Excelsior mining ditch. Wooden flumes (boardwalks) cross the steep drainages; in places discarded wood from the historic flumes can be seen. A full mixed forest shades the way—this area is uncharacteristically green for California.

At the 0.4-mile platform overlook, visitors view the South Yuba River far below in the canyon. There are benches and a trail register at this point. Staying on the Independence Trail, it remains little changed; it is still a rich, varied forest tour.

At 1 mile, an extensive trestle-supported flume wraps around the head of the steep, rock-walled gorge of Rush Creek, offering a falls vista. Buckeye and alder adorn the gorge. Springtime finds the 15-foot falls its most scenic, as it curves through the gorge, cascading into a couple of pools. A switchbacking ramp descends to the creek, and a picnic deck marks the end of the flume.

The trail continues along the Excelsior, touring an area recovering from the fire of 1988. Already it is remarkably green with an understory that sometimes overtakes the trail. The environment can get humid here. Leaving the Rush Creek drainage at 2 miles, hikers find an upstream view of the South Yuba River. As the trail closes in on Jones Bar Road (2.5 miles), more snags are seen.

For a loop tour, follow Jones Bar Road downhill to the right. At the 3.2-mile fork, bear left downhill. In another 0.1 mile, the trail arrives on a river bench above the South Yuba; a couple of paths lead to the water. Gold panning is allowed, and the rock rubble recalls the mining effort of old.

To return to the Independence Trail, follow the jeep trail heading upslope; it soon merges with the route not taken at 3.2 miles. Ahead, hikers cross Rush Creek via a scenic cable footbridge. They then cross over the jeep road, following the steep, rocky trail uphill for a few steps, to take the path angling left; be alert for this direction change. The narrow, uneven trail ascends steeply 0.2 mile, then eases for the final push to the Independence Trail at 3.75 miles. Go left for CA 49.

*Access:* Find the trailhead off CA 49 6.1 miles northwest of Nevada City.

## Empire Mine State Historic Park

**Hours/Season:** 9:00 A.M. to 6:00 P.M. May through October; 10:00 A.M. to 5:00 P.M. November through April

**Facilities:** Picnic area; visitor center/museum; historic mine area; hiker, horse, and bicycle trails; restrooms

**For Information:** (916) 273-8522

**Access:** The park is on East Empire Street in Grass Valley.

At this park, visitors have an opportunity to view, side by side, the genteel existence of the mine owner and the hard-bitten, sterile mine yard of what was one of California's oldest, biggest, and richest hardrock gold mines (1850–1957). Before touring the grounds, plan on visiting the park's museum. Its exhibits serve as a primer, introducing gold mining, the Empire Mine, its owners, and its Cornish workers.

At the museum, visitors can learn how extraction methods advanced over the years, see a model of the Empire Mine's 367 miles of underground passages and shafts, and enter the gold room filled with hundreds of core samples and a vault with the "genuine stuff."

In addition to the Empire Mine, the park offers picnic sites near the museum and across the street. Visitors also can enjoy open space with old mining roads and trails to travel. Some of these routes bypass historic mine sites recalled by foundations, rusting equipment, and tailings. Travelers should be aware, though, that a 7-acre area is closed due to heavy-metals contamination; heed posted signs and keep out. Trail brochures are available at the museum.

### Attractions and Activities

**Mine Yard–Bourn Estate Walking Tour.** The numbered legend and descriptions in the park brochure and the many plaques about the mine yard provide visi-

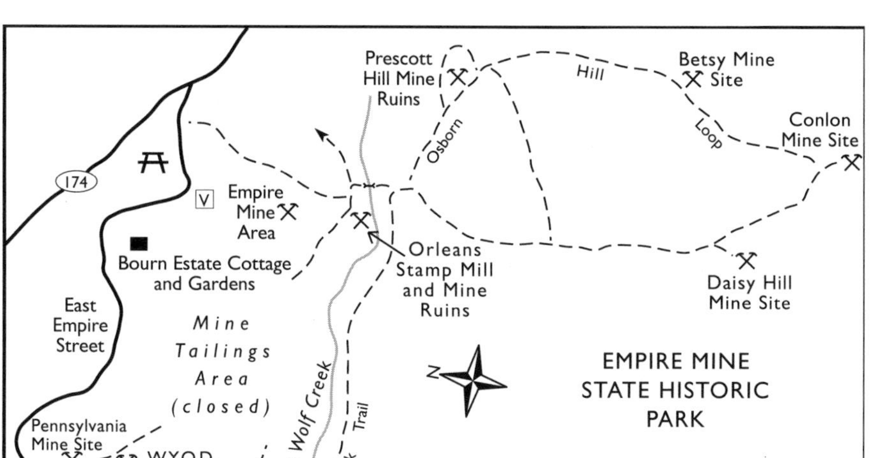


tors with an understanding of how the various structures were used in the extraction and refining of gold. The mine-yard structures were all built between 1898 and 1914, and remodeled as needed until the 1950s. The office buildings are built of stone, while the operational ones are made of corrugated tin. The mine yard itself is an open dirt flat, barren of vegetation. The mine office is set up as a walk-in museum. Elsewhere, visitors can peer through doorways and windows.

Touring the grounds, visitors can view the support operations: the carpentry, machine, and electrical shops and the dry room, where the miners changed out of their wet, grimy clothes at the end of a shift. They can also view the stamp mill and furnaces associated with refining, but the most interesting part of the tour is the main Empire Mine shaft, where visitors can look into the cold, dank darkness of a miner's existence.

Looking down the steep, open shaft and breathing the dusty air draws one into the miner's life better than all the word panels together do. The miners entered this small portal folded together on skips (long, flat cars). Then, at a rattling rate of 600 feet per minute, they descended 4,600 feet below ground. An ambitious park project for the future is an underground tour, during which an electric train would take visitors 100 feet below ground through an 800-foot tunnel. Other points of interest, today, are the headframe, compressors, and hoists.

Leaving the mine yard, visitors enter another world of tiered grounds, grand lawns, brick walkways, rose gardens, fountains, and arborways—this is the Bourn estate. The mine owner's gable-roofed stone and brick "cottage" was built in 1897 and has the look of an English country manor.

Daily from mid-April through mid-October, guided afternoon tours are offered at the Bourn Cottage. It has 4,600 square feet of living space and all the conveniences: electricity, hot and cold running water, and servants' quarters. The tour shows the first-floor rooms with their period furnishings and hand-planed redwood interior.

*Mine yard displays, Empire Mine State Historic Park*

A clubhouse, reflection pool, lily pond, and greenhouse complete the estate setting.

*Access:* Entry to the yard and estate is via the museum.

**Hardrock Trail–Osborn Hill Loop.** This 3.1-mile tour lends itself to both shuttle and round-trip hiking.

From the staging area at the west end of the park, follow the gravel road bearing right. Numbered posts along the Hardrock Trail correspond to descriptions in the Walking Trails brochure. In 0.1 mile, the mostly open trail passes the Pennsylvania Mine site, where there are some old foundations and concrete structures and the old mine is slowly being reclaimed by nature.

Stay on the gravel road, touring a ponderosa pine forest with oak and shrubs. Ahead is the W.Y.O.D. (Work Your Own Diggins) Mine with its tailings mounds and old foundations. Beyond it, the roadway changes to dirt, and the side trails are posted for allowed use.

At the road fork at 0.4 mile, go right, staying on the Hardrock Trail. At 0.6 mile, it crosses Sand Dam. What once was a settling pond below the dam is now a tree-filled flat. At the end of the dam, take either the path or the road, as they again merge. The forest now shows cedar and black oak with fewer pines. Beware of the poison oak in the understory tangle.

At 1.2 miles, going right adds the Osborn Hill Loop to the hike; continuing straight returns to the Empire Mine area. To add the loop, continue uphill on a mining road, following the signs. The sides of the road have full, mixed forest. At 1.4 miles, hikers may forgo taking the Prescott Hill Mine Trail, as the Osborn Hill Loop also passes the mine. The Prescott Mine covers a much bigger area with foundations, tailings, and old timbers and is by far the most interesting on the tour.

At 1.5 miles, the Prescott Hill Mine Trail returns and the Osborn Hill Loop curves right. Continue uphill, bypassing the cutoff trail on the right. Soon, a beautiful old-growth madrone rises next to the road, and a few feet away on the opposite side is a fenced vertical shaft. After briefly following a utility corridor, the loop bears left at 1.7 miles; an arrow points the way.

Just beyond is the spur to the Betsy Mine. Overgrown with poison oak, this is one mine to avoid. Elsewhere, mountain misery, wild geranium, and starflowers add to the forest floor, and wild turkeys may be seen. At 2 miles, the loop tops out, and at 2.1 miles a junction appears. The Conlon Mine lies 0.1 mile to the left, featuring high mounds of discarded rock; the loop continues to the right.

Continuing on the loop, hikers descend through an open forest with manzanita, skirting the rubble of the Daisy Hill Mine. At 2.6 miles, the loop closes, and at 2.7 miles hikers return to the Hardrock Trail; go right.

A little past the Little Wolf Creek footbridge crossing sits a T junction. There, go left, remaining on the Hardrock Trail, heading toward the Orleans Stamp Mill. Reaching the old foundations of the stamp mill, travelers can see the rooftops of the mine-yard buildings. Proceed on the old road to the mine yard (3.1 miles). Round-trip hikers may turn around here.

*Access:* Begin at the horse staging area, west of the visitor center on East Empire Street. Trail hours are sunrise to sunset.

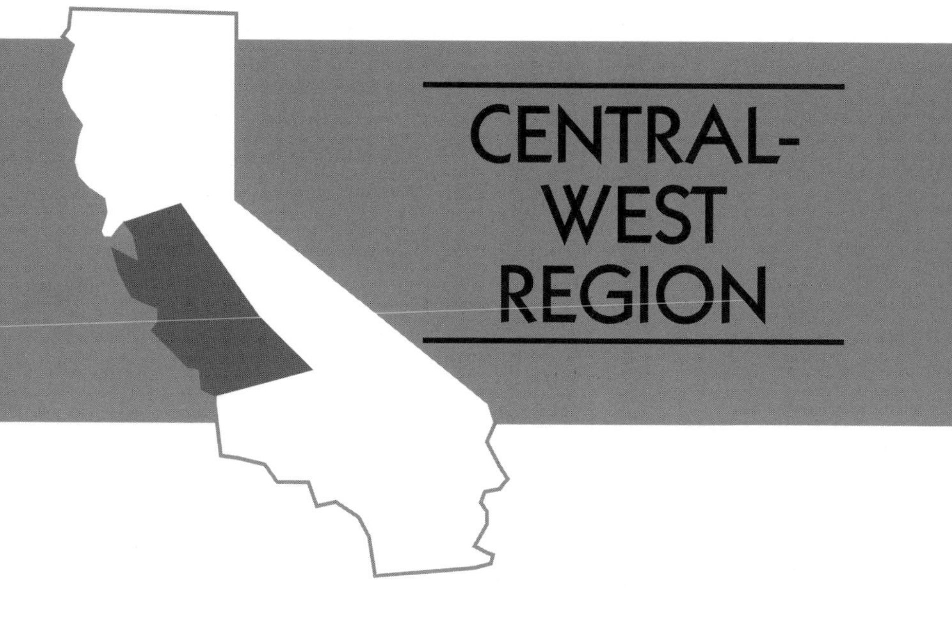


## Delta Meadows River Park

**Hours/Season:** Daylight hours
**Facilities:** Primitive boat launch, hiker trail, nonflush toilets (summers only), *bring water*
**For Information:** (916) 777-7701
**Access:** From Walnut Grove, go 0.5 mile north on CA 160. After driving over Cross Channel Bridge, take a right, followed by a quick left at the sign to enter the park on a gravel road. The gravel road follows a former railroad grade for 1.25 miles, accessing park lands.

This primitive, minimally improved park accesses Railroad Slough, one of the last remaining wild areas in the entire Delta slough system. Although it is a day-use area, houseboats may anchor here. Due to the park's proximity to the historic town of Locke, a number of vacationers seek that privilege; a 30-day mooring limit per calendar year is enforced.

The quiet backwater is a favorite of naturalists, especially during the winter months, when the crowds are gone. River otters roll and play in the water, chomp crayfish, and run along shore. Beavers, too, may be spied in the early morning, and the birdwatching is rewarding. Explore by foot or canoe.

### Attractions and Activities

**Delta Meadows Trail.** This mostly level trail hugs the slough's shoreline for 1 mile, occasionally rolling up the slope, where a rush of alders or the erosion of the

Opposite: *Point Montara Lighthouse*

bank suggests it. Near the boat ramp, the trail can be muddy, but for most of the way it is a grassy footpath. Galls from the oaks litter the path.

This is a trail for slow touring. Along the way, hikers have an opportunity for wildlife sightings: beaver, otter, muskrat, heron, kingfisher, hawk, and jay. Gray squirrels are numerous. Frequent splashes, wing flaps, and lecturing squawks call hikers to halt and seek the source. Across the way, wildlife paths divide the tule bulrushes, and cottonwoods bow to shore. By summer, ripe blackberries offer visitors and wildlife a tasty treat.

*Access:* The trail begins at the primitive boat launch located on the side road to the right 0.2 mile into the park.

**Boating/Canoeing.** A primitive boat launch suitable for small or hand-ported boats accesses Railroad Slough. The park service plans to offer guided canoe trips on a trial basis; visitor response will determine whether the program is adopted. A series of small side sloughs extends the range for paddlers.

*Access:* Go 0.2 mile into the park on the gravel road. The ramp is off the side road to the right. *Beware: The side road can be muddy and impassable after heavy rains.*

## Benicia State Recreation Area

**Hours/Season:** Daylight hours, with vehicle access to the picnic area from 8:00 A.M. to sunset

**Facilities:** Picnic area, hiker and bicycle trails, fitness trail, restrooms, nonflush toilets

**For Information:** (707) 745-3385

**Access:** For the main entrance, follow I-780 west from Benicia, take the Columbus Parkway exit, and go left on Rose to reach the park. In Benicia, an east access is located at the west end of West Military Road.

Along South Hampton Bay and Carquinez Strait, this 720-acre recreation area is highly popular with the walkers, joggers, cyclists, dog owners, and rollerskaters of neighboring Benicia and can become crowded in the early morning and after-work hours. The flat paved trail traversing the park draws the exercise-conscious, while the hiker-only trail appeals to naturalists. The park consists of wild fields, an estuary/marsh, and a bay shore, with areas for birdwatchers and fishermen wishing to pursue their interests. An occasional fox is seen in the fields.

The park contains a fine, extensive picnic area at its west end along Dillon Point Road. Some sites occupy the pine- and bottlebrush-shaded grassy slope, while others line the marsh and strait shore. Visitors may hike, cycle, or drive to the picnic area. At the park's main entrance, a large grassy area with pine and eucalyptus trees invites visitors to spread a blanket and relax, but here and elsewhere in the park, the drone from the interstate highway intrudes.

### Attractions and Activities

**Jogging/Bicycling Trail.** This 5-mile round-trip trail travels between the east end of the park and Dillon Point, overlooking the park terrain.

Next to Benicia, separate, parallel paved lanes serve the pedestrian and cyclist, as the tour skirts an open field of willows, fennel, and mixed grasses. At 0.4 mile, a bench offers looks across the broad expanse at Carquinez Strait. At 0.5 mile, the individual paths merge, and a foot trail heads left into the field.

The now-single-lane paved exercise path travels nearer to the freeway, isolated by a eucalyptus tree buffer. In a quarter mile more, it bypasses a marshy bottom, with cattails, rushes, and wetland grasses. In autumn, the marsh presents a swaying, textured mosaic of yellow, green, and russet hues.

As the trail reaches the main park entrance, visitors find the basic conveniences of a bench, chemical toilet, and a drinking fountain (behind the entrance signboard). Vehicles now share the route, but cyclists and pedestrians continue to dominate traffic.

*Pedestrian trail, Benicia State Recreation Area*

The road now skirts the large, eucalyptus-shaded lawn, bypasses the park residences, and rounds field, marsh, and strait to reach Dillon Point. Travelers again find basic conveniences along the way. The developed picnic area at Dillon Point offers an ideal place for a snack and a cool-down before heading back.

*Access:* Begin at the east entrance off West Military Road for a complete east-west linear tour of the park.

**Hiking Trail.** This 1.2-mile trail tours field and marsh, offering nature study. From the 0.5-mile mark on the Jogging/Bicycling Trail, go south on the earthen path closed to dogs and bicycles. It passes through a mixed grass field, quickly bypassing a trail to the right, which becomes overgrown. At the following fork, bear right, keeping the same general line of travel. A marsh, edged by pickleweed and cordgrass, is now east of the trail, while thistle and a few wildflowers mark the untamed field west.

The trail travels slightly higher ground than the marsh it rounds. Killdeer, meadowlark, towhee, and dove may be seen or heard. Where the trail splits at 0.4 mile, take either of the two forks since they soon merge. Traveling the wide path along a powerline corridor, hikers continue to overlook the marsh with its pockets of standing water and views toward Carquinez Strait and Dillon Point.

Where the trail forks at 0.6 mile, return to the Jogging/Bicycling Trail and follow it right, to avoid a soggy section of trail. At 0.7 mile, take the unmarked earthen trail to the right to resume the marsh tour, heading toward the strait.

By 0.9 mile, hikers find spurs—some open, some overgrown—leading to bay overlooks, where mallards, cormorants, and egrets may be surprised. At 1.2 miles, the trail emerges at the southwest corner of the West Military Road parking lot.

*Access:* Begin on the Jogging/Bicycling Trail, heading west from the West Military Road access.

## Benicia Capitol State Historic Park

**Hours/Season:** 10:00 A.M. to 5:00 P.M., except major holidays
**Facilities:** Picnic sites, historic buildings, restrooms
**For Information:** (707) 745-3385
**Access:** The Capitol Building is at the corner of First and G streets in Benicia.

Benicia was California's fourth capital city, and from 1853 to 1854, this building served as its seat of government. Monterey (the capital city during the Mexican period), San Jose, and Vallejo were the first three capitals. Sacramento, the current capital, is the fifth one. Of the early capitol buildings, Benicia's is the only one still standing.

This two-story brick building has a Greek-temple design; two Ionic columns frame its doorway. It took only three months to build, for it had no plumbing, lighting, or other contemporary refinements. Because the bricks were inadequately kilned, the exterior has a distinctive salmon color. The grounds of the Capitol Building are landscaped, with red brick walkways.

### Attractions and Activities

**Self-guided Capitol Building Tour.** Today, visitors can peer into the Capitol Building rooms and return to 1853. The Senate Room has both original and period furnishings. Atop the desks are inkwells and quills, the senator name tags, candles, and felt hats. On some of the desks, visitors will note copies of the *Columbia Gazette* from 1853. Brass spittoons dot the aisles. As fire was a key concern, smoking tobacco was not allowed. At the head of the room are a United States flag and picture of George Washington.

The upstairs Assembly Room has a similar presentation. Elsewhere in the building, original and duplicated archives, old photographs, a state-seal press, and an early-day copying machine await discovery.

**Fischer-Hanlon House and Carriage House.** Next door to the capitol, the Fischer-Hanlon House is an example of a Gold Rush–period home, complete with furnishings common to the day. It represents the lifestyle of an upper-middle-class family and is shown by guided tour on weekend afternoons.

Out back, the carriage house holds an antique buggy, road cart, and butcher wagon. It is generally open to public viewing during park hours.

## Brannan Island and Franks Tract State Recreation Areas

**Hours/Season:** Year-round

**Facilities:** 102 developed campsites, 32 boat-in slips with walk-in campsites (reservations recommended), picnic areas, visitor center, boat launch, swimming area, restrooms, pay showers (Brannan Island); none (Franks Tract)

**For Information:** (916) 777-6671

**Access:** From the CA 12–CA 160 junction, east of Rio Vista, go south on CA 160 to reach Brannan Island State Recreation Area in 3.3 miles. Franks Tract on the False River is accessible only by boat and easily reached from the marinas at Bethel Island. It also may be reached from Brannan Island following water routes east and south.

These two recreation areas offer convenient boating and fishing access to the miles and miles of waterway in the Sacramento–San Joaquin Delta. The rivers, marshes, sloughs, and channels offer great opportunities for exploration; the rich Delta farmland creates a relaxing backdrop. The many recreational boats, houseboats, and fishing boats attest to the Delta's appeal. Franks Tract, an immense

*Boat dock, Brannan Island State Recreation Area*

lake created by broken levees, wins favor with waterskiers. Its watery expanse is interrupted only by 300-acre Little Franks Tract, a native marshland, providing habitat for fox, raccoon, otter, mink, and nesting birds.

Brannan Island State Recreation Area is bordered by the Sacramento River and Three Mile and Seven Mile sloughs. Three Mile Slough links it to the San Joaquin River. At the park, visitors can launch their boats from a six-lane ramp or set up camp, picnic, swim, or fish. Seven Mile Slough, where the swimming area is located, is closed to boats. As private land borders its far side, keep to the park shore.

A visitor center near the entrance has information about Brannan Island and the Delta, as well as a few cultural and natural-history panels. At the campground, planted willow, pine, and eucalyptus bring some shade to the mostly open, grassy flat. Noise from CA 160 rolls across the terrain. Rabbits abound in the early morning and evening hours, as do their predators. Stitching together the park's camp areas is an informal 0.5-mile path following the levee above Three Mile Slough.

## Attractions and Activities

**Fishing.** Striped bass (which run in spring and summer), sturgeon, catfish, and bluegill challenge anglers, with the productive waters of Franks Tract winning favor. Most of the fishing is done by boat.

**Birdwatching.** The Delta's mild climate, shelter, and plentiful food supply attract a sizeable winter bird population, but year-round, birders are tempted to reach for their binoculars. Herons, cormorants, various hawks, meadowlarks, pheasants, mockingbirds, kites, and burrowing owls are just some of the sightings.

# MOUNT DIABLO STATE PARK

**Hours/Season:** Entries are gated from sunset to 8:00 A.M.; campers should plan a daytime arrival

**Facilities:** 60 developed semi-shaded campsites; horse camp; picnic sites; museum; observation tower; hiker, horse, and mountain-bike trails; an all-ability trail; restrooms; nonflush toilets

**For Information:** (510) 687-1800 or (510) 837-2525

**Access:** From I-680 at Danville, take the Diablo Road exit and head east. In 0.7 mile, turn right, remaining on Diablo Road. In another 2.1 miles, turn left to enter the park. The summit is in 10 miles. The park may also be entered from North Gate Road in Walnut Creek.

This 19,000-acre mountain park in the San Francisco East Bay area is ideal for the active visitor and a fine escape from the city. Numerous interlocking trails weave around the mountain for a variety of tours. Rock City, the park's collection of wind-shaped sandstone, appeals to both photographer and rock scrambler. A trail up Sentinel Rock affords a lofty overlook of the area. Oak and laurel woodlands, stands of Digger pine, grassland, and chaparral habitats bring bounty and diversity to the vistas and tours. In April and May, a myriad of wildflowers decorates the park.

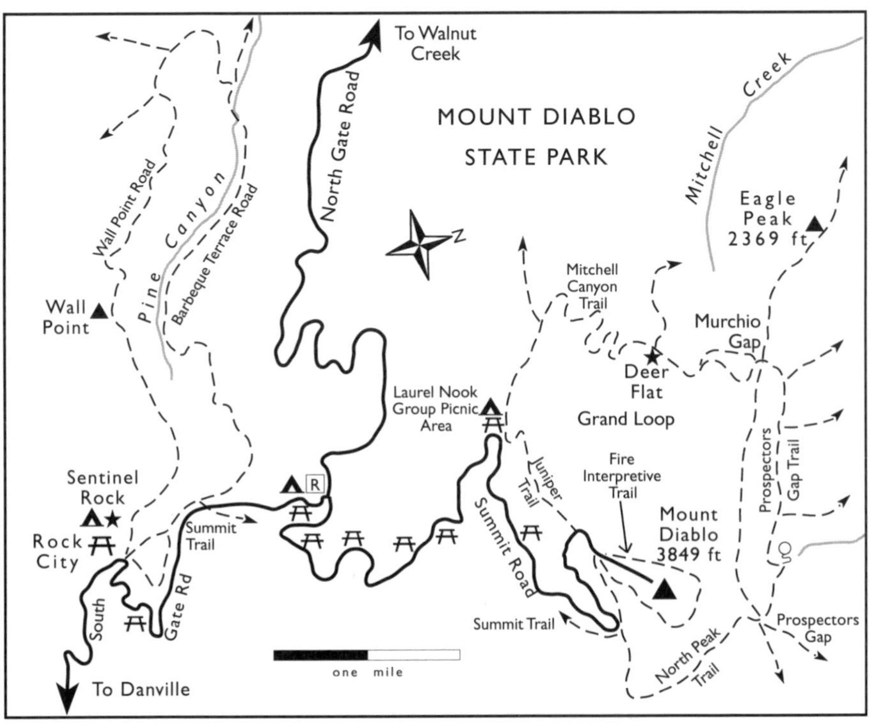

Formed through a serial process of subduction, lateral motion, and uplift, Mount Diablo atypically embraces its oldest rocks at the top. While not especially high (summit elevation 3,849 feet), the mountain boasts sweeping vistas. Clear-day views encompass a remarkable 40,000-square-mile area. According to park staff, geographers have determined that only the summit view from Africa's Mount Kilimanjaro exceeds it.

## Attractions and Activities

**Summit Drive.** The paved, winding 10-mile summit route passes through exciting mixed habitats and overlooks the valleys and communities below. As it climbs, the road tours areas of older and older rock formations. Marking the way, quiet, dispersed picnic sites welcome a stop for lunch or a closer look. At the top, clear days reward with far-reaching views.

*Access:* The drive begins off Diablo Road, following South Gate and Summit roads to the peak. A similar drive may be enjoyed via North Gate Road.

**Summit Observation Tower and Museum.** The stone observation tower has both a window-enclosed area and an open-air deck that present the 360-degree view. Vistas sweep from the Farallon Islands to the Sierra Nevada, from Mount Lassen to the gleam of the Lick Observatory atop Mount Hamilton. Closer landmarks include North and Eagle peaks and Devils Pulpit. At times, coastal fog swirls around the summit for a wild and different look.

A visitor center is housed in the building. Through displays, dioramas, art, and videos, it introduces the mountain's unique geology, islandlike presence, and natural and cultural history. As you leave the building note the shell fossils in the tower stones; these rocks were quarried from the mountain.

*Access:* Find the tower at the Upper Summit parking area, where there is a 20-minute limit to parking.

**Fire Interpretive Trail.** This 0.7-mile self-guided trail travels a contour just below the summit, slowly unrolling a 360-degree view. Brochures may be purchased at the headquarters.

The initial distance is paved, open to wheelchairs, with vista platforms overlooking the Bay Area and destinations as far west as the Farallon Islands, as far north as Mount Lassen. In 1977, a wildfire swept this rugged mountain habitat; recovery is now nearly complete. In spring, wildflowers dot the rock outcrops and sprinkle the slope.

At 0.25 mile, a narrow gravel trail replaces the paved one, as the tour rounds the brushy, open eastern slope. After crossing a saddle below the rock monolith of Devils Pulpit, glance uphill to find the summit tower.

On the south side of Mount Diablo several secondary trails appear; keep to the contouring route. A few juniper dot the open rock and grass slope. The trail ends at the handicapped parking area opposite the starting point.

*Access:* Begin above Lower Summit parking area, on the left-hand side of the one-way Summit Road loop.

**Grand Loop.** This rolling 6-mile trail encircles upper Mount Diablo, marking both substantial elevation gains and losses. Counterclockwise from Laurel Nook picnic area, it strings together the Juniper, Summit, North Peak, Prospectors Gap, and Mitchell Canyon trails. Dirt roads and paths make up the hiker/horse route, with much of it open to mountain bikes. On the north side of the mountain, a 1.8-mile round-trip detour tops Eagle Peak.

The Grand Loop tour passes through laurel and oak woodland, high chaparral, dry grassland, and areas of open pine forest, as it slowly reveals a 360-degree vista.

Mount Diablo

At 0.9 mile, near the entrance to the Lower Summit parking area, pick up the Summit Trail on the right.

Where it takes a switchback next to Devils Elbow (a sharp turn on Summit Road), continue the tour on the North Peak Trail. It passes below the rock monolith Devils Pulpit. At 1.7 miles, hikers are greeted by a straight-ahead view of craggy North Peak; at 2.3 miles stands wind-whipped Prospectors Gap (elevation 2,950 feet).

From there, follow the Prospectors Gap Trail, which descends sharply toward Deer Flat, offering views to the north and west. Keep following the signs to Deer Flat. At 3.8 miles you will reach Murchio Gap, where hikers have the option of cresting Eagle Peak for the view.

This side tour travels the steep-sided hogback between Mitchell Canyon and the Back Creek drainage and offers views of the Sacramento–San Joaquin Delta, Mount Zion, the communities below, Mount Diablo, and North Peak. A message tin is stashed on the summit (elevation 2,369 feet).

After an Eagle Peak detour, resume the loop at 5.6 miles, heading toward Deer Flat (6.2 miles). The flat is a scenic oak grassland. Mistletoe adorns the leaf-bare branches of the oaks. From the flat, take the Mitchell Canyon Trail, an exposed wide dirt road, uphill to Juniper Campground.

At 7.25 miles, go straight, crossing over a saddle to tour the south-facing slope, overlooking a grassy flank of Mount Diablo. Pass through the campground to conclude the tour at Laurel Nook (7.8 miles).

*Access:* Begin at the marked trailhead at the Laurel Nook group picnic area, off Summit Road 2.5 miles uphill from the headquarters junction.

**Summit Trail–Barbeque Terrace and Wall Point Roads Loop.** This demanding 6.6-mile loop explores some of the remote country of this vast mountain park, visiting areas of woodland, grassland, chaparral, and wind-shaped rock.

From the northeast side of South Gate Road, a counterclockwise tour begins heading right on the Summit Trail, a dirt fire road climbing a grassland slope. Views are to the south. At the junction where the trail approaches Summit Road, go left, still climbing via the Summit Trail.

In spring, buttercup, blue-dick, wallflower, and shooting star decorate the sides of the trail. After rains, the path can be gooey and troublesome. By 0.6 mile, hikers gain a Rock City overlook, just as a foot trail replaces the single-lane road.

The trail now follows a pine-oak ridge, bearing right past a remnant of barbed-wire fence. The bountiful poison oak deters any off-trail jaunts. Where the trail again meets Summit Road, bear left on the foot/horse trail indicated to Barbeque Terrace; do not cross the road.

This trail descends a grassy slope and follows along a barbed-wire fence, reaching the hiker gate to Barbeque Terrace Road at 1.2 miles, just before the group camp.

As this part of the park is a working ranch, secure the gates behind you.

The dirt ranch road now steeply descends toward Pine Canyon, touring grassland and later oak woodland. Ground squirrels, bluebirds, and deer divert attention. By 2 miles, the still-descending trail enters Pine Canyon, following its drainage downstream. At 2.7 miles, it bypasses a spring-fed pool, reflecting the boulder and oaks that rim it. Overhead sail paragliders and hang gliders; they take off near Juniper Campground.

At 3.1 miles, the trail crosses the Pine Canyon drainage and passes through a gate. In another 0.2 mile, take the gate on the left for a hefty climb out of the drainage. This slope shows a congested forest of smaller oaks. At the triangle junction at 3.8 miles, follow the route to Wall Point, bearing left.

Where the trail travels atop a ridge, the north side shows chaparral, the south side oak grassland. Vultures tilt their wings as they glide past. Ahead, at the Emmons Canyon Road junction, the loop bears left, touring above a fire-darkened area. The view is of rounded and bald Wall Point peak.

After a steep peak ascent, the fire road tops out at 5.2 miles, and a 0.1-mile side trail tags the Wall Point summit for a 360-degree view. In another half mile, the loop reaches a saddle, with views out chaparral-clad Dan Cook Canyon. The head of Pine Canyon affords yet another fine vista. Views of Sentinel Rock and Rock City cap the journey.

At 6.5 miles, unmarked trails to the right lead to Sentinel Rock, Grotto picnic area, and the Live Oak Campground. Hikers may choose to detour, or go straight to close the loop at 6.6 miles.

*Access:* Start at the trailhead on the east side of South Gate Road, between Little Rock and Arroyo picnic areas and opposite some park buildings. It is about 3.5 miles uphill from the Danville entrance or 2 miles downhill from the headquarters junction.

## Candlestick Point State Recreation Area

**Hours/Season:** 8:00 A.M. to the posted evening hour
**Facilities:** Individual and group picnic areas, fishing piers, hiker and bicycle trails, fitness trails, restrooms, outdoor showers
**For Information:** (415) 557-4069
**Access:** From US 101, take the Candlestick Park exit; the recreation area occupies the bay shore opposite Candlestick Stadium.

This park includes both developed and undeveloped areas bordering more than 3 miles of the San Francisco Bay shore. Close to US 101 and bounded by Harney Way, Jamestown Avenue, and Hunter Expressway, the park ambience suffers from road noise, but the grounds offer a fine exercise area with both paved and dirt routes paralleling the shoreline and two fitness trails, one designed for seniors. In the morning hours, dog owners frequently walk their animals.

Two piers lead fishermen out to the deeper bay waters, where surfperch, flounder, and halibut may be caught. Benches line the larger pier off Sunrise Point; a fish-cleaning sink at its end serves anglers.

Churned by the notorious Candlestick winds, the park waters attract advanced windsurfers, drawing both sport enthusiast and spectator. On shore, shelters protect the dispersed picnic tables overlooking the bay. The windchill and a shoreline of mudflats and riprap discourage swimming or sunbathing at this bay park.

At the west end of the park, small planted trees promise future shade for the unkept grassy field, while at the park's center visitors find a more mature area, with groomed lawns, cypresses, pines, and flowering trees. Terns, gulls, herons, pelicans, surf scoters, and various mudflat feeders make for good birdwatching. In the open north field, jackrabbits can be spied. Cross-bay views throughout the urban park are engaging.

As the recreation area continues to develop, additions will include a wetland observation area and boat ramp.

## Bethany Reservoir State Recreation Area

**Hours/Season:** Daylight hours

**Facilities:** Picnic sites, boat launch, California Aqueduct Bikeway access, non-flush toilets, *bring water*

**For Information:** (209) 826-1196 or (209) 874-2056

**Access:** The park is located between Byron and Tracy off Byron Highway. From Byron, go 4 miles south on Byron Highway and turn right (west) onto Bruns Road. Follow Bruns Road for 3 miles, and turn left for the reservoir.

Located in the northwestern San Joaquin Valley, Bethany Reservoir is a small, irregularly shaped water body formed by a low rock-levee dam. It hosts the quiet recreation of the windsurfer and fisherman; high-speed boats and waterskiing are not allowed. A consistent wind is the area's hallmark, witnessed by the many "windmill farms" erected on the surrounding rolling hills. Their whirring, like the drone of some strange science-fiction insect, carries to the site.

*Windmill farm, seen from Bethany Reservoir State Recreation Area*

Day-use areas are found at either end of the dam. The one to the south is more developed, with a paved parking area and boat launch. The one to the north is primitive; its parking area is rough and potholed. Save for a few planted trees at each area, the reservoir's shoreline is open. Some covered picnic tables overlook the lake.

### Attractions and Activities

**The California Aqueduct Bikeway.** The aqueduct offers cyclists a carefree but exposed ride along the riprap bank of the reservoir and the outtake canal. Hundreds of gulls speckle the glistening water, while rolling, grassy hillsides spread out from the route. Winds steal conversation and add to the workout. The length of the ride depends on the cyclist's endurance and schedule. This long-distance route begins following the reservoir's shore for about 1.5 miles and continues south to San Luis Reservoir, some 70 miles distant.

*Access:* Begin at the southern day-use area, near the boat launch.

## San Bruno Mountain State and County Park

**Hours/Season:** 8:00 A.M. to sunset (as posted)
**Facilities:** Picnic area; hiker, horse, and mountain-bike trails; restrooms
**For Information:** San Mateo County (415) 363-4020
**Access:** From the junction of Bayshore Boulevard and Guadalupe Canyon Parkway in Brisbane, go 2.3 miles west on the parkway to reach the entrance station. Or go 2.5 miles east of I-280 at Daly City / Colma.

At the northern end of the Santa Cruz Mountains, this vital 2,700-acre San Francisco Peninsula open space represents a last refuge for several plants and animals, and the urban dweller as well. Rising out of a civilized sea, the mostly coastal-scrub-clad mountain affords top-notch San Francisco and East Bay views, with clear-day looks stretching from the Farallon Islands to Mount Diablo. However, the summit communication towers deny a full 360-degree view.

Visitors may hike or drive to the summit vantage, but parking spaces are few. The mountain and / or its surrounding area may be hugged by fog any time of year, and winds often assail the top.

The rugged terrain of San Bruno Mountain affords hiking, horseback riding, and cycling opportunities. Horses are restricted to the trails touring the parkland on the south side of Guadalupe Canyon Parkway, while cyclists are restricted to the north-side trails. Nowhere in the park are dogs allowed. Brochures containing a map are available at the parking lot.

With some fourteen species of rare plants, a healthy bird population, and a kaleidoscope of butterflies, including the endangered Mission blue and San Bruno elfin species, there is ample study to engage the naturalist. Picnickers find a relaxing setting, with both sun-drenched and partially shaded tables rimming a central lawn. Enfolding the area is a border of eucalyptus and cypress trees.

### Attractions and Activities

**Ridge Trail.** This 4.2-mile round-trip hiking tour follows a dirt and loose gravel fire road as it rolls southeast along the summit ridge serving up views. Mileage posts mark off 0.5-mile increments.

It begins with a quick plunge away from the communication towers area, offering early views of the South Bay and Santa Cruz Mountains. At the 0.1-mile junction with the Summit Loop, hikers find an outstanding San Francisco city view. If hikers go no farther, it is worth snaring this vista. Keep to the fire road to continue the ridge tour.

As the fire road rolls between saddles and rises, the ridge features a coastal scrub-grassland mix, with coyote bush, fern, blackberry, and a sprinkling of wildflowers. Where a utility line crosses overhead, the view sweeps the steep southern flank, furrowed by Poison Oak and Tank ravines. Ahead, overlooks provide views of a quarry on San Bruno's north side. At one time, it was proposed that the entire mountain be knocked down for fill.

By 0.8 mile, over the left shoulder, hikers have views of the city, Angel Island, and Mount Tamalpais. Grasshoppers enliven a fall tour while, almost anytime, lizards and mice rustle unseen in the vegetated mat. Before long, views of the airport explain the many flight patterns over the mountain, and hikers also see Candlestick Point State Recreation Area. Effortlessly, hawks soar by at eye level.

While some side routes descend the ridge, keep to the fire road, touring the backbone. It again passes under some wires on a rocky rise, approaching the 2-mile mark.

Ahead, where the fire road makes a sharp descent, bear left off the Ridge Trail, following a secondary track. This short side trail leads to a vantage, capping the tour with one last new view, overlooking a South Bay marina. Although visitors may continue on the Ridge Trail, this marks a good turnaround point.

*Access:* Begin at the summit parking area (on the south side of the park), reached by taking the parkway underpass.

**Saddle Trail–Old Guadalupe Trail Loop.** This 2.6-mile loop, open to foot and bicycle travel, has but a 150-foot elevation change, offering a comfortable tour with its own series of fine views. It travels graveled and paved surfaces, with distance markers in place.

Wrapping around a side ridge, travelers tour an area of coastal scrub often displaced by gorse—a dense, thorny, yellow-flowering shrub. Over-the-shoulder views are of San Bruno summit (elevation 1,314 feet). A eucalyptus grove claims its slope above Guadalupe Canyon Parkway.

At the 0.5-mile mark, a bench welcomes a leisurely appreciation of the 180-degree view spreading before it. The view spans Brisbane Lagoon to Mount Tamalpais and includes Candlestick Point, the ballpark stadium, the Cow Palace, the San Francisco skyline, the city's famous pastel-painted rowhouses, the Bay Bridge, and Angel Island.

Resuming a counterclockwise tour, rounding the north slope travelers bypass

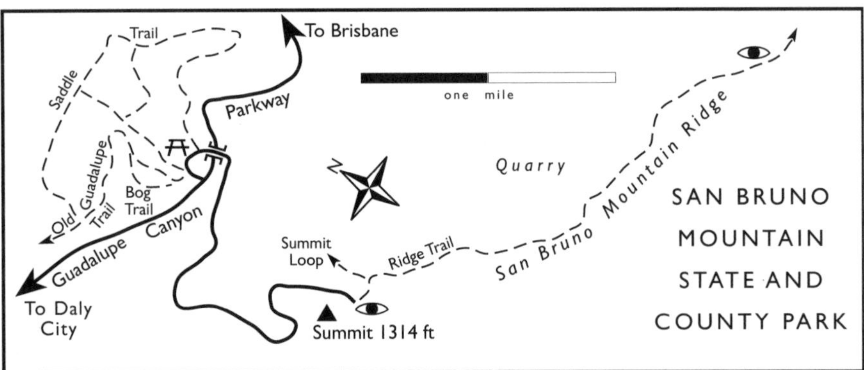

more of the invasive gorse, and the trail climbs slowly and steadily. Among the wildflowers are monkey-flower, California poppy, lupine, and campion. Keep to the graveled trail, as side paths branch to nearby rises. At 1 mile, the route passes beneath some pines, as homes nudge toward the park.

At the upcoming junction, go straight to continue the loop; a left here leads to a day camp and offers a shorter loop option. Eucalyptus now crowd out much of the view, but looks at San Bruno Mountain return. Coyote bush and grass regain their footing. Topping a rise near the boundary at 1.5 miles, travelers gain views west of the city, along with ocean glimpses.

Where the gravel path next descends to a eucalyptus grove, the Saddle Trail ends, and the Old Guadalupe Trail continues the journey left. Its paved, mostly flat, tree-and shrub-framed lane affords easy travel. At 2 miles, it tours above a willow-crowded bog; foot trails branch right to the wetland. Keep on the Old Guadalupe Trail to end the tour. The trail comes out near the picnic-area bike racks at 2.6 miles.

*Access:* On the north side of Guadalupe Canyon Parkway, begin by passing through the picnic area; the marked trailhead is at its far right corner.

## Pacifica, Gray Whale Cove, and Montara State Beaches—Point Montara Light Station

**Hours/Season:** 8:00 A.M. to sunset (Pacifica and Montara); 9:00 A.M. to sunset (Gray Whale Cove); 4:30 P.M. to 9:30 A.M. (Point Montara Light Station)

**Facilities:** Restroom, outdoor shower (Pacifica); picnic tables, beach stairway, nonflush toilet, *bring water* (Gray Whale Cove); hiker, horse, and mountain-bike trails; volleyball court; nonflush toilets; *bring water* (Montara); historic light station, hostel-style overnight accommodations, rustic hot tub (Point Montara Light Station)

**For Information:** City of Pacifica (415) 738-7381; Gray Whale Cove concessionaire (415) 728-5336; the state park district (415) 726-8819; the hostel (415) 728-7177

**Access:** Find these parks along a 5-mile stretch of CA 1 between Pacifica's Linda Mar District and south Montara.

This section of California coast offers beach recreation, a clothing-optional experience, inland rides and hikes, and overnight stays at a scenic 1875 light station. Along this stretch, chilly ocean temperatures limit one's stay in the water. While all three beach areas boast beautiful clean sand, the main recreation is found at Pacifica and Montara state beaches.

Pacifica State Beach features a picturesque 0.75-mile crescent of golden sand, bound by headlands and facing a broad, yawning cove. Montara State Beach is wide, mildly cupped, and laid out below chiseled bluffs for 0.8-mile. Less protected than Pacifica, powerful breakers crash to its shore, attracting surfers while turning away swimmers.

Sunbathing, jogging, beachcombing, and beachplay are popular at both. As hikers pass, gulls disperse and reassemble on the strands. In the off-season, quiet moments can be found. At each, the limited parking helps keep down the crowds.

For inland recreation, there is McNee Ranch, a 2,000-acre unit of Montara State Beach. It claims the rounded hillsides east of CA 1 between Gray Whale Cove and Montara state beaches and offers fine tours and superb coastal vantages. While fairly new and still being improved, the unit already has found favor with the mountain-biking set. In the near future, park legend boards will be in place to aid travelers in selecting their routes.

## Attractions and Activities

**Gray Whale Cove State Beach.** Snuggled by the cliffs below CA 1 and the points to its north and south, this is a privately operated, clothing-optional beach. The cove provides customers a desired level of privacy, while its broad, sparkling-sand beach affords ample blanket space. Here, the special rules, fees, and schedules of the concessionaire apply. Hopeful sunbathers may contact the concessionaire for an on-site weather report.

*Access:* Find the entry west off CA 1 between Pacifica and Montara state beaches. A parking area is located south of the entrance on the east side of CA 1.

**Point Montara Light Station.** This historic light station offers hostel accommodations and overlooks a rugged coast that claimed the lives of some nineteenth-century ships and to this day offers high-splashing excitement. The station's tidy cream-and-slate-colored buildings, traditional white lighthouse, groomed lawns, and wind-shaped, towering cypress are postcard pretty, worthy of a stop, whether or not one plans to stay overnight.

*Access:* Find the lighthouse off CA 1, in south Montara.

**Coast Trail.** This 1.4-mile McNee Ranch trail stitches together Gray Whale Cove and the north end of Montara State Beach. Contouring the coastal slope above CA 1, it offers exciting ocean views.

From Gray Whale Cove, a southbound tour begins on a wide earthen trail, ascending through a congestion of knee-high coastal scrub. The trail then rounds the hillside overlooking CA 1. Along the route, the blooms of the bush lupine, monkeyflower, and lizardtail add springtime color. The elevation of the Coast Trail recommends it for whale watching.

At 0.1 mile a bench overlooks Gray Whale Cove. A second bench at 0.3 mile overlooks the next isolated cove south—one reserved for the gulls.

As the tour continues, sage and coyote bush mostly claim the route. At 0.7 mile, a spur onto a seaward jut presents an open view of Montara State Beach, the long surf, the lacy tidal scallops, Point Montara Lighthouse, and the coastal community of Montara. Ahead, keep right, contouring past another bench. At the 0.9-mile junction, the route left is designated for bicycles; the one that leads straight ahead is for hikers and horseback riders.

Taking the latter, the route soon begins descending the inland side of the ridge, coming out at a cypress stand above the park residence road, which doubles as a public trail. Go right to reach CA 1. A Montara State Beach parking area is found on the west side of the highway, 0.1 mile south of here; use care crossing CA 1.

*Access:* Begin at the southeast corner of the Gray Whale Cove parking area or at the primitive bluff parking lot for Montara State Beach, west off CA 1, 0.7 mile south of Gray Whale Cove.

# HALF MOON BAY STATE BEACHES

**Hours/Season:** Year-round; 8:00 A.M. to sunset (day use)
**Facilities:** 55 developed campsites, en route camping, hike/bike campsites, picnic areas, hiker and bicycle trail, horse trail, restrooms, outdoor showers
**For Information:** (415) 726-8819

**Access:** Turn west off CA 1 onto Kelly, 0.3 mile north of the CA 1–CA 92 intersection in Half Moon Bay. Two more accesses are found to the north.

Four named, adjoining beach areas make up this 3-mile-long state park looking out at gaping Half Moon Bay. From south to north, they are Francis, Venice, Dunes, and Roosevelt beaches. Roosevelt Beach is primarily accessible only by residents, but public access and parking are found at each of the other three. Francis Beach is the largest and most developed, with the park campground and a big day-use picnic area. Venice Beach also has picnicking. At both, flocks of gulls vie for handouts.

A broad, light-colored, coarse-sand beach cants to the cold waters of the bay and offers the walker a long, uninterrupted avenue of sand. Long-distance hikes are possible, with public-access beaches extending beyond the state park boundary. Although swimming is not recommended at Half Moon Bay, visitors still enjoy sunbathing, surfing, fishing, kite flying, and beachplay.

Summer days bring fog to this coastline; more pleasant conditions are found in the spring and fall. While winters can be blustery, they also can bring an edge of excitement to a park stay.

### Attractions and Activities

**Beach Hike–Coastside Trail Loop.** A northbound beach journey through the park finds the canted avenue of sand backed first by a 6- to 10-foot sandbank showered in ice plant. In turn, it is replaced by a defined bluff, an area of dunes, and another bluff at Roosevelt Beach. Throughout, the coastline and bay waters afford pleasant viewing. Gulls and shorebirds provide diversion.

At the eastern boundary of the park the 2.25-mile Coastside Trail is open to hikers, joggers, and cyclists. It presents a return loop option. A separate equestrian trail runs parallel to it from Dunes Beach back to Francis Beach.

Outside the park, stables rent horses for the trail ride, but horseback riding is not allowed on the beach.

*Access:* Begin at Francis Beach.

## Burleigh Murray Ranch

**Hours/Season:** 8:00 A.M. to sunset
**Facilities:** Picnic table; hiker, horse, and mountain-bike trail; ranch outbuildings; nonflush toilet; *bring water*
**For Information:** (415) 726-8819
**Access:** Turn east off CA 1 onto Higgins–Purisima Road, 1.2 miles south of the CA 1–CA 92 intersection in Half Moon Bay. Follow this narrow paved route into the hills for 1.6 miles. Trailhead parking for ten vehicles is on the left; dogs are not allowed in the park.

One of the newer, less well-known park units, this former ranch property in the coastal hills outside Half Moon Bay offers an opportunity for solitude. The park has but one trail touring the canyon drained by Mills Creek. Long-range plans call for making it part of a greater skyline-to-the sea route. Presently, the park ranchland connects with the Peninsula Open Space and the Skyline Trail corridor at Rancho Raymundo, but no trails connect them.

The 1,100-acre park features rounded hills blanketed in grass and coastal scrub-sage. Stands of beautiful big eucalyptus dot the drainage downstream from the ranch. Upstream, more native species dominate. The ranch buildings, dating back to the last quarter of the nineteenth century, are closed to the public. The quiet of the park allows for wildlife encounters with deer, rabbit, frog, quail, hawk, and woodpecker.

### Attractions and Activities

**Burleigh Murray Trail.** Traveling alongside Mills Creek, this 5-mile round-trip trail offers a mostly wild canyon tour. As Mills Creek is the source of the local water supply, it is closed to the public.

Dense tangles of blackberry, coyote bush, thistle, and lupine frame the sides of the ranch road, with alders and willows hugging the steep-sided drainage of perennial Mills Creek. The road corridor is mostly open, with a good, flat dirt surface for easy traveling. Where it crosses over Mills Creek at 0.5 mile and again at 0.6 mile, visitors have a chance to overlook the quiet water.

After 0.6 mile, the canyon narrows, and at 1 mile the road bypasses a single picnic site, with a table and chemical toilet, situated amid the eucalyptus and alder. When the winds blow through the canyon, the towering eucalyptus moan and squeak.

Before long, the route bears left to skirt the ranch residence. It again crosses Mills Creek near the old dairy barn—a long, rustic, weathered-wood barn recessed in the hillside. Some nice stonework can be seen in its foundation and a retaining wall along one side.

This barn is an English bank barn, one of only two in the United States. By building the barn into the hillside, the rancher could easily load its upper level by wagon. Scattered about the site are various rusted farm implements.

Past the ranch outbuildings, the road is replaced by a narrowed, grassy track; nettles tilt toward the path. Uphill to the left, hikers may spy a round cave opening in a rock outcrop. By 1.6 miles, where the trail tours below the north canyon wall, its sides become shrubbier. At 2 miles, three dripping, wooden water tanks line the route, muddying the ground.

Beyond them, the little-traveled trail grows even more congested, invaded by the rush of riparian plants. With nettles and poison oak amid the profusion, shorts are not a good idea. Oaks, too, stand amid the growth.

At 2.5 miles, the trail ends abruptly at a 7-foot drop to the creek. While it is a likely site for a future bridge, it presently marks the turnaround point.

*Access:* Begin on the gated ranch road.

## San Gregorio, Pomponio, Pescadero, and Bean Hollow State Beaches

**Hours/Season:** 8:00 A.M. to sunset; no camping
**Facilities:** Picnic tables, restroom or nonflush toilets, *bring water* (all); hiker trails (Pescadero and Bean Hollow)
**For Information:** (415) 879-2170
**Access:** These beaches are found along an 8.5-mile stretch of CA 1, south of the CA 1–CA 84 junction; parking is limited.

The northern three beaches—San Gregorio, Pomponio, and Pescadero—adjoin, providing public access to a strollable 4-mile stretch of coastal sand. San Gregorio presents 0.5 mile of beach at the foot of a scenic, eroded sandstone bluff; it is divided by the braided waters of San Gregorio Creek. Pomponio State Beach adds another 1.5 miles of glistening sand, backed by bluffs and squeezed by points. It, too, is divided by a creek. Completing the line-up is Pescadero State Beach. It contributes 2 miles of sandy beach, shifting dunes, rock outcroppings, and a sea arch south of Pescadero Creek.

Along this shoreline, the cold, unpredictable waters prohibit swimming but afford a fine backdrop. Throughout the tour, vistas up and down the coast present an imposing profile of the 100-foot-tall vertical cliffs. Drift logs washed down from the coastal hills crowd the drainages. At the cliff points between Pomponio and Pescadero state beaches, high tides can turn back hikers or require them to wade.

East of Pescadero Beach is 600-acre Pescadero Marsh, one of the region's largest and most important wetlands. On the Pacific Flyway, it offers varied year-round birding, with some 230 resident and migratory species.

Coastal scrub and wild herbs, tule rushes, and other marsh plants make up much of the estuary. Along its edge, a eucalyptus grove and riparian woodland provide nesting and hiding for larger animals. Nature trails explore the marsh on either side of Pescadero Creek; a CA 1 underpass allows safe passage between Pescadero beach and marsh. On the weekends docents offer guided walks.

To the south, the two beach areas of Bean Hollow State Beach offer yet a different coastal experience, with spectacular rock-and-surf scenery and pretty pocket beaches. The honeycombed orange-sandstone cliffs, tilted rock beds, showering surf, harbor seal rookery and cormorant rock, and accessible tidepools excite visitors.

Sea lettuce, eel grass, limpets, snails, mussels, and fish invite study. Surf fishermen cast from the rocks, but need to beware of the erratic waves. The tiny, colorful, polished pebbles that give Pebble Beach its name are protected natural features; no collecting.

*Pescadero Marsh, Pescadero State Beach*

## Attractions and Activities

**North Pond Trail.** This 0.75-mile trail explores North Pescadero Marsh and the shore of North Pond.

On the east side of CA 1, turn north, traveling at the base of the dunes below the highway. Before long, the trail drifts east, passing through an area of coastal sagewort and lizardtail between the pond and marsh.

Midway, visitors reach a fine vista, overlooking the marsh and the wetland mosaic, with its areas of open water, side channels, and rush-and-reed pools. As the trail resumes, it rolls along the east shore of North Pond, passing through marsh, meadow, and scrub habitats.

In spring, sticky monkey-flower, geranium, lupine, California poppy, and iris accent the way. Wrens, hawks, herons, and ducks provide reason to raise the binoculars, while deer tracks often dot the narrow footpath. Beware of poison oak at all times, and ticks in the spring. Return as you came.

*Access:* At Pescadero State Beach, take the CA 1 underpass, following the north side of Pescadero Creek to Pescadero Marsh.

**Sequoia–Audubon Trail.** This 1-mile trail tours an old earthen dike along the edge of North Marsh, following Pescadero Creek upstream.

Journeying generally east, the trail is thin, with leg-sweeping brush and areas of tall shrubs. Blackberry and nettles grow amid the mix. Along the creek and in the marshy channel, hikers may spy turtles sunning on a bank or snag.

At 0.7 mile, a pair of benches overlooks a scenic, wide, slow stretch of Pescadero Creek, overhung by willows and eucalyptus. Where the trail forks, leading to the destination vista, poison oak grows profusely; stay left for the less threatening route.

It soon crosses over a small waterway, with duckweed, polywogs, dragonflies, and turtles. The marsh overlook is adequate, but no rival for the one on North Pond Trail. Retrace your steps.

*Access:* At Pescadero State Beach, take the CA 1 underpass, following the north side of Pescadero Creek to reach the trailhead sign.

**Bean Hollow Nature Trail.** A 1-mile nature trail connects the two Bean Hollow beach areas, touring the edge of the marine terrace and overlooking the meeting of surf and land. Coyote bush, lizardtail, blackberry, and wildflowers cloak the terrace. While close to CA 1, it does offer a nice leg stretch and chance to view the coastline.

*Access:* At Bean Hollow State Beach, find the trailheads at the south end of Pebble Beach and at the Bean Hollow Area.

# PORTOLA STATE PARK

**Hours/Season:** Year-round

**Facilities:** 52 developed redwood-forested campsites, 6 walk-in campsites, trail camp, picnic areas, visitor center, hiker trails, restrooms, nonflush toilets, showers

**For Information:** (415) 948-9098

**Access:** From the CA 35–CA 9 junction, go 6.1 miles north on CA 35, turn west on Alpine Road, go another 3.4 miles, and turn left onto State Park Road. It winds downhill 3.3 miles to the headquarters.

Tucked away in the ridges of southern San Mateo County, this Santa Cruz Mountains park escapes the notice and number of visitors received by some of the other redwood parks, yet it offers a fine stay amid the ancient trees. Stands of second-growth redwood ring the core of the park, and in the upper reaches hardwoods can be found. Drained by the forks of Pescadero Creek, the park is closed to fishing but offers a winter opportunity for seeing wild steelhead and silver salmon. While the runs are not sizeable, they are an interesting natural spectacle.

A variety of trails pass through the park, with some continuing into neighboring parks and open spaces. The unsurfaced Old Haul Road affords mountain bikers a 12-mile round-trip ride through redwoods, but it travels outside the park. Along Peters Creek, the park maintains some scenic, wooded picnic sites with stone fireplaces. At the picnic area and at camp, visitors should properly attend to and store their food, as feral cats and raccoons roam the park.

## Attractions and Activities

**Sequoia Nature Trail.** This 0.7-mile loop travels old-growth redwood flats on both sides of Pescadero Creek, visiting a record-size tree that burned in 1989; the park brochure contains descriptions of the tour.

This pleasing circuit travels a rich redwood, Douglas fir, and tanoak complex. At 0.1 mile, it bears right to reach the seasonal bridge over Pescadero Creek, a pretty waterway, with flowing-grass sides. Hazel, alder, azalea, and maple decorate its corridor. Past a spur to the Iverson Trail, hikers reach the burned-out snag of the 2,000-year-old Shell Tree; its blackened log lies behind it. The tree's absence creates a clearing for admiring the lofty tops of the surrounding big trees. The trail then curves right following Pescadero Creek upstream to the bridge for the return.

*Access:* Begin behind the headquarters past the restroom.

**Old Tree–Slate Creek Trail.** This 6.2-mile round-trip hike offers a good overview of this 2,800-acre park, visiting a stately redwood and the park's trail camp.

At 0.1 mile, the Slate Creek Trail heads left, while the Old Tree Trail continues straight, following a small drainage. Going first to the old tree, hikers pass through an area where select redwoods demand a double-take or a neck-craning look. At 0.4 mile, the trail dead ends at the old-timer: a 12-foot-diameter, fire-scarred, and lichen-mottled coast redwood, its lowest branches starting high up the tall, thick trunk.

Returning to the Slate Creek Trail junction (0.7 mile), mount the stairs recessed

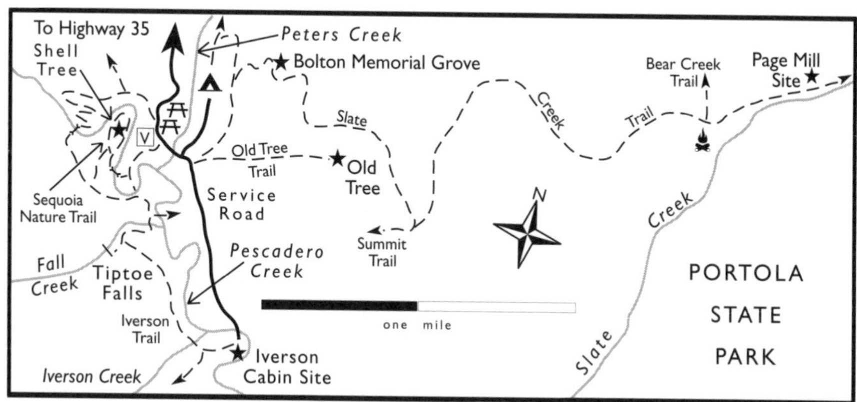

in the slope. After the initial steep climb, the trail settles into a gradual ascent, contouring the slope. Here, more Douglas firs join the redwood ranks. At 1.2 miles, the trail bears right. Where it forks at Bolton Memorial Grove, take either route since left and right options merge before long. This old-growth grove sports several big trees and makes a fine turnaround site for the redwood lover seeking a shorter tour.

Before long, the trail crosses over to the next drainage, where it again contours a redwood-tanoak slope. At 2.1 miles, it reaches a saddle junction with the Summit Trail. The Slate Creek Trail continues straight for the trail camp and Page Mill Site.

More light penetrates near the top of the ridge, as the trail rounds the redwood slope overlooking the Slate Creek drainage. At 2.7 miles, it crosses over a second saddle to tour above the Peters Creek drainage. While big redwoods still line the trail, the lower slope shows a second-growth forest with stumps. Ahead, the slope flattens, huckleberry abounds, and second-growth trees border the route.

At 3.4 miles, hikers come to the trail camp, an open flat with a couple of picnic tables and a pit toilet. Six tent sites are set back in the woods. Hikers may turn around here or continue along the Slate Creek Trail to the Page Mill Site, which is just a creekside flat, a leftover redwood, and a sign, 0.4 mile downhill. The trail continues east from there, eventually entering the Long Ridge Open Space Preserve. Another option from the trail camp tours the Bear Creek Trail–Peters Creek Loop, adding another 7 miles to the present 6.2-mile round-trip hike.

*Access:* Upon entering the group camp, look for the trailhead on the left side of the park road; parking precedes it on the right.

**Iverson Trail.** This 2.7-mile circuit rolls along the redwood slopes of Pescadero Creek, visiting a tiny waterfall and the ruins of an 1860s-built pioneer cabin.

The hike begins climbing a sun-drenched utility corridor lined by live oak, madrone, fir, and tanoak. At 0.1 mile, the trail heads left, and in another 0.1 mile it descends to a seasonal bridge on Pescadero Creek and an untouched redwood complex.

Upon crossing, hikers briefly follow Pescadero Creek downstream, returning to forest. At 0.5 mile, a small wetland meadow sits uphill from the trail; at 0.7 mile it passes the Sequoia Trail spur.

Rolling along the steep drainage slope, the trail offers Pescadero Creek overlooks. Ahead, it curves right, following often-dry Fall Creek upstream and passing through a meadow of bracken fern and horsetail reeds to its point of crossing. Soon after, a short spur heads upstream along Fall Creek for a view of Tiptoe Falls, a 10-foot cascade emptying from a small gorge or slide area into a 2-foot-deep pool.

Resuming the trail, hikers tour a redwood flat with a bracken fern floor. The route then rolls past hollow-based trees and springboard-logged stumps. After the Iverson Creek bridge, it meets a service road and follows it downhill. Before crossing Pescadero Creek, look for the cabin ruins on the right. The cabin stood until the 1989 earthquake; today, only a jumble of boards remain.

Continue on the service road, passing the park residences; redwoods line the road. At 2.4 miles hikers find an overlook of Pescadero Creek's steep sliding slope. At 2.7 miles, they return to the headquarters area.

*Access:* Begin across from the Madrone picnic area.

## HENRY W. COE STATE PARK

**Hours/Season:** Year-round; 8:00 A.M. to 4:00 P.M. weekends, with variable weekday hours (museum)

**Facilities:** 20 primitive drive-in campsites; 8 horse camps; backpacker camps; visitor center/museum; historic ranch buildings; hiker, horse, and mountain-bike routes; nonflush toilets; restrooms and water at visitor center
**For Information:** (408) 779-2728
**Access:** From US 101 at Morgan Hill, exit at East Dunne Avenue and proceed east for 13 miles. The route becomes narrow and winding leaving town; *18 feet is the maximum trailer length allowed in the park.*

At this 79,500-acre Diablo Range park, visitors have a rare opportunity to experience and explore the wild, wide-open spaces of the legendary West. This little-traveled, little-investigated park is an enigma lying so close to the greater San Francisco Bay area. The former ranch features a rugged, folded landscape of rounded ridges separated by deep-plunging drainages and enjoys a mosaic of oak savanna, broadleaf woodland, pine forest, grassland, meadow, chaparral, and riparian habitats. Spring wildflowers bring admirers, as do the leaf-color changes in fall. Spring is the favored time to visit—as summer goes by, it takes the streams with it.

The eastern portion of the park, which includes the Orestimba Wilderness, is particularly isolated and wild, requiring physical exertion and an investment of time to reach it. This region holds the park's larger reservoirs: Mississippi, Coit, and Kelly. Chaparral dominates some slopes, alternating with open grassland, but beautiful pocket woodlands exist. Many trails here are obviously secondary and are not well signed, so keep the map and compass handy and be alert for junctions.

The western portion of the park is what most visitors see. Its appearance is more chiseled than its eastern counterpart and the habitats more varied. The trails are mostly well signed, indicating either the name or destination, giving key mileages, and indicating the allowed users, but a map remains critical for determining how the trails fit together. Carry more water than the mileages dictate. With the park's terrain and climate, heat exhaustion and dehydration are genuine threats.

## Attractions and Activities

**Visitor Center Museum and Ranch Buildings Tour.** Together the park's museum and historic red ranch buildings introduce life here in the 1880s. The Coe family history dates back to 1883, when Henry and his brother first homesteaded here. Coe family heirlooms help recreate the living and dining rooms at the museum, while exhibits and displays describe ranch existence.

Next door, visitors can peek inside a typical bunkhouse, complete with lucky

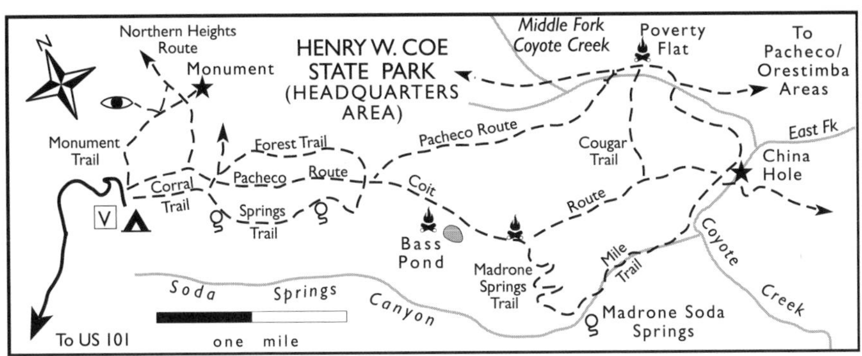

horseshoe over the bed and longjohns hanging from a hook. They can also feel the chill created by the thick rock walls of the cooler, where the ranch perishables were stored. In a shed above the campground, visitors can look in at old carriages, surreys, and working wagons in states of disrepair; old ranch and farm implements are scattered about the grounds.

**Monument Trail.** This 1.6-mile round-trip hike visits a memorial to Henry W. Coe and a vista knoll.

Hiking up Pacheco Route 0.1 mile, take the Monument foot trail heading uphill to the left. It climbs along the edge of a laurel and oak woodland, before crossing an open grassland dotted by multi-colored wildflowers. At 0.4 mile, the trail passes below an old-growth ponderosa pine, the first as the trail approaches the top of Pine Ridge.

At the 0.5-mile junction, the way to Frog Lake is straight, the Monument Trail heads right crossing over the Northern Heights Route, and a vista trail angles uphill to the left. Going first to the monument, hikers find a simple tribute, with the image of Henry Coe atop his mount and a message to enjoy these quiet hills. A nearby bench offers eastern views that stretch to the Sierra.

Back at the 0.5-mile junction, following the 0.2-mile spur to the top of a grassy knoll, hikers find another bench with views west, looking across the valley at the Santa Cruz, Gabilan, and Santa Lucia mountains. Return from the 0.5-mile junction as you came.

*Access:* Begin at the Pacheco Route trailhead, 0.1 mile uphill from the visitor center.

**China Hole Loop.** This rigorous 9.3-mile hiker loop travels canyon and ridge, passing through many of the park habitats. Similar loops exist for horse and mountain-bike riders. Beware of ticks and poison oak.

Beginning on the Corral Nature Trail (for which a brochure is available), hikers find a comfortable foot trail, touring above the thin, steep, wooded drainage of Soda Springs Canyon. Bypassing the Monument Trail junction, the nature trail continues straight, soon entering an oak savanna. A bench sits below one of the scenic, sprawled oaks. The view is of the Soda Springs headwater drainage.

At 0.6 mile is a three-way junction. While the Corral Trail continues straight, go right on the Springs Trail for the loop. This trail, too, contours a drainage slope, traveling at the grassland edge or amid the trees, where there are ponderosa pines and hole-riddled snags. At 1.1 and 1.4 miles, hikers bypass springs, where deer may be seen. The trail continues, descending moderately.

At 2 miles, the trail reaches the Coit Route (here, a major ranch road) just to the right of the Coit–Pacheco junction. Hikers seeking a shorter tour may cross the road, following the Forest Trail and the Pacheco Route back to the visitor center for a 3.7-mile loop. For the full 9.3-mile loop, go right on the Coit Route. At 2.3 miles you will reach Blue Oak Horse Camp, with Bass Pond just below it. While not scenic, the pond does support fish.

Continuing on the Coit Route, bear left as it passes through the Manzanita Point Group Camp. Opposite Camp 7 at 2.7 miles, go right on the Madrone Soda Springs Trail. Digger pine, manzanita, and California buckeye intermix with the oaks. The foot trail offers views as it works its way down the slope to Madrone Soda Springs at 3.7 miles. All that remains of the onetime resort is some rockwork, a sandstone sink, and a stone springhouse recessed in the slope.

At 3.8 miles, the trail name changes to Mile Trail, as the hike continues downstream. Laurels shade the way, together with a few bigleaf maple and black oak. Maidenhair fern, starflower, and ocean spray add to the narrow drainage. Between 4.2 miles and 4.7 miles, the trail crosses the creek a dozen times, coming out at its confluence with Coyote Creek.

*Coyote Creek, Henry W. Coe State Park*

Following Coyote Creek upstream past the Coit Route junction (4.8 miles), hikers find a more open, sunny tour. As they cross the rolling, rocky shore, turtles plop into the water. Rock-bound China Hole is just ahead where the canyon opens up. At 7 to 8 feet deep in the spring and early summer, it offers a cooling dip few can refuse. Inch-long fish investigate swimmers, and garter snakes and dragonflies can be seen.

Beyond is the confluence with the East Fork of Coyote Creek, dubbed "the Narrows" for its steep canyon at this location. Continue the hike upstream along the Middle Fork of Coyote Creek. The trail gradually becomes more defined, but remains rugged, uneven, and rocky. At the fork at 5 miles, take the lower route; the upper one dead-ends. Crossing a rocky flat at 5.4 miles, hikers will see the Pacheco Route ranch road on the opposite shore. Ford Coyote Creek and go left on the road, passing through Poverty Flat.

From the flat, continue straight on Pacheco Route, bypassing the Cougar and Middle Ridge trail junctions, crossing Coyote Creek along the way. From 5.9 to 6.1 miles, hikers find a breath-stealing climb. Afterward, the grade moderates but remains a workout. Scrub oak, laurel, and madrone toss patchy shade across the road. Where it crosses a grassy area at 7.2 miles, hikers enjoy canyon views. At 7.5 miles, bear right on the Forest Trail for a shaded trek.

Built by volunteers, this foot trail offers a fine walk through a woodland of big manzanita, Digger pine, madrone, laurel, oak, and buckeye. Buttercups, Chinese houses, irises, and gold nuggets sprinkle color through the woody complex. At 7.9 miles is an impressive, six-trunk madrone. Ahead are views of Middle and Blue ridges and the Little Fork Coyote Creek drainage. At 8.6 miles, where the trail meets the Pacheco Route opposite the Springs Trail, go right on the Pacheco Route to close the loop.

The ranch road ascends, passing through open oak grassland. After the Northern Heights Route junction, it travels below a perfect, small geologic fold at 9 miles. Past the Monument Trail junction, the Pacheco Route meets the park road; go left to end the hike.

*Access:* The trailhead is next to the fee station near the visitor center.

**Horseback Riding.** This park is well suited to horseback riding, with ample routes, but the terrain and climate are demanding. Make sure your horse is in good condition and that water sources along the way are viable and running. In this harsh region, volunteers do an admirable job keeping the springs flowing, but on occasion time, nature, and the wild pigs win out.

Horse camps may be reserved. The parking and unloading area is above the park headquarters or in the outer lot near the park entrance sign. Riders must register at the visitor center area. Ask about trail conditions before starting a journey.

**Mountain Biking.** The former ranch roads and wide-open spaces of the park have been discovered by mountain bikers, but the terrain is not for novices. The ups and downs can be physically and mentally brutal. The ranch roads that remain in use as service roads generally have good riding surfaces; secondary routes can be rough and rutted.

Remember to yield to hikers and horseback riders; a speeding mountain bike threatens the well-being of all trail users. Cross-country and wilderness cycling are prohibited. Again, carry more water than the mileage suggests and purify spring and other water sources.

**Fishing.** Some twenty park reservoirs offer unexpectedly fine fishing; all require an effort to reach. Large-mouth bass and sunfish are common to most, with bluegill, crappie, and catfish found in a few. The popular large lakes—Mississippi, Coit, and Kelly—are in the backcountry 11 miles from the headquarters; allow at least two days if you plan to fish these. Spring holds the best fishing; conditions improve again in the fall.

**Stargazing.** The open dirt knoll above the ranch headquarters is a popular site for astronomers to set up telescopes. The park's dry air, elevation, and location removed from city lights recommend it.

## BUTANO STATE PARK

**Hours/Season:** Year-round
**Facilities:** 39 developed deep-forested campsites (19 of which are walk-in sites), trail camp, picnic area, nature center, hiker trails, mountain-bike roads, restrooms, nonflush toilets
**For Information:** (415) 879-2040
**Access:** From CA 1, 5.3 miles south of the CA 1–CA 84 junction, turn east onto Pescadero Road, go 2.5 miles, and bear right on Cloverdale Road. The turn for the park is on the left in another 4.2 miles.

In the Santa Cruz Mountains, snuggled in the steep-sided canyon drained by Little Butano Creek, is this 3,200-acre park. Its redwood rain forest consists of old-and second-growth stands. Here, big Douglas fir, the spared redwood trees, tanoak, maple, and ferns weave an enchanted setting for campers and hikers, banana slugs and newts. Pygmy nuthatches, winter wrens, and chickadees further enliven the forest.

*Banana slug, Butano State Park*

Less publicized than some of the other redwood parks, Butano State Park offers visitors a better chance for solitude. There are trails for hikers and routes suitable for cyclists. The park campground is a favorite—spacious, dark, and majestic. Elsewhere at Butano, visitors enjoy the open grassland, chaparral, oak woodland, and riparian habitats.

A recent park expansion is the ridgetop site of Butano Crossing. When additional trail easements are in place, it will allow passage between Butano and Big Basin Redwoods state parks. The crossing also protects a critical flyway for the threatened marbled murrelet, a seabird that nests in the forest treetops of southern San Mateo County.

The park contains a small nature center, with a few exhibits, newsletters, and natural-history resources. On its grounds grows a fine nature garden, where native plants have been identified. In the forest, the purple calypso orchid annually draws plant aficionados; it blooms February to April.

## Attractions and Activities

**Little Butano Creek Loop.** This 1.6-mile loop travels trail and service road, exploring the Little Butano Creek drainage. It is one of the easiest hikes in this park of steep ups and downs.

The trail follows Little Butano Creek upstream, touring a redwood, Douglas fir, and tanoak complex, with bountiful ferns—a thick rush of green beneath the forest darkness. Footbridge crossings take the hiker back and forth across the shimmering, 3- to 6-foot-wide, gravel-bottomed creek. Wet years can bring mosquitos.

Oxalis, trillium, pathfinder, forget-me-not, and red clintonia add to the lush forest carpet. Some redwood stumps hint at the logging that ended here in the early 1900s. In April, the trail is alive with young newts.

Where the trail forks at 0.4 mile, take either path. The upper fork is slightly overgrown, but passable, and offers a different perspective on the forest drainage. The lower one stays with the creek, crisscrossing it to bypass a slide area. Where the forks merge, beautiful maples overhang the creek.

The trail briefly climbs and contours the slope. By 0.8 mile, it is again creekside, near a gauging station and a small spillway. Here, hikers have the option of crossing the creek and returning via a service road or retracing the trail.

Taking the service road downstream, hikers travel above the creek through a mixed forest with a fern and evergreen huckleberry understory. The road first climbs steeply, then moderates. At 1 mile, it begins to descend; keep to the service road. It bypasses a spur to the campground in a quarter mile. At 1.4 miles, it meets the paved park road; bear right for the trailhead.

*Access:* Find the trailhead along the park road, 0.3 mile downhill from the campground. There is roadside parking for a couple of vehicles.

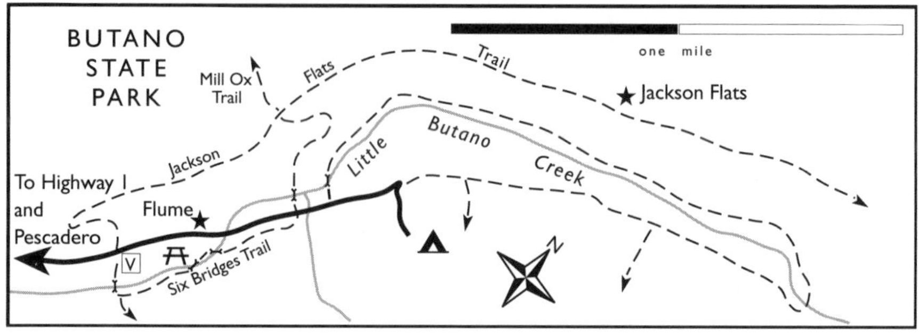


**Jackson Flats–Six Bridges Hike.** This 3.7-mile tour visits a variety of habitats and offers a glimpse at the unusual vernal wetlands that give rise to the park's newt and tree frog populations.

Passing through a flat of tall shrubs and young fir, hikers begin contouring the base of an oak-wooded ridge. Large Douglas fir, hazel, a few madrone, and poison oak live among the twisted live oaks. Fluted orange chanterelles pierce the duff, but mushroom collecting is not allowed.

After a brief climb, the trail skirts a group of large redwoods, signaling a change to second-growth redwood, tanoak, and fir. At 0.8 mile, it crosses over the Mill Ox Trail. For a 1.9-mile loop, descend here and pick up the Six Bridges Trail (described below).

Opting instead to remain on the Jackson Flats Trail, hikers resume contouring the slope. At 1.1 miles a wet slump or landslide appears, dotted in spring by pungent, yellow skunk cabbages. The slide, here and elsewhere, is likely the product of shifts along the San Gregorio Fault. Ahead, the trail crosses a larger landslide flat, with areas of ocean spray, hazel, blackberry, and nettles. Some big redwoods claim it, as well.

Looking left between the trunks of the Douglas firs at 1.4 miles, visitors can see a sizeable cattail marsh, one of the vernal wetlands. Ahead, more pocket wetlands dot the broad, forested terrace. At 1.7 miles, hikers come upon an untouched stand of magnificent redwoods, just as the trail begins to climb. This marks the turnaround for the tour; going straight on the Jackson Flats Trail allows for some long-distance treks through Butano State Park.

Returning to the 0.8-mile junction (2.6 miles), follow the Mill Ox Trail for a sharp 0.2-mile descent through second-growth redwoods and tanoaks. Newts crisscross the trail, so watch your step.

Upon crossing the Little Butano Creek footbridge and meeting the park road, go right and take a quick left on the service road there. Before long, the Six Bridges Trail crosses the service road; follow it right to return to the trailhead.

This trail rolls along the forested slope, overlooking the road and a flume and small dam along Little Butano Creek. At 3.2 miles, it crosses the park residence road and one of the footbridges of the trail's name. An open forest of fir and oak surrounds the trail; alders and maples fill the drainage.

Past the next footbridge, a spur to the right leads to the picnic area. Continue straight, crossing another bridge, staying in the riparian corridor. At the upcoming junction, the Año Nuevo Trail heads straight; go right, crossing the creek once more to end near the nature center.

*Access:* Begin on the trail heading north from the entrance station; there is parking for up to six vehicles.

# Castle Rock State Park

**Hours/Season:** 6:00 A.M. to sunset
**Facilities:** 25 primitive backpacker campsites, camp shelter, dispersed picnic tables, hiker and horse trails, interpretive shelter, nonflush toilets, water (at the headquarters/backpacker camp only, reached via 2.7-mile trail)
**For Information:** (408) 867-2952
**Access:** From the CA 9–CA 35 junction (Saratoga Gap), go 2.5 miles south on CA 35. The entrance is on the right.

This mostly wild 3,700-acre park on the western ridge of the Santa Cruz Mountains attracts with its peaceful woodlands, rugged chaparral sweeps, clear-day vistas, and outstanding eroded rock features that call to climbers. With no vehicle routes into Castle Rock State Park, visitors must expend some effort to get to know it. But this area has drawn visitors since the turn of the century—a powerful endorsement, given that travel then was by no means easy.

More than 30 miles of trail traverse the park. The 37.5-mile Skyline to the Sea Trail links Castle Rock and Big Basin Redwoods state parks, allowing hikers and equestrians to travel from these western mountain reaches to the ocean at Waddell Beach. Ongoing efforts continue to connect Castle Rock to other area parks and open spaces, extending travel options. Visitors should note that dogs and bikes are not allowed in the park, and smoking is prohibited due to extreme fire danger.

## Attractions and Activities

**Saratoga Gap–Ridge Trail Loop.** This moderate 5.1-mile loop travels wooded and chaparral slopes, attaining vistas, visiting a waterfall, and bypassing scenic sandstone boulders and outcroppings, including Goat Rock.

The trail descends alongside a drainage, passing through a varied woodland

*Goat Rock, Castle Rock State Park*

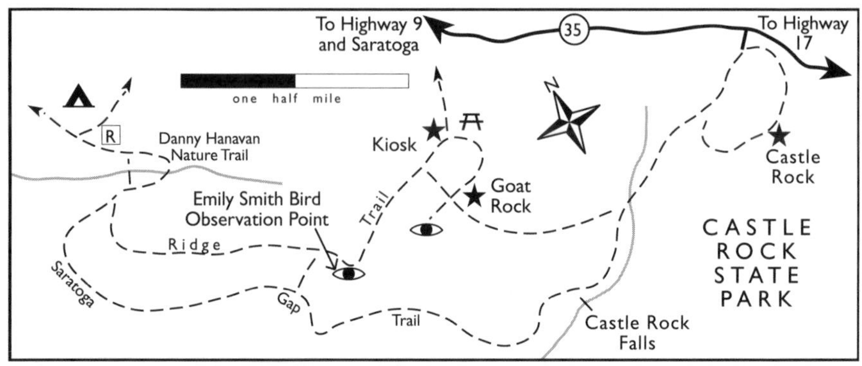


with madrone, fir, mixed oaks, laurel, and maple. Uphill to the right is a hollowed, smooth-edged boulder, a herald of more to come. Spurs branch to Castle Rock. Upon crossing a small footbridge, hikers come to the loop junction (0.5 mile). Go straight for a clockwise tour.

At 0.7 mile, hikers arrive at the wooden platform overlooking the top of Castle Rock Falls. After rains, the falls shows a pretty, misting veil; other times, it is just a trickle. Always impressive is the broad, nearly vertical, sheer-faced cliff.

The rolling trail then crosses over boulders and outcrops, as it contours a more exposed slope with areas of live oak and chaparral. Views southwest stretch to Monterey Bay. At 1.5 miles, a connector trail heads right to meet the Ridge Trail.

Keeping to the gap trail, hikers soon overlook the San Lorenzo drainage, with Ben Lomond, Pine Mountain, and Mount McAbee in the distance. In spring, yerba santa, Indian paintbrush, monkey-flower, and California poppy lend color to the tour. By 2.3 miles, the trail overlaps part of the Danny Hanavan Nature Trail, which starts at the headquarters; brochures are available at its start.

In a live oak-madrone woodland, bypass the Ridge Trail (the loop's return), and bear left to reach the headquarters area (2.7 miles). Visitors find water, picnic tables, pit toilets, and a primitive campground. Many choose to stop here for a lunch or snack before resuming the loop.

For the return, retrace the previous route or follow the nature trail back to the Ridge Trail junction. There, go left, switchbacking uphill through a mixed woodland with a fair amount of poison oak. Gray squirrel and deer may be spied, and the peeled madrone are eye-pleasing.

Where the trail reaches a ridge opening at 3 miles, hikers enjoy a 180-degree view west. As the trail continues ascending, knobcone pine and manzanita briefly appear. At 3.6 miles, the ridge-gap connector trail arrives on the right and the woodland opens up.

Just ahead, a detour right leads to the oak-grassland site of the Emily Smith Bird Observation Point. Although the view is limited, especially when the black oaks are fully leafed out, it proves a peaceful stop to watch for hawks, vultures, and jays.

Staying on the Ridge Trail, at 3.9 miles take either path to reach Goat Rock in 0.2 mile. Going straight adds a visit to the interpretive shelter, with its central pyramid display on the park's natural history. Nearby are a couple of picnic tables. From the shelter, take the foot trail to the right to reach Goat Rock.

Next door to Goat Rock is a scenic overlook from which visitors can admire the sandstone's pigeonholed west side. Benches overlook the open chaparral slope; directional boards identify the area landmarks.

Resuming on the Ridge Trail, visitors descend along the west side of Goat Rock, rounding its base. There, they can see climbers clutching the rock and hear others barking instructions. The trail then skirts beneath neighboring rocks, one with a natural arch. Posts point the way. Beyond the rocks, the trail again becomes more defined, and hikers find shade. At 4.6 miles, the loop closes next to an old-growth fir; go left.

*Access:* Begin at the information board at the west side of the parking lot.

**Climbing.** Castle Rock, the park's high point at an elevation of 3,214 feet, and Goat Rock are the two most popular climbs. Both are picturesque sandstone features with honeycomb, dimples, caves, and hollows lending to their character and their challenge. In the 1880s, a cave in Castle Rock served as a temporary home for the area school marm.

Castle Rock occupies the edge of a wooded flat and lacks a summit view. In the park interior, Goat Rock rises up some 100 feet, overlooking a steep chaparral slope, giving it greater drama. While its top affords a view, it is not the purpose of a climb.

At Castle and Goat rocks, visitors find straightforward ascents and some that challenge, requiring precarious positions or acrobatic maneuvers. Some climbers tackle Goat Rock simply for the fun of swinging out from its overhang. At the rocks, novices commonly receive instruction, broadening their abilities, while veterans hone their techniques and keep in shape. All climbers do so at their own risk, and should be properly equipped and trained in their sport.

*Access:* A 0.3-mile walk reaches Castle Rock. A mile hike via the Saratoga Gap and Ridge trails leads to Goat Rock.

## Big Basin Redwoods State Park

**Hours/Season:** Year-round

**Facilities:** 100 developed RV / tent campsites; 45 developed walk-in campsites; 36 tent cabins; hike / bike campsites; picnic areas; visitor center; nature centers; seasonal gift shop, store, and snackbar; hiker and horse trails; mountain-bike roads; restrooms; nonflush toilets; showers; dump station

**For Information:** (408) 338-8860

**Access:** From Boulder Creek on CA 9, go 9 miles west on CA 236 for the main park entry. From Santa Cruz, go 14.5 miles north on CA 1 for Waddell Beach and Rancho del Oso.

Big Basin, established in 1902, was California's first state park and remains one of its most popular. In its 18,000 acres, it contains ancient redwoods, stands of knobcone pine, oak and chaparral ridges, skipping creeks, delicate waterfalls, summit outcrops, a wetland, and the meeting of sand and surf. While the park can be enjoyed through a vehicle windshield, one should venture out to find its best qualities. Some 80 miles of trail lead the way. Paved roads and fire roads serve the mountain biker, and the 37.5-mile Skyline to the Sea Trail allows equestrians and hikers to travel from the ocean at Waddell Beach through Big Basin Redwoods State Park northeast to Castle Rock State Park.

At the headquarters area, travelers may want to visit the rustic Sempervirens Room, which offers a history on the park, sells brochures, and has a staff to direct visitors to park attractions and trailheads. Across the way, the nature center offers unique exhibits created in wood, including a relief map and habitat and geology dioramas. At the buzzing headquarters area, day parking can be troublesome; an early arrival is recommended.

## Attractions and Activities

**Waddell Beach.** This beach parallels an 0.8-mile stretch of CA 1 and is sliced by Waddell Creek, which hosts wild steelhead runs in the fall. The north end of the beach is backed by a road cut and riprap, while the southern end shows a low dune bank. At its base, snowy plovers nest. Windsurfers can sometimes be seen riding the waves. The sand is clean and invites walking, but high tides can steal the beach away from the creek mouth.

**Redwood Nature Trail.** This 0.6-mile loop is the most walked trail in the park, touring a fine grove of ancient redwoods on the flat above Opal Creek. Where it rounds above the creek, azaleas are common. Elsewhere, tanoak and huckleberry dominate.

The loop features a first-rate Chimney Tree. Stepping inside, visitors can gaze up the naturally burned flue at the upper branches. Mother of the Forest, the park's tallest tree at 329 feet, can be viewed from a distance and up close; Father of the Forest is noted for its girth. Next door, at the campfire center, visitors can explore a massive upturned redwood for a different perspective on size.

*Access:* Opposite the headquarters, at the southwest end of day-use parking, a 10-foot-tall sign marks the trail.

**Sempervirens Falls.** This tiny photogenic falls is best appreciated on a hike but can be seen from a roadside turnout 1.2 miles uphill from CA 236 by taking the park road past Huckleberry and Wasatahi campgrounds. Beware: The road is narrow and turnaround space is limited. A viewing platform presents this 10-foot charmer gently spilling over a cliff richly decorated with five-finger ferns. Following rain, a broader, heavier veil plunges down.

*Access:* From the headquarters or Wasatahi Campground, take the Sequoia Trail.

**Pine Mountain Trail.** This 4.8-mile round-trip trail climbs 1,100 feet through forest to reach the vista outcrop of Buzzards Roost and the summit of Pine Mountain.

Upon crossing Bloom Creek, bear right briefly, touring along the shore. Azalea, tanoak, and huckleberry overhang the banks. At 0.1 mile, go left, turning away from the creek; beautiful redwoods cloak the slope. Crossing over the East Ridge Trail, the route settles into a steady, moderate ascent. A tanoak midstory fills out the forest.

At 0.7-mile, the trail switchbacks left, coming out at a road; bear left. The trail resumes on the right in 100 feet. Gaps in the tree cover afford limited looks at the pine-sided mountain. At 1.1 miles, springboard notches mark the charred stumps next to the trail. Ahead, the route rounds over a few rock beds, entering an elfin forest of knobcone pine, madrone, chinquapin, oak, and manzanita. Crossing over a small ridge, it contours toward Pine Mountain. At the 2-mile junction, to the left is Buzzards Roost in 0.1 mile; to the right is Pine Mountain Summit in 0.3 mile.

With an easy ascent on hard sandstone, hikers reach Buzzards Roost, a rock outcrop capping the knoll; a small pillar marks its top. Vistas are mostly open, and by strolling along the rock visitors can piece together a 360-degree view of Big Basin, Pine Mountain, the ocean, and neighboring ridges. Winds often assail the roost.

Continuing to Pine Mountain, visitors find the trail more overgrown. Just before the summit, a flat-topped rock outcrop with a sheer drop affords a spectacular basin view. The summit is enclosed by trees. Return as you came.

*Access:* Begin near site 110 at Bloom Creek Campground, taking the footbridge over the creek near the gated road.

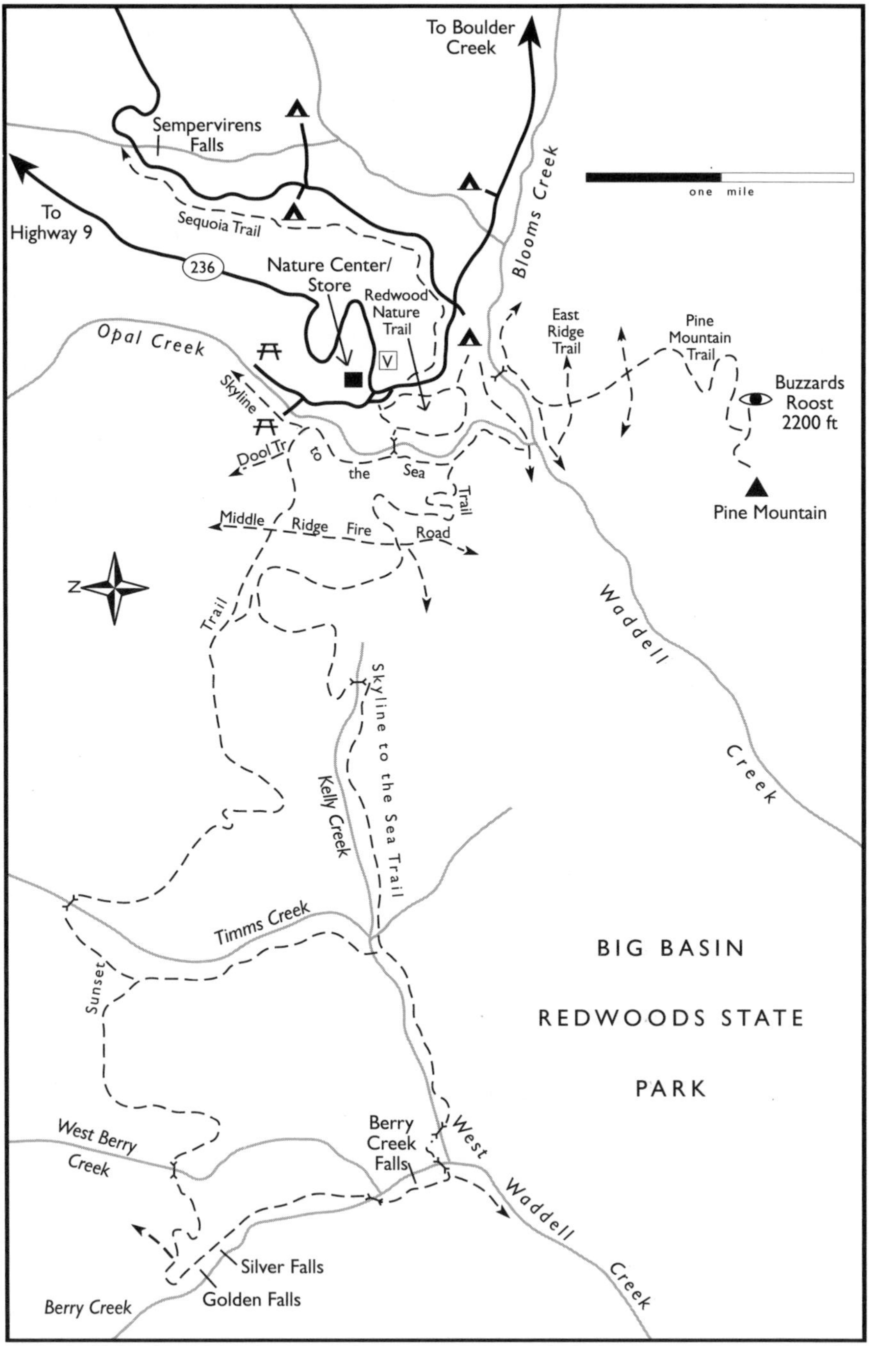

To Boulder Creek
Sempervirens Falls
To Highway 9
Sequoia Trail
236
Nature Center/ Store
Redwood Nature Trail
Blooms Creek
one mile
Opal Creek
East Ridge Trail
Pine Mountain Trail
Buzzards Roost 2200 ft
Pine Mountain
Skyline to the Sea Trail
Dool Tr
Middle Ridge Fire Road
Trail
Waddell Creek
Skyline to the Sea Trail
Kelly Creek
Timms Creek
BIG BASIN
REDWOODS STATE
PARK
Sunset
West Berry Creek
Berry Creek Falls
West Waddell Creek
Silver Falls
Golden Falls
Berry Creek

**Berry Creek Falls Loop.** This strenuous 10.4-mile loop rolls between ridge and creek, traveling rich redwood drainages and semi-arid ridges and visiting three falls: Berry Creek, Golden, and Silver.

Upon crossing Opal Creek, go left on the Skyline to the Sea Trail for a clockwise tour. The route begins passing some amazing big trees, including the Santa Clara Tree, 240 feet tall and 17 feet in diameter. A few azalea spot the complex. Ahead, bear right, keeping to the Skyline Trail. By 0.5 mile, it is climbing. Where it reaches the ridge (1 mile), next to a corkscrew-armed madrone, angle right, crossing over the Middle Ridge Fire Road to descend the opposite slope.

*Elephant seal, Año Nuevo State Reserve*

The tour remains in a magnificent redwood forest. Some benches and memorial groves mark the way. Keeping to the Skyline Trail, contouring and descending the slope, hikers cross the Kelly Creek footbridge, at 2.2 miles, and follow the creek downstream. More routes branch off, but keep to the Skyline Trail. After 3 miles, it tours above West Waddell Creek, which is lined by maples and shows some big boulders. The trail becomes more rolling.

At 3.7 miles, it passes under a redwood jumble and, soon after, crosses the footbridge on West Waddell Creek. From there, the loop ascends to a vista bench, offering a distant look at Berry Creek Falls, a 65-foot waterfall. Staying on the trail to the falls, hikers descend, cross Berry Creek, and climb to the viewing platform at 4.2 miles. It affords a direct look at the pretty, misting drop coursing over the black rock. Redwoods march up the drainage to it.

Switchbacking uphill, the trail tours alongside the scenic cascades of upper Berry Creek, before crossing and following mossy-banked West Berry Creek upstream. Some big Douglas fir punctuate this mildly ascending stretch. At 5 miles, hikers overlook the silvery rivulets of Silver Falls, tracing a 70-foot vertical cliff. In times of high water, it has a more imposing presence. Be careful when ascending the steep slippery slope next to the falls and its series of upstream sparkling cascades; use the guidewires where provided. Where the water falls in sheets over a spectacular reddish gold cliff you are at Golden Falls.

From there, the trail continues briefly upstream, then curves right, turning away from the drainage and coming to a junction post (5.2 miles). Continue straight; the loop now follows the Sunset Trail. It begins crossing a knobcone pine, chinquapin, live oak, and madrone slope. The open skyline serves up a strong contrast to the previous redwood tour, but it is not long before the trail descends back amid the evergreen giants.

Crossing a Berry Creek footbridge, the trail again climbs through the redwoods, thick with tanoak. At 6.5 miles, it tops and crosses over a ridge for a descent to West Waddell Creek. The descent grows steeper upon approaching the 7.1-mile junction. Go left, staying on the Sunset Trail. After the rustic bridge crossing of West Waddell Creek, the route ascends steadily, topping and crossing another ridge at a memorial grove at 8.4 miles.

Contouring the slope, it briefly tours an area of oak, fir, and grassland, but the tanoaks and redwoods are not gone. After the climb resumes, stay on the Sunset Trail, meeting and crossing over the Middle Ridge Fire Road at 9.5 miles. A rapid descent follows. At 10 miles, the loop continues right on the Dool Trail and crosses a redwood flat along Opal Creek, heading downstream. At 10.3 miles, cross the Opal Creek footbridge to close the loop.

*Access:* Begin on the Redwood Nature Trail, heading straight to cross Opal Creek near the restroom.

## AÑO NUEVO STATE RESERVE—PIGEON POINT LIGHTHOUSE

**Hours/Season:** 8:00 A.M. to sunset, arrive before 4:00 P.M. to see the elephant seals; guided tours: December through March (Año Nuevo); 4:30 P.M. to 9:30 A.M. (Pigeon Point Lighthouse)

**Facilities:** Picnic tables, visitor center, bookstore, hiker trails, nonflush toilets, water (Año Nuevo); historic lighthouse, American Youth Hostel cabins (Pigeon Point Lighthouse)

**For Information:** (415) 879-0227 (Año Nuevo); (415) 879-0633 (Pigeon Point Lighthouse)

**Access:** Año Nuevo is west off CA 1, 21 miles north of Santa Cruz. Pigeon Point Lighthouse is west off CA 1, 6.5 miles north of Año Nuevo.

At Año Nuevo State Reserve, a rock island, remote beaches, shifting dunes, layered cliffs, a freshwater pond, and an upland brushfield create a vital wildlife habitat, supporting marine and land species. Extending the park reaches is an undeveloped, wild area on the east side of CA 1—Cascade Ranch.

From December through March, the annual breeding ritual of the northern elephant seal plays out on the Año Nuevo shore. It is the single most popular attraction, bringing visitors from around the world. A recent breeding season census counted 3,000 adult and adolescent seals, with 600 pups born.

During these months, guided tours allow visitors to witness the battling bulls; the harem selections; the birthing, nurturing, and maturing of the pups; and the sequenced exodus to the sea. The tours are paced so that common behaviors also may be witnessed. Each tour lasts about 2.5 hours and covers about 2 miles; much of the walk is through loose sand.

A 50-foot safety margin is maintained, as bulls can reach 16 feet in length and weigh over 4,000 pounds. It also minimizes the human intrusion on the natural events. Well in advance of the breeding season, visitors should secure their tour tickets, available through MISTIX (1-800-444-PARK).

Although breeding season is easily the reserve's busiest time, natural events occur year-round. In spring and summer, the elephant seals return to molt. In April, when the females arrive, the numbers almost match those of breeding season.

Beginning in mid-August, Steller sea lions mate on the offshore rocks, and in September and October, the California sea lions rest here on their track north. Harbor seals are year-round island residents, and sea otters and gray whales are often spied in the area waters. An influx of birds, likewise, fills a calendar.

From April through November, visitors may secure free permits to enter the restricted Wildlife Protection Area to view the marine mammals. Año Nuevo Island is always off-limits to the public.

Areas of unrestricted access are found at Cove Beach and at the marked turnouts north of the main entrance, accessing bluff and isolated beach areas. Check at the visitor center in the rustic barn for other points of interest.

Between Año Nuevo and Pigeon Point, the rocky, fog-cloaked coastal waters claimed several early-day vessels, leading to the building of Pigeon Point Lighthouse in 1872. The point received its name from one such tragedy, the 1853 wreck of the *Carrier Pigeon*.

Today, American Youth Hostels operates an overnight facility on Pigeon Point. The accommodations include dormitory and family rooms, kitchen and common rooms, hot showers, and even an outdoor hot tub. Reservations are recommended for overnight stays and lighthouse tours.

## Attractions and Activities

**Pigeon Point Lighthouse.** Rising above a 35-foot cliff, the classic, stained white-brick lighthouse may be toured on Sundays, but is presently closed for restoration. It is the second tallest lighthouse on the West Coast at 115 feet. Its original multi-prism Fresnel lens remains in place but is no longer operational. An automated aerobeacon now guides sailors along this coast, using the historic ten-second flash pattern.

*Access:* Go 6.5 miles north of Año Nuevo State Reserve on CA 1.

**Año Nuevo Point Trail.** This is the trail visitors follow to view the seals, whatever the season. It accesses the Wildlife Protection Area; visitors must have tour tickets or a permit to enter.

At the initial trail fork, take either path, as they again merge after rounding the inland pond. Side paths branch off the left fork to Cove Beach. The right fork bypasses a remnant from the *Point Arena*, a schooner that smashed into the rocks at Pigeon Point.

Both wide gravel paths pass through the coyote bush and grassland of the upland field. In spring, the field is dressed in wildflower regalia. At 0.4 mile, visitors find a bench where the trail forks merge; at 0.6 mile, they arrive at the staging area.

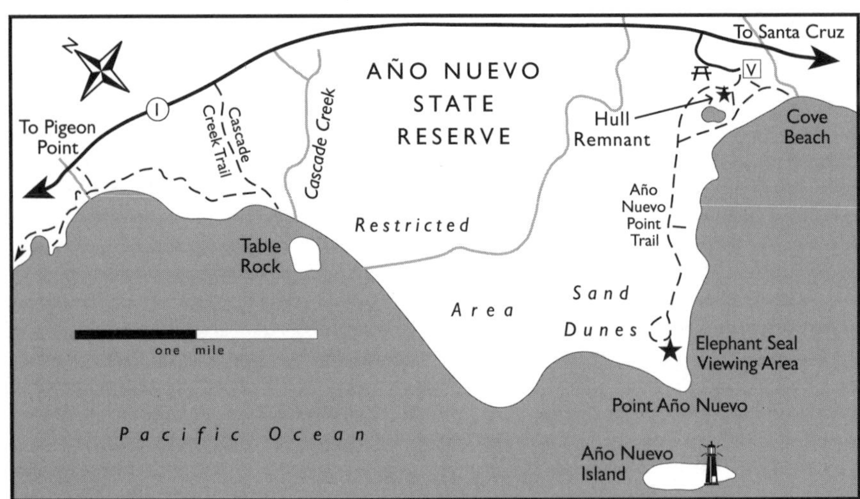

Posted here is a seal census, and displayed are life-size cutouts of the four pinnipeds seen at the reserve: the elephant seal, the Steller and California sea lions, and the harbor seal. Chemical toilets are located nearby.

During breeding season, the staging area is where docents receive tour groups and prepare them for the guided tour across the dunes. Other times of year, visitors in possession of a permit continue on their own, staying on the roped-off trail.

Bush lupine, low willows, and sea fig vegetate the dunes. At 0.8 mile, visitors secure looks at Año Nuevo Island and its former lighthouse, abandoned to the marine animals. The tightly packed sea lions and seals create a breathing shore.

A section of boardwalk follows, with hikers reaching the dunes and primary seal-viewing area at 1 mile. During the off-season, docents answer questions and supervise viewing here.

Mock bouts, snorting, snoozing, itching, and yawning are the common behaviors of the elephant seal. As the wide-eyed giants pulse their Jello-like bodies up the beach, they leave sandy trails in their wakes. Often the animals dust their backs with sand. Bring cameras, scopes, and binoculars. Return as you came.

*Access:* At the main entrance to Año Nuevo State Reserve, start at the parking lot trailhead or begin near the visitor center.

**Cascade Creek–Bluff Hike.** This 2.8-mile round-trip tour travels the coastal bluff of Año Nuevo State Reserve, offering ocean overlooks and limited opportunities to descend to the isolated beach below it.

Skirting the gate, hikers follow an old road west across the grassy bluff plateau mottled by patches of blue-eyed grass, lupine, and geranium. At 0.4 mile, the trail reaches the bluff edge near a small grove of eucalyptus and cypress. Views south are of Table Rock.

For a bluff tour, follow the footpath north through the grove. At the base of the 10-foot bluff is a little-tracked wilderness beach. When tides are cooperative, it offers an alternate way north or perhaps a return route.

The bluff trail, open to hikers and horses, stays inland, is narrow, and sometimes is encroached by poison oak. After dipping into a drainage at 0.8 mile, the trail briefly tours closer to the bluff edge, overlooking a rocky shore.

At the 1.1-mile junction, the path to the right leads to CA 1; the one to the left drops to the rocky cove at Whitehouse Creek. Angling upstream, hikers must cross the creek on rocks and logs to resume the bluff trek north. The trail remains seaward. Coastal sagewort, lizardtail, and bush lupine vegetate the remnant dunes that now top the bluff.

At 1.4 miles, the trail arrives at a small point overlooking a quiet, rounded cove to the north and a smaller one to the south. In spring, sea pinks, lavender sea daisies, blue lupine, and orange poppy complement the blue horizon. The passing otters, pelicans, and seals engage. This is a good turnaround point, as farther north multiple paths confuse the way, and ankle-height poison oak overtakes the trail.

*Access:* The trailhead turnout is west off CA 1, about 2.2 miles north of the main reserve entrance.

**Tidepooling.** With a constant, moderate climate, the intertidal life at Año Nuevo is rich and varied. Some 300 species of invertebrate have been identified. The standing pools in the rocky ledges seclude anemone, limpets, chiton, hermit crabs, and fish. Any collecting, even that of shells, is prohibited.

*Access:* Find the pools at the northern end of the reserve.

**Birdwatching.** The reserve boasts a varied resident and migratory bird population. In spring, hummingbirds engage in a courtship ritual, ducks settle on the reserve pond, and migrating orioles, vireos, and warblers pass through the area. Raptors, meadowlarks, and quail can be seen amid the brushfield vegetation. At the beach, turnstones, plovers, and sandpipers search for food to fuel their spring flights north. Loons and some seven species of gulls also may be spied.

With the arrival of fall come the sanderlings and black turnstones. Then, too, the brown pelican viewing is exceptional, as they come to feed on the anchovies.

## THE FOREST OF NISENE MARKS STATE PARK

**Hours/Season:** 6:00 A.M. to sunset
**Facilities:** Trail camp, picnic areas, historic sites, hiker and horse trails, mountain-bike routes, nonflush toilets, *bring water*
**For Information:** (408) 761-3487 or (408) 429-2850
**Access:** From Soquel Drive in Aptos, turn northeast on Aptos Creek Road *(not suitable for motorhomes and trailers)*. Reach the entry station at 0.8 mile, the gate at 3 miles. Parking is limited and can be a problem.

Among its 10,000 acres, this minimally developed park contains some of the most rugged countryside in the Santa Cruz Mountains, encompassing the watersheds of Aptos and Hinckley creeks. The park's crooked ridges and steep-sided canyons were logged during a breakneck effort in the late nineteenth century. Today, a regenerating forest, rich with second-growth redwood, Douglas fir, and mixed deciduous trees, greets guests. Fire roads, trails, and old railroad grades lead through the park.

While the terrain is rugged, several routes are remarkably well-graded, drawing a strong mountain-biking contingent and winning favor with local joggers. Mountain bikers boast that in exchange for an uphill workout on Aptos Creek Fire Road, they get a good, free 30-minute ride downhill. Horseback riders must stay downstream from George's picnic area. After rains, the entrance road is gated near that picnic area, 1.1 miles prior to the normal 3-mile gate at the Porter Family picnic area.

### Attractions and Activities

**Aptos Creek Fire Road to Sand Point Overlook.** This 12-mile round-trip tour travels the core of the park, overlooking Aptos Creek and ascending China Ridge.

Follow the wide, tree-framed dirt road traveling upstream above Aptos Creek. On the left, a fern-laden side canyon precedes the Loma Prieta Grade. Downhill from the grade, the fire road crosses broad, even-flowing Aptos Creek. Fording is

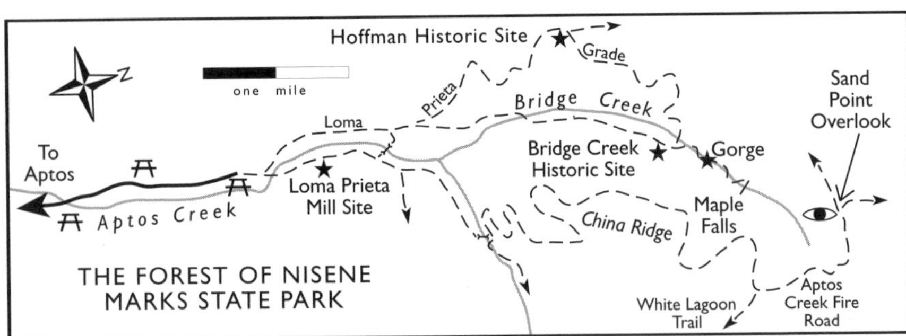

often required, with a rock-hopping crossing possible at low water.

The road then ascends, becoming more open near the Loma Prieta Mill Site, where only a foundation remains. A full woodland then returns with blackberry, sword fern, and poison oak amid the mix. Where the fire road again crosses the creek at 1.5 miles, a footbridge allows a dry crossing.

At the foot of China Ridge, a sign marks the epicenter for the October 1989 quake that measured 7.1 on the Richter scale. Hikers opting to tour the Aptos Creek foot trail upstream from here can find clues to the quake—slides, debris, snapped trees—but the fire road shows little physical evidence of the event.

Keeping to the fire road, travelers begin the long, steady, gently curving ascent of wooded China Ridge. The route alternates between sun and shade. Where it enters a curve at 3 miles, visitors find a limited view of the Bridge Creek drainage, overlooking a scrub slope. The opening is a legacy of the logging-era steam donkey used to lower loaded railcars to Aptos Creek.

*Maple Falls, The Forest of Nisene Marks State Park*

The road continues to climb with a milder gradient. On the upper reaches of China Ridge, areas of fir, oak, and madrone alternate with the redwood-tanoak complex. Below the road near the Whites Lagoon Trail junction is a small meadow. In another mile, travelers reach the overlook and turnaround point.

From Sand Point Overlook, the view again sweeps the forested Bridge Creek drainage, extending the views across Monterey Bay and adding ones of Santa Cruz and Ben Lomond Ridge. Cyclists generally continue on the fire road, which remains relatively flat, then steepens at "The Wall" for yet another workout.

*Access:* Begin at the 3-mile gate at the Porter Family picnic area.

**Loma Prieta Grade–Bridge Creek Loop.** This 7.6-mile hiker-only circuit likewise enters the heart of the park, visiting woodland, historic sites, an impressive creek canyon, and small waterfall.

Go 0.2 mile on Aptos Creek Fire Road, and bear left for the Loma Prieta Grade. It is a wide lane reclaimed by leaves and needles, with occasional rusted cables or ties betraying its original use. A typical redwood complex with scattered maples enfolds it. At the footbridge crossing at 0.4 mile, five-finger ferns adorn the bank. Where the trail opens up with nonnative vegetation, hikers find the Porter Family homesite and a junction. Stay on the Loma Prieta Grade.

At 1.1 miles is the loop junction. Go right for a counterclockwise tour, now following the grade of the Bridge Creek Trail. Oaks first claim the way. They are replaced by redwoods, as the trail overlooks Bridge Creek. Crossing over a sandstone slide, hikers can see shell fossils in the exposed rock. Throughout the park, the soft sandstones have barely consolidated, making them vulnerable to sloughing. Where hikers ford Bridge Creek at 1.8 miles, fossils also riddle the loose rock in the stream.

Scoured by slides and winter high waters, the drainage bottom holds little greenery, but the enfolding canyon's second-generation redwood forest is pleasant.

At 2.5 miles is the Bridge Creek Historic Site, just a small flat with some boards; high waters have carried away much of the ruins. Here, a creek crossing continues the loop via the Loma Prieta Grade. A detour upstream finds 30-foot Maple Falls in 0.6 mile.

This cross-country detour requires fourteen creek crossings, as it travels trail fragment, creekbed, and scenic, pinched gorge to reach the base of this delicate falls, housed in a sandstone bowl. A few maples hint at the name. Be careful climbing over the wet logs and slippery rocks, and watch out for the many newts.

Resuming the loop at 3.7 miles, hikers find a steep uphill climb along a redwood side drainage. As the trail rounds the drainage head, there are some eye-catching, charred stumps. It then contours and slowly descends. Tanoaks hug the steep slope, while redwoods retain custody of the drainages. At 5.1 miles, the trail passes through Hoffman Historic Site, a 1920s logging camp with several collapsed ruins.

Continue straight, still slowly descending on the Loma Prieta Grade. Between 5.2 and 5.5 miles, the trail rounds a sandstone cliff with an eerie drop-away slope to the Bridge Creek drainage. The forest then becomes more mixed. At 6.5 miles, hikers close the loop. Retrace the first 1.1 miles to the trailhead.

*Access:* Begin at the gate at Porter Family picnic area.

## San Luis Reservoir State Recreation Area

**Hours/Season:** Year-round; 9:00 A.M. to 5:00 P.M. (Romero Overlook Visitor Center)

**Facilities:** 79 developed tree-shaded campsites (San Luis Reservoir), 200 open primitive campsites and 53 developed campsites with hookups, designated swimming areas (O'Neill Forebay), 20 semi-shaded primitive campsites and an open primitive horse camp (Los Banos Creek Reservoir), picnic areas, visitor center, boat ramps, hiker trails, bike routes, restrooms, nonflush toilets, indoor and outdoor showers

**For Information:** (209) 826-1196

**Access:** The recreation area units are reached off CA 152. *For San Luis Reservoir and O'Neill Forebay* head west from I-5; signed accesses begin in 2.5 miles. *For Los Banos Creek Reservoir,* go east from I-5 for 2.2 miles, turn right on Volta Road, and go 1 mile. There, turn left on Pioneer Road; in 0.9 mile, it reaches Canyon Road, which heads south 4.6 miles to Los Banos Creek Reservoir.

This Central Valley recreation area includes three artificial lake bodies: San Luis Reservoir (the main one), O'Neill Forebay, and Los Banos Creek Reservoir, providing ample opportunity for boating, sailing, windsurfing, fishing, and swimming. Waterskiers can enjoy their sport at San Luis Reservoir and O'Neill Forebay. In-season waterfowl hunting is allowed in the lake wildlife areas. Multiple day-use areas are found along the shores. O'Neill contains the most developed picnic areas with lawn, shade trees, and gravelly sand beaches.

Located in the eastern foothills of the Diablo Mountain Range, San Luis Reservoir is enfolded by rounded hills of golden grass. The largest of the three water bodies, it covers 14,000 acres, with an almost treeless 65-mile shore. A basalt dam holds back this storage water brought by aqueduct from the Sacramento–San Joaquin

Delta. When drawn down, a harsh ring separates the blue from the golden hillsides and islands and peninsulas appear.

O'Neill Forebay occupies the valley flat below the dam. It covers 2,000 acres, with a mostly open 14-mile shore; its storage waters are kept fairly constant. To the southeast, Los Banos Creek Reservoir is the most scenic of the three, filling a steep-sided canyon. This lake is long and narrow, with 12 miles of shore. Golden eagles sometimes pass over the canyon. Where dirt roads travel the area, be aware that they can be very muddy following a rain.

At the Romero Overlook Visitor Center, on the north shore of San Luis Reservoir, newcomers can pick up trip-planning information and learn about the water project.

## Attractions and Activities

**Path of the Padres.** This popular guided hike is offered only on weekends during March and April; advance reservations are required. Both a reservation fee and a tour fee are charged. The size of the group is limited to twenty. The hike covers some 5 miles, with a 700-foot elevation change.

The guided tour begins with a 30-minute barge trip that travels the length of Los Banos Creek Reservoir to its headwater canyon. The hike then follows Los Banos Creek upstream. Located in the canyon are the state's largest sycamore grove and a bounty of spring wildflowers. Tidytip, larkspur, California poppy, clarkia, mariposa lily, and more adorn grass, cliff, and riparian areas.

In 1805, the padres and soldiers from Mission San Juan Bautista crossed over the pass, rounding up the resident Yokut Indians to work on the mission lands. This trail retraces their route and visits the carved, waist-deep pools where the padres bathed. A steep hike to the top of a ridge caps the journey with a view of Los Banos Grande Valley.

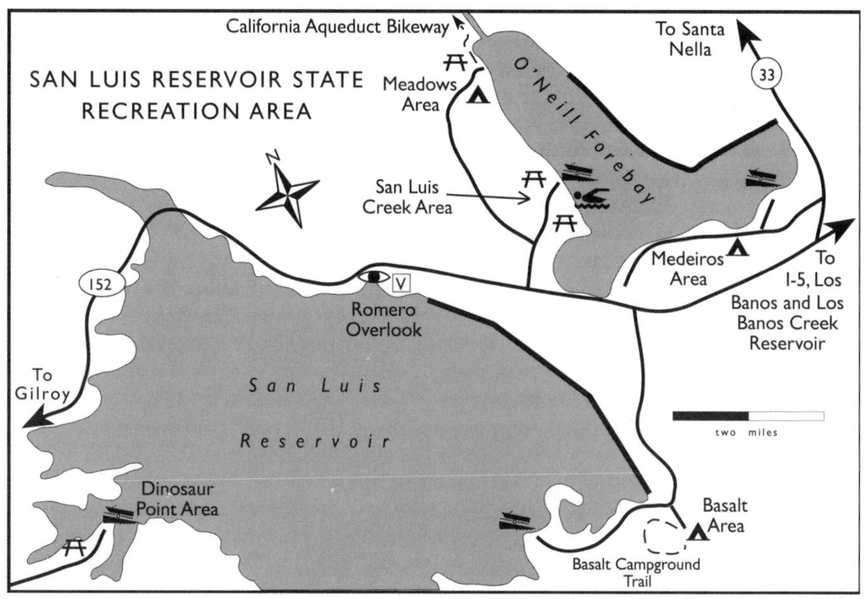

*Access:* The trip begins at the Los Banos boat launch.

**Basalt Campground Trail.** This 1.5-mile loop travels foot trail and service road, offering a hilltop vista.

The hike begins in a grassland peppered with out-of-place pines and eucalyptus. At 0.1 mile, continue straight; the path to the right leads to the entrance station. Rich knee-high grasses claim the area and drape into the trail. Early views of the main reservoir and dam hint at more to come. The trail crosses over a jeep road and under some wires as it heads straight toward a rounded hill. By 0.4 mile, it is contouring and climbing that hill.

At 0.7 mile, hikers reach a small saddle, offering views of the southwest side of San Luis Reservoir. The trail then bears left for a steep ascent to the summit (0.8 mile). Winds assault the post; the view sweeps the reservoir-forebay area, Basalt Hill, and the San Joaquin Valley. A sign identifies the vista landmarks. As hikers continue along the hilltop, they come out at a paved service road that descends through the open grassland, returning to the campground road at 1.5 miles.

*Access:* Find the trail across from the entry to Basalt Campground's north loop.

**Bicycling.** Cyclists can ride the 3-mile paved route atop the dam between Basalt Campground and Romero Point or access the California Aqueduct Bikeway. The paved bikeway follows the canal north some 70 miles to Bethany Reservoir; rest stops are spaced every 10 miles. When done, the bikeway will parallel all 400 miles of canal.

*Access:* For the California Aqueduct Bikeway, pass through the cycle access in the gate located at the end of the Meadows day-use area on O'Neill Forebay and go 0.2 mile on the graveled path following the water.

**Boating.** Boats are allowed on the waters between sunrise and sunset. The ramps for San Luis Reservoir are at the Basalt Area and Dinosaur Point. Boat access for O'Neill Forebay is at the San Luis Creek and Medeiros areas. For Los Banos Creek Reservoir, access is along the north shore.

On the open waters of the main reservoir and forebay, boaters should beware of the winds; they can rise suddenly and powerfully. Watch for the warning lights at Romero Overlook, Quien Sabe Point, the Basalt Area entrance, and Tunnel Island on San Luis Reservoir. The ones at O'Neill Forebay are placed above South Beach at San Luis Creek and at the Medeiros boat ramp. Flashing amber is a small craft warning. Flashing red means all boaters get off the water, as winds exceed 30 miles per hour.

On Los Banos Creek Reservoir, the boat speed limit is 5 miles per hour. While there are adequate winds for sailing, the canyon generally keeps them from reaching threatening speeds.

**Windsurfing.** All three lake bodies are open to windsurfing. The prevailing winds are typically out of the northwest or west.

Much of O'Neill Forebay is suitable for the novice, as well as the more experienced windsurfer, but the southwest corner is for advanced to expert riders only. Due to the wind, launching from the developed west shore is not recommended. Wetsuits should at least cover the torso and thighs to prevent hypothermia; at times, a full wetsuit may be required.

Generally speaking, San Luis Reservoir is an arena for the experienced windsurfer. When the winds exceed 30 miles per hour, only advanced windsurfers, dressed in full wetsuits with safety equipment and teamed with a buddy, are allowed on the water. The launch is at Basalt Bay, at the southeast corner of the lake.

At Los Banos Reservoir, windsurfers should exercise their own best judgment and not go out in conditions that exceed their abilities. For a 24-hour wind and weather report for these waters, phone (209) 826-9019.

**Fishing.** Boat and shore fishing are popular at all three lakes. Striped bass, catfish, crappie, and blue gill carried by canals from the Delta populate the storage waters of the forebay and main reservoir. Los Banos Creek Reservoir is stocked with rainbow trout (during fall and winter), black bass, catfish, crappie, and blue gill. Fishing is good February through August, with spring being best; all-night shore fishing is allowed.

## Henry Cowell Redwoods State Park

**Hours/Season:** Year-round; campground: subject to periodic *winter* closures; 6:00 A.M. to sunset (Fall Creek Unit)
**Facilities:** 112 developed and mostly wooded campsites, riverside picnic areas, nature center, environmental studies center, gift shop, historic sites, hiker and horse trails, mountain-bike routes, restrooms, pay showers
**For Information:** (408) 335-4598
**Access:** From central Felton, *for day use,* go 0.6 mile south on CA 9; *for the campground,* go 2.6 miles southeast on Graham Hill Road; and *for Fall Creek Unit,* go 0.7 mile west on Felton-Empire Road to reach its small parking lot.

This Santa Cruz Mountains park boasts a premier grove of ancient coastal redwoods, diverse forests and woodlands, an open meadow, and chap-

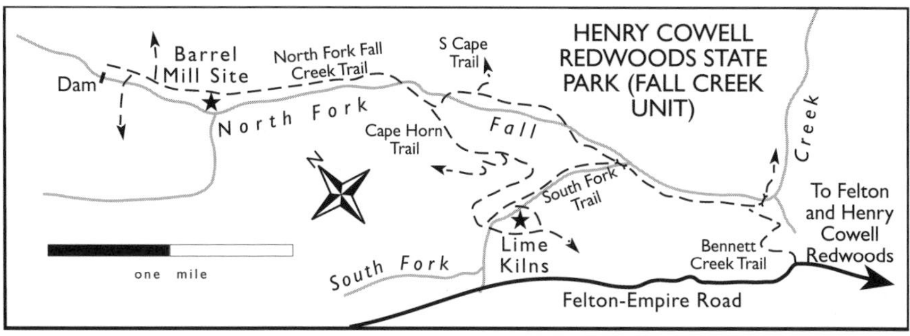


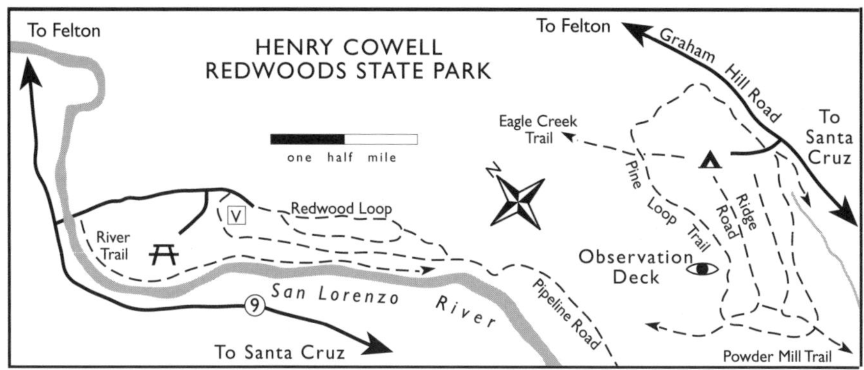

arral. The San Lorenzo River flows through it. In summer, the river is creeklike, placid, and shallow, a place where children can wade. In winter, it transforms into a fast-flowing water, hosting salmon and steelhead runs. Only then, on certain dates, is it open for fishing. Paralleling the river are the park's River Trail and Pipeline Road, a paved service road ideal for walking and jogging.

Other popular park activities are hiking, horseback riding, mountain biking, and picnicking. Across from the nature center, a private tourist train has its ticket office and station; the whistle of Steam Engine #2 calls park guests to its doors. The tour passes through forest next to the park.

Fall Creek Unit extends the park offering with a fine wooded area, drained by the forks of Fall Creek. It is open to hiking and horseback riding, but dogs and bikes are not allowed. Fern- and moss-reclaimed lime kilns and sawmill ruins record earlier times here.

## Attractions and Activities

**Redwood Loop.** This 0.8-mile all-ability loop features the park's oldest redwoods, with trees named for presidents and generals. Two presidents, Benjamin Harrison and Theodore Roosevelt, visited this grove in 1891 and 1903, respectively. Legend has it that in 1846, the hollow base of one served Lieutenant John C. Fremont as an overnight shelter. The loop features several trees that top 200 feet; the tallest one shoots up 285 feet even after having lost its 75-foot crown in a windstorm. Fire-charred and hollowed trees, snags, logs, tanoak, laurel, and hazel complete the first-rate grove. A self-guided brochure is available; log benches dot the way.

*Access:* Begin near the nature center.

**Pine Loop Trail.** Encircling the campground, this 2.5-mile hiker-horse trail visits an observation deck and an odd assemblage of trees within a small geographic area. Most junctions are marked.

A clockwise tour begins on the south side of the park road, passing below ponderosa pines, a rarity for this low elevation near the coast. Before long, areas of redwood, Douglas fir, oak, and tanoak claim the route. At 0.7 mile, it crosses over the Powder Mill Trail, entering an oak-madrone complex, which, in turn, is replaced by some unusually tall knobcone pines above a chaparral floor.

Where the trail meets Ridge Road, go left for the observation deck (1 mile). This concrete platform, one story up, overlooks the park treetops and offers glimpses at the neighboring ridges and Monterey Peninsula. Drinking fountains for both horse and human can be found at the site.

Continue the Pine Loop Trail. Past a campground spur at 1.3 miles, the route descends through areas of chinquapin, knobcone pine, chaparral, and oak. At 2 miles, go right, bypassing the Eagle Creek Trail. In a quarter mile, another spur branches right to the campground. As the Pine Trail approaches the boundary, classic sprawled oaks claim the way. The tour ends by traveling a woodland beside Graham Hill Road.

*Access:* Begin near the campground kiosk.

**Fall Creek Hike.** This 6.8-mile round-trip hike tours the riparian corridors of North and South Fork Fall Creek, visiting a mill ruin and lime kilns.

The hike begins touring the shrub-fir complex of the Bennett Creek Trail, switchbacking to the junction with the North Fork Fall Creek Trail at 0.2 mile. The bridge over the creek leads to the horse route; hikers stay left for an upstream tour on the foot trail.

Fall Creek is a pretty, clear-flowing stream, spilling over sand and cobbles. Its steep-sided evergreen-deciduous drainage is eye-catching, especially when the leaves are new or changing color. Where the trail forks at 0.5 mile, take either course since they do merge again.

Where the trail crosses the South Fork bridge at 0.9 mile, bear right, continuing the North Fork tour. Oxalis and sugarscoop shower the sides of the trail, which is now much narrower. Ahead is the first of several log crossings; be sure to use extra care when they are wet. Tanoak, redwood, maple, and fir continue to crowd the drainage.

After bypassing the S Cape Trail on the right, the trail crosses the creek and comes to the Cape Horn Trail junction (1.6 miles). This is a loop junction. Hikers may go left here for a 3.6-mile round-trip hike. (Go right to visit the mill ruins and end the North Fork tour.)

Staying on the North Fork Trail, hikers quickly angle right for a side-by-side log crossing of the creek. A dark, deep redwood forest enfolds the way. At 2.4 miles, on a flat above the creek, visitors can see the rusting ruins of Barrel Mill; a sign marks the site. Upstream from here, the canyon becomes more squeezed, and hikers must duck under tumbled redwoods overlaying the path. Bypassing the fragments of the Big Ben Trail, which angles across the North Fork Trail, hikers reach a remnant flume and tiny dam at 3.2 miles, the trail's end.

Returning to the 1.6-mile junction at 4.8 miles, follow the dirt road of Cape Horn Trail downstream, above the creek toward the kilns. The steadily climbing road quickly puts distance between hiker and creek. Bypassing the Lost Empire Trail at 5 miles, it soon rounds into the South Fork drainage for a descent.

At 5.5 miles, hikers leave the road, following the South Fork Trail through the kiln area. While the road rounds above the kilns, overlooking their thick-walled shells and low-arched openings, the trail offers hikers a view of the picturesque kiln fronts, reclaimed by moss and fern.

Following the South Fork downstream, hikers bypass the site of the cooper's house and rock piles topped by ferns and fall leaves. The trail next passes through a man-made canyon to follow the rock-studded creek shore for a fast-dropping descent to the North Fork Trail at 5.9 miles. Go right, retracing the first 0.9 mile.

*Access:* Begin at the Fall Creek parking area off Felton-Empire Road.

## WILDER RANCH STATE PARK

**Hours/Season:** 8:00 A.M. to sunset; 10:00 A.M. to 4:00 P.M. Wednesday through Sunday (visitor center)

**Facilities:** Picnic areas; visitor center / bookstore; historic ranch buildings; hiker, horse, and mountain-bike trails; nonflush toilets; water (at entrance only)

**For Information:** (408) 426-0505

**Access:** Leaving Santa Cruz city limits, go 2 miles north on CA 1.

Straddling CA 1, this 3,900-acre park offers recreation amid a back-country of rounded grassland ridges, mixed woodlands, and dark, moist drainages of second-growth redwood and laurel. On its seaward side, visitors find a Mexican-era adobe and historic dairy ranch dating back to the late nineteenth century. Wilder Ranch boasts a spectacular coastline with vertical mudstone cliffs, sea stacks, crashing waves, and remote beaches. Across its bluff plateau is cropland, leased to private farmers. These lands account for 12 percent of the nation's Brussels sprout production.

Wilder Ranch is a premier mountain-biking park, perhaps the best in the state system. The gently rounded ridges and canyons are well-suited for the sport. With mountain bikes allowed on all routes—dirt ranch roads and foot trails—riders find a uniquely open arena to explore. Off-trail riding is prohibited. As signs are few, map and compass are needed to navigate the park's dizzying web of routes. Even then, riders can find themselves on an unintended trail.

These routes also serve hikers and horseback riders, but only the inland ones are open to horses. Picnicking, photography, and wildlife observation are other pursuits, with surfers taking to the water at Four Mile Beach, reached by going 2 miles north on CA 1 from the entrance.

## Attractions and Activities

**Cultural Preserve Self-guided Walking Tour.** At Wilder Ranch, visitors have an opportunity to tour a late-nineteenth-century dairy operation. The lower story of the attractive Victorian ranch house has been restored and furnished with period pieces; it may be viewed on weekend guided tours. Established trees and gardens add to the grounds. Goats, horses, geese, chickens, and Guinea fowl enliven the ranch.

When docent-led tours are not available, a brochure guides visitors through the neatly kept ranch buildings, describing their use and historical significance. The structures are all big and functional, with modest fine touches, such as the archways in the horse stalls. In the cow barn, visitors can see old buggies and wagons; in the garage are two vintage automobiles: a 1930 Model A Ford and a 1916 Dodge Touring Car. Granaries, corn cribs, and equipment sheds are among the other structures. A farm house, which predates the Victorian home, and an 1839 adobe complete the central ranch. On the other side of CA 1, visitors view the corral where weekend rodeos were held.

*Mountain biker, Wilder Ranch State Park*

*Access:* From the parking area, take the 0.2-mile paved route indicated for the cultural preserve.

**Old Landing Cove Trail.** This 3.6-mile round-trip trail tours north along the edge of the park bluff, showcasing the 50-foot cliffs and wave-sculpted shore. A fine brochure introduces the natural history.

Crossing over a railroad track, the trail tours the coastal plateau and skirts the edge of a cultivated field to reach the bluff. At 0.5 mile, it overlooks the estuarine wetland of Wilder Creek. At 0.7 mile, it is above Wilder Beach Natural Preserve, where snowy plovers nest; the beach is closed to the public.

The trail then curves north, touring the bluff edge and overlooking the aquamarine water. Along the way, travelers overlook the cliff nesting sites of pigeon guillemots and cormorants.

At 1.1 miles, travelers view a long, flat sea bridge, a park trademark. Cormorants and gulls roost on a nearby rock; a sea stack can be seen to the north. At 1.3 miles, a side trail descends to the beach at Old Landing Cove. There, visitors discover a fern grotto in the north wall. The dripping hollow secludes chain and deer fern with accents of monkey-flower. Swallows nest beneath the overhang. In the late 1800s, schooners anchored in this protected cove while taking on loads of lumber and lime for West Coast markets.

Continuing north along the bluff, hikers find a vista looking down and across a thin channel at a flat rock claimed by harbor seals. Binoculars bring the scene to life; sometimes as many as 100 seals occupy the rock. At 1.5 miles a coastal point affords a second look at the seal haul-out, and at 1.8 miles, steep, slippery paths descend to Sand Plant Beach, an isolated sandy curvature.

Return as you came or continue north, touring the Ohlone Bluff Trail to Four Mile Beach at the park's north end (another 3.6 miles). The route continues showcasing the spectacular coastline; sea otters and brown pelicans are passersby. At the deep drainages, the trail detours inland, traveling along the railroad track or following farm roads. It passes Strawberry and Three Mile beaches before ending at Four Mile Beach.

*Access:* From the parking area, take the trail near the display board.

**Wilder Overlook Tour.** This 4.5-mile round-trip trail has a 500-foot elevation change. Its destination provides the best vista in the park, with open views of the Wilder Ranch hillsides, the historic area below, and Monterey Bay.

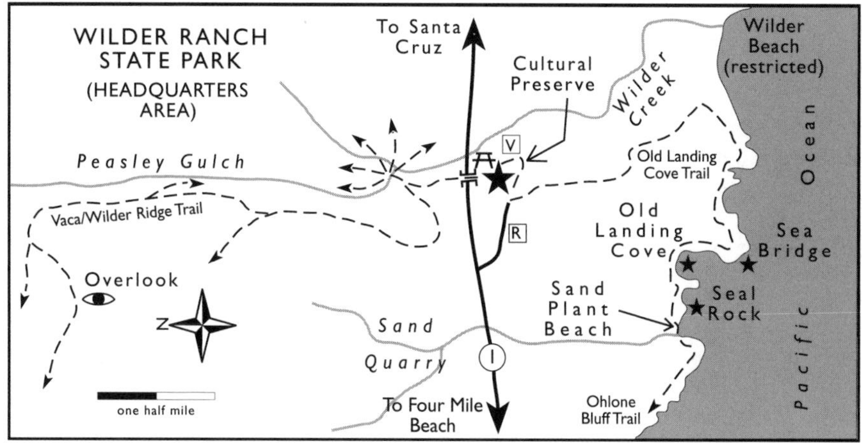

After taking the route to the Cultural Preserve, continue on the gravel road passing through the historic ranch to the CA 1 underpass at 0.3 mile. From the tunnel, continue on the ranch road past the corral to the trail junction at 0.5 mile. There, take the Vaca / Wilder Ridge Trail, hooking back to the left for a steady climb.

This ranch road passes through grassland and above a cultivated field. Noise intrudes where it briefly tours above a sand-and-gravel operation. Overlooks are of Wilder Ranch, the coastal plateau, and the park shoreline. Ahead, it offers views of Wilder Ridge. At just over a mile, on the left, ducks and coots ply a rush-rimmed stock pond.

At 1.2 miles, the road approaches Peasley Gulch; its green-filled drainage contrasts the golden hillsides. Patches of thistle intersperse the sometimes shoulder-tall grasses. In places, the drainage trees are close enough to offer shade. As the route continues to climb, side routes branch from it; keep to the main ranch road.

Rounding onto the ridge, at 2.2 miles hikers find the 100-foot detour left to Wilder Overlook. The site is just an open, dirt flat at the edge of the ridge, offering a sweeping view down the grassland flanks and across the bluff to the ocean. Looks south stretch to the Monterey Peninsula. Far below is Wilder Beach. Return as you came.

*Access:* Take the paved route to the Cultural Preserve.

## Natural Bridges, Lighthouse Field, and Twin Lakes State Beaches

**Hours/Season:** 8:00 A.M. to sunset (Natural Bridges); 7:00 A.M. to 10:00 P.M. (Lighthouse Field); daylight hours (Twin Lakes)

**Facilities:** Picnic areas and restrooms (all), visitor center, nature trails, outdoor shower (Natural Bridges); footpaths (Lighthouse Field); volleyball courts (Twin Lakes)

**For Information:** (408) 429-2850 (Natural Bridges and Twin Lakes); City of Santa Cruz, (408) 429-3777 (Lighthouse Field)

**Access:** In the city of Santa Cruz, find these beaches off West Cliff and East Cliff drives.

Different offerings are found at each of these beach parks looking out at Monterey Bay.

Natural Bridges State Beach receives its name from a nearby scenic, eroded-rock feature but is perhaps best known for its wintering monarch butterflies. The landmark natural bridge can be admired from the bluff parking lot that overlooks it or from the attractive, deep-crescent beach—0.2 mile long and equally wide, well-used by sunbathers, swimmers, and surfers. Where the shoreline is rocky, tidepools await. Set back from the beach is a large picnic area shaded by eucalyptus and Monterey pine. A few tables line a small riparian corridor. The visitor center has regular hours during butterfly season (October through February); otherwise it is open weekends.

Found along a 0.5-mile stretch of West Cliff Drive, Lighthouse Field is not a beach at all, but a city open space creating a buffer between the coastal bluffs and a residential area. It takes its name from the picturesque red-brick lighthouse across the street, where the Santa Cruz Surfing Museum is located. Offshore is "Steamer Lane," acclaimed for its gigantic breakers, stirring both surfer and wave-watcher. Loud barks announce a sea lion colony on the nearby rocks. Shapely cypress accent

the grassland field, and there are paths for strolling or exercising the dog. The sound of surf and the taste of the sea breeze carry to the site.

Twin Lakes State Beach is a bustling, urban beach comprised of two 0.5-mile-long, broad sandy strands on either side of Santa Cruz Harbor, a jetty-lined, small-craft harbor. Bluffs line much of Seabright Cove (the western strand), with cave-hollowed Lorenzo Point forming its western terminus. At the park's eastern terminus is a 30-foot sandstone cliff, showing shell fossils. Views from both beach areas are of Monterey Peninsula and the municipal pier.

At the park, fishermen cast from the jetty, as sea kayakers emerge from the harbor. Sharing the waves are riders of surfboards, outrigger canoes, and catamarans. On the beach, a heated volleyball match often takes place. At the nearby marina are shops and eateries. By midday, streetside parking is hard to find.

### Attractions and Activities

**Monarch Butterflies.** Each October through February, the monarch butterflies return to and winter at the inland eucalyptus groves at Natural Bridges State Park. An all-ability boardwalk leads to the trees where the monarchs gather. Next to the visitor center is a milkweed garden. The monarch caterpillars feed on this toxic weed, receiving a lifetime of protection from predation. Mimic species—painted ladies and red admirals—benefit indirectly from this protection. They, too, can be seen at the park.

**Schwan Lagoon.** Part of Twin Lakes State Beach, this bulrush-ringed lagoon hosts small sailboats and invites birdwatching, although domestic birds generally outnumber wild ones.

## SANTA CRUZ MISSION STATE HISTORIC PARK

**Hours/Season:** 10:00 A.M. to 4:00 P.M. Thursday through Sunday
**Facilities:** Picnic tables, visitor center, historic building, nonflush toilet, *bring water*
**For Information:** (408) 425-5849
**Access:** In Santa Cruz, the park is on School Street between Emmet and Adobe.

This park features the lone remaining original building from Mission Santa Cruz. The restored adobe contains seven complete rooms and a partial ruin, with a veranda running the length of the building. The original edifice had seventeen side-by-side rooms. It was built by Ohlone and Yokut Indian workers between 1822 and 1824 and served as the residence for Native Americans who converted to Catholicism. After the secularization of the mission, the adobe housed Californios and Irish-American immigrants. It was continuously occupied for an amazing 159 years, before becoming part of the California state park system.

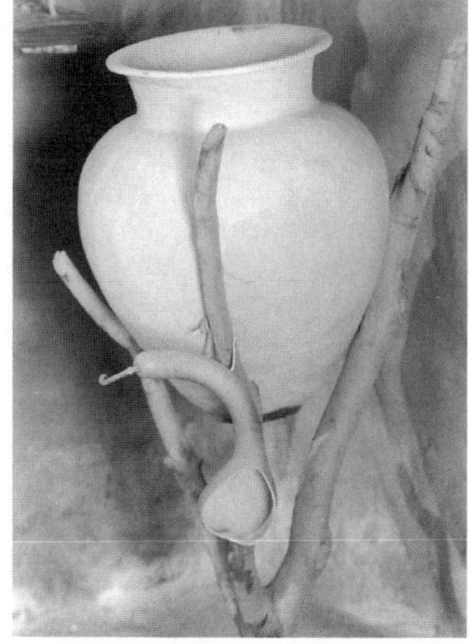

*Jug, Santa Cruz Mission State Historic Park*

The adobe can be seen by self-guided or docent-led tour. At the orientation room, visitors may request to see a video on the restoration process or one on Native Americans.

### Attractions and Activities

**The Mission Adobe Tour.** Touring the various rooms, visitors can witness both the original adobe construction—thick walls, dirt floors, rawhide-lashed beams—and the later modifications—wooden floors, glass windows, finished ceilings. The furnishings reflect how the various inhabitants lived during different time periods. At each entry is a listing of the families who occupied the room and when.

Lights in one dark, smoke-stained chamber reveal an area of counting marks and places where the Indians' fingerprints were preserved in the plaster they applied to the adobe. In another, where a family of six Indians lived, a recording tells the story of a Yokut Indian family. Not far away, by contrast, is a room reflecting the fineries and contemporary touches enjoyed by wealthy merchant Felipe Armas.

Behind the adobe is a lawn area with trees planted by the various residents. The stone water filter on display makes for interesting viewing.

## NEW BRIGHTON AND SEACLIFF STATE BEACHES

**Hours/Season:** Year-round (New Brighton); 8:00 A.M. to 10:00 P.M. (Seacliff)

**Facilities:** 112 developed tree-shaded campsites, picnic area, beach-access trail, restrooms, indoor and outdoor showers, dump station (New Brighton); 26 RV sites with hookups, picnic area, interpretive center (open summers), food concession, pier, pedestrian walkway, restrooms, indoor and outdoor showers (Seacliff)

**For Information:** (408) 475-4850 (New Brighton); (408) 688-3222 (Seacliff)

**Access:** From CA 1 at Capitola, *to enter New Brighton State Beach,* take the Park Avenue exit, go south 0.1 mile, and turn left; in another 0.1 mile, turn right; *for Seacliff State Beach,* go south on CA 1, take the Seacliff Beach/Aptos exit, and head south 0.4 mile.

These two state beaches look out at Soquel Cove and Monterey Bay. Both offer long, beautiful strands of soft, clean sand for strolling and relaxing. The predictable waves along this shoreline make it nice for swimmers; surfers gather farther out. At Seacliff, the walkway and beach draw an equal following of joggers.

New Brighton is a tiered park, with just over a half mile of beachfront. Its scenic, cypress- and pine-forested campground and picnic area occupy a tall-grass coastal terrace. A 0.2-mile access trail, consisting of stairs and a developed path, connects the campground and beach; beware of the poison oak pushing toward the path.

At the park's west end is the day-use parking area for China Cove, reached by driving under the train trestle. Its name traces back to the 1870s, when Chinese fishermen occupied this beach, setting up villages of driftwood lodges, launching their boats, and drying their catches for sale. Today, surf fishermen continue the legacy.

Although New Brighton State Beach ends in a half mile, hikers can extend the tour east, staying on public beach below the high-tide line. Beyond the park, private residences line the blufftop. Views are of Monterey Peninsula and the Seacliff pier.

To the east, Seacliff Beach is a linear park nearly a mile in length, sliced by Aptos Creek at its eastern end. At the western end of the beach-level parking is the en route RV campground. Relative to other state parks, it is a pricy overnight stay, but it is close to the beach for moonlit walks. Strung along the length of the beach are picnic sites, both open and covered.

The park includes additional day-use parking on a bluff flat above the west end of the beach. An attractive multi-landing stairway ties it to the shore facilities. It is lit for the evening return to the vehicle.

The far east section of Seacliff State Beach, posted as Rio Del Mar State Beach (reached through Aptos), is the only area where visitors may enjoy the beach with their dogs. The animals must be leashed at all times, and owners may not take them west of the Aptos Creek Pedestrian Walk Bridge. Nowhere are dogs allowed on New Brighton State Beach.

### Attractions and Activities

**Pier.** Central to Seacliff State Beach is its unusual pier, comprised of a traditional wooden plank fishing pier extended by a scuttled ship, the *Palo Alto—1919*. The far end of the ship is closed to the public; it has been set aside for the pelicans, cormorants, and gulls. Visitors can view the seabirds through the heavy grate divider. Out from the pier, loons and harbor seals attract attention.

Fishermen line the open ship and pier, casting for croaker, surfperch, flounder, and sole. Benches and fish-cleaning sinks aid their endeavors.

## MANRESA AND SUNSET STATE BEACHES

**Hours/Season:** Year-round

**Facilities:** 64 walk-in tent campsites, picnic sites, beach-access trails, restrooms, indoor and outdoor showers (Manresa); 90 developed campsites, hike/bike camp, picnic sites, beach-access trails, model glider port, restrooms, indoor and outdoor showers (Sunset)

**For Information:** (408)761-1795 (Manresa) or (408) 763-7062 (Sunset)

**Access:** From CA 1 south of Aptos, take the Sunset and Manresa beaches/Larkin Valley Road exit, and go south on San Andreas Road. The units are reached along or just off San Andreas, taking Sand Dollar, Sunset Beach, and Beach roads.

Despite their location between the Santa Cruz and Monterey population centers, these two beach parks looking out on central Monterey Bay have a nice, out-of-the-way feeling about them. Tall bluffs, alternately eroded and vegetated, back the canted, soft sand beach at Manresa. At Sunset State Beach, vegetated dune hills overlook the mildly sloped, clean coastal strand. Manresa comprises some 2 miles of beachfront; Sunset includes 3 miles. Agricultural fields make up much of the neighborhood.

Manresa State Beach offers a fine getaway. Here, the surf is more ragged and pronounced. While beautiful to watch, it is not recommended for casual swimmers. Signs warn of rip currents and deep holes. Surfers and surf fishermen, however, find these waters suited to their needs. The sands, scoured by the ocean, are fine for sunning, but the slope threatens the ankles of would-be joggers. Marbled godwits and willets share the beach.

At the Manresa Uplands Campground, tenters find a first-rate coastal grassland. While presently lacking in shade, planted native trees promise a future reprieve from the sun. In spring, the grassland explodes with color. California poppy, lupine, dandelion, and thistle add to the show.

At the main area of Sunset State Beach, the two day-use areas are bookends to the campground, which is set back from the coast. Steep beach-access trails mount and descend the stabilized dunes, connecting the pine-shaded campground areas to shore. The southern day-use area offers easy beach access. Atop the dunes, sunset watchers find choice seats for viewing the orange-hued sky. Lucky viewers may spy dolphins riding the waves.

Sunset Beach serves a wider range of pursuits, with boogie-boarding, fishing for surfperch, kite flying, sunning, swimming, and waveplay. The waves roll to shore in a rhythmic pattern, and the beach welcomes strollers and joggers.

Coastal scrub, wild cucumber, and fern vegetate the dunes. From March 15 through August 15, beachgoers should avoid the flat area between the high-tide line and the base of the frontal dunes, as this is where the rare snowy plover chooses to nest.

South of the main area lies the Palm Beach Unit of Sunset Beach. This day-use area features a dozen picnic sites cradled in a eucalyptus bowl and open beach for family fun.

### Attractions and Activities

**Model Glider Flying.** Enthusiasts of radio-controlled model gliders make use of a place atop the dunes at Sunset Beach. The port has a landing area, picnic table, and bench. The site presents a first-rate coastal view, overlooking Monterey Bay, the Peninsula, and the coastline sweeping north to Santa Cruz.

*Access:* Take the trail topping the dunes opposite South Camp at Sunset State Beach.

## ZMUDOWSKI, MOSS LANDING, AND SALINAS RIVER STATE BEACHES

**Hours/Season:** Daylight hours
**Facilities:** Beach-access trails, nonflush toilets (all); en route camping, picnic sites (Moss Landing); hiker and horse trail (Salinas River)
**For Information:** (408) 384-7695
**Access:** From CA 1 at Moss Landing, exit at Struve Road (then take Giberson Road) for Zmudowski Beach, at Jetty Road for Moss Landing, and at Potrero or Molera road for Salinas River Beach.

Between the Pajaro and Salinas rivers, these three state parks line up along Monterey Bay for about 4 miles of beachfront. They offer visitors a wild, wind-buffeted coastal experience. Dunes back the beaches; agricultural lands, sloughs, and estuaries border the parks. These parks boast the most unspoiled dunes on the central California coast. Efforts are ongoing to keep the sands free of exotic vegetation. Along the harbor at Moss Landing, visitors can sit and watch the sea lions laze on an isolated tongue of sand. Pelicans are often seen in their midst, while sea otters commonly paddle in the harbor calm or ride the untamed ocean waves.

These parks offer surfing, windsurfing, clamming, fishing, horseback riding, and hiking opportunities, but the rough coastal waters prove dangerous to swimmers and waders. Horseback riders can tour all three beaches, as well as a designated horse trail through the dunes at Salinas River State Beach, but they must clean up after their animals. Seasonal closures of the beaches may occur to protect the snowy plover, which nests along the beach at the base of the foredunes.

### Attractions and Activities

**Dune Trail.** This 2-mile, round-trip hiker-horse trail links the two beach accesses at Salinas River; riders must travel single file. Posts mark the route along the back edge of the dune. As no formal trails cross to the ocean, respect the dune's integrity and keep to the trail.

Sand verbena, lizardtail, beach sagewort, California poppy, lupine, and Indian paintbrush are among the natural dune vegetation. Most of the views look east over a marshy wetland and agricultural fields. Terns sweep the channel waters; hawks patrol the cropland. At times, the sinking-sand trail tops a rise affording looks over the glistening ocean. The sound of the surf is a pleasing constant. At 1 mile, round-trip travelers have the option of retracing the dune trail or returning via the beach.

*Access:* Begin at the Potrero or Molera trailhead; equestrians find better parking for trailers at Molera.

## San Juan Bautista State Historic Park

**Hours/Season:** 10:00 A.M. to 4:30 P.M., except major holidays
**Facilities:** Picnic tables, historic buildings, restrooms
**For Information:** (408) 623-4881
**Access:** Find the park in the town of San Juan Bautista, off Second Street.

The historic district of the park remains a compact, distinct island in the sea of contemporary shops and businesses of San Juan Bautista. Radiating out from the plaza's open grass square are the historic 1797 Mission San Juan Bautista, owned and still used by the Catholic Church, and the crisply painted, adobe and wood-frame structures of the park, recording the Mexican and American periods. Here, visitors can learn about the bustling days of the 1860s and early 1870s, when San Juan Bautista was a trade and transportation center, and they can learn what became of the Breen family—survivors of the 1846 Donner Party ordeal.

A visit begins at the two-story Plaza Hotel, on the corner of Second and Mariposa streets. There, entrance fees are collected and brochures are available.

### Attractions and Activities

**Historic Area Self-guided Tour.** Representatively restored rooms can be seen at the Plaza Hotel, the Castro-Breen House, and Plaza Hall. Viewing is from behind a cord or through glass; coded photos locate items of interest. Plaques and the tour brochure describe the structures, introduce their former owners, and point out colorful facts.

In the hotel, visitors find a museum in the works and the restored hotel dining room, adjoining barroom, and upstairs parlor, all with detailed furnishing. The lower story originally housed the soldiers who guarded the mission.

Next door is the Castro-Breen Adobe. Exhibits tell the story of the Breen family, their remarkable journey west, and their rise in status, following young John's success in the gold camps. Among the furnishings are memorial hair wreaths, whale-oil lamps, Judge James Breen's desk, and the tiny, brutally fitted shoes of the women. General José Castro's office features an imposing Spanish-style wooden desk beneath a Mexican flag.

The two-story, cream-colored Plaza Hall features the restored living quarters of a leading citizen. The first story was built with adobe bricks salvaged from the Indian women's dormitory at the mission. Restored are the bedrooms, children's room, parlor, kitchen, and dining room. In the parlor, live birds occupy an antique cage.

Passing through the double-wide doors of the Plaza stable, visitors find finely painted stages, a fringe-topped surrey, an Amish buggy, and a beer wagon. Harnesses and tack dress the walls. Out back is the smithy, with wheelwright tools, forge, and bellows.

While not part of the state park, the historic Mission does open its doors to park visitors; a small donation is requested.

# MARINA STATE BEACH

**Hours/Season:** 8:00 A.M. to a half hour after sunset
**Facilities:** Picnic sites, hang glider station, hiker trail, restrooms
**For Information:** (408) 384-7695
**Access:** From CA 1 at Marina, exit at Reservation Road and go west; the road ends at the beach.

Picnic tables line the edge of the parking area overlooking this steeply canted, coarse sand beach met by unpredictable waves. Dunes back the beach, affording nature study, and the westward-looking park offers fine sunset viewing. While swimming is unsafe, fishing is popular. But what sets apart this Monterey Bay beach is its hang-glider station.

## Attractions and Activities

**Dune Nature Trail.** This 0.3-mile self-guided nature trail provides an unrivaled introduction to the rare and common plant species of the dunes. Boardwalks make up most of the trail, with sand ladders and stairs bridging boardwalk segments; the initial portion is wheelchair accessible. The plaques and example species pair up without confusion. Travelers learn not only each plant name but when it blooms. Lizardtail, beach sagewort, sea pinks, and more embroider the sands.

At 0.2 mile, benches look out at Monterey Peninsula. At 0.3 mile, where the trail curves next to the beach, travelers have the option of returning via the beach or retracing the boardwalk trail. As this is a snowy plover nesting habitat, avoid tracking the frontal dunes and upland beach from March through mid-August.

*Access:* The trail begins at the southeast corner of the parking lot, across from the restroom.

**Hang Gliding.** The park's favorable conditions for hang gliding draw both enthusiasts and spectators. Atop the dune at the northwest corner of the parking area is a sloped takeoff platform. Its lip directs the wind under the glider's wing. At the hang-glider store, souvenirs may be purchased and information on the sport exchanged.

# Fremont Peak State Park

**Hours/Season:** Year-round

**Facilities:** 25 primitive wooded campsites, picnic area, telescope, historical monuments, hiker trails, nonflush toilets, water

**For Information:** (408) 623-4255

**Access:** From CA 156 at San Juan Bautista, turn south at the sign for the park, go 0.4 mile, and bear left on San Juan Canyon Road. Stay on this road for 9.7 miles to reach the park.

The Spanish called this prominent Coast Range peak above San Juan Bautista "Gabilan," meaning hawk, but an event in 1846 caused it to be known forever after as Fremont Peak. It was here that an American flag was first raised over Mexican-held California.

Defying General José Castro's order to vacate Mexico's Alta California, Captain John C. Fremont led an Army survey party to this peak, built a log fort, and raised a modified version of the United States Army Corps of Engineers flag. A Mexican-American standoff followed. After the pole flying the American flag blew down, Fremont took it as a bad omen and complied with Castro's order. While the standoff lasted only 3 days, it set the stage for events to come in California.

Besides its place in history, Fremont Peak is rich in natural beauty. Magnificent stands of live, valley, and black oaks, along with Coulter pines, grace the picnic areas and campground. Claiming the upper reaches of the park are scrub oak, coyote bush, toyon, and manzanita. The drier, southern-exposed hillsides wear a grassy mantle, green in spring and golden the rest of the year. Wildflowers sprinkle the sides of the park's 4 miles of trail. As poison oak finds a niche almost everywhere, be careful in your travels.

## Attractions and Activities

**Fremont Peak Trail.** A 0.6-mile trail wraps its way to the summit of Fremont Peak, elevation 3,169 feet.

Following the gated, paved road next to a John C. Fremont historical monument, hikers go only a few feet before coming upon another one honoring the man. In less than 0.1 mile, take the old gravel road to the right; a sign indicates it as "trail." The paved route dead-ends at some broadcast towers.

Near a pair of wooden water tanks hikers find an overlook bench. It offers views of the immediate area and points north. Beyond it, a footpath leads the way. Lupine, Chinese houses, larkspur, California poppy, wallflower, and owl's clover color the open slope, hugged by only a few shrubs and oaks.

At 0.3 mile, rounding a rocky side of Fremont Peak, the route grows fuzzy. Keep a low, contouring course above the fence that now wraps around the slope; do not climb up the rocks. Beware the many thick pockets of poison oak along the way.

Views are to the west as hikers cross a grassy slope dotted by metamorphic rock outcrops. At the T junction at 0.4 mile, either fork works. The left fork climbs more directly; the right one angles up the slope. They meet on a flat saddle at 0.5 mile. A nearby bench allows visitors to survey the area to the south and west.

The climb to the summit begins rounding the right-hand side of the peak; the final few feet require a rock scramble. Once atop, visitors find a commemorative flagpole and marker, noting the first time an American flag flew over California.

Views include the flanks of Fremont Peak, the surrounding valley, Monterey Bay, and neighboring coastal mountains. On clear days, visitors can see the Sierra Nevada to the northeast. Return as you came.

*Access:* Begin at the scenic overlook parking area below the peak.

**Stargazing.** The uncommon clarity enjoyed at Fremont Peak invites astronomers. Housed in a simple structure on the mountain is a 30-inch Challenger telescope. An astronomy program is offered at the park, during which times the observatory is open to the public. Programs generally start at 8:00 P.M., beginning with a half-hour talk by a guest speaker and concluding with a look through the telescope. Visitors set up their private telescopes outside. All flashlights must have a red cover to preserve night vision. The evenings of the Perseid meteor showers in August are often a great time to travel up the mountain. For a program schedule or more information, phone the Fremont Peak Observatory Association, (408) 623-2465.

*Access:* The marked road to the observatory is on the left after you enter the park.

## MONTEREY AND ASILOMAR STATE BEACHES

**Hours/Season:** Daylight hours

**Facilities:** Nonflush toilets (Monterey Beach); conference center, hiker trails (Asilomar)

**For Information:** (408) 384-7695 (Monterey Beach); (408) 372-4076 (Asilomar)

**Access:** Reach *Monterey State Beach* off Sand Dunes Drive at the Monterey/Seaside city limit or along Del Monte Avenue in Monterey. In Pacific Grove, access *Asilomar State Beach* along Sunset Drive; the Asilomar Conference Center is on the east side of Sunset.

*Tidepool, Asilomar State Beach*

Visitors to this coastal area find entirely different offerings at these two state beaches.

Monterey State Beach is a long, sandy walking strand curving around a 2-mile stretch of Monterey Bay. It extends north from the municipal wharf to the Sand Dunes Drive access. Quiet waters lap the shore. Otters, surf scoters, and grebes float in the bay, while willets and godwits share the beach with joggers and sunbathers. Often, near the wharf, the barking of sea lions can be heard. On the dunes at the north end of the beach stands a wooden cross, recalling the one Father Crespi erected near here in 1769, when the Portola expedition entered Monterey Bay.

Low dunes and residences alternately back the beach. Save for an occasional piece of glass, this is an exceptionally clean, inviting urban beach. The number of visitors is controlled by the limited amount of parking. There is only street parking off Del Monte, and the parking area off Sand Dunes Drive is modest in size.

By contrast, Asilomar State Beach consists of a beautiful, ragged, wave-sculpted rock and cliff shore, marked by areas of rich tidepools, hideaway beaches, and high-shooting waves. Situated within the Pacific Grove Marine Refuge, all marine life, rocks, and shells are protected. Fishing, however, is allowed, as long as anglers possess a valid California state fishing license.

Opposite the state's Asilomar Conference Center, a broad, sandy beach adjoins Moss County Beach to the south. A rough, unpredictable surf makes this area unsuitable for swimming and wading, but a reliable, strong wind challenges the kite flier. A crosswalk links the beach and conference center grounds. Managed by the Pacific Grove–Asilomar Operating Corporation, the state conference center houses meeting and dining rooms, guest accommodations, and recreational facilities. For more information, phone (408) 372-8016.

At both the conference grounds and Asilomar State Beach, State Park rangers offer interpretive programs.

### Attractions and Activities

**Asilomar Dunes.** Sixty acres of white sand dunes border the west side of the Asilomar conference-center grounds. Completely restored to their native vegetation, they support both endangered plants and animals. A boardwalk traverses the dunes, allowing visitors a closer look at this sensitive habitat; keep to the boardwalk.

*Access:* Find the trail's start at the Asilomar conference center.

**Asilomar Coast Trail.** Overlooking this breathtaking coastline, a 1.2-mile trail journeys along the bluff at Asilomar State Beach. The route is open to hikers and joggers but closed to bikes; a separate paved bike path along the road offers cyclists a similar offering. From the foot trail, side trails detour to white, crystalline coves, tidepools, and a dramatic meeting of land and sea. Lupine, sea daisies, sand verbena, and beach sagewort frame the sides of the trail and its segments of boardwalk.

*Access:* Start opposite the Asilomar conference center or begin at the northern access, which is just south of the Sunset Drive–Jewell Avenue intersection (look for the entry in the low wooden fence).

## MONTEREY STATE HISTORIC PARK

**Hours/Season:** 10:00 A.M. to 5:00 P.M., except major holidays (Orientation Center); check there for a current listing of the days and times for the other sites and tours

**Facilities:** Orientation center, historic buildings, museums, restrooms

**For Information:** (408) 649-7118

**Access:** From CA 1 in Monterey, take the Pacific Grove/Del Monte Avenue exit and follow the signs toward Fisherman's Wharf. Sites are scattered throughout downtown; the Orientation Center is located in the Maritime Museum of Monterey, off Custom House Plaza.

Scattered amid contemporary Monterey are the restored and preserved nineteenth-century adobe structures recalling the Mexican era—a time when Monterey prospered as a center of shipping, enterprise, and government. Other sites record the change from Mexican to United States rule. At Custom House, the 1846 raising of the Stars and Stripes marked the outbreak of war, and in Colton Hall (city owned and operated), the delegates of the First Constitutional Convention laid the groundwork for California statehood. Home tours introduce some of the prominent citizens and reveal much about the life and times of early Monterey. The French Hotel pays tribute to its most famous boarder, Robert Louis Stevenson.

A visit begins at the Orientation Center, where a video tells the story of Old Monterey, the guided walking tours originate, and self-guided brochures to the historic district are available. The house tour tickets may be purchased here or at the individual sites: Casa Soberanes, Larkin House, the Cooper-Molera Complex, and Stevenson House. With the tour number limitations, visitors should sign up early. Special events sponsored by the Old Monterey Preservation Society turn back the clock.

## Attractions and Activities

**Path of History Walking Tour.** The park offers much to see with dozens of buildings and sites spread over several blocks of downtown Monterey. Among the highlights is California's First Theater, along Pacific Street. In the mid-1800s, this small adobe lodge and saloon hosted its first plays, produced, oddly enough, by some United States Army officers. The tradition of performance continued, and Friday and Saturday nights, this historic theater still presents the Troupers of the Gold Coast in nineteenth-century melodramas. Today, as in the past, the seat-cushion rentals remain a value.

Museum offerings are found at both the Monterey Custom House and Pacific House, located off Custom House Plaza. Started in the 1820s, Custom House is where the cargo duties were collected. Today, it has a room representing a typical ship's cargo. Amid the inventory are burlap bags stamped either grain or cacao, kegs of brandy and gin, bolts of fabric, fur pelts, storage chests, farm and work tools, cookware, and china—the necessities and refinements for frontier life. Pacific House has displays, exhibits, and artifacts devoted to early Monterey and to Native American history.

At the Stevenson House, visitors can view several items that belonged to R. L. Stevenson or his family back in Scotland. On the guided tour, you can learn about his controversial courtship of Fanny Osbourne and his life as a writer.

At the front of the Old Whaling Station, where Portuguese whalers boarded in the 1850s, a sidewalk of diamond-cut whalebone catches the eye.

While wandering between historic-district buildings or waiting for scheduled tours, visitors can relax amid the many historic gardens, enjoy the benches and tables at the open, tiered Custom House Plaza, and take advantage of the shops and eateries of present-day Monterey. Some historic adobes also house small shops; Casa Gutierrez features a Mexican restaurant.

# Carmel River State Beach—Point Lobos State Reserve

**Hours/Season:** 7:00 A.M. to 10:00 P.M. (Carmel River Beach); 9:00 A.M. to 5:00 P.M. (Point Lobos)

**Facilities:** Hiker trail, restrooms (Carmel River Beach); picnic sites, museum,

information station, diver's access ramp, hiker trails, restrooms (Point Lobos)
**For Information:** (408) 624-4909
**Access:** *Carmel River State Beach* is reached off Scenic Road or CA 1 at the south end of Carmel. *Point Lobos State Reserve* is west off CA 1, 2.5 miles south of Carmel. *Point Lobos State Reserve has no access for trailers, and dogs are not allowed.*

These adjacent park units are among the most highly photographed and painted in the state park system. Carmel River State Beach brings together a concave, mile-long curvature of beautiful white sand and the clear, blue-green deep of Carmel Bay. To its south, Point Lobos State Reserve captivates with its wild, ragged-cliff shore, its tranquil aquamarine coves, and the exciting clash of rock and surf. Point Lobos is also the finest site on the California coast for observing marine mammals and ocean birds. In 1960, its offshore waters became this country's first underwater marine reserve.

Carmel River, San Jose Creek, and a low coastal-scrub slope divide the mile-long beach. Most times, the river and creek are wadeable or dry, and a trail travels the slope, giving beachgoers access to the entire area. Off its south end is a dangerous surf zone and collapsing floor that can catch waders and swimmers unaware. While divers commonly enter the bay here, it is not recommended for novice swimmers. Overall, Carmel River State Beach is better suited for sunning, walking, and admiring. Where the Carmel River arrives, the bay lagoon and wetlands invite birdwatching.

*Granite Point, Point Lobos State Reserve*

While the bluffs of Point Lobos State Reserve make up the southern boundary of Carmel River State Beach, no access between the parks exists. To maintain the integrity of the reserve, the daily visitor numbers are strictly controlled and limited to 450 people. During peak times, new arrivals may need to wait for other visitors to leave before gaining entry.

Point Lobos State Reserve is a park to be seen from underwater, along the trail, and through binoculars. The rocks off Point Lobos (Sea Lion Point) support a colony of California sea lions. It is from these barking sea wolves that the reserve receives its name. Harbor seals and sea otters are commonplace in the park's marine reserve. The seal pups arrive in April and May, while the otters give birth mainly in winter and stay with their pups for up to eight months. January is traditionally the best month for whale viewing, with the south shore offering the best sighting opportunities.

Brandt's cormorants claim Bird Island, while pelagic cormorants prefer the cliffs. Guillemots, oystercatchers, and brown pelicans are also seen.

## Attractions and Activities

**Whalers Cabin Museum.** Few clues remain to the nineteenth-century enterprises that took place at Point Lobos; one is the 1850s-built Chinese fishing cabin that now serves as the park museum. Despite irregular hours, it is worth pursuing. Inside are some interesting discoveries and fun facts about the succession of Native Americans, Chinese, whalers and abalone divers, coal miners, and Hollywood film-

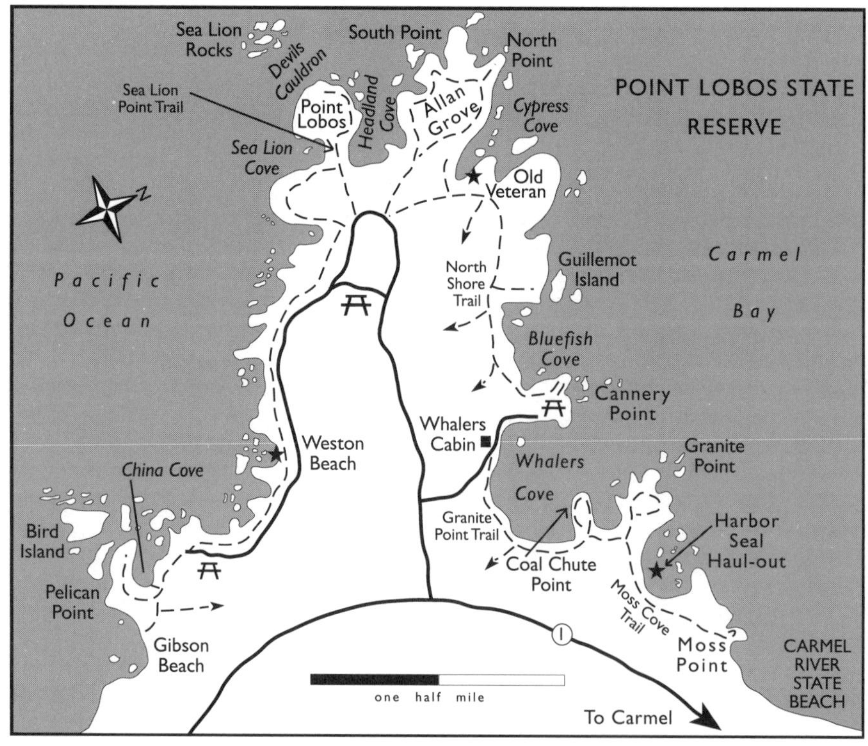

makers who have come to these shores. Out back are skeletal pieces from a whale. A brochure about the cabin and its collection adds to one's appreciation and understanding.

*Access:* Find the museum uphill from the Whalers Cove parking lot at Point Lobos State Reserve.

**Perimeter Trail.** With its side loops and spurs, this linear 6.5-mile hiker trail travels and probes the shoreline of Point Lobos State Reserve from its northern boundary overlooking Carmel River State Beach to its southernmost reaches at Bird Island. With seven convenient access points located along the park road, visitors can customize the length of their tours. The following are but three hiking options.

**Northern Perimeter Hike.** This 2-mile round-trip hike stitches together the Granite Point and Moss Cove trails for some spectacular coastal views of Point Lobos State Reserve and Carmel River State Beach.

It begins on a cordoned path rounding Whalers Cove, a beautiful, protected water, with Window Rock rising near shore. Buttercup, sea daisies, and wild geranium ornament the bluff grassland in April. Then, too, harbor seals and sea otters can be seen swimming with their pups in the incredibly clear water.

As the trail exits from a stand of Monterey pine, it forks. To the left, a small loop tours Coal Chute Point for additional Whalers Cove views. Beware of the poison oak here and elsewhere on the tour. From the loop junction, the trail resumes north, following the sculpted shore, passing through coastal scrub. At 0.4 mile, going left leads to the Granite Point Loop, which overlooks a craggy shore and beautiful open water.

From this loop, the Moss Cove Trail continues the journey, heading north across a marine terrace—once used for pasture, now returned to meadow—presenting a showy floral display in the spring. As it passes Moss Cove, look for the harbor seals commonly sunning on the low, flat rocks. At 0.9 mile, one final loop overlooks Carmel River State Beach. Return as you came.

*Access:* Start on the Granite Point Trail, which heads north near the Whalers Cabin.

**Sea Lion Point Trail and Cypress Grove Loop.** The 0.3-mile Sea Lion Point Trail and the 0.8-mile Cypress Grove Loop spotlight two of Point Lobos State Reserve's star features—a noisy California sea lion colony and one of only two naturally growing Monterey cypress groves in the world (the other is found on Cypress Point across Carmel Bay).

The Sea Lion Point Trail passes through a coastal sage-poison oak habitat overlooking Headland Cove. Harbor seals can be seen pulsing up the beach or sunning at the foot of a cliff. At 0.1 mile, bear right and descend the stairs. Cobbly conglomerate outcrops comprise the headland. At the foot of the stairs, again bear right to overlook Sea Lion Rocks at 0.3 mile. Morning lighting is best for viewing; by afternoon, visitors can only make out shiny silhouettes. Admire, but stay clear of the furious surf. Return as you came.

Cypress Grove Loop tours the Allan Memorial Grove; brochures are available at the trailhead. After passing through a shrubby corridor on the Cypress Grove Trail, go left at the loop junction to quickly enter an old-growth stand of the rare, gnarled trees. Tall grasses blanket the floor. The cypresses near the cliff show bizarre, weathered shapes.

Ahead, a silver, polished cypress log marks Sea Lion Rocks Vista, which looks out at Headland Cove and the churning waters of Devils Cauldron. Exiting the trees at 0.2 mile, hikers reach the granite outcrop of South Point for a sweeping coastal view. In winter, whalewatchers favor this site. At North Point, shapely cypresses add to the view; a rich orange algae decorates the trunks.

After viewing Cypress Cove, the loop closes, and hikers may return to the trailhead or follow the North Shore Trail 0.25 mile to view Old Veteran—an impressive, ancient Monterey cypress clinging to the cliff.

*Access:* Both hikes begin at the Information Station parking area. The trailhead for Sea Lion Point is at the southwest end of the parking lot; the one for Cypress Grove Loop is at the north end.

**Bird Island Trail.** This 0.8-mile round-trip hike passes two gorgeous coves en route to Bird Island Vista. A rock arch is visible as the trail heads uphill; coastal scrub and Monterey pines line the way. At 0.1 mile, the beautiful jade-green waters and white sand beach of China Cove captivate travelers. A stairway later descends to the dreamy, secluded site. The primary trail continues south, coming to a junction overlooking Gibson Beach. Bear right for Bird Island; a left leads to the Gibson Beach access.

Despite the house visible above it, Gibson Beach is a stunning, white sand crescent looking out on a broader cove. In the quiet waters, sea otters anchor in kelp or dive for food. At the trail fork at 0.3 mile, going right leads to Bird Island Vista; going left leads to a view of Pelican Point. Normally, a loop is possible, but a break in the rock ruptured the trail in 1993. Each viewpoint overlooks a narrow, turbulent channel marked by sea caves. Return as you came.

*Access:* Begin at the reserve's southernmost parking and picnic area.

**Diving.** Scuba divers, snorkelers, and visitors with diving boats must register at the Point Lobos entry station. Divers are admitted to the reserve in pairs, and both must present proof of certification. Only Whalers and Bluefish coves are open to diving. These underwater realms hold a rich array of life, with kelp forests, corals, fish, and mollusks and the occasional sea lion, seal, or otter. Even the close-by passing of a whale has been witnessed.

*Access:* Entry is at Whalers Cove, Point Lobos State Reserve.

## GARRAPATA STATE PARK

**Hours/Season:** Daylight hours
**Facilities:** Hiker trails, nonflush toilets, *bring water*
**For Information:** (408) 624-4909
**Access:** Find the park along a 4-mile stretch of CA 1, 4 miles south of Carmel's southern city limit or 14.7 miles north of Andrew Molera State Park.

This undeveloped 2,800-acre park features rocky shores, a cliff-secluded sandy beach, multiple coastal vantage points, and a strenuous hike in the Santa Lucia Mountains wilds. Deep in Soberanes Canyon, groves of towering coastal redwoods shade the creek and trail, and throughout the park visitors find an incomparable wildflower show, colorful and varied, stretching from the coastal bluff and shady canyon floor to the grassland and chaparral ridges.

Offshore, the guano-iced Lobos Rocks host barking sea lions, with sea otters, cormorants, and oystercatchers further enlivening the area. On Saturdays in January, park rangers lead whale-watch tours along the Garrapata shore to see the close-passing gray whales. Rock fishing, tidepool discovery, and surf watching are other pastimes. Numbered trailhead gates paired with roadside turnouts along CA 1 provide park access. A Garrapata State Park brochure may be purchased at Andrew Molera State Park to the south.

## Attractions and Activities

**Garrapata Beach Trail.** A corded-off 0.2-mile trail crosses the scrub-vegetated plateau and descends the bluff to the beach. There, a half mile of wild, beautiful, light-colored sand invites the stroller. Rocks protrude in a string off the ends of Garrapata Beach. While the ocean mesmerizes with its white-lapping surf and aquamarine clarity, be alert, as irregular waves can come in suddenly, sweeping you off your feet. The water here is unsafe for swimming and wading.

*Access:* Begin at gate 32 on the west side of CA 1, 7.6 miles south of Carmel River State Beach.

**Soberanes Point Trail.** This 1.7-mile round-trip trail strings together coastal views from the bluff, Soberanes Point, and the saddle and twin summits of Whale Peak. A 0.2-mile trail travels the bluff north, offering some additional rocky shore overlooks.

At the initial junction, go left (south) for the main tour, passing through a cypress grove to reach the coastal scrub of the bluff. The sounds of crashing waves and barking sea lions accompany the early distance. At the 0.1-mile junction, go right for Soberanes Point and a counterclockwise tour, rounding the coastal flank of Whale Peak.

In spring, the yellow blooms of the lizardtail and the lavender sea daisy decorate its slope. At the 0.25-mile junction, again go right descending to the point. Rounding its edge, visitors may spy sea arches, pocket beaches, magnificent coastal cliffs, sea palm forests, aquamarine pools, nesting gulls (in spring), and sea mammals.

Where the trail works its way back to the base of Whale Peak at 0.5 mile, continue right to round the next point extension. It offers views south of Garrapata Beach, a distant Point Sur, and the tidepool rocks below the 50-foot cliff. The trail then swings back toward CA 1, bypasses gate 15, and ascends the back of Whale Peak.

At the 1.1-mile junction, a 0.3-mile round-trip detour leads to Whale Peak Saddle, a viewing bench, and short paths to the tops of North and South summits. Each summit presents nearly 360-degree viewing. Resuming the hike, visitors descend through coastal scrub, closing the loop at 1.6 miles. The hike ends 0.1 mile farther north.

*Access:* Begin at gate 13 on the west side of CA 1, 5 miles south of Carmel River State Beach.

**Rocky Ridge Saddle–Soberanes Canyon Loop.** This demanding 4.5-mile

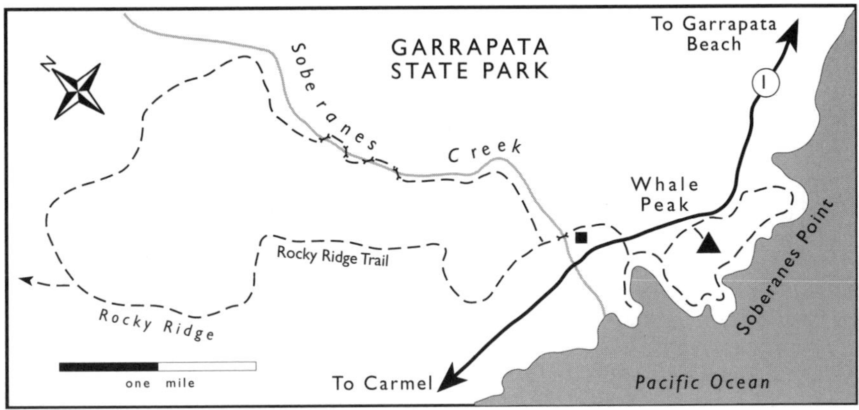

round-trip tour has a 1,700-foot elevation change, with a steep climb to the ridge saddle and an even steeper plummet to the canyon bottom, but the vistas and setting reward the effort. An additional 1.4-mile round-trip hike to the highest point in the park (elevation 1,977 feet) may be added by taking the peak spur from the saddle junction.

From the east side of CA 1, follow the old ranch road uphill. It rounds a barn and crosses small Soberanes Creek, coming to the loop junction. To the left is the ridge saddle trail, to the right is the canyon trail. Go left for a clockwise tour remaining on the old road. Views are of Lobos Rocks and Whale Peak. At 0.2 mile, keep an eye out for the foot trail angling uphill to the right; it continues the hike. While marked, the signpost is placed a short way uphill from the road, and the coastal chaparral partially hides it.

The trail now climbs a grassland slope dotted by coyote bush, lupine, and sage. By 0.4 mile, it is above Soberanes Canyon, offering looks at this impressively steep, tight canyon. Coastal redwood stands mark its upper reaches. Throughout the climb, hikers find only a narrow ocean vista, overlooking the Garrapata shore. From 0.5 to 0.7 mile, the trail charges up and over a granite bed. It then leaves the canyon, contouring and climbing. Quail and rabbits startle and stir in the scrub. Hikers should beware of ticks and poison oak.

By 1.3 miles, the trail is climbing toward a high rocky-faced peak, with steep side ridges and chiseled drainages. Clarkia, California poppy, larkspur, yellow buckwheat, and owl's clover spangle the grasses. Ahead, a detour to a rock outcrop on the coastal edge affords a fine vantage overlooking the ribbed foot of the slope. Hikers who choose this for their turnaround point will not feel cheated; it is a fine ending and sampling of the Santa Lucia Mountains offering.

As the ridge-saddle trail continues climbing, patches of granitic rock and sand claim the path. By 1.75 miles, hikers overlook Malpaso Canyon to the north. Here, the trail forks; go left for the main trail, contouring the slope overlooking the canyon. A secondary trail travels the top of the ridge, offering clear-day views of both Soberanes and Malpaso canyons. In a broad, grassy saddle at 2 miles, hikers come to the Peak Trail junction; go right, following the Soberanes Canyon Trail for the loop. Ground squirrels range the area.

The canyon trail quickly enters its descent, marked by sharp pitches. By 2.5 miles, hikers have views out the drainage at Whale Peak, but soon after the trail is following a fast-plunging side ridge into Soberanes Canyon. Numerous redwoods mark the canyon head and its side drainages.

At 3 miles, the trail enters the creek-influenced canyon habitat. Laurel, redwood, ferns, oxalis, nettles, and poison oak abound here. The canyon shade is welcomed after the exposed ridge tour. Soberanes Creek is 3 to 4 feet wide, spilling over a rocky bed. While there are many good-size redwoods in the drainage, none is massive in proportion. The rolling downstream tour shows some steep rises and dips, sometimes drawing out of the canyon shade.

After 3.4 miles, the trail enters a comfortable grade alongside the creek. Ahead, it crosses the creek four times via footboards. Marking the trail's return to the open scrub is a picturesque, wind-shaped redwood. Willows grow along the creek, which is now separated from the trail.

At 4.3 miles, a thick patch of ancient cacti captures attention. In spring, their large pads sport bright yellow blooms. Just beyond, the loop closes, and the hike ends in another 0.1 mile.

*Access:* Begin on the east side of CA 1, opposite gate 13, 5 miles south of Carmel River State Beach.

# POINT SUR LIGHT STATION STATE HISTORIC PARK

**Hours/Season:** Shown by guided tour Wednesdays 10:00 A.M., Saturdays 10:00 A.M. and 2:00 P.M., and Sundays 10:00 A.M. (weather permitting); arrive a half hour before tour time and allow 2 to 3 hours; groups are limited to 15 vehicles
**Facilities:** Small visitor center, historic light station, nonflush toilets, *bring water*
**For Information:** (408) 625-4419
**Access:** The park is west off CA 1, 19 miles south of Carmel and 0.25 mile north of Point Sur Naval Facility. *Parking prohibits trailers and motorhomes.*

Point Sur Light Station, consisting of the historic 1889 lighthouse and its community of related buildings, sits atop a volcanic rock promontory attached to shore by a short neck of land. As private lands and beaches surround the point, the only access is by docent-led tour. Visitors unable to meet the tour schedule can see the station from turnouts on CA 1. Plus they now have the option of taking a video tour of the facility while visiting Big Sur Station, a joint-agency visitor center, east off CA 1, 6 miles south of the light-station gate.

## Attractions and Activities

**Light Station Guided Tour.** The tour begins with the group driving as a convoy to the designated parking area below the point. From there, the light-station visitors climb some 300 feet in elevation and 0.5 mile to the seaward brow of Point Sur and the light tower. Winds and fog often claim this section of coast, but clear days offer

*Point Sur Lighthouse*

exceptional viewing of Molera Point, the offshore kelp beds, and the high-spraying water meeting the rocks. Sea daisy, Indian paintbrush, and lizardtail dot spring color on the Point Sur cliffs. Sometimes, the passing of a gray whale adds to a tour.

The lighthouse, built of stone blocks, includes the lamp tower and engine and oil rooms. At its center, the tower stands 40 feet tall. Its large Fresnel lens is no longer in place, and modern aero and radio beacons have replaced the kerosene lamps and steam fog whistles. As the tour travels up the spiral staircase and onto the lighthouse balcony, visitors learn about the lighthouse, its operation and maintenance, and about the legendary shipwrecks along this coast.

Another set of stairs climbs from the lighthouse to the complex atop the rock. At one time, four families lived up here, well-isolated until the opening of CA 1 in 1937. Visitors learn about their self-sufficiency: how they received supplies from sea, how they grew vegetables and raised stock, and how they educated their children.

One story has it that the keepers' families had to tie down their chickens because of the winds. The information and nature of the tours will vary depending on tour size, the group's level of interest, and the docent in charge.

While the buildings remain intact, most have yet to be stabilized for entry. The main keeper's house is the only other structure open to the public. It is just a shell, hinting at the former living quarters and at life here. Other buildings include the assistant keeper's stone house (the impressive three-story, gable-roofed building seen from CA 1), a blacksmith shop, pumphouse, and now-tilting barn.

Tours wrap up at the visitor/hospitality center, where old photos depict the historic light-station years. Posted information sheets describe the early shipwrecks, the Fresnel lens, the transportation of goods to the light station, and the geology of Point Sur. Among the few exhibits is baleen (whalebone). Tours conclude as they began, with the group leaving as a convoy.

*Access:* Meet at the locked gate on CA 1, 0.25 mile north of the naval facility.

## ANDREW MOLERA STATE PARK

**Hours/Season:** Year-round
**Facilities:** Walk-in, open meadow camp area serving upward of 100 tents (reservations not accepted); picnic area; horseback-riding concession; hiker, horse, and mountain-bike trails; nonflush toilets; water
**For Information:** (408) 667-2315
**Access:** Find the park off CA 1, 22 miles south of Carmel; *access is unsuitable for trailers.*

At nearly 4,800 acres, this minimally developed coastal park straddling CA 1 and cut by the Big Sur River offers exploration of riparian, beach, meadow, and coastal bluff and hills topography. It features an exciting 2.5-mile shoreline and a vast, mostly untried area east of CA 1. In summer, temporary bridges cross the river, easing travel on the park's west side. As not all routes are open for horse and mountain-bike use, riders should study the map and heed signs.

Managed for naturalness, the park boasts a vital wildlife population. Visitors enjoy such sightings as deer, raccoon, fox, and boar; otter, seal, and sea lion; lizards and snakes; and land, shore, and sea birds. Ocean fishing from the beach is a year-round activity, while the river is open to steelhead fishing on certain dates in winter. In January, whalewatchers search the watery plain for the spouts and backs of migrating gray whales.

## Attractions and Activities

**Beach and Headlands Trail.** This 2.8-mile round-trip hike takes visitors to Molera Point headland, offering coastal overlooks of the beach, Cooper Point, and the great ocean expanse. It also affords beach access.

Following the north side of the Big Sur River downstream, the trail (a former ranch road) tours a semi-open riparian habitat, with willows, sycamores, a few big live oak, and ample poison oak. At 0.3 mile, it passes through the long open meadow of the campground, where tables, grills, pit toilets, and water meet the campers' needs. Beyond it, a short uphill spur leads to Cooper Cabin, a three-room, hand-split redwood shake cabin amid a eucalyptus grove. Built in 1861, it is the oldest building on the Big Sur coast.

The hike continues, heading downstream along the ranch road. By 0.9 mile, the roadside border consists of willow, coyote bush, poison oak, and morning glory. At 1.1 miles, going right on the path labeled "footbridge" leads to a junction: To the left is a summer bridge to the beach; to the right is the Headlands Trail.

Going right, hikers mount the stairs above a small wetland. In 0.1 mile, a bench overlooks the beach, the vegetated bluff, the bay curvature, and Cooper Point. Going right on the cordoned loop, hikers round the edge of Molera Point, securing looks north at a beach and the jutting flat rock at the foot of the headland. Looks west follow, with cormorants and gulls roosting on a nearby rock. The circuit concludes with an impressive look south of the Andrew Molera coast. Sage, succulents, and lizardtail vegetate the headland; in spring, yellow blooms set it ablaze.

Returning to the beach junction, hikers cross the Big Sur River coming out on the sands next to the river mouth. Low tides reveal a long walkable beach below the bluffs to the south, while high tides often leave only a small patch of beach next to the river mouth. Travelers must be attentive to the tide table and to the possibility of sleeper waves. This is not a tour for dallying. Along the way, beachgoers may note a purple stain on the sand, a product of almondite leaching from the cliffs.

*Access:* Begin at the trailhead at the center of the parking lot.

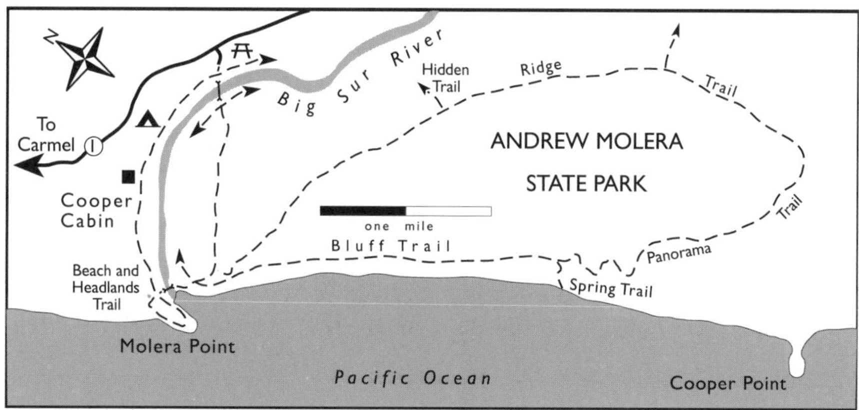

**Bluff–Panorama–Ridge Loop.** This strenuous 9-mile round-trip trail tours atop the open bluff for coastal overlooks and traces the seaward ridge, visiting a scenic oak woodland and pleasant redwood grove. Portions of the route are open to horse and cycle use. A detour on the Spring Trail offers beach access and an alternative 6.6-mile round-trip tour.

The hike begins following the Beach and Headlands Trail. Arriving at the 1.1-mile junction, go left, crossing the summer footbridge over the Big Sur River. There, veer left traveling the upper end of the beach to climb the bluff. By 1.4 miles, the trail journeys south atop the bluff, overlooking the coastline and the rounded east hills. At the Bluff–Ridge trail junction (the loop junction) at 1.6 miles, bear right for a counterclockwise tour.

As the Bluff Trail travels a grassy 2-track, over-the-shoulder looks find Point Sur Light Station, Molera Point, and the park beach. To the south, the view is of Cooper Point. A grassland plateau patched by bush lupine, coyote bush, and coastal sage enfolds the trail. Paintbrush, thistle, and poppy lend spring accents.

At 2.8 miles, lizardtail chokes the thin path of the trail, brushing the legs of travelers. Emerging from the thicket, hikers come to a bluff-edge vista, overlooking a rock where harbor seals haul out. Pelicans pass by in rolling flight. Afterward, the trail crosses an old dune, dipping into a drainage.

At 3.2 miles, the 0.25-mile Spring Trail descends to the beach, suggesting a detour or an alternate return when the tide is low and will remain so for the 2-mile beach hike north. Almondite is commonly seen where the Spring Trail arrives at the beach.

Opting instead for a ridge return, hikers follow the Panorama Trail left. It drops into the next drainage before climbing toward the ridge. As it switchbacks up, hikers find a good view north of Point Sur. By 3.7 miles, the trail climbs alongside an unusual low-growing hedgerow of wind-buffeted redwoods. From 4.2 to 4.4 miles, hikers ascend through a humid shrub corridor. Beware of poison oak and nettles amid this tunnel of ceanothus and coyote bush. A grassy slope greets the hiker on the other side.

By 4.9 miles, the trail climbs close to the south boundary fence. Here, it affords first-time views of the rugged Big Sur coast farther south. A few hillside houses can also be seen. Near a stand of cypress at 5.2 miles, hikers find the Ridge Trail and a bench at which to catch their breath.

Following the descending Ridge Trail north, hikers soon enter a shady oak grove, picturesque with its tangled trunks. The oaks briefly give way to a rich, dark stand of redwood, laurel, and tanoak. By 6 miles, the trail pulls into the open for good. Go straight at the junction here.

Where the Ridge Trail crosses a long saddle at 6.6 miles, hikers have the best views east of the coastal mountains, with their tree-filled drainages and the Big Sur Valley. Deer and vultures may be spied on this open tour; gold nuggets (yellow lilies) spangle the grasses. At the Hidden Trail junction at 6.9 miles, head straight to continue the loop. The Hidden Trail offers an alternative return to Big Sur Valley. If you take it, return to the parking lot via the River Trail.

Staying on the Ridge Trail, hikers top one final vista rise, before making a steep descent to the bluff (7.8 miles). At the 8-mile junction, go left to reach the Bluff Trail in a few feet, and follow it north. Upon crossing the upper beach, hikers return to the Beach and Headlands Trail junction. Retrace the ranch road upstream to the parking area (9.2 miles).

*Access:* Begin on the Beach and Headlands Trail, which leaves from the center of the parking lot.

## PFEIFFER BIG SUR STATE PARK

**Hours/Season:** Year-round
**Facilities:** 218 developed native-tree-shaded campsites, hike/bike camp, motel/cabin facility, concession-run lodge, picnic areas, nature center, restaurant, store, gift shop, laundromat, softball field, hiker trails, restrooms, showers, dump station
**For Information:** (408) 667-2315
**Access:** Find the park off CA 1, 26 miles south of Carmel.

For many, this popular state park serves as a base for discovering the breathtaking beauty of the greater Big Sur coast and the inland wilds of the Santa Lucia Mountains. While this particular park embraces no ocean frontage, it is within easy reach of those that do, and its system of short trails offers a fine snapshot of the region's inland offerings: giant coastal redwoods, clear-coursing streams, and lofty vantages of an exciting, rugged terrain. Due to the concentration of people and the park's community-like atmosphere, though, locating solitude can be a challenge.

The most impressive redwoods are located in the campground and the developed heart of the park, with the oldest grove located right next to the ranger station. A charming waterfall, river boulders and pools, scenic oak woodlands, and a homestead cabin suggest visitors take to the trails. The crystalline waters of Big Sur River support rainbow trout and steelhead; the river is open to fishing only at certain

*Big Sur River, Pfeiffer Big Sur State Park*

times of the year. Just south of the park is the Big Sur Station, a joint-agency office dispensing information for additional outings in the Big Sur area.

## Attractions and Activities

**Gorge Trail.** A 0.1-mile trail from camp takes hikers to the south shore of the Big Sur River, just below a steep-sided gorge. Alder, maple, willow, and laurel frame the river. Where the trail ends at the mouth of the gorge, hikers find a scenic boulder-accented pool and tiny coarse-sand beach. The swirling-clear river waters captivate and invite. A trail on the north shore also arrives at this same spot; it is accessed via a summer footbridge from camp or from the park's group picnic area.

Additional pools await upstream, but from here, travel is by rock hopping and wading. The cooling pools and sizeable round boulders for sunbathing prove a summer siren difficult to refuse, but use care scrambling over the wet rocks.

*Access:* Start in the upper campground loop, near sites 202 and 218.

**Nature Trail and Homestead Cabin Hike.** These two short trails introduce the area's natural and cultural history. The 0.6-mile round-trip Nature Trail tours a woodland immediately above the park road, introducing some of the common area plants. Brochures are available at the trailhead or from park personnel. The 0.5-mile round-trip hike to the cabin follows an oak-shaded, paved fire road away from the group picnic area for 0.2 mile. From there, take the gravel lane on the left to reach the rustic home site.

Ringed by a weatherworn picket fence is the small, wooden cabin where the Innocenti family raised six children. Peering in the windows, visitors can see a table and stove in the simple, dark room. Downhill to the left is an Indian cemetery, just a small flat marked by a sign. Return as you came.

*Access:* The Nature Trail starts opposite the family picnic area. For the cabin, follow the Gorge Trail, leaving the east side of the group picnic area parking lot north of the softball field.

**Pfeiffer Falls–Valley View Loop.** This 1.8-mile loop tours a fine redwood grove, visits a delicate 60-foot waterfall, and mounts a ridge for an open view of the park's Big Sur coast–Santa Lucia Mountains neighborhood.

At the trailhead, visitors find a redwood display and an 800-year-old redwood slab, its rings paired with corresponding events in history. Immediately afterward, the trail enters the redwood splendor, paralleling tiny Pfeiffer-Redwood Creek. At 0.1 mile is the loop junction. To the left is Valley View; straight ahead is the falls.

Continuing straight on an upstream tour, hikers overlook the glistening ribbon of the creek. Some big trees rise above the trail, while the fire-hollowed ones (goose pens) invite youngsters inside. Near a wooden bench, the Oak Grove Trail heads right; the falls trail again heads straight. Tanoak, sword fern, oxalis, and chain fern bring touches of green to the moist canyon bottom. After four footbridge crossings, hikers come to the second loop junction at 0.4 mile.

The Valley View Trail heads left here, crossing the creek; the spur to the falls heads up the stairs to a vista platform. Pfeiffer Falls is small, even at flood stage, but pretty, with its white streamers rolling down a black cliff. Five-finger ferns and moss add to its quiet charm. Redwoods march up the drainage to it.

When ready to continue the loop, follow the Valley View Trail across the bridge for a switchbacking ascent of the slope. The redwoods give way to a tanoak-laurel woodland. As the trail leaves the Pfeiffer-Redwood drainage, it comes to a junction at 0.7 mile. The 0.3-mile spur to the view heads uphill to the right; the loop continues on the downhill trail.

Taking the spur to the view, hikers switchback uphill, topping a small ridge mantled with live oak. They then follow the ridge for an easy walk to the vista. Poison oak and monkey-flowers grow amid the understory species. At 1 mile the small loop gains the vista. From the open, rock-studded edge of the ridge, visitors overlook the redwood-forested Big Sur drainage, but not the river itself; coastal views include Point Sur.

From the vista, return to the 0.7-mile junction at 1.3 miles, and take the trail heading down the canyon slope toward the lodge. The quick, steep descent passes from oak and laurel woodland back into redwood forest, ending with a footbridge crossing of the creek at 1.7 miles. Go right for the nature center and lodge.

*Access:* Begin next to the nature center.

## JULIA PFEIFFER-BURNS STATE PARK—LIMEKILN CREEK STATE PARK

**Hours/Season:** Daylight hours (Julia Pfeiffer-Burns); year-round (Limekiln)

**Facilities:** 2 hike-in environmental campsites (stays must be pre-arranged), picnic sites, hiker trails, restroom (Julia Pfeiffer-Burns); campground (being refurbished), historic site (Limekiln)

**For Information:** (408) 667-2315

**Access:** Find *Julia Pfeiffer-Burns State Park* off CA 1, 37 miles south of Carmel or 12.9 miles north of Lucia. Find *Limekiln Creek State Park* off CA 1, a couple of miles south of Lucia or about an equal distance north of the CA 1–Nacimiento Road junction.

Along the Big Sur coast, Julia Pfeiffer-Burns State Park features the picturesque cove where McWay Creek showers over an 80-foot cliff to the ocean. An arch marks the foot of the rocky point cupping the cove. The ocean, grading

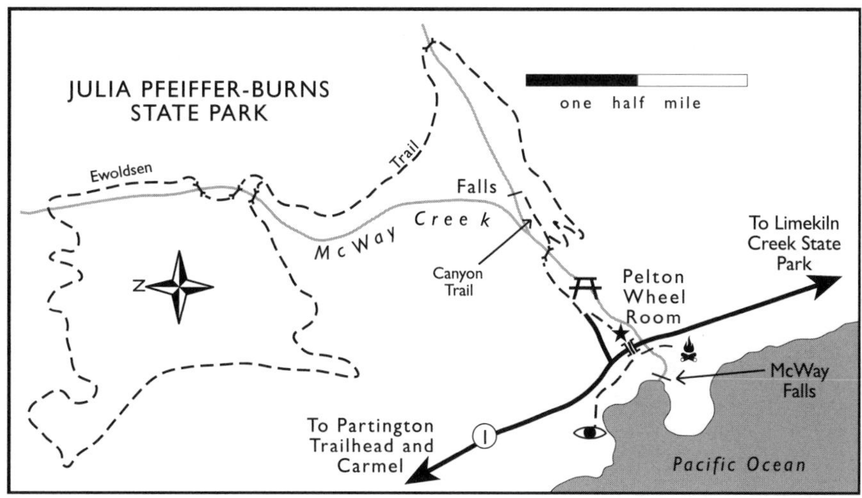

from aquamarine to cobalt, holds visitors spellbound, as colorful kelp streamers sway in the designated marine sanctuary.

The park's 3,600 acres also stretch inland. They enfold steep, rugged, redwood-lined creek canyons, oak-studded slopes, and open grassland and chaparral ridges. In spring, the various habitats put on a first-rate wildflower show. When fog is absent, the lofty coastal promontories reward the effort of a climb with spectacular views. The park is named for a local pioneer who prized this remote area where land and sea collide.

South of Julia Pfeiffer-Burns State Park, at the edge of Los Padres National Forest, the Big Sur coastal traveler will find one of the more recent additions to the California State Park System—Limekiln Creek State Park. This holding includes a redwood canyon; a small, sheltered beach; a waterfall; and the historic kilns from which the site receives its name. A campground already on the acreage at the time of acquisition is being upgraded and likely will be concession-run.

Because of Limekiln's newness at the time of this writing, visitors should contact the Monterey District at (408) 667-2315 for specifics about its attractions, recreational opportunities, and facilities.

## Attractions and Activities

**Waterfall Overlook–Pelton Wheel Trail.** At Julia Pfeiffer-Burns, this 0.5-mile round-trip trail follows the McWay Creek Canyon downstream, crossing under CA 1 to the ocean cliffs across from Saddle Rock.

The hike begins with a stairway descent. At the bottom, going left for a short distance leads to the Pelton Wheel Room and exhibit; going straight leads to the overlook. Opting for the detour left, visitors learn about the McWay homestead and the workings of a Pelton wheel—an early means of power generation.

Back on the overlook trail, they travel a corridor of wild berries, willow, sage, and poison oak, as riparian and chaparral species intermingle. From the trail's end, visitors overlook the scenic, protected McWay Falls cove, with its inaccessible beach and white watery veil falling to a wondrous blue sea. Nolina, succulents, and exotics dot the sharply dropping, eroded cliffs. Return as you came.

*Access:* Begin across from the restroom at Julia Pfeiffer-Burns State Park.

**Ewoldsen Trail.** This strenuous 4.3-mile round-trip trail makes a loop through Julia Pfeiffer-Burns State Park and undergoes a 1,600-foot elevation change as it travels redwood-forested McWay Canyon to the open ridge and back.

Hiking upstream along McWay Creek, visitors pass an unusual redwood showing a sharply bowed trunk-size branch with a sagging elbow. Other genetically twisted trees grow in the area. Upon passing through the picnic area and crossing the bridge below a homestead barn, hikers come to the Ewoldsen Trail junction at 0.2 mile.

From here, the Canyon Trail continues upstream along McWay Creek, reaching a small falls in a narrow, green canyon in another 0.1 mile. Staying on the Ewoldsen Trail, hikers switchback upslope for a fast elevation gain. Experiencing the physical effort it takes to come eye-level with the redwood tops, hikers better appreciate the height of these trees.

Ferns, oxalis, trillium, and starflower occasionally color the open forest floor. Tanoak and laurel grow amid the redwoods. At 0.4 mile, the Ewoldsen Trail overlooks the cascade at the end of Canyon Trail. At the footbridge ahead, chain, five-finger, and lady ferns decorate a side creek. After passing through a corridor of redwood sprouts (0.6 mile), the trail travels a coastal scrub and oak slope, where

*McWay Falls, Julia Pfeiffer-Burns State Park*

lizardtail, bracken fern, monkey-flower, and poison oak are found. Views are out McWay Canyon. Soon, the redwood tour resumes.

At 1.1 miles go right per the sign at the loop junction. The demanding climb resumes, heading up the canyon. Some scenic, mossy rock walls and fire-blackened redwoods add to the tour. The stair-stepping creek is pretty. Where the trail crosses it at 1.5 miles, hikers find an easy step over the much-narrowed creek.

The trail now climbs steeply up and out of the main canyon to again tour an oak and scrub slope, with views out McWay Canyon. After a brief return to the redwoods, the trail then switchbacks into a grand oak woodland topping the ridge. Fog can create a moody aura.

Where the trail tops out at 2.3 miles, the path heading north (when complete) will take Ewoldsen Trail hikers all the way to the Partington trailhead at the park's north boundary. For the loop, bear left following the ridgetop onto a grassy, open seaward slope.

A steep descent follows, touring the spine above a CA 1 landslide; chaparral replaces the grassland. Views extend past highway to ocean, nearby offshore rocks, and multi-blue waters. On clear days, the post affords a fine whale-watching vantage.

At 2.8 miles, the trail leaves the ridge, curving into the oak woodland of McWay Canyon. A steep, steady, angling descent leads hikers back into the redwoods. At 3.2 miles the McWay Creek footbridge closes the loop. Retrace the initial 1.1 miles to the trailhead.

*Access:* The trailhead is found at the east end of the Julia Pfeiffer-Burns State Park picnic area parking lot.

**Diving.** In the waters off Partington Cove, at the northern end of Julia Pfeiffer-Burns State Park, underwater caves and natural bridges, as well as intriguing life forms, captivate divers, but due to the challenging nature of these waters, only experienced divers are allowed entry. A permit is required; contact the park for more details.

*Access:* The access for Partington Cove is on CA 1, 2 miles north of the main entrance to Julia Pfeiffer-Burns State Park.

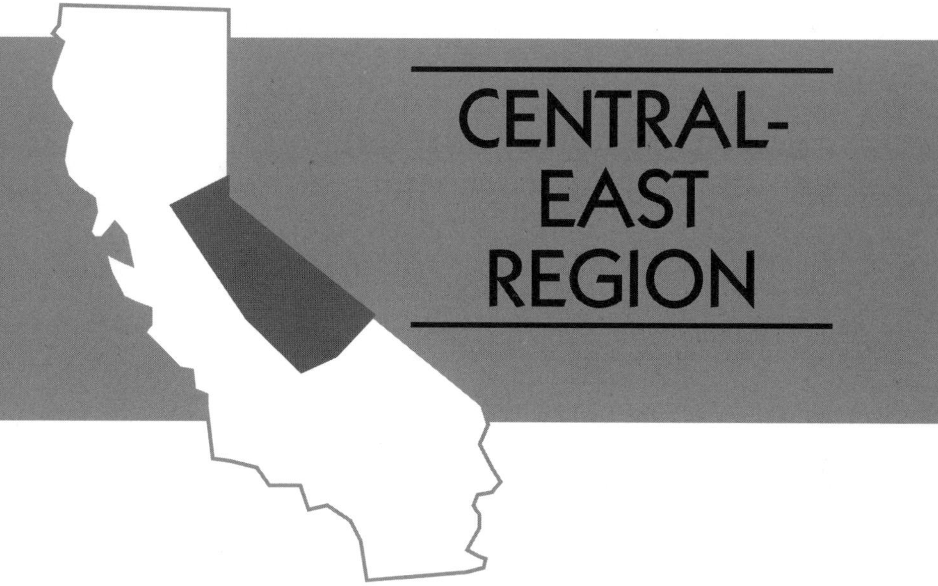


## Donner Memorial State Park

**Hours/Season:** Year-round; Memorial Day weekend through mid-September (campground); 10:00 A.M. to 4:00 P.M. (museum)
**Facilities:** 154 developed campsites, picnic area, museum and bookstore, monuments, swimming area, hiker trails, Nordic trail, restrooms, showers
**For Information:** (916) 587-3841
**Access:** From I-80 at Truckee, take the Lake Tahoe/CA 89 South exit and head north 0.1 mile. There, turn west on Donner Pass Road and stay on it, crossing back over I-80 to reach the state park in another 1.4 miles.

This park commemorates the most haunting and heart-wrenching episode in the history of western migration—the story of the Donner Party. In late October 1846, the trail-broken and fragmented party stopped here to rest, after having endured the hardships of what was purported to be the Hastings Shortcut. It was a fatal decision, as the most fearsome snowstorm in ages quickly settled into the Sierra Nevada, stranding the pioneers.

During the winter of 1846–47, the party endured cold, starvation, death, a heroic struggle to snowshoe out, and ultimately cannibalism, before four separate rescue missions led what remained of the party to safety. When the ordeal ended, only 47 of the 89 had survived.

The park itself occupies a 350-acre flat on the south side of 3-mile-long Donner Lake. Lodgepole and Jeffrey pines and white fir forest the area, while large glacier-deposited boulders mark the flat. The mountain setting is beautiful, but the high-

*Jeffrey pine cones, Grover Hot Springs State Park*

way noise intrudes upon the relaxation and the solemn nature of the place. Guests enjoy camping, picnicking, hiking, swimming, and fishing, with Nordic skiing in winter.

## Attractions and Activities

**Emigrant Trail Museum.** Here, visitors can view a 25-minute video telling the story of the Donner Party, with several of the exhibits devoted to their experience. Other exhibits and displays pay tribute to the westward migration, the Truckee Stage Stop, the building of the Central Pacific Railroad and Summit Highway, the Chinese work crews, and the Native Americans.

**Donner Memorial.** A moving monument dedicated to the American pioneer stands where the Donner Party passed their tragic winter. The bronze piece features a pioneer family: father, mother, infant, and child, atop a stone pedestal 22 feet high—the exact height of the snow that fateful winter. On it, an inscription captures the fortitude and spirit of the pioneer.

*Access:* The memorial is located north of the museum.

**Nature Trail.** A 0.5-mile self-guided nature trail introduces the park forest and its streamside and meadow vegetation; brochures are available at the museum. Along it, travelers bypass the site of the Murphy family cabin, marked by a large boulder that formed one wall. On it, a plaque bears the names of the pioneers who perished and those who survived.

As the trail parallels Donner Creek upstream, visitors learn a little about the area's glacial geology. At 0.2 mile, the trail crosses over the creek to follow the opposite bank downstream. Where it again crosses the creek to close the loop, look over the bridge to find freshwater clam shells dotting the sandy-bottomed creek.

*Access:* Begin at the south side of the museum.

*Campground, Donner Memorial State Park*

**Lakeside Interpretive Trail.** This trail travels 1.2 miles along Donner Lake's south shore, touring the open lodgepole pine corridor between it and South Shore Drive.

The route strings through the picnic area and offers convenient lake access. Its soft earthen bed is ideal for walkers and joggers. Along it, eighteen graphic panels introduce the natural and cultural history of the area and describe some key events. From the east end of the trail, near the dam, hikers gain views of Donner Peak and Mount Judah. Ground squirrel, Steller's jay, kingfisher, and merganser are typical sightings.

*Access:* Begin at either China Cove or the Donner Lake Dam.

**China Cove Swimming Area.** Named for the Chinese workers who camped here during the building of the Central Pacific Railroad, the cove today holds a fine swimming area. The pleasant, protected cove has a pebbly beach and lake floor. As the water deepens gradually, it provides areas for wading, waterplay, and swimming. A buoy-rope marks off the good-size area. With summer water temperatures seldom topping 62 degrees Fahrenheit and no lifeguards, swimmers should be careful and limit their stays in the water.

*Access:* At the west end of the park.

**Boating and Fishing.** The 860 acres of Donner Lake also serve sailors, boaters, jet skiers, and anglers. While the park itself lacks a launch site, a public facility at the lake's north end provides park guests a convenient access. The lake is planted with trout and has stocks of kokanee and Mackinaw. Anglers, however, enjoy only variable success.

**Nordic Skiing.** The parking area near the Emigrant Trail Museum is an official winter Sno-park area; the required use permits may be purchased at the museum. Within the park a 2.5-mile groomed ski trail is maintained. The area's flatness is ideal for beginners.

## Tahoe State Recreation Area—Burton Creek State Park

**Hours/Season:** End of May through Labor Day (Tahoe); daylight hours (Burton Creek)

**Facilities:** 39 developed lakeside and hillside campsites, 6 picnic sites, pier, restrooms, showers (Tahoe); hiker and mountain-bike routes, Nordic trails, *bring water* (Burton Creek)

**For Information:** (916) 525-7982

**Access:** Find Tahoe State Recreation Area at the northeast end of Tahoe City, straddling CA 28. For Burton Creek, go 1.5 miles east of the recreation area on CA 28, and turn north (left) on Old Mill Road. Go 0.4 mile and turn left onto Polaris. In another 0.5 mile, near North Tahoe High School, an unmarked dirt road enters the park.

Tahoe State Recreation Area, on the northwest shore of Lake Tahoe, offers separate trailer and tent camping areas on either side of CA 28, along with a 100-yard-long rocky beach and pier, accessing this prized mountain lake. Primarily though, it serves visitors as an overnight base, with lake recreation calling them elsewhere.

*Mountain biker, Burton Creek State Park*

Lodgepole pines with a few willows and alders vegetate the 13-acre park. A small picnic area occupies the open grassy slope above the beach. From the pier, park guests can enjoy a Lake Tahoe view, access the clear, rocky-bottomed lake for swimming, or try fishing.

The undeveloped 2,000-acre state park drained by Burton Creek offers inland recreation amid forest, riparian, and meadow habitats. Two natural preserves frame the upper and lower creek course, and the area is wild enough to support black bear.

Miles of abandoned dirt road run through Burton Creek State Park, serving hiker, mountain biker, and jogger. Before arriving though, visitors should stop at the Tahoe State Recreation Area Ranger Station to review a map of this park, as there are many unmarked junctions. In winter, Nordic skiers take over the roads.

## Attractions and Activities

**Burton Creek Loop.** A moderate 4.75-mile loop introduces the area, passing through mostly fir-pine forest.

From the Polaris access, a dirt road heads southwest into the park, bypassing the state park sign at 0.1 mile. At 0.25 mile is the first junction; go left, heading downhill another 0.1 mile. There, go right for a counterclockwise tour of the loop. The route passes through an open forest of white fir and Jeffrey pine, with patchy showings of manzanita and chinquapin.

By 0.6 mile, it is removed from, but generally follows, 2-foot-wide Burton Creek with its thin riparian strip. Areas of willows, grass, and wildflowers mark the course, while lodgepole pines and snags rise above it. A field of mule's ears marks the 1-mile junction; continue straight.

The road becomes somewhat rockier and before long is climbing away from the drainage. Coming upon another junction at 1.8 miles, go left for the loop, crossing a Burton Creek bridge. A small dam, barely visible upstream, serves as the demarcation between the Antone Meadows and Burton Creek natural preserves. This area below the dam is part of the latter.

A quarter mile ahead is another junction. There, go straight, remaining on the loop. Stumps dot the fir and lodgepole pine forest, and a large sugar pine may be seen next to the trail. At 2.4 miles, stay on the main road as it bends left, slowly descending.

Continuing straight at the 3.6-mile junction, travelers find the pines create a more open forest, affording limited looks at Lake Tahoe, where the road curves. At the crossing of rocky Burton Creek, the route bottoms out. Ahead, at the 4-mile junction, go left.

A moderate climb brings the loop to a close at 4.4 miles. Go right here and again at the next junction to return to the trailhead at 4.75 miles.

*Access:* Near the school, take the dirt road off Polaris.

**Nordic Skiing.** The park ski trails are groomed by the Tahoe Nordic Center, which charges a use fee for the service; the center is reached off Village Road. As snowmobiles are not allowed in the park, skiers enjoy carefree travel.

# Sugar Pine Point State Park

**Hours/Season:** Year-round; 11:00 A.M. to 4:00 P.M. July 1 through Labor Day (mansion tours)

**Facilities:** 175 developed forested campsites; picnic area; nature center; historic buildings; pier; hiker, bicycle, and mountain-bike trails; Nordic trails; restrooms; pay showers (available summers only); dump station

**For Information:** (916) 525-7982

**Access:** From the junction of CA 89 and CA 28 in Tahoe City, go 9.3 miles south on CA 89 for the campground. The day-use area and Hellman-Ehrman Mansion are another 0.6 mile south.

This 2,000-acre park on the west shore of Lake Tahoe encompasses nearly 2 miles of waterfront, a few untouched ancient cedar and sugar pine trees, wet and dry wildflower meadows, and an impressive lily pond wetland. Besides the park's natural offerings, visitors may tour the turn-of-the-century, Queen Anne-style Hellman-Ehrman Mansion, the summer residence of a successful frontier banker. Rock and white sand beaches and a split-level pier invite sunning, swimming, wading, picnicking, and relaxing.

The cobalt-aquamarine waters of Lake Tahoe mesmerize, while cross-lake views applaud Nevada's mountainous shore. The clear waters of General Creek, which feeds into the lake, offer fishing mid-July through mid-September.

## Attractions and Activities

**Guided Hellman-Ehrman Mansion Tour/Self-guided Grounds Tour.** Given on the hour, the popular 40-minute tour begins on the slate porch of the Hellman-Ehrman Mansion. This three-story summer home is imposing with its granite stonework and chimneys, round towers and turrets, and gabled roof. Overlooking the sloped lawn, the front porch affords a grand view of Lake Tahoe, the beach, and pier.

Indoors, visitors gaze upon the beautiful hardwoods, Spanish chandeliers, and the stone and tiled fireplaces. The furnishings are all representative of the day. As

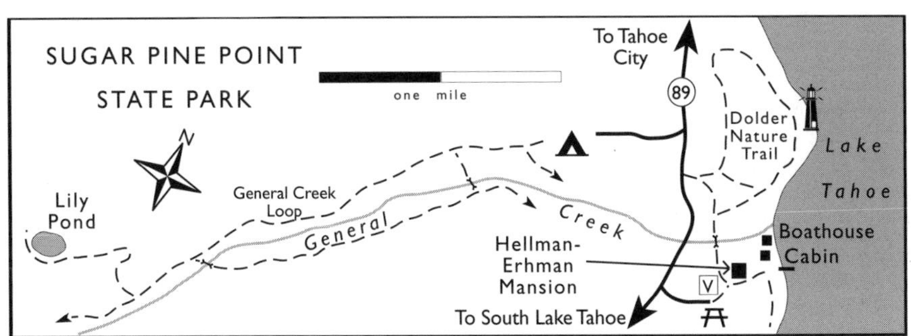

*Water tower/steam generator building, Hellman-Ehrman Mansion, Sugar Pine Point State Park*

the tour rounds the exterior and passes between rooms, visitors learn about the owners' summertime routine and lifestyle.

The bedrooms upstairs are modest relative to the downstairs rooms. Visitors are permitted to view these quarters on their own; plaques tell who used the rooms. As the tour leaves the mansion, visitors may note a fishing pole, riding crop, and croquet set.

The support buildings, like the mansion, are all painted brown, blending with the lakeside forest. Close by is the Children's House, where the family's children lived with their nanny. The youngsters only entered the main house for dinner and special occasions. The water tower/steam generator building, with its five-story tower, calls the visitor to its door. The lower story holds a small nature center/visitor center.

Some of the more interesting buildings are found north of the mansion. They include the 1872 hand-hewn cabin of General Phipps, the first permanent white settler at Lake Tahoe and the one responsible for saving some of the park's big trees on his 160-acre homestead. At the North Boathouse, visitors can see the children's boat and the launch *Tahoma*. The ice house with its thick walls and saws and ice hooks is another stop.

Hiking the trail south from the mansion, visitors pass the old bathhouse, pumphouse, and South Boathouse. The rocky point just south of this boathouse proves a fine escape from the crowds. Big near-shore rocks invite visitors to enjoy the lake from atop them.

*Access:* Begin at the day-use parking area.

**Dolder Nature Trail.** This 2-mile round-trip hiker- or skier-only trail travels the forest of the lakeshore natural preserve, north of Hellman-Ehrman Mansion.

Following the paved path, travelers quickly cross General Creek for a tour of forest and sandy meadow habitats. Plaques introduce the area history and natural features. The trail itself is mostly sunny.

Bypass the dirt foot trail on the right at 0.2 mile to take the one at 0.3 mile; the paved trail continues to the campground. The tour now crosses a sandy flat for 200 feet and then turns left for the start of the nature-trail loop. Ahead, it becomes forested and semi-shaded, with areas of lupine and manzanita dressing the otherwise open floor. Beautiful red-trunked incense cedars, some with snag tops, add to the tour. The area's few remaining sugar pines are also seen.

At 0.8 mile, turn right, remaining on the loop. Woodpeckers and Steller's jays call for attention. Where the trail curves south, a 7-foot-diameter old-growth ponderosa pine stands to its right. The loop now tours closer to the lake separated only by a thin forest buffer. At 1.4 miles, a 30-yard detour to shore finds the lighthouse, a small beacon atop a white picket tower 30 feet high.

As the loop resumes, some big cedars usher the way, and hikers find lake views.

At 1.6 miles, the trail is above a beautiful sandy beach cove, well worth seeking out. A sign cautions swimmers about the cold water. At this point, hikers may return via the beach, via the thin forest trail straight ahead, which comes out on the paved trail at the 0.2-mile junction, or by heading uphill to the right to the paved trail. All eventually lead back to the mansion at about 2 miles.

*Access:* Begin at the Hellman-Ehrman Mansion grounds, taking the paved trail heading north between the nature center and restrooms building.

**General Creek Loop–Lily Pond Trail.** From the campground, this 5.2-mile tour combines the 3.6-mile General Creek circuit (open to hikers, mountain bikers, and skiers), with a 1.6-mile round-trip hike to Lily Pond. Visitors starting at the day-use area add another 2 miles to the total round-trip distance.

Hikers who start the tour on the gated dirt fire road heading away from camp find an open fir-pine forest framing the route. Day-use travelers arrive on the left near the trail's start. Another trail originating from outside the park comes in on the right. Keep to the fire road heading upstream.

At 0.3 mile go straight at the loop junction for a counterclockwise tour. A dry Sierra meadow peppered by summer wildflowers is near the junction. Farther along, many of the lodgepole pines exhibit beetle-kill. At times, rocks stud the roadbed, but generally it offers an easy walking and riding surface. As the route enters a mild incline, a rough former jeep trail branches right.

At 1.1 miles, the fire road passes through an area of bunchgrass and mule's ears, while some big Jeffrey pines divert the eyes skyward. At 1.7 miles, the General Creek Loop (now trail width) turns left; the trail to Lily Pond heads straight.

Continuing toward Lily Pond, the rolling trail passes through more meadow openings and forest. At 2.1 miles, above a scenic aspen grove is the junction where cyclists and hikers part company. To the left is the trail to Lost Lake (outside the park); cyclists may follow it or return to the General Creek Loop. To the right is the hiker-only trail to Lily Pond.

After a steep 0.1-mile climb, the Lily Pond trail begins rounding the forested shore. At 2.5 miles, it comes out in a moist meadow, with a granite boulder suggesting a seat and an open view of the large pond, with its wildflower meadow and bulrush shore, lily-pad surface, and a stand of ghost trees along its bank. Garter snakes sometimes sun on the rock and slither through the tall grass. While the mosquitos may be maddening, the destination is impressive.

Back at the General Creek junction (3.3 miles), resume the tour following the trail-width section of the loop to the opposite creek shore. A boardwalk advances the route, as it passes through a wet meadow. Cyclists should ride on the boardwalk or walk their bikes through this sensitive area. Upon crossing the creek, the loop is once again on a fire road for the downstream leg of the tour. General Creek is shallow and slow flowing; 6-inch trout can be seen flashing between its small pools.

From 3.75 to 4.25 miles, lodgepole-pine rails line the fire road, as it passes through a broad bunchgrass meadow dotted by lodgepole and Jeffrey pines. The road then returns to forest. At 4.8 miles, turn left crossing the bridge to return to the start of the loop at 4.9 miles.

Go right for both the campground (5.2 miles) and the day-use parking lot (7.2 miles). Day users bear right before entering the campground, retracing the way you came.

*Access:* Begin at the end of the campground near site 150. Day users start at the parking lot near the campground entrance station, taking the trail that rounds the south side of the campground to reach General Creek Loop in 1 mile.

**Nordic Skiing.** The park offers more than 12 miles of marked ski trails, some of them groomed. Possible tours are the General Creek Loop, the preserve nature trail, the loops both north and south of the mansion, and the closed areas of the campground. The mild gradients recommend them for families and beginners. Ski tours are offered weekends, January through March.

## D. L. Bliss and Emerald Bay State Parks

**Hours/Season:** Memorial Day Weekend through September; 10:00 A.M. to 4:00 P.M. July 1 through Labor Day (Vikingsholm tours)

**Facilities:** 288 developed forested campsites (RVs over 18 feet and trailers over 15 feet must stay at Emerald Bay; neither park can accommodate RVs over 21 feet or trailers over 18 feet); 20 primitive boat-in campsites, with mooring buoys and dock; visitor center; Vikingsholm Castle; pier; swimming areas; hiker trails; restrooms; nonflush toilets; showers

**For Information:** (916) 525-7277

**Access:** From the junction of CA 89 and CA 28 in Tahoe City, go south on CA 89 16.1 miles for D. L. Bliss, 18 miles for the Vikingsholm trailhead, and 19.9 miles for Emerald Bay's Eagle Point Campground.

Together, these adjoining state parks preserve 1,830 acres of the highly scenic southwest curvature of Lake Tahoe, including 6 miles of waterfront. Due to its superb beauty and unspoiled state, Emerald Bay has been recognized as a National Natural Landmark. In its waters is the lone island of Lake Tahoe—Fannette Island. The parks' shorelines feature rugged granite slopes and rock promontories, mixed evergreen forests, and the white sand beaches of Lester and Calawee Cove to the north and Emerald Bay to the south.

At the west side of Emerald Bay, tucked away in the ancient forest is a Norse-styled fortress built in 1929. The exacting workmanship of carved and hand-hewn wood, cut stone, forged latches, and hand-painted Scandinavian designs recreate a

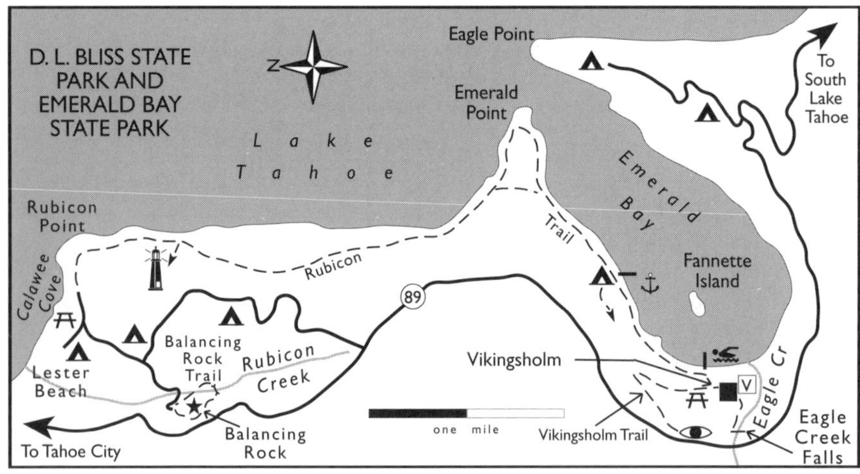

chieftain's castle dating back to A.D. 800. Atop sparsely forested Fannette Island is a stone structure, where Vikingsholm guests occasionally took afternoon tea. It may still be visited by boaters today; launch sites are found outside the park at private facilities. From February 1 through June 15, though, the island—a protected nesting site for Canada geese—is closed to visitors.

*Balancing Rock, D. L. Bliss State Park*

## Attractions and Activities

**Vikingsholm Trail and Tour.** A 1-mile dirt fire road with a 600-foot elevation change switchbacks downhill to Vikingsholm and the Emerald Bay shore. For some, the exposed uphill return is brutal; carry water and take rests as needed. From the trailhead vista, visitors overlook a granite-, shrub-, and tree-mantled slope at Emerald Bay, Fannette Island, Eagle Point, and the boats moving in and out the bay. They can also glimpse upper Eagle Creek Falls.

Tours of Vikingsholm are offered on the half hour, with the last one leaving at 3:30 P.M. Tickets may be purchased at the visitor center, found near Eagle Creek at the bottom of the hill. The center's photographic history of the castle and its interesting mistress, Mrs. Lora J. Knight, provides a fine background for the tour.

The fortress from another time and place seems strangely appropriate here, with the walls built around the ancient cedars and pines. The tour begins in the open-air courtyard, with the park staff offering a history of the place, the architecture, its owner, her noted guests, and their summer routine. Crossed serpents (a Viking symbol) and braided eaves mark the courtyard entrance, while trees pierce its center and a small creek runs through it. At its sides are the sod-roofed wings of the building, holding the main kitchen, the servants' and caretaker's rooms, garage, and workshop.

The main castle is representatively furnished, with many original Scandinavian-painted pieces, but the craftsmanship of the building is truly outstanding. The parlor and dining rooms have a strong rustic appeal. The carved dragon beam suspended from the ceiling is another Viking symbol noting an area of male domain. When upstairs, visitors may note the latches on the outside of the bedroom doors. In A.D. 800 the chieftains commonly locked their guests in for the night.

With each tour approaching the maximum size of 49, and with the fortress's narrow halls and stairways, visitors have only a limited chance to glimpse the many unusual features of Vikingsholm.

*Access:* Begin at the trailhead on the east side of CA 89. Parking cannot begin to serve visitor numbers, so try to arrive early; spillover parking lines CA 89 to the south.

**Eagle Creek Falls Trail.** From Vikingsholm, this 0.4-mile round-trip hike passes through a mixed forest, crisscrossing a small side drainage. At 0.1 mile, it passes beneath a beautiful old-growth fir with a 7-foot diameter. Topping a low ridge at 0.2 mile, visitors find a vista.

The 120-foot falls is beautiful and wide, comprised of skipping and streaming waters coursing down a steep, broad, broken-faced, dark cliff. An upper falls is set back on the next higher rise. The loud rush drowns out voices. Visitors play in the pools created by the falls and scale the rocks at its sides. In early summer, the snow-melt creates a thundering wall of water. Return as you came.

*Access:* Begin near the courtyard entrance to Vikingsholm.

**Balancing Rock Trail.** This 0.4-mile self-guided nature trail visits the trademark feature of D. L. Bliss State Park, a 130-ton balanced rock. As far back as the late 1800s, visitors have sought out this feature for their souvenir photographs. A brochure available at the trailhead introduces the area geology and plants.

The small loop rounds a rock knoll, proceeds past Balancing Rock, crosses Rubicon Creek below a rock-pinched cascade, and returns to the trailhead. Manzanita and huckleberry oak hug the slopes, while white and red fir and Jeffrey, ponderosa, and lodgepole pines make up the open forest.

*Access:* Find the trailhead past the park residences at D. L. Bliss State Park; parking is limited.

**Rubicon Trail.** This 4.8-mile linear trail rolls along Lake Tahoe's southwest shore and links the two state parks.

From Calawee Cove, the route south travels some 100 feet above shore, rounding beneath firs, crossing over boulders, and passing between shrubs of manzanita and huckleberry oak. At Rubicon Point (0.25 mile), hikers can overlook the cliff plunging into the blue-green clarity of Lake Tahoe. As granite steps advance the trail at 0.4 mile, hikers will notice a small balancing rock to the south. Ahead, a spur branches to the lighthouse; keep to the lakeside tour.

Views build to the south and east. Where trails branch right at 0.9 mile, continue straight, entering a full, shaded forest of pines and fir. Lake views are now gone, save for the sun's glint on the water. The creeping skeletons of dead shrubs overlay the forest floor.

At 1.7 miles, the trail is again on an open slope. The high-mountain setting complements the vast blue of the lake. The trail briefly tours closer to shore, only to head uphill, rounding the drainage of a thin, vertically cascading creek lined by alder. A vista rock outcrop waits ahead. Once again nearing the water, the trail tours the scalloped cove north of Emerald Bay.

At 2.7 miles, the Emerald Point Bypass Trail heads right; bear left to round the forested flat of Emerald Point. Some big ponderosa and Jeffrey pines punctuate the forest. After rounding the point, the trail travels the forested edge of Emerald Bay, but small beach areas suggest detours.

Contributing to the bay view are Eagle Point, the granite southwest skyline, Fannette Island, and the boat-camp dock. At 3.4 miles, the Bypass Trail rejoins the main trail, and by 3.9 miles, the Rubicon Trail passes through the boulder-dotted, old-growth-forested flat of the primitive boat-in camp.

Higher upslope, a paved service road from CA 89 and Vikingsholm parallels the trail. Views now are of Fannette Island and the shoreline jut of Parson Rock. After arcing over Parson Rock, the trail comes to the 4.6-mile junction post, above a white sand beach. Vikingsholm lies another 0.2 mile ahead; CA 89 is uphill. Travel through forest or along shore to the castle.

*Access:* Begin at the Calawee Cove Beach parking area or reverse the hike, starting at Vikingsholm.

# AUBURN STATE RECREATION AREA

**Hours/Season:** Year-round, with some closures due to fire danger or wet, impassable roads

**Facilities:** 41 primitive river or lakeside campsites; an open river-bar camp area; 22 boat-in campsites; marina and boat ramp; raft put-in and take-out sites; hiker, horse, and mountain-bike trails; off-road area; nonflush toilets; *bring water*

**For Information:** (916) 885-4527

**Access:** From Auburn, go 1 mile south on CA 49 for the headquarters. The recreation area has multiple accesses off CA 49, Auburn-Foresthill Road, and I-80.

This semi-developed 30,000-acre recreation area enfolds some 30 miles of the Middle and North forks of the American River and owes its existence to the controversy surrounding the building of Auburn Dam. While the issues are debated, the unfettered waters serve up premier raft and kayak adventures, tempt anglers with wild trout, and excite gold fever in the recreational panner. Held back by a small dam on the lower North Fork, Lake Clementine extends the recreation. The long, thin canyon lake offers boating, fishing, waterskiing, and swimming, but has limited access.

Enclosing the river forks is a spectacular, untouched canyon, sheltering deer, bear, and mountain lion. Trails and primitive roads explore its reaches, welcoming travel on foot, horse, and mountain bike. The primitive camps offer solitude and a base from which to explore.

The rugged Sierran foothills bring together mixed chaparral, live and black oak, Digger and ponderosa pine, California buckeye, and willow and alder riparian areas. Large scenic boulders shape and squeeze the river forks. They create prized swimming holes and challenging whitewater runs.

## Attractions and Activities

**Western States Pioneer Express Trail.** A 10.8-mile segment of the long-distance Western States Trail, linking Sacramento and Carson City, Nevada, tours along the Middle Fork American River. Its first 7.1 miles (Quarry Road Trail) is multi-use; across the river, it becomes a hiker/horse-only route.

An upstream tour follows the wide dirt road downhill from the parking area and around a gate. This marks the start of a contouring journey, some 80 feet above the Middle Fork American River. Deep pools entice travelers off the trail, as the river alternately shows still pools and shallow riffles. The good surfaced road is popular with joggers.

At 1.7 miles, the trail enters the quarry, ascending to the upper excavated flat. Where the road forks, bear right keeping to the main route. At 2.1 miles, it again rounds a gate. Although the Western States Trail stakes occur at 0.25-mile intervals, they are notably absent at the junctions.

Past the quarry, keep to the main road. Unmarked side routes regularly branch to the river, while others journey up the slope. At 2.4 miles, a side trail to the river offers a brief look at the wild and woolly Murderer's Gorge Rapid before it halts at an upstream bar. The wide road of the main trail remains open, bordered by live oak, toyon, and small Digger pine.

Cross-river looks soon include Mammoth Bar, Auburn's off-road area. At 3.2

miles, the trail briefly nears the river. Where it draws away, a fine grove of madrone claims it. After a steady ascent, the trail tops out at 4.1 miles and enters a more wooded stretch. In the fall, the buckeye show off their dried leaves and heavy suspended fruit.

Where the route descends, views return. At 5.1 miles, the trail heads across a river bar. In the soft dirt, the early morning traveler may spy bear tracks. Farther along, the bar becomes more heavily cobbled.

Rolling away from the bar, the route tours a moister corridor with maples, black oaks, and fir. At the crest of a small ridge, a steep side trail closed to bikes heads right. The Western States Trail continues straight, reaching a scenic oak grouping, picnic table, and pit toilets at 6.3 miles.

The steep side trail is actually a branch of the Western States Trail. It remains on the south side of the river, passing through the old Sliger gold mine and along the dirt access road to the Cherokee Bar camp. It then reconnects with the Western States Trail, with a river crossing at Ruck-A-Chucky Campground.

Staying straight on the Western States Trail, travelers descend from the picnic site and travel the length of cobble-congested Main Bar, arriving at a river fording at 7.1 miles. A crossing is possible during low water; mountain bikers must turn back here.

Following the fording, the trail remains along or just above Poverty Bar for the next 1.5 miles, but a thick border of willow and alder denies river access. Fir, blackberry, and wild grape are common in the riparian corridor.

Climbing and contouring the slope upstream, the foot trail is either open or semi-wooded, with oak, buckeye, Digger pine, toyon, and poison oak. Much of the way, hikers have open or filtered views of Cherokee Bar, the even-flowing river, and the upstream canyon.

At 10.5 miles, the trail comes out on a dirt road; go right for a continuation of the Western States Trail and to reach Ruck-A-Chucky Campground (10.8 miles).

*Access:* Go 0.4 mile south from the CA 49 bridge over the American River and turn left for trailhead parking.

**Ruck-A-Chucky Falls Hike.** This easy 3-mile round-trip hike contours above the Middle Fork American River, for a falls overlook and river access. A sign at its start shows 1.5 miles to Canyon Creek and 4 miles to Fords Bar.

This upstream journey begins on a onetime road, some 200 feet above a pictur-

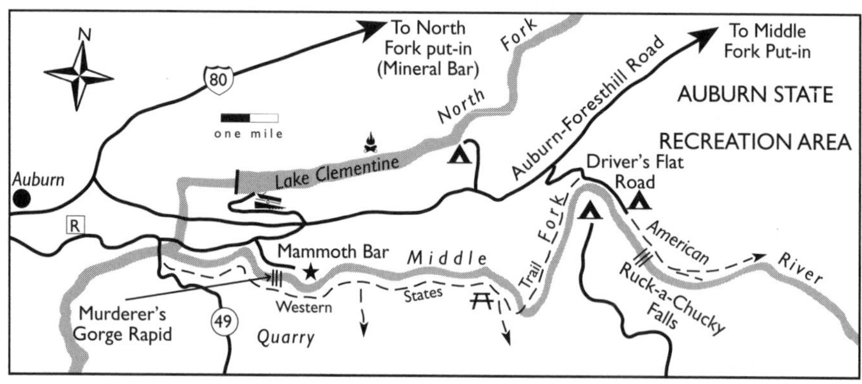

esque segment of the Middle Fork. Dark, slow waters mirror the light-colored bedrock and alternate with riffling, fast-water stretches. The steep, wooded slopes show pine, mixed oaks, laurel, and toyon. Heron, dipper, and kingfisher share the waterway with rafters. The exposed trail affords exceptional views.

At 0.7 mile, a steep 0.2-mile side trail descends to the rocky shore below Ruck-A-Chucky Falls. Beware, the area's river-polished, gray-green rocks are slippery. Here, an angler may be seen, or even a crayfish fighting its way to the shallows.

Keeping to the main trail, hikers soon overlook the squeezed river channel, the abrupt surging drops, and the rounded river boulders of Ruck-A-Chucky Falls. By contrast, the waters upstream bend calm and dark.

At 1.2 miles, the trail passes a shallow mining adit. At the upcoming junction, go right to end the hike riverside. The trail to the left goes to Fords Bar.

At 1.5 miles, after passing through a willow- and blackberry-narrowed passage, hikers arrive at a small sandy beach and a quiet, deep swimming hole, opposite often-dry Canyon Creek. A sandy floor gently slopes to the middle of the river, while downstream the rapids sound. Retrace the way, when ready.

*Access:* Begin at the end of Ruck-A-Chucky Campground, reached by taking Driver's Flat Road off Foresthill Road.

**Rafting.** Neither the North nor Middle Fork American River is a beginner run; both require established whitewater technical skills. Rafters should note the existing flow, know their craft, be realistic in judging their capabilities, and portage their craft when in doubt. Both private and commercial rafts run these waters.

The more difficult of the two, the North Fork presents a 9.5-mile run from Iowa Hill Bridge to Ponderosa Way Bridge, encountering Class III, IV, and V rapids. Named rapids include Chamberlin Falls (a 10-foot linear drop into a roiling pool), Staircase Rapids, and Bogus Thunder. Shirttail Canyon marks where the Class IV rapids end and the Class II ones begin downstream. Most rafters treat this as a 1-day tour; it is best staged when flow levels are between 1,500 to 3,000 cubic feet per second.

The 15-mile Middle Fork American River run between Oxbow and the ruins of Greenwood Bridge at Ruck-A-Chucky Campground may range from a full-day to a 3-day trip. The ride strings together several Class IV rapids, as well as some Class II and III. Named rapids include Tunnel Chute and Ruck-A-Chucky Falls, both of which require mandatory portage. If rafters decide to extend the trip beyond Greenwood Bridge, they should take out at Mammoth Bar. Just downstream, the sharp-walled Murderer's Gorge Rapid is a proven life-taker.

Prior to a trip, rafters should acquire the *Boating Trail Guide to the North and Middle Forks of the American River;* phone the Whitewater Management Office at (916) 885-5648. The publication includes a map showing the put-in and take-out sites, the rapids and their class ratings, and emergency exit roads. The brochure also includes safety and permit information.

For flow information, phone (916) 322-3327. For river camping permits, contact Auburn State Recreation Area headquarters.

**Prospecting.** Personal, recreational gold seeking, utilizing a gold pan or recreational suction dredge or motorized sluice, is allowed within the recreation area. Searches must be conducted within a permanently running streambed, without disturbing surface soils. Muddy water from the panning must dissipate within 20 feet, and dredges must not obstruct navigable waters. Check at the headquarters for open areas and what restrictions apply.

Near Mineral Bar Campground, visitors can see rubble displaced by placer mining, during the Gold Rush era.

# MARSHALL GOLD DISCOVERY STATE HISTORIC PARK

**Hours/Season:** 8:00 A.M. to sunset, except major holidays; 10:00 A.M. to 5:00 P.M. (visitor center)
**Facilities:** Picnic areas, visitor center/museum, historic buildings and sites, restrooms
**For Information:** (916) 622-3470
**Access:** From the US 50–CA 49 junction at Placerville, go 8 miles north on CA 49. The park is in Coloma.

This park commemorates the January 24, 1848, gold discovery made by James Marshall while supervising the building of Sutter's Mill. That discovery awakened the country and the world to the whereabouts and prospects of a place called California. Nearly 70 percent of Coloma, the town which sprang up around the find, lies within the historic park. Some of the original buildings still stand; elsewhere, there are only historical markers.

The park museum and visitor center is a good place to begin tracing the Marshall gold discovery. Films and exhibits take you back in time, and the orientation maps for the self-guided tour may be picked up here. At the entry, rangers post which buildings are open for viewing. Among the more unusual exhibits are a tree-trunk grave marker and a gold nugget from 1848.

In addition to preserving this critical landmark from California's past, the park also serves the South Fork American River recreationist. In summer, the waterway becomes a congested highway of commercial and private rafts. Park guests, too, enjoy cooling off in the clear waters. Others swept up in gold fever can try panning along the east shore, opposite the sawmill area. The tree-shaded North Beach picnic area offers spectators a pleasant spot to sit and take in the river mania.

## Attractions and Activities

**Historic Area Self-guided Tour.** While this park does not lend itself to a neat point-to-point walking tour, it does welcome a series of short park-and-walk explorations. Historical panels identify the sites and relate the tale.

Exploring the museum area, a tour begins at the mining display, with its stamp mills, ore cart, and mining cabin. Close by, at the lower end of a picnic area are two boxy stone buildings with heavy iron doors. One houses the Wah Hop Store featuring the typical items purchased and used by the town's Chinese population. Next to it, in what was the Man Lee Store, is information on the various means of mining, including a mock mining tunnel. A bedrock outcrop at the north end of the picnic area shows a couple of dozen Indian mortars, cups worn into the rock by the grinding of acorns.

Across CA 49 from the museum, along the South Fork of the American River, travelers discover a replica of Sutter's sawmill, an open-sided mill where demonstrations are given periodically. A platform allows a closer inspection. In a small building nearby are some of the original mill timbers. Also at the site is a replica of the cabin used by the Mormon Battalion work crew.

Continuing downstream toward North Beach, visitors pass the original mill site and the discovery site located on a ditch returning to the river—the mill's tailrace.

Touring the town area immediately south of the museum, visitors get to know a little about Coloma, her residents, and businesses. Among the visited townsites is the ruin of the old jail (1857 to 1862). Throughout Coloma, abandoned orchard trees hint at the area's agricultural basis following the rush.

Off Cold Springs Road, at the far south end of town, visitors can explore the pioneer cemetery, where many 49ers were buried. Families, prostitutes, and murderers all share the same hill. The oldest marker dates back to 1850. Some of the graves were never marked, while others have long lost their wooden crosses. Across the way is an old winery.

From Cold Springs Road, making a loop via Monument and Church roads, tourists find the statue of James Marshall atop the hill where he was buried. His figure overlooks the American River, pointing to where he found gold. Among the pedestal designs is an emblem with a gold pan, shovel, pick, and rifle above the discovery year.

Continuing along the loop, the roadway changes to one-way. It is steep and narrow, with tight curves, not recommended for trailers or large RVs. Along it are the Marshall cabin and the historic Catholic church and cemetery. The cabin construction hints at Marshall's skill as a carpenter, and the interior shows furnishings handcrafted from manzanita wood. A mining ditch runs past the cabin.

*Access:* Major parking areas are found near the visitor center/museum, the sawmill, and North Beach, all off CA 49; the Pioneer Cemetery off Cold Springs Road; and Monument picnic area off Monument Road.

**Monroe Ridge Trail to Vista Point.** This 1.5-mile round-trip hike samples the southern end of the 2.3-mile trail crossing the west ridge behind the park. Brochures are available at the trailhead. The well-graded, switchbacking trail makes the 300-foot elevation gain a comfortable undertaking.

The hike begins amid Digger pine, oak, toyon, and madrone, ascending to a scrubbier complex of manzanita, live oak, and California buckeye. By 0.3 mile, gaps

*Rafters, South Fork American River, Marshall Gold Discovery State Historic Park*

in the cover afford looks at the Marshall Monument and snatches of Coloma. Lizards rustle in the dry grass.

By 0.6 mile, the trail rounds onto the south-facing slope. At 0.7 mile is a trail post indicating "vista point." Continue past it along the ridge to a picnic table (0.75 mile), from where you see out across the Lotus Valley. While the views are not outstanding, the ridgetop site is pleasant and offers a different perspective on the area that changed California history. Return as you came or continue along the ridge route.

*Access:* Find the marked trailhead across from the Monument picnic area parking lot.

**Rafting.** The park's North Beach picnic area is a popular put-in and stopover site for rafters on the South Fork American River, but it may not be used as a raft takeout site. Self-registration rafting permits are available at the park.

## Lake Valley State Recreation Area—Washoe Meadows State Park

**Hours/Season:** Year-round

**Facilities:** Concession-run golf course, clubhouse, and restaurant; Nordic ski and snowmobile rentals; restrooms (Lake Valley); informal hiker and mountain-bike trails, *bring water* (Washoe Meadows)

**For Information:** (916) 525-7277 (Lake Valley); (916) 525-7232 (Washoe Meadows)

**Access:** From the CA 89–US 50 junction in South Lake Tahoe, go south on US 50 for 3 miles for the recreation area. For the meadows, continue south on US 50 for another 0.4 mile and turn west on Country Club Road. In 0.4 mile, near the intersection of Country Club and Bakersfield roads, gated dirt fire roads enter the park. An alternative approach to Washoe Meadows is at the corner of South Lake Tahoe Boulevard and Sawmill Road. Park in the U.S. Forest Service lot, cross Sawmill Road, and climb over the wire fence to enter the park.

Along the Upper Truckee River, these adjoining parks bring together an 18-hole golf course, complete with driving range, and some undeveloped forest and meadow reaches. Lake Valley Recreation Area enjoys a beautiful Sierran valley setting, with the granite butte of Twin Peaks overlooking the Lake Tahoe Golf Course clubhouse. To the southwest rises the ragged ridge of Angora, Echo, and Flagpole peaks, and to the northwest towers Mount Tallac.

Washoe Meadows State Park, which borders the Lake Tahoe Golf Course, preserves a wild space along the Upper Truckee River for hiking, jogging, mountain biking, and nature study. Its broad meadows boast a bounty of spring and summer wildflowers, while the river affords a peaceful backdrop. In places, the high peaks to the southwest can be seen above the tops of the lodgepole pines. Informal river paths and about 5 miles of fire road offer tried routes for discovery.

Although the undeveloped park is well set up for travel, it does lack an established public access. Its jigsaw-piece border touches several area roads, allowing good local access, but visitors to the region must go in search of the park. Winter affords the easiest access, for then visitors can ski from the golf course into Washoe Meadows.

## Attractions and Activities

**East Shore Trail.** This 1.2-mile round-trip tour offers a peek in the door at Washoe Meadows.

Following the fire road through a corridor of willow and lodgepole pine, hikers quickly emerge in a dry, bunchgrass meadow, with lupine and yarrow. Where the 2-track ends, trails fork in three directions. The golf course is to the right, while the Upper Truckee River is straight ahead and to the left. Going straight, hikers reach the river in 0.1 mile. It is a scenic, braided stretch, with gravel bars and grassy islands, channeled waters, and silvered logs.

Hiking upstream, visitors overlook areas of mirror-still waters and riffling flows. While mostly shallow, a few deep holes exist. Where an unusual multi-branched lodgepole pine leans over the water, the trail merges with the other river path and continues upstream. On the opposite shore, a fire road travels through forest. A river wading is necessary to reach both it and the bulk of the Washoe Meadows acreage.

The East Shore Trail now travels inland from the river's edge. Wildflowers, willow clumps, and lone-standing pines accent the beautiful golden-green grassy expanse. Some noise from the highway carries to the site. Side paths branch to the water. Where the trail tours a forested stretch, spurs branch left to the neighborhood roads. Remain on the upstream trail.

At 0.5 mile, bear right, following the path along the river's willow edge. The trail soon comes out in another big, beautiful meadow. A ditch now separates the trail from the river. While the footpath continues, plan to turn around at the meadow, as a private resort lies ahead.

*Access:* Begin at the far left access gate at the junction of Country Club and Bakersfield roads; there is summertime-only roadside parking.

**Golfing.** The golf course grounds are flat or mildly rolling, landscaped with native pines. The Upper Truckee River and its side waters contribute to the beauty while providing natural hazards on this championship-caliber course. Golfers find their shots carry far at the 6,000-foot elevation. Canada geese sometimes "play through."

*Access:* Begin at Lake Valley State Recreation Area.

**Winter Sports.** These adjoining parks combine to create a 750-acre playground for Nordic skiers. The mostly gentle terrain is ideal for the newcomer to the sport. At Lake Valley Recreation Area, visitors find ski equipment and snowmobile rentals; a use fee is charged for the groomed ski trails.

# FOLSOM LAKE STATE RECREATION AREA

**Hours/Season:** Year-round

**Facilities:** 3 developed campgrounds with 169 total sites; environmental campsites; picnic areas; historic building; primitive and developed boat launches; marina; snackbars; boat and beach rentals; designated swimming areas; equestrian center; hiker, horse, bicycle, and mountain-bike trails; restrooms; nonflush toilets; showers; dump stations; water at developed areas

**For Information:** (916) 988-0205

**Access:** Between Folsom and Auburn, the recreation area is encircled by US 50,

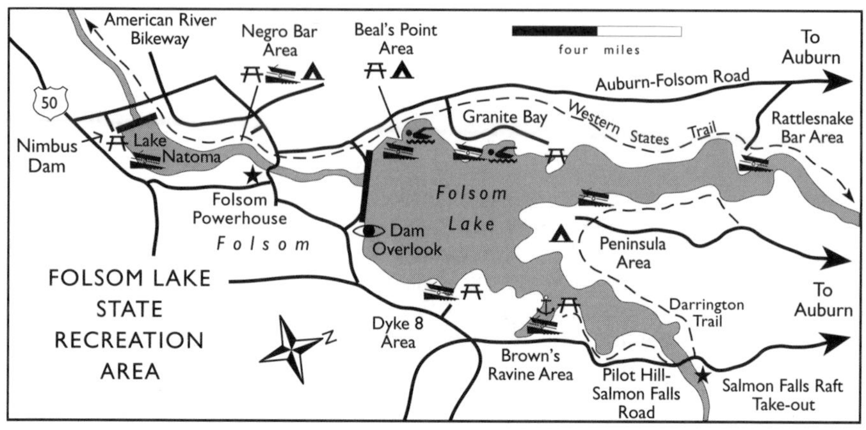


Auburn–Folsom Road, and Pilot Hill–Salmon Falls Road, with multiple marked access sites.

Capturing the waters of the American River, this 18,000-acre reservoir and its 75 miles of shore provide boating, fishing, swimming, hiking, and horseback and mountain-bike riding opportunities. Its Skunk Hollow Area is the final raft take-out site for the South Fork American River. Near Nimbus Dam on Lake Natoma (a smaller downstream reservoir within the recreation area), a first-rate aquatic center offers safe boating classes and lessons in sailing, windsurfing, kayaking, and canoeing.

Low valley terrain surrounds much of Folsom Lake, while steep canyon walls enclose its river arms. Area habitats include chaparral, grassland, riparian, and pine-oak forest. Although the metropolitan sprawl approaches the reservoir, visitors can still find remote wilds in the canyon arms and places to be alone in the primitive dispersed-use areas.

Campgrounds are at Beal's Point and Peninsula on Folsom Lake and at Negro Bar on Lake Natoma. Most of the sites are semi-wooded, with the campgrounds offering similar services. Peninsula Campground is the more remote and wooded, but lacks a shower facility. Situated between the North and South Fork American River arms, it may be reached by driving 10 miles off CA 49 at Pilot Hill or by boat.

Visitors find a fine, expansive day-use facility at Beal's Point—a broad, landscaped peninsula, with a sandy beach, buoyed swimming area, and lifeguard services. A rental concession offers a full range of lake recreation equipment from shade canopies and volleyball sets to sailboards and canoes. Food services are also available.

Canada geese winter at Folsom Lake, while herons maintain rookeries at Anderson Island Natural Preserve and on Lake Natoma's south shore. Coveys of quail commonly race through camp or across the trails. Vultures, hawks, and eagles claim the sky.

## Attractions and Activities

**Folsom Powerhouse Tour.** This 1895 powerhouse, one of the oldest hydroelectric facilities in the country, remains remarkably intact inside and out. In this tall, red-brick, windowless structure, visitors can see its impressive prisoner-cut stone interior and the vintage penstocks, generators, and Tennessee marble switchboard. On the grounds, a trail leads to the drained forebays. A display board near the powerhouse explains the features involved in power generation.

In 1895, this powerhouse marked the first long-distance transmission of high-voltage electricity for commercial use. It served Sacramento some 22 miles distant. The pioneering effort gave life to the Grand Electric Carnival seen across the valley.

On the tour, visitors are walked through the rooms, tracing the creation of electricity. A fire-damaged generator is an interesting discovery. In this 100-year-old facility, safety systems were nonexistent.

Bats now occupy the dark recesses of the powerhouse turbine rooms. Only their high-pitched voices betray their presence. These bats are Mexican free-tails, and unlike other bats that migrate to warmer winter locales, they hibernate at the site.

The grounds are open year-round, the powerhouse noon to 4:00 P.M., Wednesday through Sunday.

*Access:* Find the powerhouse on the upper east side of Lake Natoma, off Riley Street.

**Folsom Dam Tour.** Holding back the waters of the American River is this impressive 340-foot-high concrete dam. Together with its earthen wing dams, it spans 9 miles, and it contains enough concrete to build a sidewalk from San Francisco to New York City. The Bureau of Reclamation offers Folsom Dam tours at 10:00 A.M. and 1:00 P.M., Tuesday through Saturday; each lasts just over an hour.

*Access:* Tours begin at the base, enter the dam, and visit the tower and powerhouse. For more information, phone (916) 989-7275.

**Recreation Area Trails.** While lake recreation remains the park's primary draw, its shore offerings are rising in popularity. The growing trail system serves hiker, horseback rider, bicyclist, and mountain-bike rider, with close to 100 miles in all. Several premier long-distance routes pass through the recreation area.

The 32-mile-long paved *American River Bikeway* travels from Beal's Point at Folsom Lake to Discovery Park in Old Town Sacramento. It offers a fine, carefree ride south from the park, touring the southwest corner of Folsom Lake and the west shores of Lake Natoma and the American River.

For nearly 35 miles, the *Western States Pioneer Express Equestrian Trail,* linking Sacramento and Carson City, Nevada, travels the wooded and grassy west shore of Folsom Lake. From the Granite Bay Horse Assembly Area, a 20-mile ride north travels along the scenic North Fork American River to the Auburn staging area; a 14-mile tour south passes along the Folsom and Natoma lakeshores to the Nimbus Overlook assembly area off Hazel Avenue. Stables lying outside the park offer guided trail rides.

The *Darrington Trail,* open to mountain bikers and hikers, travels 7.8 miles from the Skunk Hollow trailhead (at Salmon Falls Bridge on Pilot Hill–Salmon Falls Road) to the Peninsula Campground. Rated an intermediate to advanced ride, the single-track trail traces the lake's South Fork American River shore, traversing wooded stretches and crossing intermittent creeks. But, with much of the trail being open, carry plenty of water.

**Boating.** Folsom Lake offers ample room for all kinds of boating: trolling, speedboating, waterskiing, jet-skiing, sailing, and windsurfing.

Lake levels range from a high elevation of 466 feet in early summer to a low of 426 feet in early winter. As the lake recedes, the launch ramps migrate with it, but at times the drop can exceed their reach. With this fluctuation, boaters need to be alert to low-water hazards.

*Marina at Brown's Ravine, Folsom Lake State Recreation Area*

Paved ramps at Dyke 8, Granite Bay, Rattlesnake Bar, and Peninsula Campground, as well as a protected, full-service marina at Brown's Ravine, serve boaters. The marina offers wet and dry slips, a gas dock, courtesy docks, a marine supply store, and snackbar.

Fully self-contained vessels with sleeping quarters may be moored overnight for two consecutive nights. Boaters wishing to do so must register at Granite Bay or Brown's Ravine; a map of the designated areas may be picked up at that time. Boaters may also boat in to Peninsula Campground to camp on shore in a designated site.

Long, narrow 500-acre Lake Natoma has a 5-miles-per-hour boat speed for its entire length, with no motorized boats allowed between Nimbus Dam and Willow Creek. Negro Bar is the developed access on this lake. Willow Creek and Nimbus Flat offer primitive launch sites.

**Fishing.** Folsom Lake presents anglers a healthy, varied fishery of trout, bass, kokanee, catfish, sunfish, crayfish, and even sturgeon, at its lower depths. Fishing from shore or boat is open year-round; Lake Natoma adds more opportunity for angling. Below Nimbus Dam at Nimbus Shoals, special conditions apply, so consult the current fish and game regulations.

## Sacramento's State Park Units

**Hours/Season:** Most are open daily, except major holidays, 10:00 A.M. to 5:00 P.M.
**Facilities:** Restrooms
**For Information:** (916) 445-7373
**Access:** All are within Sacramento.

Seven park units within the city of Sacramento unravel the story of early California, its politics, and its players. Both guided and self-guided tours introduce these sites. To join any tour, plan on arriving at least one hour before closing.

**California State Capitol Building.** Surrounded by a 40-acre park, the Capitol Building houses a working government in a nineteenth-century setting of classic architecture. Central to the building is the richly detailed 120-foot dome; contributing to the Capitol Building elegance are rich woods, tiles, marble, and fine art. The building serves as a tribute to the restoration process, in which teams, drawing from old records and photographs, undid one hundred years of remodeling, returning the interior to its original look. The exterior is Greek and Roman in style.

A visit begins at the basement tour office, where visitors can sign up for a guided tour or pick up a brochure for a self-guided one. The basement also holds a museum, theater, and a legislative bill room, which has complimentary copies of pending legislation.

On the first floor, visitors can look back into time at the government offices of 1906. The furnishings, coal-burning stoves, old vaults, and fixtures recreate the period. In the central office of Governor Pardee, telegrams carry word of the San Francisco earthquake.

The second floor holds the leadership offices, and the third floor houses the assembly chambers, blending historic furniture with contemporary speaker systems and technology. When legislature is in session, visitors can observe the process from the gallery. Interesting bits of California history are found throughout the building.

*Access:* Find the Capitol at 10th and L streets.

**Governor's Mansion.** Built in 1877 for hardware magnate Albert Gallatin, this Victorian mansion housed thirteen California governors' families from 1903 to 1967. The building is shown by guided tour. The rooms remain as they were when the Reagans vacated the premises in 1967. The mansion holds the actual furnishings used by the governors' families, as well as any personal items they may have added to the collection.

Within the rooms are items ranging from antiques to a television set. The portraits of the first ladies, who oversaw the household, decorate one hallway.

*Access:* The mansion is located at 16th and H streets.

**Leland Stanford Mansion State Historic Park.** The four-story Victorian home of Leland Stanford (former California governor, businessman, and railroad chief executive officer) stands out amid contemporary high-rises. It offers the public an unusual opportunity to look at an ongoing restoration and see the meticulous detective work that goes into returning this structure to its 1872 appearance. Some rooms will reflect an earlier period.

On the plaster walls, date rings surround careful sandings, tracking the paint color changes over time. Posted nearby are old photographs of the furnished rooms; each one carefully marked to show which Stanford pieces remain in the park collection. Cuts in the wall reveal clues to remodelings, or record events such as the flood of 1862. Throughout the tour, the incredible woodwork, marble fireplaces, and etched glass recall the home's former splendor and hint at the days to come. The park hopes to complete the project by the year 2000.

It is shown by guided tour on a limited basis. Tours are given on Tuesdays and Thursdays at 12:15 P.M. and on Saturdays at 12:15 and 1:30 P.M., but call before planning a visit. The phone number is (916) 324-0575.

*Access:* The Stanford Mansion is at the corner of 8th and N streets.

**Sutter's Fort State Historic Park.** High, exterior white walls of adobe brick encompass the rectangular compound of Sutter's Fort. In 1840, John Sutter became a naturalized Mexican citizen and a year later received a Mexican land grant. He constructed his fort and broke ground for crops about a mile from the American River. It was the beginning of his dream settlement—New Helvetia (New Switzerland)—the beginning of Sacramento.

During its day, Sutter's Fort was a critical supply outpost. It sent aid to the stranded Donner Party, and it outfitted the 49ers. Ironically, it was the discovery of gold at Sutter's Mill that led to the eventual demise of the fort. Sutter's workers rushed away to the gold fields, his business partners cheated him, squatters overtook his land, and the lawless miners raided his fields and butchered his livestock.

Today, visitors tour the fort compound, residences, and workshops restored to their 1846 appearance. Exhibits and audio-wands with recorded messages relate the story of John Sutter and fort life. A gun room, trading post, smithy, cooperage, and textiles room reveal the enterprises of the day.

On living-history days, docents in period costume demonstrate musket drills, candledipping, weaving, and other frontier skills. The doctor's quarters is particularly interesting with its terrifying assemblage of surgeon's tools.

*Access:* The fort is located at 2701 L Street.

**California State Indian Museum.** Next door to Sutter's Fort, this museum reveals aspects about the life of the California Indians, past and present. Prior to the Europeans' arrival, some 300,000 Native Americans belonging to some 150 tribes occupied what is now California. By the mid-1800s, their numbers were greatly reduced.

This museum honors the many Indian cultures, and their ongoing role in California, through film, photographs, artifacts, and exhibits. Displays address the role of women, examine customs, and describe various ceremonial dances—their purpose, garb, and regalia. Others look at musical instruments; the role of tobacco; handgames, money, and gambling; the use of natural resources and the importance of baskets; and the value of boats. Along the walls, photographs offer a look at the old ways and life today.

*Access:* The museum is at 2618 K Street.

**Old Sacramento State Historic Park.** This riverfront shopping district nestled between the freeway and the Sacramento River successfully ties together the city's past and present commerce. The old-time storefronts and wooden business signs, the veranda-covered boardwalks, old-fashioned lampposts, and passing stagecoach tours transport visitors back in time. It is like stumbling onto a movie set, while you shop, dine, museum hop, or stroll.

In addition to the stage tours, there are docent-led walks and self-guided walking tours of the district. Pick up a brochure at the visitor center on Front Street. Among the points of interest are the Lady Adams Building, the district's oldest, having survived the fire of 1852. Others include the reconstructed Central Pacific Passenger Building (part of the California State Railroad Museum), the reconstructed Eagle Theatre, the B. F. Hastings Building (now a museum), and monuments to the Pony Express and the engineer behind the transcontinental railroad. Riverboats and steam trains further capture the spirit of Old Sacramento.

*Access:* Take the J Street exit off I-5, and follow the signs to Old Sacramento.

**California State Railroad Museum.** This museum boasts a premier, growing collection of restored, spic-and-span locomotives and passenger cars from the 1860s to the 1960s. Among them are the *Governor Stanford* and the *C. P. Huntington*, which were initially fired up in Sacramento back in the 1860s.

The roundhouse occupies one end of the Great Hall. There, a restored 1929 sleeping car, the *St. Hyacinthe*, allows visitors to experience a night ride, complete with rocking motion, the sounds of the crossings, and lights briefly breaking the black of night. At the opposite end of the hall is an elaborate, full-scale diorama of a Sierra Nevada construction site for the transcontinental railroad.

Visitors can wander among the exhibits and also admire them from above on the second floor. A slide program, movie, or visit to the library adds to one's understanding of railroading. Docents lead tours daily at 1:00 P.M.

Not far from the museum, visitors may tour the 1876 Central Pacific Passenger Station and Freight Depot. For those with an irrepressible urge to climb aboard on summer weekends, an hourly excursion train departs from the depot; a separate fee is charged. In the off-season, it operates on the first weekend of the month, from noon to 3:00 P.M.

*Access:* The museum is located in Old Sacramento on I Street.

## Grover Hot Springs State Park

**Hours/Season:** Year-round
**Facilities:** 76 developed forested campsites; picnic area, which doubles as a 17-site winter camp area; hot-springs pool, swimming pool, and pool house; hiker trails; restrooms; showers
**For Information:** (916) 694-2248
**Access:** From CA 89 in Markleeville, turn west on County E-1/Hot Springs Road to reach the park in 3.4 miles. *In winter, the maximum vehicle length is 15 feet.*

On the eastern flank of the Sierra, Grover Hot Springs enjoys a magnificent setting. Its high-elevation forest and broad, glacier-carved meadow are cupped by the forest and the exposed volcanic mud slopes of Hawkins and Markleeville peaks; the actual summits are not visible from the park. Although the park itself proffers only a few miles of trail, it provides a hiker gateway to the forest and wilderness lands of its regal neighborhood.

The park alone is better suited for its Nordic skiing and snowshoeing. The flat or gently rolling meadow and the winter-closed loops of the campground are ideal for families and beginners. Capping a day in the snow, visitors have the uncommon luxury of stepping into the park's famed hot-springs pool.

The park's natural hot springs and the developed concrete pool it feeds are indeed its primary draw. The thermal waters emerge from the ground at a temperature of 148 degrees Fahrenheit. Unlike its sulfurous counterparts though, this spring's mineral makeup renders it virtually odorless, but the chemistry does contribute to the yellow-green hue of the hot-springs pool. At its above-ground origin, the springs also create a natural salt lick, drawing wildlife to the area.

### Attractions and Activities

**Pool House.** Visitors may choose between the waist-deep, 102-degree-Fahrenheit hot-springs pool and a larger swimming pool kept at a comfortable 75 degrees. Despite the solid wooden fence enclosing the pools, the open-air cathedral allows visitors to smell the mountain air, feel the breeze, and gaze up at the treetops. Swimsuits are required. Visitor conveniences at the pool house include restrooms, showers, and changing areas.

Generally, the pools are open from 9:00 A.M. to 9:00 P.M. daily, except in winter. Visitors should phone for the existing winter schedule as it varies from year to year. The pools are closed for major holidays and for periodic maintenance and cleaning, including the last two weeks of September. Again, a phone call before visiting may prevent an unnecessary trip. A use fee is charged.

**Transition Nature Trail.** This 1.25-mile, self-guided hiker loop is an excellent park orientation tour. A brochure may be purchased at the entrance station.

A clockwise tour begins following Hot Springs Creek upstream. Small cascades and boulders accent the clear, cool-water creek, while alders and willows overhang it. Carrying the runoff from the pools, the creek does not betray its hot-springs beginnings. During fishing season, the creek is planted with catchable-size trout. Above the trail is a small knoll—a moraine left behind by the glacier that caused the meadow's formation.

The meadow sweeps away to the forested foot of Hawkins Peak Ridge. Mullein, wind-shaped juniper, and snags alone pierce the golden-green expanse. Passing through it, visitors may see aster, lupine, goldenrod, and buttercup. At 0.3 mile, where the trail travels through a Jeffrey pine stand, the vanilla smell can be so strong that hikers can almost taste it.

Ahead, arrow posts point hikers away from the creek and through the meadow to the forest at its upper end. From the meadow, open views to the southwest find the slope of Markleeville Peak. From the upper end of the meadow (0.6 mile), the trail swings back toward camp. At 0.75 mile, near a lightning-struck tree, the Transition Trail nears the wide dirt lane of the Burnside Trail, eventually merging with it.

At 1 mile bear right, leaving the Burnside Trail. Winds launch waves through the tall grass. The loop closes near the start at 1.25 miles.

*Access:* Begin on the north side of the Hot Springs Creek bridge between the campground and picnic area.

## Chaw'se Indian Grinding Rock State Historic Park

**Hours/Season:** Year-round; 11:00 A.M. to 3:00 P.M. weekdays and 10:00 A.M. to 4:00 P.M. weekends (museum)

**Facilities:** 23 developed semi-open campsites, an environmental (bark house) group camp, picnic sites, museum and gift shop, recreated Miwok village, hiker trails, restrooms, showers

**For Information:** (209) 296-7488

**Access:** From the CA 49–CA 88 junction in Jackson, go 7.7 miles east on CA 88, turn left on Pine Grove–Volcano Road, and go another 1.4 miles to reach the park.

Centerpiece to this 135-acre park is a large, flat limestone outcrop exhibiting more than 1,100 mortar holes (chaw'ses) and some 360 barely visible petroglyphs. This rock is more richly laden with grinding cups than any other in North America, and it is one of only two sites known to exist where the native peoples deliberately decorated their work stones. Some of the carved designs date back two to three thousand years. A couple of lesser outcrops showing grinding cups are located nearby and elsewhere in the meadow.

*Mortars, Chaw'se Indian Grinding Rock State Historic Park*

## Attractions and Activities

**Chaw'se Regional Indian Museum.** The museum reflects the shared lifestyle of ten Sierra Nevada tribes, including the Miwoks from this site. Displays, a film, and artifacts introduce the people, their customs and beliefs, and their way of life. The touch table is particularly interesting. Its collection includes a flicker cage, a two-piece arrow with reusable shaft, and hand games and musical instruments. The museum itself is attractive, consisting of a large, round, high-ceilinged room with a window to the sky.

**Grinding Rock and Recreated Miwok Village.** A wide, 0.1-mile concrete walkway leads from the museum to the grinding rock and a recreated Miwok village with four bark houses, a granary, and game field. More bark houses and the ceremonial roundhouse are located slightly downhill.

A platform extends out over the rock, allowing a better look at the pockmarked surface and the now-faint carvings of wiggly lines and spoked wheels. While a low rail fence rings the stone, visitors may circle the enclosure to acquire a better angle for viewing and photographing the rock, given the shadow and light. The wildflower-dotted, rolling grass meadow and magnificent valley oaks at the site further recall the days of the Miwok Indian. Acorn woodpeckers fly between the trees.

Each September, the Miwok people celebrate the harvest thanksgiving at the Chaw'se Big Time. The event features a Native American soccer game, traditional music and dance, food, and crafts. The public is welcome.

*Access:* Begin at the museum.

**South Nature Trail.** This 0.5-mile, self-guided trail travels the park's meadow, wood, and riparian areas. A first-rate brochure points out the native plants and describes their use by the Miwok people; it may be purchased at the trailhead or museum.

At the tour's start, big valley oaks shade a reconstructed village site with a granary and eight more of the tepee-shaped bark houses, made of long strips of cedar bark tethered to a pole frame. A footbridge crossing over a small creek leads into the choked forest near the boundary.

As the trail ascends, a more varied forest of pine, cedar, and madrone enfolds the trail. Past an old mining ditch is a particularly pretty multi-trunked madrone. The nature trail concludes near the campground. Return to the trail's start and the museum.

*Access:* Downhill from the museum, take the dirt path away from the Ceremonial Roundhouse and Practice House.

# Calaveras Big Trees State Park

**Hours/Season:** Year-round; normal hours: 10:00 A.M. to 4:00 P.M. daily, off-season hours: 11:00 A.M. to 3:00 P.M. weekends (visitor center)
**Facilities:** 129 developed forested campsites (fewer in winter), picnic areas, visitor center, hiker trails, restrooms, nonflush toilets, showers, seasonal dump station, water at North Grove and Oak Hollow areas
**For Information:** (209) 795-2334
**Access:** The park entrance is off CA 4, 2.5 miles west of Dorrington and 2.7 miles east of Arnold.

Located on the western slope of the Sierra Nevada, this 6,300-acre park boasts two ancient sequoia groves, with more than a thousand of the mammoth trees gracing its skyline. The park also holds the stump of the Discovery Tree. In 1853, promoters felled this tree, making a dance floor of the stump, a bowling alley of the trunk, and a traveling display of the stripped-bark shell. The deed so riled John Muir that he wrote "The Vandals Then Danced Upon the Stump!" For a time, Calaveras's North Grove was thought to be the lone growing place for this magnificent tree, drawing both scientists and dignitaries to its door.

In addition to the big trees, the park enjoys the beauty of the Stanislaus River. It flows through a mixed-forest corridor, coursing over bedrock and around large boulders. The surface shows alternating smooth black waters and white-water riffles and rapids. Summer guests enjoy both fishing and cooling off in the pools.

## Attractions and Activities

**Forest Blooms.** The park forest reveals a beautiful midstory of dogwood, with pockets of azalea along the creeks. In spring, the floral display is so popular, the park has a postcard notification system, alerting visitors to the event. In autumn, the red-hued dogwood leaves and berries again bring enchantment to the groves.

**North Grove Trail.** This 1-mile self-guided loop is the most-traveled trail in the park. A brochure may be purchased at the trailhead or at the visitor center, where visually impaired visitors may borrow a tour audiotape. The 600-foot Three Senses Trail starts next to the North Grove loop.

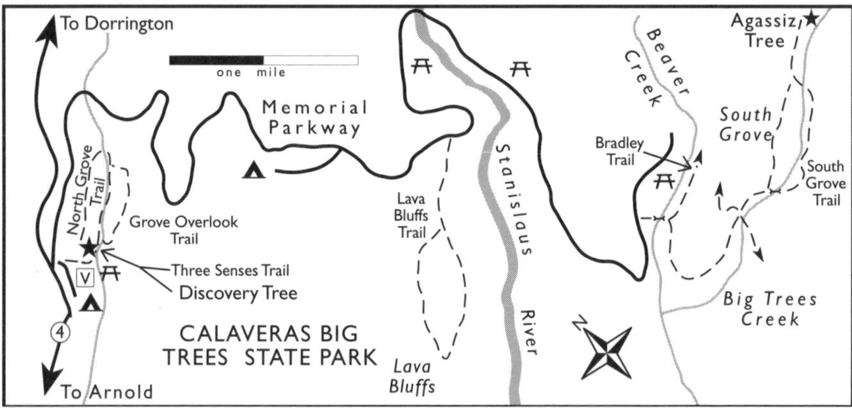

*Agassiz Tree, Calaveras Big Trees State Park*

The loop begins near the 24-foot-diameter stump of the Discovery Tree; stairs lead to its top for a humbling perspective. It took five men twenty-two days to drill the circumference with auger holes, and several days more to fell the tree. A nearby kiosk offers a pictorial history of the grove.

On a clockwise tour, a platform takes visitors up close to a split-trunked giant. Farther along, they can see how the sequoia grows intermixed with trees of the ponderosa pine belt. Dogwood and hazel weave a midstory, while starflower and pathfinder dot the ground. The brochure only points out a few of the giant trees; many more occupy the grove, dwarfing even the big sugar pines.

A walk-through tree, the nearly perfect Abraham Lincoln Tree, and the stripped Mother of the Forest snag (a second victim of promoters) are among the tour features. Near the Mother is a side route to the Carson-Emigrant Trail.

At 0.6 mile, visitors may either continue on the loop trail, traveling the boardwalk alongside the tumbled Father of the Forest, or go left on the Grove Overlook Trail. Remaining on the loop, near the Mother and Son, visitors find a canted-backed bench for comfortably admiring the treetops—one of the best features of the tour.

*Access:* Begin at the day-use parking near the entrance. A 0.1-mile walk on a wide dirt lane leads to the loop.

**South Grove Trail.** This 5.25-mile round-trip hike loops through the park's larger, more remote grove and visits the Agassiz Tree, the park's biggest. Purchase trail brochures at the visitor center or trailhead, and carry water for the tour.

The trail passes through a bunchgrass meadow to the Beaver Creek footbridge. The creek is about 15 feet wide, flowing over a bedrock floor. Climbing away from it, at 0.2 mile hikers come to the Bradley Trail junction. The 2.5-mile Bradley Trail journeys left, touring an area previously logged, while the South Grove Trail continues straight.

Keeping to the South Grove tour, hikers soon round over a ridge, following the Big Trees Creek drainage upstream. Dogwood and hazel have a spotty forest presence. Where the trail approaches the creek at 0.9 mile, azaleas are abundant.

Ahead, the trail crosses a fire road, and at 1.1 miles, it crosses over an old logging railroad grade, an ominous reminder of what might have been. At 1.25 miles is the loop junction; go right, crossing the footbridge, for a counterclockwise tour.

Ascending from the creek, hikers encounter the first giant sequoias. Pathfinder, clintonia, and prince's pine decorate the forest floor. Dogwoods become more common. Hikers may note the peculiar size difference between the tiny cones of the giant sequoia and the long, heavy ones of the sugar pine. When panning the forest, the rounded crowns of the many ancient sequoias stand out.

At 2 miles, where the trail again crosses the creek, the hollowed log next to the trail offers a different look at the forest. Here, too, the spur to the Agassiz Tree heads right; the loop continues downstream.

Opting for the side trip, visitors are rewarded with seeing many more of the big trees. At 2.2 miles, hikers may stand inside the burned-out Chimney Tree and look out its top at the sky. Remarkably, the tree still lives. In another quarter mile, the trail passes a pair of merged giants. The formal trail then ends at the Agassiz Tree (2.8 miles), named for a Swiss naturalist. Beyond it, volunteer-constructed trails extend the exploration for another couple of miles. Ranked among the ten largest sequoias, the Agassiz Tree is 25 feet in diameter and stands 250 feet tall.

Return to the loop (3.6 miles) and continue downstream along Big Trees Creek. While still present, the sequoias become fewer in number. Ahead is a nice group of three. Next to them is an uprooted, hollow stump. Maple, hazel, and oak grow along the creek. The trail passes through a fine azalea patch, before the loop closes at 4 miles. Retrace the initial 1.25 miles.

*Access:* Find the trailhead parking lot off Memorial Parkway, 8 miles south of the North Grove area.

**Lava Bluffs Trail.** This 2.9-mile round-trip trail travels the upper forested slopes of the Stanislaus River drainage, crossing a lahar meadow. It is best hiked in the early morning and in the spring. Carry water.

The hike begins rounding a dry forest slope with ponderosa pine, cedar, and live and black oak; rocks stud the trailbed. As the trail rolls between rises, the forest floor shows an open mat of evergreen needles or thick areas of mountain misery. Openings afford cross-canyon views.

At 0.3 mile is the loop junction. Going right begins a counterclockwise tour, traveling the more demanding leg first. Manzanita grow in the open forest, and quail sometimes flush from hiding. Where the trail dips to El Venado Creek (often dry), hikers find dogwood and fir. At 0.8 mile is the first open view out and across the Stanislaus River; lava bluffs and cliffs mark the canyon slope ahead.

The trail next rounds and descends at the bottom edge of a steep lahar meadow. An array of wildflowers intersperses the grasses, while the rounded rock debris makes footing difficult. Poison oak dots the trail sides, and woodpeckers can be heard in the nearby trees. After passing under a ledge of consolidated volcanic rock, the trail returns to a pine-oak forest.

At 1.5 miles is the vista junction. Here, a 50-foot side path leads to an uninspired look at the lava bluff. It used to be the site of the Stanislaus River bed, until lava filled it in, and the river cut its present-day canyon.

Stay left for the loop, soon touring a fragment of an 1850s water ditch. Where the trail leaves the ditch, it becomes more rolling; twice more, it will return to the ditch. Along lower El Venado Creek (2.2 miles), hikers see a beautiful patch of chain fern and dogwoods. For the next 0.2 mile, the trail ascends, remaining in mixed forest.

The loop concludes, contouring above the Stanislaus River. Return as you came.

*Access:* Find the trailhead parking lot off Memorial Parkway, 4.5 miles south of the North Grove area.

**Winter Sports.** When snow claims the park, North Grove Trail and the miles of park road call to Nordic skiers and snowshoers. Rangers occasionally lead tours.

## BODIE STATE HISTORIC PARK

**Hours/Season:** Summer hours, 9:00 A.M. to 7:00 P.M.; winter hours, 9:00 A.M. to 4:00 P.M.
**Facilities:** Picnic sites, historic buildings, museum, nonflush toilets, water
**For Information:** (760) 647-6445
**Access:** On US 395, go 7 miles south of Bridgeport and turn east onto CA 270 to reach the park in 13 miles. *The road is not recommended for trailers. Off-season visitors should phone the park for current road conditions.*

Bodie, a wild boom town of the 1880s, owes its start to the 1859 gold discovery of Waterman S. Body, from whom it derives its name. During its heyday, the town boasted a population approaching 10,000 and a scandalous reputa-

*Bodie*

tion. It is said that the firebell, which tolled the ages of the deceased, was seldom silent as sickness, hardship, and reckless living whittled at the camp numbers. Holdups and street frays were commonplace. "Justice," as rendered by the Vigilante 601 Committee, likewise rang the bell.

Some 65 saloons and gambling halls lined the town's mile-long Main Street, while Bodie's new elite emulated San Francisco society. The Miners' Union and the Masons and Odd Fellows lodges hosted balls and other gatherings. A Catholic church and a Methodist church steered the town's devoted.

Three major fires swept through Bodie, leaving behind the town as it is seen today. Cradled in this desolate high-desert place, devoid of trees and dusted by sagebrush, the ghost town's rustic wooden buildings capture the wholehearted endorsement of photographers. The shootists in the streets of Bodie today carry 35mm cameras.

At an elevation of 8,400 feet, Bodie endures a bitter climate, so bring extra clothing and come prepared for weather changes.

## Attractions and Activities

**Self-guided Mining Town Tour.** Visitors may set their own course or follow a self-guided walking tour. Brochures are available at the park, Memorial Day through Labor Day; off-season visitors should phone and request one prior to visiting. During the summer, history talks add to one's appreciation of the park.

At this remote mountain mining camp, it is easy to step back in time. Some 100 buildings, nearly five percent of the original town, still stand, maintained in a state of "arrested decay." A few allow access, but most are viewed through their windows or from the sidewalks and streets.

One senses the desperate day-to-day existence while standing in a room with only newspaper to hold back the wind or when reading the grave markers, where names were passed on from infant to infant until one lived long enough to own it. The shelves at the general store reveal the self-reliance of the townspeople; the red-light district hints at their boredom. The old Miners' Union Hall now houses a museum.

Looking at the west slope of Bodie Bluff, visitors can see the Standard Mine and Mill—responsible for the 1878 Bodie gold rush—now in disrepair. The stamp mill, however, may be viewed in a guided-tour setting.

With a history of fire and the town's "tinderbox" condition, smoking is prohibited. Visitors should beware of the nails, broken glass, rusted cans, and splintered wood that are a part of the ghost town's character.

**Standard Stamp Mill Guided Tour.** Offered during the summer, this tour lasts about an hour. With the tour group's size limited to twenty, upon arriving at the park interested parties should pick up a reservation token at the museum. The tour skirts the mill exterior before venturing inside. Typically, the narrative revolves around gold mining, the life of a miner, and the milling and refining process.

**Snowmobiling/Nordic Skiing/Snowshoeing.** During the winter, these methods of transportation represent the only means of reaching the park, throwing open the door to a whole different experience. Winter shows the frontier ghost town in all its isolation.

Snowmobilers must remain on the designated marked routes. Winter visitors should always contact the park in advance of a visit to learn about current conditions. Normal snowfall can be 3 to 6 feet deep, with drifts up to 20 feet. The wind-chill factor can be devastating.

# COLUMBIA STATE HISTORIC PARK

**Hours/Season:** Generally 10:00 A.M. to 5:00 P.M., except major holidays
**Facilities:** Picnic sites, historic town, nature trail, restrooms
**For Information:** (209) 532-4301
**Access:** From downtown Sonora, follow CA 49 north for 2.3 miles. Bear right on Parrotts Ferry Road and go another 1.6 miles to reach the park.

This park offers visitors a unique opportunity to tour an actual Gold Rush town and to see, feel, hear, taste, and smell it. The blacksmith shop rings with the clang of pounded metal. At the candy kitchen, visitors can sample the sweet taste of old-fashioned licorice or horehound drops. Visitors can ride into town on the hard wooden seats of an authentic stagecoach, or they can catch gold fever and pan for flakes and dust.

The paved, tree-lined streets of town are open to pedestrian, horse, and stage travel only. Buildings are about evenly split between walk-in or window-viewing museums and concession-operated businesses that convey the mood and services of the gold town of old. Covered boardwalks connect the Western-style fronts of the red-brick buildings. Old-style wooden signs announce the enterprises, while horse hitching rails serve patrons.

Picnic sites are located along the landscaped boulevards of the parking lot and dispersed through town. Near the old schoolhouse, visitors find a nature-trail loop. Horse rentals are available for guided rides on the area trails or for passing through town.

*Gold panning trough, Columbia State Historic Park*

## Attractions and Activities

**Columbia Walking Tour.** At the corner of Main and State streets is the park visitor center and museum, where visitors can view a Gold Rush slide show and look at the exhibits and displays on mining, Columbia and her townspeople, and the restoration process. There, too, they can purchase a brochure for the self-guided tour or perhaps join one of the docent-led ones. The brochure includes a town map with each building numbered and paired with a number-coded description, allowing visitors to tour Columbia in random order, going where they please.

Many of the buildings have plaques noting how they were previously used. Some have audio messages telling the visitor about the room and the items being viewed. With so many historic items on display, the building interiors are protected by carbon dioxide; it chokes a fire and prevents water damage. The heart of Columbia had a long history of fires, with major ones in 1854, 1857, and 1861.

Housed in the French bakery is an exhibit devoted to the Chinese. They accounted for one-sixth of Columbia's total population, occupying the west and later the north end of town. Here, visitors can see traditional items from an apothecary and herb shop, as well as items from a temple of worship.

Peering in the shop windows of town, visitors can see the butcher block and meat hooks, the fear-raising tools of the dentist, and the stocked shelves of the drugstore. Displayed are such items as jitter tablets and mustard plaster, and behind the counter are canisters holding raw pharmaceutical powders. While touring the town, visitors also have an opportunity to view a fancy-painted Conestoga freight wagon and the 1852 *Papeete*, a hand-pump fire engine.

Within Columbia are two currently operating hotels, possessing old-style Victorian charm—the City Hotel and the Fallon Hotel and Theater. Performances are still held at the Fallon Theater on a regular schedule.

A replica of the miners' boarding house, Eagle Cotage (sic), together with a miner's cabin, a remnant mining ditch at the north end of town, and the big limestone rocks unearthed by hydraulic mining at the south end of town, recall the activity that gave rise to Columbia. The assayer's office does likewise, with its ore bags, acids, and crucibles.

# MONO LAKE TUFA STATE RESERVE

**Hours/Season:** Daylight hours
**Facilities:** Reserve office at visitor center, hiker and all-ability trails, *bring water*
**For Information:** (760) 647-6331
**Access:** The reserve is east off US 395 at Lee Vining.

On an arid plain in the shadow of the Sierra Nevada, this park unit preserves and protects an ancient lake and a bizarre gallery of tufa (pronounced "toofah") towers—cavelike formations brought to the light of day. The formations owe their presence to nature and the thirst of a city. Nature is the artist; a thirsting Los Angeles the cause of the unveiling.

Mono Lake is fed by underground springs and five streams and has no outlet other than evaporation. Over time, minerals have concentrated in the lake, making it three times more saline and eighty times more alkaline than the ocean. The lake chemistry combined with the percolating springs created the calcium carbonate towers, mushrooms, and spires. For thousands of years, they grew undetected, but stream diversions changed all that.

The state reserve protects the lake and its historic lakebed; the National Forest Scenic Area extends the area of protection to include the outlying craters and bordering high desert. Although tufa formations can be found in similar environments around the world, nowhere are they so prevalent and varied. Each tower marks an underground spring.

The lake's unusual chemistry supports an equally unusual wildlife population of brine shrimp and flies. The flies, which blacken the alkaline ring of the lake, earned it the name "Mono"—Yokuts Indian meaning "brine fly." Together, the flies and shrimp create an unmatched foodbank for nesting and migrating birds.

Off US 395 north of Lee Vining is the Mono Basin Scenic Area Visitor Center, where visitors can learn more about the lake's natural history and find out about ongoing ranger-led activities. At several sites rimming the lake, short trails tour the marshy shore and pass between or overlook the tufa structures.

## Attractions and Activities

**Mono Lake Boardwalks.** For visitors with limited time, two fine boardwalks introduce Mono Lake and its unusual tufa gallery. One is found at Mono Lake County Park on the northwest shore, the other is at Old Marina on the west shore. At each, winds send waves through the thick shore grasses, while the blue lake waters reflect the white tufa. Photographers will want their cameras handy to capture the towers' shapes and textures.

*Access:* Both are located east off US 395 north of the visitor center and Lee Vining.

**Mark Twain Interpretive Trail.** Through the words of Mark Twain, an early-day visitor, this 1-mile trail presents facts about the lake. Along the way, it weaves past some of the lake's finest examples of tufa. Towers here range from 200 to 900 years old; a few at the lake are an impressive 13,000 years old. As the towers are extremely sensitive, do not mount or otherwise mar them.

This trail also bypasses a small hot spring, offers looks at Panum and Mono craters to the south, and visits an impressive collection of sand tufas near Navy Beach. At Navy Beach, freshwater springs have percolated through the briny lake sands, forming intricate straws, tubes, plates, and columns, revealed over time by the wind. As these natural sandcastles and futuristic miniatures are extremely delicate, and many lie yet unseen beneath the sand, tread lightly.

*Access:* The trail starts at the South Tufa Area, 10 miles southeast of Lee Vining.

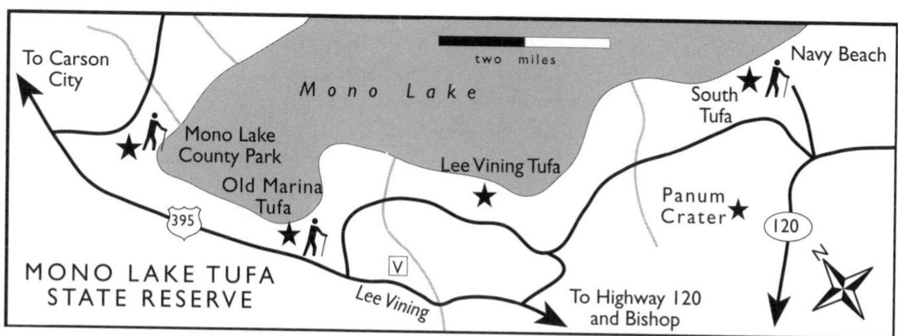

*Tufa towers, Mono Lake Tufa State Reserve*

Take US 395 south from Lee Vining, turning east on CA 120. From CA 120, follow the dirt roads north to the South Tufa Area–Navy Beach.

**Canoeing.** Canoes offer visitors a closer look at some of the near-shore tufa formations and different angles on the reflecting waters. But the lake's size is imposing—13 miles wide and 8 miles long—and winds pose a real threat, so confine your touring close to shore. From April 1 to August 1, steer away from Negit and Paoha islands, located along the north shore, where a 1-mile safety distance is enforced to protect the nesting birds.

*Access:* While there are no launch sites, the parking area for Navy Beach offers the shortest portage to the lake. It is on the south shore, reached off CA 120.

**Swimming.** The buoyant Mono Lake waters offer carefree waterplay, but due to the salinity, be cautious about eyes and any cuts. Also, it is advisable to test the shoreline where you plan to enter the lake, as sinking mud is common. Navy Beach offers perhaps the most reliable swimming spot. After a swim, be sure to rinse well in fresh water.

**Birdwatching.** Mono Lake is a historic nesting and stopover site along the Pacific Flyway. It attracts more than 80 different bird species. In July and August, some 150,000 phalaropes dine on the Mono Lake brine flies. When they leave, an estimated 800,000 eared grebes take their place, remaining through October. About 90 percent of the state's California gull population is born at Mono Lake. The rich food supply ensures them a healthy start. The alkali flats of the east shore serve the nesting needs of the snowy plover, supporting a colony of about 400 of these rare birds; stay away April through August.

# Railtown 1897 State Historic Park

**Hours/Season:** Daily, except Thanksgiving Day and Christmas Day; excursion trains run on weekends, March through November

**Facilities:** Picnic area, historic building and trains, gift shop, restrooms, nonflush toilets, water

**For Information:** Sierra Railway Company, (209) 984-3953

**Access:** At the east end of historic Jamestown (3 miles west of Sonora), turn south off CA 108/CA 49 onto 5th Avenue for the park.

This park celebrates the glory days of the iron horse and steam locomotion. Preserved here are the general offices, roundhouse, and maintenance buildings of the Jamestown station of the Sierra Railroad that served the Mother Lode mines and lumber mills of the Sierra foothills. The shortline railroad operated from 1897 to 1955 and is once again a working line, hauling freight on weekdays and passengers on summer weekends. It is one of only two surviving, original shortline facilities in the United States still in use.

Above the station house, a black-and-white sign announces the stop: "Jamestown Elevation 1476 Feet." From the passenger boarding deck, visitors can view some historic steam engines and antique passenger cars. At the station house, they can arrange for a roundhouse tour or purchase a ticket for the weekend excursion train.

The picnic area occupies a large central lawn with a few shade oaks. It is ringed by the brick-red-painted buildings of the station yard. At one corner, an interpretive board explains how steam locomotion works.

## Attractions and Activities

**The Roundhouse Tour.** "Roundhouse" is the descriptive name for the building where the locomotives are stored and serviced. This guided tour begins with a 15-minute film in the old freight shed. Afterward, visitors pass through the station yard, viewing the turntable, the still-operational six-track roundhouse, and the blacksmith and carpenter shops. In and about the roundhouse are rail cars of different vintage in different states of repair.

At a back storage shed jammed with motion-picture props, visitors can view old station signs and a wooden cow-catcher pilot (the rack or grill on the front of a locomotive that pushes obstacles aside). This intact shortline railroad and the park's historic rail cars have appeared in some 200 Westerns and been featured in such films as *Back to the Future III.*

*Rail station signs, Railtown 1897 State Historic Park*

**Excursion Train Ride.** The basic train trip is on the *Mother Lode Cannon Ball.* This steam train travels 12 miles round-trip to Chinese Station, touring the oak grassland of the Sierra foothills—Gold Rush Country. Docents on board relate the rail line's history and answer questions. During visitor season, the *Cannon Ball* departs every hour and a half, 10:30 A.M. to 3:00 P.M.

For information on the line's other tours, its specialty train rides, and its current fares and schedules contact the Sierra Railway Company.

## Caswell Memorial State Park

**Hours/Season:** Year-round
**Facilities:** 66 developed wooded campsites, picnic sites, hiker trails, restrooms, showers
**For Information:** (209) 599-3810 or (209) 847-2056
**Access:** From CA 99 at Ripon, follow Main, which later becomes West Ripon Road, west for 4.4 mile and turn south on Austin Road to reach the park in another 1.4 miles.

Located along the Stanislaus River, in the San Joaquin Valley, this park, once part of a pioneer homestead and early-day ranch, was little altered over the years and continues to feature many scenic, ancient valley oaks and a dense riparian habitat. Some of the grand oaks measure 60 feet tall and have girths exceeding 15 feet. The Stanislaus River is a sleepy, gentle-bending host. The area welcomes fishing, swimming, hiking, canoeing, birding, and lounging at camp.

Tangles of wild grape and blackberry and shrubs of wild rose and currant weave thick borders between the campsites and along the trails. When following angler paths or touring the trails, beware of nettles spilling into the way; some reach a remarkable height. At times, mosquitos can be a nuisance.

### Attractions and Activities

**Loop Trail.** Following mowed tracks and jeep trails west downstream along the Stanislaus River, hikers can craft a 1.5-mile loop touring the riparian shore. Side routes extend the exploration.

The nature trail enters a mixed woodland with impressive valley oaks and a dense understory. Wild grape climbs the oak trunks, while box elder, Oregon ash, willow, cottonwood, and an introduced fig contribute to the area richness. Ahead, hikers reach a river view.

At 0.3 mile, a 0.4-mile side loop journeys closer to the river. As it is often overgrown with nettles and fails to offer good river access or views, it may be one to bypass. Keeping to the main trail, hikers find another junction in 200 feet; bear left for the loop. Nettles can invade the main trail, as well.

Before long, the trail is atop an 8- to 10-foot river bank overlooking a horseshoe bend, with views up- and downstream. In this deceptively smooth-flowing waterway is a fair amount of current. Although the trail stays along the river, the vegetation swallows any view. At 0.6 mile, some large cottonwoods overlook the trail.

Where side trails branch to the right and left at 0.9 mile, keep to the same route of travel. Ahead, the corridor opens up, and the trail meets a main jeep track at 1.1 miles. Going left on it, hikers follow the park perimeter, reaching a dead end in 0.8 mile; going right brings the loop to a close. Where the gravel 2-track comes out at a gate, turn right to return to the day-use parking area at 1.5 miles.

*Stanislaus River, Caswell Memorial State Park*

*Access:* Begin at the west end of the day-use area, taking the trail indicated "nature trail."

**Fishing.** When fishing the muddy-bottomed Stanislaus River, the best time to cast a line is in the summer. The catches are bass, catfish, bluegill, bullhead, and buffalo carp.

**Swimming.** Near the day-use area is a small, open, sandy beach sloping to the river. Elsewhere in the park, the vegetation restricts river access. With the hot valley summers, swimming is a popular pursuit, but swimmers and waders need to be alert to the river's uneven floor and submerged branches.

**Birdwatching.** In the park's rich riparian and oak habitats, birders find numerous species to zoom in on with binoculars. Woodpecker, wood duck, heron, egret, swallow, kingfisher, hawk, jay, hummingbird, and oriole are just a few. Isolated at the west end of the park is a heron rookery; coveys of quail scurry about the campground.

## TURLOCK LAKE STATE RECREATION AREA

**Hours/Season:** Year-round
**Facilities:** 67 developed campsites, picnic sites, boat launch, fishing dock, swimming areas, restrooms, showers
**For Information:** (209) 874-2008
**Access:** From Modesto travel 21 miles east on CA 132 and turn south onto Roberts Ferry Road. Go 1 mile and turn left (east) onto Lake Road. The reservoir day area is reached in 1.2 miles, the river campground in 2 miles.

This San Joaquin Valley park offers picnicking and watersport on 3,500-acre Turlock Lake and camping and nature study along a short stretch of the Tuolumne River. Turlock Lake has a jigsaw-piece 26-mile-long shoreline, with humpbacked islands and jutting peninsulas. Low, rolling grass foothills enfold the reservoir; a private ranch can be seen at its east end. At the picnic areas, cottonwoods and sycamores provide shade. Away from the developed areas, trees are absent from shore. The lake is at its prettiest when water levels are high. From the Lake Overlook parking lot, visitors gain a fine overview.

The Tuolumne River is a pretty, clear-flowing, shallow waterway, spilling over a gravel and rock bed. Willow, cottonwood, cattail, and grass vegetate its banks. The broader riparian shore features a thick tangle of oak, willow, and fig trees intertwined with wild grape, blackberry, and mock orange. When pushing to shore, anglers should beware of nettles and poison oak. From mid-July to October, the ripe blackberries summon pickers with buckets cinched to their belts. Mosquitos can be a seasonal nuisance.

Along the Tuolumne River, visitors may note tailings (mounds of discarded rock) left behind from gold-mining days. Some 115 bird species have been identified at the park, including woodpecker, jay, hummingbird, finch, oriole, and bluebird, all commonly seen along the river corridor.

## Attractions and Activities

**Boating.** Controlled by the irrigation district, the lake level can drop dramatically. In summer, when water needs are great, the surface acreage can be halved. Year-round, the exposed lake may be subject to wind.

The lake is open for speedboating and waterskiing, as well as for trolling. Boating hours are from sunrise to sunset. There is no overnight moorage or boat-in camp. The recreation area does have a four-lane boat ramp, with ample boat-trailer parking.

**Fishing.** At Turlock Lake, boat and bank anglers fish for trout, bass, bluegill, crappie, and catfish. Rainbow trout are planted here in the early spring. On the Tuolumne River, trout are the sought-after species. From October 1 through December 31, the salmon spawning season, fishing is not allowed, but visitors can watch this dramatic natural event played out on the rocky bed of the river.

**Swimming.** The lake has two developed swimming areas: One at its northwest corner, the other is nestled in a small bay created by the land jut at Peninsula picnic area. The second is the more scenic.

# George J. Hatfield and McConnell State Recreation Areas

**Hours/Season:** Year-round (Hatfield); 2:00 P.M. Friday through 2:00 P.M. Monday (McConnell)

**Facilities:** 21 developed tree-shaded walk-in campsites, picnic sites, restrooms (Hatfield); 17 developed tree-shaded campsites, picnic sites, restrooms, showers (McConnell)

**For Information:** (209) 826-1196

**Access:** *For George J. Hatfield State Recreation Area,* from CA 33 in Newman, travel northeast on Merced Street, which becomes Hills Ferry Road, J-18, and North

Kelley Road, before reaching the recreation area in 3.3 miles. *For McConnell State Recreation Area*, from CA 99 at Delhi, take the Shanks Road exit and go east 0.4 mile. From there, go south on Vincent Road for 0.3 mile, and turn left on El Capitan Way. Continue 2.9 miles, and turn right on Pepper Street, which turns into McConnell Road, entering the park in another 1.6 miles.

These San Joaquin Valley parks, situated along the Merced River, are very similar in offering and appearance. Both have camping, picnicking, fishing, and small, natural beach areas for swimming access. Mature valley oak, cottonwood, and willow are common to both. At McConnell, sycamore, fig, and evergreen also shade the sweeping lawns of the developed area. Open areas at each park welcome play.

Wide and cloudy, the gentle-bending Merced River flows past these parks. Along its shallow edges, small fish and tadpoles may be spied; bullfrogs bellow from places unseen. Anglers pull in catfish, bass, and perch. At the beach areas, visitors find a gentle slope to the water. Elsewhere, steep banks and willow thickets line the river. Swimmers should be cautious about the submerged branches and trunks and the deep holes that riddle the bottom of the Merced River.

Hatfield State Recreation Area fills a horseshoe bend, enjoying 1.5 miles of river frontage. Much of McConnell's 70 acres lie inland from its river front. Away from the developed areas of the parks, visitors find the mosquitos fiendishly hungry.

## Wassama Roundhouse State Historic Park

**Hours/Season:** 11:00 A.M. to 4:00 P.M. Monday, Wednesday, and Saturday
**Facilities:** Picnic tables, cultural site, nonflush toilets, *bring water*
**For Information:** (209) 822-2332
**Access:** From the junction of CA 41 and CA 49 in Oakhurst, go 5.3 miles north on CA 49 and bear right on Roundhouse Road/Road 628. The park is on the right in 0.4 mile.

This Sierran foothills park preserves a sacred Miwok Indian site. Since the 1860s, a ceremonial roundhouse has stood here; earlier roundhouses were burned following the death of a tribal chief. The present one, built in 1985, continues to be used for traditional ceremonies. The roundhouse is where the dead are mourned, the spirits are summoned, and the harvest is celebrated through song and dance.

Beautiful big valley oaks, which attracted the earliest people to this location, similarly draw the contemporary traveler.

### Attractions and Activities

**Roundhouse Walking Tour.** Approaching the roundhouse, visitors may view the sweathouse used for cleansing and religious purposes. Bowed branches shape its frame. During ceremonies, water is poured on a heated rock pile at the hut's center to produce steam. Three bark houses also contribute to the attraction.

On the other side of the roundhouse is a noteworthy rock outcrop. Worn into the granite are some two dozen grinding cups. In a few, a pestle rock has been placed to hint at their use. Some measure 6 inches deep.

*Wassama Roundhouse*

The roundhouse itself is a large, circular wooden building, with an opening to the sky to release smoke and reveal the stars. Low doorways lead into it. As both the sweathouse and roundhouse remain sacred in their use, visitors are asked to keep behind barriers. An Indian burial site occupies the rise above the area.

## GREAT VALLEY GRASSLANDS

**Hours/Season:** Daylight hours
**Facilities:** Primitive boat launch, hiker trails (closed dirt or gravel roads), *bring water*
**For Information:** (209) 826-1196
**Access:** From the junction of CA 140 and CA 33 in Gustine, go 5.4 miles east on CA 140 and turn south before the bridge to reach the boat and fishing access. From the junction of CA 140 and CA 165, travel south 1.2 miles on CA 165. South of the San Joaquin River, park lands now butt the west side of a 3-mile stretch of CA 165. Parking is along the highway. *Be careful not to block any gates and beware of the soft shoulder.*

This wild 2,700-acre San Joaquin Valley park enfolds two former state park units—Fremont Ford and San Luis Island—and features a native bunchgrass expanse, vernal pools, riparian woodlands, and a stretch of the San Joaquin River, its oxbows and sloughs. It is a rare, untouched region in a sea of otherwise cultivated lands. Neighboring reaches include state and federal wildlife areas, creating an impressive open space for plants, birdlife, and animals—a naturalist's treasure trove.

Great Valley Grasslands invites discovery by foot or small boat; bring binoculars, as the birdlife is rich and varied. Even driving south along CA 165, visitors can appreciate the look and texture of this unusual prairie grassland, where antelope, grizzly, and elk once roamed.

## Attractions and Activities

**Grasslands Hike.** Following a gravel levee road for most of the way, visitors can make a 6-mile loop through the grassland. As the route is open and sunny, carry plenty of water.

Walking the levee, visitors overlook the grassland mosaic of highs and lows and golden and green hues. If fortunate, one may spy the delta coyote thistle, long thought extinct, but rediscovered here in 1976. It only grows along a 20-mile stretch of the San Joaquin River.

Before long, hikers overlook the river, with its cattail and willow shore, but a thick riparian border soon hides it from view. Rush, bunchgrass, and wildflowers intermix in the grassland, while mice and lizards rustle beneath the mat. Mosquitos raise havoc early in the year.

At 0.4 mile, a solitary oak marks the grassland to the south, as does a big vernal pond, artificially dammed by the road levee. Red-winged blackbirds, stilts, coots, and migrating waterfowl animate the pond. As the road stretches west, distant views are of the Coast Range. Where it curves north is another vernal pool, and silence prevails.

With another bend west, river views return. Here, a fence separates the levee from the river. At 1.1 miles is the loop junction; continue straight for a counterclockwise tour, still paralleling the San Joaquin.

At 2.4 miles, the road turns sharply south away from the river. National wildlife refuge lands sweep west, while the state grasslands spread east. After 2.9 miles, both areas show pockets of willow-crowded wetland.

At 3.6 miles, the levee turns east toward CA 165. Still, all one hears is the wind in the grasses. By the next half mile, the route is again fully surrounded by state grassland. As it continues its arrow-straight course, the levee gradually tapers to grassland level.

At the T junction at 4.5 miles, the loop turns left toward the San Joaquin River, following a flat gravel track across the grassland bottom. It is generally walkable, except following heavy rains. At 4.9 miles, hikers return to the 1.1-mile junction; go right to reach the trailhead. Hawks, quail, avocets, and killdeer continue to divert attention.

*Access:* Begin at the gate on the west side of CA 165, 0.25 mile south of the San Joaquin River.

**Fishing.** At the primitive boat launch and fishing area off CA 140, visitors find a riprap-reinforced bank and sandy bars from which to fish. Catfish and bass are commonly landed. The much-narrowed San Joaquin River flows slow, smooth, and cloudy here.

# MILLERTON LAKE STATE RECREATION AREA

**Hours/Season:** Year-round

**Facilities:** 139 developed savannalike campsites; boat-in campsites and overnight mooring area; picnic areas; marina and boat rentals; boat launches; historic building; swimming area; hiker, horse, and mountain-bike trails; restrooms; nonflush toilets; dump station

**For Information:** (209) 822-2332

**Access:** From the junction of CA 41 and CA 145, northeast of Fresno, go 3.2 miles east on CA 145, coming to a junction with Road 206. Stay on CA 145 for the campgrounds; Road 206 rounds below Friant Dam, accessing the south-shore day-use areas and marina.

On the eastern outskirts of the central valley, 300-foot-high Friant Dam captures the clear-flowing waters of the San Joaquin River, creating this 15-mile-long lake. Oak-studded, rounded grassland ridges and hills enfold the water body, which brings cool, splashing fun to this sunbaked area. Swimming, fishing, waterskiing, jet skiing, and sailing are all popular Millerton Lake pursuits.

The shoreline fluctuates with the demand for water. When levels drop, islands form, and a sloped rim with a bouldery north shore is revealed. On warm weekends and holidays, the lake's popularity soars, sending a myriad of wakes across its surface. A closed area along the south shore provides swimmers with a safe place to swim.

The picnic areas are mostly natural. Scenic oaks, Digger pines, and planted trees afford some shade; lake views are common to most sites. Trails take visitors to skyline vistas and wrap around the recreation area's dry, grassy hillsides. The squeezed eastern arm of the lake features chaparral and a wilder, more rugged canyon character. Trails have yet to be extended into it, although long-range plans call for one to encircle the lake.

## Attractions and Activities

**Millerton Courthouse.** With the building of Friant Dam, much of the early Central Valley history was swallowed up. Flooded were the ancestral home of the Northern Foothill Yokuts, Camp Barbour (a military post where a treaty ended the Mariposa Indian War), and the gold-mining town of Millerton (once the Fresno County seat). The lone feature that was saved was the Millerton Courthouse.

Dismantled and reconstructed on Mariner's Point, the 1867-built two-story brick and granite courthouse is now open to the public. Interpretive panels and exhibits help tell its story, and sometimes the Friends of Millerton conduct special tours of this relic from the Gold Rush.

*Access:* Find the courthouse on Mariner's Point on the south shore near the dam.

**Buzzard's Roost Trail.** This 1.2-mile round-trip hiker-only trail has a rugged 500-foot elevation change, but it rewards with a fine Millerton Lake–Sierra foothills vista.

It begins by crossing over a multiple-use trail for an immediate climb without

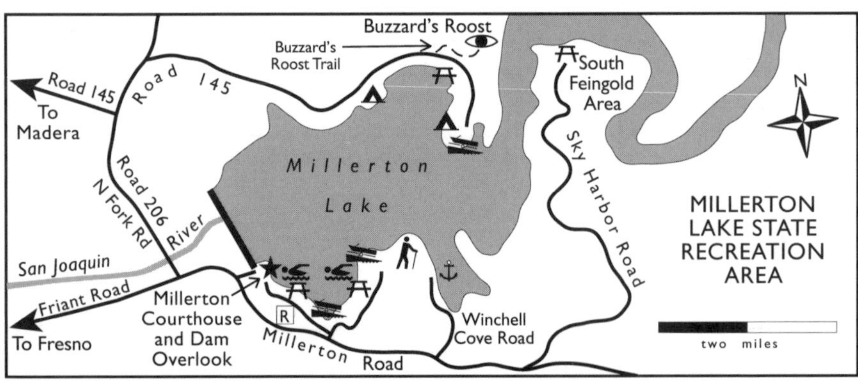

switchbacks. Digger pines and lichen-encrusted boulders punctuate the oak-grassland slope. Where the mostly open trail dips in and out of a side drainage, the gradient eases but remains steep, passing through knee- to waist-high grasses.

By 0.2 mile, the trail rolls alongside a livestock fence. After the narrow hiker passage in the fence, a large rock outcrop affords the first expansive Millerton Lake view from Friant Dam to just past the park's Meadow Campground. Buzzard's Roost is visible on the next rise.

At 0.6 mile, the trail tops the granite outcrop of Buzzard's Roost, appropriately named, as the big black scavengers commonly circle above and below it. The view spans 270 degrees, with the ridge to the north, the lake to the south, and the San Joaquin Valley stretching west. Return as you came.

*Access:* On the north shore, find the marked trail on the north side of Road 145 at a creek drainage, between Dumna Strand and Valley Oak campgrounds. One of the dispersed picnic sites lies across the road to the west.

**Boating, Sailing, and Waterskiing.** The narrow upper-canyon portion of the lake is closed to any skiing, but boat speeds up to 35 miles per hour are permissible. Boat ramps occupy both the north and south shore, with a developed marina along the lake's south shore. As the shoreline shifts, the boat launches and lake-access routes migrate with it. Watersport equipment and boat rentals may be found at the marina and at a concession located at ramp 1. Of particular interest to sailors and windsurfers, a special "Wind Talker" line, giving current wind and weather conditions, is in place; phone (209) 822-6276.

**Birdwatching.** From late November through mid-March, bald eagles may be seen soaring above the lake, as they make Millerton their winter home. For information on bald eagle tours conducted at the lake, contact the park. Roadrunners and quail may be spied running through the picnic areas or along the trails. Vultures and hawks are other common sightings.

*Jet skiers, Millerton Lake State Recreation Area*

## Hearst San Simeon State Historical Monument—Hearst Memorial State Beach

**Hours/Season:** 8:00 A.M. to 3:00 P.M. except major holidays (Hearst Castle); daylight hours (beach)
**Facilities:** Visitor center / museum, historic mansion and grounds, gift shop, food concession, restroom (Hearst Castle); picnic area, pier, concession-run tackle shop, hiker trail, restroom, outdoor shower (beach)
**For Information:** (805) 927-2000 (both)
**Access:** Entrances for the monument (Hearst Castle) and the beach are found on opposite sides of CA 1 at San Simeon.

High on a coastal hill overlooking the ocean sits the grand palace of newspaper magnate William Randolph Hearst. Designed by Julia Morgan, Hearst Castle (built between 1919 and 1947) is today a museum of fine architecture, Gothic and Renaissance art, antique furnishings, and elegant landscaping. Entertained within its hallways and rooms were world and national leaders and Hollywood greats. Name dropping and legend help move the tours from room to room.

In contrast to the opulence on the "Enchanted Hill," Hearst Memorial State Beach captivates with quiet beauty. San Simeon Point to its north protects the main beach area. Its small cove features an attractive white sand beach for sunbathing, calm waters for swimming and wading, and a fishing pier that angles out over the ocean. The far north end of the beach attracts nudists.

Opposite: *Torrey pines, Torrey Pines State Reserve*

*Neptune Pool, Hearst San Simeon State Historical Monument*

At the concession-run tackle shop, fishing licenses may be purchased, equipment rented, and fishing boats chartered. Picnic tables occupy the eucalyptus grove north of the pier and the broad grassy slope above the beach.

## Attractions and Activities

**Guided Hearst Castle Tours.** The main house, twin-towered La Casa Grande, boasts 115 rooms, including 14 sitting rooms, 41 baths, two libraries, a theater, and a wine cellar with more than 3,000 bottles of rare vintage wines. It also features a dazzling 200,000-gallon indoor Roman pool lined with Venetian glass and gold. Many of the rooms have antique stone fireplaces, rich tapestries, beautiful wood furniture, rare art, and antique ceilings.

A trio of Mediterranean-style guest houses, floral gardens, sculptures and fountains, cypresses and palms, and an enormous outdoor swimming pool—the Neptune Pool—complete the grounds. As visitors approach the "Enchanted Hill," the castlelike grandeur is striking, as is the contrast between the meticulously groomed 127-acre estate and the scrub and wooded wild of the Santa Lucia Mountains.

The park offers four basic tours, exploring different aspects of the mansion, with Tour 1 being the introductory one. A fifth tour, an evening one offered in the spring and fall, was recently added to the line-up. Each lasts about 2 hours.

As annually some one million people visit the castle, reservations are recommended year-round. MISTIX handles this service: phone (800) 444-7275 or (800) 444-4445. Wheelchair-accessible tours may be arranged by contacting the park directly at least 10 days in advance.

Be advised, the tours involve considerable walking and stair climbing, and strollers are not allowed. Buses shuttle groups from the visitor center to the castle. During the 15-minute bus ride, an audiotape sets the stage for a tour.

*Access:* Begin at the visitor center for Hearst San Simeon State Historical Monument, on the east side of CA 1.

**Bluff Trail.** West off CA 1, north of its main cove, Hearst Memorial State Beach presents two bluff-top coastal accesses, stitched together by a 0.5-mile hiking trail. From atop the bluff, travelers can admire a wild, rocky coastline, where harbor seals haul out and cormorants roost. Here, too, sea otters may be seen passing close to shore; bring binoculars. Low tides uncover a rocky flat that teems with intertidal life. Piedras Blancas Lighthouse can be seen to the north.

*Access:* Go north on CA 1 from Hearst Castle and the main area of Hearst Memorial State Beach to find these accesses. One is at 2.7 miles, the other at 3.3 miles.

## San Simeon State Park

**Hours/Season:** Year-round
**Facilities:** 116 developed landscaped campsites, 68 primitive hilltop campsites, picnic areas, hiker trails, cartop-boat launch, restrooms, nonflush toilets, showers, dump station
**For Information:** (805) 927-2068
**Access:** Find the beach and inland park parcels off CA 1 near Cambria, 5 miles south of San Simeon.

Three general areas comprise this state park: Santa Rosa Beach, Leffingwell Landing, and the San Simeon Creek–Washburn area. Besides its drift log- and cobblestone-strewn dark, coarse sand beaches, the park offers low coastal knolls and bluffs, near- and on-shore rocks, vital tidepools, a ragged surf, and an inland forest and lagoon. At the park, moonstone agates are the sought-after prizes of the beachcomber.

### Attractions and Activities

**Coastal Trail.** Stringing the length of the state park between Santa Rosa and San Simeon creeks is this 2.25-mile foot trail troubled by erosion and breakaway segments. It tours both bluff and beach parcels.

Hiking the bluff north from Santa Rosa, travelers round a point at 0.2 mile and begin following a canted beach, marked by foamy scallops. By 0.4 mile, the trail again tours the low bluff. At 1 mile, hikers arrive at Leffingwell Landing, where they find a restroom and picnic area atop a small knoll and a tidepool area, with benches overlooking the shore. It is a beautiful meeting of land and sea, with cliffs, rocky tongues, and churning waters.

The trail then continues north from the end of the parking area, bypassing other picnic sites and a small launch where divers and fishermen can portage their boats to water. Ahead, it parallels CA 1, and at 1.9 miles the trail overlooks a small beach cove of cobbles and dark sand.

At low tides, hikers can cross the beach and round the cliff to its north, extending the hike on a short sandy spit created by San Simeon Creek. Again, when waters are low, hikers can cross to the north side of the creek, where a 0.25-mile walk leads to a guano-iced bird rock. In spring, the blue breeding pouches of the cormorants catch the eye. Swallows and gulls share the sky. Makeshift driftwood wind shelters dot the beach.

*Nearshore rock, San Simeon State Park*

*Access:* Begin at the Santa Rosa Beach parking lot.

**Whittaker Ranch Trail.** Nearing completion, this 3.5-mile trail explores the inland bounty of San Simeon State Park. Touring the rolling hills, it encircles the camp areas, passing through coastal scrub, riparian woodland, and Monterey pine forest, serving up Santa Lucia Mountains vistas. Where the trail is wheelchair accessible, it affords a close-up view of the park's seasonal wetlands. Scenic overlooks, interpretive panels, and benches are offerings along the way.

*Access:* As this trail is in its infancy at this writing, inquire at the park for trailhead information and the availability of a trail map.

**Surf fishing.** Anglers can pull in barred surfperch year round, but concentrations increase in December and January. Walleye perch is another common catch, and in late summer three kinds of croaker add to the action. Anglers should be watchful of irregular waves and a strong backwash that can sweep them off their feet.

**Wildlife Watching.** At the lagoon, visitors may spy the red-legged frog or Southwestern pond turtle (both proposed for endangered species listing), as well as many shorebirds. From November through March, the bluffs of the park afford a good vantage for viewing the gray whale migrations. Year-round, they offer sightings of the playful sea otter, as the park lies within the 100-mile length of the National Sea Otter Refuge. From October to March, the park eucalyptus trees and Monterey pines host wintering orange-and-black monarch butterflies.

## Cayucos and Morro Strand State Beaches

**Hours/Season:** Year-round

**Facilities:** Picnic tables, pier, playground equipment, restrooms, outdoor shower (Cayucos); 104 developed beach campsites, picnic tables, restrooms, outdoor shower (Morro Strand)

**For Information:** San Luis Obispo County, (805) 781-5200 (Cayucos), (805) 772-2560 (Morro Strand)

**Access:** Cayucos State Beach is in the town of Cayucos; parking is along Ocean Front Road. South of Cayucos, Morro Strand State Beach has accesses off CA 1 for the next 5.6 miles. The campground access is at Yerba Buena Street.

These two state beaches face Estero Bay, offering views south to Morro Rock and north to the Santa Lucia Mountains, curving with the coastline. Cayucos State Beach is a small-town family beach with a 0.3-mile sandy strand and a scenic old-time fishing pier. A low seawall separates it from the shops and businesses of the coastal community. The area is fine for swimming, wading, sunning, and surfing; a summer lifeguard oversees the proceedings.

*Cayucos Pier, Cayucos State Beach*

Morro Strand State Beach consists of two long, residential beach fragments. Combined, they offer 3 miles of coastal sand for strolling, kite flying, and surf fishing. The steady breezes common to this area call to windsurfers and their spectator following. The waves curl to shore in strings of simultaneous breakers. At this beach, no lifeguard is on duty.

The Morro Strand Campground (formerly called Atascadero State Beach Campground) is a congested, squeezed parking area for camper rigs. Landscaping fills the dividers, and a low, coastal-scrub slope isolates it from the residential area. Seaward, low dunes shield it from the brunt of the ocean breeze.

Despite its limited tent areas, people do devise places and means to pitch them. Primarily though, the camp offers a convenient place to sleep, while taking in the activities along the southern end of Morro Strand.

## Attractions and Activities

**Cayucos Pier.** Built in 1875, the fishing pier is wheelchair accessible, lit for night fishing, and offers benches for admiring the water. When the surf is high, the rolling waters wrap around the pier pilings, splash well up its sides, and cause the structure's end to tremble. Next door to the pier is a wind-protected picnic area behind the art center.

**Morro Strand Beach Hiking.** The southern 1.7 miles of beach is more accessible to the public. Here, beachgoers find a broad strand backed by sand bumps, mounds, and low dunes, with the residential area set back from shore. Creeks divide the strand, sometimes requiring wading or uphill detours. The length of the beach disperses visitors.

Homes line the much thinner northern beach. With limited street parking, it is better suited for local use, although surf fishermen frequent the public access off 24th Street. At that site, a few picnic tables dot the sea fig–topped dune, nudging the beach.

# Morro Bay State Park

**Hours/Season:** Year-round; 10:00 A.M. to 5:00 P.M., except major holidays (Morro Bay Museum of Natural History)

**Facilities:** 135 developed tree-shaded campsites (20 have hook-ups), hike/bike campsites, picnic area, museum, marina, public golf course, cafe, boat/bike rentals, hiker trails, fitness trail, frisbee/disc golf course, restrooms, showers, dump station

**For Information:** (805) 772-2560

**Access:** In Morro Bay, reach the park taking State Park Road off Main Street or South Bay Boulevard.

Morro Bay is perhaps the most civilized park in the entire California state park system. In addition to its natural offerings of Morro Bay, Morro Rock, and a blue heron rookery, the park has within its borders an 18-hole golf course, a marina, and the acclaimed Morro Bay Museum of Natural History.

Rising 578 feet, dome-shaped Morro Rock is the area's prominent landmark. The monolith guided early-day mariners and calls to contemporary travelers as well. An ancient volcanic plug, it is one of nine forming a bumpy skyline between San Luis Obispo and Morro Bay. Today, Morro Rock is recognized both as a natural preserve and a state historical landmark. The sea otters frequenting its surrounding waters add to its appeal as a visitor destination.

Between October and March, the park's eucalyptus groves house the orange-and-black Monarch butterfly, a delicate winter migrant. Year-round, birdwatching is rewarding, with the park—indeed, the entire town of Morro Bay—designated a bird sanctuary.

## Attractions and Activities

**Morro Bay Museum of Natural History.** This museum, located on the bay at White Point, has an ambitious, year-round calendar of interpretive programs and walks, explaining the natural and cultural attributes of the area. Inside, visitors enjoy first-rate exhibits that are both accessible and educational, addressing coastal life forms, habitats, and the natural elements that shape this area.

Youngsters can get their hands wet at the Discovery Center tidepool, where docents instruct them on the proper handling of intertidal life, as well as inform them about the many creatures, their diets, and their eating, moving, and defense mechanisms. A schedule of videos covering different natural history topics runs throughout the day. The museum's large picture windows overlooking the bay, the spit, and Morro Rock bring the outdoors inside. A separate admission fee is charged.

*Access:* Reach it off State Park Road, 0.4 mile northwest of the park campground entrance.

**Black Hill Trail.** This 0.3-mile trail zigzags up the western face to top Black Hill (elevation 661 feet), another of the nine volcanic plugs found between San Luis Obispo and Morro Bay. Grasses and coastal scrub vegetate the slope, with the initial trail segment bordered by cypress and pine. In spring and summer, a few wildflowers dot the sides of the trail.

At 0.1 mile, hikers find a nice overlook of the channeled estuary. As the trail climbs, the view continues to open up and broaden. Finally, the summit greets hikers with a spectacular 360-degree, coastline-to–Santa Lucia Mountains vista, featuring Morro Rock and Morro Bay, Valencia Peak, and the El Chorro Creek Valley. Only the strong wind gusts chase away visitors; return as you came.

*Access:* At the golf course, take Black Hill Road off Park View Drive, and follow it to its end where there is parking for six cars. The road is closed from 7:00 P.M. to 6:00 A.M.

**Birdwatching.** The park boasts three prime birding sites: the Heron Rookery, Morro Bay, and Morro Rock.

From January through June, at the *Heron Rookery Natural Preserve* north of White Point, visitors can observe the mating, nesting, and nurturing behaviors of the great blue heron. Situated next to the bay, the preserve's eucalyptus grove is ideally suited for a rookery. It is protected, has ample nesting material, and is near an abundant food supply. Recently though, roosting cormorants have taken over much of the grove, outnumbering herons.

The rich tidal flat of *Morro Bay* nourishes not only the great blue heron, but sizeable migratory and resident seabird and shorebird populations. Landbirds inhabit the bay's marshy edge, further adding to the sightings. In all, this vital habitat supports some 250 bird species, with 100 commonly seen. When the incoming tide fills the bay, bobbing sea otters float side by side with loons and grebes. Near the marina, informal foot trails allow visitors to roam the bay shore.

*Morro Rock*, at the mouth of Morro Bay, is the seasonal home for a pair of peregrine falcons. These exciting hunters nest safe from harm, high on the rock ledges. Gulls are ever-present, encircling the crown of Morro Rock and stealing the sea otters' dinners.

*Access:* The Heron Rookery Natural Preserve and the bay are reached off State Park Road; Morro Rock is reached taking Coleman Drive off Embarcadero in the town of Morro Bay. The Heron Rookery also may be reached by trail from the Morro Bay Museum of Natural History, hiking north 0.25 mile along the bay.

**Morro Bay Golf Course.** Operated by San Luis Obispo County, this attractive 18-hole golf course occupies the lower slopes of Black Hill. Eucalyptus, pine, and cypress define the fairways. While playing a round, golfers enjoy fine ocean-bay vistas. Afternoon winds can play havoc with shots, increasing the challenge. For more information, phone the clubhouse, (805) 772-4341.

*Access:* The golf course is located off Park View Drive.

**Disk Golf.** The park also has an 18-hole frisbee golf course, where players shoot the plastic flying discs at white numbered posts standing 4 to 6 feet high. As in traditional golf, players keep score for each hole/post. While the straightforward course covers only a small area, the coastal wind is again an obstacle.

*Access:* The course is located adjacent to the campground, alongside the fitness trail.

## Montaña de Oro State Park

**Hours/Season:** Year-round

**Facilities:** 50 primitive wooded campsites, horse camp, picnic sites, visitor center, hiker and horse trails, mountain-bike routes, nonflush toilets, water

**For Information:** (805) 528-0513

**Access:** From Los Osos, follow Los Osos Valley/Pecho Road west and south, reaching the core of the park in 5 miles.

This park enjoys 7 miles of wild coastline with rugged headlands, remote beaches, surf- and weather-sculpted offshore rocks, shifting dunes, and a long, sandy spit. Elsewhere, wooded creek canyons, coastal live oak groves, chaparral, and stands of Bishop pine characterize the 8,000-acre park. Valencia Peak, rising 1,347 feet, is the dominant land feature. The park's name, meaning "mountain of gold," is readily understood in the spring, when California poppy, mustard, bush monkey-flower, buttercup, and tidytip blaze the peak, bluff, and rolling slopes in orange and yellow.

The small, half-moon beach at Spooner's Cove is the longest, most accessible one to stroll. Multi-colored seaweed and algae accent its tideline, while shell fragments invite a stooped investigation. Seen from the Bluff Trail, the descriptively named

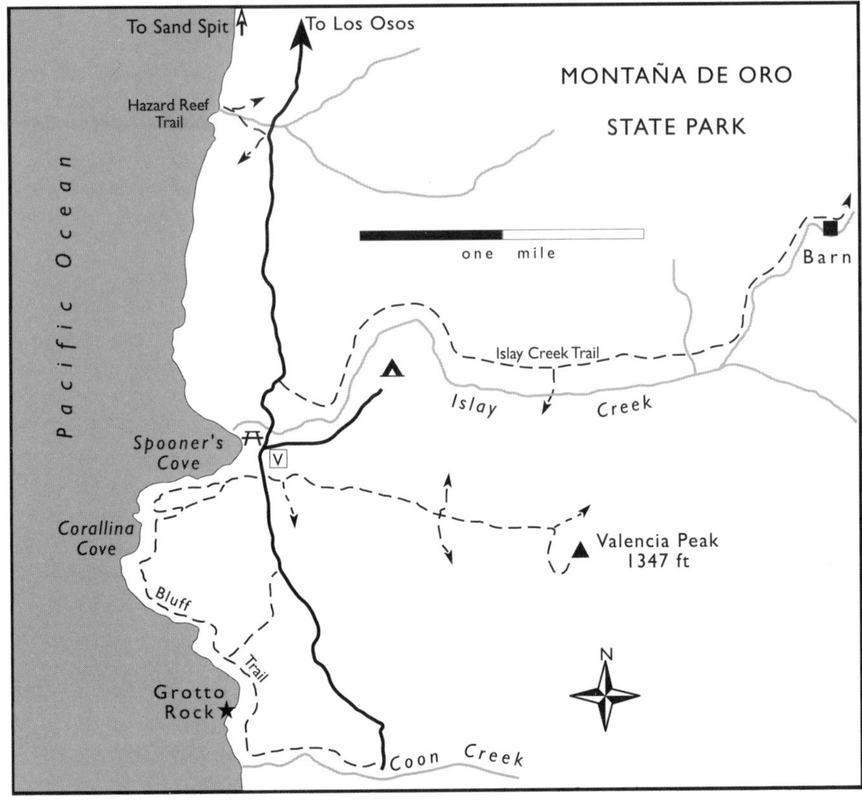


near-shore sea stack of Grotto Rock is the park's photo signature.

The ranch house visitor center offers a park-related rotating natural history exhibit, a video, a few old photographs, and some leftover items from the ranch days. It also holds a small bookstore, where park brochures may be acquired. Below it is the highly scenic primitive campground, nestled in a wooded creek valley just inland from the coast. Thick, flowing grasses carpet the floor. Campers should stow their food and gear properly, as the shiny-eyed raccoons maraud at night.

## Attractions and Activities

**Bluff Trail.** This hiker path meanders some 2 miles, overlooking the park's dramatic wave-sculpted shore, including picturesque Grotto Rock. A few side paths descend the 50-foot bluff to small, rocky beaches and isolated tidepools; other such areas are inaccessible.

Along the way, hikers may see strings of brown pelicans, crimson-billed oystercatchers, sea lions and harbor seals, and the ever-favorite sea otters in the kelp bed just offshore. Seemingly stranded squirrels chide from niches far below in the sharp-dropping cliffs. Pigeon guillemots fly out from cliff-side nest holes, in this, their southernmost nesting ground. Birdwatchers and wildlife enthusiasts rarely leave the trail unhappy.

Pleasing constants are the booming surf and the hypnotic blue water. In spring, a wildflower tapestry tops the bluff plateau, and at sunset park guests make their way here for the orange-colored show. This is a trail to travel again and again; carry binoculars, cameras, and field guides.

*Access:* Reach the trail via access spurs off the south end of the park road; the northernmost trailhead is across from the visitor center.

**Valencia Peak Trail.** This 4-mile round-trip tour crosses a broad marine terrace then switchbacks uphill, crossing older, more eroded terraces masked beneath the dense chaparral-grassland. Spring and summer wildflowers dot the slope. Throughout the trek, breathtaking coastal views engage, while the ocean roars below. Off the trail, poison oak grows in pockets.

The summit rewards with an outstanding 360-degree view, featuring the far-stretching coastline from Point Sal in the south to Piedras Blancas in the north. Morro Rock, Los Padres National Forest, and the bumpy western skyline fill in the view.

November through February, the summit affords the best seat in the park for spying the spouts of migrating gray whales. Swallows sweep the peak's bald top, as red-tailed hawks and turkey vultures soar overhead. Even on foggy days, Valencia Peak may poke through the cloaking mist for an exciting vista. Return as you came.

*Access:* It begins off the park road, 100 yards south of the campground turnoff.

**Hazard Reef Trail–Wild Spit Hike.** This trail travels above a eucalyptus-lined drainage, reaching a reef vista, tidepool rocks, and a long sandy beach at 0.3 mile. Surfers, anglers, beachcombers, and naturalists frequent this path. In October, when the eucalyptus are in bloom, monarch butterflies congregate in the drainage. These orange-and-black migrants browse the blossoms by day and cluster on the trees at night to keep warm.

Hiking 1.5 miles north along the beach and atop the sand dunes leads to a 4-

*Grotto Rock, Montaña de Oro State Park*

mile-long wilderness spit, offering additional exploration with its beach, central dunes, and Morro Bay shore. The pristine spit has recently been named a natural preserve. In places the shifting sands reveal shell middens (disposal sites) left behind by the Chumash Indians, who first occupied this area. Placed in half-mile increments along the spit, numbered orange posts mark off the beach distance. The remote strand holds ample opportunity for solitude and reflection.

As Morro Bay Spit is a vital nesting site for the rare snowy plover, avoid tracking the oceanfront dune where the tiny birds nest from March to September. This sandy tongue is also home to owl, northern harrier, deer, and bobcat. At its tip, hikers look out at Morro Rock, another natural preserve, where peregrine falcons nest. Boaters pass in and out of the protected bay channel, while surfers sometimes paddle across to the spit. Return as you came or consider a bay-shore return, if the tide is out.

*Access:* Begin at the parking lot on the west side of the park road, 0.9 mile north of Spooner's Cove.

**Islay Creek Trail.** This 4.2-mile round-trip tour travels a fire road and is open to all users. Contouring at the foot of a grassland-chaparral slope, the road overlooks the congested riparian habitat of year-round Islay Creek, a protected spawning water where fishing is prohibited. Occupying the other side of the steep creek drainage is the park campground, with Valencia Peak rising above it. Monkeyflower, poppy, and morning glory decorate the slope. With poison oak common, keep to the fire road. The trail maintains a mild grade.

At a wooden guard rail at 1 mile, travelers can overlook a 5- to 6-foot waterfall changing course as it spills through a curvature in a rock outcrop. In wet years, the flow is pretty and white. Along the route, the road cut typically reveals a horizontally layered sedimentary bed. At 1.1 miles though, the bed is tilted, indicating some past geologic event.

Ahead, rock outcrops dot the slopes, and views into the upper canyon reveal the headwater forks of Islay Creek. At 2.1 miles, next to a side creek drainage, hikers arrive at an abandoned, tin-roofed barn with missing sideboards. Although the road continues, this marks the end of this tour. Quail can be seen scurrying through the barn. Return as you came.

*Access:* Find the gated fire road on the east side of the park road, 0.2 mile north of Spooner's Cove.

**Tidepooling.** The jagged, layered rocks turned on their sides and jutting into the sea at Corallina Cove house some of the best tidepools on the California coast. The shimmery pools seclude pink and yellow nudibranchs (shell-less mollusks), purple urchin, orange and brown starfish, red feathery seaworms, and green and white anemone. Iridescent seaweed and coralline algae add to the display. Out of reach on the offshore rocks, harbor seals slumber, occasionally eyeing the two-legged intruders.

*Access:* Reach the stairway to Corallina Cove, hiking south 0.75 mile along the Bluff Trail from its northern terminus.

## Los Osos Oaks State Reserve

**Hours/Season:** Daylight hours
**Facilities:** Hiker trail, *bring water*
**For Information:** (805) 528-0513
**Access:** From the town of Los Osos, go 0.7 mile east on Los Osos Valley Road.

*Oak grove, Los Osos Oaks State Reserve*

This 85-acre reserve protects the area's last remaining stand of California coast live oaks. Many of the mature oaks stand no more than 6 to 8 feet tall, yet they are 700 years old. The dwarfism is a product of the mineral-depleted soil of the ancient, relict sand dune on which they grow. In other parts of the grove, the old oaks reach 20 to 30 feet tall. All of them reveal twisted, contorted shapes, accented by stringy beards of lichen. Three forms of lichen can be seen here and nowhere else.

When the Spanish explorers first passed along this stretch of coast in 1769, the California grizzly roamed the area lowlands, hence the name Los Osos, meaning "the bears." Prior to that, Chumash Indians inhabited this coastal region, supporting themselves by gathering and fishing. Middens, areas of discarded shell and chert, record their presence; a portion of the reserve nature trail passes through one of these sites, while touring amid chaparral. In the nineteenth century, this isolated, tangled woodland sheltered outlaws and no-goods, until a posse ran them out in a Western shootout.

## Attractions and Activities

**Nature Trail.** About 0.7 mile of trail, in three interlocking lobes, explores the beauty of this remaining coast live oak grove—a phantasmagoria of twisted and bowed shapes. Circuits between 0.4 and 0.6 mile long are possible. They visit both the tall and dwarf oak communities and chaparral and grassland habitats. The many scenic oaks may inspire a leisurely tour, but beware of the poison oak, which abounds, frequently pushing trailside.

At the start of the trail, a big, sprawled oak with a braced limb extends a scenic welcome to a captivating tall-oak grove. Where the trail branches, go left per the arrow post. Overhead, twisted branches weave a shady cathedral. Side, forward, and over-the-shoulder views offer different perspectives on the oaks. After 0.1 mile, sandy and grassy open pockets separate the tangles of dwarf oak. Here, sand verbena, sage, and bush lupine add color. Brief, limited views are of Los Osos Valley and the Santa Lucia Mountains.

At the 0.25-mile trail junction, going right leads to a magnificent shady oak showcase immediately ahead. Going left adds the less-traveled third lobe to the tour. But as it has side paths that confuse and the poison oak is even more intrusive, it is better to go right.

Entering the shady grove, hikers reach a three-pronged fork. To the left is the conclusion of the third lobe tour; the center fork offers a 0.2-mile return to the trailhead, with dispersed oaks, pretty spring and summer wildflowers, and areas of ducking required; the right fork offers a slightly shorter return, fully shaded, passing beneath more of the big, contorted oaks. The choice of return is yours.

Docents from the Morro Bay Museum of Natural History regularly lead walks at Los Osos Oaks State Reserve, relating the area's natural and cultural history; contact the museum for a schedule.

*Access:* Begin at the west end of the parking area; dogs are not allowed in the reserve.

## TULE ELK STATE RESERVE

**Hours/Season:** 8:00 A.M. to sunset; 1:00 P.M. to 5:00 P.M. Sundays (visitor center)
**Facilities:** Shaded picnic area, visitor center, viewing benches, displays, restrooms
**For Information:** (805) 765-5004
**Access:** Between Gorman and Buttonwillow on I-5, take the Stockdale Highway exit, go west for 1.2 miles, and turn south onto Morris Road. Go another 1.5 miles, and turn west on Station Road to reach the reserve in 0.2 mile.

This 950-acre reserve provides a sanctuary for descendants of the lone surviving herd of tule elk. The reserve land itself represents one last tract of the elk's native habitat, though it is no longer in good shape. In the 1800s, commercial hunting and the rapid spread of agriculture brought about the near demise of this Central Valley species, which once numbered in the tens of thousands.

By 1895, only 28 animals remained. Today, some 40 tule elk wander the reserve grounds, while others have been successfully introduced to the Owens Valley (at the foot of the Sierra in east-central California) and the Cache Creek area in Colusa County.

### Attractions and Activities

**Elk Viewing.** The tule elk is the smallest of three elk subspecies native to western North America. The male stands just over 4 feet tall at its shoulder and weighs 550 pounds.

These elk may be seen grazing, resting in the distance, or wallowing in a mud hole or artificial pond to cool off. During the dry season, which is much of the year, daily feedings supplement the natural forage. These afternoon feedings bring the elk within close viewing range of the public.

The tule elk are most active in late summer and early autumn, when bugling,

antler thrashing, herding, and other behaviors accompany the rut. Calves arrive in April and May and nurse until September. An on-site caretaker is generally available to answer questions.

Binoculars are necessary to fully enjoy a visit. A raised viewing platform allows visitors to overlook a natural rise and pan the reserve for elk. At the east boundary, a rough, dirt road travels alongside the reserve property fence line. Visitors may walk this to increase their opportunity for a tule elk sighting. Egret, kestrel, and meadowlark often divert attention.

## Pismo State Beach—Pismo Dunes State Vehicle Recreation Area

**Hours/Season:** Year-round

**Facilities:** 2 campgrounds with a total of 184 developed sites (42 at Oceano have hook-ups), golf course, pier, beach-access trails, nature trails, restrooms, showers, dump station (Pismo State Beach); primitive beach camping for 500 vehicles (four-wheel-drive recommended), vehicle access to beach and dunes, hiker trails, nonflush toilets, *bring water* (Pismo Dunes SVRA)

**For Information:** (805) 489-2684 (Pismo State Beach); (805) 473-7230 (Pismo Dunes SVRA)

**Access:** The parks are found off CA 1 between Pismo Beach and Oceano. Beach-access ramps are at the west ends of Grand and Pier avenues. North Beach Campground is at the southern city limit of Pismo Beach; Oceano Campground is off Pier Avenue in Oceano.

A 7-mile-long state beach stretching from the north end of Pismo Beach to just south of Oso Flaco Creek and a first-rate dune field backing much of it to the south draw visitors to this stretch of California coast. Some 5.5 miles of the beach are open for driving, with 3.5 miles open to off-highway vehicles. At Pismo Dunes State Vehicle Recreation Area (SVRA), campers set up sites right on the beach above the high-tide line.

North of the Grand Avenue access ramp, the state beach is closed to vehicles, and beachgoers enjoy tranquil pursuits, such as sunbathing, swimming, beachcombing, and sand sports. The 950-foot Pismo Beach Pier welcomes a stroll over the ocean or the casting of a line; it is lit for nighttime fishing. Surfing is restricted to the waters south of the pier.

*Dune boardwalk, Pismo Dunes State Vehicle Recreation Area*

From October to March, the eucalyptus grove south of North Beach Campground hosts wintering monarch butterflies, drawing naturalist and photographer.

The 2,500-acre SVRA has ample

room for off-road driving, but it also boasts Pismo Dunes Natural Preserve and a natural area surrounding the Oso Flaco lakes for carefree hiking and nature study. Birding, surf and freshwater-lake fishing, and horseback riding are other SVRA pursuits.

## Attractions and Activities

**Pismo Dunes Natural Preserve.** Closed to vehicles, the preserve houses more than a square mile of undisturbed, shifting sand. Here, animal tracks, wind patterns, and sand by the shoeful await, as visitors are free to roam at will. These closed dunes also afford a fine sunset vantage.

*Access:* Find the preserve south of Arroyo Grande Creek.

**Guiton Trail.** This easy, 1-mile trail rounds man-made Oceano Lagoon; ask for a brochure at the Oceano Campground entry station.

A clockwise tour skirts the edge of the campground, overlooking the west bank of the lagoon. In the first 0.1 mile, it bypasses a fishing platform for the disabled. Bass occupy these waters, as do ducks, muskrat, and beaver. A natural vegetation of willows and riparian species frames the open water. Poison oak grows amid the mix. At 0.6 mile, the route crosses over a bridge to tour the undeveloped eastern shore, which is less open for views and fishing access. At 1 mile, the loop closes.

*Access:* Next to Oceano Campground, begin at the west side of the Pier Avenue bridge over Oceano Lagoon. Day visitors park alongside the road.

**Oso Flaco Beach Trail.** Operated by the Nature Conservancy, this moderately easy 1-mile trail skirts Oso Flaco Lake and meanders through the Nipomo Dunes to arrive at the beach. Closed to off-road vehicles, the area welcomes quiet appreciation.

The hike begins following a gated, paved lane overhung by cottonwoods and willows, passing between Oso Flaco and Lower Oso Flaco lakes. Here, rabbits abound, supporting a population of great horned owls and hawks. The freshwater lakes and surrounding marsh attract terns, egrets, cormorants, and ducks. Bulrushes and willows encircle lakes; white dunes rise above them.

At 0.25 mile is the sign for the beach trail. Arrow posts point the way across the dunes and past Oso Flaco Lake. Wind, a creative force in this landscape, can sandblast travelers; windbreakers and sunglasses are a good idea. By 0.5 mile, a boardwalk leads the way through a vegetated area at the outskirts of the primary dune field. A bridge that will connect it with the causeway is under construction.

Where the trail climbs a tall sand ridge, it offers a north-south view, spanning Point Buchon to Point Sal. Arriving at the beach, hikers pass between a couple of wind fences (markers for the return trek). The broad, lengthy beach invites in both directions. Shorebirds run and feed along the tideline. Return as you came.

*Access:* Go 9.5 miles south from Oceano on CA 1 and turn west on Oso Flaco Lake Road to reach the trailhead in 3.1 miles. Watch for debris on the farm road. The area is open 6:00 A.M. to 6:00 P.M. There is a fee for parking.

**Clam Digging.** Historically, the Pismo clam brought this area fame, but within recent years, it has all but disappeared from the tide zone at Pismo State Beach. Rangers believe it will not be until later this decade that the clam will return in sufficient numbers to bring back the sport.

Any attempt at clamming in the meantime still requires a valid state fishing license for persons 16 years and older. To be harvested, the clams must measure at least 4.5 inches in diameter; carry a gauge for measuring them. For the per-person limit, consult the current state fishing regulations.

Clams that are not taken must be properly reburied, with the top end and brown bump up and the hinge facing the ocean. At no time may clams be taken from a 0.3-

mile area north of Grand Avenue—the Pismo Invertebrate Reserve.

**Golfing.** The Pismo State Beach Golf Course is a 9-hole, par 3 course, but with different colored tees for the front and back 9, it allows 18-hole play. At the attractive course, golfers find rewarding coastal views and the challenge of the ocean breeze. For more information, phone (805) 481-5215.

*Access:* Find it off Grand Avenue.

## Point Sal State Beach

**Hours/Season:** Daylight hours
**Facilities:** None
**For Information:** La Purisima Mission State Historic Park, (805) 733-3713
**Access:** From CA 1, 1.7 miles south of Guadalupe, go 8.9 miles west on Brown and Point Sal roads to reach the hillside parking areas. *In places, the route is rough and unpaved; in winter, rains may make it impassable.*

Abutted by the steep flanks of the Casmalia Hills, this is one of California's more remote and wilder beaches. Here, steep cliffs, sections of rocky shore, and a 0.4-mile-long pristine curvature of sand intermingle. Often, it is an open canvas free of footprints for days at a time. Neither seaweed nor shell fragment mars the beach.

Point Sal and a layered cliff to the south frame this scenic U-shaped cove. At times, a halo of clouds rings the hills overlooking the beach. This is a good place to escape with your thoughts, fish, or watch for seabirds. The unruly surf makes it too treacherous to swim, but engages with its power.

Harbor seals sometimes haul out on the secluded beach, and seabirds regularly roost on the rocks. Giant coreopsis and other sunflowers color the bluff in spring.

From the parking lot, steep unmaintained paths descend to the beach. As it is easy to slip, wear sturdy shoes with a tread. The width of this beach depends on the tide.

## Fort Tejon State Historic Park

**Hours/Season:** Daylight hours; 10:00 A.M. to 5:00 P.M. (historic buildings)
**Facilities:** Picnic area, visitor center/museum, historic fort, restrooms
**For Information:** (805) 248-6692
**Access:** Take the Fort Tejon exit off I-5, 36 miles south of Bakersfield or 77 miles north of Los Angeles. The park is on the west side of the freeway.

In the Tehachapi Mountains near the summit of the Grapevine Grade, the tranquility of this historic site proves the ideal escape from the freeway parade of vehicles, led by straining diesel trucks. Four-hundred-year-old sprawling oaks shade the lawns and native grassland. Picnic tables invite the taking of a lunch.

Established in 1854 to protect the Indians of the San Joaquin Valley and enforce civil law, this U.S. Army post was home to the First Dragoon. The fort also housed the first and only Camel Corps of the U.S. Army, but the experiment was abandoned with the approach of the Civil War.

The naturalist offerings at the park go beyond the beauty of the ancient valley oaks. Overhead, golden eagles and red-tailed hawks engage in aerial combat, while woodpeckers and western bluebirds vie for attention beneath the leafy canopy. Rabbits and black-tailed deer, too, are commonly spied.

In spring, California poppy and mustard seemingly set aflame the surrounding rounded hillsides. More often though, they are cloaked in parched golden grass and accented by the fingery shadows of the wooded canyons. While there are no established trails, visitors are free to roam the park grounds. When touring, beware of the many ground squirrel holes that threaten ankles.

### Attractions and Activities

**Peter le Beck Oak.** Among the park's many grand old valley oaks is one of historical note—the Peter le Beck oak, first recorded in an 1853 survey report. It bears this carved notice: "Peter le Beck killed by a X bear, Oct. 17, 1837."

*Access:* Find it at the north side of the parade ground.

**Historic Fort Tour.** At the original fort, some twenty adobe buildings rimmed the parade ground. Today, all that stands are the officer and orderly quarters, a restored barracks, and a few corner foundation ruins. Together with a small museum, they tell the story of Fort Tejon.

Inside the buildings, mannequins reveal the dress of the day. The furnishings convey the stark existence: a couple of prized books, small trinkets from home, and what could be constructed for comfort. On the first Sunday of each month, life returns to the fort, with volunteers in period dress engaged in the chores and routine of the 1850s.

**Civil War Reenactment.** During the Civil War, fifteen of the fort's officers rose to the rank of general. Eight wore blue, seven gray. Now, a regular part of the park's summer program is a reenactment of a Civil War battle. Contact the park for more details.

## La Purisima Mission State Historic Park

**Hours/Season:** Daily, except major holidays; generally 10:00 A.M. to 5:00 P.M. (historic buildings)

**Facilities:** Picnic sites, visitor center, small museum, historic mission, bookstore, hiker and horse trails, restrooms

**For Information:** (805) 733-3713; for volunteer-led tours, (805) 733-1303

**Access:** At the CA 1–CA 246 junction east of Lompoc, go east on CA 246 for 1.8 miles and turn left on Mission Gate Road. The park entrance is at the junction of Mission Gate and Purisima roads in 0.4 mile.

In a 968-acre pastoral setting, this state historic park preserves La Purisma Mission—the most completely restored Franciscan mission in California's string of twenty-one. The restored mission actually represents the second La Purisima settlement. The earthquake of 1812 destroyed the first, which was located some 4 miles away in what is now Lompoc.

Through exacting efforts, builders duplicated the mission. They handcut beams and handturned adobe bricks, handcrafted the nails and tiles, and precisely matched the paints. The only variance in construction was the inclusion of earthquake safety features, well hidden within the buildings. Altogether, some thirty-seven restored and furnished rooms take visitors back to the mission year 1820.

The grounds, likewise, recall the mission period, with burros, four-horned churro sheep, and other livestock; historically accurate gardens; and the planted fields below the chaparral mesas. During living-history days, volunteers in period dress enliven the settlement, recreating the daily chores and remembering the mission people. At the chapel, each December 8, a ceremony of *luminarias* (lights) celebrates the mission's founding.

The visitor center introduces the mission through dioramas, artifacts, exhibits, and a pictorial history. Next door at the bookstore, brochures for the self-guided tour may be purchased. Besides touring the mission site, visitors can enjoy a 14-mile network of park trails that explore the chaparral hillsides. True to the mission setting, the trails all bear Spanish names.

## Attractions and Activities

**Self-guided Mission Tour.** This walking tour visits the primary mission buildings and grounds, covering a distance of 0.75 mile.

The La Purisima Mission site, which housed the padres, soldiers, and hundreds of Chumash Indian workers, is extensive and impressive. The mission chapel and cemetery is an early stop. In the pink-hued bell tower, two of the three original bells hang; the third is wooden.

Some of the rooms look as though the mission residents just stepped away. Chamber sizes and furnishings hint at a mission hierarchy, from the Indians to the lowly soldiers to the officers to the padres. Plaques add to the information of the brochure.

Throughout the mission, visitors can witness the exacting reconstruction in the bricks, the windowsills and doorways, and even the benches. At the south end of the main residence, visitors can see how the padres fortified the structure against earthquake with a heavy stone buttress; it withstood the test of a century. The mission's water system is another study in ingenuity.

The storeroom holds items used daily—ropes, farm tools, dishes, woven mats,

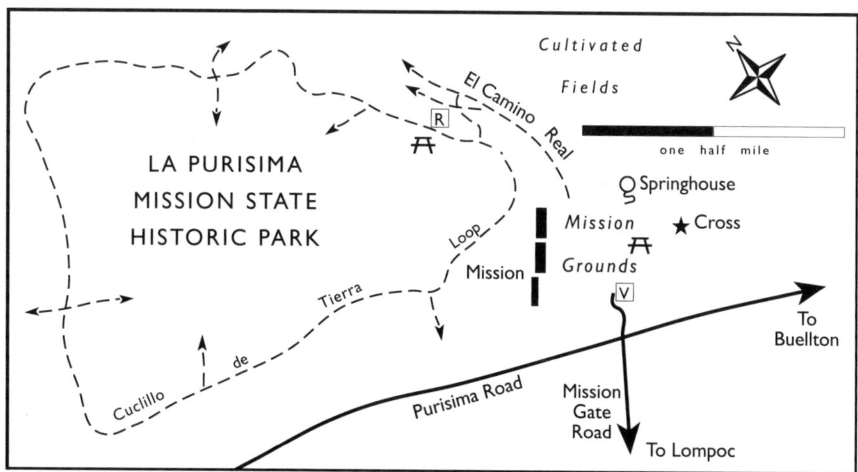

and blankets—while the leather shop reeks of hides. Quail and rabbits dart through the stock pens and between the garden plantings. A sundial, a traditional Indian hut, and other discoveries can be made while touring the grounds.

*Access:* Begin near the visitor center, crossing the footbridge to its west.

**Cuclillo de Tierra Loop.** This 2.75-mile round-trip tour circles the top of the west mesa, passing through the rare Burton Mesa chaparral habitat. Carry water.

To begin, go north on El Camino Real, touring the foot of an oak-grassland slope. Valley-bottom agriculture spreads east from the route. Past the Huerta Mateos Trail junction, go left on the unmarked paved road, heading uphill to the mesa top (0.25 mile).

Coming out at a gate and a junction near the park residences, go left on a paved route for a clockwise tour, passing through a grassland-chaparral transition habitat. Spring blooms add to the enjoyment, with owl's clover, cacti, sage, bush lupine, phlox, and thistle.

At 0.6 mile, where the paved route curves downhill, take the dirt road to the right for the loop. It soon enters an area of full chaparral intermixed with a few live oaks. Views are of Lompoc and the Santa Ynez River. At 1.2 miles, as the route curves north, sounds from a nearby public road intrude. Keep to the dirt road of Cuclillo de Tierra, bypassing all other mesa routes.

In another mile, the loop swings southeast, remaining open and shadeless, with limited views of the eastern valley. At 2.2 miles, stay straight, bypassing Las Canerias Trail. Ahead, the Cuclillo de Tierra Trail bears right at a scenic, twisted live oak.

Keep to the right, skirting both the park residences and the La Purisima offices; pavement returns. At 2.5 miles, hikers close the loop. Turn left to reach the gate and the downhill route to the mission area.

*Access:* Begin near the blacksmith shop, heading north on El Camino Real.

## CHUMASH PAINTED CAVE STATE HISTORIC PARK

**Hours/Season:** Year-round
**Facilities:** None
**For Information:** (805) 968-3294
**Access:** From US 101 at Santa Barbara, exit onto CA 154 and head northeast for 5.9 miles. Turn right on Painted Cave Road; the cave is on the left-hand side of the road in 1.9 miles. *The route is winding and climbing and narrows to one lane, not recommended for trailers or RVs. There is minimal roadside parking for one or two vehicles.*

This tucked-away site is a little difficult to spot, even with the state park sign, so keep an eye on the odometer. A short, rocky footpath leads to the gated cave in a large, honeycombed sandstone outcrop. Inside the dim recess is a spectacular array of ancient Chumash Indian art. Speculation has it that the black circle ringed in white on the cave's west wall represents the total eclipse that occurred November 24, 1677.

Viewed through the grate, the art is first rate, with bold patterns and wheel-like designs. The recess has protected the black, red, and white pigments over time. The mineral paints were made with animal fats for a base. Two main groups of designs can be seen; some are superimposed over earlier creations.

With limited turnaround space, travelers may wish to continue out Painted Cave Road to Camino Cielo and head left (west) to CA 154. Other archaeological resources exist in the area; do not disturb them. In any off-trail travels, beware of the poison oak.

## GAVIOTA STATE PARK

**Hours/Season:** Year-round
**Facilities:** 52 developed campsites; hike/bike campsite; picnic sites; historic area; pier with boat hoist; hiker, horse, and mountain-bike routes; restrooms; indoor and outdoor showers; *bring drinking water*
**For Information:** (805) 968-3294
**Access:** From US 101, about 20 miles northwest of Goleta and 10 miles south of Buellton, take the Gaviota State Park exit.

A rugged, inland wild makes up much of this nearly 2,800-acre beach park. The fire roads and trails webbing the oak-grassland and chaparral habitats of the park's undeveloped coastal mountains afford fine vistas and solitude, winning favor with equestrians and mountain-bike riders. As poison oak grows freely, and mountain lion and bear roam the backcountry, travelers should stay on the trails and keep a watchful eye on children. A listing of trails may be reviewed at the entry kiosk.

The beach itself is a winner. The broad 0.1-mile-long sandy cove stretching between Gaviota Creek and the 595-foot pier is ideal for sunning and swimming. A train trestle backs the beach. On the other side of the pier, visitors find a much narrower strand below a sheer, tilted-layer cliff; it is only walkable during low tides. Mussel shells cling to the rocks, seabirds occupy the cliff nooks, and swallows nest under the pier.

### Attractions and Activities

**Las Cruces.** Off CA 1, visitors find the last remnant of Las Cruces, a once-booming stage-route settlement serving trail-weary travelers and area rancheros. During its heyday, it boasted a stage station, store, saloon, restaurant, hotel, and blacksmith

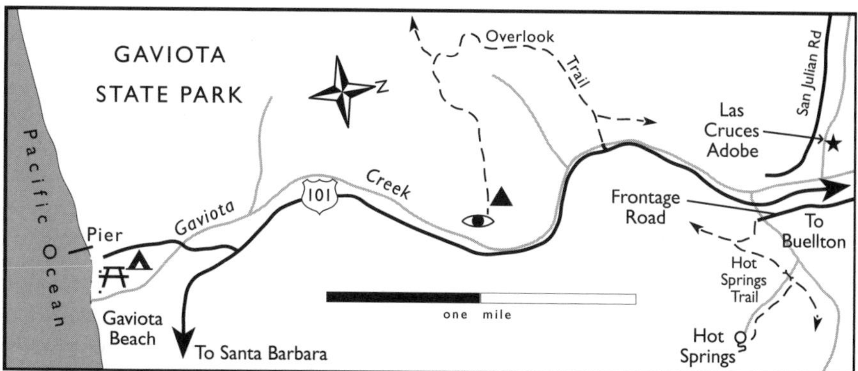

shop. Today, all that remains is the rubble from a century-old barn and an 1860 adobe that served as a hotel, bar, and brothel. A huge cactus patch is near the barn.

The adobe is fenced off, and a history panel introduces the site. The name Las Cruces, meaning "the crosses," traces back to the early 1800s, when the friars placed crosses on the area's unmarked Indian graves.

*Access:* From the main park, return to US 101, go 2.4 miles north, and take the Lompoc/CA 1 exit. Go 0.6 mile north and turn left on San Julian Road. On the left in 0.5 mile is a sign; a parking lot is 0.1 mile farther, on the road indicated as having a "narrow tunnel."

**Overlook Trail.** This 3-mile round-trip fire road excursion climbs 600 feet to a coastal overlook and explores the inland countryside. Beware of ticks.

Passing through a mixed area, with live oak-grassland and chaparral, visitors soon round a gate, coming to a T junction. There, go left. Grasses now push up through the steeply climbing 2-track. Look left to find the destination peak, dressed in chaparral and dotted by rock outcrops. Sounds from US 101 intrude.

The grade eases, as the fire road passes through a rolling, tall-grass meadow. At 0.4 mile, a scenic grove of beautiful multi-trunked oaks enfolds the route. On the north-facing slope, a shrubby floor replaces the grassland.

As the climb resumes, the views build, including more of the Upper Gaviota Creek drainage and the backcountry mosaic of grassland and chaparral. At the 0.9-mile trail junction, bear left, continuing uphill. The poison oak growing beneath the route's shade oaks suggests you bypass them. More views come as the route proceeds through low chaparral.

At 1.2 miles, the trail reaches the ridge at a low saddle for a view in two directions. The ocean view features the Gaviota Creek mouth, the offshore oil platforms, and the Channel Islands. The backcountry view features the high chaparral peaks and grassland valleys of the Upper Gaviota drainage.

The fire road ends at some towers just below the summit; bushwacking is needed to reach the top. But as the views are similar to those at the saddle, travelers may wish to just turn around and return as they came.

*Access:* The trailhead is off US 101 South. From the main park entrance, return to US 101 and go 2.4 miles north, taking the Lompoc/CA 1 exit. From there, get on US 101 South, go 0.9 mile, and turn right for the trailhead.

**Hot Springs Trail.** This 0.4-mile fire-road route leads to a pair of pleasant, small, warm-water pools. Climbing moderately, the road passes between a sycamore-lined creek and an oak-grassland slope. Fiesta flower, thistle, and mustard add springtime color.

Midway, oaks spread over the route, offering shade. Bird songs and the clicking of insects accompany the hiker. At the T junction, go left for the hot springs. Scenic oaks and sycamores continue to line the route, and the poison oak becomes more abundant.

At the 0.25-mile junction, go right on the foot trail, following Hot Springs Creek upstream to the pools (0.4 mile). A shrub and blackberry thicket lines the final leg.

The slight smell of sulfur announces the two pools linked by a small cascade. Between them grows a small palm; willows shade their sides. The upper pool is the nicer one, with small, primitive benches. Each is a couple of feet deep, with warm water percolating up through the rock and mud bottom. Nudity is prohibited.

*Access:* At the Lompoc/CA 1 exit, 2.4 miles north of the main park exit on US 101, take a sharp right on the frontage road to reach the trailhead parking lot in 0.3 mile; it is a fee lot.

**Fishing.** Both surf and pier fishing are popular. The pier extends over a sandy ocean bottom attractive to California halibut, barred surfperch, and Pacific mack-

erel. With the pier being lighted, campers can enjoy night fishing; day visitors must leave at sunset.

**Boating.** Local fishermen make extensive use of the pier's self-operated boat hoist, which is generally open sunrise to sunset, except for the first Wednesday of the month, when it is closed for servicing. Boat owners must have their own sling, with a ring that fits the hoist, and they must hand-pull the boat trailers to and from the lowering site, as no vehicles are allowed on the pier.

Divers and surfers likewise launch here to reach the preferred spots off Point Conception, to the northwest.

## REFUGIO AND EL CAPITAN STATE BEACHES

**Hours/Season:** Year-round
**Facilities:** 85 developed campsites, playground and horseshoe pits (Refugio); 140 developed campsites, en route campsites, dump station (El Capitan); hike/bike campsite, picnic sites, seasonal store, hiker and bicycle trails, restrooms, pay showers, outdoor showers (both)
**For Information:** (805) 968-3294
**Access:** Reach the parks off US 101, 10.5 miles and 8 miles northwest of Goleta, respectively. Exits are marked.

Occupying part of the 1795 Spanish land grant awarded Ortega (the first *comandante* of El Presidio de Santa Barbara), these two beach parks offer tree-shaded campsites within easy walking distance of the beach. The sites at Refugio are closely spaced on a flat right above shore. Dividing the campground is Refugio Creek. The bluff sites at El Capitan are more spacious and nicely wooded, with the loop nearest the ocean more open.

A 2-mile bike path along the bluff stitches together these two state beaches, and at the developed area of El Capitan, periodic stairways descend to shore. The railroad tracks that bypass both campgrounds carry day and night trains. The early-morning whistles often startle campers awake.

The character of both beaches varies seasonally. Winter storms and the spring runoff steal most of the sand, leaving behind narrowed, cobbled shores. Usually by June, though, the natural processes have restored the sands, and the beach parcels once again invite sunbathing and waterplay.

Swimming, surfing, sea kayaking, and surf fishing are other pastimes at the parks. Divers and snorkelers enjoy discovery off Refugio Point, although the offshore kelp beds have yet to recover from the storm of 1981.

*Palms, Refugio State Beach*

## Attractions and Activities

**Refugio Beach and Point.** Refugio Beach is a beautiful, broad 0.75-mile crescent of fine sand and cobblestones, cut by the waters of Refugio Creek. The tide determines how much of the bluff-lined, 0.5-mile stretch east of the creek can be traveled. Cobbles dominate the east end of the crescent.

At the west end of Refugio State Beach rises Refugio Point, a low, off-white bluff extension. A 0.2-mile trail climbs to its end, where a picnic table overlooks the water. Above the beach, a row of scenic, stout palms ushers travelers to the trail. The palms are a park trademark.

Views from the point include three Channel Islands: San Miguel, Santa Rosa, and Santa Cruz. They also feature the offshore wells, the tilted sedimentary beds of the cliff, and the surfers awaiting the next wave.

**El Capitan Beach.** This beach often features cobbles below its 100-foot bluffs. At times, the tides lap at the cliffs. Other times, a good expanse of sand greets park visitors. In spring, bush sunflowers and mustard color the bluff slopes.

Landmark for this beach is the flattish bulge of El Capitan Point. Low boulders and rocks are strung off it, suggesting tidepooling. The point itself is fine for reflection, admiring the Channel Islands, watching for marine mammals, or casting a line. The best surf is also found off the point, judged by the gathering of surfers.

Low, white cliffs curve east away from El Capitan Point. At times, beachgoers catch a whiff of the natural tar seep or find the sticky goo attached to their feet.

**El Capitan Nature Trail.** A pleasant 0.3-mile nature trail explores inland from El Capitan Point, touring the El Capitan Creek drainage. Magnificent twisted sycamores, old oaks, and woodpeckers are there to discover. A guide to the trail may be borrowed at the entry station. Beware of the poison oak intertwined with the exotics and low-growing vegetation along the trail.

*Access:* Begin near the El Capitan State Beach entrance station.

**Fishing.** Surf fishing from these beaches is best two hours before and after high tide. Surf perch is a prized year-round catch, while the flatfish are most often caught between December and March.

# El Presidio de Santa Barbara State Historic Park

**Hours/Season:** 10:30 A.M. to 4:30 P.M.
**Facilities:** Visitor center, historic buildings, *bring water*
**For Information:** (805) 965-0093
**Access:** Find the park at the intersection of Santa Barbara and East Canon Perdido streets in Santa Barbara.

This park unit preserves the last of four royal fortresses built by Spain to protect her California claim. Established in 1782, it took the Spanish colonists and Chumash Indians five years to construct. Much of the original was lost in the earthquakes of the 1800s and the rise of modern-day Santa Barbara, but La Caneda Adobe, the chapel, and a portion of the Comandancia have been restored or reconstructed.

Across the street stands the unassuming whitewashed adobe, El Cuartel—the second oldest building in California. It housed a soldier's family. While it is temporarily closed for restoration, visitors can look through the window and see its spartan furnishings.

## Attractions and Activities

**El Presidio de Santa Barbara Tour.** Inside La Caneda Adobe, visitors can view a model of the original presidio quadrangle, with its buildings and a defense wall encircling an open court. The chapel was centrally placed opposite the main gate. Among the buildings were barracks, family housing, warehouses, a jail, and defense bastions. A 15-minute video explains the presidio's historic significance, while the museum artifacts and exhibits introduce the people and the time.

*Mission altar, El Presidio de Santa Barbara State Historic Park*

The two-story chapel has an uneven red tile floor, colorful hand-painted borders, and a high ceiling. Much of the altar is of seventeenth- and eighteenth-century Spanish design, with the altar frontal dating back to 1578. Elsewhere in the presidio, visitors can see a hand-chiseled loom, a beehive oven (*horno*), and a crude ox cart.

The area has undergone archaeological excavation since the 1960s. Digs may be seen behind the main adobe and off Santa Barbara Street, where future plans call for additional reconstruction. Near a pepper tree at the back of the presidio, visitors can see the original foundation that supported the 10-foot-high, 4-foot-wide adobe defense wall.

# Carpinteria State Beach

**Hours/Season:** Year-round
**Facilities:** 262 developed campsites (86 have full hookups, another 33 have electricity and water), picnic area, visitor center, restrooms, pay showers, outdoor showers, dump station
**For Information:** (805) 684-2811
**Access:** From US 101, take the downtown/Casitas Pass Road exit at Carpinteria and follow the signs through town, entering the park in 0.6 mile.

Carpinteria Creek divides this nearly mile-long, east–west beach in half, with the broader west end showing more sand, and the east end showing more cobbles. The east end also holds a rocky tidepool area and a natural asphalt seepage.

It is this naturally occurring beach tar that attracted the Chumash Indians to the area long ago. With the tar, they could build watertight driftwood vessels seaworthy enough to reach the Channel Islands across Santa Barbara Channel. In turn, the boat-building Indians led the Spanish to name this area "La Carpinteria"—the car-

*Beachcombers, Carpinteria State Beach*

penter shop. More recently, the natural seepage has brought offshore drilling platforms.

Low dunes, a boulder riprap slope, and a section of bluff border this family beach. Activities are many, with swimming, surfing, boogie-boarding, tidepooling, surf fishing, sunbathing, strolling, and sandplay. On the west-end beach, beachcombers, strollers, and joggers enjoy a broad, flat, tide-washed strand. Above the high-tide line is a reliable patch of sand, where blankets and chairs can be left.

Surfers prefer the water off the "tar pits" area. The catches in the fishermen's buckets include barred perch and corbina. At low tide, sea stars, crabs, and urchin are among the intertidal species discovered amid the rocks; all such species are protected.

At the small visitor center, park guests can view similar marine species in a tidepool aquarium, without getting their feet wet. Other exhibits are devoted to the Chumash Indian. Outside, a Chumash garden features the plants historically used by the Indians.

Passing trains on a nearby track occasionally shatter the calm of the surf and awaken campers.

## EMMA WOOD, SAN BUENAVENTURA, MCGRATH, AND OXNARD STATE BEACHES

**Hours/Season:** Year-round

**Facilities:** 61 primitive beachside campsites, en route campsites, hike/bike campsites, nonflush toilets, with restrooms, outdoor shower, and water at the south area only (Emma Wood); large picnic area, snackbar, beach rentals, pedestrian/bicycle path, fitness trail, volleyball courts, pier, restrooms, outdoor shower (San Buenaventura); 174 developed coastal-plain campsites, picnic sites, hiker trail, restrooms, pay showers, dump station (McGrath); picnic area, ball field, volleyball courts, pedestrian/bicycle path, restrooms, outdoor showers (Oxnard)

**For Information:** (805) 654-4610

**Access:** These four Ventura County beaches are reached off US 101, beginning 2 miles northwest of Ventura and ending at Oxnard; state beach signs mark the exits and routes.

Lined up along the southern Santa Barbara Channel, three of the beaches offer similar sandy strands, while the fourth, Emma Wood, is narrow and cobblestone riddled. In winter, high tides can steal its beach altogether, lapping at the old seawall. Views from the Channel Coast beaches are of Channel Islands.

In the city of Ventura, 2-mile-long San Buenaventura is the premier state beach playground for this area. Protecting it from erosion, riprap groins extend into the ocean, creating a broader, harder-packed area of sand for sunbathing, strolling, relaxing, and having fun.

Oxnard State Beach is a similar active urban beach on a much smaller scale. It has a broad 0.25-mile beach backed by dunes and a pretty, landscaped picnic and sports area. Joggers and rollerskaters enjoy the pedestrian way passing through and around the park.

Tolerable ocean temperatures and reliable wave sets attract swimmers and surfers to the channel coastline, but stiff currents and riptides off 2-mile-long McGrath State Beach reserve it for the surfer. In summer, cool ocean breezes sweep the beaches, sending kites aloft and raising goose bumps on sunbathers. Summer lifeguards oversee the activity at all but Oxnard State Beach.

At McGrath State Beach, the campground has sites suitable for all means of camping. It also affords greater comfort than the primitive camp facility at Emma Wood North, where the side-by-side sites are mostly suited to RVs, drinking water is unavailable, and US 101 and the Southern Pacific Railroad pass next door. What attracts campers to Emma Wood North is its closeness to the cobbly shore.

## Attractions and Activities

**Ventura Oceanfront Bike Route.** This developed route runs the length of Ventura, stitching together Emma Wood and San Buenaventura state beaches. Annually, the Century Bike Race takes place along it.

*Access:* The route has multiple accesses within Ventura and at the two state parks.

**Fishing.** Ocean fishing is popular, as is pier fishing off the 1,700-foot San Buenaventura Pier. Perch, corbina, bass, and bonita are among the year-round catches. In March, June, July, and August, on the first to fifth night following a full moon, grunion runs occur on the sandy shores. The tiny silvery fish are scooped by hand; a valid fishing license is required.

**Birdwatching.** For this activity, McGrath State Beach receives particular note. Different sightings are possible at its Santa Clara River Estuary Natural Preserve, toured by a 0.75-mile nature trail; at McGrath Lake, a small freshwater lake reached by hiking the beach south; and along the park's entire coastal shore. Songbirds, raptors, shorebirds, and seabirds build the count. A sighting of the endangered California least tern or Belding's savannah sparrow may reward a patient watcher at the nature preserve.

# Los Encinos State Historic Park

**Hours/Season:** 9:00 A.M. to 5:00 P.M. Wednesday through Sunday, except major holidays

**Facilities:** Picnic tables, visitor center, historic buildings, restrooms

**For Information:** (818) 784-4849

**Access:** From US 101 at Encino, go south on Balboa Boulevard and turn left (east) onto Moorpark Street; the park is at 16756 Moorpark.

This 5-acre San Fernando Valley park preserves the center of operations for Rancho del Encino (Oak Ranch), which was worked from 1849 to 1915. A natural warm-water spring on the property brought ranchers here. Prior to their

*Adobe ranch house, Los Encinos State Historic Park*

arrival, a Native American village occupied this site for the same reason. The ranch house served as a hospitality stop for travelers on the El Camino Real, "the Royal Highway," a primary transportation route connecting the Franciscan missions.

A guided tour of the adobe ranch house and a self-guided tour of the grounds tell the story of nineteenth-century ranch life and the various owners. Areas of lawn, old oaks, olives, palms, a citrus grove, and a historical garden unite for an attractive, relaxing setting. Ducks and migratory waterfowl splash about in the small spring-fed reservoir. Dispensers sell duck food so children may feed them.

## Attractions and Activities

**Rancho Tour.** The linear, single-story, nine-room adobe ranch house effectively represents a timeline for the ranch, with each of its side-by-side rooms recalling one of the owners. Period furnishings decorate each of the living compartments. Among the historical items is the bedroom set of Don Vicente de la Ossa, who built the original adobe. One small area in the structure allows visitors to see how the 2-foot-thick mud brick was held together by straw.

Next door is the two-story Garnier building, a living quarters built by the second owners. Presently, it holds the park visitor center, with a few historical displays. Elsewhere on the grounds, the self-guided tour takes visitors past a geometric-shaped spring house, a limestone sheepherder's hut, and a food storage shelter. The brochure describes the various trees and plantings seen on the way.

# SANTA SUSANA MOUNTAINS

**Hours/Season:** Daylight hours
**Facilities:** Historic site and marker, informal hiker trails, *bring water*
**For Information:** (818) 880-0350
**Access:** From the CA 118-CA 27 junction at Chatsworth, go south on CA 27 (Topanga Canyon Boulevard) for 1.5 miles, turning west on Devonshire. Chatsworth City Park, gateway to the state land, is at the end of the road in 0.5 mile.

This undeveloped wilderness state park enfolds three sides of Chatsworth City Park, with the bulk of the state lands stretching north and west. The park applauds the rugged beauty of the Santa Susana Mountains, with their rounded, fractured boulder outcrops and their chaparral-cloaked hillsides.

Traversing the state park land is the historic Santa Susana Stage Route (1859–1890), both a destination and a passageway for the contemporary traveler. A web of well-traveled informal trails unites the various rock outcrops, affording first-rate Santa Susana Mountains and San Fernando Valley vistas, as well as some fine rock scrambles. Posted signs warn that this is mountain lion country; one can easily picture them here.

## Attractions and Activities

**Stagecoach Trail.** This informal 2.5-mile round-trip tour heads west following a fire road along the southern border of Chatsworth City Park, skirting an open lawn. A few oaks line the way. From the start, wonderful looks at the light-colored, blocky rock outcrops of the Santa Susana Mountains engage. At 0.2 mile, bear left, switchbacking up the slope, coming to a paved route. Follow it right (west), toward the power station at 0.4 mile.

At the fence around the power station, follow the dirt trail that heads left. The well-trodden path parallels cable markers up the steep chaparral slope. Sage, laurel sumac, greasewood, and wildflower annuals weave the hillside tapestry. As the trail climbs, it passes a few boulders. Over-the-shoulder views of the city of Chatsworth and the San Fernando Valley build.

Scanning the rock face of the hillside to the south, hikers may spy a large white square. Below it is the contouring course of the historic stage road—the hike's goal.

At 0.6 mile, where a couple of side trails streak straight uphill, stay on the primary trail as it curves left. Ahead, it meets the stage route, now worn down to the bedrock. Here, visitors can overlook a long segment of what must have been a bone-rattling, white-knuckle ride.

Go right, following the stage route uphill to find the white-and-red tile marker placed by the Daughters of the Golden West (0.9 mile). Pale orange monkey-flowers color the sides of the trail. Uphill from the marker, rainy-season hikers may discover tadpoles in the puddles created by the tiny, unreliable springs.

The old stage route ends atop a rise, for an area overview. Going right on one of the good informal trails leads to an even better vantage (1.25 miles). Return as you came.

*Access:* Begin at the parking area at Chatsworth City Park.

# Point Mugu State Park

**Hours/Season:** Year-round

**Facilities:** 50 developed wooded campsites, 80 primitive beach campsites, trail campground (lost to fire, but plans to rebuild), picnic areas, hiker and horse trails, mountain-bike roads, restrooms, nonflush toilets, indoor and outdoor showers, dump station

**For Information:** (818) 880-0350 or (805) 488-5223

**Access:** Find the park accesses along a 1.7-mile stretch of CA 1, starting 4.1 miles south of the Point Mugu Naval Station in Port Hueneme.

This state park's 15,000 acres bring together the beauty and recreation of the Santa Monica Mountains and the Pacific Ocean. Revelers in the outdoors can seek solitude in the rugged chaparral wilds of Boney Mountain Wilderness, explore rich valley grasslands, travel along a magnificent sycamore-lined drainage, enjoy views from atop a coastal ridge, play in the Great Dune, and admire the crashing waves and the passing of gray whales. The chaparral, coastal scrub, and native bunchgrass habitats put on a splendid spring wildflower show, and the monarch butterfly finds a suitable winter habitat here. The followers of Audubon rarely leave disappointed.

Swept by fire late in 1993, the park's rejuvenation was underway within a matter of weeks. Following the first post-fire growing season, the coastal scrub and grassland habitats were again vital, showing few clues to the fire.

## Attractions and Activities

**Sycamore Cove and Thornhill Broome Beaches.** Lining CA 1, these Point Mugu State Park beaches suffer some highway intrusion, but generally the surf crowds out the noise. Quarter-mile-long Sycamore Cove is the more developed beach. Nearly all 1.1 miles of Thornhill Broome's oceanfront is backed by primitive La Jolla Beach Campground.

Both slant steeply to the water, with a flat sandy area behind for blankets and sunbathing. Here, the waves crash close to shore, and an underwater rift creates cold upwellings. Combine these with a steep drop-off, and beach newcomers should ask a lifeguard about swimming safely here. Surf fishing remains popular at both Sycamore Cove and Thornhill Broome beaches.

Between the naval base and the Point Mugu land feature is another 0.2-mile strand, accessed via a large dirt parking area. This primitive area extends a similar beach offering, removed from the crowds.

*Access:* Sycamore Cove and Thornhill Broome beaches are marked accesses off CA 1.

**Overlook–Sycamore Canyon Loop.** This 10-mile fire road loop travels the ridge between Big Sycamore Canyon and La Jolla Valley and returns via the canyon.

Lining the wide, dirt road of the Big Sycamore Canyon Trail are jimson weed,

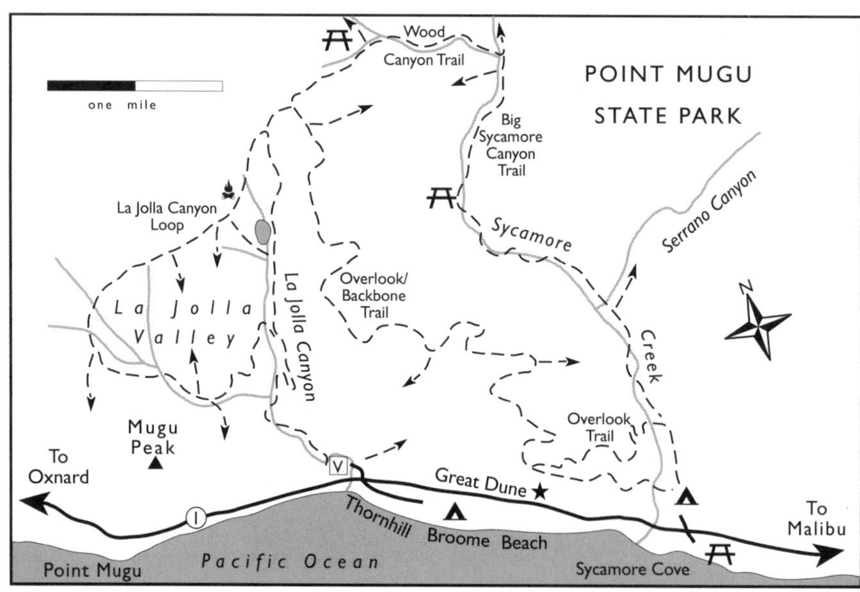

sumac, and elderberry, along with several nonnative species: castor bean, milk thistle, and tobacco weed. The latter's tubular yellow flowers call in the hummingbirds. The mild grade of the canyon road welcomes a family bicycle ride.

At 0.4 mile, the Overlook Trail heads left, crosses intermittent Sycamore Creek, and climbs for a clockwise tour. Laurel sumac, buckwheat, poison oak, and other native species cloak the slope above this road. Coastal views build, as hikers continue along the ridge.

On the upper slope, the *Yucca whipplei* stalks push up beside the road, and occasionally a roadrunner may be spied. By 1.8 miles, the route adds Boney Mountain and Serrano Valley views. Continuing, it alternates between areas of coastal scrub and chaparral and slips back and forth between ocean and inland views. At 3.1 miles, it merges with the Backbone Trail—the long-distance Santa Monica Mountains route, yet to be completed.

*Wood Canyon rest, Point Mugu State Park*

At 4 miles, the trail tops a saddle affording early looks at La Jolla Valley Grassland and the Laguna Peak Radar Station. A slow descent through chaparral follows. Bypassing the Wood Canyon View Trail on the right at 5.25 miles and La Jolla Valley Loop (another fire road) on the left at 5.3 miles, the descent quickens, dropping away from the ridge. Where the road bottoms out is the Wood Canyon Trail junction (6.2 miles). Bear right, following Wood Canyon downstream.

At its creek crossing, water usually lingers, supporting tadpoles and frogs. Live oaks enclose the canyon, with sycamores appearing near the Big Sycamore Canyon Trail junction at 7 miles. Go right on this major fire road for a leisurely walk out the broad canyon.

Lots of 6-foot-tall milk thistle and twiggy wreath plant line the route, and at times the tall, grand sycamores offer shade. Starting at 8 miles, the trail crosses Sycamore Creek seven times. In spring, these upper crossings may require wading but become stone-step crossings later in the year. The last two are normally dry except after rains.

At 8.8 miles, a scenic woodpecker-drilled sycamore precedes the Serrano Canyon Trail junction. Remaining on Big Sycamore Canyon Trail, travelers close the loop at 9.6 miles, and end the tour at 10 miles.

*Access:* Begin at the Sycamore Canyon Campground, taking the gated dirt road near site 10, upstream.

**La Jolla Valley Loop.** This 8-mile hiker loop travels a rugged, narrow canyon, bypasses a seasonal waterfall, and tours the lush grassland of the nature preserve. The coreopsis (giant sunflower), ceanothus, and myriad wildflowers decorate it in spring.

Heading up La Jolla Canyon, hikers bypass the restroom and cross the canyon drainage. Exposed rock punctuates this canyon, with coreopsis dotting one slope, yucca and prickly pear the other. Rabbits abound. At 0.7 mile, the trail again crosses the drainage, passing through an old quarry site, for a rugged climb through the now-pinched canyon. A thin foot trail leads the way.

The trail crosses the small seasonal falls at the flat between its two 15-foot drops. Willows and boulders accent the creek. Vegetating the canyon are candelabra-branched coreopsis, toyon, and poison oak. The sandstone outcrops show small hollow openings.

After the trail levels, passing through a ceanothus-live oak corridor, it comes to the start of La Jolla Valley Loop; go right for a counterclockwise tour. After bypassing a shortcut to the camp, hikers overlook a bulrush-rimmed pond. At the edge of the grassland is the 2.7-mile junction; go left for the loop.

Ahead, the route skirts the edge of the oak-secluded sites of La Jolla Valley Walk-in Camp (facilities lost in fire of 1993) and overlooks the grassy sea. Leaving the camp area, stay right, keeping to the right-hand edge of the valley grassland. Mustard corridors and chaparral at times claim the 2-track. Elsewhere, hikers see tufts of the 5-foot-tall native grasses for which the area is known. Ticks are a springtime concern, and the mosquitos can be bad amid the trees.

At 4.4 miles, the trail crosses over a drainage, rounds an oak grove, and crosses a second drainage, coming out amid the beautiful shoulder-tall grasses below Mugu Peak. At the junction here, go left, passing through the flowing grasses, as the trail to the right rounds the peak.

At 5.1 miles, the loop crosses an oak drainage and begins touring a transition grassland-scrub habitat. At 5.6 miles, side trails enter from the left and the right; keep to the loop, curving toward La Jolla Canyon.

The trail rounds and climbs, and where it tops out, hikers find ocean and La Jolla Canyon views. A descent follows, and with one last wooded drainage crossing, the loop closes at 6.6 miles. Retrace the initial 1.4 miles.

*Access:* Begin at the La Jolla Valley trailhead, following the gated dirt road up La Jolla Canyon from the parking area.

## MALIBU CREEK STATE PARK

**Hours/Season:** Year-round; 12:00 P.M. to 4:00 P.M. weekends (visitor center)
**Facilities:** 60 developed tent campsites; picnic sites; visitor center; hiker, horse, and mountain-bike trails; restrooms; nonflush toilets; showers
**For Information:** (818) 880-0350 or (805) 488-5223
**Access:** From the junction of CA 1 and Malibu Canyon Road, go 5.8 miles north on Malibu Canyon Road/Las Virgenes Road for the park. From US 101 at Calabasas, go 4 miles south on Las Virgenes Road.

This 7,000-acre park is a showplace for the rugged grandeur of the Santa Monica Mountains and the bending beauty of equally wild Malibu Creek, slicing through them. Featured here are rough, chiseled chaparral hillsides, rolling oak grasslands, a marshy 20-acre lake, and eye-catching rock outcrops, canyons, and gorges. The varied terrain caught the attention of Twentieth-Century Fox, which established a movie ranch here.

Today, the area has been turned over to the adventurer and the naturalist. To see the park, one must walk, horseback ride, or bike in, following dirt fire roads and trails. The only car touring is what one can see from Malibu Canyon Road and its few turnouts. But, the earned rewards—a deep rock pool, sweeping mountain and ocean vistas, and natural sightings of deer, eagle, roadrunner, and quail—call visitors back again and again.

## Attractions and Activities

**Visitor Center.** The picturesque ranch house of the visitor center overlooks a slow, yawning stretch of Malibu Creek. Inside are maps and handouts, natural-history and cultural displays, and a photographic record of the park's film history. Outside, pleasing old sycamore trees shade a couple of picnic tables that, in turn, invite an appreciation of the area. Water and chemical toilets are the amenities.

*Access:* Reached by a pleasant 0.5-mile stroll, traveling upstream from the day-use parking area on Crags Road.

**Crags Road–Upper Canyon Tour.** This fire-road route offers a variety of destinations. It accesses the serene setting of the visitor center at 0.5 mile, the Gorge and Rock Pool at 0.8 mile, Century Lake beginning at 1 mile, and the "M*A*S*H" set at 2 miles, with the untamed upper park beckoning beyond that.

The route descends from the main day-use parking lot, crosses Las Virgenes Creek, and heads upstream. Oak grassland covers the south-facing slopes, while chaparral clads the north-facing ones. At 0.25 mile, follow Crags Road across Malibu Creek and continue up the canyon, passing through the open grassy flat. Side routes branch off it, and along it dispersed picnic tables invite the opening of a

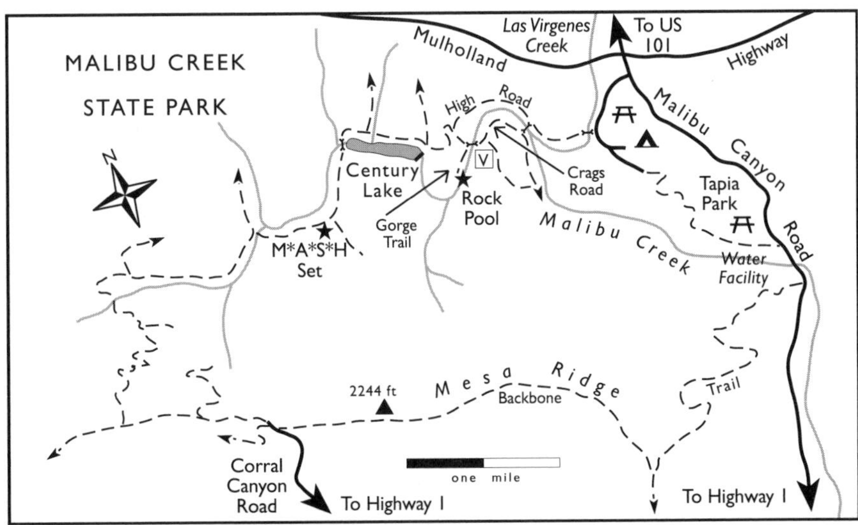

*M*A*S*H jeep, Malibu Creek State Park*

basket lunch. Before long, the rambling white ranch house of the park visitor center suggests a stop to learn more about the park.

Leaving the visitor center area, travelers resume the upstream tour, crossing Hunt Bridge back over Malibu Creek, coming to the Gorge Trail junction at 0.6 mile. Following it left, visitors find three oak-shaded picnic sites in 100 yards, a technical climbing area in 0.1 mile, and the popular Rock Pool in 0.2 mile.

The climbers, connected by rope and clinging to the pock-marked, vertical pink cliffs draw a spectator gallery. While these rocks require technical skills, others in the park serve both the free and technical climber. More of the colorful cliffs frame Rock Pool, the depth of which depends on the season and rainfall. Hot summers can render it dry.

Forgoing the Gorge Trail detour, the canyon tour resumes by following Crags Road upstream, bypassing another picnic site and the High Road junction. At 1 mile, the route overlooks the dam of Century Lake and the steep, narrow outlet gorge. It then tops a rise and descends, skirting this willow-lined, marshy lake.

Upon crossing the concrete bridge just upstream from Century Lake (1.3 miles), cyclists may be turned back by the chunky, loose rock surface of the road, which continues for the next 0.5-mile. Others choose to carry or push their bikes over the rough section. Red rock cliffs and ridgetops now punctuate the chaparral slopes.

Bypassing the Lost Cabin Trail, visitors finally arrive at the "M*A*S*H" site—a favorite destination. A rusting ambulance and jeep provide a photo opportunity that few can resist, as they pile on board for a souvenir shot. Return as you came, or venture deeper into the park. Various routes lead to hilltop overviews of the park wilds and the Pacific Ocean; carry a map and compass.

*Access:* Begin at the main day-use parking lot at the west side of the developed park, following the paved and dirt fire road upstream toward the visitor center.

**Backbone Trail to Corral Canyon Road.** This 6-mile one-way journey is open to foot, mountain bike, and horse travel. It offers a fine introduction to the rugged park terrain and a frequently changing vista. Carry water.

Soon after leaving the corridor of Malibu Canyon Road, hikers, riders, and cyclists share the route of this sometimes eroded, westwardly bound fire road. As it climbs steadily, it passes through areas of thick, classic high-chaparral vegetation. Atop a rise at 0.5 mile, travelers gain their first full look at Brents Mountain, a light-colored conical-rock peak with a ragged northeast ridge.

Ahead, the route descends and rounds above a small reservoir. At 0.75 mile, another fire road descends to the right; bear left, wrapping and climbing the slope. With the climb come additional views of Brents Mountain, the northern reaches of the Malibu Creek drainage, and the Santa Monica ridges rolling north and east. Above the road, a few small oaks mount the slopes.

As the route rounds onto the south-facing slope of Mesa Ridge (1.2 miles), an impressive overlook of the steep chaparral drainage of Malibu Creek greets the traveler. Coreopsis, lupine, monkey-flower, and phlox contribute to the spring kaleidoscope. Saddle flats afford brief north-south vistas, including early ocean views. At 1.9 miles, the trail passes through a small grove of shade oaks—a rare escape from the summer sun. Still, the Backbone Trail climbs.

At 2.9 miles, the trail bypasses a fire road on the left coming to a junction with the Mesa Peak Fire Road. Bear right, continuing the Mesa Ridge tour, exchanging inland views for coastal ones. Saddle crossings again expand the view. At 3.4 miles, the trail makes a steep climb to top a rise. Along this stretch, a study of the road will reveal eroded turret shell fossils sprinkling the trailbed. As the tour continues, the views are out Corral Canyon.

At 4.1 miles, the trail tops out, with looks at the park's dramatic rock canyons and gorges. In another mile, it travels an area where vertical rock outcrops shoot out from the hillsides. Weathering carves small caves, hollows, and nooks in the hard sandstone. The rocks invite scrambling and photography.

Past the rocky area is Corral Canyon Road, at 5.7 miles—the turnaround site for round-trip travelers. If a shuttle was pre-arranged, follow Corral Canyon Road uphill to the graveled trailhead parking area at 6 miles. From there, still more routes probe the park backreaches, saluting the wilds of the Santa Monica Mountains.

*Access:* Begin at the paved trailhead parking area 1 mile south of the park entrance, off Malibu Canyon Road. Hikers follow the Backbone Trail from the parking area; cyclists and horseback riders start on the fire road just to its south. The routes merge in 0.1 mile.

## Topanga State Park

**Hours/Season:** 8:00 A.M. to sunset

**Facilities:** Trail camp, picnic sites, visitor center, hiker and horse trails, mountain-bike roads, restrooms, nonflush toilets

**For Information:** (310) 455-2465

**Access:** From US 101 at Woodland Hills, take the Topanga Canyon Boulevard exit, head south for 7.8 miles, and turn left on Entrada Road. Remain on it to enter the park in another mile.

Topanga State Park is one of several gateways to the Santa Monica Mountains National Recreation Area—a rugged 50-mile-long coastal mountain corridor. What is, at once, so amazing and so appropriate about this mostly untouched wilderness range and natural area is its Greater Los Angeles location. The steep, chiseled canyons, faulted and folded ridges, and challenging chaparral wilds bring prized solitude, adventure, and escape to the urban dweller and visitor.

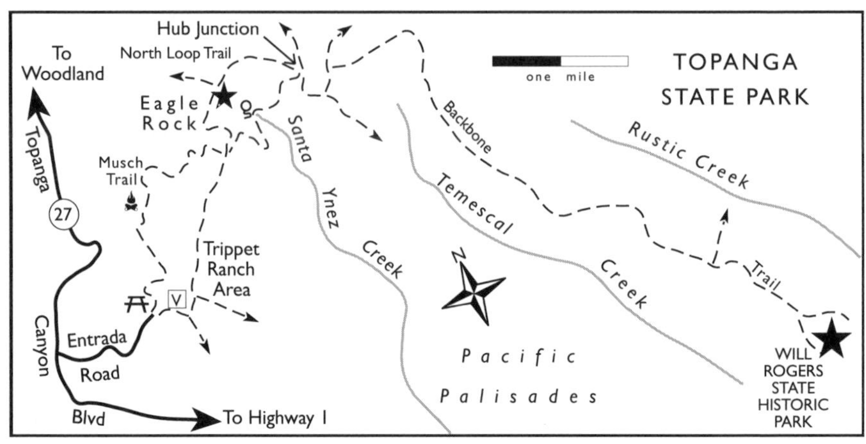


Topanga is an activity park, welcoming enthusiasts of hiking, horseback riding, and mountain biking, but it also appeals to the naturalist. Oak woodland, grassland, and chaparral habitats make up the park. The eroded rock outcrops and expansive coastal-valley vistas add to the excitement of its various tours.

## Attractions and Activities

**Eagle Rock Loop.** This 7.25-mile figure-eight loop, with a 900-foot elevation change, travels fire road and trail, visiting the park's most prominent land feature.

Upon leaving Trippet Ranch parking, at the first junction go right on the fire road ascending a grassland slope dotted by large coastal live oak. Bearing left at an arrow marker, travelers come to the 0.2-mile junction; here, the tour heads left. Early views are to the west overlooking the grassland, Trippet Ranch, and the visitor center. At the Santa Ynez junction, travelers find views east out Santa Ynez Canyon.

By 0.7 mile, the trail climbs steadily. Sage, laurel sumac, and sugarbush often line the ridge route. Where it travels amid rock outcrops, visitors will note the many cobbles weathering from the rock. At 1 mile, the tour offers the first look at Eagle Rock.

At 1.4 miles, travelers reach the three-pronged Eagle junction. The fire roads to the right and center form a loop; the Musch Trail, a footpath, heads left. Take the center fork, the North Loop Trail, for a clockwise tour of Eagle Rock. Where the fire road crests at 1.9 miles, a rock-scrambling detour to the right tops the hard sandstone outcrop for a fine panorama, with Backbone Ridge, Temescal Canyon, and ocean and valley vistas. Shelves and hollows mark Eagle Rock. Ravens, swallows, and vultures soar below the vantage.

Leaving the landmark rock, go right to resume the figure-eight tour. Over-the-shoulder looks offer a different perspective on the monolith. Keep to the main fire road, bypassing an unmarked dirt road and Garapito Canyon Trail. Other views are of the San Fernando Valley and Santa Susana Mountains.

At 2.9 miles, travelers find the Hub junction, with a chemical toilet and trash can. Here, the fire road to the left leads to Mulholland Highway, while the far-right one leads to the Roger's and Backbone trails. The near-right trail angling downhill continues the figure-eight tour, overlooking the upper Santa Ynez drainage.

At 3.5 miles, the trail skirts a road washout, and a half mile farther a vegetation change from the familiar chaparral signals the arrival at Eagle Springs. Soon, the

*Eagle Rock, Topanga State Park*

trail affords good upward looks at Eagle Rock and its impressive cliff. The massive outcrop dwarfs the people atop it. At 4.5 miles, the upper loop of the figure-eight closes at Eagle junction. To close the lower loop, follow the footpath of Musch Trail downhill to the right.

The open trail steadily descends the chaparral-clad slope. Thicker, taller vegetation frames the small drainages crossed along the way. The one at 5.3 miles has a few sycamores, but it also has poison oak. Where the trail switchbacks through a grassland dotted by mariposa lily and blue-dicks, deer may be seen.

At 6 miles is the eucalyptus-shaded hiker/horse camp with corrals, water, and flush toilets. Beyond it, the trail crosses over a one-lane gravel road; arrows point away from an employee residence. After briefly merging with a jeep road, the trail veers left, contouring a slope with a downhill grade. At 7.2 miles, go left on the paved lane. The tour ends just ahead, near the parking lot restroom.

*Access:* Begin at the southeast corner of the Trippet Ranch parking area.

**Backbone Trail.** This 9.8-mile hiker/horse link between Topanga State Park and Will Rogers State Historic Park (SHP) is just one segment of a burgeoning long-distance trail that will travel the entire length of the Santa Monica Mountains crest from Griffith Park to Point Mugu State Park. Presently, the trail is underutilized, overgrown in places, and marred by unmarked junctions, but volunteers are hoping to change all that.

To reach the Backbone Trail, from the Hub junction on the Eagle Rock Loop (2.9 miles), follow the far-right fire road toward Roger's and Backbone trails. In a half mile (3.4 miles), take the footpath on the left; it is the Backbone Trail. The route of varying width is rugged and often overgrown, and travelers need to beware of the patchy presence of poison oak. Early views are of West Los Angeles; later the shrubby corridor denies all views.

At 6.6 miles, where the trail passes beneath a scenic shade oak, go right, descending the thick chaparral of the canyon slope. At 7.3 miles, travelers gain looks at Santa Monica Bay, Marina del Rey, and the Palos Verdes Peninsula. Beyond the shade of another coastal live oak, the trail crosses over a rock slide (or unstable rock slope).

At the trail fork at 7.9 miles, go right, traveling the ridge and crossing over a bridge platform. At 8.2 miles, keep an eye out for a footpath angling left. It continues the hike, steeply descending to Will Rogers SHP. Stay left, as spurs branch to vistas. At 9 miles, the trail enters the SHP near Inspiration Point; follow the Inspiration Point Trail left toward the nature center and the developed park, ending the one-way tour at 9.8 miles.

*Access:* Reach it via the Eagle Rock Loop at Topanga State Park or via Will Rogers SHP.

## Leo Carrillo State Beach

**Hours/Season:** Year-round

**Facilities:** 138 developed inland campsites, 32 beach campsites for self-contained vehicles under 8 feet in height, hike / bike campsites, picnic sites, visitor center, summer store, snackbar / rental concessions, hiker trails, restrooms, nonflush toilets, indoor and outdoor showers

**For Information:** (818) 880-0350

**Access:** Find the main entrance east off CA 1, 0.1 mile south of the Mulholland Highway–CA 1 intersection. An underpass connects the park's inland and beach sides.

This park's 1.5 miles of rocky points and sandy strands can be enjoyed up close, with the surf washing at your heels, or from 1,000 feet above, atop a coastal hill. A grassland-coastal scrub habitat blankets much of the inland park, where the springtime blooms are hard to beat both for color and assortment. Mulholland Highway passes through the park's Arroyo Sequit Canyon, disturbing the quiet of its main campground and the naturalness of its canyon.

The popular shore welcomes a variety of activity—surfing and wind surfing, skimboarding, tidepooling, surf fishing, beachcombing, and relaxing. Sequit Point, a land jut marked by sea caves, separates the park's North and South beaches. Cormorants roost atop the rocks broken away from it.

In the protected waters near the point and amid the kelp beds beyond it, divers and snorkelers find an interesting discovery of colorful fish and varied ocean species. Visitors can travel to the top of Sequit Point for a better vantage on the coastal stage. When gray whales pass closer to shore in February and March, it can be a fine place to sit.

### Attractions and Activities

**South Beach.** This is the park's most scenic beach, featuring a clean, cobbly sand curvature looking out at the cove, Sequit Point, and the near-shore rocks. Its lone detractor is CA 1, which passes directly above it. South Beach also maintains the best facilities, attracting a greater proportion of park guests. While the state beach extends only 0.5 mile south, the sandy strand continues, entering Nicholas Canyon County Beach.

**North Beach.** This Leo Carrillo beach shows a long strand with a cant to the water. It is partially backed by the park's limited recreational-vehicle campground, with bluffs rising above it farther north. It is a fine area to walk or jog and perhaps find a little more quiet.

**Yerba Buena Beach.** The northernmost of the strands comprising Leo Carrillo State Beach is separated from the others by an area of private land. Attractive to surfers, this 0.25-mile-long primitive sandy beach looks out at consistent sets of well-shaped, green-curling waves. Parking for it is along CA 1.

**Nicholas Flat–Willow Creek Loop.** This 1.7-mile loop joining the lower Nicholas Flat Trail and the Willow Creek Trail offers a reliable tour, granting a fine vista from atop a bald point overlooking the ocean. Hikers may extend the journey, remaining on the Nicholas Flat Trail. But be forewarned; when it is not on a regular maintenance schedule, thick shrubs strangle its upper stretches. Ask a ranger about current conditions before attempting a tour.

A clockwise tour of the loop follows the Nicolas Flat Trail left from the initial junction. Angling up the canyon slope, the trail overlooks the campground. Tall grass, laurel sumac, sage, a few cacti, and *Yucca whipplei* cloak the slope, while wildflowers abound. At 0.25 mile, the trail grows steep, but the climb quickly rewards with looks out Arroyo Sequit Canyon of the beach and ocean. Quail often spook into flight.

Although the fires of 1993 swept over the slope, few clues remain. The new growth of the laurel sumac has nearly hidden the fire-silvered bush skeletons, and the wildflowers are plentiful and varied.

Where the trail arrives at a saddle (0.8 mile), uphill to the right 200 feet is the Willow Creek Overlook (elevation 590 feet). This small point affords looks at the shore, Arroyo Sequit Canyon, Point Dume, West Anacapa and Catalina islands, and the kelp beds offshore. Like Sequit Point, it offers an outstanding vantage for spying gray whales' spouts.

Returning to the saddle, hikers may either follow the Willow Creek Trail down the opposite slope for the loop, or resume the hardy ascent, staying on the Nicholas Flat Trail. In another 1.4 miles, the latter tags a pair of vista rises, overlooking the coast, the park, and the truly rugged Santa Monica Mountains; eventually, it enters Nicholas Flat, a high, open grassland.

Taking the loop alone, hikers switchback down a chaparral slope marked by yucca and prickly pear cactus. By 1.2 miles, the descending trail contours the hillside, serving up views of Leo Carrillo's sculpted coves, the near-shore rocks, and the poised riders on surfboards and sailboards. The loop closes by slicing through the tall grasses and mustard; be alert for ticks in the spring.

*Access:* Find the trailhead near the park entrance kiosk; it is marked by a trail post indicating no dogs or bikes allowed.

## Robert H. Meyer Memorial State Beaches

**Hours/Season:** 8:00 A.M. to sunset
**Facilities:** Picnic tables, beach-access trails, nonflush toilets, *bring water*
**For Information:** (818) 880-0350
**Access:** This park's three separate beach accesses are found west off CA 1, beginning 0.2 mile south of Decker Canyon Road or 4.7 miles north of Kanan-Dume Road.

Three small beach parcels comprise Robert H. Meyer Memorial State Beaches: El Pescador, La Piedra, and El Matador. Each holds a similar offering with a small off-highway gravel parking lot, a couple of picnic tables, ocean viewing from atop the bluff, and a steep access trail to the beach. The clean, sandy strands look out at a beautiful stretch of ocean with near-shore rocks, offshore kelp beds, and Point Dume to the south. Small mesh barriers mark off the 0.1-mile stretches of state beach at both El Pescador and La Piedra.

El Matador, the largest of the three narrow beaches, stretches for 0.4 mile at the base of a 100-foot bluff. A fluted alluvium slope shapes its coastal cliff; at the other two, the cliff is mostly vegetated. El Matador is also the most scenic, having large on- and near-shore block outcrops, with wave-carved feet. When the water is not swirling through the low caves and arches, youngsters enjoy exploring them. If you venture south past the state boundary, stay below the high-tide line, as the area above it is private.

All three beach areas are popular sites for sunning, swimming, surfing, and waterplay, but come early on weekends and summer days, as the parking lots fill quickly.

## Point Dume and Dan Blocker State Beaches

**Hours/Season:** Year-round
**Facilities:** Hiker trails, restrooms, outdoor shower (Point Dume); nonflush toilets, *bring water* (Dan Blocker)
**For Information:** Los Angeles County Department of Beaches and Harbors, (310) 305-9545
**Access:** Reach *Point Dume State Beach,* turning west off CA 1 onto Westward Beach Road, just south of Zuma County Beach. In 0.5 mile, visitors reach its county-operated fee parking lot. *Dan Blocker State Beach* lines CA 1, beginning opposite Corral Canyon Road, 4.4 miles south of the Westward Beach Road intersection; the parking is roadside.

These two state beach areas along the Malibu Coast offer swimming, surfing, sunbathing, waterplay, surf fishing, and diving. The headland jut of Point Dume separates two beach areas: Westward Beach, a mile-long, broad, open sandy strand that adjoins popular Zuma County Beach to the north, and Paradise Cove, the breathtakingly pretty, isolated white-sand curvature to the south.

Dan Blocker State Beach boasts a narrow, clean sandy strand below a 20-foot embankment along a 0.75-mile stretch of CA 1. Its north end is rocky where Corral Creek empties to the ocean. Its broader south end is more congested, having the easier access.

At both parks, the beaches slope to meet aquamarine waves breaking close to shore, but the waters off Dan Blocker State Beach break more gently. Summer lifeguards keep an eye on swimmers at both areas.

### Attractions and Activities

**Point Dume Natural Preserve.** The rocky north face of 215-foot Point Dume attracts the technical climber, while a mile of trail calls the beachgoer to roam.

The Point Dume trail system climbs from Westward Beach to tour the headland

bluff. Guide wires keep travelers on the trail, protecting the rare coreopsis (giant sunflower) and other native vegetation: sand verbena, California poppy, grasses, and coastal scrub. Side trails lead to the residential neighborhood, and a stairway descends to the rocky north end of Paradise Cove, but winter storms can swallow this rocky approach, denying access to the stunning cliff-protected beach.

Atop Point Dume, visitors find fine ocean vantages and whale-watching posts. Views stretch north to Point Mugu and south across Santa Monica Bay. To the east rise the rugged, chaparral-clad Santa Monica Mountains. Below the vantage sites are Paradise Cove, the rocky cliffs where cormorants roost, Westward and Zuma beaches, and the glorious Pacific blue stretching to the horizon.

The habitat of the bluff is wild enough to support red fox. Dogs are prohibited, so leave them at home.

*Access:* Find the Point Dume trailhead and its climbing face at the south end of Westward Beach.

## Malibu Lagoon State Beach

**Hours/Season:** 9:00 A.M. to sunset; 6:00 A.M. to 6:00 P.M. (pier); 11:00 A.M. to 2:00 P.M. Wednesday through Saturday (Adamson House)
**Facilities:** Picnic sites, historic place, museum, gift shop, pier, beach- and lagoon-access trails, volleyball nets, restrooms, nonflush toilets, outdoor shower
**For Information:** (310) 456-8432 or (818) 880-0350
**Access:** For the Malibu Lagoon estuary, turn west off CA 1 opposite Cross Creek Road, 1.6 miles south of Malibu Canyon Road. Parking for Surfrider Beach and the Adamson House is 0.3 mile farther south.

Surfrider Beach, the Malibu Lagoon estuary, Malibu Pier, and the historic Adamson House unite to create this state beach. Surfrider Beach and Malibu Pier are legendary sites along the Malibu coastline, popularized in film. It was here that surfing was first introduced to California in 1926. Summertime brings set after set of perfectly shaped waves rolling to shore—the combined product of ideal winds, currents, and upwellings. Riders enjoy a quick start and a long signature ride. Windsurfers, kayakers, and boogie-boarders share the bounty.

At the Malibu Lagoon access, at the north end of the park, visitors find a small attractive lawn area with picnic tables, a central natural-history kiosk, and short trails leading to both the beach and the lagoon. The beach trail arrives at the 50-yard-long northern extension of Surfrider Beach, often separated from the main beach by the outlet of Malibu Creek. By summer, though, the mouth of the creek is either dammed or presents an easy wade, allowing connection.

*Malibu Pier, Malibu Lagoon State Beach*

## Attractions and Activities

**Malibu Pier.** This is a scenic, old-fashioned wooden pier with twin white towers at its end. Benches line its sides, and fishing poles stand at attention in the rod holders along its rail. Gulls sit atop the light poles. From the pier, travelers can look out at Surfrider Beach to the north. A section of private property separates the pier and the beach. From the pier, daily sport-fishing trips may be chartered year-round.

**Adamson House Tour.** This National Register residence, built in 1929, likewise sets apart this state beach. It blends Moorish and Spanish-Mediterranean architecture, featuring the decorative tile produced by Malibu Potteries (1926–1932). Hand-carved teak, hand-painted murals, and lead-framed bottle-glass windows further contribute to its elegance.

The interior is shown by guided tour. A self-guided tour presents a look at the home's exterior, courtyard, and grounds; plaques identify the points of interest. Exceptional ocean views are found throughout the property. The home's seven-car garage is now an adjoining museum of Malibu history. The site, Vaquero Hill, once held a Chumash Indian village.

**Estuary Trails.** A maze of short, often overgrown foot trails travel the estuary shore, overlooking the arms of the lagoon and its main water body. Eared grebes, ruddy ducks, scoters, brown pelicans, killdeer, sanderlings, and other waterfowl and shorebirds frequent the lagoon. A tour also offers an opportunity to view the plants of this chemical desert: salt grass, pickleweed, bulrush, and succulents.

The fire of 1993 did pass through some brushy areas at Malibu Lagoon and north of CA 1, temporarily altering the look of the area and clearing the way for regrowth—a process already underway.

*Access:* Take the path leaving the south end of the Malibu Lagoon day-use area opposite Cross Creek Road.

# Las Tunas and Topanga State Beaches

**Hours/Season:** Daylight hours
**Facilities:** Nonflush toilets, *bring water* (Las Tunas); picnic tables, restrooms (Topanga)
**For Information:** Los Angeles County Department of Beaches and Harbors, (310) 305-9546
**Access:** From the junction of CA 1 and Topanga Canyon Boulevard, go 1.2 miles north on CA 1 for Las Tunas, 0.2 mile north for Topanga. Parking for Las Tunas is along the dirt shoulder of CA 1.

Snuggled below a rock-reinforced 15-foot bluff, Las Tunas State Beach is a small, unattractive beach strip with sandy patches and rocky areas. A near-shore rock affords surf fishermen a casting edge, and remnant pilings extend from the beach into the water. Atop them, cormorants fan their wings dry.

While sunbathers can usually find enough sand for their blankets, this is not a good beach for swimming or waterplay. Nonetheless, scuba divers find much to discover offshore while exploring an easy-to-reach reef.

At Topanga State Beach to the south, a stairway descends from the parking lot to a frequently rocky patch of beach near the mouth of Topanga Creek. Farther from the creek, beachgoers find more open sand.

A riprap point marks the southern end of the cove. To the north, the beach wraps around a flat-topped bluff. A single tilted palm tree punctuates the strand, while seagulls splash and bathe in the freshwater stream.

Above the beach are a few picnic tables. Despite the nearby planted eucalyptus trees, most of the tables sit in the open. The sound of the surf wins out over the noise of CA 1, and the limited amount of parking keeps beach numbers down. Topanga State Beach is fine for swimmers and surfers, but joggers should look elsewhere.

## Will Rogers State Historic Park

**Hours/Season:** 8:00 A.M. to 5:00 P.M., except major holidays; the house opens at 10:00 A.M.

**Facilities:** Picnic area, visitor center and store, historic ranch, polo field, hiker and horse trails, restrooms

**For Information:** (310) 454-8212 or (818) 880-0350

**Access:** The park is at 14235 Sunset Boulevard in Pacific Palisades, 4.6 miles west of I-405.

Today, the 186-acre Santa Monica ranch estate of Will Rogers gives park visitors a glimpse of the private side of this colorful turn-of-the-century cowboy philosopher, who had a way with a rope and a phrase. Visitors learn about the man and his accomplishments through video, snapshots, quotes, and a peek in the door at his private ranch. The grounds are magnificent, immaculate and restful, overlooking the Pacific Ocean. At the back door are the rugged Santa Monica Mountains.

### Attractions and Activities

**Ranch Tour.** The guided tour of Will Rogers' family home is offered on the hour, while the audiowands for the self-guided grounds tour are available for visitors to pick up at their leisure.

Although the ranch house is big—two stories and thirty-one rooms in all—it has a rustic simplicity. Visitors are allowed to view only the large, open, roped-off living quarters, with its high wooden rafters, Indian rugs, wagonwheel light fixtures, and couch swing. The furnishings are authentic and look as they did when the Will Rogers family lived here (1928–1935). Mementos and memorabilia are everywhere.

Central to the living room is a mounted calf, missing its ears after years of roping. The calf was given in self-defense—presented to Will Rogers by his family and friends to keep him from roping them.

The ranch stables still house the horses of celebrities. Buried in front of them are two of Will Rogers' favorite mounts, Bootlegger and Soapsuds. The blacksmith shop is another of the stops on the self-guided tour. Once the ranch has been fully explored, the park's sweeping groomed lawn suggests the spreading of a blanket for a picnic lunch or an afternoon nap.

**Polo Matches.** The polo fields continue to host sport just as they did in the 1920s and 1930s. Every Saturday at 2:00 P.M. and Sunday at 10:00 A.M., conditions allowing, a match takes place.

**Inspiration Point Trail.** This 1.9-mile round-trip hike ventures into the wilder parts of the park, lassoing a Pacific Ocean–Santa Monica Mountains vantage.

The trail begins climbing a eucalyptus-shaded lane. Interpretive posts mark the route; ask for a brochure. At 0.7 mile, where the Bone Canyon Trail branches left, stay on the fire road, continuing straight ahead. In another tenth of a mile, a 0.3-mile loop branches left to Inspiration Point. To the right, a long-distance route travels Backbone Ridge to Topanga State Park.

Taking either path left, hikers soon come to Inspiration Point, a broad, open vista knoll with benches overlooking the Santa Monica coastline, Will Rogers State Historic Park, the canyons and ridges of the Santa Monica Mountains, and the hazy outline of Westwood and downtown Los Angeles. Laurel sumac, greasewood, and sage cloak the vista slope. Complete the loop, and return as you came to the heart of the park.

*Access:* Begin heading right near the old nature center (no longer in use).

## Will Rogers, Santa Monica, Dockweiler, Manhattan, and Redondo State Beaches

**Hours/Season:** Year-round
**Facilities:** 158 en route campsites, mini-mart (Dockweiler); piers (Santa Monica, Manhattan, and Redondo); picnic tables, bikeway, volleyball courts, restrooms (all)
**For Information:** Los Angeles County Department of Beaches and Harbors, (310) 305-9546
**Access:** Spaced along a 15-mile coastal stretch from Pacific Palisades to Redondo Beach, these five Los Angeles area state beaches are reached via CA 1 and city streets. *Will Rogers* is near the CA 1–Temescal Canyon Road intersection; *Santa Monica* is in the city of Santa Monica; *Dockweiler* is west of CA 1 via Imperial Highway and Vista del Mar; *Manhattan* is in the city of Manhattan Beach, west off CA 1 to Highland Avenue; and *Redondo* is west off CA 1, at the south end of Redondo Beach.

On southern Santa Monica Bay, these urban beaches dot a single lengthy strand interrupted only by Marina del Rey. They all boast broad, beautiful sandy shores meeting a rolling surf. Some show a slight bank or slope where the water breaks, making an uneven footing for the wader or jogger. A coastal bluff rises above Dockweiler; stairways access the strand.

Neighboring shops and residences crowd the beach corridor but do not spoil the sun and ocean fun. As these state beaches serve both the tourist and the Greater Los Angeles population, expect them to be crowded. Nonstop activity abounds with swimming, surfing, boogie-boarding, jogging, and the latest game crazes. Off-season visits find fewer numbers and greater room to roam.

Some swimmers consider Redondo to have rough waters, and skin divers prefer the underwater realm off Will Rogers State Beach. Dockweiler hosts fewer numbers, but it suffers air-traffic noise, lying in the take-off pattern from Los Angeles International Airport. Sound sleepers may take advantage of its year-round en route camping. The sites offer convenient access to both coastal and city attractions.

During peak visitor times, lifeguards monitor activity. Due to the number of visitors, alcoholic beverages and fires (except where rings are provided) are prohibited.

## Attractions and Activities

**Piers.** Three of the state beaches—Santa Monica, Manhattan, and Redondo—have piers. Ocean storms have stolen the end of the Santa Monica Municipal Pier (built in the 1920s), but it remains a favorite with its arcades, carousel, and food services. At Manhattan and Redondo state beaches, classic fishing piers, complete with circling gulls and roosting pelicans, invite visitors to stroll out over the ocean. Marine exhibits are found at the Manhattan Beach Pier, while floodlights allow night fishing off Redondo's Monstad Pier.

**South Bay Bicycle Trail.** This 19.1-mile route runs between Will Rogers and Redondo state beaches, stringing together the state, municipal, and county beaches of southern Santa Monica Bay, with a detour through Marina del Rey. It combines carefree pedaling with ocean breezes, the sound of the surf, and convenient beach access throughout, making it the most popular bike path in Southern California. It is perfect for the family.

While the route is intended for bicycle use only, cyclists must remain alert for rollerskaters, joggers, and walkers who take advantage of the lane where walkways are absent.

*Access:* Reach the route at any of the five beaches.

**Grunion Hunting.** During the summer at high tide on the first to fifth night following a full moon, grunion, silvery 6-inch fish, beach themselves to spawn in the sand. The event finds pairs of grunion hunters along the flatter beaches. While one person locates the fish with a flashlight, the other dives after them, scooping up the slippery quarry by hand. Nets may not be used.

Some nights, great numbers of grunion beach themselves in a madcap spectacle. Other nights, only a few fish come to shore. A fishing license is required. Protected grunion runs occur in April and May. On the nights of the open runs, the beaches have special-use hours.

*Access:* The grunion come to shore at all five beaches.

# Kenneth Hahn State Recreation Area

**Hours/Season:** Daylight hours

**Facilities:** Picnic areas, man-made pond and streams, a wheelchair-accessible fishing platform, informal hiker trails, walking paths, playground, restrooms

**For Information:** County of Los Angeles, (213) 298-3660

**Access:** In Baldwin Hills, the park entrance is off La Cienega Boulevard, 1.7 miles south of I-10.

This 1,300-acre, multi-tiered metropolitan open space welcomes picnicking, fishing, hiking, jogging, and relaxation. Residential areas approach its northern boundary, while the nodding pumpers of a working oil field can be seen to the west. Bus service accesses the park.

Planted lawn and eucalyptus trees rim the catfish-stocked fishing pond, while cattails and a few boulders accent the water plied by domestic ducks and geese. Below the pond, red-winged blackbirds flit from rush to rush in a natural drainage.

At the east end of the park is a large, grassy bowl planted with young trees—

Janice's Green Valley. While relatively new, it promises future shade. Much of the east end of the park is a work in progress; among the proposed additions is an archery range.

### Attractions and Activities

**Olympic Forest.** This area of the park salutes both the 1932 and 1984 Olympic Games in Los Angeles, with planted trees representing the participant nations.

In 1932, during the tenth Olympiad, the Olympic Village occupied what is now the park. Despite the Depression, 1,500 athletes from forty nations competed. When Los Angeles again hosted the games in 1984, some 140 nations sent athletes.

At the entry, a kiosk notes each tree species, its scientific and common name, and its native country, continent, and habitat zone. Walkways tour the forest plantings. The area offers pleasant strolling.

*Access:* Follow the signs through the park to the forest.

**Baldwin Hills Trail.** This 0.5-mile trail/service road climbs 400 feet, topping the ridge above the developed park. Along the knobby ridge, it reaches four vista sites, each offering a slightly different perspective on the neighborhood. Views sweep downtown Los Angeles, the various residential areas, the nearby oil fields, the ocean, the Santa Monica Mountains, and the attractive park grounds. Coastal-scrub vegetation blankets the hills. Return as you came.

*Access:* Take the turn for Olympic Forest, and hike the gated service road between the two westernmost parking areas.

## ROYAL PALMS STATE BEACH

**Hours/Season:** Daylight hours
**Facilities:** Restrooms
**For Information:** Los Angeles County Department of Beaches and Harbors, (310) 305-9546
**Access:** The beach is in San Pedro, at the south end of Western Avenue.

*Royal Palms State Beach*

On the Palos Verdes Peninsula, this bluff-backed 0.25-mile-long ribbony beach of rock and sand curves around a sculpted shore. To the north and south small headland features rise up. At the north end of the beach, a small grove of palms and ruins recalls the Royal Palms Hotel, built here in 1915.

The scatter of rocks on shore extends into the near-shore waters, suggesting tidepool exploration, while farther out the deep holds intrigue for scuba divers and snorkelers. Sea hares, urchins, colorful seaweeds and kelp, and the unexpected keep explorers coming back. An underwater diving trail leads the way.

Because of the rocks, this is not a good swimming or sunbathing beach. Fishermen, however, find success here, and the bluffs prove a good sunset and whale-watching post. The park looks out at Catalina Island and adjoins White's Point County Beach to the southeast.

## BOLSA CHICA AND HUNTINGTON STATE BEACHES

**Hours/Season:** 6:00 A.M. to 9:00 P.M.

**Facilities:** 50 self-contained vehicle campsites (Bolsa Chica); picnic sites, snackbars, beach rentals, paved bikeway, wheelchair access to beach, restrooms, outdoor showers (both)

**For Information:** (714) 536-1454 (both beaches)

**Access:** From I-405, exit at Seal Beach Boulevard and follow it west to CA 1. There, go 4.3 miles south on CA 1 to reach the Bolsa Chica State Beach entrance (south of Warner Avenue). The Magnolia Street entry to Huntington State Beach is another 4.8 miles south on CA 1.

Looking out at the open ocean, these popular, nearly mirror-image, linear urban beaches in or surrounded by the city of Huntington Beach afford similar recreational offerings. Both are flat, wide, and shadeless. Bolsa Chica State Beach stretches for 2.5 miles. Huntington State Beach measures 2 miles long, with the Santa Ana River serving as its southern terminus. Both afford ample space for picnics, sunbathing, beachcombing, and shore sports, with the Pacific Ocean calling the swimmer, surfer, and surf fisherman. The beach lengths can easily accommodate the crowds of summer.

Both sport relatively clean sandy strands, sprinkled with small clam shells and shell fragments. Although the beaches show a mild cant to the water, the waves break with less vigor here than they do farther up the California coast. Surfers find the area's well-shaped waves and long rides to their liking. Oil platforms and Catalina Island alone interrupt the blue expanse.

*Kelp, Huntington State Beach*

Across CA 1 from each is a sensitive coastal wetland, supporting shorebirds and waterfowl; these are managed by the California Department of Fish and Game. At the Bolsa Chica Ecological Preserve, the much larger and more extensive of the two, beachgoers may tour its 1.5-mile loop trail. At Huntington State Beach, there is also a 5-acre natural preserve along the Santa Ana River, protecting a nesting area for the California least tern.

A paved bikeway connects these two parks and continues south all the way to Dana Point, for a distance of some 20 miles. Grunion runs occur along this shore, attracting a midnight crowd armed with flashlights and buckets. The tiny silvery fish are hand scooped as they come to shore to spawn. Check the current California state fishing regulations to see the timing and learn which runs are open for harvesting.

## Corona del Mar State Beach

**Hours/Season:** 6:00 A.M. to 10:00 P.M.
**Facilities:** Picnic sites, snackbar, beach rentals, volleyball nets, restrooms, outdoor showers
**For Information:** City of Newport Beach, (714) 644-3151
**Access:** In Corona del Mar, find the park at the south end of Newport Bay; a parking lot entrance is at the intersection of Jasmine and Ocean Boulevard.

This pretty, light-colored sand curvature below the cliffs of residential Corona del Mar offers swimming, sunbathing, surfing, and diving. The wide 0.5-mile-long beach affords ample area for blankets, while its mild cant and tide-compressed sand welcome walking or jogging. At its north end, anglers line a rocky jetty, tossing their weighty lines into both Newport Bay and the ocean.

Both the services area and the parking area show some landscaping with palm trees. A small, sheltered picnic area off the north end of the parking lot occupies a patch of lawn dotted with pines and bordered by a scenic, contorted rock outcrop. The outcrop, with its ragged and pointed shapes, is unsafe to climb. Where it extends and breaks up into the bay, pelicans roost on it.

## Crystal Cove State Park

**Hours/Season:** 6:00 A.M. to sunset; 9:00 A.M. to 5:00 P.M. (headquarters)
**Facilities:** Historic cottages; beach-access trails; hiker, horse, and mountain-bike trails; restrooms; nonflush toilets; outdoor showers; *carry water for backcountry outings*
**For Information:** (714) 494-3539
**Access:** Leaving Corona del Mar, go 1.3 miles south on CA 1 for Pelican Point, 3 miles south for Reef Point, or 3.2 miles south for El Moro Canyon and the headquarters. Park lands are on both sides of CA 1.

This park unites a 3.5-mile-long, cliff-sheltered beach, a 1,000-acre underwater marine reserve, and some 2,400 acres of scrub and chaparral in the San

Joaquin Hills. It is a premier destination for both divers and mountain bikers. The walkable beach features sandy coves, bluff-backed strands, tidepools, and interesting cliff-eroded rock features. From atop the bluff, visitors can admire the coastline and watch for the passing of gray whales from November through February.

The inland backcountry offers miles of trail open to all users. Joggers and mountain bikers find this realm to their liking, with routes offering both challenge and exercise. Although the creek is often dry, Lower El Moro Canyon is pleasingly wooded with sycamore and live oak.

Presently, though, the park's backcountry is in a state of recovery. The fire of October 1993 swept away 90 percent of its vegetation, consuming the park's environmental campsites. But the hardy coastal sage-scrub environment will return to full vitality with time.

## Attractions and Activities

**Beach Hike.** This 3.2-mile one-way tour travels most of the park's flat sandy beach. The platform chairs of the lifeguards are regularly spaced along the beach.

From the northernmost parking lot follow the bike/pedestrian way north along the bluff for 0.3 mile to descend via a steep concrete pad to the beach (0.4 mile). While the beach extends north to a scenic sandstone point marked by a sea cave, this tour description features the hike south.

Touring below a 50-foot bluff, hikers travel a mostly wild (particularly in the off-season), drift log– and seaweed-strewn beach. The sedimentary rocks and cliffs have a layered, platelike look. Low rock outcrops protrude above the surf as the well-shaped, crystalline waves curl to shore. Where the trail rounds Pelican Point at 0.7 mile, hikers find tidepool rocks off the point. A few driftwood wind shelters dot the beach.

At 1 mile is the next bluff-to-beach access trail; they now come at regular intervals. Chemical toilets are located near each. Egret, turnstones, and a multitude of shorebirds can be seen along the beach, and harbor seals are common passersby.

Beginning at 1.6 miles, the picturesque beach cottages of the Los Trancos Historic Area line the way. While they interfere with the wildness of the tour, they do

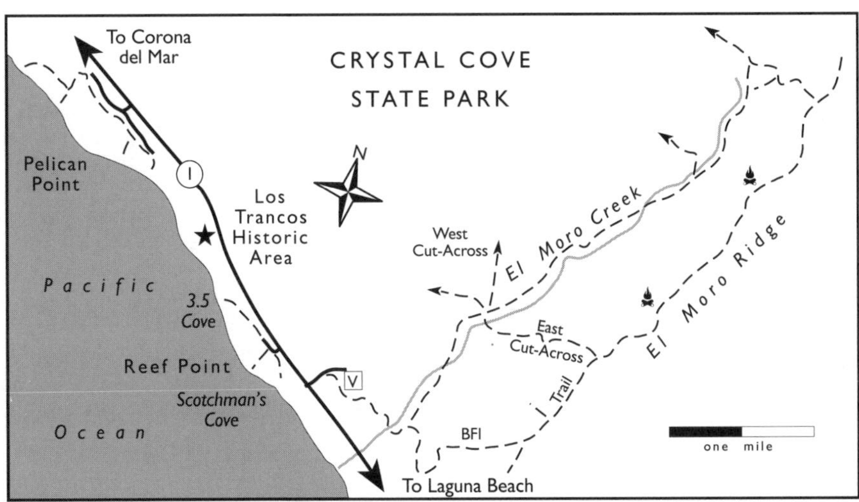

not detract from the beach. Rounding a jut at 2 miles, many more rocks punctuate the surf and beach, as the natural setting returns. Here, hikers will note some unusual big rock discs eroding from the cliff and wedged in the sand; they resemble prehistoric wheels.

The tidepools briefly end at 3.5 Cove, at the north end of the Reef Point access. Rounding Reef Point, hikers travel Scotchman's Cove, which is frequented by surfers. This area attracts greater crowds than the northern reaches of the beach. At 3.2 miles is the final access ramp. Travelers may ascend here, return as they came, or continue strolling to the beach's southern terminus, at the mouth of El Moro Canyon.

*Access:* Begin at Pelican Point's northernmost parking lot.

**El Moro Ridge and Canyon Tour.** This multiple-use route travels 9.75 miles on dirt road and trail and has an 800-foot elevation change. While signs are mostly absent, the ridge and canyon shape easy avenues to follow. To further ease navigation, pick up a trail brochure indicating the routes and their difficulty levels at the headquarters/visitor center.

On the east side of CA 1, the tour begins on a dirt road wrapping around the grassland slope above the southwest boundary. At 0.4 mile, it crosses dry El Moro Creek; at 0.5 mile is the start of the loop. A counterclockwise tour follows the trail-width route to the right to reach El Moro Ridge. Dubbed "BFI," this trail climbs steeply, passing through a scrub habitat of coyote bush, artichoke thistle, and mustard. Wildlife sightings may include tarantula, roadrunner, quail, deer, rabbit, and coyote.

By 0.75 mile, the trail affords ocean views, and by 1 mile it ascends and rolls along the backbone of the ridge. Broken patches of pavement interrupt the now

*Spiderweb, Crystal Cove State Park*

gravel road. The loop remains open and sunny. Adorning the roadside vegetation, the many spider webs add to a tour. At 1.8 miles, approaching a boundary fence, bear left to continue the ridge leg of the loop. The grade eases and stands of fence remain, as the road passes through a grassland-chaparral mosaic. Bear right, keeping to the ridge at the East Cut-across junction at 2.5 miles.

At 3.1 miles and at 4 miles, the trail bypasses the former sites of two environmental camps. Prickly pear and cholla cactus appear amid the vegetation, as the trail resumes its rolling way. At 4.8 miles, go left on the side trail leaving the ridge, as the road ahead soon leaves the park. The loop now begins its descent to the canyon bottom, touring a narrow, loose dirt path through lemonadeberry, sugarbush, laurel sumac, and monkey-flower.

At the 5.4-mile junction, either way presents a steep descent to the canyon bottom. For the less severe descent, go right and take the next left. Going left at 5.4 miles finds a suicidal, wheel- and body-bashing descent, reserved for the expert.

Once on the El Moro Canyon floor (5.8 miles), travelers enjoy a gradual, leisurely descent to close the loop. Sycamore, live oak, tall chaparral, toyon, and some poison oak line the canyon. The drainage itself typically brims with greenery. Keep to the canyon avenue, as side routes branch left and right.

At 7.2 miles, where the trail descends steeply and enters a sharp curve, cyclists should walk their bikes. Views out the canyon now add to the tour. On slopes, a zonal scrub-chaparral vegetation pattern is apparent. At 8.25 miles, the canyon route bypasses the East and West Cut-across trails. Leaving the canyon, the loop closes at 9.25 miles, and the hike ends at 9.75 miles.

*Access:* Begin downhill from El Moro Canyon Headquarters, heading south next to the propane tanks.

**Diving.** The park's underwater marine reserve attracts snorkelers and divers. Its incredible diversity, with reef, rock, kelpbed, and open-water species, make it one of the top diving areas in California. Coralline algae, eel grass, sea cucumber, sea urchin, iridescent and camouflaged fish, and sand shark are just a beginner's list of sightings; more await the accomplished diver.

As the park lies within the Irvine Coast Marine Life Refuge, all marine invertebrates are protected. For questions about fishing, ask a ranger or lifeguard.

*Access:* Popular entry points are at Reef Point and Los Trancos Historic Area; ask a ranger or lifeguard about specific underwater areas to investigate.

## Doheny State Beach

**Hours/Season:** Year-round
**Facilities:** 120 developed beachside campsites, picnic areas, visitor center, snackbar, pedestrian walkway, bike trail, volleyball nets, restrooms, indoor and outdoor showers
**For Information:** (714) 496-6172
**Access:** South of Dana Point, turn west off CA 1 onto Dana Point Harbor Drive; the park is in 0.1 mile.

Divided by San Juan Creek, this park has a wide mile-long sandy beach. The south jetty of Dana Point Harbor shapes its northern boundary. Swimming, sunbathing, beachplay, and fishing engage park guests, with surfers preferring the waters off the jetty.

*Picnicking, Doheny State Beach*

Set back from the beach, a beautiful green lawn with eucalyptus, palm, and other shade trees invites the laying out of a blanket for a picnic lunch or a nap in the shade. For those seeking sunshine and an ocean view, a series of open concrete tables lines the upper edge of the beach. The park visitor center calls people indoors to view its five aquariums and indoor tidepool that together show some of the area marine life.

Across the creek is the park campground, a mostly sterile, paved area with low bushes dividing the sites, but it provides campers with convenient beach access—always a prized commodity. More day-use facilities lie beyond it. While state lands end, the popular urban beach extends south, adjoining Capistrano Beach Regional Park, creating a long highway of public sand to stroll. Only the occasional train on the nearby railroad track disrupts the coastal spell.

Central to the park, San Juan Creek is a pretty little estuarine area with bulrushes and cattails lining its shores and small vegetated islands breaking its flow. Egret, herons, ducks, and gulls may be observed here. Beginning near the estuary is the county bike trail, which strings north to Bolsa Chica State Beach some 20 miles distant.

## San Clemente State Beach

**Hours/Season:** Year-round
**Facilities:** 160 developed campsites (nearly half have hook-ups), picnic area, beach-access trail, restrooms, showers, dump station

**For Information:** (714) 492-3156

**Access:** From I-5 South, take the Avenida Calafia exit in San Clemente and head west. From I-5 North, exit at Cristianitos Road, head west and north for 1.1 miles, and turn west on Avenida Calafia.

Jam-packed on a coastal bluff plateau away from the ocean edge, the park's campsites offer access to a 1-mile stretch of beach at the south end of San Clemente. Grass and eucalyptus landscape the campsites. Nearby, a bowl-cut drainage overlooking the ocean holds the day-use picnic area and campfire center.

The picnic area is sterile and utilitarian, just an open area with ramada-covered tables, barbecues, and trash cans. At its corner, the 0.2-mile paved beach trail descends to the ocean shore. Between the bluff and the beach is a railroad track that must be crossed.

Public beach stretches north to the San Clemente Pier and south to a scenic sandy point. Private homes overlook the beach beyond the state park boundaries. Abutting the state beach are scenic, 50-foot, fluted sandstone bluffs. From atop them, park guests enjoy a superb sunset vantage, looking out at Catalina Island.

The canted, loose-sand beach gives strollers and joggers a workout. Swimming, fishing, and scuba diving are other area activities; surfers prefer the waters off the north end of the beach.

## SAN ONOFRE STATE BEACH

**Hours/Season:** Year-round

**Facilities:** 221 developed compact coastal campsites, 20 en route campsites, 20 walk-in campsites, 12 hike/bike campsites (the Bluffs Campground); 150 developed landscaped inland-valley campsites, of which 67 have water and electricity hook-ups (San Mateo Campground); picnic areas; beach-access trails; volleyball court; restrooms; nonflush toilets; outdoor showers; hot showers at San Mateo Campground; dump station; *bring water at the Trestles*

**For Information:** (714) 492-0802

**Access:** From I-5 south of San Clemente, take the Basilone Road exit and head west and south to reach the Bluffs in 2.8 miles. Surf Beach is reached off this route. For the park's San Mateo Campground and Trestles Bridge, go 0.9 mile north on I-5 from the Basilone Road exit and take the Cristianitos Road exit. Head east 1 mile for camping. A paved trail to the Trestles starts next to the southbound I-5 on-ramp.

Surfing at this park is legendary, attracting an enthusiastic, year-round following from across the United States. Three separate beach segments, together with an inland coastal-valley parcel, make up San Onofre State Beach.

The core of the park, the Bluffs, incorporates a 3.5-mile stretch of untamed, pristine beach, backed by abrupt cliffs and an eroding coastal terrace. Its campground is actually the old coastal highway. Sites sit side by side on the wide paved strip, but surfers find it to their liking.

Leaving the south end of the Bluffs is a long-distance, paved bike trail, passing through Camp Pendleton to Oceanside. Temporary closures may occur due to military activities.

## Attractions and Activities

**The Bluffs Beach.** Six primary beach-access trails, varying from 0.1 to 0.3 mile long, cross and descend the bluff, accessing this wide, unbroken sandy strand. Dogs are allowed on the southernmost end. To the north, the sight of the San Onofre Nuclear Power Plant intrudes on an otherwise natural stage.

The bluff succeeds in isolating the beach from the parallel corridors of interstate highway and rail. Surfing, fishing, strolling, relaxing, and beachplay are popular park pastimes. Drift-log shelters dot the strand. Between beach-access trails #1 and #6 is a pleasant 2.6-mile avenue of sand to stroll or jog on.

*Access:* Reach via trails from the Bluffs Campground or the day-use parking areas at its north and south ends.

**Surf Beach.** To the north of Bluffs Beach is the park's more popular day-use area—Surf Beach. It stretches 0.6 mile between the power plant and a military facility. Thatched cabanas dot the upper beach. Footballs, frisbees, and other beach missiles sail overhead, while the sand volleyball courts are seldom quiet. Offshore, surfers in neon-colored wetsuits wait, read, and ride the shapely waves curling to shore. Low tides reveal a cobble shelf off the sandy beach.

*Access:* Follow the beach access signs that begin 1 mile north of the Bluffs entrance station. The route rounds past a military facility, leading to a bluff-backed, sometimes-rough dirt parking strip that stretches for the full length of the beach.

**Trestles Beach.** At the southern end of San Clemente is the park's famous Trestles Beach. Passing under a low railroad trestle, beachgoers arrive at the primitive, wide, canted beach of "surferdom." Beautiful, well-shaped waves call the

*Surfer, San Onofre State Beach*

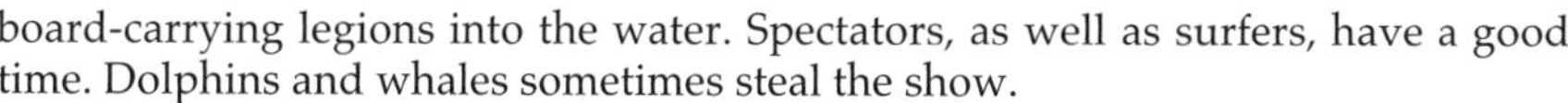

board-carrying legions into the water. Spectators, as well as surfers, have a good time. Dolphins and whales sometimes steal the show.

Inland from the beach is the San Mateo Creek Natural Preserve, a vital riparian corridor, although the trees have been marred by graffiti.

*Access:* Reach via a 0.6-mile bike trail from the Cristianitos Road / I-5 ramp or a 1.5-mile trail from San Mateo Campground. Where the bike and campground routes meet, follow the sign to Trestles Beach–San Mateo Creek Natural Preserve.

## Carlsbad, South Carlsbad, Leucadia, Moonlight, San Elijo, and Cardiff State Beaches

**Hours/Season:** Year-round

**Facilities:** 226 developed campsites, dump station (South Carlsbad); 171 developed campsites (San Elijo); summertime concession-operated grocery / beach equipment rental and laundromat, restrooms, indoor and outdoor showers (both South Carlsbad and San Elijo); restrooms, nonflush toilets, outdoor showers (at the developed accesses of the other state beaches)

**For Information:** Carlsbad and Cardiff, (760) 220-5400; South Carlsbad, (760) 438-3143; San Elijo, (760) 753-5355; City of Encinitas for Leucadia and Moonlight, (760) 623-2740

**Access:** These beach parks are accessed off old US 101 (now County Route S21), between Carlsbad and Solana Beach. Off-road parking lots and day-use roadside parking serve the various state beaches.

Together, these six northern San Diego state beaches offer access to 9 miles of prized ocean frontage. The mild-temperature Pacific waters and predictable waves win popularity with swimmers, surfers, and wave dodgers. For divers and snorkelers, a nearby reef off San Elijo and the waters off South Carlsbad invite exploration.

The mix of cobblestones and sand can vary greatly beach to beach and according to the season and tide. Generally, low tides reveal some sandy real estate sloping to the water. In winter, cobbles alone may shape the beach. Most of the beaches are backed by 30- to 100-foot-tall, eroding sandstone bluffs. Where the bluff is absent, County Route S21 intrudes on the experience.

Surf fishing is another area pastime, but due to the cobbles and cant of the beaches, strolling and jogging are generally out. Both anglers and committed hikers need to keep an eye on the tides. While the cobbles deny easy walking, they do create an exciting, thunderous backwash.

A popular way to cap the day is by viewing the sunset from atop the bluffs. For visitors taking in the show from the beach, fires may be built in existing fire rings only.

Of the beaches, Leucadia is but a small residential access, used primarily by local surfers. Moonlight Beach has the best sunbathing area—a broad half-moon of sand, with a lone palm tree. The others are linear, sometimes narrow strands. Summer lifeguards are on duty at all of the beaches, except Leucadia.

The South Carlsbad and San Elijo campgrounds are both elongated bluff-top camps. While each is home to planted palms, cypress, and privacy buffers, the sites remain open, so bring a shade source. Half the campsites overlook the water; all are exposed to the traffic sounds of S21.

*Beach access, San Elijo State Beach*

Attractive wooden stairways descend from the camps to the beach. Trails and walkways link San Elijo and Cardiff state beaches, which meet at San Elijo Lagoon. Due to the popularity of both camps, summer stays are limited to seven days.

### Attractions and Activities

**The Carlsbad Boulevard Seawall Walkway.** A broad, 0.5-mile walkway travels the coastal slope overlooking Carlsbad State Beach. Together with the parallel beach strand and city walkway above it, the route offers loop tours for morning exercise walks and jogs. At regular intervals, stairways descend from the walkway to the beach. The low bluff shields both from the city.

*Access:* In the city of Carlsbad, the walkway parallels Carlsbad Boulevard between Pine and Tamarack avenues.

## Torrey Pines State Beach and State Reserve

**Hours/Season:** 8:00 A.M. to sunset
**Facilities:** Picnic tables, restrooms, outdoor showers (beach); visitor center, hiker-only trails, restrooms (reserve)
**For Information:** (619) 756-2063 (beach); (619) 755-2063 (both)
**Access:** From I-5, take the Carmel Valley Road exit, head west 1.5 miles, and turn south following North Torrey Pines Road. Go another 1.7 miles to reach the

reserve and visitor center parking. Los Penasquitos Marsh and beach parking are passed along the way.

Three adjacent but distinct park reaches make up the Torrey Pines complex: the state beach, the Torrey pine–clad reserve bluffs, and the Los Penasquitos salt marsh and lagoon. United, they form a thriving natural area amid an urban setting.

Sandstone cliffs isolate much of the state beach to the south. To the north, it is quickly replaced by Del Mar City Beach. Los Penasquitos, one of the last remaining saltwater estuaries on the Southern California coast, is inaccessible, but an ample road shoulder allows birders to set up spotting scopes.

The reserve is one of two sites in the world where the Torrey pine lives naturally; the other is Santa Rosa Island, part of Channel Islands National Park. Here, the stiff-needled pine grows on the rolling coastal bluffs and in the steep-sided ravines. In places, the picturesque tree grows beautifully grotesque, sculpted by the ocean breeze. Torrey pines range from 10 to 100 feet tall, with the ancient ones being more than 150 years old.

Years of drought followed by insect infestations have stolen many of the reserve's Torrey pines from Razor Point to the Guy Fleming area. To restore the pines, the park service is mimicking nature, with limited clearing, prescribed burns, and plantings.

In January, the reserve bluffs give whale watchers a much sought-after vantage, and in March and April, they are spangled with wildflowers. Spring also can bring young sea lions to shore, so grant them a wide safety margin. Trails tour both the primary reserve and its northern extension, which is reached via residential streets.

At Torrey Pines State Reserve, the pueblo-styled visitor center presents some outstanding, well-designed exhibits, despite its spatial constraints, and visitors can acquire trail maps, brochures, and nature guides. With no picnicking allowed at the reserve, hold all lunch plans for the beach. Dogs are not allowed either, so leave them at home.

## Attractions and Activities

**Torrey Pines State Beach.** Split by Los Penasquitos Creek, Torrey Pines State Beach stretches south 4.5 miles from Del Mar City Beach. At its northern end, the state beach is backed by North Torrey Pines Road. To the south, the reserve's broken, golden-hued sandstone cliffs butt the strand. Low tides allow hiking, but even then, the sea can steal beach parcels, turning back walkers.

Consult a tidetable before beginning a beach hike or planning a lengthy stay at the base of the cliffs. The dependable surf attracts a board-carrying following. At times, dolphins, too, ride the waves.

*Access:* Reach it from the parking areas off Carmel Valley and North Torrey Pines roads or from the reserve's Beach Trail.

**Beach Trail to Flat Rock.** This popular 0.8-mile trail links the reserve bluff to a cliff-and-tide isolated beach. Along the way, a 0.1-mile detour leads to a scenic coastal overlook. Signs mark the junctions.

The hike begins following the well-trampled route between guide wires, touring an area of sage, greasewood, monkey-flower, and other shrubs. Cross-bluff views overlook the Pacific blue, the eroded reserve sandstones, and the beetle-killed pines of Razor Point. Cacti spot the area. Stay on the Beach Trail.

Spring is wonderful, with sea dahlia, wild hyacinth, Indian paintbrush, and

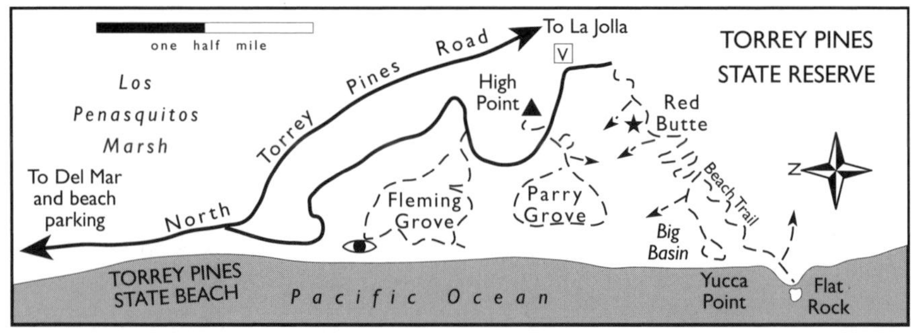


nightshade adding to the color palette. Benches dot the route. Next to one at 0.4 mile, detour right for Yucca Point, briefly following the path indicated to Big Basin and Razor Point. A few feet down the trail, bear left for the destination point, well-named for its many yucca. The Yucca Point Trail then swings a loop overlooking the water. Views south include Flat and Mussel rocks, Scripps Pier, Hang Glider Point, and La Jolla. Eastern views are of the reserve.

At 0.6 mile, return to the Beach Trail for a descent to Flat Rock. At 0.9 mile, the Broken Hill Trail ascends the stairway south; the Beach Trail works its way out through the drainage, rounding a trail cut into the sandstone cliff to reach Flat Rock (1 mile). The route continues rounding the cliff path to Mussel Rock and the beach areas to the south. What hikers can visit depends on the tide.

Flat Rock, too, is an aptly named feature. This eroded rock 20 feet offshore presides over a sandy pocket beach less than 0.1 mile long. Here, the banded, light-colored cliffs rise 80 to 100 feet. Within the cliff fossil beds, oyster shells date back 50 million years. Explore farther south or return as you came.

*Access:* Begin at the southwest corner of the second visitor center parking lot, next to the restroom.

**Guy Fleming Trail.** This 0.7-mile loop explores the reserve's chaparral and Torrey pine habitats and offers area overlooks.

Hikers begin in chaparral, quickly coming to the loop junction. Going clockwise, they find themselves amid North Grove, where plaques indicate the trailside vegetation. It is a diverse habitat with Torrey pine, California holly and laurel, coastal cacti, black sage, and yucca. Weakened by years of drought, some of the pines have been attacked by the bark beetle.

Where the trail contours the mesa, hikers gain ocean views, and the cactus and yucca become abundant. At 0.25 mile, a side trail leads to a vista. To the south, the view features La Jolla and Scripps Pier; to the north is Torrey Pines State Beach. North Overlook, which is visited later, offers a more open view of Torrey Pines State Beach, the coastal community of Del Mar, and Los Penasquitos Marsh. Beyond it, the loop swings inland, returning to the pine grove and passing a fluted sandstone outcrop, before drawing to a close.

*Access:* The trail begins on the west side of the road, 0.3 mile north of the visitor center; it has some parking.

**Parry Grove Trail.** This 0.5-mile loop begins with the interlocking rings of a native plant garden and explores the reserve's coastal scrub and Torrey pine habitats.

At the garden's end, the main trail descends via the stairway to the right; a side trail leads to a bench overlooking the Canyon of the Swifts and the coastline south. At the base of the stairs, a clockwise tour descends slightly, passing through a coastal sage scrubland, with sumac, greasewood, lemonadeberry, and cacti. Later it tours a dense pine grove. In places, the light sandstone cliffs of the Canyon of the Swifts contrasts the green of the pines and the chaparral.

At 0.2 mile, a bench overlooks the ocean. The Torrey pines lining the trail are now smaller and fewer in number. Although the trail contours the ocean slope, views are limited. Turning inland, hikers return to the main pine grove, where bushy chaparral claims the floor.

*Access:* The trail starts on the west side of the road, 250 yards north of the visitor center; park at the center.

**Birdwatching.** The long estuary flat of Los Penasquitos shows areas of open water, shores of pickleweed, bulrush thickets, and meandering channels. It is home to the rare light-footed clapper rail and host to the California least tern and numerous migratory birds. Elsewhere in the reserve, California quail, pinyon jays, raptors, and great horned owls may be spied.

*Access:* Observe the estuarine area from the side of Carmel Valley Road; observe reserve wildlife from the trails.

## SILVER STRAND STATE BEACH

**Hours/Season:** Year-round; 8:00 A.M. to sunset (day use)
**Facilities:** 120 en route recreational vehicle campsites, picnic areas, snackbar and beach equipment rental facility, volleyball courts, restrooms, outdoor showers
**For Information:** (619) 435-5184
**Access:** Turn west off Silver Strand Boulevard (CA 75), 4.5 miles south of downtown Coronado.

This outstretched beach park on the sand spit forming San Diego Bay has a dual offering. It boasts 2.5 miles of ocean frontage and 0.5 mile of bay shore. Despite having four huge parking lots, the park is remarkably uncrowded and succeeds in dispersing its visitor numbers.

Its ocean strand is beautiful, wide, and inviting, with fine, hard-packed sand, ideal for strolling, jogging, and sandcastle building. It shimmers clean, showing only a few kelp streamers and a scattering of shell fragments.

Set after set of perfectly shaped waves complement the fantasy beach. Without a lot of riptides, the area is great for boogie-boarding, surfplay, and surfing. Surf fishing also engages park guests. Point Loma dominates views north, while Imperial Beach Pier and the Coronado Islands command the looks south.

From the parking area, pedestrian tunnels pass beneath Silver Strand Boulevard, reaching the wind-protected Bayside Picnic Area. Here, ramada-covered tables are strung along the length of the bay shore, while a few open tables dot the beach curvature at Crown Cove. Views include the privately owned and moored boats and the U.S. navy vessels across the way. The bird sightings and shell discoveries differ from those on the ocean shore.

Both the ocean and bay offer swimming and waterplay, with lifeguards on duty Easter week through Labor Day. For visitors seeking a more private ocean beach experience, the long strand south of the park entrance is little traveled.

*Equestrians, Border Field State Park*

## BORDER FIELD STATE PARK

**Hours/Season:** 9:30 A.M. to 4:00 P.M. / 5:00 P.M. / 6:00 P.M. (varies seasonally), Thursday through Monday
**Facilities:** Picnic area, visitor center, monument, hiker and horse trails, hitching posts and corrals, restrooms, nonflush toilets, water
**For Information:** (619) 575-3613
**Access:** From I-5, take the Coronado Avenue exit. For the beach, go straight from the off-ramp on Hollister Street for 2.3 miles and turn right on Monument Road to enter Border Field in another 1.8 miles. For the Tijuana Estuary Visitor Center, head west from the off-ramp on Coronado Avenue / Imperial Beach Boulevard. In 2.5 miles, turn left on 3rd and then follow Caspian Way east to the visitor center.

On the Mexican-American border at the extreme southwest corner of the continental United States, Border Field State Park is part of the greater Tijuana River Estuary. Appropriately, a good starting point is the interagency-run Tijuana Estuary Visitor Center on Caspian Way. The center dispenses information on Border Field, Tijuana Slough, and the national estuarine program. Visitors can pick up information on the flora and fauna, travel the center's nature trail, and learn about guided walks offered at the state park and elsewhere within the estuary.

At Border Field State Park, visitors discover three areas of interest: the monument bluff, the broad, sandy beach, and the coastal plain threaded by the Tijuana River. The top of the monument bluff features a manicured-grass flat with picnic tables and a wide concrete walkway traveling its edge.

Border Field's 2-mile-long beach and coastal plain offer fine, uncrowded hiking and horseback-riding opportunities. Within a couple of miles of the park are several stables that rent horses. Surf fishing and swimming are only intermittently popular, as the shoreline is periodically fouled by sewage and debris carried out of Mexico by the Tijuana River.

Backing the beach, the low, flat, vegetated dunes of the park are closed for restoration and revegetation. Near the mouth of the Tijuana River, these dunes provide summer nesting habitat for the endangered California least tern.

Nature study abounds, with some 350 bird species identified at the estuary. The vegetation is remarkably varied, even by slight changes in elevation or dryness. Willows, giant reed, tamarisk, alkali heath and weed, cordgrass, and pickleweed are among the species of the coastal plain. Springtime travelers find a colorful wildflower display.

While the trail along the beach is straightforward, the ones through the coastal plain are not. Confusing the travel are the secondary trails created by illegal immigrants in their patterns of flight.

## Attractions and Activities

**Monument Bluff.** Along the bluff perimeter, signboards in English and Spanish point out the vista and explain the estuary ecosystem. Views south find the congested Tijuana business district, a bullfighting ring, and a lighthouse, while views north overlook the Border Field beach and the estuarine reserve with its marsh, dune, river, wash, and slough habitats.

In the wire-mesh fence that separates Mexico from the United States is the marble obelisk monument surveyed and placed by both countries, following the end of the Mexican-American War. It can be viewed from both nations.

Often small-scale commerce is conducted next to it, as Mexican merchants sell food from their pushcarts. This is also an area where families separated by the border gather to talk. Immigration and Naturalization Service (INS) officers maintain a high profile here and throughout the park.

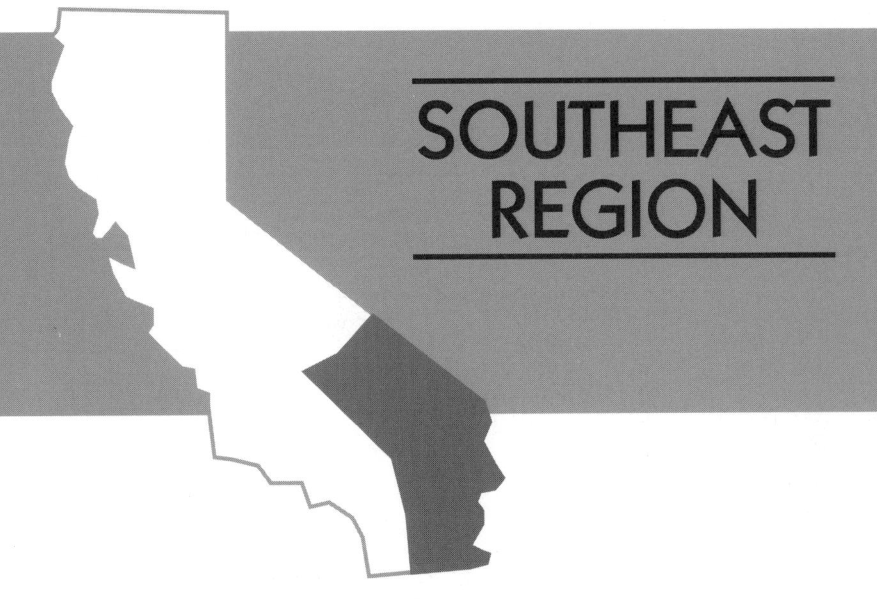


## Colonel Allensworth State Historic Park

**Hours/Season:** 10:00 A.M. to 4:00 P.M., except major holidays; year-round (campground)
**Facilities:** 16 primitive valley flat campsites, picnic tables, visitor center, historic town, restrooms, nonflush toilets
**For Information:** (805) 849-3433
**Access:** From the junction of CA 43 and J22 (8 miles west of Earlimart and US 99), go 2.1 miles south on CA 43 and turn right onto Palmer Avenue to enter the park.

In the southern San Joaquin Valley, this park unit offers visitors a unique opportunity to step back in time and view the interworkings of an experimental African-American town—the town of Allensworth. It was the first of its kind in the United States and the only one in California fully founded, financed, and governed by African-Americans. Visitors can peek in the windows of homes and businesses, walk the streets, and hear the recollections of people who actually grew up, lived, and worked here.

Colonel Allen Allensworth, a former slave, chaplain, and the highest-ranking African-American officer of his day, established this model town in 1908. Its purpose was to allow emancipated African-Americans the freedom to dwell and succeed in a supportive atmosphere. It was also seen as a preparatory arena, giving them the education and skills they would need to compete in the white-dominated world beyond Allensworth.

The experiment was a success. What brought about the town's demise was a

Opposite: *Mariposa lilies, Chino Hills State Park*

*General Store, Colonel Allensworth State Historic Park*

drop in the water table, coupled with the untimely, accidental death of the colonel. With no crops to sustain them and no strong leader to guide them, the townspeople simply drifted away.

Today, Allensworth is quiet, but the restored town stands in tribute to its visionary and the 300 or so African-American pioneers who lived and worked here with him.

## Attractions and Activities

**Allensworth Town Tour.** Park visitors are free to explore the blocks of this town on their own and at their leisure. For groups, guided tours may be prearranged. A 30-minute video at the visitor center provides some of the town's background. Photographs, documents, and mementos contribute to the telling of its story.

Although smaller, the town looks much as it did. The passing years, however, have greatly altered its setting. Gone are the gushing artesian wells, the flourishing crops, and the productive trout streams, but the meadowlarks do still sing.

The homes and buildings are all neat, simple, boxy, and utilitarian. Their furnishings show the interests and amusements of the people. Music and books were both cherished and important; the school and church were central to townspeople's lives. The railroad station was a vital link for the community, bringing goods and communication both to and from town. The old platform may be seen near the visitor center. Historic wagons, equipment, and outbuildings further recall the era.

A plaque next to the boardwalk leading to each house or building identifies the owners, their occupations, and how the structures were used over time. At a few places, pushbutton recordings help visitors better appreciate the daily life and concerns of the townspeople. Plans call for more of Allensworth to be either restored or reconstructed. Dispersed picnic tables invite a stop.

# Red Rock Canyon State Park

**Hours/Season:** Year-round
**Facilities:** 50 primitive campsites, picnic sites, hiker trails, jeep trails, nonflush toilets, water
**For Information:** (805) 942-0662
**Access:** From Mojave, go 25 miles north on CA 14. Park lands straddle the highway.

Picturesque badland-character cliffs and canyons of white clay, orange and red sandstone, brown lava, and pink tuff comprise this park. The eroded walls are tiered, fluted, and columnar. Caprock layers, tilted outcrops, and striated colorations add to their appeal. The low-angle sun of early morning and evening animates the landscape with shadow and light, giving photographer and artist the desired image. The pink- and red-stained colonnade formation of Red Cliffs Natural Preserve, on the east side of CA 14, is an accessible, "don't miss" stop.

The campground occupies a Joshua tree basin sloping away from the park's scenic White House Cliffs. While the open sites afford no shade, they present stargazers with a big-screen view of the constellations. Antelope ground squirrels inhabit the campground. Bats, vultures, and ravens are other often-seen residents.

The presence of early Native Americans is evidenced by the mortars scattered throughout the area. In the late 1800s, a reliable spring in Red Rock Canyon served the mule trains hauling silver and supplies between the Cerro Gordo mines and Los Angeles. Today, hikers, naturalists, photographers, and four-wheel-drive enthusiasts frequent the canyon, reveling in its solitude and beauty. When exploring the park, carry water.

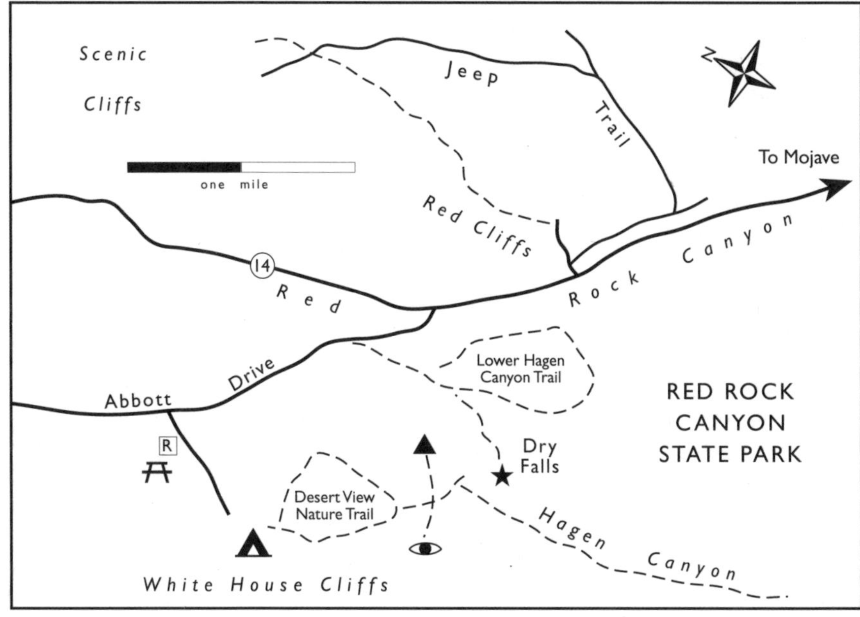

## Attractions and Activities

**Red Cliffs Natural Preserve Hike.** While the main colonnade formation may be viewed from the parking area, this hike offers a closer look at the preserve.

It begins paralleling the cliffs to the north, topping a low saddle at 0.2 mile. There, hikers gain a different perspective on the almost perfect Red Cliffs columns, with their alternating color bands.

Following abandoned jeep tracks and crossing washes, hikers can explore the next basin north. Small stands of Joshua trees mark the basin floor. Overshadowing it to the east are the rugged El Paso desert mountains. To the west at 0.5 mile is a pink tuff hillside with a boulder-rubble base. As hikers begin to pass a new area of red-striped badland, the Scenic Cliffs rise straight ahead.

At the preserve boundary at 0.8 mile, hikers may follow the old jeep trail into the Scenic Cliffs bowl or mount one of the low rises for a better vista. The view brings together the eroded claybeds, desert mountains, and arid basin floor. Only the occasional jet trail disturbs the area's wildness. Return as you came.

*Access:* Begin at Red Cliffs parking area, on the east side of CA 14.

**Desert View Nature Trail.** This 0.5-mile round-trip hike introduces the high-desert plantlife, wildlife, and geology; nature trail brochures are usually available at the trailhead. Midway is the trail climax—a ridge-top vista overlooking the park neighborhood. Where the trail tops out hikers find options for additional exploration.

Numbered cairns mark the interpretive sites, as the trail meanders and climbs away from the campground. It advances via foot trail and a section of stairway. At 0.25 mile, it tops the ridge at marker #12. Northern views overlook the campground basin. Southern ones sweep the San Gabriels, Hagen Canyon, and Cantil Valley.

Here, too, is a three-way junction. To the left (east), a 0.2-mile hike tops a crusty,

*Joshua tree below Red Cliffs, Red Rock Canyon State Park*

cindery 10-million-year-old volcanic rise for a view of the El Paso Mountains and the state park lands to the east. To the right, hikers may walk the narrow spine of White House Cliffs, where a skyline breach signals them to stop in 0.2 mile. The tour offers dramatic looks down the eroded cliffs at the campground, with Hagen Canyon on the opposite side. Keep away from the unstable edge.

Going straight from the three-way junction leads to Upper Hagen Canyon and an overlook of the dry waterfall separating it from its lower canyon counterpart. At the 0.1-mile fork, going left leads to where the volcanic cliffs pinch off Hagen Canyon in a 100-foot vertical drop. Going right enters the upper canyon basin.

When touring the upper canyon, follow the main wash to the right; a smaller wash travels along the canyon's southern wall. Hagen Canyon displays impressive, fortresslike rock formations, with red caprocks balanced on eroded clay pedestals. In 0.8 mile, the hike ends at a box canyon with a 10-foot wall of red-rock blocks backed by a higher cliff.

For all of the side trails, return as you came. When ready to return to the campground, descend from the ridge and complete the nature trail loop.

*Access:* Begin near campsite 50.

**Lower Hagen Canyon Trail.** This tour travels the washes and the vegetated basin flat of Lower Hagen Canyon, affording looks at the colorful rock formation and a different perspective on the dry falls between Upper and Lower Hagen canyons.

From the south end of the parking area, the hike begins traveling a wash upstream. In 0.1 mile, a trail post directs hikers out of the wash and across the arid basin. Keep an eye out for more of the 3-foot-tall wooden posts, with arrows indicating the line of the trail.

Touring close to the north wall, hikers can appreciate the red-banded cliffs and tilted outcrops. After a rain, the blood-red bands have a fiery intensity.

At 0.4 mile, where the primary trail crosses back over the main wash, hikers may wish to make a detour, following the wash up-canyon another 0.4 mile to view the dry waterfall. Here, low beds of light-colored rock are sandwiched between the volcanic walls that eventually squeeze together, forming a box canyon. The detour concludes with a square-on look at the streaked 100-foot vertical cliff (the dry falls).

Forgoing the detour, upon crossing the wash, hikers tour below a scenic section of cliff, showing both strong erosion and strong coloration. A few of the drainages are stained red from the rock up-canyon. As the loop returns, traveling closer to the southern wall, grayish cliffs replace the colored ones.

Approaching a large, rounded, pink outcrop at 0.7 mile, the trail curves north, crossing another wash, to close the loop. Retrace the initial trail, re-entering the main wash at 1 mile, and returning to the trailhead at 1.1 miles.

*Access:* Begin at the dirt crescent parking area off Abbott Drive, just northwest of CA 14.

## Tomo-Kahnie State Park

**Hours/Season:** Plans call for spring and fall weekend tours; reservations required

**Facilities:** Cultural sites

**For Information:** (805) 942-0662

**Access:** This park is located off CA 58 in Sand Canyon, east of Tehachapi. Access is controlled; entry is via guided tour only.

This exciting new addition to the California state park system has cultural, geologic, and biologic significance. Visually striking, this park unites high desert and pinyon-juniper forest habitats and features caves, overhangs, and wind-eroded rock features. But most importantly, it protects and preserves a sacred Native American site.

It was here, according to legend, the land gave birth to the Kawaiisu Indians, and it was here that they flourished. As such, the rangers are working cooperatively with tribal members to develop a sensitive management strategy for this area.

Pictographs decorating the caves and rock overhangs, bedrock mortars, and village house rings recall the history of the Kawaiisu. Buried beneath the surface is a hallowed treasury of Native American artifacts.

Tour groups, limited to twenty individuals, meet near the park, with tours lasting about 90 minutes.

## PROVIDENCE MOUNTAINS STATE RECREATION AREA

**Hours/Season:** Year-round, with daily guided cavern tours from September 16 to June 15; call for schedule
**Facilities:** 6 primitive closely spaced tent/camper sites, visitor center, caverns, hiker trails, restrooms
**For Information:** (805) 942-0662
**Access:** From I-40 at Essex, take the Mitchell Caverns exit and head north 15.3 miles to reach the visitor center.

While the limestone formations of Mitchell Caverns Natural Preserve are the highlight of this remote high-desert mountain location, the setting is nothing less than striking. The precipitous, craggy rhyolite mountains, bouldery slopes dotted by cactus and yucca, and vast desert expanse spilling away from the mountain create an overwhelming presence—majestic and forbidding.

Cavern tickets are purchased at the small, scenic rock-and-concrete visitor cen-

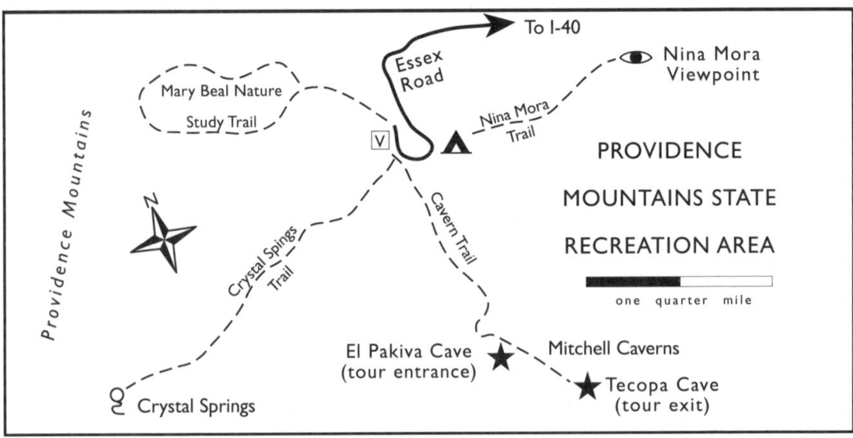

ter. As the maximum tour size is twenty-five, plan an early arrival to ensure yourself a slot; groups of ten or more must make advance reservations.

At the center, visitors may bide their time by studying the few displays on Native American artifacts, insects, mining, cave formations, and the days of Jack and Ida Mitchell. The Mitchells originally owned this site, built the rustic stone buildings, and operated the first cavern tours.

Outside are benches, a cactus garden, a broken cave formation, and a grand vista of the Eastern Mojave expanse. Vista boards point out the key features. The nearby nature trails also beckon, but be alert in your wanderings, as rattlesnakes reside here. With desert bighorns ranging the high country, you may want to carry binoculars.

*Cave tour, Providence Mountains State Recreation Area*

## Attractions and Activities

**Mitchell Caverns Guided Tour.** This 1.5-mile round-trip tour travels rocky trail, narrow cave passages, and stairs, visiting Tecopa and El Pakiva caves. A tunnel connects the caves, while lights and railings facilitate travel and discovery.

The tour is paced so that visitors get to know a few chambers intimately, as the ranger points out the common and unique formations and challenges the imagination. Information about the geologic and human history of the cavern, the windflow patterns, and the structural changes enhance a tour. Native Americans were known to have used these caves some 10,000 years ago; soot near the entrances records where they built fires.

Highlights consist of a single room bringing together stalactites, stalagmites, and columns (a 1 in 40,000 occurrence); coral pipes, which are known to exist in only seven caverns: six in the United States and one in Hungary; and three cave shields, including what has been declared the finest example anywhere. Bell canopies, popcorn, soda straws, and flowstone contribute to the beauty of the chambers. Interesting stops are the Queen's Chamber, Hollow Floor Room, and Bottomless Pit.

The Bottomless Pit is only 60 feet deep but gained its reputation in one of Jack Mitchell's flashy tour demonstrations. He would pitch a torch into the pit, and when it flickered out into blackness because of a lack of oxygen, tour members surmised the pit had no floor.

*Access:* Tours begin at the visitor center.

**Mary Beal Nature Study Trail.** This rocky, 0.5-mile self-guided loop offers a first-rate introduction to the high-desert flora. It traverses an alluvial plain below the Providence Mountains, where the slope is congested with diverse vegetation. Mojave and banana yucca, old-man prickly pear, buckhorn cholla, felt thorn, and other arid species attract the eye of the nature photographer.

Along the route, air pockets (vugs) riddle many of the volcanic boulders. Detours lead to benches nestled amid the desert showcase. Roadrunners and antelope ground squirrels commonly are spied.

*Access:* Begin near the visitor center and employee residence.

**Nina Mora Trail.** As it tours a creosote, yucca, cactus, and desert shrub-cloaked side ridge, this rocky, 0.5-mile round-trip trail passes a small Spanish grave marker. Barrel cactus punctuates the slope, and small animal burrows riddle the sides of the trail. At 0.25 mile, a white granite ring marks the end of the tour. Views are of the Providence Mountains, the Clipper Valley, and Wild Horse Mesa. Return as you came.

*Access:* Begin at the campground.

**Crystal Springs Trail.** This 0.75-mile trail twists up the rocky slope behind the visitor center, offering superb looks up at the rhyolite spires and turrets of the Providence Mountains. The view sweeps nearly 3,000 feet of the mountains' 7,000-foot elevation. Although the views draw attention, be sure to keep an eye out for cacti encroaching on the path.

The trail ascends steadily. By 0.25 mile, it is touring amid the rhyolite cliffs, with outcrops on either side of the upper canyon drainage. Here, too, pinyons make an appearance, and a few trail markers keep hikers on track. As the climb continues, hikers lose the last reminders of civilization and are swept up in the isolation of the mountain.

Midway, hikers gain a nice view through the V of the canyon at Wild Horse Mesa and the mountains in Arizona. Ahead, the trail crosses over a rocky drainage, and the climb intensifies. At 0.6 mile, hikers can see a pipe running along the drainage wall to the north. A pinyon shades the end of the trail, where the canyon grows more brushy.

The hike never actually reaches the spring, but willows hint at its closeness. Mainly, this trail gives visitors an opportunity to experience the mountain and a greater chance for seeing wildlife. Return as you came.

*Access:* Head uphill at the start of the Cavern Trail.

**Winding Stair Cave.** Exploration of this cave located north of Mitchell Cavern is restricted to experienced spelunking groups and requires a special entry permit. The cave has a vertical orientation that requires a 320-foot drop, accomplished in a series of free falls, varying from 50 to 180 feet.

*Access:* Contact the park for entry permits and access details.

## ANTELOPE VALLEY CALIFORNIA POPPY STATE RESERVE—DESERT WOODLAND STATE PARK

**Hours/Season:** Daylight hours with visitor center open mid-March through mid-May (California Poppy Reserve); daylight hours (Desert Woodland)

**Facilities:** Picnic tables, visitor center, hiker trails, flush toilets (when visitor center is open), nonflush toilets, water (California Poppy Reserve); none (Desert Woodland)

**For Information:** (805) 942-0662

**Access:** From CA 14 in Lancaster, go west on Avenue I, which becomes Lancaster Road, to reach both parks. In 13.2 miles, visitors arrive at the California Poppy Reserve. The core of Desert Woodland State Park is found another 7 miles farther west; state park boundary stakes mark off its undeveloped lands, which straddle Lancaster Road.

The adaptable and abundant California golden poppy rightfully earns the title "state flower," and in 1976 it won a permanent home here, at the heart of the most consistent poppy-producing land in the state. In profusion, the California poppy challenges the sun with its orange brilliance. During the bloom, naturalists, photographers, and painters converge on the reserve.

From mid-March through mid-May, owl clover, tidy-tip, alkali goldfield, pygmy lupine, and filaree sprinkle through the orange-petaled prairie fire. The timing and extent of the show depends greatly on the current and preceding months' weather. Year-round the grassland slopes of Antelope Buttes offer peaceful touring and fine vistas; some 7 miles of trail lead the way.

Open only during the bloom season, the reserve's Jane S. Pinheiro Interpretive Center features some of the artist's 150 wildflower watercolors and is itself a point of interest, being a state-of-the-art energy-conservation building. On the hill above the center, the few shade-covered picnic tables do a revolving business in spring. Visitors are reminded to beware of snakes while touring the reserve.

Farther west, wildflowers also grace the congested Joshua tree-juniper woodland of Desert Woodland State Park. Once a prominent western Antelope Valley feature, these native woodlands have all but disappeared, claimed by farms and an ever-sprawling population. This park represents one of the few remaining wooded parcels still intact.

The Joshua tree-juniper complex is eye catching, unusual in profile and texture. The trees stand only about 10 feet tall. Weaving the understory are buckwheat, annual grasses, sage, rabbitbrush, cotton-thorn and box-thorn, and a few cacti. When roaming, be alert to the many low-growing Joshua sprouts, as their radial bladelike leaves can send a pointed message. Views are of the Tehachapi Mountains to the north, the Sierra Pelona to the south.

Presently, this 500-acre park is undeveloped, and visitors are free to stroll at will or follow one of the abandoned jeep tracks entering the park. Rabbits, birds, and lizards divert attention. Future plans call for the development of a formal parking area and a nature trail, complete with interpretive signs. Meanwhile, this state park offers a quiet look at a rare natural habitat.

## Attractions and Activities

**Antelope Loop.** This is the California Poppy Reserve's longest loop option, traveling 3.25 miles and climbing 200 feet. It combines vistas and an appreciation of the grassland habitat.

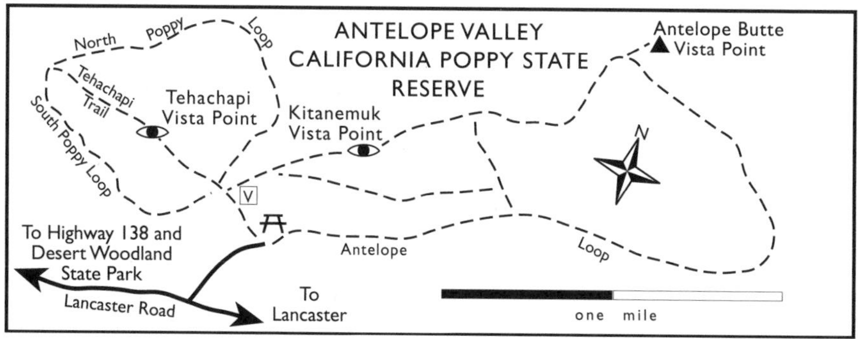

The hike begins following an old 2-track east along the fence line, with looks south at the distant San Gabriels and the immediate hills shaped by the San Andreas fault. Burrows riddle the grassland, while a succession of spring wildflowers adorns the landscape. Stink bugs, meadowlarks, and lizards are co-travelers.

The trail meanders north and east, reaching a bench and a junction at 0.6 mile. To the left lie two shorter loop options back to the visitor center; stay right to tour Antelope Loop. It affords fine solitude, with eastern looks at Lancaster and Saddleback and Piute buttes.

At 1.4 miles, hikers follow a narrow footpath up a deceptively gentle-looking slope to top a saddle at 1.6 miles. A few shrubs and buckwheat intermingle with the grasses of the slope. Views to the north build on those to the south. Just ahead is the Antelope Butte Vista Point, with a 360-degree panoramic view of the Sierra Pelona Mountains, the San Gabriels, Antelope Valley, Lancaster, the Tehachapis, Fairmont Butte, and the western rises of Antelope Buttes.

As the trail loops back on the north side of Antelope Buttes ridge, bunchgrasses claim the higher slope. Before long, the trail is atop the ridge, tracing it west. At 2.3 miles, hikers come to a bench and a junction. Here, one of the shorter loop options from the 0.6-mile mark tops the ridge and joins the tour west back to the visitor center. The second one travels a parallel course, rounding the south slope below; it is at times visible from the ridge route.

At 2.75 miles, ridge travelers come to the Kitanemuk Vista Point. It, too, offers a 360-degree view, with sweeping looks west and butte-obstructed views east. The trail now descends the south slope. Below the windmill, the second of the shorter loops and a spur from the picnic area arrive on the left. Continue downhill to end the hike at the visitor center (3.25 miles).

*Access:* Begin at the northeast corner of the poppy reserve parking lot.

**Tehachapi Vista Point Trail to North and South Poppy Loops.** The 0.6-mile Tehachapi Vista Point Trail is common to both the North and South Poppy loops of the reserve trail system. The loops measure 1.7 miles and 1.2 miles, respectively.

The Tehachapi Trail begins as a concrete all-ability trail, reaching a vista bench at 0.1 mile. Beyond it, the trail remains wide, but is no longer wheelchair accessible. Steadily, it ascends Godde Hill, topping it at 0.3 mile. Here, Tehachapi Vista Point offers a 360-degree view dominated by Antelope Buttes.

The hike then continues west, bypasses a bench, and comes to a junction at 0.6 mile. To the right is North Poppy Loop; to the left is South Poppy Loop. Both offer opportunity for wildflower appreciation.

*North Poppy Loop* travels a moister slope, which may account for a difference in floral species and/or an altered bloom calendar from that witnessed elsewhere at the reserve. Wrapping around the northern foot of Godde Hill, it offers fine looks at Fairmont Butte to the immediate north.

At 0.8 mile, stay right, following the main track slowly, contouring and climbing the slope. At 1.2 miles, hikers come to a memorial bench and a long boardwalk across a sometimes soggy drainage. From there, the trail sidewinds up the slope heading south toward the windmill, just visible over the rise. The loop closes, returning to the concrete walk.

Opting instead for the *South Poppy Loop*, the hike continues contouring the south slope of Godde Hill, passing through the wildflower-spangled annual grasses. Views to the south feature the nearby undulating hills. By 1 mile, the visitor center comes into view. At 1.2 miles, the loop ends just west of the concrete walk.

*Access:* The Tehachapi Vista Point Trail begins just west of the reserve's visitor center entrance.

# ANTELOPE VALLEY INDIAN MUSEUM

**Hours/Season:** Generally 11:00 A.M. to 4:00 P.M. weekends, October through June; guided tours by appointment on Tuesdays and Thursdays
**Facilities:** Picnic tables, museum, bookshop, nature trail, restrooms, water
**For Information:** (805) 942-0662
**Access:** From CA 14 at Lancaster, go 17 miles east on Avenue K and turn south on 150th Street East. Go another 2 miles and turn east on Avenue M. The museum is north off Avenue M in 0.8 mile.

This place is sure to cause you to do a double-take when driving down the road. It is not often you see a pale green Swiss chalet sticking out of a rocky butte in the middle of the desert. Inside, the museum continues to bombard the senses with its many Native American and aboriginal artifacts and its unusual, artistic housing—an exhibit in itself.

Howard Arden Edwards, a self-taught artist, is the creator of the building and a procurer of many of the artifacts. He homesteaded 160 acres here at Piute Butte and began building the home in 1928. The building was later bought by anthropologist Grace Oliver, who greatly expanded the collection and opened the home as a museum. Today, the state park continues her mission.

## Attractions and Activities

**Museum Tour.** Visitors are free to roam the museum at leisure, with docents stationed in each room to answer questions and point out "don't miss" features.

*Antelope Valley Indian Museum*

A visit begins in Kachina Hall, named for the brightly painted Kachina panels decorating the vaulted roof and the room's impressive Kachina doll collection. It also displays many fine pots, baskets, and blankets from various Southwestern tribes. Rustic Joshua tree-styled furniture decorates the former dining room; rocks of the butte shape one wall.

Upstairs is the California Room, reached by ascending an expanded natural rock fissure. In this desert locale, this room's boulder floor and A-frame ceiling would cause it to simmer, but a cooler keeps it pleasant. The exhibits are first-rate, displaying many daily-use items of the California tribes. A manicure kit, fishing tools, and examples of braiding are among the items. Paired with some exhibits are Mr. Edwards' interpretations as to their use or significance.

The Southwest Room, back on the lower level, equally bulges with discoveries. At the chalet, no space is overlooked. Stashed in every nook, on every ledge, and in every floor corner are mortars and pestles and other artifacts.

Atypical of the rest of the house is the Great Basin Room, a late addition by the park service. It has the orderly, clean look of a conventional museum.

**Joshua Cottage.** Separate from the chalet, this cottage attracts and involves restless youngsters of all ages with its touch table. In this room, visitors can examine the foods from the desert, grind corn, and try their hands at starting a fire with either a bow or a pump drill. Although the fire-starting demonstration seldom reaches the stage of smoke, let alone fire, everyone gets the idea.

**Nature Trail.** A 0.5-mile nature trail also appeals to the restless. It travels the desert grounds and skirts the base of a rock jumble behind the museum; ask at Kachina Hall for a brochure.

*Access:* The trail leaves from the parking area.

**Rock Scrambling.** The linear-fractured, jumbled rock behind the museum beckons the more adventurous to come wonder and climb. It resembles the formation at Joshua Tree National Park (located to the southeast)—one of the best rock-climbing sites in the nation. A white guano icing hints at raptor roosting sites amid the rocks. From atop the rocks, visitors gain fine vistas of Lovejoy Buttes and the San Gabriel Mountains. As this is snake habitat, watch where you put your hands and feet.

*Access:* Reach the jumble via the nature trail.

## SADDLEBACK BUTTE STATE PARK

**Hours/Season:** Year-round

**Facilities:** 50 semi-primitive creosote-plain campsites, picnic area, hiker trails, restrooms, nonflush toilets, water

**For Information:** (805) 942-0662

**Access:** From CA 14 at Lancaster, take the 20th Street West/Avenue J exit, go 0.4 mile north on 20th, and turn east on Avenue J. Go 18.7 miles on J to reach the park.

This park enfolds a 3,000-acre desert wild that is being encroached upon by the rapidly growing, ever-sprawling Antelope Valley. It includes one of the area's landmark buttes and a fine Joshua tree forest. In spring, the many desert wildflowers are an added draw. The butte's summit (elevation 3,651 feet) is a popular hiker destination, one frequented by area Boy Scouts. The summit vista sweeps

*Joshua trees, Saddleback Butte State Park*

360 degrees, with looks at the San Gabriel Mountains, the neighboring buttes, the High Mojave Desert, and the valley floor.

The park's campground, picnic area, and trails are most popular fall through spring. Summertime visitors should take a cue from the desert wildlife and go out only in the early morning and evening hours. While shade is generally absent, some of the campground and picnic sites have ramada-covered tables.

Overnight guests will find the park still affords some pretty good stargazing, even with the approaching lights of civilization. The dagger-leafed, ragged-armed Joshua tree is a favorite subject of photographers. It lends a fine silhouette to a sunrise or a sunset-lit sky.

In your desert travels, be aware that the sidewinder and the Mojave rattlesnake are among the residents of Saddleback Butte.

## Attractions and Activities

**Joshua Trail.** This 0.5-mile nature trail loop has nine stops introducing the features and residents of the desert; a brochure is generally available at its start. It is a good park sampler for visitors with limited time.

The tour begins mounting the rock outcrop to the west of the headquarters for a neighborhood view. It then drops to the desert floor, encircling the outcrop. Yellow-capped posts mark the route. The tour boasts stately Joshua trees, spring wild-

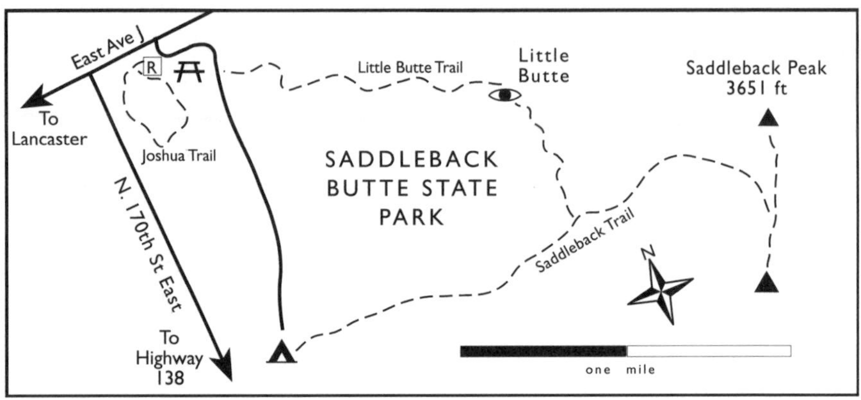


flowers, and chances to observe desert animal tracks, burrows, and the actual residents: jackrabbits, lizards, hawks, vultures, and loggerhead shrikes.

*Access:* This hike begins at park headquarters.

**Saddleback–Little Butte Loop.** This 5.2-mile round-trip tour has a 950-foot elevation change and shows off much of the park. From the campground, yellow-capped posts guide hikers along the wide track of loose sand. Direct looks at Saddleback Butte may be had the entire way. A few ancient Joshua trees mark the grassland-creosote plain. Off the trail, the soft sand records last night's travelers: insect, kangaroo rat, and rabbit. Many of the burrows are active, sheltering ground squirrels and burrowing owls. Hikers find a mild gradient, as the trail slowly ascends the alluvial fan.

At the 1-mile junction, the Little Butte Trail heads left. The Saddleback Trail continues climbing toward the granite-studded butte; stay on it for the 5.2-mile round-trip tour. Feldspar riddles the boulders and outcrops. A chukar may sound from its hideout. The climb intensifies just before reaching the saddle (elevation 3,348 feet) at 1.7 miles; views are to the east and west.

From the saddle elevation marker, one last yellow-capped post points the way to the summit. A narrow, rocky path then twists its way skyward to tag the northeast hump of the butte (2 miles). Views include Piute Butte, the southwest hump of Saddleback Butte, the San Gabriels, the Tehachapi Mountains, the scattered desert communities, and the compass network of roads crisscrossing the broad desert floor.

A summit message tin allows travelers to record their achievement. As smog from the valley can quickly erode the view, an early morning arrival is best.

To continue the tour, descend the butte, return to the 1-mile junction, and turn north on Little Butte Trail. Again, the route follows a wide sandy path, though one less tracked. Desert annuals spring up in its bed, and animal tracks can be seen in the trail. Lizards slip from hiding place to hiding place.

By 3.2 miles, hikers are touring the open Joshua tree forest, with some wonderfully bizarre and beautiful trees. A few golden cholla dot the forest floor; each of the large ones cradles a cactus wren nest in its spiny arms. At 3.5 miles, the trail tops the small bump of Little Butte, for a nice overlook of the Joshua tree expanse and views of Saddleback and Piute buttes.

The walk back toward the picnic area remains mostly flat and easy. This flatter portion of the tour also offers the better wildflower show, with desert primrose, goldfields, yellow coreopsis, and desert candles among the blooms. At 4.5 miles, the trail meets the park road near the picnic area. Go left on the road to close the loop at the campground (5.2 miles).

*Access:* Begin at the day-use/trailhead parking area at the campground.

## Placerita Canyon State and County Park

**Hours/Season:** 9:00 A.M. to 5:00 P.M., except major holidays
**Facilities:** Picnic area, nature center, historic sites, hiker trails, playground equipment, restrooms
**For Information:** (805) 259-7721
**Access:** From the junction of I-5 and CA 14, go northeast on CA 14 for 3.1 miles, exit at Placerita Canyon Road, and turn right. The park entrance is in 1.6 miles.

Operated by the County of Los Angeles, this canyon park offers a shady retreat with oak woodlands, chaparral hillsides, and a sycamore-lined clear trickle of a creek. It also boasts a first-rate nature center, with live exhibits. A rehabilitated red-tailed hawk, lizards, snakes, a desert tortoise, tarantula, and beetles attract the curious eyes of young and old alike. Inside the center are interactive educational displays on the planet, climate, geologic faults, and microclimates that truly entertain as they teach.

The canyon's history traces back to the discovery of gold in 1842. In bygone days, the placers were worked using pan, sluice, and dry-wash methods. Today's would-be panners must seek in reaches outside the park.

After the gold ran out, Placerita Canyon served as a working ranch. It now attracts the urban dweller with its natural features and the wildness of its terrain. The fully oak-shaded picnic area, overlooking the creek, offers a relaxing stop between trails.

### Attractions and Activities

**Heritage Trail.** This easy 0.5-mile round-trip trail begins following a concrete walkway and bypasses a couple of big sycamore trees, before reaching Walker

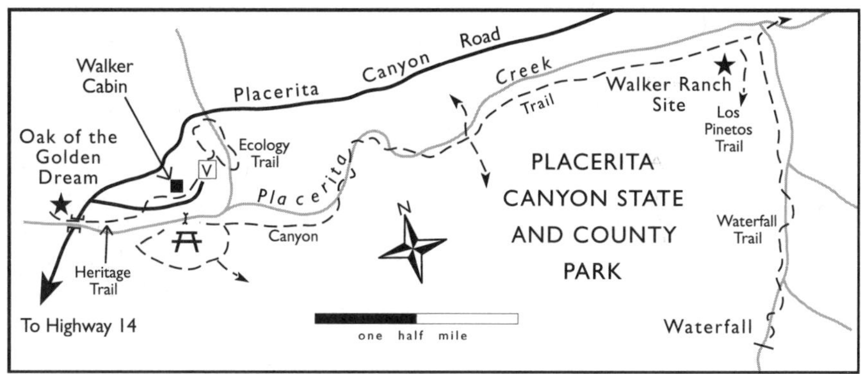

Cabin. Viewed through window grates, the interior of the rustic, one-room cabin shows time-period furnishings. Outside its door rests an old iron cart. After crossing over the park road, the trail continues downstream alongside the creek, passing through a mural-decorated tunnel under Placerita Canyon Road.

At 0.25 mile is the "Oak of the Golden Dream," site of the 1842 gold discovery. While gathering onions under this ancient tree, Francisco Lopez espied gold particles clinging to the bulb root hairs—this find preceded Marshall's famous discovery at Sutter's Mill by six years. But the landmark, hollow-footed live oak alone is noteworthy for its scenic quality.

*Access:* Begin at the nature center parking lot.

**Ecology Trail.** This 0.5-mile, thirteen-station self-guided nature trail introduces the canyon vegetation; brochures are available at the nature center.

At the initial trail fork past the center, go left following the wide, earthen path through an oak woodland. The loop begins beyond an Indian camp replica. Again, go left, for a clockwise tour.

The nature trail explores a dense chaparral-oak transition habitat, where woodrat nests, darting lizards, and galls on the scrub oaks number among the discoveries. At 0.25 mile, it crosses a small drainage, coming to a junction. Going uphill to the left hikers find a stairway to a vista in a few hundred feet, but poison oak overgrows the trail. The loop bears right, quickly crossing back over the drainage. At the next junction, go left to return to the center.

*Access:* Start behind the nature center.

**Canyon Trail.** This mostly shaded 5.5-mile round-trip trail follows and crisscrosses the park creek, working its way upstream to a canyon waterfall.

*Walker Ranch fireplace ruin, Placerita Canyon State and County Park*

At the trailhead sign reading "Walker Ranch 2 miles," take either path, as they again merge. The rolling trail begins wide and easy, then narrows as Placerita Canyon becomes more squeezed.

Sycamore, live oak, and willow line the drainage, but in places chaparral dominates. The entire way, hikers need to beware of poison oak. The lower creek is 6 to 18 feet wide. In spring, when it is full, the hike is at its prettiest, but it is also more demanding with additional wadings or rock hoppings. At times, late-season visitors may find the creek dry.

At 2 miles, where the hike enters the oak flat of Walker Ranch, follow the old jeep track upstream. The route bypasses some chemical toilets, a picturesque fireplace ruin of folded metamorphic stone, the trailhead for Los Pinetos Trail, scattered picnic tables, and a drinking fountain with sulfurous-tasting water. From the east end of the flat, follow the Waterfall Trail upstream. In a few feet, where a nature trail branches left toward the creek, keep to the Waterfall Trail, crossing a small, grassy meadow.

At 2.3 miles, the trail mounts the slope to the right, touring an area of oak, hollyleafed cherry, and sage. Just below is the creek. In another 0.2 mile, the trail is next to a pretty stairstepping stretch of water. Here, the tree-draped channel is 3 to 5 feet wide; more creek crossings follow. At times, hikers catch a whiff of sulfur, explaining the taste back at the drinking fountain.

Where the canyon forks at 2.7 miles, follow the right fork upstream a short distance. A few defaced alders precede the 15-foot falls, skipping over a cracked granite surface. Ferns dot its rocky sides, as maples bend over the site. The tight viewing space accommodates only a few hikers at a time. Although the waterfall makes a pleasant destination, the picturesque canyon truly recommends this hike.

*Access:* Start at the east end of the picnic area.

## SILVERWOOD LAKE STATE RECREATION AREA

**Hours/Season:** Year-round; day-use hours vary by season
**Facilities:** 136 developed campsites, picnic areas, marina/boat launch, fish-cleaning station, swimming beaches, snackbar/rental concessions, hiker and bicycle trails, restrooms, showers, dump station
**For Information:** (760) 389-2303
**Access:** From the CA 138–CA 173 junction (8.1 miles east of I-15), follow CA 138 east for 2.5 miles to the Silverwood Lake exit and go left to enter the park. Or follow CA 173 north for 2.3 miles to reach the dam.

This aqueduct-fed reservoir brings lake recreation to the north slope of the San Bernardino Mountains; its waters journey some 600 miles from their origins in the Feather River Basin. The attractive hourglass-shaped lake has a 13-mile shoreline and a surface area of almost a thousand acres. Quiet arms and coves welcome fishing boats, while the north end of the lake hosts waterskiing.

The neck of the lake is a no-ski zone, allowing traffic to flow between the two lake ends. There are designated swimming areas at Sawpit Canyon and Cleghorn Cove, as well as a hike/bike-to beach area—Serrano Beach. The Pacific Crest National Scenic Trail (PCT) travels the western slope overlooking the water.

Steep chaparral slopes enwrap much of the lake, with the tree-covered mountains of San Bernardino National Forest rising in the backdrop. Riparian areas,

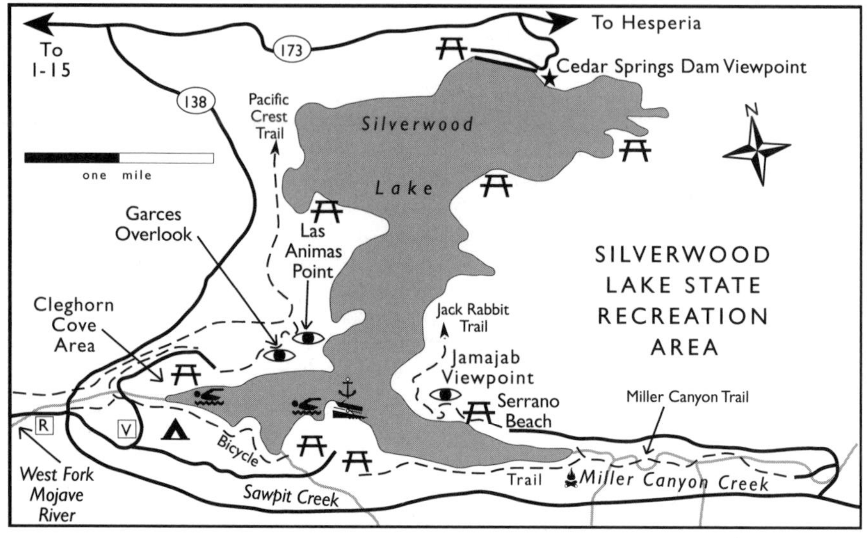


oak woodlands, pine- and fir-studded grasslands, and transition habitats also contribute to the lake border for a rich plant and wildlife diversity.

Cormorants congregate on a platform near the intake towers at the south end of the lake. In winter and spring, visitors can expect to find a major section of Miller Canyon, including Serrano Beach, closed to the public to protect an active bald eagle nest next to the lake. During that time, lakegoers can see eagles making passes over the lake.

## Attractions and Activities

**Miller Canyon Trail.** This 1.7-mile hiker trail journeys downstream along Miller Canyon Creek, crisscrossing the stream. While rock hopping is possible in summer, wading may be necessary in winter. Sycamore, alder, ponderosa pine, and a few cedar provide partial shade on the route. The park's paved bicycle route offers cyclists similar access to the area.

At 0.4 mile and 0.8 mile, respectively, hikers visit the Devils Pit and Lynx Point vista sites. At Devils Pit, a large granite outcrop and a jumble of boulders shape picturesque cascades and pools. At Lynx Point, visitors can look out Miller Canyon at the lake.

At 1.2 miles, the foot trail merges with the bike route for the final 0.5 mile to Serrano Beach. It is a thin, canted rock-and-sand beach with a small, sycamore-shaded picnic area above it.

Staying on the paved route as it leaves Serrano Beach, travelers may continue west for 0.3 mile to a lake vista. From there, the unmaintained Jack Rabbit Trail, an earthen footpath open to hikers only, switchbacks down through the thick chaparral for a rolling, contouring journey. The open trail remains good for 0.5 mile, then deteriorates, but not before it delivers a fine vista overlooking the southern end of the lake neck. Return as you came.

*Access:* The trail leaves the Miller Canyon group site.

**Las Animas Point Trail.** This 0.75-mile trail begins open to bicycle and hiker use and offers fine Silverwood Lake vistas.

Touring a tight border of oak and chaparral above the Cleghorn Cove beach, the trail gradually begins to climb. At 0.25-mile, it reaches the ramada-covered picnic table at Garces Overlook, where the views include the Sawpit Canyon Area, the lake's West Fork Mojave River Arm, and the nearby mountains. At this site, cyclists must lock up their bikes and continue on foot.

The trail grows steeper, advancing via quick, sharp switchbacks. Where it begins contouring the manzanita- and greasewood-clad slope, the PCT sometimes can be seen above it. At 0.7 mile, the PCT is 100 feet to the left; Las Animas Point is to the right. The gazebo at Las Animas Point affords the finest lake vista, overlooking the south end, the neck, and much of the main lake body to the north, including the Cedar Springs rock dam. Here, too, one can also search for eagles and ospreys. Return as you came.

*Access:* Begin at the east end of Cleghorn Cove day use.

**Bicycle Trail.** Some 6 miles of paved bicycle trail wrap around the southern end of the lake from Cleghorn Cove to Miller Canyon and Serrano Beach. The route passes through developed and open lake areas, often traveling close to shore. Between Black Oak picnic area and the closed intake area, the route travels a service road well removed from the lake. Much of the tour is semi-shaded with mixed oaks, pines, and firs. The bike camp occupies a scenic flat above the southeast arm of the lake. Watch out for blind curves and dirt patches.

*Access:* Reach the trail at various points along the south end of the lake.

*Silverwood Lake*

**Boating/Waterskiing.** The lake has a maximum speed of 35 miles per hour, with a 5-miles-per-hour limit near swimmers, developed shores, fishing areas, and the Miller Canyon and Cleghorn Cove lake arms. In the ski zone, traffic is one-way, counterclockwise.

Boats may land anywhere, except the buoyed-off areas at the spillway and inlet on the main lake, the outlet in Miller Canyon, and the no-powerboat zones at both the eastern end of Miller Canyon and the western end of Cleghorn Cove. Boat-in picnic sites dot the north end of the lake; bring water and remember that fires, barbecues, and cook stoves are not allowed.

**Fishing.** Anglers enjoy success from both boat and shore. The lake supports catfish, bass, bluegill, crappie, and trout. In the past, trout stocking was commonplace, but a moratorium now exists on the practice. Striped bass are caught in the spring and summer near the dam and in Miller Canyon, with trout hooked year-round. Coves afford the best warm-weather fishing, while the dam offers night fishing. To weigh catches and find out other Silverwood Lake fishing secrets, visit the marina.

## Los Angeles State and County Arboretum

**Hours/Season:** 9:00 A.M. to 4:30 P.M., except Christmas Day; trams run at selected hours weekday afternoons and every 45 minutes beginning at 10:00 A.M. on weekends

**Facilities:** Picnic grounds, historic buildings, greenhouses, bookshop, cafeteria, narrated tram tours, walkways, restrooms

**For Information:** (818) 821-3222

**Access:** In Arcadia, at 301 North Baldwin Avenue, just south of I-210.

Located at the base of the San Gabriel Mountains, this 127-acre arboretum provides an escape to cultivated beauty and bygone days. The arboretum boasts a world-representative tree and plant collection, arranged by geographic region. Among the species are South African aloes, bamboos, a rare 35-foot Boojam tree (native to remote central Baja California), American coastal redwoods, Australian acacias, and flowering fruit trees. In fall, color accents the grounds.

A 2-mile self-guided walking tour or a guided, shade-covered tram tour introduces the collection. Upon entering the complex, look for the fliers that announce the upcoming calendar of events and the seasonal highlights that may be observed in the garden. The grounds and facilities are handicapped accessible.

In addition to touring the grounds, visitors can discover a bit of area history. Wickiups—crude huts made of reeds, mats, and brush—are from the days of the Gabrielino Indians, while the restored Hugo Reid adobe ranch house recalls the days of the original Mexican land grant. The arboretum's Queen Anne Cottage and Coach Barn chronicle "Lucky" Baldwin's time here at Rancho Santa Anita. The elegant white cottage may look familiar; it has appeared in film and television.

### Attractions and Activities

**Santa Anita Depot.** The hundred-year-old Santa Anita Depot, which was moved to the arboretum in 1970, completes the area history lesson. It features railroad memorabilia and is restored to look like a functioning station. Tours are offered Tuesdays and Wednesdays, 10:00 A.M. to 4:00 P.M., and in the afternoon on the first Sunday of the month.

*At the Tropical Greenhouse, Los Angeles State and County Arboretum*

**Arboretum Self-guided Walking Tour.** The wide walkways, wooden benches, and open lawns suggest a relaxed pace for this 2-mile tour. Ancient, native oaks interweave the geographic tapestry of the grounds, while man-made streams, carp ponds, a spring-fed lake, and Meyberg Waterfall complement the setting.

Visitors are free to wander off the path to read a species label or seek out a secluded bench. Peacocks and peahens stroll the grounds, while herons, grebes, coots, and egrets frequent the lake.

Stops of interest include the greenhouses. The Begonia Greenhouse explodes with bold-shaped leaves and brightly colored flowers, Spanish moss, and ferns, while next door the Tropical Greenhouse draws visitors inside with its outstanding orchid collection and many bromeliads. A small pond, running stream, and moisture contribute to its junglelike atmosphere.

At the far end of the arboretum, the aquatic garden atop Tallac Knoll calls visitors to climb the stairway at Meyberg Falls. The garden features hibiscus, tropical plants, and interlocking pools of water lilies, hyacinths, and other aquatics. The southeast slope of the knoll supports one of the area's last stands of native Engelmann oak. An herb garden with more than 100 plants, the spring-flowering trees of the Asiatic and North American areas, and the Drought-Tolerant Garden may also be enjoyed.

## PIO PICO STATE HISTORIC PARK

**Hours/Season:** 10:00 A.M. to 5:00 P.M. Wednesday through Sunday, except major holidays
**Facilities:** Picnic tables, historic building, restrooms
**For Information:** (310) 695-1217 or (310) 454-8212

**Access:** From I-605, take the Whittier Boulevard exit in Whittier. The park is on the west side of the freeway, at 6003 Pioneer Boulevard.

This 3-acre park features the adobe mansion of Governor Pio Pico, the last governor of California under Mexican rule and an influential leader during the Mexican-American transition period. The mansion, central to Pio Pico's 9,000-acre cattle ranch—El Ranchito—served as his country residence from 1852 to 1892. In 1892, he lost the property in a questionable business deal.

Throughout its history, the adobe has suffered the ravages of flood. A more recent threat to its well-being came from the 1987 Whittier Narrows Earthquake, which closed the adobe's doors to the public. Although stable now, the home remains closed as it undergoes historic restoration. In the meantime, the public can still view the adobe exterior or prearrange to go on a special behind-the-scenes tour with a state park interpreter. To do so, phone the park in advance of a visit.

Picnic tables dot the open east lawn and rest beneath shade trees on the north side of the adobe. Situated next to I-605, the park grounds are noisy, yet provide an oasis in the urban setting.

### Attractions and Activities

**The Pio Pico Adobe.** The two-story white adobe structure is constructed in the shape of a hooked L that wraps around a central red brick patio, onto which the doors open. From the patio, an exterior stairway ascends to the second level. Impressive prickly pear hedges border the edge of the house and the property.

Historians believe that five of the rooms are from the original adobe, but much of the house has changed since Pio Pico's time. Years of remodeling and even flawed restoration attempts have altered its appearance.

When fully restored, the house will look much as it did in the 1870s and will be open again for public tours on a regular basis. A preview, however, is possible by making advance arrangements.

## Chino Hills State Park

**Hours/Season:** 8:00 A.M. to sunset

**Facilities:** 8 primitive campsites; picnic sites; small visitor center; hiker, horse, and mountain-bike routes; equestrian staging area; a designated model-plane glider point; nonflush toilets; water

**For Information:** (909) 780-6222

**Access:** From the junction of Freeways 60 and 71, go south on 71 for 5.8 miles and turn right on Pomono-Rincon Road. Go 0.8 mile and turn left on Soquel Canyon Road. In another mile, turn left on Elinvar Drive. Where it ends in 0.2 mile, go left on Sapphire Road to find the park entry on the right. *Following rain, this dirt road entering the park may be closed to vehicles.*

Chino Hills is an impressive wild island in an urban and suburban sea. Its 12,000 acres feature chiseled, sycamore-lined creek canyons; broad valley bottoms; steep, rounded grassy slopes; oak-filled drainages; and one of the largest remaining stands of native Southern California black walnut. The vistas sweep north to the San Gabriels and east to Mount San Jacinto. But the park's trademark is its luxuriant grasslands.

Equestrians and mountain-bike riders would be hard pressed to find a better Southern California destination. The park contains some 30 miles of interlocking ranch road for long, varied, challenging tours. As the junctions are frequent and not all marked, secure a map at the entrance or at the headquarters visitor center. Taxidermic examples of wildlife, topographic maps, and a natural-history table make up the visitor center's small display room; the facility is open on an irregular basis.

Throughout the park, ticks are a concern in spring. Grass seeds are the hiker's nemesis in summer. The best time to visit Chino Hills State Park is during the milder temperatures of late fall through early spring.

## Attractions and Activities

**Aliso Canyon–Scully Ridge Loop.** This rugged 5.3-mile loop begins open to all users, but the congested vegetation of the ridge turns back all but the most determined of riders. Touring creek drainage and ridge top, the loop offers a fine survey of the park's terrain and habitats.

Past the campground, the trail quickly crosses Bane and Aliso creeks to follow Aliso Canyon downstream. Willows line the water, but the ranch road remains open. Red-winged blackbirds are common in the canyon.

At 0.5 mile, go right for Scully Ridge and remain on the ranch road. As it bypasses the Water Canyon Trail, the route climbs steadily, rounding toward the ridge. Along the grass and chaparral slope, mustard, thistle, sage, and a smattering of wildflowers are among the mix.

At 1 mile, the Bobcat Ridge Trail journeys right; the loop bears left, continuing southeast on the Scully Ridge Trail. Just ahead, where a utility route heads right, the Scully Ridge Trail becomes a narrow path, overgrown and sometimes overtaken by a jungle growth of mustard.

By 1.4 miles, travelers are touring the ridge. Where the trail passes through open grassland, views are of Aliso and Brush canyons and the San Gabriels to the north. Past a large shade oak, the route begins rounding above Brush Canyon.

From Scully Ridge, hikers have several loop options back to Aliso Canyon. For the shortest one, at the initial Brush Canyon Trail junction (2.7 miles), go left 200

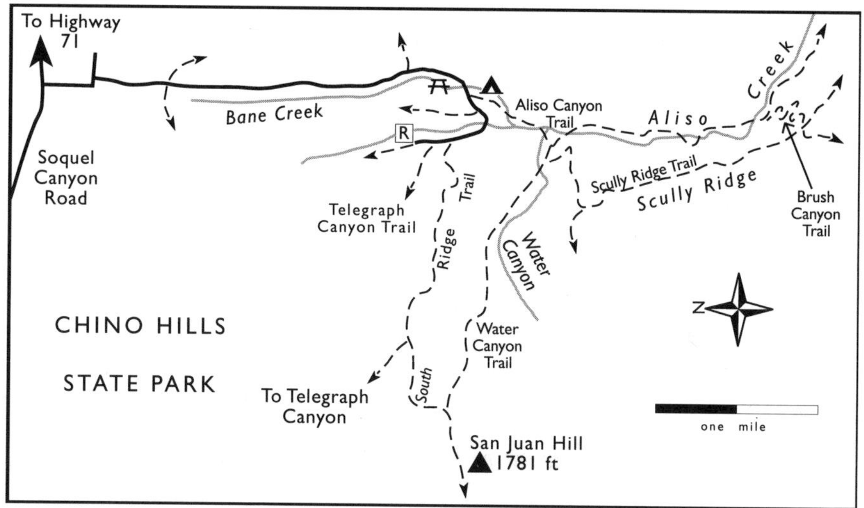

feet on the Scully Ridge Trail, and there bear left on the Brush Canyon Trail as it descends to Aliso Creek.

Initially, a heavy mustard border claims this switchbacking descent. The trail then emerges, passing through chaparral, before reaching the canyon bottom at 3.6 miles. Cottonwood, willow, and live oak line the banks of Aliso Creek; a dirt ranch road (Lower Aliso Canyon Trail) now continues the loop upstream.

This route crisscrosses the normally low creek several times; tadpoles occupy the pools in the spring. A lush grassland fills the flat valley bottom. At 4.8 miles, the loop closes at the Scully Ridge junction. Travelers come to the campground and tour's end at 5.3 miles.

*Access:* Begin at the campground on Bane Canyon Road, 2.3 miles from the park entrance; take the gated ranch road past the corrals.

**Water Canyon–San Juan Hill–South Ridge Loop.** For this tour, travel the loop clockwise (in the described order), as the Water Canyon–South Ridge junction is otherwise impossible to find. This circuitous route combines ranch road and foot trail.

The hike shares its initial 0.5 mile with the Aliso Canyon–Scully Ridge Loop, described above. From the ranch road of the Scully Ridge Trail, go right on the Water Canyon Trail. After crossing Water Canyon's thin creek, the trail then follows it upstream. Willows line the banks, while a grassland slope rises above the 12-inch-wide trail.

At 1.2 miles stands a prickly pear cactus grove, where the cacti grow over 7 feet tall, and the old pads become trunks for the new growth. Farther upstream, a couple of scenic sycamores mark the corridor. Tarantulas can sometimes be seen in the grassland habitat, though lizards, hawks, and vultures are more commonly spied.

At 1.5 miles, near a small, typically dry pond, the loop heads uphill to the right toward the utility lines on the ridge. As it climbs, the view broadens, looking out Water Canyon and across the park hillsides at the surrounding communities. The tall, thick grasses brush hikers' legs.

Finally, at 2.2 miles, the path pokes through mustard, arriving at the South Ridge Trail. Bear left on this ranch road to visit San Juan Hill (elevation 1,781 feet). At 2.5 miles stands the corner post that indicates a 0.1-mile 2-track to the San Juan Hill summit; a small monument marks the top. The 360-degree view overlooks the Los Angeles Basin and the untamed park. When the haze is absent, visitors discover the San Gabriel Mountains to the north. Utility lines intrude on views east.

Back on the South Ridge Trail, head right for a hefty downhill to close the loop. Grassland canyon views accompany the descent. At 3.7 miles begins a spur to the popular Telegraph Canyon Trail; again keep right, continuing east along the South Ridge Trail.

By 4.5 miles, the descent eases, and down-canyon views feature the park headquarters and ranch area. At 5.1 miles you will reach the paved park road. Go right to close the loop at the campground (5.5 miles); go left to find the park headquarters and visitor center in 0.3 mile.

*Access:* Begin at the campground past the corrals.

## California Citrus State Historic Park

**Hours/Season:** 8:00 A.M. to 3:00 P.M.
**Facilities:** Picnic area, activity center, interpretive gazebo, amphitheater, walkways, hiker trail, restrooms

**For Information:** (909) 780-6222
**Access:** In southwest Riverside, from Highway 91 take the Van Buren Boulevard exit, go 1.3 miles south, and turn east on Dufferin to reach the park in 0.1 mile.

*Oranges, California Citrus State Historic Park*

Opened August 1993, this state park unit is sparkling new and not fully realized, but the picnic grounds are inviting. Announcing the park at the corner of Dufferin and Van Buren Boulevard is a king-size orange outside a charming, though nonworking, cream-colored fruit stand—a fine entrance sign for this park saluting the citrus industry's role in California history.

Presently, the park features a palm tree-lined drive, groomed lawn, and young, planted eucalyptus trees that promise future shade. Wide walkways tour the grounds, passing between the arborways and gazebos. The attractive wooden-shake activity center will one day host weddings and reunions.

At the interpretive gazebo, visitors find interesting exhibits devoted to the citrus industry and the Gage Canal. One particularly interesting display includes the historic logos and labels of the various growers. At the small amphitheater, talks and films are presented.

Nearby, a short trail leaves the picnic grounds to top a small knoll overlooking a neighboring newly planted citrus orchard, as well as the surrounding expanse of mature groves. When the trees are in bloom, a sweet aroma saturates the air.

Future plans call for this 400-acre park holding to include a packing house and workers' camp. When completed, they, too, will be open to the public.

## Lake Perris State Recreation Area

**Hours/Season:** Year-round; 6:00 A.M. to 10:00 P.M. May through October, 6:00 A.M. to 8:00 P.M. November through April (day use); 10:00 A.M. to 2:00 P.M. Wednesdays and 10:00 A.M. to 4:00 P.M. weekends (museum)
**Facilities:** Developed open campground with 167 tent sites and 264 hook-up sites; 50 primitive horse campsites with corrals and troughs; picnic areas; museum; marina; tackle shop; boat ramps; designated swimming areas; waterslide; hiker, horse, and mountain-bike trails; restrooms; nonflush toilets; showers
**For Information:** (909) 940-5608
**Access:** The park is southeast of Riverside. From I-215, take the exit for the Ramona Expressway and follow it east 2.5 miles. There, turn north on Lake Perris Drive to reach the park in 1.1 miles.

This park couples the water sport and recreation of the reservoir with the exploration of its surrounding rocky hills and arid uplands. Activities include picnicking, swimming, boating, windsurfing, fishing, hiking, cycling, horseback

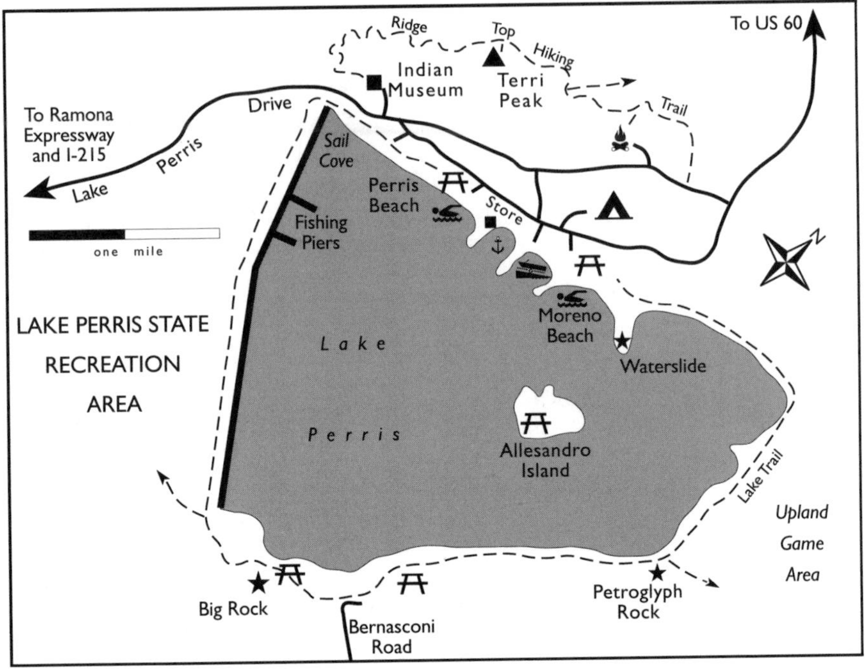


riding, and rock climbing. The park even has a waterslide and an area for scuba diving. Under a tight set of restrictions, in-season small-game hunting is allowed in the Upland Game Area.

The water filling the reservoir comes from the High Sierra, journeying 600 miles south along the California Aqueduct system. Piercing the shimmery blue waters, cone-shaped Allesandro Island extends the lake area recreation with boat-in picnicking and a trail to its summit.

Summers find great crowds flocking to the reservoir's refreshment. Naturalists favor the off-season for its quiet and improved wildlife watching.

## Attractions and Activities

**Regional Indian Museum.** Housed in an eye-catching, copper-colored geometric building below rocky Terri Peak and the Armada Mountains is the first of a series of regional Indian museums to grace the state park system. It introduces the earliest peoples to have lived in this Mojave desert region, describing and depicting their customs and lifestyles. Visitors learn about the Cahuilla, Cupeno, Chemehuevi, Serrano, Luiseno, and Vanyume peoples during three periods: pre-European, Hispanic-Anglo, and present. An attractive desert mural depicts the area wildlife. Fire starters, rattles, pipes, and pestles and mortars are among the artifacts.

*Access:* The museum is on the north side of the park road 0.5 mile past the entrance station.

**Lake Trail.** Parallel 9-mile trails encircle the reservoir. The mostly paved route close to shore is open to mountain biker and hiker use; the dirt track below the dam and farther away from shore is open to horses.

Beginning from the north end of the dam, a counterclockwise tour crosses (or skirts) the 2.25-mile dam with its two fishing piers; rolls through the rock jumbles and Big Rock Area at the foot of Bernasconi Hills; passes through the semi-developed Bernasconi day-use area on the southeast shore; travels a 2.5-mile wild stretch just away from the willowy east shore, bypassing Petroglyph Rock (actually a pictograph); and concludes by touring the highly developed north shore.

Vistas sweep the reservoir, Allesandro Island, and the surrounding desert hills and mountains. Jackrabbit, coyote, and kangaroo rat may be spied in the arid scrub. Some 100 species of bird have been identified at the lake, including roadrunner, burrowing owl, white pelican, and eagle. Chemical toilets and tables dot the route.

*Access:* Reach the loop from the park's day-use areas or horse camp.

*Lizards, Lake Perris State Recreation Area*

**Ridge Top Hiking Trail.** For the adventurous, who enjoy a desert challenge, this long-distance skyline trail crosses and stitches together the mountain groups ringing Lake Perris: Big Rock, the Bernasconi Hills, and the Apuma, Russell, and Armada mountains. A popular day-hike sampling of this route is the 1.4-mile Terri Peak Hike, elevation gain 1,000 feet.

For it, follow the dirt path climbing west from the museum, touring above a small drainage. Views along the way are of rocky Terri Peak, the copper-colored Regional Indian Museum, and the lake basin. Fringe-toed lizards scurry over the rocks, while deer tracks mark the narrow path. Views build to the west and north as the second half of the climb grows more rugged.

At 1.1 miles, the trail follows the ridge east to the peak. At the junction, go right to gain the summit (elevation 2,600 feet) for a 360-degree vista of the lake, March Air Force Base, and the valleys north. Return as you came or continue on the Ridge Top Trail.

*Access:* For Terri Peak, begin on the unmarked path climbing from the west end of the Regional Indian Museum's parking lot.

**Boating.** Boats travel in a counterclockwise pattern, with a maximum speed of 35 miles per hour, 5 miles per hour next to shore. Sail Cove, at the northwest corner of the lake, is reserved for sailboats, sailboards, and other nonpowered boats. Elsewhere on the north shore, three ramps with a total of fifteen lanes serve powerboaters. A concession-operated marina presents a boat-rental service, gas dock, slips, and storage.

**Fishing.** The Lake Perris waters support bass, rainbow trout, bluegill, channel catfish, and a healthy number of "crawdads." The park brochure explains where and how to fish for each of these.

**Swimming.** Along its 9-mile shoreline, swimming is only allowed off Moreno and Perris beaches in the buoy-marked areas. Lifeguards are on duty during peak visitor times.

**Rock Climbing.** The Big Rock Area at the south end of the dam offers a variety of practice routes where climbers can hone their skills. From atop the granite rocks and walls, climbers gain fine neighborhood vistas. Climbers should note the state does not provide or maintain any fixtures to facilitate climbing on Big Rock. Use of this area and any fixtures that may be present is strictly at your own risk.

*Access:* For the shortest hike to Big Rock, follow the Lake Trail clockwise from the south shore day-use area, off Bernasconi Road.

# MOUNT SAN JACINTO STATE PARK

**Hours/Season:** Year-round; trams leave on the half hour beginning at 10:00 A.M. Monday through Friday, 8:00 A.M. weekends and holidays (Note: The tramway typically has a ten-day maintenance shutdown starting the first Monday in August.)

**Facilities:** 33 developed wooded campsites, 50 primitive wooded campsites, 4 wilderness camp areas, picnic sites, nature and Nordic centers, hiker and horse trails, mule-ride concession, restrooms, nonflush toilets, showers, with additional services available at the Palm Springs Aerial Tramway terminals

**For Information:** (909) 659-2607; for the tram, phone (760) 325-1391 (recording) or (760) 325-1449 (person)

**Access:** The peak is reached via trails from the Idyllwild area (26 miles south of I-10 on CA 243), or via the Palm Springs Aerial Tramway (at the north end of Palm Springs, turn off CA 111 onto Tramway Road and go 3.7 miles).

Mount San Jacinto and its 13,500-acre wilderness offer a premier backcountry experience. At an elevation of 10,804 feet, Mount San Jacinto is the second highest peak in Southern California, lifting its traveler above the problems of cities, freeways, and smog into crisp mountain air. From its summit, hikers find a grand 360-degree view sweeping hundreds of square miles from the desert to the ocean.

The tramway climbs alongside the mountain's Chino Canyon, spectacularly craggy and precipitous, with its stark gray-white rock and steep, vegetated year-round creek. It offers an impressive first acquaintance with the imposing, granite-

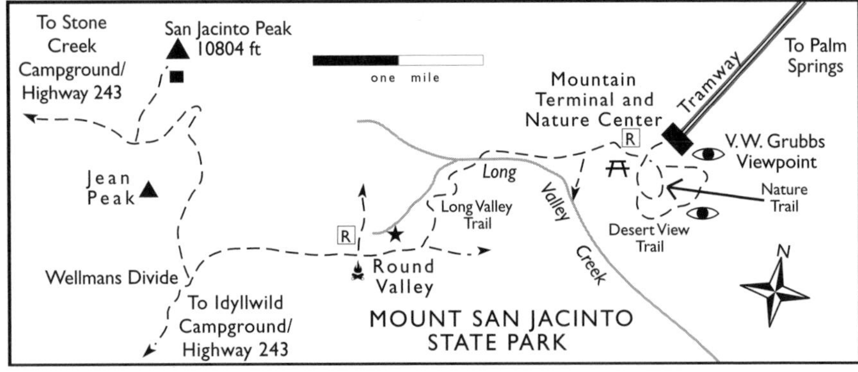

ribbed giant. The 14-minute ride between the valley and mountain terminals travels 2.5 miles of cable, climbing more than a vertical mile. The rise from the desert floor gives little clue to the pristine subalpine landscape on top.

Mountain travelers enjoy a beautiful high-country setting of sparkling creeks, wildflower meadows, granite outcrops, and mixed forests, with lodgepole and limber pines claiming the highest reaches. The park welcomes hiking, wilderness camping, nature study, and photography; and from mid-November to April, Nordic skiing and snowshoeing.

Both day hikers and campers need wilderness permits to travel beyond the Long Valley/Mountain Terminal Area. Day hikers may self-register atop the mountain at the Long Valley Ranger Station, a quarter mile west of the mountain terminal. Backpackers must pick up permits in person at the park headquarters at Idyllwild, or write for them, prior to a visit.

*Tramway, Mount San Jacinto State Park*

At the western foot of the mountain, at the center of Idyllwild is the park's fully developed campground, with oak, pine, and manzanita vegetating the sites. A mortar rock lies within camp; it shows more than a dozen deep-worn grinding cups. Stone Creek Campground, about 5 miles north of town, is less developed, occupying a similar pine-manzanita complex; keep an eye out for the sign.

## Attractions and Activities

**Mountain Terminal.** At the Mountain Terminal (elevation 8,516 feet), guests may ascend the stairs from the terminal deck to V. W. Grubbs Viewpoint, from where signs point out landmarks. Along the deck, 20-power telescopes allow zooming in on the neighborhood in view. Inside, on the lower floor of the terminal, a small nature center shows a film on the tram project and makes available brochures for the nature trail.

The Mountain Terminal restaurant is a popular destination through the evening hours. Nighttime travelers enjoy the desert sky and the lights of the cities.

**Desert View Trail–Nature Trail Hike.** The 1.5-mile Desert View Trail stitches together modest overlooks along the mountain's edge for a 270-degree view. It interlocks with the 0.75-mile Nature Trail, which forms an interior loop.

For both, begin by heading left from the walkway. In a short distance, this mutually shared segment crosses over the mule-train trail. At the next unmarked junction, hikers again go straight; the big, vanilla-fragrant Jeffrey pines form an open forest. At 0.1 mile, the Desert View Trail heads left; the Nature Trail heads right, touring the lush green meadow of Long Valley Creek.

Opting for the Desert View Trail, the path narrows, becoming more rock studded as it climbs. Mountain bluebirds and Clark's nutcrackers are common. Spurs to the left branch to the vista overlooks. The first two peer over the abrupt northeast escarpment at the desert floor. The best view is at 0.7 mile, looking out at an impressive, close-by, fractured-rock dome, with high rugged mountains to its south. Mountain mahogany grows along the ridge.

The trail then descends, swinging back through the boulder-studded forest. At 1.1 miles is the Nature Trail junction. To the right is the start of the Nature Trail; to the left are its closing numbers. Either way, the hike concludes at the terminal walkway at about 1.5 miles.

*Access:* Begin at the steep concrete walkway leaving the mountain terminal.

**Peak Hike.** This 10.4-mile round-trip hike offers the shortest possible route to the summit, climbing 2,300 feet in elevation.

At the junction past the ranger station, go right on the Long Valley Trail, passing through the boulder-studded high-elevation forest, with its helter-skelter shade. After the trail crosses a creek on side-by-side logs (0.6 mile), it climbs, skirting a few small false hellebore meadows.

At the 1.7-mile junction, bear right for Round Valley, soon edging its big meadow swath; side paths lead to hidden campsites. At 2 miles are pit toilets, and at 2.1 miles hikers come upon a water spigot and junction post. For the peak, go left toward Wellmans Junction, resuming the climb in a lodgepole pine–white fir forest.

After crossing over the upper drainage at 2.7 miles, the tour becomes more open with boulders and lupine patches between the trees. At 3.1 miles the route reaches the junction at Wellmans Divide. Here, visitors gain the first good views of the journey, with a look at the Salton Sea and views of the Mount San Jacinto Wilderness to the south and west. Winds wash up and over the divide, shaping the nearby trees.

Head right, contouring the chinquapin-mantled, boulder-studded slope of Jean Peak. Views are to the south and east, before the trail returns to fuller forest. At 4 miles, the trail again contours a boulder-chinquapin slope, and at 4.9 miles it tops the saddle between Jean and San Jacinto peaks. Go right for the summit. Past the historic stone cabin, the trail gives way to a rock scramble to the top (5.2 miles).

From the summit's rounded granite jumble, visitors can view the San Bernardino Mountains, the dusky desert mountains and plains, and the hazy ridges straining toward the glare of the Pacific Ocean. The silver platter of the Salton Sea shimmers to the southeast, but the plunging sides of the peak itself surpass all views. Return as you came, or make a loop or shuttle tour.

*Access:* Begin at the Long Valley Ranger Station, 0.25 mile west of the terminal.

## INDIO HILLS PALMS

**Hours/Season:** Daylight hours

**Facilities:** Hiker and horse trails, with restrooms and water available at Coachella Valley Preserve

**For Information:** The Nature Conservancy, (760) 343-1234

**Access:** From I-10, take the Thousand Palms / Ramon Road exit and head east on Ramon for 4.3 miles. There, turn north on Thousand Palms Canyon Road to reach the Coachella Valley Preserve's Thousand Palms Oasis Visitor Center and state park lands in 2.1 miles.

Part of the greater Coachella Valley Preserve, this 2,200-acre wilderness park includes rugged canyons and hills and an arid plain. It both represents and celebrates an unblemished portion of the Colorado Desert. Located along the San Andreas Fault, it features wide-open spaces and oases of Native California fan palm.

Five palm groves lie within the park: Horseshoe, Hidden, Pushawalla, Biskra, and Macomber. Ground waters released by the San Andreas Fault nurture these oases, some of which are linear groves, conspicuously painting in bold green the line of the fault. One need not be a geologist to see it at Horseshoe Palms.

Altogether some 21,000 acres of choice desert make up the Coachella Valley Preserve. It is jointly managed by state and federal agencies and by the Nature Conservancy. The isolated state park lands are reached only via primitive trail, starting from the adjacent Nature Conservancy lands. The preserve trails are open to foot and horse use, though some routes, such as the Horseshoe Palms Trail, have sections too narrow and rugged for horses.

This is an area to be seen and enjoyed in the early morning light and in the cooler weather months. Water is a traveler's best friend; smoking is prohibited in the preserve.

*Horseshoe palms, Indio Hills Palms*

## Attractions and Activities

**Horseshoe Palms Trail.** This semi-cross-country hike navigates between landmarks and follows a stretch of historic Indian trail; wear boots.

It begins on a tracked path angling southeast across the desert flat. Sagebrush, creosote, brittlebush, and desert annuals decorate the dry, rocky soil. Crossing over Thousand Palms Canyon Road, hikers come to a junction at 0.2 mile. Go right for Horseshoe, Pushawalla, and Hidden palms—the state park groves.

Hikers now must make their way along and over washes, heading toward the steep, diagonal foot trail mounting the rocky ridge to the southeast. Cholla and barrel cactus intermingle in the desert mix; tamarisk grows in the wash.

At the ridge, a hefty 0.1-mile climb on an unstable, rocky trail puts hikers atop Bee-rock Mesa. Views sweep Thousand Palms, the Coachella Valley Preserve, Mount San Jacinto, and the Little San Bernardino and Santa Rosa mountains. The cleared areas at the center of the mesa record Malpais Indian encampments, dating back thousands of years. From the Bee-rock Trail junction at 0.5 mile, hikers may opt for either the mesa or ridge tour to Horseshoe Palms.

The *mesa tour* follows a narrow, well-tracked path heading right, crossing the mesa slope. Creosote bushes remain but become more dispersed as new plant varieties enter the mix. In another 0.5 mile, the trail grows fainter in the rocky terrain near the foot of Indio Hills. Keep the same general line to top a side ridge (1.2 miles from the trailhead) overlooking Horseshoe Palms; a short, rugged descent then leads to the grove.

Horseshoe Palms Oasis runs along the foot of Indio Hills for an impressive 0.5 mile. The stark, chiseled ochre hills lend a striking contrast to the verdant oasis. Palm trees can reach a height of 60 feet, with fronds measuring 6 feet across. Some may be nearly 200 years old. Dry fronds make an ideal nesting material for birds and animals. Veiled rustlings are commonplace.

The rare shade suggests a lingering stay. When ready, return as you came or extend your discovery by hiking up the wash to Pushawalla Canyon and heading north to its palm grove, or by hiking down the wash to Hidden Palms Grove. Be sure to carry plenty of water for these half- to full-day travels.

Opting instead for the *ridge tour* at the Bee-rock Trail junction, hikers travel the spine, where a stiff breeze mitigates the heat and views are nonstop. Looking north across the wash, hikers discover the tucked away grove of Indian Palms. The utility poles to the south point out Hidden Palms. Yellow, purple, and white wildflowers sprinkle the ridgetop.

On the right in 0.7 mile, cairns indicate a rough connecting route to the mesa tour; it comes out at the Horseshoe Palms side-ridge overlook. Stay on Indio Hills ridge for a loftier vantage on this scenic grove. All about, swallows zip and swoop as hikers pace off the grove's length. Dizzying looks down the steep flanks reveal the palms.

In another 0.2 mile, the trail tags the ridge high point. Where the hike halts at the end of the ridge (1.7 miles from the trailhead), eastern views find steep-sided Pushawalla Canyon, with the tops of its palms barely visible. From the ridge post, hikers also look into the wild heart of the Indio Hills Palms park unit. Return as you came.

*Access:* Start at the Thousand Palms Oasis Visitor Center parking lot. A sign indicates the route to Indian, Horseshoe, Pushawalla, and Hidden palms oases.

# Salton Sea State Recreation Area

**Hours/Season:** Year-round
**Facilities:** 150 developed tamarisk- and ironwood-shaded campsites (15 of which have hook-ups), 800 primitive shoreline sites (bring a shade source), ramada-covered and open picnic sites, visitor center, boat launch and wash, fish-cleaning stations, swimming beach, nature trail, restrooms, nonflush toilets, indoor and outdoor showers, dump station, *water except at Salt Creek*
**For Information:** (760) 393-3059
**Access:** From Indio, go south on CA 111 for some 20 miles to reach the park.

Salton Sea is a vast, open, cobalt-blue water with mountains rising to the west and the desert flat sweeping east. A briny smell is noticeable on first approach, due to the high salinity of the water. At times, millions of tiny, washed-up barnacles form a white ring on the beach. Elsewhere, a crusty, crystalline rim meets the sea. For waterplay, swimmers and waders may want to don an old pair of sneakers to protect their feet. Much of the shore is exposed and shadeless.

The Salton Sea owes its 1905 birth to a burst dike that sent Colorado River waters plunging to the desert floor, some 230 feet below sea level. When the dike was repaired, this landlocked, 35-mile-long and 15-mile-wide desert sea remained, growing saltier than the ocean over time.

*Picnic shelters, Salton Sea State Recreation Area*

Swimming, fishing, boating, waterskiing, and birdwatching are the primary Salton Sea pastimes. In a few places, long walks along shore are also possible, with an occasional wading between segments of beach. The state recreation land occupies an 18-mile length of the northeast shore, while the 36,500-acre Salton Sea Wildlife Refuge borders the southern end of the watery expanse.

## Attractions and Activities

**Ironwood Nature Trail.** This easy, self-guided 1.2-mile one-way trail journeys south, traveling just east of the Salton Sea shoreline. The tour is flat.

Brochures are available at the visitor center or camp host site. While plants migrate and sometimes die off, this trail remains a first-rate introduction to the desert habitat. Descriptions and plants match up with minimal confusion, and the recurrence of vegetation allows hikers to test their newfound knowledge. Quail, jackrabbit, lizard, and even a desert iguana (in spring or fall) may divert attention from the brochure.

Spurs branch to the sea; one of the most passable begins near post 6. Where the lakeshore opens up, hikers find nice cross-lake views of the mountains to the west.

At post 10, arrows indicate the trail veers left. Here, too, the path becomes less formalized, crossing open sand; just follow the footprints and posts. For a time, the trail travels close to the highway and the railroad tracks beyond it.

At 0.8 mile, near post 22, bear left for the final leg to Mecca Beach Campground. For many, its fine swimming beach suggests a cooling plunge before the return trek.

*Access:* Begin near site 32 at the Headquarter's Los Frijoles Campground. The trail concludes near the fish-cleaning station at Mecca Beach Campground.

**Boating.** Boaters are cautioned that strong winds buffet the area and lake levels do change, revealing hazards, particularly at the shallow north and south ends of the sea. A wind-warning light on the harbor entrance jetty advises boaters as to their safety. Spring marks an unsettled time, when the winds can launch waves up to 5 feet high.

The man-made bay at Varner Harbor has a two-lane boat ramp and dock. Cartop boats may be launched from shore. Posted speeds and rules apply.

**Fishing.** The lake fishery has changed over time, as the salinity of Salton Sea has increased. Today, orangemouth corbina, Gulf croaker, and sargo are the sought-after ocean transplants. Tilapia, an unwanted guest from the irrigation canals, also provides sport and is best eaten skinned and filleted.

While boat fishing is popular, shore anglers enjoy great success off the riprap bank of the harbor jetty and at Sneaker Beach. Fishing remains good year-round, although summer "green tides" can suffocate fish trapped in the algae blooms. Fishing tips are offered in the park brochure; check with the park service about any health advisories that may affect the fish. Nighttime fishing is allowed.

**Birdwatching.** The state park distributes a map showing birdwatching locations in the Salton Sea area, as well as a bird checklist, allowing you to track your successes. The checklist also indicates the seasonal presence of the various birds, so if you are interested in spying a particular species, you can time your watch for when you will have a greater likelihood of success.

Within the park, the best areas for seeing waterbirds are at Salt Creek (between CA 111 and the sea) and the shore area south of Bombay Beach. For landbirds, check out Mecca Beach Campground and the Whitefield Stream and Wash on the east side of CA 111. The sightings are varied and may include roadrunners, stilts, geese, northern harriers, burrowing owls, cedar waxwings, and mockingbirds.

# Palomar Mountain State Park

**Hours/Season:** Year-round
**Facilities:** 31 developed forested campsites (3 are wheelchair accessible), picnic sites, pond, hiker trails, restrooms, coin-operated showers
**For Information:** (760) 765-0755
**Access:** From I-15, go 21 miles east on CA 76 and turn north on Route S6/South Grade Road. Then, go another 9 miles, following Routes S6 and S7 (State Park Road) into the park.

Located on the western flank of Palomar Mountain, this mile-high park enjoys rich forests and woodlands, expansive meadows, a small fishing pond, cool mountain air, and some surprising weather changes. A "don't-miss" attraction at the park is a group of prized ancient live oaks along the French Valley Trail. These trees boast 10-foot diameters and thick, outstretched limbs—there are mighty oaks, and then there are the Palomar oaks.

Early Native Americans hunted and gathered seeds and nuts on Palomar Mountain. They built both villages and temporary camps; three permanent Luiseno villages have been identified within the park. Sturdy wickiup huts and a central, semi-buried sweat house typically comprised a village.

The presence of the Spanish is reflected in the mountain's name, "Palomar," meaning "place of the pigeons." At the time of their arrival, thousands of the birds nested here. In the 1850s, cattle rustlers found the mountain's isolated meadows ideal for hiding stolen stock.

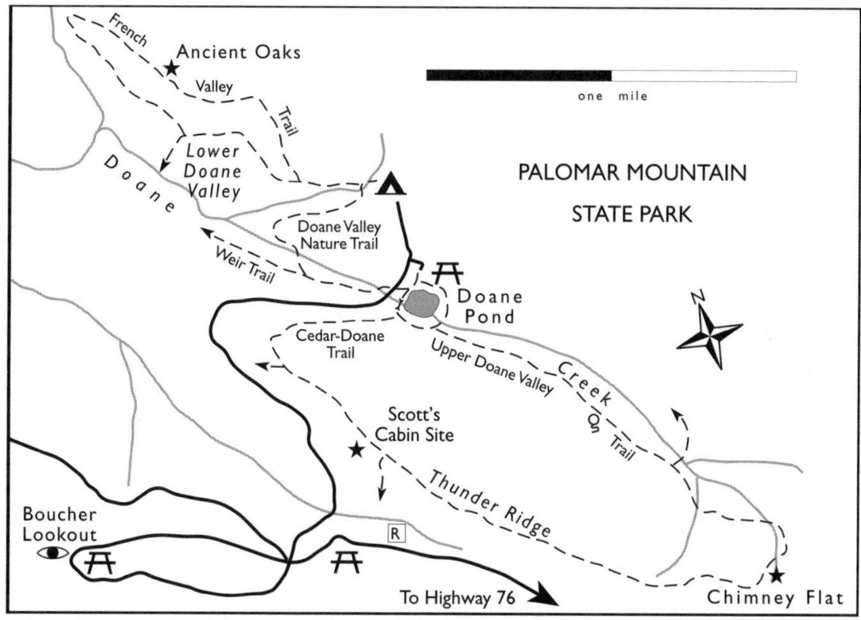

## Attractions and Activities

**Palomar Observatory.** While not part of the state park, the observatory suggests a trip to the top of the mountain (elevation 6,100 feet), where one of the world's largest telescopes is housed. Its museum is open to the public 9:00 A.M. to 4:00 P.M. daily; contact the California Institute of Technology, (619) 742-2119.

*Access:* From the junction of Routes S6 and S7, continue 8 miles north on S6 to the observatory.

**Doane Valley Nature Trail-French Valley Hike.** Stitching together the Doane Pond area and the campground, this 2-mile hike unites the park's fine nature trail, native grass meadows, and famed oaks.

Starting below Doane Pond, hikers cross Doane Creek and briefly tour a mixed forest, before crossing over the park road. From there, the trail continues downstream, crisscrossing the creek. At 0.25 mile, stay straight for the nature trail; to the left is the Weir Trail. For a nature trail, the early distance is semi-rugged, with stone-hopping crossings and a rolling grade.

A bench at 0.4 mile overlooks a forked-top cedar. Afterward, the trail enters a grassy meadow and tours a slope charred from the 1987 fire. Most of the mature trees survived, while the young ones were culled. Many silver snags sport black hollows. Ahead, the trail edges a meadow, where bunchgrasses abound.

To the right 100 feet at the 0.8-mile junction is the campground; to the left are French and Lower Doane valleys. To visit the park's prized oaks, go left, followed by a right at the 1-mile junction on French Valley Trail. Hikers now pass through a live oak–ponderosa pine habitat, overlooking the meadow expanse of Lower Doane Valley.

At 1.2 miles, the trail reaches the first massive live oak, with a huge boulder cradled in its belly. The tree has a 10-foot diameter and thick, heavy arms. Beware of the poison oak growing in its shadow. The trail next descends through a ponderosa pine-meadow habitat, bypassing several acorn woodpecker-drilled trees.

Greeting hikers at 1.4 miles is a group of the amazing oaks, growing around and atop boulders. The photogenic oaks are huge, majestic, and sometimes interwoven—some of the best seen anywhere. They rightfully call the tour to a halt.

Retracing the route to the campground (2 miles), hikers come out near sites 24 and 25; the return to the Doane Pond parking lot is via the park road. Alternatively, visitors can explore the park's back reaches, venturing beyond the oaks; carry a trail map and a compass.

*Access:* At the southwest corner of the Doane Pond parking area, descend the stairs to cross the outlet creek.

**Upper Doane Valley–Scott's Cabin Loop.** This 3.5-mile circuit has a 700-foot elevation change and explores meadow and forest.

Reaching Doane Pond, cross over the outlet footbridge and follow the west shore toward Thunder Spring. Mixed oak, cedar, and fir shade the way. Ahead, the trail travels the forest-meadow edge, paralleling the fine thread of Doane Creek upstream. White alder and few false hellebore line the drainage. On the left at 0.3 mile, a grinding stone beneath a live oak shows mortars 5 inches across and 2 inches deep.

A false hellebore patch along the trail signals Thunder Spring is just ahead (0.6 mile). Past the spring is a trail junction on the bank of Doane Creek. For the loop, continue upstream toward Chimney Flat. The drainage is now steep-sided and bordered by tall alders. Bracken fern and annuals adorn the meadow grasses.

At the head of the meadow (0.9 mile), bear right, continuing upstream toward Chimney Flat. Here, a congestion of currant crowds the creek, while dogwood trees accent the fir and mixed oak forest. Ahead is a log crossing of the creek, followed by a quick, strenuous uphill. Above the trail are fenced private and state lands. Beyond a huge cedar, the trail crosses back over the creek, arriving at Chimney Flat, a big, rolling bracken fern meadow (1.4 miles).

Stay on the trail, passing through the meadow for Scott's Cabin. It is soon replaced by an abandoned jeep road, enfolded by mixed forest; beware of the poison oak along its sides. At 1.9 miles, after crossing over a maintenance road, an eroded footpath continues the tour, traveling a grass and bracken fern meadow punctuated by cedars, oaks, boulders, and twisted logs.

At 2.2 miles, the tour returns to forest, descending Thunder Ridge. Acorn woodpecker holes riddle the snags. Past the Silvercrest picnic area junction, the trail bypasses Scott's Cabin on the left. All that remains of the 1880s homestead cabin is its square shape, defined by the first few rows of logs.

The descent then continues to the 2.9-mile junction, where the loop heads right on the Cedar-Doane Trail, still descending and contouring the forest slope. It concludes with a steep downhill along a drainage to reach Doane Pond and the parking area (3.5 miles).

*Access:* Begin at the Doane Pond parking area, following the trail to the pond.

**Fishing.** At the meadow bottom of Upper Doane Valley, Doane Pond is open to fishing year-round. It is stocked with trout in winter and spring. Bluegill, bullheads, and catfish are the other catches. This pleasant, small, cattail-rimmed pond is an ideal first fishing spot for children. Picnic tables border the lake.

## ANZA-BORREGO DESERT STATE PARK

**Hours/Season:** Year-round; 9:00 A.M. to 5:00 P.M. daily, except summers, when it is open on weekends and holidays only (visitor center)

**Facilities:** 144 developed campsites (52 of which have hook-ups), primitive campsites, horse campsites, open camp areas, picnic sites, visitor center, historical sites and markers, hiker trails, jeep trails, restrooms, nonflush toilets, showers, dump station, water at developed areas

**For Information:** (760) 767-5311

**Access:** Locate the park 8 miles north of I-8, at Ocotillo (east of San Diego). CA 78 and County Routes S2, S3, and S22, all access the park.

Anza-Borrego is one of the premier desert parks in the country and one of the biggest state parks in the lower forty-eight states. Its 600,000-acre expanse applauds the Colorado Desert in all its finery. Sculptured badlands, parched mountains, rugged canyons, varied cactus, native fan palm oases, elephant trees, and far-reaching views make up this disquieting, alluring land.

Elevations vary from 6,000 feet along the eastern escarpment of the Peninsular Range to the badlands at sea level. Some 300 Peninsular bighorn sheep range a quarter of the park. ("Borrego" is Spanish for bighorn sheep.)

Pictographs, grinding stones, and ancient village sites record the presence of early Native Americans. The historic routes of the 1774 Anza Expedition, the Mormon Battalion, and the Butterfield Stage remain locked in the land.

When conditions are right, the desert explodes with the fire-red flags of the ocotillo, the pink blooms of the beavertail cactus, and showers of yellow brittlebush. The annual bloom is so popular the park established a wildflower hotline at (619) 767-4684 and a postcard-notification system. The floral event begins in mid-February and runs through the first half of April, with March marking the peak.

Anza-Borrego affords uncommon solitude and welcomes great outdoor adventure, with hiking, automobile and four-wheel-drive touring, horseback riding, mountain biking, birdwatching, stargazing, photography, and nature study. More than 500 miles of jeep trail invite exploration. For desert travel, make sure your vehicle is in good shape, with a usable spare and a full fuel tank; carry extra water, food, blankets, a good map, and a compass; be aware of your personal limitations; and respect the desert sun. Boots are recommended for all desert hikes.

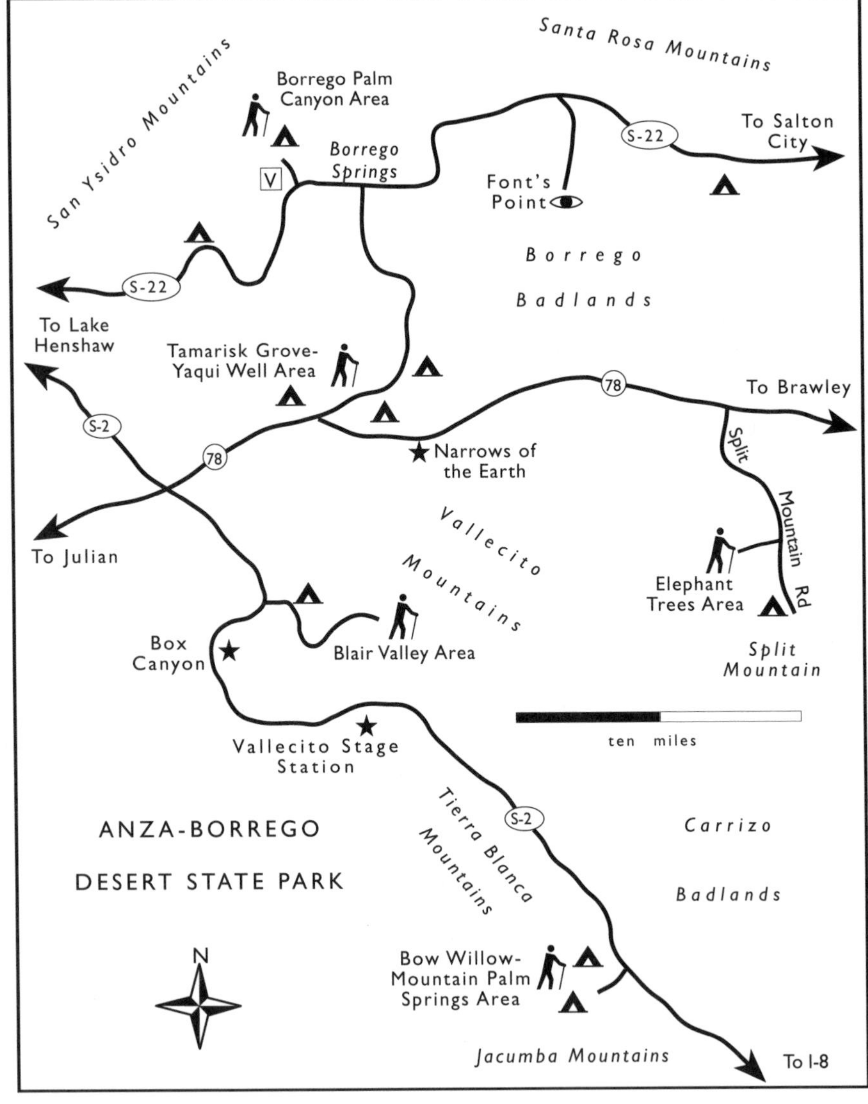

Despite its size, this desert park is remarkably accessible, with various self-guided nature trails and driving tours doing a good job of introducing it. Obtain brochures at the visitor center, 1.6 miles west of Borrego Springs off County Route S22.

The center itself is impressive. Semi-buried and landscaped with cactus, it offers a theater, exhibits, bookstore, identification guides, posted road conditions, and other vital information. A 0.6-mile nature trail explores the creosote scrub habitat between it and Borrego Palm Canyon Campground.

Five areas and their related drives and trails form a fine composite picture of Anza-Borrego. They are the Bow Willow–Mountain Palm Springs Area, the Borrego Springs Area, the Blair Valley Area, the Tamarisk Grove–Yaqui Well Area, and the Split Mountain Road–Elephant Trees Area.

## Attractions and Activities

### BOW WILLOW–MOUNTAIN PALM SPRINGS AREA

**Erosion Road Tour.** This 18-mile car tour along S22 introduces the volatile geologic history of the desert through landmarks and descriptions. The tour points out the work of the San Jacinto Fault, the scouring effect of wind and storm on the Borrego Badlands, and a "continental divide" feature.

Just over a third of the way is a side trip for four-wheel-drive vehicles to Font's Point. It travels 4 miles of dirt road reaching a promontory with a sharply eroded cliff and exceptional views of the Borrego Badlands. The vantage itself is a dizzying spectacle. Elsewhere on the Erosion Tour, a roadside turnout offers a Borrego Badlands view, though with less flare.

*Access:* Go east on S22 from the Visitor Center junction.

**North Fork Trail.** This is one of several short hikes leading to palm oases. It begins up a sandy wash, dotted by white granite boulders and riddled by footprints of human and beast. Five kinds of cactus, along with ocotillo, desert holly, brittlebush, and sage, color the route. Entering the canyon, the wash narrows, and hikers alternately cross a sandy floor or scramble over rocks. At 0.4 mile is North Grove, featuring some twenty shaggy-trunked palms in a shady hollow. Insect buzzings and bird rustlings animate the grove.

Continuing up the canyon to the right leads to Mary's Bowl at 0.6 mile. This fan-palm grove features trees of varied height, some with denuded trunks, others sporting woolly skirts. Some of the boulders take on interesting shapes where the granite has not entirely eroded out.

Keen eyes may spot an elephant tree above Mary's Grove. It stands 3 to 4 feet tall and has darker leaves than the surrounding vegetation. Better examples are found at other places in the park. Return as you came.

*Access:* Begin at Mountain Palm Springs Primitive Camp, west off S2, 17.2 miles north of I-8. Follow the wash heading north (to your right as you enter camp).

**South Fork Trail to Torote Bowl.** This more demanding hike explores the rugged desertscape, visiting oases and elephant trees.

The hike passes a display kiosk, and heads west up the wash, touring a bouldery canyon of the Tierra Blanca Mountains. At the trail fork, bear right; pygmy palms quickly come into view. Cacti and desert shrubs and annuals accent the tour; springtime puddles support tadpoles. At 0.25 mile, the trail enters the fire-charred Pygmy Grove. Its trees stand half as tall as the other palms; there are about fifty in all.

Leaving the grove, the trail alternately travels a wash or the low ridge to its left. The open, sunny trek reaffirms the charm of the oases. Soon, Southwest Grove comes into view; take either the wash or the ridge route to enter this good-size palm grove at 0.7 mile. Detours to the right lead to an elephant tree or an alternative destination, Surprise Palm Grove. To reach Torote Bowl, a more extensive area of elephant trees, go straight, touring the length of Southwest Grove.

Stone steps lead out of the canyon as the tour climbs a rugged desert slope. Wooden stakes briefly mark the rocky route. At 1 mile, a sign indicates that Bow Willow Campground lies to the left; to the right is Torote Bowl. Views east are of Carrizo Badlands. The trail to the bowl remains open, hot, and rocky.

At 1.4 miles, hikers top the ridge at Torote Bowl Overlook; an elephant tree stands next to the sign. About two dozen of the short, unusual trees pepper the western slope. The stocky trunk of this desert tree resembles an elephant's leg, suggesting the name. The vista east broadens, overlooking the neighboring palm groves and the distant desert. Return as you came.

*Access:* Begin at Mountain Palm Springs Camp; follow the wash that lies straight ahead as you enter camp.

## BORREGO SPRINGS AREA

**Palm Canyon Trail.** In bygone times, the year-round flow of Palm Creek supported an ancient Cahuilla Indian village and early-day ranching. Today, it draws hundreds of park visitors. A moderately easy 1.5-mile trail journeys up the canyon to its hidden palm oasis.

The tour begins as a self-guided nature trail. Impressive high-desert mountains enfold the area. In spring, brittlebush blazes the landscape yellow. By 0.5 mile, the canyon takes shape. When the creek is full, a nice series of cascades greets the hiker, and before long the palm canyon destination comes into view.

At 1 mile, a stone-step creek crossing continues the journey. On the opposite shore, an alternative path heads downstream; hikers may loop back here or consider it for the return.

Continuing upstream, hikers come upon a 10-foot waterfall spilling between room-size boulders. There is also a nice view out the V of the canyon. At 1.2 miles stands the first big palm. Afterward, the trail crosses the drainage, touring a boulder area above the palm corridor.

At 1.5 miles, it again dips to the creek at a second similar falls with a nice pool at its foot. Palms offer shade; cottonwood and alder grow here, too. Return as you came, keeping an eye out for rattlesnakes.

*Access:* Begin at the day-use parking area of Borrego Palm Canyon Campground, off S22.

## BLAIR VALLEY AREA

**Southern Emigrant Road Tour.** This 26-mile tour traces an early-day transportation route. Historical markers and the car-tour brochure tell the story of the hardships endured and challenges met at that time. Present-day travelers visit such places as Walker Pass, where passengers had to walk and sometimes even had to push the stage; Box Canyon, where visitors can overlook the actual wagon ruts made by the Mormon Battalion and the Butterfield Stage; and Vallecito Stage Station, where visitors can escape the desert sun in this faithfully reconstructed sod building. Spectacular desert scenery completes the tour.

*Access:* Go south on County Route S2 from the Scissors junction (the CA 78–S2 junction).

**Morteros Trail.** Long ago, the nomadic Kumeyaay tribe based itself here to gather pinyon nuts, agave, and mesquite beans in season. Morteros, depressions worn in the granite, record where women pounded the nuts and seeds into meal.

Follow the wide sandy path toward the rocky desert hillside. The route crosses a varied desert floor of agave, cholla, yucca, juniper, creosote, and ocotillo. At 0.2 mile, morteros dimple a granite boulder next to the trail. Generally, stones rest in a couple of the depressions, hinting at how they were used.

Go a few strides farther and take the side trail on the right. It leads to a triangular stone with morteros 6 inches deep and 6 inches in diameter. At 0.25 mile, the trail ends at a canyon vista. Return as you came.

*Access:* Go 6 miles southeast on S2 from the Scissors junction (CA 78–S2), turn left for Blair Valley, and go 3.7 miles on jeep trails, following the signs to "Morteros." *Blair Valley's jeep trails are open to high-clearance vehicles, but ask at the visitor center before attempting. Roads have sandy stretches and deep channels; passing may be tricky when two conventional vehicles meet.*

**Pictograph Trail.** This trail features a Native American rock art site; more than fifty exist in the park. It also offers a grand desert vista.

After meandering through a pocket of large granite boulders, the trail enters a bowl, slowly ascending a wash. Juniper, creosote, yucca, and agave grow on the hillsides; desert stars spangle the sandy floor. At 0.5 mile, the trail tops a saddle or low pass and begins descending via another sandy wash.

At 0.7 mile, the huge, rounded boulder next to the trail reveals the red and yellow pigment art of the ancient Indians. A natural rock overhang protects the geometric designs, which have grown faint with time.

Past the rock, the trail journeys east into the bowels of Smuggler Canyon. As the canyon closes, it funnels hikers out a narrow gap, where the wash slices through the hillside, coming to a 100-foot drop—a dry waterfall (1.25 miles).

The site affords a grand vista of both the dramatic gap and far sweeping desert, with Vallecito Valley and the southern high-desert mountains. Smooth granite boulders afford seating; bats come out at dusk. Return as you came.

*Access:* Go 5.2 miles on Blair Valley jeep trails, following the signs to Pictograph Trail. (Heed the road caution in the Morteros Trail access description.)

**Ghost Mountain Trail.** This trail climbs rocky Ghost Mountain to reach the 1932 homesite of the Marshall South family, who resided in this out-of-the-way setting for sixteen years.

The trail begins in the desert bottom. As it climbs, agave dominate the hillside. Dotted by their tall floral stalks in the spring, Ghost Mountain calls to mind a birthday cake with candles. Switchbacks advance the narrow, often rocky trail. Overviews of the desert are quickly gained.

At 0.5 mile, the trail tops a ridge, where hikers find a limited view north at Borrego Springs. The trail then follows the ridge toward a granite-riddled rise. Stone steps up the rise lead to a flat and, just ahead, the granite-adobe ruin of the South home (0.75 mile).

Parts of the water system, some standing walls, a chicken-wire–supported door frame, and rusting bed frame are among what remains. Tiers hint at the onetime hilltop garden. Views are open, but not 360 degrees. Return as you came.

*Access:* Go 3.2 miles on the Blair Valley jeep trails, following the signs to Ghost Mountain. (Heed the road caution in the Morteros Trail access description.)

**Mountain Biking.** The Blair Valley jeep roads invite mountain biking. The roads are relatively flat, with only a patchy presence of the deep, loose sand that hampers the going. The area foot trails suggest getting off the bike for a closer look. Jackrabbits, kangaroo rats, and roadrunners may be noted along the way.

Other popular rides are found at Grapevine and Coyote canyons, but there are

*Cholla patch, Anza-Borrego Desert State Park*

many suitable jeep trails in the park. When planning a tour, it is advisable to avoid the wash routes, as they are often too sandy, wearing out the rider.

Riders must keep to the jeep trails; do not stray, looking for a better surface. Always carry more water than you think you will need.

## TAMARISK GROVE–YAQUI WELL AREA

**Yaqui Well Trail.** This trail tours an arid slope reaching a well and its vital wetland habitat.

Alongside County Road S3, a palm and cottonwood mark the start of the hike. In the morning, owls may be seen changing roosts from the tamarisk trees across the way to the cottonwood overhead. The hike briefly follows a rock-framed path passing through a creosote scrub area next to the road.

As it climbs, the trail grows rockier; cactus and ocotillo replace the shrubs. Cholla dominates the upper slope. Plant identification plaques can be seen along the route, but several are old and no longer legible.

At 0.3 mile, Yaqui Well Campground comes into view. Back on the sandy floor, the trail bypasses a couple of ancient ironwoods, with clumps of desert mistletoe in their branches. At 0.75 mile, the trail squeezes through a deep mesquite grove, reaching Yaqui Well, marked by a sulphurous smell.

A 10-foot-diameter circle, dense with cattail reeds, marks the well. Hummingbird, phainopepla, sage thrasher, and other species may be spied by the patient guest. Visitors may either return as they came or continue along the trail, entering Yaqui Well Camp at 0.85 mile.

*Access:* Find the trailhead off S3, opposite Tamarisk Grove Campground.

**Cactus Loop Trail.** This often rocky trail ascends a drainage, where ocotillo and six kinds of cactus may be seen: two kinds of cholla, beavertail, fishhook, hedgehog, and barrel.

In this cactus gallery, each variety adds its signature bloom in turn. The narrow drainage invites a close-up appreciation of the vegetation. Ahead looms a high-desert mountain, ranged by bighorn sheep; a scope is needed to locate them.

At 0.2 mile, the trail leaves the drainage, mounting a low ridge. In the morning, a sunlit army of jumping cholla dazzles the eye, calling photographers to their trade. Brittlebush weaves among the cactus. Views east sweep across the broad desert floor to the staircased hills and mountains in the distance. The noise from County S3 is now more apparent.

At 0.4 mile, the trail crosses a small depression on the ridge and descends the slope overlooking the next drainage east, larger and more rugged than the last. Barrel cactus populate its floor. At 0.75 mile, the trail comes out on S3, just east of where the trail started. Go right to close the loop.

*Access:* Begin off S3, across from the Tamarisk Grove Campground entrance.

**Kenyon Overlook Trail.** This tour offers close-up looks at the desert vegetation and vistas south and east.

From the open camp flat, the hike follows a rock and dirt path, rounding the boulders of the slope to tour the foot of a desert hill. Cactus, creosote, ocotillo, and agave are among the vegetation. At 0.4 mile, a brief detour left leads to a rocky bump, with a 180-degree vista south.

Continuing straight another 0.2 mile, hikers find the 100-foot spur to Kenyon Overlook on the left. The vista features the agave-dotted Mescal Bajada (adjoined alluvial fans), with Salton Sea just visible to the east. Sunset Peak rises to the southeast. From the vista, return as you came or continue on the path coming out at a parking area off S3.

*Access:* Begin at Yaqui Pass Primitive Campground, off S3, north of Tamarisk Grove Campground.

**Narrows of the Earth Trail.** For this self-guided 0.4-mile nature trail, brochures are usually available at the trailhead; if not, obtain one at the visitor center.

The tour pairs physical features with geologic explanations, helping travelers better understand the impact of faults, differential erosion, and other geologic events. The trail is easy, following a sandy wash, but hot, touring the tight canyon. Pencil cholla grows where the trail loops back to the trailhead.

*Access:* From the junction of S3 and CA 78, south of Tamarisk Grove, go 4.6 miles east on CA 78. The unmarked trailhead is on the right.

## SPLIT MOUNTAIN ROAD–ELEPHANT TREES AREA

**Elephant Trees Loop.** This 1-mile self-guided nature trail introduces some of the northernmost examples of the elephant tree. Hundreds of these unusual trees dot the alluvial fans of the Vallecito Mountains, yet scientists did not discover them here until 1937.

As the trail tours Alma Wash, the brochure points out the area vegetation and the unique characteristics of each species. The bright white sand suggests travelers don sunglasses. Rock barriers and arrows keep travelers on track.

The first elephant trees are on the left at 0.3 mile; one squeezes a barrel cactus with its limbs. More of the stocky, gnarled trees dot the expanse behind the pair.

At 0.5 mile, the trail crosses the wash and begins to loop back, bypassing another elephant tree, the biggest one yet. Desert annuals, shrubs, and cacti contribute to the tour. Foot-long lizards can sometimes be seen scurrying across the wash or cooling off on a branch.

*Access:* From the junction of Borrego Springs Road and CA 78, go 6.5 miles east on CA 78 and turn right for Split Mountain Road. In another 5.7 miles, turn right for the Elephant Trees Area. *The road ahead has 0.8 mile of loose, mounded sand, dirt, and rock; high clearance is needed. Drivers of two-wheel-drive vehicles should avoid the route on weekends, as problems can result when two conventional vehicles meet on the road.*

**Fish Creek/Split Mountain Area.** The park service offers periodic jeep tours through this exciting geologic area; they are limited to four-wheel-drive vehicles. The tour reveals the red-rock realm of fault-divided Split Mountain and its rugged, arid neighborhood.

*Access:* Tours leave from Fish Creek Primitive Camp on Split Mountain Road. Check the park newspaper for a schedule of tours and sign up at the visitor center.

## San Pasqual Battlefield State Historic Park

**Hours/Season:** 10:00 A.M. to 5:00 P.M. Friday, Saturday, and Sunday
**Facilities:** Picnic sites, visitor center / museum, historic monuments, amphitheater, hiker trail, restrooms
**For Information:** (760) 220-5430
**Access:** At Escondido, go southeast from I-5 on CA 78, following the highway signs through town. In 9 miles, the San Pasqual Monument is on the left; in another 0.4 mile, turn left for the park museum.

Situated in the chaparral and weathered-granite foothills of the Peninsular Range, this 50-acre park overlooks the valley where a scene from the Mexican-American War played out. On December 6, 1846, a bloody hand-to-hand confrontation took place between the outnumbered, weary, and ill-prepared American troops sent to occupy California and the organized ranks of Mexico's Captain Pico. It was followed by a four-day standoff at Mule Hill.

During the standoff, Edward Beale, Kit Carson, and an Indian scout stole across Mexican lines to summon support from Admiral Stockton's fleet at San Diego Bay. By the time the reinforcements arrived, the ordeal had come to a quiet end.

*Beale-Carson plaque, San Pasqual Battlefield State Historic Park*

### Attractions and Activities

**Museum.** The park's attractive museum offers an excellent presentation of the battle through video, displays, maps, and exhibits. Colorful panels introduce the Mexican and American leaders, the maneuvers, and the outcomes. The descriptions are both in Spanish and English. Next to a picture window overlooking the actual battlefield, a lightboard shows the actions and reactions of the Mexican and American troops.

The museum also pays tribute to the valley's Kumeyaay Indians. After the secularization of the missions, the tribe established a successful self-governing village here.

**Trail.** This 2-mile round-trip trail has a 250-foot elevation change and links the museum and monument sites. A 0.5-mile nature loop launches the tour; a brochure for it may be purchased at the museum.

The dirt path travels an area of buckwheat, laurel sumac, prickly pear cactus, grasses, and wildflowers. The brochure identifies the plants, as well as some Indian mortars and an Indian shelter.

Where the trail forks, go right for a counterclockwise tour of the nature trail. At 0.2 mile is a ramada-shaded bench overlooking the valley and battlefield. At 0.25 mile, hikers may go left for the nature loop alone or continue ahead on the uneven trail to the monument.

The trail to the monument tops the ridge at 0.6 mile. Another vista bench offers views out the valley and across the San Diego Wild Animal Park. Red-tailed hawks and vultures soar by at eye level. Where the trail descends, it passes through a scenic buckwheat-laced cactus patch, accented by yellow blooms in spring and red fruit in fall.

The monument area, at 1 mile, features an open grass slope and planted shade trees, encircled by a low wall. Centrally located is a large granite boulder bearing the names of the soldiers who died in the Battle of San Pasqual, December 6 through 10. Return as you came following the second half of the nature trail.

*Access:* Begin the walk next to the bronze plaque of Beale and Carson hailing Stockton's ship.

## Picacho State Recreation Area

**Hours/Season:** Year-round

**Facilities:** 54 undeveloped semi-shaded campsites, primitive boat-in campsites, picnic sites, boat ramps and securing posts and docks, fish-cleaning station, historic sites, hiker trails, nonflush toilets, sun-heated shower, dump station, water

**For Information:** (760) 393-3052

**Access:** From I-8 at the California-Arizona border, take the Winterhaven Drive/ Fourth Avenue exit and head north. In 0.4 mile, turn right onto County Route S24, go 0.2 mile, and turn left on Picacho Road. The pavement ends in another 4 miles; the remaining 17.2 miles to the park are often narrow and winding, with stretches of washboard and potholes. During dry weather, though, the route is passable for conventional vehicles, motorhomes, and trailers; drive cautiously.

Along the Colorado River, in the far southeast corner of the state, this 7,000-acre desert wild calls to the adventurous. It boasts grand solitude, challenging terrain, spectacular canyon and wash scenery, varied wildlife, four-wheel-drive back reaches, and first-rate river recreation. The craggy volcanic plug, Picacho Peak—landmark for the area—lends the park its name.

Much of the exploration is by foot, hiking cross-country up the washes or following abandoned jeep tracks; ask at the headquarters for recommended routes. A four-wheel-drive vehicle is needed to access the trailhead for such treasured sites as the Little Grand Canyon Area. Wild burros, desert bighorn sheep, coyotes, and mule deer range the park recesses.

The Colorado River has always played a vital role in the area's history. The Quechen Indians crossed it, using logs, rafts, and crude pottery vessels to harvest the fertile flood plain. Years later, the river brought early-day explorers and carried the paddlewheelers transporting people and supplies to the remote gold camp of Picacho (population 2,500). The Colorado River has long since reclaimed the town. Today, what it serves up is refreshing river sport.

Kinder temperatures grace this area from mid-October to the end of April. Beginning in April and continuing through midsummer, the mosquitos can raise havoc, especially near the river and backwater lakes; come prepared with repellent and netting.

## Attractions and Activities

**Stamp Mill Trail.** This 1-mile, one-way self-guided trail climbs a rocky hillside and crosses a stark gray outcrop and red volcanic slope. It overlooks the Colorado River, the nearby mounds of multi-colored tuff, the Trigo Mountains of the Arizona shore, and the onetime townsite of Picacho. Brochures are available at the trailhead.

As the trail ascends from the park road, early views are of eye-catching Picacho Peak. In March and April, desert wildflowers, beavertail cactus blooms, and flowering shrubs decorate the route. Benches welcome rests and enjoyment of the area.

Midway, a brief detour leads to the Picacho jail, a cramped hollow cut in the tuff. It alternately held the town's desperados and explosives. At the wash at 0.7 mile is a junction. To the right are Railroad and Ice Cream canyons. Bear left to finish the stamp mill tour.

At 0.9 mile, hikers come upon the Upper Mill ruin, with its rusting equipment, brick and rock walls, coiled wire, and broken porcelain. It was constructed in 1896, and at one time provided work for 700 men. A short way beyond it, the trail halts above Lower Mill, Picacho's first stamp mill. All that remains of it is the building's standing shell.

Brown-striped lizards measuring a foot long roam the wash between the mill sites; their tails leave signatures in the sand. Return as you came.

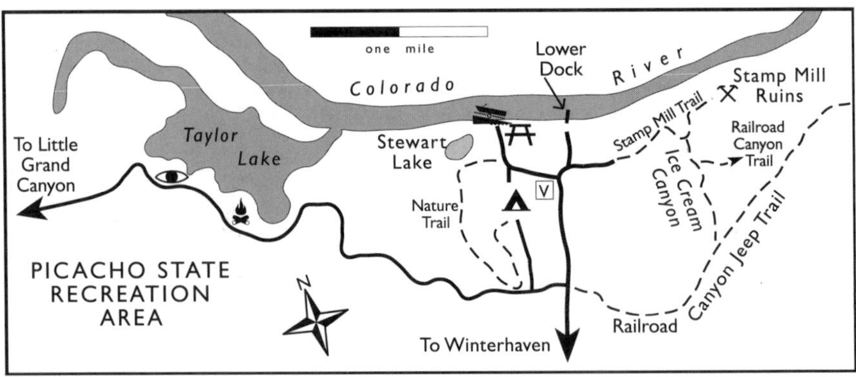

*Beavertail cactus, Picacho State Recreation Area*

*Access:* Find the trailhead off the road to Lower Dock; an old ore cart marks the site. There is parking for two vehicles.

**Ice Cream Canyon Trail.** Follow the first 0.7 mile of the Stamp Mill Trail and turn right for this route, exploring one of the park's scenic canyons.

The trail briefly follows the wash bank upstream, before dipping to its floor. Pink and green tuff walls enclose the lower canyon. In 0.2 mile, steps cut into the green tuff ascend the canyon slope on the left; this is the Railroad Canyon Trail. Stay in the wash for the Ice Cream Canyon Trail.

The hike alternately crosses beds of tuff and areas of loose rock, exploring the colorful canyon. Cholla, barrel, and fishhook cactus ornament the nooks and cracks of the canyon walls. Ironwood trees afford patchy shade. Farther up the canyon, harder volcanic outcrops appear. Hummingbird and phainopepla are co-travelers.

At 1 mile, a 4-foot rock fall must be crossed. Watch your hand placements here, as this is rattlesnake country. The immediate cliffs measure 50 feet tall, the surrounding ones 400 feet tall. At 1.3 miles, where the canyon opens up, a side drainage on the right pinpoints an exceptional view of some conical peaks. As the canyon curves left, the opportunity for bighorn sheep sightings exists.

Ahead, the canyon again pinches, before opening up to a dramatic basin. Chiseled desert peaks—each a big outcrop—radiate out in all directions. Paloverdes dot the bowl. Continuing ahead, hikers meet the Railroad Canyon Jeep Trail (1.7 miles). Return as you came or continue exploring via the jeep trail.

*Access:* Start at the Stamp Mill trailhead, off the road to Lower Dock.

**Stewart Lake Nature Trail.** This 1.5-mile loop encircles the red-rock outcrop towering above the campground. The beginning 0.5 mile is a nature trail; brochures are available at the trailhead.

Following the nature-trail segment first, hikers opt for a counterclockwise tour. After passing through a mesquite-tamarisk corridor, the trail contours the rock base. At 0.3 mile, a bench overlooks the tamarisk-overtaken Stewart Lake; only a few pockets of standing water remain. Better views are of the Colorado River and the cliff behind you.

Rounding the outcrop, hikers learn the names of area vegetation. At the end of the nature tour, the trail climbs. Painted arrows point the way.

At 0.8 mile, the trail serves up a great view of White Wash, with its exciting fire-red outcrops. The eroding volcanic slope traversed by the trail allows only a few annuals to gain their footing. A coyote's howl or a burro's "yee-aah" sometimes may be heard. As the trail advances along a ridge, desert views continue to intrigue.

At 1 mile, the trail meets the park road; bear left traveling alongside it. The trail resumes on the left in less than 0.1 mile. Over-the-shoulder views are now of Picacho Peak, while the ones ahead find a skyline arch marking the outcrop above camp. At 1.4 miles, where the trail dips into a wash, go right to return to the campground near site 40.

*Access:* Begin near campsites 15 and 16.

**Canoeing/River Running/Boating.** A 76-mile stretch of the Colorado River between Blythe and the Imperial Dam has been designated for recreation. Along it, Picacho borders a 12-mile segment. The California Department of Boating and Waterways has prepared a boating trail guide for this area, complete with maps, land ownerships, take-out points, boat-in camps, and safety suggestions.

The river current averages 5 miles per hour. Snags, brush, and submerged sandbars are some of the boating obstacles. It is recommended that river canoeists travel in groups with a minimum of three boats. Backwater lakes, such as Taylor Lake, offer additional exploration.

Thick cane, tule rush, and willows line much of the broad, muddy river and its backwaters. A Colorado River tour is visually striking, with the verdant green flood plain contrasting the corridor's stark desert mountains. Winter bird migrations add to the discovery.

**Fishing.** River dams led to the elimination of many native fish species, but the Colorado River still serves up fine sport, with catfish, crappie, bass, and bluegill. Bank and boat fishing are equally popular. Ask at the park for angling hints.

## CUYAMACA RANCHO STATE PARK

**Hours/Season:** Year-round

**Facilities:** 181 developed semi-forested campsites, horse campsites, picnic sites, nature center, headquarters museum, historic sites, hiker and horse trails, mountain-bike routes, restrooms, showers, dump station

**For Information:** (760) 765-0755

**Access:** On CA 79, go 9 miles north from I-8 or 14 miles south from Julian to reach park headquarters.

Situated in the Peninsular Range, this 25,000-acre park houses the nearest forest recreation to San Diego. Yellow pines, incense cedar, and mixed oaks create an unexpectedly rich and inviting habitat. The onetime ranch also encompasses chaparral mesas, upland meadows, intermittent streams, scenic outcrops, stony peaks, and access to man-made Lake Cuyamaca; more than half the area is wilderness. Unusual for Southern California, this area also undergoes seasonal change, with spring blooms, summer thunderstorms, autumn color, and winter white.

The park invites exploration on foot, horse, or mountain bike. Birdwatchers find unusual variety due to the park's location between the coast and the desert and due to its elevation range and terrain. Owls, wood ducks, sage sparrows, and even brown pelicans can be seen. Sweetwater River and Lake Cuyamaca offer fishing, but with less favorable results.

## Attractions and Activities

**Museums.** A small interpretive center at the Paso Picacho Campground and picnic area has a few natural-history exhibits, most impressive of which is its collection of area conifer cones.

At the headquarters area, visitors find a first-rate exhibit hall devoted to the Kumeyaay Indian tribe, who occupied this area and resisted its development. Among the exhibits are baskets, stone tools, a throwing stick, and yucca sandals. Panels introduce the people and their culture. Other displays and artifacts are devoted to the era of the white settlers. Outside the museum, the 0.5-mile Indian Trail leaves near the parking lot flagpole and travels to an ancient village site.

**Stonewall Mine Ruins Tour.** In 1870, gold was discovered in the area above Lake Cuyamaca. Most successful of the mines was the Stonewall Jackson Mine, which gave rise to a company mining town, Cuyamaca City. In its heyday, it boasted a population of 500. In 1892, the mine closed, and the city failed soon after.

Today, all that remains is a fenced area encircling a stone foundation, the filled-in shaft, and some rusty, abandoned mining equipment. Piles of tailings spot the grounds. On a knoll, the Miner's Cabin Museum displays old photographs of the town and the mine. Nearby is a pine-shaded picnic area.

*Access:* Turn east off CA 79, 0.9 mile north of Paso Picacho Campground.

**Stonewall Peak Trail.** This 2-mile hiker trail climbs 900 feet, topping Stonewall Peak (elevation 5,730 feet) for a 360-degree view.

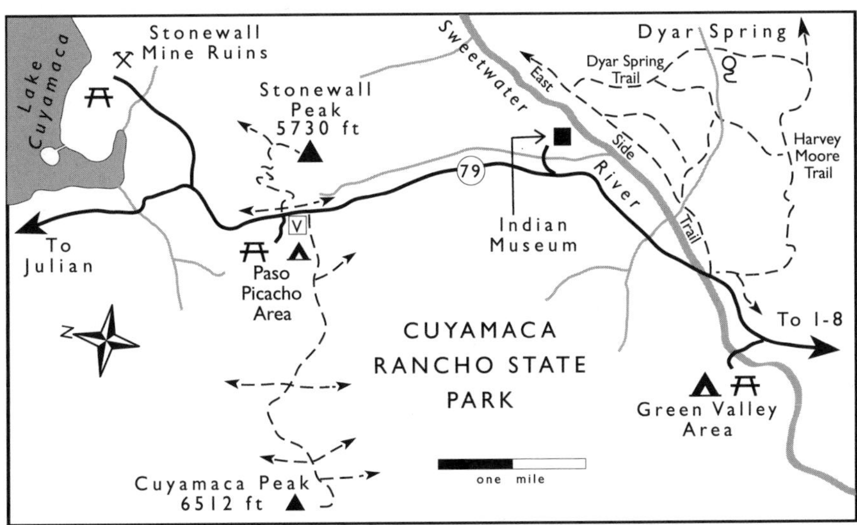

*Dyar Spring Trail, Cuyamaca Rancho State Park*

The tour begins following a dirt road across a grassy-floored, pine-oak slope, active with quail and woodpeckers. Soon after bypassing the trail junctions for Los Caballos and Cold Stream, the dirt road is closed off for the domestic water supply. Bear right on the footpath, gaining views of the destination's white stony top.

Comfortable, steady switchbacks advance the trail, touring the west and northwest slopes. The route is mostly shaded, passing through mixed oak-woodland and live oak-chaparral habitats. At 0.4 mile, the trail offers views of Cuyamaca and Middle peaks; later, it serves up a view of Lake Cuyamaca. Granite outcrops border the trail. Amid a cedar stand at 0.7 mile is a stone bench. Fence sections discourage shortcutting.

Where the trail tags the summit ridge at 1.75 miles, a path on the left descends to Los Caballos Horse Camp. For the final approach to the peak, a handrail and steps guide hikers up the exposed stone ridge.

Views west extend past Cuyamaca and Middle peaks into San Diego County; views north include Lake Cuyamaca, North Peak, and a distant higher peak; and the ones south find chaparral-clad mountains. To the east lies the Colorado Desert. Return as you came.

*Access:* Find the trailhead off CA 79, opposite the entrance to Paso Picacho Campground and picnic area.

**Cuyamaca Peak Trail.** This 2.7-mile paved fire road climbs 1,700 feet, reaching the top of the park's tallest peak (elevation 6,512 feet). The straightforward, steadily climbing route is open to hikers and cyclists. The latter group has a 15-miles-per-hour limit and must yield to other travelers. As several trails cross over this route, and some allow horses, proceed with caution and courtesy.

The fire road offers a pleasant workout, climbing from chaparral into a mixed woodland of pines, oaks, and cedars. Morning tours offer a chance to see deer. At 1.4 miles, an area of bracken ferns lines the road. Farther up the slope, the trees show fuller skirts, and the Coulter pines wear magnificent big cones.

After 1.8 miles, gaps in the tree cover grant the first view, looking east at Lake Cuyamaca and Stonewall Peak. At 2.1 miles, hikers find open views west, overlooking the steep chaparral slope. Here, a stiff wind washes over the saddle.

Sugar pine, lichen-etched fir, and boulder outcrops interwoven by manzanita line the final leg of the journey. At 2.7 miles, the trail reaches the summit. Following the road spur left leads to the former lookout site, while remaining on the main fire road leads to some summit buildings and a tower.

Neither site alone affords a full 360-degree view. Together they offer an impressive panorama that sweeps the Pacific Ocean, Mexico, and the Salton Sea, and the steep drop of the western slope is breathtaking. Return as you came.

*Access:* From the Paso Picacho day-use area, follow the paved road open to authorized vehicles, as it heads behind the park residences to reach the gated fire road. Campers may begin near site 37, saving 0.3 mile each way.

**East Side–Dyar Spring–Harvey Moore Loop.** This 5.75-mile loop travels a rolling terrain, passing through riparian, meadow, chaparral, and woodland habitats.

On the south shore of the Sweetwater River, it begins following the East Side Trail upstream. It tours a meadow, oak, and pine bench, overlooking the less-than-scenic waterway. At 0.5 mile is the first of several Juaquapin Trail junctions. Afterward, the trail crosses Juaquapin Creek, which is generally small or dry.

By 1.2 miles, the trail tours a fire area, mostly confined to the drainage. While the riverbank is disturbed, open, and lined by silver snags, the slope shows living trees with a few charred trunks. Trails crossing to the other side of the river are now closed because of the fire. Continue upstream.

At 1.7 miles, opposite the headquarters, take the Dyar Spring foot trail uphill. The trail begins as a narrow, rugged, and steep climb, then calms as it contours a canyon drainage slope. Soon, hikers gain views north, looking out the Sweetwater drainage at Stonewall Peak. Black oak, pine, and chaparral line the trail.

At 2 miles, hikers again enter a fire zone. Here the impact was minimal, and the recovery is fast underway. Switchbacking up the head of the drainage, the route grows rockier, and poison oak spots the area. At 2.5 miles, hikers arrive at upper Juaquapin Trail; following it right offers shorter loop options. For the full 5.75-mile loop, go left toward Dyar Spring. Suggesting time out for a snack are the beautiful shade oaks at the junction.

Before long, the Dyar Spring Trail offers looks at the opposite slope, a meadow bowl, and Cuyamaca, Middle, and Stonewall peaks. After crossing the Juaquapin headwater, the trail travels the right-hand edge of a broad meadow below a tree-covered ridge. Majestic live oaks dot the meadow.

At 2.9 miles is Dyar Spring, captured in a pipe. The now-deep channel of the trail continues along the edge of the meadow plateau; it is later replaced by a 2-track. Oak transition habitats separate the meadow plateaus.

At 3.8 miles lies the Harvey Moore Trail, which the loop now follows to the right toward Sweetwater Crossing. While it is a wide dirt lane framed by oaks and manzanita, shade is rare. Pancake cactus fills the rock cavities, and upon closer inspection the rustlings in the leaf mat prove to be mouse, lizard, bird, or horned toad. The trail descends steadily. Scrub oak and ceanothus add to the chaparral; in places, nolina dots the slope.

At the 4.7-mile junction, continue straight on the Harvey Moore Trail, rounding a chaparral slope. After 5 miles, the descent steepens. By 5.5 miles, hikers reach the shady woodland bottom, as the loop draws to a close past the spur to Green Valley Campground.

*Access:* Begin at the CA 79 trailhead parking area at the southeast corner of Sweetwater bridge, 1.3 miles south of the headquarters.

# Old Town San Diego State Historic Park

**Hours/Season:** 10:00 A.M. to 5:00 P.M., except major holidays; 10:00 A.M. to 4:00 P.M. (Mason Street Schoolhouse Museum)

**Facilities:** Visitor center, historic buildings, pedestrian-only roads and walkways, restrooms

**For Information:** (619) 220-5422

**Access:** From I-5, take the Old Town Avenue exit; the park is at San Diego Avenue and Twiggs Street. Parking areas rim the Old Town quarter.

Old Town San Diego marks and commemorates two events from California history: the first permanent Spanish settlement on the California coast in 1769, and the start of the American period in San Diego and California in 1846. The beginning of Old Town traces back to when retired soldiers from the area presidio (the Spanish fort) received land grants and settled here. It then grew with the disbanding of the presidio, at the start of the Mexican era in 1821.

Along the streets of Old Town San Diego, restored and reconstructed Mexican adobe and prefabricated American wood-frame buildings stand side by side, housing museums, shops, and eateries. Both plain dwellings and showier residences make up the quarter. The park encompasses twenty historic structures, seven of which are original. Efforts are being made to eliminate the contemporary trappings, so the bygone era of 1821 to 1872 can be revisited true to the time.

## Attractions and Activities

**Old Town San Diego Tour.** The historic district covers a 13-acre area (six square blocks) within present-day San Diego. The visitor center/park headquarters is in the Robinson-Rose Building at 4002 Wallace Street. There, visitors may view a model of the town as it looked in 1872.

Self-guided and staff-led walking tours introduce the buildings and explain their place in history. Brochures are available at the visitor center and various locations throughout the park. The free guided tours begin at the center at 2:00 P.M. and last for 1 hour.

The most famous building, La Casa de Estudillo, was built in 1827 by the former commander of the presidio. At his residence, visitors can peek into the life of a wealthy citizen during the Mexican era. An entry fee is charged, but the price includes admission to the Seeley Stables, where a fine collection of horsedrawn carriages may be admired.

At Seeley Stables (once the site of the San Diego-to-Los Angeles Stage), visitors can also examine Western and Native American artifacts and view a slide program on the hour, beginning at 11:00 A.M. The program offers a good primer on San Diego history, the stagecoach era, and the California Gold Rush.

Elsewhere on the walking tour, visitors view places from the Mexican-American War, such as La Casa de Machado y Silvas, where the Mexican flag was reportedly hidden as U.S. troops approached the town, and the Central Plaza, where the U.S. flag was first raised in 1846. One of the adobes, the reconstructed Wrightington Adobe, served as an American hospital following the Battle of San Pasqual.

At the *San Diego Union* newspaper building, a painstaking restoration of the building, an identical press, and the time-representative furnishings successfully erase the passage of a century. Similarly, the town's first tobacco shop has been reconstructed to its 1868 appearance inside and out, right down to the biting-sweet smell.

Videos, demonstrations, and brief grounds tours further add to one's understanding of the various buildings and life in Old Town. Between sightseeing stops and shopping, the serene, tree-shaded lawn of the Central Plaza invites visitors to take a needed break.

# INDEX

# D



# E



# F



# G

# N



# O



# P

## R



## S

## T



## U



## V



## W



## Y



## Z

## ABOUT THE AUTHORS

Formerly from California, Rhonda (author) and George (photographer) Ostertag have hiked and traveled extensively in the western United States. Rhonda is a free-lance writer specializing in travel, outdoor recreation, and nature topics. George has participated in several environmental impact studies, including the California Desert Bill. Their work has appeared in more than fifty national and regional publications, including *Westways, Backpacker, Trailer Life, Western Outdoors,* and the *Los Angeles Times.* They are the author/photographer team of *50 Hikes in Oregon's Coast Range and Siskiyous, Day Hikes from Oregon Campgrounds,* and *100 Hikes in Oregon* (all from The Mountaineers). The Ostertags now reside in Wilsonville, Oregon.